A DELICATE RELATIONSHIP

A DELICATE RELATIONSHIP

The United States and Burma/
Myanmar since 1945

Kenton Clymer

CORNELL UNIVERSITY PRESS   ITHACA AND LONDON

First published 2015 by Cornell University Press
Printed in the United States of America

Library of Congress Cataloging-in-Publication Data

Clymer, Kenton J., author.
    A delicate relationship : the United States and Burma/Myanmar since 1945 / Kenton Clymer.
        pages cm
    Includes bibliographical references and index.
    ISBN 978-0-8014-5448-6 (cloth : alk. paper)
    1. United States—Foreign relations—Burma. 2. Burma—Foreign relations—United States. 3. United States—Foreign relations—1945–1989. 4. United States—Foreign relations—1989– 5. Burma—History—1948– I. Title.
    E183.8.B93C55 2015
    327.7309591—dc23   2015020019

Cornell University Press strives to use environmentally responsible suppliers and materials to the fullest extent possible in the publishing of its books. Such materials include vegetable-based, low-VOC inks and acid-free papers that are recycled, totally chlorine-free, or partly composed of nonwood fibers. For further information, visit our website at www.cornellpress.cornell.edu.

Cloth printing   10 9 8 7 6 5 4 3 2 1

Contents

Preface

In addition to the scholarly reasons for writing this book, there is a personal one. In 1987, when my wife, Marlee Clymer, and I were in India where I was research-ing a book on US interest in India's independence, like the British before us we fled to the cool hill station of Shimla (Simla) for a month during New Delhi's extreme heat in June. In Shimla I worked at the Indian Institute of Advanced Studies. One of the long-term fellows at the institute was Michael Aris, an Oxford professor of Himalayan studies with a particular interest in Bhutan. At that time I was teaching at the University of Texas at El Paso, perhaps the only place out-side of Bhutan where the buildings are all constructed in the beautiful Bhutanese style. A few days later, Michael's wife, Aung San Suu Kyi, arrived, and we became friends, going on picnics together, eating out in restaurants, our children playing with their children of about the same ages. I had vaguely heard of Suu Kyi's father, Aung San, the leader of Burma's independence struggle who was assassinated in 1947, but knew little of Burma's history.

We also shared some tense days when stories appeared in the Indian press in-dicating that the government was suspicious of the activities of the few foreigners at the institute and was probably going to arrest them. One day I returned to our room to find eight Indian policemen there. They were impeccably dressed and very polite, but they asked for our passports.

Suu Kyi loved the challenge. I had a very different reaction. A stay in an Indian jail loomed, I feared. I booked a telephone call (as was necessary in those days) to the American embassy, which sent a Chevrolet Suburban van, along with Foreign Service officer Susan Jacobs, to demand the return of our passports and rescue us if need be. Ultimately the passports were returned, and there was no need to shorten our stay in Shimla. But Suu Kyi's reaction was revealing.

By this time I had come to know much more about Aung San Suu Kyi. In particular I had learned that her mother, Daw Khin Kyi, had served as Burma's ambassador to India. But she, Michael, and their children lived in Oxford, and there were as yet no hints that she would become famous as the leader of the Burmese opposition to Ne Win's oppressive dictatorship. But within months Suu Kyi was back in Rangoon to care for her mother who had suffered a debilitat-ing stroke. She was there when the revolutionary events of 1988 took place and ultimately accepted the mantle of leadership that her ancestry demanded. She did not leave Burma again for well over two decades and spent much of those years under house arrest. Consequently I followed events in Burma with interest and determined eventually to write something about the history of United States relations with that country. This is the result.

A note on nomenclature. Burma derives its name from the predominant ethnic group, the Burmans (or Bamars). The British took over Burma in three successive wars in the nineteenth century and used that name for their colony. When Burma achieved independence, the new rulers retained the name. However, in 1989 the ruling military junta changed the official name to Myanmar and also changed the names of many cities and roads. Thus, for example, the capital Rangoon became Yangon. Normally name changes of this sort have not resulted in much controversy. But not in Burma. Because the change of names was instituted by what was perceived to be an illegitimate and oppressive regime, the opposition forces continued to use the older names, as did the United States government. Thus what name to call the country has a political dimension. Those who most strongly supported the opposition and condemned the military government used Burma, while those with a different perspective generally preferred Myanmar. Not surprisingly this has also caused division in the ranks of scholars and public policy analysts, who often sparred with each other over a variety of issues, including the efficacy of sanctions and the nature of the government. There are honorable people on both sides of this debate. In this book Burma is used for the years before 1989. After that Myanmar and Burma are used interchangeably, reflecting the mixed usage in the United States. As the country has opened up, Myanmar has been increasingly accepted. The term "Burmese" applies to all of the people of country, not just the Burmans. As for Chinese names, the newer pinyin transliteration is usually used (thus Mao Tse-tung is Mao Zedong), but I have sometimes used the older Wade-Giles spelling in cases where it is still commonly used. Thus Chiang Kai-shek is used rather than Jiang Jieshi and Kuomintang rather than Guomindang.

All authors have persons and institutions to thank for inspiration, assistance, and support. Aside from the inspiration of Michael Aris and Aung San Suu Kyi, I have many to thank. I began this study at the University of Texas at El Paso, which was always supportive of my work. President Diana Natalicio kindly asked Marlee and myself to represent the university at the memorial service for Michael Aris in Oxford. After I moved to Northern Illinois University in 2004 the Department of History, the College of Liberal Arts and Sciences, the Center for Southeast Asian Studies, and the Center for Burma Studies all supported me in various ways, including with a sabbatical leave in 2009. Northern Illinois University provided a generous subvention for this book. I also appreciated the assistance of my colleagues who are Southeast Asian specialists, especially Eric Jones,

Trude Jacobsen, Theraphi Than, Clark and Arlene Neher, Danny Unger, Judy Ledgerwood, Kheang Un, and Catherine Raymond. Southeast Asia librarian Hao Phan responded to my requests for materials. My former colleague Alicia Turner, a Burma specialist now at York University, was kind enough to review a portion of the manuscript.

In 2011–12 the Woodrow Wilson International Center for Scholars invited me to spend the academic year working on the book, and I am very grateful to my colleagues and staff members there. At the risk of inadvertently leaving someone out, I want particularly to thank Robert Hathaway, then the director of the Asia program at the Center, who helped me in numerous ways; and Marvin Ott, a senior scholar there who shared very valuable insights about China's policies and American involvement in Burma. Other center people to be singled out include Xia Yafeng (who helped arrange a visit to East China Normal University's Center for Cold War Studies), Christian Ostermann, Susan Leverstein, Michael Kugelman, Lindsay Collins, Arlyn Charles, Kim Conners, Louisa Clark-Roussey, Fabio Rugge, Mike Van Dusen, Zahid Hussain, Douglas G. Spelman, Julia Clancy-Smith, Robert Baum, Jill Jonnes, Jackie Hagan, Ren Xuefei, Dennis Kux, Elizabeth Wishnick, and Eric Arneson. I am also grateful for the important assistance provided by the four student interns assigned to me at the center: Ngo Khien Thien, Taiyi Pan, Daniel Fong, and Nay Min Oo. William Roger Louis kindly invited me to present my work at one of the weekly meetings of the National History Center's seminars, which met at the Center.

There are too many other persons in Washington who assisted me in various ways to name them all. But I must single out David I. Steinberg of Georgetown University, the dean of Burma Studies, who invited me to Burma conferences even before I was in Washington, encouraged my work, and strengthened the manuscript in ways too numerous to mention. Karl Jackson and William Wise of the Johns Hopkins School of Advanced International Studies kindly invited me to take part in SAIS's Southeast Asian studies activities and to join their Burma Studies Group. Bill Burr at the National Security Archive provided leads on relevant documents, as did Matthew Jagel, a Ph.D. student at NIU. Murray Hiebert of the Center for Strategic and International Studies' Southeast Asian Program invited me to Burma-related events at CSIS. Donald Jameson shared his knowledge about Burma with me. Sally Benson provided us with housing in Dupont Circle and also introduced me to persons with Burma connections.

Our daughter, Megan Haddock, who has been interested and involved in Burma matters for several years and who worked with Burmese student refugees in Mae Sot, Thailand, provided both inspiration and contacts with Burmese opposition figures. She also wrote an important article on one of the most famous Burmese prisoners, Min Ko Naing. Sue Newhall, author of an excellent memoir about the "Burma Surgeon," Gordon Seagrave, and her husband Dr. Joe Newhall, of Bradenton, Florida invited me for several visits and provided important information and photographs about Seagrave. Lynn Hamilton sent me relevant clippings.

The staffs at the US National Archives and of all of the presidential libraries that I visited were invariably courteous and well informed. I am particularly grateful to Herb Pankratz, David Haight, and Carolyn Cain at the Eisenhower Library; to Michael Devine, director of the Truman Library; and Sarah Haldeman at the Johnson Library. In addition, both the Eisenhower and the Kennedy libraries kindly provided me with travel grants. Betsy Dunbar of the American Baptist Historical Society archives in Atlanta helped me navigate the papers of the American Baptist Mission in Burma.

The staff at the National Archives of Australia, and in particular Caroline Connor, could not have been more helpful. Daw Khin Khin Mya, Deputy Director at the Myanmar National Archives, was particularly helpful to me on the two occasions I was able to do research there. I am also grateful for the assistance of U Toe Hla, vice chairman of the Myanmar Historical Commission.

Professor Dr. Margaret Wong, head of the Department of History at Yangon University, kindly invited me to teach a short course in December 2013 on the history of United States relations with Burma/Myanmar since World War II. Teaching mostly History Department faculty members gave me a good opportunity to try out some of the findings in this book. Doctor Chaw Chaw Sein, head of the International Relations Department, invited me to speak to the new class of undergraduate students (the first admitted to the university since 1988). These were challenging, yet exciting opportunities to interact with faculty and students who have, for too long, been denied the opportunity to have international scholarly contacts. I am grateful for Open Society Foundation funding of my teaching assignment in Yangon, and to an NIU delegation, and in particular my colleague Tharaphi Than, for helping to arrange this. It was also a great pleasure to meet Lilian Handlin and Paula Helfrich in Yangon. I can't say enough about the kindness and helpfulness of Saw Kalya Aye, manager of the Classique Inn (and a graduate of the International Relations Department at Yangon University), where we have stayed several times. Also in Yangon friends Jim and Debbie Aung Din Taylor provided numerous insights about Burmese developments. In addition to allowing me to interview him about his years as the American consul at Mandalay, David Harr and his wife San Harr have over the years educated me about Burma.

I am also extremely grateful to those in the United States and in Burma who consented to interviews. A list of those interviewed is included in the bibliography, and I thank them all. One of the most striking interviews was with U Thet Tun, a well-known Burmese economist and diplomat who, although in fragile health himself, drove over to the Classique Inn to meet with me the day after his wife had suffered a serious stroke. I appreciate the assistance of NIU colleague U Saw Tun for helping arrange interviews.

The two external reviewers for the press made valuable suggestions that have improved the book. Finally, much thanks to the entire staff at Cornell University Press and especially to Michael McGandy who encouraged this project over the years. Gavin Lewis did a superb job copyediting the manuscript, including probing questions of substance that improved the book.

An earlier version of chapter 3 was published as "The Trial for High Treason of the 'Burma Surgeon,' Gordon S. Seagrave," *Pacific Historical Review* 81 (May 2012): 245–91, and portions of chapters 4 and 6 were published in "The United States and the Guomindang (KMT) Forces in Burma, 1949–1954: A Diplomatic Disaster," *Chinese Historical Quarterly* 21 (May 2014): 24–44. These are included in this book with permission of the publishers.

Finally I must say how much I owe to my lovely wife, also a Burma aficionado, who organized my notes and documents, put up with the long hours I spent alone in the archives and my study, and urged me to apply for various grants. The book would have taken a lot longer to complete had it not been for her encouragement and help at every stage.

Abbreviations

AFPFL	Anti-Fascist People's Freedom League
ASEAN	Association of Southeast Asian Nations
BCP	Burma Communist Party
BNA	British National Archives
CAT	Civil Air Transport
CIA	Central Intelligence Agency
CIF	Chinese Irregular Forces
D-	Democrat of [US state]
DEA	Drug Enforcement Administration
FSO	Foreign Service Officer
IBMND	Intelligence Bureau of the Ministry of National Defense
IBRD	International Bank for Reconstruction and Development
JCS	Joint Chiefs of Staff
KKY	Ka Kwei Yei/Ka Kwe Ye
KMT	Kuomintang
KNDO	Karen National Defense Organization
KNU	Karen National Union
NLD	National League for Democracy
NUF	National United Front
OCB	Operations Coordinating Board
PLA	People's Liberation Army
PRC	People's Republic of China
PVO	People's Volunteer Organization
R-	Republican of [US state]
SEATO	Southeast Asia Treaty Organization
SLORC	State Law and Order Restoration Council
SSA	Shan State Army
SUA	Shan United Army
TAMS	Tippetts, Abbott, McCarthy, and Stratton
UNLF	United National Liberation Front
USAID	US Agency for International Development
USIS	US Information Service

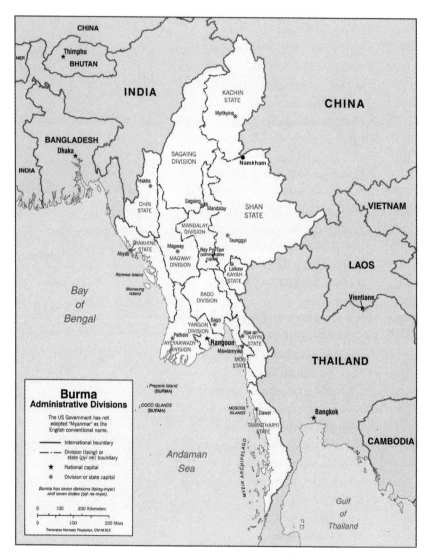

Burma/Myanmar's administrative divisions

INTRODUCTION

The story of American relations with Burma since 1945 is an important one that has until now not been told. Study of Southeast Asia, and particularly American relations with the region, has blossomed in recent decades, largely because the War in Vietnam focused attention on it. Despite being the largest country in mainland Southeast Asia, however, and occupying an important geographical position between the two most populous countries in the world, India and China, Burma is an outlier, a country largely ignored in historical study about its relations with the United States.

A small group of scholars has written important historical works about Burma, and there have been many studies of contemporary relations between the United States and Burma, mostly by international relations specialists and journalists. But serious historical studies of the relationship are scarce. There is, in fact, no comprehensive historical account of American relations with Burma. This lack of historical scholarship is probably because after 1962 military dictator General Ne Win kept Burma decidedly neutral in the Cold War, played little role in the Vietnam war and generally isolated the country (even discouraging tourism—for a time visas were valid for only twenty-four hours), so that it was mostly ignored by the American public, except for occasional stories about narcotics trafficking and ancient Buddhist monuments. To be sure, in 1976, Harvard University Press published *The United States and Burma* by the eminent historian and diplomat John Cady. Despite its title, however, the book is mostly about Burma, not the relationship with the United States.

American relations with Burma reveal persistent and often contradictory elements on both sides, which interacted to produce both fluctuation and continuity in that relationship. On Burma's side, these elements included anti-imperialist isolation versus the need for outside help, military regimes versus democratic oppositions, nationalist integration versus minority separatisms, placating versus resisting Communist China, and policies driven in different directions by personal rivalries among politicians and military men. On the US side, the issues involved were democratic values and human rights concerns versus Cold War calculations and commercial interests, racial prejudice versus "winning friends and influencing people," letting loose the Nationalist Chinese versus reining them in, its own problems of placating versus resisting Communist China, and policies driven in different directions by institutional rivalries among agencies and constituencies within the government. The result was that the relationship was almost always a very delicate one.

Burma's Importance

The story of the United States–Burma relationship is also important to tell, since without it our understanding of the American relationship with Southeast Asia in general across the decades is incomplete and distorted.

After 1947 the overwhelming context of global international relations was the Cold War which emerged when the Grand Alliance of World War II disintegrated and the United States and the Soviet Union, along with their respective allies, became bitter rivals. When in 1946 and 1947 George Kennan proposed a policy of containment of Soviet expansive tendencies, his attention was on Europe, but by the end of the decade containment grew to global proportions, particularly after Mao Zedong won the Chinese Civil War in 1949. This traumatic development for the United States led to almost frantic efforts to prevent the rest of Asia from coming under communist control.

In American eyes Burma was one of the two most threatened Southeast Asian countries (the other being Vietnam). Burma might well be the first domino to fall, thus giving China a great strategic advantage, as well as dominion over a source of significant natural resources. Burma shared a very long border with China, its governing class was suspiciously leftist in its political orientation, and within weeks after it attained independence on 4 January 1948 a communist insurgency arose that appeared at times on the verge of victory. Communist control would not only endanger the rest of Southeast Asia but also threaten neighboring Pakistan and India. The United States hoped to lessen the chances of this occurring.

By the 1960s the war in Vietnam had become the greatest American concern in Southeast Asia. Burma remained important, however, for the United States hoped that as a large, neutral country, it would support the adventure in Vietnam, or at least would resist Chinese pressure to criticize American actions. Furthermore, China's policy toward Burma remained a major source of anxiety for the United States, since China was wooing Burma with significant aid, and also settled a complicated border dispute on generous terms. When Ne Win visited Washington in 1966 the Lyndon Johnson administration pulled out all the stops to ensure the warmest possible reception for Burma's military dictator and to heal previous rifts in the bilateral relationship. In the end Ne Win refused to take sides on Vietnam, much to China's irritation, and Burma-China relations became antagonistic for the rest of the decade.

In 1971, when the United States changed its policy toward China, Burma became less of a Cold War concern. The United States did not cease to watch developments in Burma from a Cold War perspective, in particular because the Burma Communist Party (BCP) was still engaged in a revolutionary struggle against the government while receiving support from China. From 1971 to 1988, however, the primary focus of American interest in Burma was control of narcotics. President Richard Nixon had become deeply worried about cheap drugs, increasingly produced in the Golden Triangle area of Burma, Thailand, and Laos, reaching American soldiers in Vietnam, as well as by the epidemic of illegal narcotics flooding into American cities. In response, Nixon initiated the War on Drugs.

The War on Drugs was bipartisan, and both the Jimmy Carter and the Ronald Reagan administrations tried to encourage Burma's government to stop the traffickers. They received some cooperation, and provided assistance and equipment to reduce the opium crop. At a time that Ne Win had cut off close connections with outside countries, the antinarcotics discussions provided one of the very few ways to have close contact with Burmese officials.

By the 1980s, the antinarcotics campaign was becoming controversial. Critics charged that American-supplied equipment was being used against ethnic insurgents as much as against drug traffickers and that chemical spraying was seriously endangering human life, particularly in minority areas. The Reagan administration hit back hard at the human rights campaigners, however, and continued its antinarcotics practices.

In 1988 everything changed with the dramatic events of 8 August that came to be known as the 8888 Revolution. Several thousand protesters were killed, and Burma became the center of popular American attention to Southeast Asia. Because there were so few concrete American interests in Burma by this point, human rights, which had been only a secondary concern at best in American policy, suddenly became its main focus. This was heightened by the emergence of the charismatic and articulate opposition leader, Aung San Suu Kyi, the daughter of independent Burma's founder, Aung San. In 1991 she was awarded the Nobel Peace Prize, and she has had a committed following in the United States. As Burma scholar David I. Steinberg points out, from 1989 to January 2010 Suu Kyi was mentioned in the *Congressional Record* 1,598 times. "No living foreigner," he writes, "has shaped contemporary United States policy toward a single country more than Aung San Suu Kyi."[1]

The 8888 uprising and its aftermath, including the junta's refusal to recognize the results of an election that it had sponsored in 1990, led to a vigorous debate about how to improve the awful human rights situation in Burma/Myanmar. Although US administrations resisted imposing strong sanctions, fearing that they were too inflexible and would constrain their freedom of action, the debate was all about sanctions. Eventually public and Congressional opinion forced their enactment—in an effort to bring about "regime change." When that did not seem to produce positive results, the Barack Obama administration embraced "pragmatic engagement" to bring about "regime modification." That ultimately proved to be more successful (although sanctions played an important, if indirect, role in bringing about change). Indicating the level of American interest in recent developments in Burma, Hillary Clinton visited the country in November 2011, the first secretary of state to do so since 1955. A year later Obama himself came to Yangon, the first US president ever to visit the country while in office, and he made a stirring speech at Yangon University. Many other factors contributed to the changes in Myanmar, but the US role was not without influence.

The focus on human rights did not completely shut out other American concerns. Despite objections from activists, the administrations of the 1990s continued to work with the Burmese government on narcotics control, for example. With the Cold War nearly over and with sentiment strong to cut off virtually all ties with the junta, however, human rights issues dominated American discussion about Burma, and eventually American policy as well.

Burma and the US Role in Southeast Asia

In some ways American policy was much the same across the region. The effort to prevent communist expansion, for example, characterized US policy toward all of Southeast Asia and beyond. It is not widely understood, however, that before Vietnam consumed American attention, the United States considered Burma to be of equal, or near equal, importance. This newly independent state, not yet recovered from the devastation of World War II and beset by numerous internal difficulties of the first order, was thought to be very vulnerable to a communist takeover. Focusing only on the fascinating developments in Vietnam in the 1940s and 1950s, for example, distorts the larger picture that American diplomats saw in Southeast Asia.

At the same time Burma differed from other Southeast Asian countries in terms of American connections and interests, perhaps most importantly in the existence of an unusually large and influential American missionary community, with roots going back to 1813. In no other Southeast Asian country were the missionaries so prominent. Burma was the first Southeast Asian country to experience an American missionary presence. The first missionaries, American (Northern) Baptists, arrived even before the British began their conquest of the country. Except for a small number in Siam, there were few if any American Christian missionaries in other Southeast Asian countries in the nineteenth century. When the United States annexed the Philippines in 1899 Protestant missionaries entered the Philippines in significant numbers, and American Roman Catholic priests joined their Spanish brethren who had been in the islands since the sixteenth century; but there were far more Americans of other professions in the Philippines than in Burma. A very few American missionaries went to Vietnam and Cambodia in the early part of the century, but it was only in Burma that the missionary presence was the single most important focus of attention prior to World War II.

In the mid-twentieth century much of the publicity about Burma came from Gordon S. Seagrave, the celebrated "Burma Surgeon," sometimes compared to Albert Schweitzer. A fourth-generation Baptist missionary, together with his wife Marion Seagrave in 1922 he rebuilt a moribund hospital in Namkham on the border with China and made it into the most important hospital and nurses' training center in northern Burma. Still, it might have remained obscure had it not been for Seagrave's efforts to publicize his work in a series of books. During World War II, Seagrave and his nurses became heroes for their work with the Allied forces, exploits recounted in his most popular books, *Burma Surgeon* (1943) and *Burma Surgeon Returns* (1946). When the Burmese government put him on trial in 1950 for high treason for allegedly assisting an insurgency of the Karen minority people, Burma was again the subject of American attention and diplomatic involvement. There was no other American quite like Seagrave in Southeast Asia.

Burma also provides a good case study of how the United States reacted to neutral countries. The closest comparisons in Southeast Asia are American relations with Indonesia and Cambodia, with which the United States also had delicate relationships. In all three cases the United States demonstrated that, despite Cold War rhetoric about the immorality of neutralism, it could work with neutral countries. The United States funded and trained the Cambodian armed forces, for example, and provided economic assistance to Indonesia. However, there were differences. Under Sukarno Indonesia adopted a much more demonstrative, hardline anti-American posture. Unlike the Burmese government, furthermore, Sukarno sought international involvement, became a leader in the nonaligned movement, and was a near ally of China. Eventually the United States engaged in covert actions designed to destabilize his government, and it bears some responsibility for his overthrow in 1965 and the vicious massacres that followed. Cambodia's leader, Norodom Sihanouk, was not as outspokenly anti-American as Sukarno sometimes was, though he could make American blood boil with some of his comments, and American covert activity was used, at times, to destabilize his government also. In Burma the United States also employed covert actions, and at the policy level working with antigovernment forces was allowed under some circumstances, but this never reached the same level of involvement as in Cambodia or Indonesia, and there was no American responsibility for a bloodbath. Thus more than with Cambodia or Indonesia, American policy toward Burma ultimately demonstrated flexibility when it came to working with neutral countries during the Cold War.

As with Indonesia and Cambodia, Burma's neutral posture led to debates in the United States about how to respond. Some wanted nothing to do with countries that did not align themselves with American Cold War objectives. Furthermore, there was much sympathy with those ethnic minority groups with substantial Christian populations and who had fought on the Allied side in the war and who were not interested in entering the new Union of Burma without strong guarantees of autonomy; some insisted on complete independence. But in the end the Americans generally concluded that they must accept Burma's neutrality and socialism and support the central government. Better a neutral Burma than a Burma absorbed into the communist bloc. In 1955 that famous denouncer of neutralism, Secretary of State John Foster Dulles, traveled to Burma and personally invited the socialist, neutralist Prime Minister U Nu to visit the United States. In addition the United States extended some economic and military aid to neutral Burma to help keep it independent.

A unique feature of American policy toward Burma was covert support for the remnant Kuomintang (KMT) Nationalist Chinese forces who had fled to northern Burma as the communists swept to victory in China in 1949. This ultimately foolish involvement soured and complicated the already delicate bilateral relationship, but it does confirm a larger continuity across Southeast Asia: the fear of Communist China was an important driver of American policy across the region.

Burma's Past

Americans knew about Burma first from the missionaries; secondly from accounts of British colonialism there, most notably George Orwell's novel *Burmese*

Days (1934); and finally as a result of World War II, especially through Seagrave's popular accounts of the war. Still, Burma's history of course goes back for millennia and helps explain even modern developments, such as the actions of Burma's leaders today or the difficulties that Burma has had in creating a fully integrated country.

A highly developed, complex culture emerged in Burma thirty-five hundred years ago. It was one of the first regions to grow rice, make bronze, and domesticate chickens and pigs. By the early Christian era the people in the major river valley, that of the Irrawaddy, had developed a complex irrigation system, necessary because of the semi-arid climate. There were walled cities and large palaces. Most of the people became Buddhists, probably as the result of Buddhist expansion from southern India and Sri Lanka, though indigenous beliefs continue to influence religious observance, particularly the veneration of the *nats* (spirits).

The name "Burma" comes from the majority ethnic group, the Burmans, but the Burmans were actually relatively late on the scene. Prior to their arrival in about the eighth century AD, the region consisted of several kingdoms and city-states composed of non-Burman peoples. There were strong kingdoms in Arakan (the western part of contemporary Burma) and the Mon territories (in the south), with their own distinctive histories and culture and their own stories about the origins of the country. Today, however, the Burman story of the origins is widely taught. Schoolchildren learn that the first Burmese kingdom was founded in the ninth century BC at Taguang, near the present-day city of Mandalay, by a Sakiyan prince, Abhiraja, traveling eastward. (Sakiya was a clan of the ancient Vedic period [1750–500 BC] to which the Buddha belonged, in what is today the northeastern part of the Indian subcontinent. The Buddha's father Suddhodana was ruler of the clan.) The Abhiraja story may well be apocryphal, the result of an effort in the eighteenth century to tie Burma's founding closer to Buddhism, but it is widely believed.

Between the eighth and tenth centuries a Sino-Tibetan people from the Nanzhao Empire in what is today Yunnan, China, moved into Burma. They are generally understood to be the first Burmans. They called themselves the *Myanma*, or strong horsemen, and established their capital at Pagan (Bagan). Gradually they expanded, assimilating other peoples, and over time developed a language script and system of numeration. In 1989 the military junta in Rangoon, recalling this early history and appealing to nationalist sentiment, renamed the country Myanmar.[2]

From the eleventh to the thirteenth centuries, Pagan was one of the most impressive of the Asian civilizations. Led by King Aniruddha (Anawrahta), who seized control about 1044, the kingdom's area greatly expanded, including through the conquest of the Mon kingdom of Thaton to the south, so that it extended more or less to the Burma's current borders. The Pagan Empire, and the

Khmer Empire in Cambodia were the strongest powers in Southeast Asia. Several thousand Buddhist temples were built at Pagan itself, two thousand of which have survived where they are among the wonders of the ancient world. In 1287, however, Pagan fell to Kublai Khan's Mongols. Although Pagan was reduced to little more than a village, Burma was never fully integrated into the Mongol Empire. There emerged a number of smaller, often warring, principalities, one of which was the first Shan Kingdom of Ava, near present-day Mandalay. In the sixteenth century, however, King Bayinnaung from the small Burman kingdom of Toungoo, working with Portuguese forces, reunited the country, except for Arakan. He captured Ava, and even defeated the Siamese. His "exploits in expanding Burman power are unequaled in Burmese history," and it is not surprising that he is, as Thant Myint-U writes, "the favorite king of Burma's ruling generals."[3]

After Bayinnaung's death, the kingdom gradually weakened, and in 1754 Aung Zeyya (or Alaungpaya), the founder of the Konbaung Dynasty, managed to establish control over upper Burma. His successor, King Hsinbyushin, established his capital at Ava and then, in a battle still remembered with bitterness in Thailand, sacked and destroyed the Siamese capital of Ayutthaya in 1767. Thereafter the Siamese moved their capital to Thonburi and then to Bangkok.

The first major contact with the British occurred during the reign of King Bodawpaya (r. 1782–1819). In 1784 Bodawpaya conquered Arakan, which bordered on British India and thus brought Burma into direct contact with the British, but Bodawpaya's fruitless battles with Siam (which had retaken Ayutthaya) weakened the kingdom. King Bagyidaw replaced Bodawpaya in 1819 and invaded Assam in 1821, thus threatening British Bengal. This set the stage for the first Anglo-Burmese War (1824–26), which led to the British annexation of much territory in the southern part of the country.[4] It was not easy. Of the forty thousand British troops, some fifteen thousand died, more from disease and heat stroke than from wounds. A second Anglo-Burmese War in 1852 resulted in further concessions. And finally Britain took it all, destroying Ava in the third Anglo-Burmese War in 1885. The last Konbaung king, Thibaw, who traced his ancestry to the Pagan kingdom, and by extension back to the Sakiyans, was ignominiously forced into exile in India.[5]

Now Burma became a province of British India, an administrative arrangement that "was to have dire consequences for the Burmese." Burma was, in effect, a backwater in the British Empire, a colony of a colony. British Indian administrative structures were introduced that were alien to Burmese society and disrupted traditional institutions. Because the British considered the Burmese backward, they brought in Indian civil servants to administer the country. Indians and Chinese dominated the colonial economy. Many Burmese farmers were deeply in debt to the Indian *chettyars* (moneylenders). As Steinberg writes, "until late in the colonial period, the Burmans were cut out of the rewards, but not the dire effects, of the political and economic changes that had begun to have such an impact in the country."[6]

Only in 1935 did Burma get its own constitution under which "Burma had what looked a lot like a real government." The new structure was implemented in 1937, and Dr. Ba Maw, who had been educated in England and France, and was well known in Burma because he had defended a nationalist rebel, Saya San, at his trial in 1931, became the country's first prime minister. Real power still lay with the British, however.[7] Ba Maw was later jailed for sedition but was freed when Japan took over in 1942, and served as prime minister in the supposedly independent state of Burma under the Japanese. He fled to Japan ahead of the advancing Allied troops, where he was captured and interned by the Americans after the war. Later he was allowed to return to Burma.

Another unfortunate result of British rule was to exacerbate the differences between the Burmans and the minority ethnic groups. The British were not responsible for the often antagonistic relationships (though the Burmans often accused them of a divide-and-conquer policy), but they did worsen the situation. For example, they recruited troops primarily from the minorities and governed them with separate administrative structures. In addition, during British times Christian missionaries converted far more of the ethnic minorities than they did of the devoutly Buddhist Burmans, thus creating a new cultural divide, so that it has proven extremely difficult to create a common sense of nationality. Today the government recognizes over 130 ethnic groups, though not the large and unfortunate Rohingya people in Rakhine State, which the government refuses to acknowledge. In sum, there have been kingdoms and states, but there has not yet been a unified nation of Burma.

The United States and Burma to 1945

A study of American interest in Asia begins with the age of Columbus and the Elizabethans—or even before, since the revival of Europe in the fourteenth and fifteenth centuries was related to the stimulus of the oriental trade. Columbus and the other explorers were out to find a new passage to India, to the fabled wealth and wonders of the east by going west. What Columbus found was America (although he himself always believed he had landed in Asia; thus he named the inhabitants "Los Indios"). Thereafter the American colonists were concerned primarily with immediate matters of survival, but the hope somehow to touch Asia going westward was never entirely subdued. As early as the seventeenth century some British American colonists recognized the commercial possibilities of trade with China and India, and with the arrival of independence in 1783, American merchants sought worldwide markets. The famous *Empress of China* departed from Philadelphia in February 1784, thus beginning the China trade of a newly independent United States. Less well known is that soon thereafter the two-hundred-ton *United States* also weighed anchor from Philadelphia. Destined for China, the ship went instead to India, the first American ship to call there.

Between 1784 and 1815 between thirty and fifty American ships called annually at Indian ports, and many thousands of people in New England grew dependent on the India trade for their livelihood. In the first thirty-five years of the national existence of the United States, the value of the Indian trade probably exceeded that of the China trade. Some towns, like Salem, Massachusetts, were transformed by the trade with India.[8]

By at least the early 1790s some of these ships were also stopping in neighboring Burma, where they traded with the independent Burmese kingdom years before the British presence was significant. Initially the trade was almost entirely in teak. Trading in Burma could be dangerous. In 1793 King Bodawpaya commandeered one of Elias Haskett Derby's ships, *Astrea*, for his war with a neighboring kingdom; the captain and one officer became hostages until Bodawpaya's troops were successful.[9]

Trading for teak remained the primary American commercial interest in Burma for many years. In the latter part of the nineteenth century American petroleum interests tried to enter Burma, but the British successfully resisted, and after a quarter of a century John D. Rockefeller's Standard Oil Company gave up in a rare defeat. Herbert Hoover was more successful. In 1904 he learned of a long-abandoned Chinese silver mine in northern Burma and decided to revive it. After nearly a decade of frustration, the Bawdwin Mine was a considerable success, due to "Hoover's energy, audacity, and driving commitment." A very few other American commercial interests were also present in Burma, with Coca Cola establishing a presence there in1927. But generally speaking American economic relations with British Burma were, as Warren Walter Darkow put it, "merely casual."[10]

More Americans knew about Burma because of the presence of the Baptist missionaries. The founder of the mission, Adironam Judson, and his wife, former party girl Ann Hasseltine, were not originally Baptists. Judson, in fact, was an important figure in founding in 1810 the American Board for Commissioners of Foreign Missions, a Boston Congregationalist organization that became the foremost American Protestant missionary society in the nineteenth century. The American Board wanted Judson to go to India. The Judsons went first to Calcutta where they were met by the famous British Baptist missionary William Carey, whom Judson greatly admired. The British were hostile to American missionaries, however, nor did they want them in Burma because of their tense relations with that country. The English missionaries also advised against going to "savage" Burma, so the Judsons left Calcutta and made their way to Madras, also a part of British India. In June 1813, fearing arrest there, they took passage on the first available boat, the Portuguese bark *Georgiana*, which, by chance, was going to Rangoon. The boat was unseaworthy and nearly shipwrecked along the way, but they landed in Rangoon in July 1813. In the meantime Judson had concluded that the Baptist view of the sacrament of baptism was the correct one and consequently severed his relationship with the American Board. In 1814 the Judsons became official missionaries of the American Baptist General Convention for Foreign Missions.[11] Thus began the remarkable Burma Baptist Mission, the most influential American institution in Burma well into the twentieth century.

The Baptists were not the first Christian missionaries in Burma. Portuguese and Italian Roman Catholics had preceded them by over a century. For the most part the Catholics were tolerated and treated well, though (and perhaps because) they had few converts. Among their most notable representatives was Father Vincentius Sangermano, whose knowledgeable accounts of Burma are still cited. An English Protestant mission, which included William Carey's son Felix, was founded in 1807. Like some Catholic missionaries, Felix Carey won favor with the court at Ava, even receiving a title from the king for his services. But the

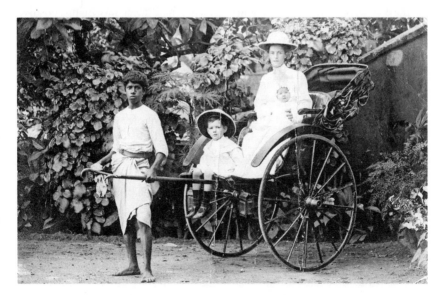

FIGURE 1.   Herbert Hoover Jr. and his baby brother Allan Hoover with their nurse and rickshaw driver in Burma, 1907. Courtesy of Herbert Hoover Presidential Library-Museum. Photo 1907-01.

British missionaries had little success and were happy to turn the their work over to the Judsons.[12]

During his first six years in Burma Judson devoted his energies to learning the language and translating religious texts. In 1819 he founded a guest house on the outskirts of Rangoon, began to preach, and achieved his first conversion from among the few curious Burmese who stopped by to hear him. King Bodawpaya tolerated the mission, but in 1819 his grandson, Bagyidaw, succeeded him. Bagyidaw was less tolerant of non-Buddhist religions, and when in 1820 Judson formally requested permission to preach Christianity, an angry Bagyidaw banished him from the kingdom. Judson hung on in Rangoon, however, and the following year, when Dr. Jonathan Price, a Baptist medical missionary famous for his delicate eye surgery, arrived, Bagyidaw invited him to Ava and Judson was the interpreter. This time Judson's reception was much friendlier, and the king even gave him some property for a church.

With the first Anglo-Burmese War (1824–26) the missionary presence in Burma became difficult. Judson and other missionaries were accused of being spies and imprisoned for twenty-one months in very harsh conditions in Oung-pen-la Prison.[13] In 1826, however, Judson and Price helped negotiate a peace agreement that included the cession of significant amounts of territory to the British. The missionaries were delighted to be under British protection, and the latter were pleased with the missionaries' contribution to the peace. Thereafter the attitude of the British toward the missionary presence in Burma was highly positive. However, Bagyidaw was also grateful to the missionaries for ending the war and invited them to remain in Ava. Price did so, and the king honored him with a Burmese title for his services to the crown. Judson, on the other hand, worked with the British to establish their capital, Amherst (now Kyaikkami). Rangoon remained in Burma proper (that is, non-British Burma). Judson moved his mission headquarters to Amherst and offered a prayer of thanks for the "rule of civilized authority and Christian toleration."[14]

For the immediate future, then, the American Baptists conducted most of their work in British Burma. Judson completed his famous Burmese-English dictionary in1826 and his Burmese translation of the Bible in 1834. More missionaries arrived, and missionary schools and medical clinics increased. The missionaries were incredibly dedicated and planned to live their entire lives in Burma, but for many years they had few converts.

Meanwhile in Burma proper the situation for the missionaries deteriorated after Bagyidaw abdicated in 1837. His successor, Tharrawaddy, banished all missionaries from Ava, and not surprisingly the missionaries welcomed the second British attack on Burma in 1852. Assisted by many Christian Karens (or Kayins)—one of the major ethnic minorities in Burma among whom the missionaries achieved many conversions—the British quickly annexed Pegu, a royal city and an area rich in rice cultivation.

Perhaps as a result of British successes, the new king, Mindon, like the Siamese rulers, decided that he must modernize his country and open it to Western influences if he was to be able to resist the British. He very much wanted to establish diplomatic relations with European countries and the United States and in 1857 engaged an American Baptist missionary, Eugenio Kincaid, to lead an official Burmese mission to the United States to deliver a letter to the president. Accompanying the mission was a delegation of Burmese men whom Mindon hoped to enroll in American institutions to learn engineering and shipbuilding.

James Buchanan responded to Mindon in the first communication to a Burmese ruler from an American president, expressing the hope that Burma's sovereignty would not be further diminished. Mindon received the letter with great ceremony. He also wanted the United States to establish a consulate in Mandalay and urged the missionaries to encourage this. But the American Civil War intervened, and nothing materialized from this early contact. In any event, during Mindon's reign the missionaries worked in Burma proper with relative freedom. His successor, Thibaw, was less solicitous, and the missionaries were glad when the British defeated him, completing their conquest of Burma in 1885. In general, although the missionaries were sometimes tolerated and even established friendships with high-level Burmese officials, in the nineteenth century they never felt secure in Burma proper and supported British efforts to expand their rule.

The missionaries' impact on the majority Burman population was limited in terms of converts. Prior to World War II only about 2 percent of the entire population was Christian, and most of these were among the minority populations. About 20 percent of the Karens, for example, were Christians. The missionaries probably contributed to a sense of Karen nationalism, and much of the Karen leadership was Christian. Burma scholar John Cady asserted that Baptist work with the Karens and Kachins had brought about "an amazing transformation of these peoples." The missionaries may also have had a broader, if indirect, influence on the majority Burman population, particularly through their many schools. By World War I the Baptists alone were operating 708 schools, and in 1920 their Judson College merged with an existing government college to create Rangoon University (today Yangon University). Cady believed that Burmese concepts of popular sovereignty, local self-government, and democracy came in part from "the democracy of the Baptist congregations." Cady, who sought Christian overseas service and taught history at Judson College from 1935 to 1938, may have overstated the importance of the missionaries. But their influence should not be underestimated either.[15] Louis Walinsky, who served in Burma for several years in the 1950s as an economic adviser, wrote in 1962 that the missionaries were "quiet, self-effacing, dedicated people who . . . lived close to the people they served so well. Their schools and hospitals were of the best, and they were held in high regard."[16]

During World War II Burma was important to the United States primarily because it was one of the few routes into besieged China. Because the Japanese were in control of the Chinese coastline, in 1937 China began to construct a road to Burma—an heroic engineering feat, with the Chinese constructing the road "with their fingernails." Opened in 1939, it was a lifeline to the Chinese forces, though not one of importance to the United States until May 1941 when the Americans began to supply Lend Lease equipment to China.[17] Responding to Japanese demands, British Prime Minister Winston Churchill, who considered the Asian theater of minor importance, closed the Burma Road in July 1941; but three months later he opened it knowing that this would please the Americans. The increased shipments of goods resulted in congestion and delays, but by late 1941 strong American intervention had improved the situation significantly.[18]

After the attack on Pearl Harbor on 7 December 1941 Japanese forces swept quickly through all of Southeast Asia, including Burma, which was important to Japan as a barrier against Allied attacks into Southeast Asia and also as a launching point for a possible invasion of India. Americans were involved in the immediate resistance to the Japanese, with General Claire Chennault's Flying Tigers air force, based in Rangoon, delaying the Japanese long enough for the British to distribute fifty thousand tons of Lend Lease equipment to their ground forces. General Joseph Stilwell, then assigned to Chiang Kai-shek's government in Chongqing (Chungking), was given command of Chinese and American troops in the Burma theater. The first foreigner since Marco Polo to command Chinese military forces, Stilwell had the job of keeping China in the war. All of this was complicated by the fact that Burma remained a British responsibility, and Chinese forces in Burma were also under the command of Sir Harold Alexander.

In March 1942 Rangoon fell to the Japanese, and the Allied forces began a difficult and costly retreat. Stilwell wanted to counterattack, but the British were committed to a scorched-earth withdrawal toward India, and Chiang would not permit the use of his forces, despite Stilwell's theoretical command. Stilwell was frustrated. As he put it, he had been "struggling with the Chinese, the British, my own people, the supply, the medical service. . . . Incidentally with the Japs."[19] After the Japanese took the northern Burmese city of Lashio in April 1942, Stilwell joined the retreat and walked out of Burma, along with Gordon Seagrave and his Karen and Kachin nurses.[20] By the time Stilwell reached the safety of Imphal, India on 20 May, the Japanese had completed their conquest and closed the Burma Road. The only remaining supply route into China was the hazardous trans-Himalayan air route.

Stilwell resolved to reopen the Burma Road, but it took nearly two years before he could launch a major offensive. This was due largely to Burma's low priority from the British perspective. The Americans thought Burma was important to their goal of keeping China in the war and ultimately prevailed—though only after alternative strategies, such as diverting supplies to Chennault's air force in China, failed. The appointment of Vice Admiral Lord Louis Mountbatten as Supreme Allied Commander in the region (with Stilwell technically his deputy) was also instrumental in equipping an invasion force to retake Burma. Administratively, Stilwell was in a nearly impossible position, with responsibility to Mountbatten, Chiang Kai-shek, and the US Joint Chiefs of Staff. After many delays, however, the Allied offensive began in January 1944. Among the American forces Stilwell commanded were the famous three thousand "Merrill's Marauders." Like the British Chindits, the Marauders were involved in long-range penetration movements. In August the Allies captured the important north Burma city of Myitkyina after a brutal seventy-two-day siege.

The one force that was unambiguously under American command was the Office of Strategic Services (OSS) Detachment 101. This clandestine unit began with only 21 men who arrived in Burma in June 1942. By July 1945 there were nearly 1,000 Americans in the unit, as well as 10,000 hill people. Initially concentrating on intelligence gathering, late in 1943 under Lt. Col. William Peers' leadership Detachment 101 developed a guerrilla warfare capability. The unit contributed significantly to the Myitkyina campaign. For the remainder of the war it engaged mostly in guerrilla operations.[21]

After Myitkyina the Japanese were on the defensive. In January 1945 the Ledo (or Stilwell) Road opened from Assam, India through Myitkyina, Bhamo, and Namkham in Burma before connecting with the old Burma Road at Mong-Yu Junction near Wanting in southern China. There was now a supply line into China. On 21 March Mandalay fell to British troops, and in May they entered Rangoon. The war was over so far as Burma was concerned, but the country was devastated.

American interests in the war in Burma were of course entirely unconnected with the Burmese people themselves. But Americans viewed the ethnic minorities favorably, the result of long-time missionary work and their heroic assistance to the Allies, something Seagrave publicized in his books. The Burmans, on the other hand, were viewed with suspicion. An American report on the Burma campaign in 1942 commented there was a "considerable pro-Jap element in Burma." Indeed, the Japanese were succeeding because the people provided them with intelligence. This was mostly because the Burmans disliked the British and hoped that the Japanese would give them independence. "They take a very short view of things and it is doubtful whether many of them are awake to the ultimate issues or look far ahead," the report stated. Later the Americans reached similar conclusions about the Burmese during the Cold War, asserting that they did not fully understand the existential threat posed by the communists. The Buddhist monks were an object of particular suspicion. "Most of the seditious and subversive activities takes place under cover of the yellow robes," the report asserted.[22] President Franklin D. Roosevelt expressed a famously low opinion of the Burmese, writing to Churchill in April 1942 that he had "never liked the Burmese" and was glad that Churchill had to deal with the likes of "He-Saw, We-Saw, and You-Saw." Of course this came at a time when FDR was pressuring Churchill strongly over British repression in India, and perhaps he intended to soothe the prime minister's feelings.[23]

The fact that many important Burmese leaders, including the most important nationalists devoted to independence, joined the Burma Independence Army (later the Burma Defence Army and then the Burma National Army) and fought with the Japanese, hoping for independence, only enhanced American suspicions. Among these pro-Japanese nationalists were the future leaders of Burma including Aung San, U Nu, and Ne Win. Although they ultimately switched sides and joined the Allies, even toward the end of the war the president was uncertain about "how we will handle that situation" in Burma.[24]

Overview

With the end of World War II, however, the United States had no choice but to grapple with "that situation" in Burma, and the subsequent discussion examines how it tried to do so. The first chapter treats the period after World War II until Burma's independence in January 1948. In Burma, as elsewhere in Southeast Asia, the United States had to respond to the pressures of nationalists who were pressing for early independence— which the Americans favored for Burma, although not without ambivalence. They were nervous about Aung San, Burma's emerging leader. He was young, had fought against the Allies, and had leftist political leadings. They also had a sympathetic understanding of the minority people, many of whom were Christians, who had fought so valiantly for the Allies, and who were suspicious of a united country dominated by the Burman majority. But as the Grand Alliance disintegrated and the United States began to focus on the communist threat, it became even more committed to independence under Aung San's leadership.

The next ten chapters explore American policy toward Burma during the height of the Cold War. Chapter 2 discusses Burma in the two years immediately following independence, when the country was beset by almost insurmountable difficulties: recovery from the war, the outbreak of communist insurgencies, and the beginning of major ethnic civil strife—all without the stabilizing hand of Aung San, who had been assassinated six months before independence. Basically, the United States determined that it was in its own interest, as well as in Burma's interest, to respond first to the communist menace. In American eyes this was the existential threat to Burma and to the American policy of keeping all of South and Southeast Asia free. This meant supporting the government of Burma, despite sentimental attraction to the minorities.

Chapter 3 examines the first crisis in American-Burmese relations: the trial for high treason of Gordon Seagrave, accused of assisting the Karen insurgency. The trial brought to the surface a number of underlying issues and tensions. It revealed dramatically Burmese suspicions about the American missionary community's loyalty to the new central government, while the negative and impassioned reaction among the American public demonstrated Cold War fears and suspicions about the trustworthiness of nonwhite, former colonial people. American policy was tested, but in the end the United States came down squarely against the ethnic insurgencies because they distracted attention from the fight against the communists. The trial also demonstrated that the goals and interests of the American missionaries were not entirely the same as those of the US government. Thus Seagrave—despite his credentials as a widely known war hero, a strong anticommunist, and a Christian humanitarian—could not comfortably serve the United States government as a popular representative of American goals in Southeast Asia.

Chapters 4 and 6 introduce a more important crisis, one that lingered on for many years: covert American support for the remnant KMT forces that had fled to northern Burma. The major American rationale was to distract China's attention from the Korean War. From the beginning all American ambassadors to Burma considered this beyond foolish, and eventually the Americans helped arrange partial KMT withdrawals to Taiwan. But the KMT did not disappear, continued to receive support from Taiwan, engaged in narcotics smuggling, and remained a troublesome irritant in Burma's relations with the United States.

Chapters 5 and 7 focus on other Cold War issues in Burma's relations with the United States. These include efforts to send economic and military assistance to Burma's government to combat communist rebels and provide some resistance should there be a Chinese invasion. The often tortuous negotiations reveal the limits of American influence on Burma, the result of Burma's insistence on pursuing a determinedly neutral course in the Cold War. American diplomats, if not the general American public, thought Burma's government was privately anticommunist but often naive and insufficiently energetic.

Chapter 8 examines Burma's efforts to reach a border settlement with China. When the effort stalled for a time, the United States took this as evidence of

China's perfidy, and when the issue was ultimately resolved in a fashion favorable to Burma, this left the United States in an uncomfortable position. Even as the negotiations continued, however, General Ne Win forced democratically elected Prime Minister U Nu out of office in 1958 in what the American ambassador termed "a polite coup." This produced a common dilemma: ostensibly supportive of democracy, anticommunism took precedence in American policy. Although U Nu was widely popular in Burma, the United States considered him soft on communism and a poor administrator. Thus it privately welcomed Ne Win's action, since this seemed to promise a more forthright anticommunist stance and a strong administration that could tackle Burma's many problems. The American military was so pleased it was ready to hand-carry heavy weapons to the general.

Gradually the Americans became uncomfortable with Ne Win's heavy-handed administration and were not displeased when he agreed to hold elections after eighteen months in office. To Ne Win's distress, U Nu easily won. Nu was quite certain that the United States had privately supported his opponent, and chapter 9 analyzes the renewed delicate relations with the United States that ensued. The same complaints that had dogged U Nu in his previous administrations soon emerged again. Critics thought that they detected a significant decline in government efficiency, and Rangoon began to revert to its previous disorderly state. The KMT issue emerged again and threatened to disrupt the bilateral relationship, and U Nu seemed too forgiving of the communists. On the other hand, the new president, John F. Kennedy, made a serious effort to respond to U Nu's concerns and devoted much attention to resolving the KMT issue.

More important for the future of US-Burma relations, however, was Ne Win's disastrous visit to the United States a few months after he stepped down as prime minister. Ne Win and his wife Daw Khin May Than were subjected to several indignities (the most important of which was an apparent racial slur against her while her husband was a patient in Walter Reed Hospital), and this led him to turn very strongly against the United States. This was very evident when he again took over the government in 1962, this time in a hard coup followed by the promulgation of the "Burmese Way to Socialism," a nationalist, autarkic, and authoritarian social and economic regime that is discussed in chapter 10. Ne Win immediately ordered American foundations out of Burma and suspended the Fulbright program; soon he began to nationalize foreign property and institutions, including all of the mission hospitals and schools; he ended negotiations for an American-funded highway from Rangoon to Mandalay; and in general he closed his country to foreign influences as much as possible. There was little the Americans could do to influence events.

To repair the damage, the United States finally managed to persuade Ne Win to visit Washington in 1966. The invitation was explicitly intended make amends for the previous visit, but Ne Win's hosts also hoped to persuade the Burmese not to join China in condemning the American war in Vietnam. Chapter 11 shows how the Americans handled the visit very well and achieved their objectives in subsequent years, although Ne Win continued to keep his country isolated.

By the end of the 1960s Burma was no longer a major factor in Cold War politics. The United States was already warming its frigid relationship with China, something dramatically apparent with President Richard Nixon's visit to Beijing in 1972. This did not entirely end US suspicions of Chinese intentions in countries like Burma, where the United States continued to keep a wary eye on the Chinese-backed communist insurgency. But thereafter until 1988 control of narcotics, to be jointly achieved by the two countries, became the center of American policy toward Burma. As shown in chapter 12, narcotics control was important in itself, but the joint program was one of the very few ways that Americans could connect with Burmese officials and thus have some avenues of influence on Burmese policy.

The United States had learned to live with Ne Win. He had destroyed democracy, was xenophobic, and was driving the economy into the ground, but there was no danger of his allowing the communists to gain ground, much less take over the country. He posed a long-run threat to the country's stability, perhaps, but the United States was willing to overlook his despotism and his disastrous economic policy for the moment. Human rights was not a major American concern.

That ended in 1988, when the country erupted in a popular uprising against the government. Chapter 13 explores the American response: because the United States had so few concrete interests in Burma by this point, and Cold War fears had largely evaporated, human rights became the center of American discussion and debate about the country. This was not necessarily the intention of either the Ronald Reagan or the George H.W. Bush administration. But all agreed that the Burmese junta had acted brutally, and the emergence of Aung San Suu Kyi as leader of the opposition made it virtually certain that human rights would be central to the policy debate. But just how to bring about change in Burma divided the executive branch from the Congress. Presidents from Ronald Reagan to Bill Clinton resisted calls for mandatory sanctions, while Congress supported them. Only in 1997 did Clinton sign a serious sanctions bill for the first time.

Whether imposing sanctions was wise policy was strongly debated, although it is clear that they had popular and Congressional support. Whether wise or not, once implemented they did not produce "regime change" in Rangoon, and ultimately the Barack Obama administration moved toward "pragmatic engagement," the subject of chapter 14. Keeping the sanctions in place while also engaging at high levels with the government of Myanmar, helped bring about significant changes in Burma's government, or at least they coincided with the changes. The sanctions themselves assisted in the process in an unintended way: they drove Burma closer to China—too close for comfort—and the Burmese responded by seeking closer relations with the West. The United States appointed a new ambassador, Secretary of State Hillary Clinton visited the country, and President Barack Obama became the first sitting president ever to come to Burma. The relationship was finally one of friendship, if still delicate.

BURMESE NATIONALISM AND THE PATH TO INDEPENDENCE

After the sudden end of World War II in August 1945, there were swaths of devastation across Southeast Asia. Manila was perhaps the most destroyed city in the region, but Rangoon and Burma in general suffered dramatic damage. As Supreme Court Justice William O. Douglas wrote:

> Her cities were first bombed by the Japanese, then by the Allies. During the Japanese occupation, there was misery everywhere. Over 2 million acres of rice land went out of production because there was no export market for Burma's surplus. The Japanese killed and ate over 2 million carabao [water buffalo], the faithful work animal of the peasant. They required the exchange of all British currency for yen. When the British returned, they repudiated the yen. Thus everyone—from the lowliest to the highest—ended up with no money. Burmese buildings stood gutted by fire; the docks and wharves were battered; the mines were flooded; transport was almost at an end.[1]

But the war also furthered nationalism in Burma and other colonial areas around the world, and how the United States decided to respond would have momentous consequences in the postwar period. Nationalist movements developed across the region well before the war. The Indian National Congress challenged British rule as early as the late nineteenth century and inspired nationalists in Southeast Asia. In Indonesia, Sukarno and other nationalists sought independence from the Dutch as early as the 1920s. Filipino nationalists initially fought

Spain, then militarily resisted the subsequent American occupation in 1899 and, once the war was over, demanded independence. In 1919 Ho Chi Minh asked the Versailles Conference to free Vietnam from French rule, and when he was ignored, he worked to throw the French out, ultimately going to war with them in 1946.

Burma was no exception. Nationalist sentiments reached back to the early twentieth century and culminated in student unrest and strikes in the 1930s. Out of this emerged the "Thakins," student leaders who challenged the British and formed Burma's new leadership. Although the specific circumstances differed from country to country, in general the nationalist movements were responses to the colonial power's introduction of new governing institutions that jarred uncomfortably with traditional ways. A new "rational," modern bureaucratic state, intended to create wealth in the service of the metropole's larger strategic interests, intruded in numerous ways. In Burma British rule severely diminished the role of the village headmen as they became appointed agents of the state, no longer able to mediate between the village and the center of power. Rural people resented the imperial government's disparagement of traditional medical practices which were dismissed as quackery. They disliked being forced to be vaccinated for smallpox, instead of being inoculated by their indigenous healers. Similarly, they objected to the state's creation of forest reserves, from which they were barred. By the 1890s land was increasingly alienated to moneylenders. Overall, as historian Mary Callahan writes, "colonial rule brought to Burmese society unprecedented changes, most of which benefited British and other foreign commercial interests at the expense of the majority of the indigenous peoples."[2]

The United States looked at the anticolonial struggles with mixed emotions. There was a genuine anticolonial tradition in the United States, dating from the independence struggle against Britain, that aroused a feeling of identity with colonial peoples attempting to claw their way out from under imperial rule. During the war President Franklin Roosevelt's position on colonialism was strongly negative, for example. His personal encounters with colonial rule in Africa had disgusted him, and he thought colonialism was one cause of the war. He did not want the French to return to Indochina after the war, sparred with the British over India and Hong Kong, and even questioned Dutch intentions to return to Indonesia. The Atlantic Charter that he championed called for self-determination.

But there was another American tradition. By the narrowest of definitions the United States had itself become an imperial power after the Spanish American War, annexing the Philippines, Puerto Rico, and Guam, exercising a protectorate over Cuba, and intervening numerous times in Latin America. The ancient foe, Great Britain, the world's leading imperial power, was now a virtual ally, and during World War II an actual ally. Colonial issues, therefore, produced ambiguous and ambivalent American responses. Even Roosevelt was uncomfortable with the idea of immediate independence in most colonial regions, although his idea of international trusteeship, if paternalistic, promised eventual independence.

But FDR died in April 1945, before the end of the war. His successor, Harry S. Truman, was less in the anticolonial tradition, and in any event as the Grand Alliance fell apart in the years after the war, fear of communist expansion competed with, and ultimately trumped, anticolonial impulses in American policy. By the end of the decade, the United States was supporting the French against Ho in Vietnam. In Indonesia, the Americans were ambivalent, though eventually they came down against the Dutch because the nationalists there had proved their anti-communist credentials. How the United States dealt with these issues in Burma is the subject of this chapter.

Burmese nationalist activities went back at least to 1910 when local land associations protested various practices that were injurious to rural interests, protests that culminated in 1930 in the Saya San Rebellion. The British quickly suppressed the uprising and hanged San, but it furthered nationalist ideas. Nationalism also had urban roots, notably the activities of a Buddhist monk, U Ottama, who was drawn to the Indian National Congress and was jailed in the 1920s for anti-British activities. U Ottama's actions demonstrated that devotion to Buddhism was a central feature of Burmese nationalism, as with Cambodia nationalist movements in the 1930s. In Burma this was partly a response to British religious insensitivity; their insistence on wearing shoes in Buddhist pagodas was especially offensive.

Nationalist ideas also centered in the universities. In 1920 when University College joined with Judson College to form Rangoon University, students struck against what they regarded as antinationalist rules. It is not insignificant that the students also occupied the Shwedagon Pagoda, thus highlighting the connection of Buddhism and nationalism. The most significant of the student nationalist activities took place in the 1930s. The students had had their eyes opened at the university to the outside world and had time to think, read, and discuss, and they were attracted to the many revolutionary and nationalist movements taking place around the world. Socialism had a very wide appeal because it posed a challenge to colonial capitalism that seemed to exploit their country, with the economic benefits flowing to foreigners. Mohandas K. Gandhi attracted Burmese nationalist support, though Gandhi's pacifism and Hindu overlay made him less attractive to some than more radical models like the Irish Republican Army and Soviet communism's challenge to the West.

Aung San was the student leader who emerged in the 1930s to lead the country to independence. He was in some ways a strange person to become a revolutionary leader. From a middle-class background (his father was a lawyer), unable to speak until he was eight years old, he nevertheless possessed, as Thant Myint-U writes, "a hard to explain charisma" as well as both idealism and determination: his heroes were Abraham Lincoln and Mexico's Benito Juárez, and he was expelled from the university for refusing to reveal the name of a student who had written an inflammatory article, though the university administrators later backed down. He and the other talented nationalist student leaders took on the name "Thakin" (master, sahib), a term usually used for the British that indicated that the students were now in charge of their own future. And indeed they were. In a few years the Thakins would be the leaders of an independent Burma.[3]

World War II strengthened nationalisms all across the colonial world. It had shown, if it was still necessary to show, that the Europeans were not invincible: they could not even protect their colonial possessions. Furthermore, to varying degrees the Japanese were welcomed. Many nationalists looked back with admiration to the Russo-Japanese War of 1904–5 when for the first time an Asian power had defeated a European one. Once Japan had conquered Southeast Asia, it had sometimes brought nationalists into the colonial governments; they were not keen to see the former colonialists return. In Burma, however, the situation was more complex. Japan proclaimed Burma independent, and Ba Maw served as prime minister, while Aung San was minister of defense and U Nu was foreign minister. But unlike in Indonesia, where Sukarno worked with the Japanese and then, following the war, led the nationalist forces against the Dutch, Ba Maw's service as prime minister under the Japanese discredited him.[4] The other Burmese nationalists, including Aung San and U Nu, and other members of the famous "Thirty Comrades" whom Aung San had recruited and the Japanese had trained in anticolonial activities, also sided with the Japanese. However, they later turned against them, formed the Anti-Fascist People's Freedom League (AFPFL), and ultimately joined the Allies. The Burma National Army, now on the Allied side, proved particularly valuable in the final stages of the war.[5] With the end of the war, they demanded an end to British rule. Ba Maw fled to Japan where, after the war, the Americans captured him.

The United States and the Political Struggle for Independence

If the United States had a certain sympathy for nationalism and took pride in freeing the Philippines in 1946, the British did not favor anything like immediate independence for their colonies. On 17 May 1945 the British government of Burma (still in exile in Shimla, India) issued a White Paper promising Burma "complete self government within the British Commonwealth" with "status equal to that of the dominions." However, the governor would have substantial control for an indeterminate interim period, although he was expected to consult Burmese opinion and establish an Executive Council. There might also be a "small Legislative Council" established on an interim basis. The British unconvincingly argued that this plan was "fully in accordance with the Atlantic Charter."[6] The White Paper was clearly much too conservative for Burmese nationalists. It did not provide for eventual independence and left the non-Burman areas under direct British control; there was never a chance they would accept it.

When soon thereafter American forces began to withdraw from Burma, some Burmese concluded optimistically that this reflected American disapproval of British colonial ambitions. Some Americans, however, thought the British position was entirely reasonable. Major Coulter D. Huyler Jr., for example, the US military observer in Bombay, in one of the earliest detailed reports about communism in Burma, believed that the "wait and see" policy of the British was eminently sensible and that the Burmese minorities were not at all ready for self-government. American Burma expert John Cady agreed with Huyler's assessment of the tribal people, but like most informed Americans, he was critical of the limited British approach. Cady advised his superiors in the State Department that the White Paper presented "an overly optimistic view of prewar Burman-British relations."[7]

After Aung San's shrewd decision to switch his allegiance to the British, London began to interpret the White Paper more liberally. Leo Amery, secretary of state for India and Burma, told Parliament that the government wanted to move as quickly as possible to self-government. He hoped that the Burmese would join the British Commonwealth, asserting that being in the Commonwealth did not mean "independence minus certain prerogatives" but rather "independence plus." The change was significant enough that even Labourites like Sir Stafford Cripps, Gandhi's friend, applauded it. The change in emphasis was evident when Sir Reginald Dorman-Smith, the governor of Burma, arrived in Rangoon on 20 June 1945 and met with Burmese leaders, including Aung San. Dorman-Smith was not unsympathetic to Burmese desires, but he leaned toward arresting Aung San for treason, something Lord Louis Mountbatten, the Allied Commander, insisted would be disastrous. Instead, Mountbatten granted Aung San's army Allied status and offered to appoint him a major general.[8] Mountbatten was instrumental in keeping the situation from unraveling.

Generally speaking, the American government was pleased with the changed British approach. Cady, the best informed American, thought that it made perfect sense for the British to deal with Aung San and others, despite their service with the Japanese. The United States had few economic interests in Burma, but it did have an interest in seeing colonial areas move toward "self-government and eventual independence."[9]

Still, not all went smoothly. Dorman-Smith refused Aung San's demand that the AFPFL be given eleven of the fifteen posts in the new Advisory Council (subsequently the Executive and Legislative Councils), and after talks broke down none of the posts went to AFPFL members. The councils were thus filled with Burmese who did not represent the majority opinion and were viewed increasingly as illegitimate. Cady took a dim view of the new Legislative Council, which met for the first time in January 1946. Acknowledging that the council members were not "stooges of the Governor's party," he declared that they nevertheless had "no authority whatever over the formulation of policies or their execution." In the following weeks the AFPFL and other organizations attempted, with much success, to discredit the councils. Though Aung San cautioned people to avoid violence, there were lots of guns in the country, and violence was a real possibility.[10]

Assistant Secretary of State Dean Acheson's request for a cabled summary of an AFPFL convention held in Rangoon 17–23 January 1946 indicated growing American interest in Burma. In particular he wanted to know about any "remarks concerning US" and instructed the consulate to request immediately additional funds for cabling expenses if needed.[11]

The consulate reported about the convention in detail. It was held at a time when there was much anger that the British government had refused to receive an AFPFL delegation. Dorman-Smith intervened and offered to make arrangements for Aung San and Than Tun (who was married to the sister of Aung San's wife and was head of the Communist Party of Burma) to go to London, if they wished. This may have defused the anger, but the AFPFL nevertheless condemned Britain for not giving the Burmese any reason to fight for the Allies during the war, compared British imperialism to fascism, condemned the White Paper's vagueness, accused the British of intending to reestablish their "pre-war economic stranglehold," and expressed solidarity with the Indonesian and Indochinese resistance movements.[12] Nothing significant, it appears, was said about the United States.

An "aggressive and optimistic tone" characterized the convention's pronouncements, reported US consul Glenn A. Abbey, reflecting, he felt, the general attitude of the country. Freedom from British rule was coming, the Burmese sensed, but they distrusted the governor and, despite their optimism, feared that they might yet be cheated out of their independence. Abbey also reported that Aung San's position as the foremost leader of the independence movement was unassailable. He hoped that an armed clash could be prevented but was concerned that if the present rift with the governor was not healed, there could be a break.[13]

Aung San was immensely popular, Abbey stating that if there were an election he might garner 80 percent of the vote, but Abbey also had reservations about him. He passed along to the State Department Dorman-Smith's view that Aung San was an "impetuous, unstable, inexperienced young man who had never had anyone say 'no' to him in his life." Abbey also noted that an American war correspondent considered him "a callow youth."[14]

Meanwhile, the governor's advisory councils were of no account to Burmese nationalists, particularly when it appeared that the British government had no intention of turning defense or foreign affairs matters over to them. Such irritants might have been resolvable had the councils been representative and had real power, but this was not the case. As the American consul in Rangoon put it succinctly, the Burmese did "not trust British intentions."[15] Increasingly, therefore, the nationalists demanded the election of a Constituent Assembly that would draft a new constitution giving authority to the Burmese.

The increasingly rancorous situation suggested one of two possibilities: government repression or government concessions. Given the problems associated with the former, Abbey thought that concessions were more likely, perhaps beginning with a reorganization of the councils. The Americans concluded that the government was "no more popular now than it has been heretofore"; this would not change until the Burmese gained "increased authority and direction."[16]

Relations did in fact grow more tense. The AFPFL created the People's Volunteer Organization (PVO), whose members, most of them former soldiers, received training in "military drill, guerrilla warfare, and . . . automatic weapons." The government arrested a number of PVO members. Several AFPFL supporters were killed in a clash with police on 18 May 1946 at Tantabin, near Rangoon, and the AFPFL and the government could not agree on a process to investigate the incident. "It is clear that compromises by either the Governor or by the AFPFL are imperative," reported Abbey to the State Department on 23 May 1946. There was a growing feeling of "desperation" among AFPFL followers, he reported.[17] In Abbey's view Aung San had acquitted himself well; it seemed foolish that London should still try to exclude him from the government.

Then suddenly on 4 June Dorman-Smith announced that he would return to London for medical treatment. This was not a diplomatic illness (although the British government did want to recall him) but the result of severe amoebic dysentery. Some prominent Burmese hoped that he would be able to persuade the government to adopt a more liberal attitude. Abbey's own assessment of Sir Reginald was that, despite angry criticism from all sides, he had accomplished much.

Dorman-Smith's replacement was Sir Henry Knight, a respected member of the Indian Civil Service but a man who had long wanted to retire and who had no experience in Burma. Some Burmese took the optimistic view that the appointment of Sir Henry presaged a change in British policy. The American consulate was less optimistic. Abbey doubted that "the volatile forces of the AFPFL" could be "held in check" much longer, and in fact, had it not been for heavy monsoon rains, there would probably have already been more demonstrations.[18]

Sir Henry, who had wanted to serve only a month, was replaced in August 1946 by Sir Hubert Elvin Rance. A major general in the British Army and Mountbatten's protégé, Rance had been Burma's director of civil affairs since 1945, and now he would be the last British governor of Burma. The Burmese nationalists were angered when Indian constitutional developments proved to be more advanced than in Burma, and it was therefore not surprising that the AFPFL called for a general strike for 23 September 1946. In addition, a "mammoth demonstration" was announced for 29 September to protest the White Paper. Government officials considered the situation "very grave" and even foresaw a possible coup led by Aung San. This, one official pointed out, was consistent with communist methods.[19] In an effort to avert the strike, Rance announced that the government was prepared to grant Burma the same status as India. The British had decided that compromise was the only course.

The British concessions worked, and the AFPFL entered the government. Aung San (for whom Rance "had quite a liking"), became councilor for defense and external affairs, although he did not have complete control of either area. For the moment, the crisis was over. "We are pulling out of Burma and I believe in turning things over to them," Rance told the American consul general. This was "the best news that has come from Burma in a long time," stated the London *Times*.[20]

Problems remained, however. The detested White Paper remained technically in force, and Aung San himself led the scheduled demonstration against it on 29 September. It was "the biggest of its kind yet held in Rangoon," with an estimated fifty thousand participants. More importantly, the British sense of debt to the hill people had not diminished, and they wanted to protect them in any future constitutional arrangement. As Dorman-Smith put it, the Kachins, the Chins, and the Karens deserved Britain's highest thanks. "We owe to these loyal and courageous people to give them every assistance on the most generous scale," he said. To many Britons this meant that the "hill tribes must not be placed under jurisdiction of future Government of Burma." If the British continued to take this position, which Aung San would certainly reject, a peaceful resolution was in jeopardy.[21]

The hill people were in fact apprehensive about an independent Burma. Some of the Shan leaders even spoke of amalgamating with Shan areas in southern China. At the end of October 1946 the new American consul general, Earl L. Packer, raised the concerns about the Shans with Aung San directly. Aung San said he knew that the Shan sawbwas (their hereditary leaders) were worried, and while he considered them not very progressive and thought some of their stated demands unrealistic (such as access to the sea), he favored autonomy for them. At the same time, however, he complained that the British "were obviously trying to hold on to the Shan States for ten years or so," something he could not accept.[22]

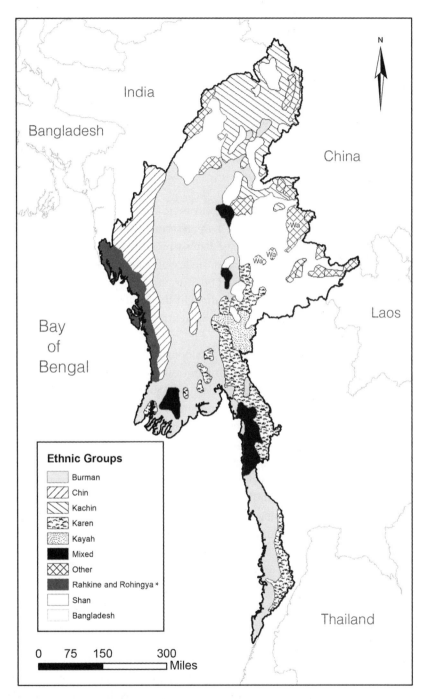

Major ethnic minority groups in Burma/Myanmar.
*The government of Myanmar does not recognize the Rohingyas as an indigenous ethnic group.

Another unsettled issue was whether Burma would remain in the British Commonwealth. The opinion among British and American observers in October 1946 was that Burma would do so because powerful countries surrounded it, and Commonwealth membership might provide some protection. The American consul general questioned Aung San about this point at length, but the Burmese leader saw little advantage in joining the Commonwealth—though he himself was not necessarily averse to the idea.[23]

American Intentions

Meanwhile the British were suspicious of American intentions. Prior to the war they quite correctly described American interests in Burma as mostly "sentimental" because of the importance of the Baptist mission. Even after the war the care of the missions was a major responsibility of American diplomats. In August 1948 of the 190 Americans resident in Burma, all but 28 were missionaries. But in the postwar period the British thought the United States was scheming to dominate Burma's economy. "It was apparent that the Americans were using their military organisations as a means of impressing themselves on the people of the country with a view to the future development of commercial connexions." They were getting ready to pounce if Britain weakened.[24]

It was an exaggerated view that revealed more about British fears than about American intentions, but it was not wholly without substance. The Americans did want to gain more influence in postwar Burma, though initially this was understood in cultural terms and in terms of advocating for democratic institutions. Packer placed much faith in educational exchanges as a way to further these aims. The Americans thought British payments for Lend Lease equipment would fund the exchanges, and one of the more contentious negotiations with the British after the war concerned the amount owed. There was much frustration, and sometimes anger, on both sides, and at one point an American colonel who was involved in the negotiations simply seized several Lend Lease jeeps, arguing that he had waited long enough for the British to agree on a price. In 1947, however, an agreement was reached by which the funds due to the United States were used to support Americans studying in Burma, particularly through the new Fulbright program, and to fund scholarships for Burmese students studying in the United States. The Fulbright program had an early start in Burma, with an agreement finalized on 22 December 1947, even before independence. In the first competition, eight slots were to be awarded to American professors to teach at Rangoon University and the State Training College for Teachers, while five other awards were for Americans to conduct postdoctoral research in Burma.[25]

American economic penetration of Burma was not entirely ignored either. Socony Vacuum and National City Bank already had representatives in the country, and in October 1946 Packer told Rance that he hoped to increase American trade with Burma. He hoped that the Open Door principle would apply once Burma was independent and was presumably gratified when Aung San stated that he did not intend to turn "things over completely to the British."[26] The United States also sought air transit rights through Burma for both commercial and military aircraft without taxes or customs duties of any kind, particularly at Rangoon's Mingaladon Airport.[27] Cultural exchanges were important, but profit and economic advantage figured into American policy as well.

To make a favorable impression on the Burmese public, the United States opened an impressive Information Room in Rangoon, complete with photographs "showing American way of life," a library of up-to-date books (largely scientific in nature), and a fifty-seat theater. A British official who attended the opening ceremonies in March 1946 was met by a "beautiful American blonde and two attractive Burmese girls." After viewing the room and observing the many Burmese and Indian officials who attended, he observed with scarcely suppressed envy, "this show has got everything." The British, he added with regret, had nothing comparable. "American stock is going up; ours . . . never very high . . . is falling to pre-war levels." This was, he concluded, a small matter, "but how important."[28] Well into the future American public relations efforts in Burma alarmed the British.

These observations revealed the difficulties that the British were facing in the postwar world. Weakened by the war, facing nationalist pressures around the world, and now having to deal with a friendly, but ascendant and putatively anti-colonial United States, the British were very much on the defensive. This was evident in British irritation about American celebrations of Philippine independence in July 1946. Soon after independence the *New Times of Burma*, published by the British government of Burma's Public Relations Department, published an anonymous letter indicating that the Philippines was not really independent after all. The Americans suspected that the letter was officially inspired, and the State Department commended Richard Usher, the American vice consul who had reported it, observing that "the friendship shown by Burmese leaders to Philippine independence is a matter to be carefully noted."[29]

Meanwhile, American interest in Burma reached its highest level yet. As Packer told Aung San at the end of October 1946, Burma and other Southeast Asian countries were of greater interest to the United States "than ever before." This was partly the result of American military investment in the area during the war but were perhaps more directly the result of concern that disturbances in the region would have "repercussions elsewhere." Burma's "strategic position" regarding air routes, its position as a buffer state between India and China, and its potential to become a major rice exporter also interested the United States. Another concern was that failure to move ahead quickly with acceptable constitutional arrangements would only strengthen the communists in Burma, a matter of growing concern to the United States.[30] Cold War fears were emerging; soon the fear of communist expansion would be the hallmark of American policy in Burma and elsewhere in Southeast Asia.

Final Status Negotiations

The British, however, were not quite ready to let go. Burma was not India, they stated, and future plans would be "affected by way Burmese politicians measure up to their new responsibilities" as members of the Executive Council. Paternalism was still apparent, more so in the Burma Office in London than among British officials in Burma.[31]

Although the State Department wanted more movement on the political front, the American embassy in London seemed content with British plans. This irritated the State Department, which declared that the intransigence of the London authorities would give "communists and others splendid opportunity fish in troubled waters," and in December 1946 it ordered the embassy to again indicate American interest in a "peaceful transition" to self government. Ten days later the State Department urged the London embassy to press the British government for an "early and positive decision on matter of declaring or acknowledging" a Burmese national government.[32]

That same day the British made an important change of course. Among other things they declared, in a concession to Burmese opinion, that the Burmese could decide if they wanted to remain in the Commonwealth, and they invited a group of Burmese politicians, including Aung San, to come to London to try and resolve differences. (Privately, the government seemed to have decided that the only possible way to keep Burma in the Commonwealth was to give it the right to opt out.)[33] The United States publicly welcomed the new British statement, but Winston Churchill, by then in opposition, condemned it.

Although the Burmese nationalists agreed to go to London, they were skeptical that anything positive would result. They feared that the British were stalling for time, and they vowed not to talk but to present their demand for "an interim government with full powers to prepare for constituent assembly elections"; they would also insist that the hill regions be given to Burma because they did not want the British to have "a base of operations against us." More colorfully the AFPFL accused the British of planning to "suck blood out of these places for economic purposes" while pursuing a divide-and-conquer policy. Packer inter-preted this as an "adroit maneuver to demand more than British can now grant in hope British will grant other demands submitted."[34]

The talks proceeded well. Gilbert Laithwaite, the assistant under secretary of state for India (his previous appointment had been private secretary to the re-actionary viceroy of India, Lord Linlithgow) was "increasingly impressed" with Aung San's "ability and strength of character."[35] The British acceded to Burmese demands, and a final agreement was about to be reached on 27 January 1947 when two of the Burmese delegates, U Saw and Ba Sein, suddenly announced that they could not accede to the proposed agreement. The suspicion was that they would try to use their dissent to gain political advantage at home, and it was feared that Churchill and those Conservatives who shared his fierce hostility to "liquidating the British Empire" in Parliament would undoubtedly seize upon this division to attack the government. Nevertheless, the delegations (minus U Saw and Ba Sein) announced an agreement the following day. The British agreed to the election of a Constituent Assembly (rather than a Legislative Assembly, as they had initially proposed) which now gave Burma the same constitutional sta-tus as India. The agreement did not set a specific date for independence, and the precise status of the non-Burman regions was not settled; but a procedure was agreed upon for resolving these important matters. The Americans were pleased, saw no legitimate basis for U Saw's and Ba Sein's dissent, and commended Prime Minister Clement Attlee's "deft handling of the opposition."[36]

Reaction in England to the Anglo-Burmese agreement was mostly positive, with all newspapers (except for the Communist *Daily Worker*) praising it. By contrast, reaction in Burma was mostly unfavorable: the Burmese-language press concluded that the promises of independence were vague and that the agreement was too much like the detested White Paper of 1945. Former Prime Minister Ba Maw thought Aung San had made a "grave error in political judgment." Aung San clearly had his work cut out for him, and when the American consul general called on him on 10 February 1947 he found him "very tired and not very com-municative."[37] Perhaps this was because Aung San was then dealing with the diffi-cult issue of the relationship of Burma's ethnic minorities at the second Panglong Conference. Due largely to the force of Aung San's personality, the conference temporarily settled the future relationships of the Shans, Chins, and Kachins with the central government; but the Karens were divided. Some pro-Union Karens re-ceived government positions, but a significant number of Karens did not want to join the Union of Burma and instead formed the Karen National Union. They did not attend the conference, boycotted the April elections, and threatened rebellion.

In any event, Aung San's leadership was fully vindicated by the elections for a Constituent Assembly that were held in April. The AFPFL won an overwhelming victory, taking 248 of the 255 seats. Trust in Aung San and the London agreement was confirmed, and the assembly began work on a new constitution.

Even before the elections the United States had considered the advisability of opening diplomatic relations with a still dependent Burma. With the election and the likelihood of full independence in the near future, the United States looked forward to the establishment of formal diplomatic relations. There was some hesitation, largely because suspicions remained about Aung San's character. Some regarded him as "an embryo Hitler" who would likely use strong-arm tactics against his opponents. Perhaps it would it be wise for the United States to move cautiously. Packer was more favorable, however, and argued that sending an ambassador to Rangoon would serve American interests. The State Department agreed and recommended that the president approve the establishment of relations. The United States had already concluded an agreement for the sale of surplus Lend Lease equipment to Burma for use in postwar rehabilitation, and an agreement to start scheduled air service by American carriers was reached. There could be a upsurge in American trade with Burma, once imperial preferences ended. Truman approved the recommendation.[38]

When shortly thereafter Packer saw Aung San, he asked first about the communists and defense, and then asked what his attitude was going to be toward foreign investment. He then inquired about his attitude toward the missionary organizations and the related question of whether Burma would adopt an official state religion. This nicely encapsulated American concerns at the moment. Aung San's responses were reassuring.

Assassination

All appeared to be going well. The Constituent Assembly had approved a resolution of independence, was working on a new constitution, and a goodwill mission to London had succeeded in advancing the independence date. The issue of the ethnic minorities had been partially resolved, and even the Karen separatists were quiet for the moment as the AFPFL put Karens in responsible positions in the new government. Then on 19 July 1947 four Burmese gunmen wearing British Army uniforms and armed with Sten guns stormed into the Executive Council chamber and assassinated Aung San and six other council members, as well as some other people. Another assassination team attempted to kill U Nu, a Thakin and an important independence leader, but did not find him. Aung San's assassination was a tragedy of immense proportions for Burma, and the United States expressed its shock and sympathy.

Some immediately suspected U Saw, but as Packer reported, responsibility was "anyone's guess."[39] U Saw was soon arrested as a precautionary measure. A considerable supply of arms was found in his house, but he had not yet been connected conclusively to the shootings. One of the surviving council members, Tin Tut, attributed the murders to a long-standing political vendetta. Though Tin Tut did not say so, U Saw apparently blamed Aung San for an earlier attempt on his life. Sir Gilbert Laithwaite reserved judgment but did suggest that the amount of arms found at U Saw's house was quite extraordinary. Also pointing to U Saw was the report that after the shooting the assassins drove their jeep to his house, where they changed clothes.[40]

There was much skepticism that U Saw could have masterminded the plot by himself. Perhaps he was a scapegoat. U Saw and his supporters claimed that the guns at his home were planted there by AFPFL or PVO men shortly before the assassination. Some even suggested that the assassination was instigated from within the AFPFL. Others asserted that the communists were responsible. A usually reliable British Army source informed an American official that the radical Red Flag Communists were the "principal originators," though U Saw and Ba Maw were also complicit.[41]

The communists, in turn, accused the British.[42] Although the government itself was certainly not involved, two corrupt British Army officers were implicated. Captain David Vivian and an army major were arrested for accepting bribes to procure the weapons for U Saw from the British arms depot. However U Nu, who took control of the government, did not expose their role or publicize their arrest, fearing that this would lead to riots and perhaps delay or derail independence.[43]

Early in August 1947 a confidential source, a member of the Burmese cabinet, told Packer that all important conspirators in the assassinations had now been arrested. The evidence pointed to U Saw, who had become rich due to money presumably received from landlords who resented Aung San's plans to nationalize land. U Saw apparently thought that in the resulting chaos he would be called upon to lead the country. But there was no chaos. Ultimately some eight hundred persons were arrested.[44]

The trial of U Saw and nine other defendants began on 24 September 1947 before a special tribunal at Insein Prison, presided over by the highly respected jurist U Kyaw Myint. On 30 December, five days before Burmese independence, U Saw and eight other defendants were convicted and sentenced to be hanged. In the end U Saw and five others were executed (on 8 May 1948), while three had their sentences commuted to life imprisonment. It was assumed that Vivian would get the death penalty, although he ultimately received only a five-year sentence and in 1949 escaped from Insein Prison during a Karen uprising.[45] Ba Maw and several other detainees were not charged.

The assassinations did not change the timetable for independence, 4 January 1948. U Nu, who took over leadership after Aung San's death, became prime minister. He was a respected, deeply religious man whose capacity, according to the American legation, was as yet uncertain. One of the Thakins at Rangoon University, elected as president of the university's important Student Union in 1935, he was involved in several disputes with the administration. Soon expelled from the university, he and other nationalist students led a famous student strike that lasted for two months early in 1936. The university then agreed to most of their demands (including the reinstatement of the expelled students). During the war Nu served as foreign minister in Ba Maw's government under the Japanese.

For the moment Nu was able to control the various factions of the AFPFL because of the memory of Aung San, and he also had the strong backing of the British. However, he felt overwhelmed with the sorry state of Burma, still not at all recovered from the ravages of World War II. As he put it in his autobiography, "he, who had never learnt to drive and had seen a motor car only once or twice at a distance, was expected to take the wheel and drive it over the worst road imaginable."[46]

Despite the very difficult times, the United States and Burma agreed to exchange ambassadors in September 1947, prior to independence. U So Nyun represented Burma in Washington, and Earl L. Packer, the current consul general, became the American chargé d'affaires in Rangoon pending the appointment of an ambassador. Still, the United States was nervous about Nu, questioning whether he would rein in the Burmese communists. His anticapitalist, socialist ideology also concerned the Americans.

Communism

American nervousness with Nu reflected concern with communism that went back before independence was imminent, even before the Cold War became the defining factor in international relations. This was evident in March 1946 when the State Department requested a complete report "as soon as possible" from the US consulate "on Communist movement with special reference Anti-Fascist League." Communist activities in India and Burma had raised US concerns during the war, although since the communists supported allied objectives, concerns were muted. The intelligence agencies even employed some communists during the war, and P.C. Joshi, the head of the Communist Party of India, also shared much information about the communists in Burma with an American major in return for what he hoped would be employment with the OSS.[47]

Although Joshi did not get hired, in June 1945 he provided a wealth of information to Major Coulter D. Huyler.[48] Among the more important assertions was that Aung San was "an ardent Communist and a reputable Burmese national." Although the communists claimed Aung San (and he had helped found the Communist Party of Burma prior to World War II), it is evident that the independence leader defied easy categorization. Indeed, in 1940 the Burmese communists themselves had concluded that he was "too reactionary for our use . . . thoroughly pro-Japanese . . . an anarchist and Trotskiist [sic]. . . . He is dangerous."[49]

The Burma Communist Party did, however, claim to exert considerable influence over the AFPFL, but this was exaggerated. In any case, in June and July 1946 the league began to reorganize itself and reduce its relationship with communist elements. Than Tun, leader of the BCP, resigned (Aung San said he had been fired) as general secretary of the AFPFL, although he remained on the Executive Committee. This troubled the American government, and the consulate's monthly review of 13 August 1946 was largely devoted to a detailed analysis of communism in Burma.[50]

Soon after Aung San entered the government in September 1946 he strongly criticized the communists at a large rally at Rangoon's Shwedagon Pagoda. The AFPFL then ousted communists from its Executive Committee, and Thein Pe, a communist leader, "denounced Aung San and colleagues as tools of policy of repression and collaborating with imperialism." The next month the AFPFL expelled the communists altogether; Aung San stated that "they had dug their own graves" with a series of blunders that had given aid and comfort to the British.[51]

The Americans were pleased, and hoped that the communists would not be allowed into the government, but neither Aung San nor U Nu would close the door entirely to future communist participation, stating that they had "no fundamental differences" with them. At the end of February 1947 Communist leader Than Tun announced that the party would contest elections in April 1947 but would not oppose the AFPFL. The Americans were further disturbed that Than Tun and Thein Pe had gone to India to consult with Joshi. Although the State Department did not think that the Burmese communists had direct contact with Moscow, Joshi did. Their Indian mentors, wrote one official, provided the Burmese communists with "the proper Party line expeditiously."[52] Hence there could be at least indirect influence from the Soviet Union on the Burmese communists, and if they did become part of the government, they might well establish closer communications with Moscow.

By this time the Cold War had begun. In Burma the American fear was that, as Loy Henderson put it, that the communists were "already laying foundations of a structure which will be devoted to preventing any kind of real self-government in Burma other than one dominated by communists and one, therefore, which will be basically hostile to the United States." Henderson urged Packer to produce "a very careful report" on Burmese communism and "watch with greatest care all communist activities" in the country.[53]

As Henderson wanted, the American consulate general kept track of communist activities as best it could. For example, it reported that on 5 April 1947, shortly before the elections, Aung San had delivered a major radio broadcast in which he vigorously attacked the communists. Despite this, doubts persisted about whether Aung San was truly anticommunist. Than Tun continued to visit Aung San at his residence, for example.[54] The elections, however, returned an overwhelming majority for the AFPFL: 166 seats, versus only 7 for the communists. The Americans nonetheless feared that the communists would reconcile with the AFPFL. U Kyaw Nyein, the member for home affairs in the government, assured them that this was only a remote possibility. Still, when Packer met with Aung San himself, the very first matter he raised was whether the communists would come back into the AFPFL. Aung San responded that they wanted to do so but only to "to stab him in the back." The possibility of their reentering the AFPFL, he told the consul general, "was completely dead."[55] Three days later Packer interviewed U Mya, the Member for Finance and Revenue and soon to be chairman of the Constituent Assembly, and again the first question he posed was about possible communist readmission to the AFPFL. Clearly this was a matter of central importance to the Americans. Mya thought there was no possibility of readmission immediately, though he did not close the door to eventual reentry. Packer gave the minister a *Newsweek* account of "communist tactics in the National Maritime Union in the United States."[56] Overall, however, the responses from Burmese leaders, especially Aung San, must have cheered the State Department.

Suspicions were not entirely obviated, however, for a month later the State Department expressed concern over the tentative design of a new Burmese flag which, they concluded, was similar to the Malayan communist flag. Was this intentional, the department wanted to know? And when Aung San was assassinated, Packer reported that if the communists were not involved in the assassination, they would likely "take advantage" of the situation. Within two weeks Packer was reporting that the communists were seeking a reunion with the AFPFL.[57]

One reason that the Americans thought that the Burmese might be susceptible to communist blandishments was because they suffered, as one diplomatic dispatch once put it, from a "lack of acumen with respect for business" as well a "lack of political and administrative experience." Aung San himself even now talked about nationalization of industry, at least eventually, which seemed suspiciously like communism. Other Burmese in the government tried to reassure Packer, informing him that any changes would be slow and carried out rationally, but the Americans were worried. They were not reassured when in October

U Nu, "spoke favorably of Russia's economic system" and even seemed to suggest that Burma would be better off it were closely tied to the Soviet Union (as Packer put it, as "a satellite state"), a view Packer attributed to a woeful Burmese ignorance of Soviet realities.[58]

Independence At Last

In October Nu and Attlee signed a treaty canceling loans and paving the way for a final vote in the British Parliament on the Burma Independence Bill. Churchill vigorously denounced it with arguments based, as the American embassy reported, on the "white man's burden" concept. The extreme nature of his speech repelled even some Conservatives, and the bill passed comfortably, with some Conservative support.[59]

To represent the United States at Burma's Independence Day ceremonies, the United States sent Edwin F. Stanton, the American ambassador to Thailand. On 3 January 1948, the day before independence, Stanton laid a wreath on the casket of Aung San. He also met with Foreign Minister U Tin Tut, an assassination attempt survivor. Tin Tut impressed Stanton as "a very keen and intelligent person" who was friendly toward the West.[60]

Actual independence came on 4 January at 4:20 a.m. (the day and time having been determined by astrologers). HMS *Birmingham*, symbolically the same ship that had recently arrived to carry away the last British governor, fired a salute. President Truman extended his best wishes and welcomed Burma "into the brotherhood of free and democratic nations." Prime Minister Nu impressed Stanton as intelligent and earnest, "obviously a dynamic and forceful personality." Stanton also clearly enjoyed seeing the French and Dutch representatives squirm when the foreign minister recognized the delegations from Vietnam and Indonesia and wished that they too could be independent.[61]

There was, however, also a note of apprehension, as all recognized that the road ahead would be difficult. Stanton, despite his many optimistic observations, noticed with foreboding all the guns in evidence. He came away with "an unforgettable impression of violence. One has the feeling that violence might flare up at any moment," he wrote.[62] It was a prescient observation.

THE LEAKY DERELICT

With independence, Burma was free but faced numerous difficulties, including divisions within the governing AFPFL, communist insurgencies, and ethnic tensions. As U Nu recalled, he "saw before him a derelict, with leaks in its gas tank and radiator, and punctures in front and rear tyres."[1] As for the United States, with the Cold War underway it was concerned about the leftist orientation of Burma's socialist leadership and wondered if the government had enough determination and ability to stop the spread of communism. Might it not be advisable to support the cause of the ethnic minorities, many of whom had fought for the Allies and were strongly anticommunist? Was it advisable to try and provide economic and even military assistance to the fledgling government? What policy should be adopted if the Americans disagreed among themselves about such matters? These were the major issues confronting the United States during the early years of Burma's independence.

By the time Burma became independent, World War II's Grand Alliance had completely collapsed, and the Cold War between the United States and its allies and the Soviet Union and its allies dominated international relations. The Cold War had not yet become entirely globalized, but in Burma, as in all of Southeast Asia, the most important American concern was whether "international communism," centered in Moscow, would extend its influence into the region. In neighboring China the anticommunist Nationalists were staggering and in danger of defeat, and there was growing concern about the future of Southeast Asia. Fear of communist advances was not the only American policy concern, but it was the most important, the one that influenced almost all other issues.

Ethnic Tensions and Other Internal Problems

Communist expansion was not so much on the minds of Burma's leaders, however. What counted for them was national unity. One of the major problems facing the new government of the Union of Burma was that, as David I. Steinberg put it eloquently, "Burma was a state without ever being a nation with an overarching ethos that promoted national unity." To journalist Hugh D. S. Greenway, the question of how much autonomy to give the ethnic minorities was "the near-lethal gene that independent Burma was born with."[2] Many of the minority peoples were hesitant to join a Burman-dominated state. Many Karens, one of the most important of the ethnic minority groups, were separatists, particularly those in the Karen National Union (KNU), led by Saw Ba U Gyi. On 3 February 1948, only a month after Burma's independence, the KNU informed Prime Minister Nu that the Karens wanted an independent state. Shortly thereafter the first reports of an armed rebellion reached the CIA. Although the reports were apparently untrue, the Burmese government was sufficiently alarmed that it sent a battalion of troops to the affected area. About the same time three thousand Karens drove through Rangoon demanding a separate state. The demonstration went off without incident, but almost immediately accusations appeared in the Burmese press that the "Anglo-Americans" were fomenting Karen unrest. The British ambassador strongly denied such charges, while the American embassy chose not to respond to these "absurd accusations."[3] Such rumors would surface again, however.

A complication for the United States was that the separatist Karen leadership was predominantly Christian (though both Christian and Buddhist Karens were split over the issue), converted mostly by the American Baptists. In 1948 there were five Baptist missionaries working in the Karen areas. The embassy believed that all of them were "discreet" and had offered no support to the separatists.[4] The Burmese government was never convinced of this, however, and it abrogated a military aviation agreement with the United States (there had been rumors of foreign aircraft dropping arms and supplies over Karen areas) and then refused a request from the National Geographic Society to undertake an expedition. In May the government put restrictions on foreign religious missions and temporarily prohibited new missionaries from coming to Burma.

Things heated up in March 1948 when the KNU gave the government one month to meet its demands for a separate state. U Nu met with the Karens for four days but without success. He then denounced the KNU and said that any separatist movements would be suppressed militarily. This, wrote the new American ambassador, J. Klahr Huddle, was the "first real AFPFL show of strength in face of various opposition movements."[5] Huddle, no friend of the KNU, was pleased.

In addition to Karen demands on the government, the Americans reported on a variety of other internal problems. Just a month after independence two cabinet members resigned due to strong disagreement between two important components of the AFPFL: the PVO and the socialists. The American embassy attributed this to class differences: the socialists were highly educated, whereas the PVO did not have the benefit of university-trained leaders. Sensing an opening, the Burmese communists launched verbal attacks on the AFPFL and some Burmese newspapers for being "tools of the Anglo-American imperialists." This resulted in a strong anticommunist response, including one by a Northwestern University–trained journalist, U Thein Tin, whom the communists characterized as "a dog fed and trained in America." Huddle believed that the communist attacks were effective, but he was pleased that a number of newspapers, some of them anticapitalist and usually unfriendly to the "Anglo-Americans," were taking on the communists editorially.[6] All of this indicated growing strains in the AFPFL. When it was originally formed, the AFPFL had been mostly leftist in its orientation, but during the war it has expanded to include those with more moderate views. Aung San had managed to hold the factions together, but now, only weeks after independence, the organization was finding it difficult to retain unity.

Things did not look good for the government. On 20 March Huddle noted the continuing crisis with the Karens, the PVOs, and the communists, along with rural unrest. The State Department was especially interested in the ambassador's observation that the communists had "redoubled noise and leader has publicly proclaimed Russia as defender pure democracy." The communists were still weaker than the AFPFL but appeared to be "gaining new adherents daily." The government leaders were "bewildered" and seemed not to know how to respond. Only seven weeks after independence, things seemed to be falling apart. U Nu himself wondered if his government would survive. It "had taken on the appearance of an old house with rotten supports," he later wrote.[7] Nu's initial hope to serve as prime minister for only six months evaporated, and he remained in charge of the country for most of the next fourteen years.

In addition to the apparent disarray in the government, the Americans became concerned that major government figures held anti-American and sometimes procommunist views. In March one Burmese informant ("a former alien employee of a United States Agency") told embassy officials that five members of the government controlled Nu. One of the "big five," U Ba Swe, whom the Americans regarded as an extreme leftist, was said to have told U Nu to prepare for a communist coup. Foreign Minister U Tin Tut allegedly nursed a grudge against an American-inflicted slight received some years before. The informant

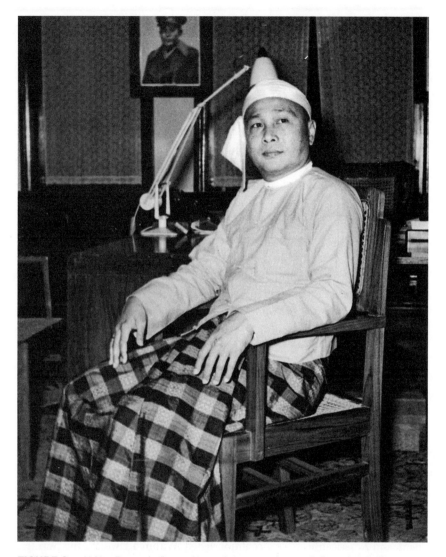

FIGURE 2.   U Nu, Burma's first prime minister and most influential civilian leader from 1948 to 1962. Note the photo on the wall of Burma's national hero, Aung San, who was assassinated in 1947. Louis J. Walinsky Papers, box 6, file 6-1, Cornell University Library. Photo by News Pix, News Photo Service, 389 Sparks St., Rangoon.

suggested better American propaganda in Burma, noting that the USIS (US Information Service) *Bulletin* was much too sophisticated to have any impact on the masses. He suggested that the United States assist some of the Burmese newspapers whose presses AFPFL-inspired mobs had destroyed.[8]

Late in March 1948 the PVO demanded, among other things, that the AFPFL seek a union of "progressive elements in country and form united front." When the State Department received this report, one official scribbled on the telegram, "looks as though communists have manipulated PVO's to work on their side." Further worrying the United States, U Nu stated that there was "no real difference" between the communists and the AFPFL, and he also reportedly approved a PVO proposal to legalize the radical Red Flag Communists. The Americans feared that this presaged an invitation to the communists to enter the government.[9]

As a result of such reports the Americans paid more attention to opposition leader Ba Maw and at least thought about his possible accession to power with American support. It is not clear how seriously the United States was about this, but it was not dismissed out of hand. Embassy officials had several discussions with knowledgeable persons, such as British Burma expert J. S. Furnivall and Edward Law-Yone, former OSS operative, translator at the American embassy, and founder and editor of the important newspaper *The Nation*. Despite Ba Maw's service for the Japanese, they evaluated him positively. In Washington, meanwhile, State Department officials met with David Tin Hla who had served with Ba Maw during the war. If Ba Maw had some encouragement from the United States and Britain, Tin Hla said, he could lead a movement to combat communism.[10] But ultimately the American embassy concluded that Ba Maw had little future in Burmese politics, though it continued to keep in touch with him and did not entirely rule out a possible reemergence. Later Ba Maw would emerge as an articulate and extreme critic of the United States and Britain.[11]

Communist Insurgency

On 26 March 1948 the communists began an insurrection against the government, and American fears of a coalition faded. Within a few days the Burmese government, after first accepting the PVO demand to work with the "progressive elements," moved forcefully against the communists, arrested a number of them, broke a communist-supported strike of petroleum workers, and closed communist newspapers. The "Commies underrated willingness and ability government take decisive action," reported Huddle approvingly, if perhaps a bit surprised.[12]

However, this was the start of a long-lasting armed communist insurgency. Train service had to be curtailed, telephone and telegraph services were interrupted, and bridges were destroyed. Significant casualties resulted. Within a month there were 158 incidents. The British government sent ammunition and three fighter bombers to Burma "more to impress insurgents," wrote Huddle, "than for actual bombing purposes."[13] The American embassy applauded the government's resolve.

The communist insurgency led to the first Burmese inquiry about possible American military aid. Huddle was supportive, but military aid was a complicated proposition since both the British and the Americans believed that Burma was primarily a British responsibility. Consequently Huddle delicately suggested to the Burmese that they turn first to that quarter. He would, he said, be happy to confer with the British about this and indeed met with the British ambassador that very evening. Both agreed that military aid was important and that the British should supply what they could. If they were unable to supply certain needed equipment, the United States could step in. But the Burmese flirtation was short lived. Two weeks later Burma's permanent secretary of the Foreign Office, James Barrington, an Anglo-Burmese who would later become ambassador to the United States, informed the American embassy that the government found it had sufficient supplies, though he thanked Huddle for his "sympathetic help."[14]

Despite the government's show of resolve, the Americans were worried about its determination to persevere. It was still not mature enough, they complained; the Foreign Office could not make decisions on even the most trivial matters without the consent of the Cabinet, and some in the government were strongly anti-British and suspicious of all foreigners. Huddle even raised the old canard about Burma's "childish" behavior. The country's attitude toward Britain, he wrote, "is a little like that of a truculent child who habitually kicks his father on the shins though dependent on him for support." In Huddle's opinion, all of this deeply embarrassed the able foreign minister, Tin Tut, but he was helpless. Similarly, Barrington was so discouraged that he reportedly considered resigning.[15]

Also, despite the current military actions against internal communists, the Americans remained concerned about U Nu's ideology, which, as Huddle put it in May, "bears considerable resemblance to the communist Party line." In a May Day address Nu praised Lenin, Stalin, and Marx, as well as the Chinese communists, even going so far as to defend Stalin's pact with the Nazis in 1939. At home his government was expropriating agricultural land and taking the economy in a socialist direction. His program, Huddle stated in a later telegram, "is frankly Communist." From the American perspective the government remained distressingly naive about the dangers of communism, a sentiment not assuaged when Nu announced Burma's intention to establish relations with the eastern European countries. Local communists were reportedly very excited at the prospect of a Soviet embassy soon to be established in Rangoon. In Huddle's view the Burmese leaders did not understand that "any state receiving Kremlin blessing must subordinate self to Moscow"; nor did Nu "comprehend that he is inviting new Russian 'imperialism' to replace old British 'imperialism.'"[16] What Huddle perhaps failed to grasp was the overriding sense of Burmese nationalism, which included a fundamental determination to see that the country's economic system was returned to Burmese control after years of imperialistic exploitation when the levers of economic power were controlled largely by foreigners.

Shortly thereafter Huddle was momentarily reassured when U Nu told him in confidence that his attempts to obtain "leftist unity" were only for domestic consumption, a way of trying to keep extremist elements in line. Should the government break up, he suggested, the situation would be much more serious. Huddle was willing to give him the benefit of the doubt, concluding that Nu genuinely hoped to establish a democratic socialist state that was not connected with international communism. But the Americans still wondered if he could accomplish his goal.[17]

Then, on 13 June 1948 U Nu spoke to an audience estimated at ten thousand people contrasting the AFPFL and the BCP, which he now denounced. He would not countenance efforts at unity with communists, except with those who renounced their ways, but the communists were not interested in unity anyway, he declared. They had decided on armed insurrection, which the government would suppress. One part of the speech that must have commended itself to the Americans was Nu's insistence that he sought friendly relations with all three major powers: the United States, Great Britain, and the Soviet Union. This contrasted, he said, with the communists who only wanted good relations with the USSR. The speech did, however, emphasize the strongly leftist orientation of the government, and this produced negative American reactions. Diplomat Henry Grady commented (inaccurately) that Burma seemed to be "behind the iron curtain."[18]

Perhaps as a result of these concerns, Foreign Minister Tin Tut quickly approved the sale of four houses to the American embassy, something the embassy had long sought. He also announced that he wanted to travel to both Great Britain and the United States to persuade them that Burma was not going communist. The AFPFL also expelled the extremist wing of the PVO (the "White Band" or "White Arm Band": in 1948 the PVO split, the Yellow Band being more moderate and supportive of the government), many of whose members had tried to join the communist insurgency. Many were arrested.[19]

However, the military situation soon sharply deteriorated. In July efforts to create a leftist unity program failed, and the White Band PVO went into armed opposition and seized significant territory in the Irrawaddy valley. Two of the five battalions of Burma Rifles mutinied. Thein Pe, a prominent leftist political leader, disappeared, apparently to join the communist insurgency (though he was soon arrested). Most Europeans fled from Bassein, although the five American missionaries there refused to leave; the American embassy urged the evacuation of women and children. The city of Maubin was attacked and the city treasury robbed. A battalion of Burmese soldiers deserted en masse and captured the town of Prome. All in all the government's position was "steadily weakening," and it could not possibly suppress the communist insurgency in the foreseeable future. In mid-August the British Foreign Office reported that two more Burmese battalions had "renounced allegiance" to the government and were advancing on Rangoon itself.[20] The priority now was to save the capital city. The British had a cruiser standing by to evacuate their citizens if needed, and the American embassy worked closely with them to develop evacuation plans.

In this context it was not altogether surprising that American officials in London agreed to speak with a former British lieutenant colonel, J. C. Tulloch, who was deeply involved with the Karens, claimed credit for organizing their rebellion, and suggested that a communist victory in Burma was imminent. In response the KNU and allied groups were about to launch a coup d'état, which would, he said, have very wide support. Would the United States secretly finance the KNU, he asked. When told that that would not happen, he asked what would be the attitude of the United States toward the new government when it emerged. He received an equivocal response.[21] Tulloch had exaggerated the degree of popular support across Burma for the KNU, and the United States was not likely to become involved in any case, since it was supporting the government in its efforts to suppress all the rebellions. But the Americans were unquestionably concerned about the future.

Burma's Arms Request

Indicating the seriousness of the situation, the Burmese government again requested arms from the United States. The Americans were more strongly tempted this time but still cautious. U Nu thought a purely commercial transaction could be arranged, and seemed surprised when the embassy informed him that the US government had to be concerned about the arms ending up in the hands of a hostile government, something that the Americans feared would certainly happen if the communists came to power. U Nu said that that would not happen as long as he was prime minister. The insurrection had clearly soured him on the communists (U Nu had "certainly learned by bitter expedience that cooperation with the Communists is impossible," reported embassy official R. Austin Acly, despite the fact that Nu's own ideological views were, at least in American eyes, not much different from those of the communists.)[22] But Acly recommended delaying actions on the arms request.

Within a few weeks the situation improved, as the communist rebellion was brought under some control, in part due to the military's Sandhurst-educated commander in chief, Smith Dun, a Karen, "purportedly named after Jimmy Stewart's character in *Mr. Smith Goes to Washington*."[23] Still, the communist insurrection gave the Karen rebels an opening to push their own demands for either complete independence, or at least autonomy. A limited insurgency broke out at the end of August 1948. The Karens were strongly anticommunist and would not consider an alliance with the communists at this point, but the communist insurrection did strengthen their bargaining position, particularly since the Burmese military was dependent on Smith Dun's abilities.

Neither the government nor the Karen rebels fully trusted either the United States or the United Kingdom. The government suspected that they might be secretly supporting the Karens. According to a British report, "some Americans," supposedly former members of the OSS, were in fact supporting the KNU. (There were unquestionably British citizens, like Tulloch, involved.) On the other hand the government again requested arms from the United States and received a sympathetic hearing. The Karens, who were "almost pathetically fond of British and Americans," were reportedly "shocked and surprised" to learn about the Burmese government's request, understandably fearing the arms might be used against them.[24]

In the end the United States declined to supply the arms. Though it supported the government, it preferred a peaceful settlement with the Karens and was open to the prospect of an autonomous Karen state. "Karens more stable and much less corrupt than Burmans," Acly wrote. "Hence prospects administrative success autonomous Karen state at least as good as Burmese prospect."[25]

The insurrections had taken their toll on U Nu. When Acly met with him on 4 September 1948 he noted a marked change in his mental and physical condition. He "looked thin, tired and run-down and showed a nervousness that I have never seen before." Then, just as things could not get much worse, on 17 September Tin Tut, who had just stepped down as foreign minister, was mortally wounded by a grenade thrown at his car. Given his moderate views, the Americans suspected that the communists or other leftists were responsible. (Later the Socialists and Yellow Band PVO faction were accused.) "Assassination removes one of the few remaining links with political realism," lamented Acly, and had dealt a "serious blow" to a democratic future for the country.[26] Furthermore the Karens had taken over some districts, such actions being perhaps the result of local initiatives rather than at the behest of the KNU.

A month after Tin Tut's assassination the new foreign minister, U Kyaw Nyein, met in New York with Secretary of State George Marshall. He stated that his government was strongly anticommunist, arguing that Burma, given its strong nationalism, its religion, and its lack of a proletariat, would never go communist. He again requested American small arms to combat the insurgents but was again turned down.[27]

But by now the American embassy in Rangoon was increasingly disillusioned with the current socialist government. American diplomats considered it unpopular and unreliable ideologically. There had been some differences of opinion on the latter score in May and June, "but by July or August everyone had come to accept the view that there is not a great deal of ideological difference between the Socialists and the Communists." The guiding American policy document, written in July, and entitled, "Government of Burma Remains Non-Communist," was now badly out of date. Given its fear of a near communist government, the embassy was pleased that Ba Maw had once again entered public life as a patron of the new National Culture Centre. Some 750 people came to the center's opening celebration at Ba Maw's residence, where the festivities resembled "an old fashioned revival meeting." Although the occasion was not overtly political, most people understood the event to be an indirect attack on the government. Soon thereafter the British ambassador told Acly that Burmese officials had accused him of encouraging Ba Maw. Acly's denial was probably correct, but privately he and the other Americans wished Ba Maw well.[28]

The Americans were less pleased when, a month later, Ba Maw ("probably Burma's most clever politician and most complete opportunist") lurched leftward. While still critical of the government, he had apparently concluded that the communists would win, not only in China but in all of Southeast Asia. The United States, he implied, would start World War III when it suited its interests to do so. By 1951, Ba Maw "continuously mouthed communist slogans," reported an embassy official.[29]

The Karen Rebellion

Meanwhile the immediate problem facing the government seemed to be the potential for escalating violence with the Karens. There were reports of Burman massacres of Karens and vice versa. On 20 November 1948 U Nu met with representatives of the Karen National Defense Organization (KNDO), the military wing of the KNU, and delivered what the American embassy called "a very statesman-like speech" wherein he "pleaded for a cessation to the madness between Burmans and Karens which was bound to lead to unspeakable misery." However, unless the government was willing to give the Karens a separate or autonomous state, which it was not, a peaceful resolution was unlikely. By early December Acly reported that "large scale civil war is possible in near future." An official in the British Foreign Office reported that in the Karen area life had reverted to medieval conditions. There were mass killings and, he said, Baptist Karens were "engaged in a bloody struggle for power with Karen Catholics."[30]

In the Burmese media the "Anglo-Americans" continued to be charged with responsibility for the unrest.

The situation deteriorated sharply when "socialist controlled police levies" massacred "at least 80 Karens" who were attending a Christmas Eve service in the Mergui district. A CIA report asserted that neither U Nu nor Karen leaders wanted violence but both were unable to control their "more extremist followers." The result, the CIA concluded, was that communal violence promised "to be more ferocious and destructive than any of the politically inspired insurrections now in progress."[31] Things were about to spin out of control. Aung San's assassination was beginning to look extremely unfortunate, since he was perhaps the only person who might have been able to hold the country together.

With the failure of the negotiations in December 1948, a full-scale Karen rebellion began in January 1949. Many soldiers, including most Karen-dominated regiments, defected from the Burmese army. The American embassy put much of the blame on Nu. He was "making a desperate bid to keep his government in power at the expense of internal injustice and international mendacity." Increasing numbers of Burman and Karen villages were sacked and burned and their inhabitants murdered. By the end of January 1949 almost all Karen students had left Rangoon University and hospitals in the capital, while Burmans had moved out of Karen districts. The situation was so bad that the American embassy formally suggested that the State Department look seriously at an international intervention to "halt genocide already going on." The State Department responded that the Convention on the Prevention and Punishment of the Crime of Genocide had not yet been ratified, and even if it had been, genocide would be difficult to prove. In any event, the department wanted to proceed cautiously to avoid any suggestion of interference in Burma's internal affairs, something about which the government was especially sensitive. Perhaps, the department thought, India might be able to help ameliorate the situation—a questionable suggestion in view of the Burmese perception of India as scarcely less imperialistic than the "Anglo-Americans."[32]

On 20 and 21 January 1949 government troops deliberately destroyed a number of American Baptist buildings in Maubin, resulting in an embassy request to the Burmese Foreign Office for a formal investigation. Then on the last day of January, they attacked the Baptist Karen location known as Seminary Hill in the Rangoon suburb of Insein (mortar shells fell "all over camp"), as well as the Karen district of Sanchaung in Rangoon itself.[33] The next day the State Department approved the emergency use of an American C-47 aircraft stationed in Thailand for an evacuation if needed.

In the wake of the Mergui atrocity, Smith Dun resigned as Army chief, which resulted in more Karen soldiers leaving. The revolt was now very serious, as the

Karens controlled several cities. Within a few weeks, thirty-one cities, including Mandalay, were controlled by one or another of the revolutionary groups. Rangoon itself was saved only because Chin soldiers remained loyal.[34]

Smith Dun's replacement was Ne Win, who would become "the most important, if not the most efficacious, figure in post-independence Burma."[35] Described by Thant Myint-U as a "playboy, tyrant, numerologist, and one time post office clerk, a man who understood his countrymen's psyche well enough to wield nearly total power for the better part of thirty years," Ne Win had come of age with the remarkable group of nationalist students in Rangoon. A colleague of Aung San, he found his calling in the military and led the Burma Independence Army. One of the reasons that he ended as a soldier was that he had failed in the coal business, done in by his competitors, all of whom where Indians. It was "a bitter lesson" and one that undoubtedly accounted in part for his later decision to oust most foreigners from the country and put the economy into Burmese hands.[36]

With Smith Dun's departure, the possibility of an "amicable settlement between Karens and Burmans increasingly remote," observed the CIA. When on 9 February 1949 the American chargé d'affaires called on U Nu at his home, "gunfire from the week-old battle between government forces and Karen insurgents" was "clearly audible." Rangoon itself was in danger, besieged not just by the KNDO but also by PVO groups opposed to the government, and was nearly taken. Two weeks later the embassy reported that the Karens could probably take Mandalay if they wished (which they later did, cooperating with the BCP), and the State Department directed the embassy to express "serious concern" about the safety of American citizens, especially in the town of Maymyo, where eight American missionaries were in danger.[37] Indeed, there was some fear that what was commonly termed a "race war" would turn into a religious one. There had been a number of incidents in which Christians had been deliberately targeted and killed. If this trend continued missionaries and Burmese Christians might be targets of undisciplined troops.

By this point it was the embassy's clear view that there was no military solution to the Karen insurgency. The embassy believed that the government did not control even half of the country. Foreign military assistance would not succeed in ending the insurgency. With aid the military might have some success driving the Karens out of various headquarters, the embassy conceded, but there was "no reason to believe that it would enable them to pacify a country-side infested with stubborn Karen guerrillas." The only solution was to create a largely autonomous Karen state.[38]

The situation continued to deteriorate, and early in March 1949 the embassy urged sixteen missionaries in central Burma to leave. The missionaries had declined previous warnings, and Acly thought that few if any would respond this time. On 8 and 9 March, however, the embassy's C-47 evacuated five Americans and a number of British citizens from Maymyo, including a Baptist missionary who had been wounded in the neck by a stray bullet.

The British Commonwealth extended an offer of good offices to help bring peace. After initially spurning the offer, the government changed its mind. On 5 and 6 April peace talks were held, the Karens attending reluctantly and suspiciously. On 7 April a deal was reached, involving the surrender of the Karen forces, but it fell apart later that same day when the KNDO refused to accept the terms negotiated. The fighting resumed almost immediately.

The American embassy sympathized with the Karens' rejection of the agreement. Though it appeared a reasonable compromise on its face, in fact it meant "the abject surrender of the Karens, without adequate safeguards, to the uncertain but probably oppressive mercy of the Burman authorities." The embassy even suggested that the government might not be acting in good faith but wanted to assuage the British because it was seeking a loan from the Commonwealth. In any event, both the Commonwealth and the British decided to extend military and economic aid, reasoning that it was in their interest to see the current government survive, even though the prospects of success appeared dim.[39]

The Americans feared that Burma might well disintegrate, with China and Thailand controlling portions of the country. For the United States, as well as for Great Britain, the most important policy goal was to try to prevent Burma from being overrun by the Chinese communists, who were then on the verge of a final victory in China. This meant that, however much the Americans might sympathize with the Karens or other minority groups opposed to the government (and the American ambassador to Burma conceded that "most of the Anglo-American community," including many "English and American missionaries and businessmen," was pro-Karen), they wanted to persuade the rebels to join forces with the government to resist the communists.

One Karen leader challenged an American official on this point. Did the American really believe that the Nu government truly opposed the communists, he asked? The American conceded that the government had no philosophical problem with communism but would oppose the communists as a "foreign menace" intent on enslaving them "with a ruthless domination which would make the Japanese regime seem like child's play." This was the position implicitly taken by the British as well when they decided to assist the Burmese government with both financial and military support. They did not relish backing away from their traditional friendship with the Karens, but the threat of Chinese communism moved them to back the regime, even though they knew that the arms they provided would be used against the Karens if no peace settlement was reached. M. E. Dening, the British Foreign Office official in charge of Southeast Asian affairs, told American diplomats that the Karens "constituted the number one problem in Burma" and that a united Burma was the only solution.[40] The British would encourage a settlement but would not demand it as a condition for supplying arms. Whether the Karens could be persuaded to settle their differences with the government and join in a united front against the communists, seemed unlikely, however.

Burma Looks Westward

Meanwhile the civil war in China was coming to its inevitable end, as Mao Zedong's forces pushed Chiang Kai-shek's forces ever farther south. The Burmese watched this development warily, concerned that the victorious Chinese would extend assistance to the Burmese communists. On the one hand this encouraged the Burmese to adopt a policy of strict neutrality in the Cold War. Given that the Burmese shared a boundary of over thirteen hundred miles with what was about to become the most populous communist state in the world, they would want to remain on at least tolerably good terms with it. Thus Burma became one of the most determinedly nonaligned, neutralist countries in the world during the entire Cold War. But Burma also needed to build up its military strength, not only to combat the various insurgencies but also to be able to present a creditable challenge to potential pressures from China. For the moment this latter concern trumped its go-it-alone attitude, and Burma took a new look at possible military assistance from Britain and the United States. A further retreat came with the socialist government's decision to allow foreign firms to participate in the development of Burma's natural resources. This "turn toward Western capitalistic aid" indicated a significant change, wrote Huddle. It involved much loss of face and consequently demonstrated considerable "moral courage," which only those who understood "oriental psychology" could appreciate. Whether or not "oriental psychology" explained the shift, Huddle was right to note its extraordinary nature. Traditionally suspicious of capitalism because of its close connection with British imperial rule in the past, from its very beginnings Burma was dedicated to some kind of socialist economy. Aung San himself set the pattern in 1947, and it continued in a general sense to inform Burmese economic policy through 1988.[41]

Given Burma's apparent new openness, Huddle wanted American firms to be ready to assist if requested. The results could be enormously significant. If something could be done "to resuscitate this promising country and improve its productivity and world utility, as well as save it for an abundant Burmese posterity," he wrote, "it should be tried." Two days later in a personal letter Huddle wrote that the Burmese had "suddenly come alive to the menace of a communistic China."[42]

The CIA was inclined to believe that the change in Burma's policy was more likely a matter of self-preservation than a change of heart. Western countries were currently the only source of assistance.[43] Whatever the Burmese motivation, Washington doubtless welcomed the change. The government's new attitude toward the West was evident in July and August 1949 when both Minister of Defence Ne Win and Foreign Minister E Maung visited Washington. E Maung told reporters that his government was "determined to halt the spread of communism in Burma," and even suggested that Burma might join an anticommunist alliance. He feared that once the communists had consolidated their power in China they would claim a portion of Burma. Ne Win, for his part, said little of substance. But it is noteworthy that his expenses were paid by a private American concern, Ameritex. And in October U Kyaw Nyein, a former foreign minister with socialist views that approached "communism itself" (according to the American ambassador), told an editor of *Time* magazine that if he were in the government he would urge taking defensive measures along the Chinese border.[44]

All of this demonstrated how important Burma was in American eyes at this time. Events in Burma, the Americans felt, would have a critical influence on the whole of Southeast Asia. If Burma (and Indochina) could be kept out of the communist orbit, the rest of Southeast Asia stood a good chance of remaining free and supportive of the democratic West. Whether the government could bring stability and prosperity to the country and would thus be able to counter communist subversion and aggression was still in doubt, however. If present trends continued, predicted an embassy official in October 1949, the result would be "a gradual sinking of Burma into a progressively primitive condition."[45]

The United States wanted to help prevent this dire prediction from coming to pass. In October policy options were presented to Secretary of State Dean Acheson. American interest in Burma was simply stated: to prevent communist encroachment in the region, there should be a stable government oriented toward the United States and the British Commonwealth, one that could maintain internal order, resist external communist pressures, and rehabilitate the society and economy. To this end the United States should be prepared to extend financial and technical assistance. It should also provide military aid and encourage the formation of a regional anticommunist pact. Finally, the United States should intensify "the use of intelligence services," step up propaganda distribution, and engage in "appropriate . . . covert activities."[46]

Shortly thereafter Ne Win (according to many Americans the man who wielded actual power in Burma) began to court the British Military Mission, which he and the government had previously demonized. A man who strongly disliked socializing, Ne Win even invited all of the British officers to dinner. The American ambassador speculated that Ne Win's recent visits to the United States and Britain accounted for his apparent change of heart—though the ambassador cautioned that he just might be playing a double game.[47]

Perceptions of Burma's Fragility

Over the next several weeks, however, the Americans found little to cheer about. There was "little reason for optimism over Burma," reported Ambassador Huddle. The British were exhibiting a "defeatist complex" toward Burma, he thought. They wanted India to come to Burma's aid, a suggestion that Huddle believed was silly. The Burmese did not like or trust the Indians, and if India did intervene in Burma, it would probably mean the end of Burmese independence. More likely, however, was Chinese absorption of Burma. If Mao Zedong were to "play his cards properly," Huddle speculated, the Chinese could engulf Burma with "peaceful penetration and gradual assimilation." The ambassador used this dire scenario to call, almost emotionally, for an intelligent and long-term constructive American policy toward the country. However dark the immediate future looked, he wrote, Burma still held promise, and its people were "too amiable and potentially capable" to be "cast aside as lost." It would take years, perhaps generations. But the Americans should persevere with "patience, tolerance, and tact."[48]

The Burmese embassy in Washington understood well how the Americans saw Burma. The United States had initially planned to give aid to Thailand, Burma, and other Southeast Asian countries but had then shifted its attention to India as the "citadel against Communist expansion." But with the collapse of China, and with India pursuing a neutralist course, the United States had swung back to providing aid for the region's countries, including Burma. The figure of $75 million for the region was said to be on the table. The entire matter would be the subject of a forthcoming conference in Bangkok of regional American diplomats in January 1950 to be chaired by Ambassador-at-large Philip C. Jessup.[49] The Burmese analysis of the American position, however, did not take into account American perceptions that Burma was very fragile.

The continuing Karen insurgency was a major cause of the fragility, and Acheson ordered Jessup to tell the Burmese that solving the Karen problem was essential to rehabilitating the country. The wisdom (as the Americans saw it) of this advice was apparent within days. The embassy reported that Chinese Communist troops were massed on the border of Kengtung State and threatening to cross into Burma to capture an estimated five thousand Nationalist Chinese stragglers who had fled to Burma. Kengtung officials had frantically asked the Burmese government to send troops to the border, but none were available. The matter was sufficiently serious that Acheson was personally informed of the situation. "I believe the situation is developing very rapidly towards a Communist orientation on the part of the Burmese Government," Assistant Secretary of State George McGhee, who had just visited Burma, informed Acheson, "or failing that, an invasion of Burma by the Communist Armies for the purpose of taking over the country."[50] It was a truly alarming report, and contingency plans were again made to evacuate Americans.

The situation was sufficiently serious that State Department officials once again prepared a lengthy memorandum with policy recommendations for Acheson. If China chose, they informed the secretary, it could take over Burma and thus gain control of a strategic location with considerable natural resources and a valuable rice surplus. This would "represent a major strategic victory for Chinese and International Communism" and put the communists in a position to gain control of other countries. In an early expression of the domino theory, Acheson was told that a communist Burma would immediately endanger "India, Pakistan, Indo-China, Malaya, and Siam." Fortunately, Burma was not yet lost and a relatively small American investment might have value. Interestingly, the memo did not suggest that such an investment would actually save Burma, but it would represent "insurance against failing to do those things within present policies and capabilities which might have forestalled Communist subversion of Burma." (No doubt this was a reaction to the withering criticism from those, mostly Republican, politicians who had so strongly objected to what they regarded that the administration's insipid China policy.) In any event, the memorandum suggested that, within the context of cooperation with the British, the United States should "utilize all available methods and appropriated funds to the maximum extent possible" to help Burma retain its independence. Before the memo got to Acheson, Assistant Secretary of State Dean Rusk crossed out the words "all" and "to the maximum extent possible." Still, the memo represented a strong plea for assistance to Burma, using funds from the Mutual Defense Assistance Act of 1949, the Fulbright Act, the Smith-Mundt Act (which concerned propaganda and public diplomacy), and the Point Four program (for development assistance).[51]

Of course, even if the United States wanted to extend assistance to Burma, it was not certain that the Burmese, who were suspicious of any foreign involvement in their country, would even request it. In fact, in December 1949 Burma was the first country outside of the communist bloc to recognize the new People's Republic of China. This was not because Burma felt an affinity with the PRC. On the contrary, the Burmese government feared a Chinese invasion and hoped to "avert communist Chinese hostility." Chinese coolness toward Burma even after Burma's early recognition and its breaking of ties with Taiwan did not alleviate this fear. In the fervor of revolutionary success, China believed—Dulles-like—that there could be no neutralism, that so-called "neutral" countries like Burma were pro-Western.[52]

Consequently it was not all that surprising that when Ambassador Jessup met with Nu on 8 February 1950 he found the prime minister open to accepting "foreign capital" in the near future. The following evening Ne Win threw a party for Jessup, attended by "all important Socialists and AFPFL leaders only." The conversation was frank and friendly, and Ne Win insisted that both the KNDO revolt and the communists would be defeated.[53]

Then, only a few days later, Ne Win's confidant, Bo Setkya, met with an American diplomat in Rangoon and made an astounding offer: Ne Win would consider fully aligning Burma with the West, provided the United States would extend long-term military and economic assistance. Setkya did not hide the fact that this offer was due in part to Burmese suspicions of British intentions, but he hoped that American assistance might also result in British aid of a sort that would be acceptable to Burma. Should the United States agree, Ne Win was prepared to begin discussions at once. The State Department responded almost immediately that it was open to exploring technical assistance of various types.[54]

A week later Ne Win repeated his interest in military aid to *New York Times* correspondent Robert Trumbull. Not only did the reclusive general speak with Trumbull at length, but he invited him on a two day "up-country" tour. Trumbull found Ne Win courteous, friendly, and frank. Ne Win indicated that he would like American assistance and trainers for the Burmese armed forces, in part because he intensely disliked the British and did not trust the British Training Mission.[55] Presumably he also remained suspicious of Chinese intentions.

It was now very clear that Burma was interested in aid, and the United States was interested in (though still cautious about) providing it. On 5 March 1950 the State Department's Bureau of Near Eastern Affairs, noting the need to provide "some tangible assurance that the U.S. has not conceded Burma to the communist sphere," proposed expending over $5 million in Mutual Defense Assistance funds to Burma, with the lion's share going to supply armed river patrol boats. The embassy, though it remained uncertain about Ne Win's ultimate objectives, felt the aid was very important for political reasons. Failure to provide it would confirm Burmese suspicions that the United States supported the Karens or in any event lacked confidence in the Burmese government.[56]

The Griffin Mission and American Aid

It happened that a special American economic assistance mission, led by R. Allen Griffin, director of the Far East Program Division of the Economic Cooperation

Administration, was just then traveling to Southeast Asia. Griffin believed that his mission was primarily a way to counter Republican and China Lobby charges that the Truman administration had taken insufficient action against communism in Asia. His assignment, recalled Griffin, would demonstrate that the administration was "going to do something about Southeast Asia." Griffin, though a Republican, liked Secretary Acheson and supported the mission's objectives. Persuaded by the British high commissioner to Southeast Asia, whom he met in Singapore, Griffin decided to include Burma on his itinerary.[57] He met with Burmese officials on 24 March 1950 and remained in Burma until 4 April. The Americans explored with the Burmese their economic and technical needs. Military aid was not a part of the mission's mandate, Griffin emphasized, and they did not discuss it.

U Hla Maung, Burma's secretary of the Ministry of Finance and Revenue, wrote later that the government welcomed the Griffin Mission "with open arms." Griffin had a very different recollection. He "had the gravest difficulty in being able to talk with the Burmese" who "were sort of like wild animals skittering away in front of us." But if some Burmese officials were uneasy about negotiating foreign assistance, they were by their own contemporary account "highly pleased" with the meeting.[58]

Interestingly, Griffin urged the United States to stop considering Burma primarily a British area of responsibility. A successful aid program, he argued, should be independent of the British. The new ambassador, David McKendree Key, agreed with Griffin with respect to economic assistance. The State Department concurred, having obtained British agreement for a "detached and independent" approach.[59]

In May the New York Times reported that the Griffin mission had recommended about $11 million in aid for Burma. About one-third of the total amount would go to agricultural projects; about one-sixth to public health; and the rest would be directed toward education, industry, transportation, communications, commodities, economic planning, and public administration planning.[60]

There is no question that by this point Burma was a matter of major concern to the United States. When Jessup reported to the State Department early in April 1950 and reviewed his travels to many Asian countries, he concluded that "Burma and Indochina are the key points." Two weeks after Jessup's report Burma's foreign minister sent him a personal letter requesting $50 million to support two projects: mass education, including translating works of "world literature" into Burmese; and rehabilitation of former insurgents by enrolling them in something like the New Deal's Civilian Conservation Corps. The foreign minister argued that a healthy society in Burma would have important positive ramifications for the economic and political health of all of Southeast Asia.

If the rehabilitation project were to fail, he warned, Burma would probably re-lapse "into that state of insecurity and frustration that has been our bitter lot for the past two years."[61] This was Burma's first formal request for economic assis-tance from the United States, and it confirmed that Burma had decided to eschew its previous isolation. It also provided the United States with an opportunity to move Burma toward (if not into) the Western sphere.

Two other matters provided some optimism about Burma. For one thing, gov-ernment forces had recently made notable progress against the rebels, including capturing the Karen "capital" of Toungoo. The government was now confident of victory in the near future. Herbert Spivack, the perceptive second secretary at the American embassy in Rangoon, was more cautious, noting that the Karen forces had not "experienced anything approximating a major military disaster." Still, the capture of Toungoo was a psychological victory. The government also appeared to have the communist rebels on the run.[62] By late May 1950 the government proclaimed optimistically that it was on the verge of "complete victory." Second, the more extreme elements in the Socialist Party, which controlled the govern-ment, were about to be purged, making it easier for the government to work with the United States and other Western powers. They would have been even more optimistic if they had known that the Burmese and the Chinese remained very suspicious of each other.

Meanwhile, however, Burma had not yet received any final word on American economic assistance and was becoming impatient. Officials were disheartened at the Griffin mission's recommendation of reportedly only $11 million, and Jessup replied in a noncommittal way to a Burmese request for $50 million. He assured them only that their request would receive "most careful consideration."[63]

In the middle of June the United States adopted a formal policy statement with respect to Burma that called for expanded economic, technical, and mili-tary assistance. The aid was frankly political. The United States hoped to help Burma achieve a stable government that would be aligned with itself, and it wanted to increase Burma's capacity to resist domestic communist insurgents and communist "infiltration or invasion from China." To this end the United States would furnish the Burmese with military supplies that were not avail-able from Great Britain, and it would also bring several Burmese officers to the United States for training. The next month the Economic Cooperation Admin-istration announced the formation of a special technical and economic mis-sion to Burma, headed by Abbot Low Moffat. Two specialists were sent out in July; Moffat himself arrived in September and remained for two years. Much of the focus was on agricultural assistance, including control of livestock diseases, soil conservation, agricultural extension work, flood control, and at least twelve other related projects.[64]

In terms of military assistance, since March 1950 the Americans had been considering offering the Burmese ten Coast Guard cutters for river patrol duty. When the idea was floated informally, Ne Win commented that in view of the urgent need for such craft the offer was a "godsend." In April Ne Win brought up the issue of other kinds of military assistance, but early in May the United States determined that it would provide only the patrol boats. The British should provide other military needs. On 12 May 1950 President Truman authorized the expenditure of $3.5 million for Burma under the Mutual Defense Assistance Act of 1949 to purchase the boats.[65]

Adoption of the June policy paper and the related decisions to move ahead with economic and military assistance marked a high point in the bilateral relationship. The agreement caused internal turmoil in Burma, as leftists attacked the government. Much to the delight of the Americans, however, Nu strongly attacked "leftist extremists," and both the government and the Burmese press (communist newspapers excepted) supported the American response to the North Korean invasion of South Korea on 25 June.[66]

Tensions Emerge

The good feelings changed dramatically in August 1950, particularly on the military assistance side, when Burma received word that a team that had planned to survey Burma's military needs would not come after all. The Burmese were told that this was because of the Korean War: the mission needed to go instead to Manila and Bangkok because the Filipinos and the Thais were sending troops to Korea, whereas Burma was not. The real reason was that the United States had learned that Ne Win, who had previously leaned toward the United States, now intended to rebuff the mission publically on its arrival. Ne Win reportedly claimed that he would not allow the Americans "to study Burmese military activities."[67]

Although Ne Win had wanted the military assistance, he objected to the lack of consultation. The Americans had simply announced that the mission would visit Burma, and it was "quite understandable," wrote an embassy official, that the government would feel that the mission "was foisted on Burma." Ne Win had no intention of allowing the mission into Burma without consultation.[68] Perhaps more fundamentally, Ne Win was angry at Nationalist Chinese activities in the north and was already very suspicious that the Americans were involved. Finally, his relations with the British Supply Mission were at an all time low, and he disliked American coordination of military aid decisions with the British.

In any event, the United States concluded that there were too many other countries that wanted American aid to justify wasting time and energy trying to push military aid on those that were raising obstacles. Discussion of military aid to Burma was therefore suspended "indefinitely," except for the already promised ten river boats. There was even an attempt to divert the boats to Burma's perennial antagonist Thailand, but Key intervened, arguing that the United States had political reasons and a moral obligation to provide the craft. These were finally authorized in November 1950, and a few Burmese naval personnel were brought to the United States for training.[69]

In the meantime Ne Win resigned from the cabinet. The reasons were primarily internal ones. Ne Win had grown increasingly disillusioned with U Nu and was beginning to explore the prospects of a military coup, but frustration with American and British policies toward Burma were probable contributing factors.[70] All in all it was a frustrating summer for Burma in terms of possible American aid.

Despite these tensions, on 13 September 1950 the United States and Burma did sign a bilateral agreement for $10 million in nonmilitary developmental assistance. The Burmese government understood this to be a first installment. Despite some criticism in Burma (from those who complained that Burma had "sold herself to the United States for a meager $10,000,000)," the agreement (which Burma ratified on 5 October) was about the only bright spot in the relationship by this point and was therefore one of the few matters that could be commented upon when the new ambassador to the United States, James Barrington, presented his credentials to President Truman the following month.[71]

Rumors of a possible coup by Ne Win surfaced in November 1950. While Ambassador Key was unable to determine whether there actually was a plot, a planned gathering of the armed forces in January 1951 provided the perfect cover for Ne Win, if he were to mount a coup. What is noteworthy is how interested the State Department was in such a possible development. How would a coup affect relations with the United States? How would it impact the economic assistance and USIS programs? With whom would Ne Win associate? Would he be inclined to support moderate or extremist tendencies? What would his leadership mean in terms of military cooperation with the United States? How would he look upon the Chinese Communists and the British? Clearly the prospect of a coup intrigued the State Department. There was certainly no suggestion that the United States ought to discourage it.[72]

Soon, however, Key threw cold water on the idea of American support. Ne Win was too irresponsible, too unstable, too "anti-occidental." "On balance," Key wrote, "we feel that seizure of power by Ne Win would be a definite blow to Burmese-US relations and would place these on a precarious footing." In light of

Ne Win's recent willingness to align Burma with the United States, this was a remarkable analysis. Neither Key nor the British ambassador had any real evidence that a coup might be in the works, and ultimately Ne Win concluded that he had enough influence in the government to make a coup unnecessary. But later in the year a formal National Intelligence Estimate concluded that a Ne Win coup was "a continuing possibility."[73]

THE TRIAL OF THE "BURMA SURGEON"

Aside from continuing American concern over international communist expansion and whether the U Nu government was sufficiently aware of the dangers, there were two other issues that emerged in 1950 that threatened American-Burmese relations. One was the growing problem of remnant Nationalist Chinese forces in northern Burma, supported covertly by the CIA, which made it difficult for Burma and the United States to maintain close and friendly relationships—an issue that is dealt with in the following chapter. The second, and not entirely unrelated problem was the trial of Gordon S. Seagrave, the iconic "Burma Surgeon," for high treason.

The Seagrave trial focused renewed attention on the unusual importance of the American missionary community in Burma, compared to other Southeast Asian countries, and revealed the deep suspicions among the Burmese that the missionaries favored the ethnic minorities and even supported their armed rebellions. Some were thought to be spies. The government's hostility toward them was unusual in Southeast Asia. The trial also revealed a subdued, almost unspoken conflict between Seagrave and the US government. The United States had determined to support the government of Burma in its fights with the minorities. Thus Seagrave, who might otherwise have been a perfect Cold War icon for the United States, could not serve that purpose since he, like other missionaries, sympathized with the minority groups and deeply disliked the U Nu government.

If the trial pointed out the exceptional missionary factor in Burma, the reaction in the American public to the trial revealed common Cold War attitudes and prejudices. Putting the saintly doctor on trial supposedly demonstrated the childish, underdeveloped nature of colonial peoples. The trial could not be a fair one. Indeed, the arrest itself demonstrated to some that Burma was already behind the Iron Curtain.

Gordon Seagrave and his Hospital

Gordon Stifler Seagrave (1897–1965) was a surgeon who practiced at a remote hospital in Burma. Adept at publicity, he wrote several books about his experiences, including *Tales of a Wastebasket Surgeon* (1938), *Burma Surgeon* (1943), and *Burma Surgeon Returns* (1946). During World War II he had to flee from the hospital, along with many of the nurses, and had served in Burma as a medical officer, first with the British Fourteenth Army and then with General Joseph W. Stilwell in the US Army as a medical officer. He rose to the rank of lieutenant colonel, and both the British and Americans decorated him. From the Americans he received a Purple Heart, a Bronze Star, and the Legion of Merit medal, and in 1943 *Life* magazine featured him. After the war he returned to his hospital. He worked selflessly, lived modestly, knew three Burmese languages, and was intimately familiar with Burmese culture—precisely the opposite of the ignorant, shallow diplomats described so graphically in Eugene Burdick's and William Lederer's influential book, *The Ugly American* (1958). He was sometimes called "Burma's Albert Schweitzer."[1] He was, furthermore, a devout Christian and anticommunist (though not fanatical about either cause). In 1961 President John F. Kennedy sent him a special letter of commendation for his service. Seagrave, Kennedy wrote, had "become a symbol to the entire world of the American tradition of humanitarian service abroad."[2] Kennedy's letter coincided with a special CBS television documentary about Seagrave, narrated by Walter Cronkite. Shortly before Kennedy was assassinated, efforts were underway for him to receive additional presidential honors. Ambassador Chester Bowles summed up the popular image of the "Burma Surgeon." He was, Bowles said, "the best American overseas."[3] Yet in 1950, to the great shock of the American public (though less so to American diplomats on the ground), the Burmese government charged Seagrave with high treason.

Seagrave was the son, grandson, and great grandson of American Baptist missionaries who had served in Burma since 1834. He was in fact the twenty-eighth member of his family to have served.[4] Born in Rangoon in 1897, Seagrave left Burma for his education, receiving an undergraduate degree from Denison University (then a prolific producer of Baptist missionaries) in 1917 and an M.D. degree from Johns Hopkins University in 1921. In 1922 he returned to Burma with a satchel full of used and broken surgical instruments (hence *Wastebasket Surgeon*), and traveled to Namkham, a town in Shan State, very close to the Chinese border. There in 1902 the Baptists had founded a hospital. Finding it in a decrepit state with almost no patients, Seagrave and his wife Marion ("Tiny") rebuilt and expanded the hospital until they had to leave in 1942. Seagrave resumed his work in January 1945, and in September that year, at the request of the British he accepted the position of chief medical officer of the Federated Shan States and North Karenni State.[5]

Seagrave used his position to restore his hospital, even at the expense of other medical facilities in the region. He maneuvered to have the medical supplies and other equipment that had been part of the "Seagrave Unit" during the war transferred to his hospital, including withdrawing them from the Taunggyi Civil Hospital in Lashio. He was chastised for his imperious behavior but refused to return the materials. "I have no intention whatsoever of transporting them uselessly back to Lashio," he wrote in response to demands from British officials. "If you desire to have these supplies returned to Lashio you may send not only an escort but also personnel capable of repacking the goods as . . . our personnel here are too busy in constructive work to repack the goods safely."[6] Seagrave got his way.

Despite his long missionary roots, Seagrave had grown uncomfortable with the Baptists. "As a missionary," he wrote, "I was a most unorthodox pain in the neck." *Burma Surgeon* revealed with surprisingly frankness his dislike of the mission's emphasis on evangelization and its limited interest in medical work. He criticized the new generation of missionaries, few of whom, he said, learned the local languages or socialized with the people among whom they worked. "The Mission thought I was directly on the road to hell," he recalled later, "and I thought they were." After the war he determined to repair the church on the hospital grounds for the use of chaplains of all denominations, "including Catholics and Hebrews." He could not have done that in peacetime, he said, because "the Baptists would have yelled." But it was still wartime, and he was "boss of this hill." He also seems to have been on good terms with Buddhist monasteries in the region.[7]

Seagrave's hospital, together with its attached school of nursing, served primarily non-Burman peoples: Shan, Karen, Kachin. The Karen rebellion provided the context for the trial, for Seagrave sympathized with the Karens. In April 1949 he wrote passionately and angrily that the Nu government was imprisoning and massacring innocent Karens and attempting to smear the Karens as communists when they were "right of center" whereas Nu's government was "very far to the left." In Seagrave's view the best solution was for Nu to resign and turn the government over to "the decent Burmese and the extremely decent Minorities" who together would "beat the day-lights out of the Burmese Communists." The government was aware of, or at least very suspicious of Seagrave's views, for Seagrave wrote that it had accused him "of being a spy for the Frontier peoples."[8]

Not surprisingly Seagrave had little sympathy with those government officials stationed near his hospital. In September 1949 he wrote to the American ambassador that they had spent the last year and a half "stirring up as much trouble as they could in our Hospital and the Nurses Training School." When the Karen rebel forces surrounded the town of Lashio, Seagrave reported with apparent approval, "there was a general exodus of all Burmese trouble makers from our area."[9]

Military Occupation of the Hospital

Soon the KNDO, led by Naw Seng, occupied Namkham and entered the hospital grounds. (Naw Seng, ethnically Kachin, had in February 1949 deserted from his post in the Burmese military, which he had joined in 1945, and gone over to the KNDO.) At the hospital his forces exhibited "perfect discipline," Seagrave wrote to the American ambassador, but soon government troops arrived and began to move up the hill toward the Karen forces. Seagrave ran toward them to warn them not to advance further or the Karen forces would fire on them. Before he reached the government lines, Naw Seng's men began firing. None of the government troops was hit, however, even though they were easy targets, and Seagrave told the ambassador that the KNDO troops were using mostly blank cartridges.[10]

As the government troops advanced up the hill, Seagrave came with them. Unlike the Karens, they fired live ammunition continuously and "promiscuously" into all of the hospital buildings and riddled the roofs with bullets. A grenade exploded near Seagrave's sister's room which, he wrote, would have killed her had she not been hiding elsewhere. "The live fire was in each case from Government troops against the hospital," Seagrave reported, "and no bullets came from Naw Seng's side even in self defense."[11]

Seagrave asserted that the decision not to injure the government forces was part of a larger Karen strategy, which he found admirable, of wanting to settle differences peacefully through negotiations. The government troops behaved very differently, Seagrave reported. Once they occupied the hospital (as the KNDO forces retreated) they beat the only Karen soldier left in the hospital grounds, a man critically ill with malaria, forcing Seagrave to use some of his precious supply of blood plasma to save the man's life. Government troops also broke into Seagrave's house and that of another American and beat up the night watchman, as well as occupying the nurses' home and the quarters of Seagrave's cook and sister and setting up fortifications near Seagrave's house. Had Naw Seng chosen to retaliate, Seagrave wrote, the hospital building would have been destroyed, but the rebels did not fire.[12]

In sum, while Seagrave had nothing to do with Naw Seng's decisions to move into Namkham or to occupy the hospital (and undoubtedly would have preferred that he not come at all since this potentially endangered the hospital), he believed that the Karen forces had acted honorably and had done nothing to injure the hospital or its personnel, or government troops. Government forces, on the other hand, had behaved badly and sometimes brutally.

The government forces soon withdrew from the grounds, but Seagrave's evident hostility to them had doubtless reinforced Burmese government suspicions about his sympathies. On 4 October 1949 a Burmese official instructed Seagrave, his sister, and his wife to meet with government officials in Rangoon. The American embassy also tried to persuade him to come to Rangoon: Ambassador Huddle wrote to him personally to this effect, the letter being given to Seagrave's sister to deliver. Fearing disruption to the hospital if he left, the doctor refused to go, although he did send his sister, Dr. Grace Seagrave, with full authority to speak for him. She had a number of interviews with officials, which the embassy helped facilitate. Seagrave's wife, who was in Rangoon attempting to leave the country, explained why her husband would not leave Namkham. He "figured rightly that if he left, the hospital would be looted and also all the Karens would be taken," she wrote. Indicative of the government's attitude toward Seagrave and its suspicions of missionaries in general, Marion Seagrave was thoroughly interrogated and searched at the airport, which frightened her. Had they found any possibly incriminating evidence, she wrote, she would have been arrested. "They think that we are spys [sic] and on the side of the insurgents."[13]

Mrs. Seagrave was correct about the Burmese government's attitude. In August 1948, for example, before the armed uprising had begun, a Karen leader told an American diplomat that "many Burmans have the false idea that American missionaries constitute a vast spy network." In November 1949 Foreign Minister E Maung told State Department officials that the attitude of the missionaries was a "major factor in creating Karen distrust" of the Burmans, and that "most Karen rebels are Baptists." Of course Seagrave himself did not really fit the missionary mold by this point. But the Burmese certainly identified him with the missionary community, referring to him in a press release "an American Missionary resident in Namkham."[14]

The situation became more serious late in December 1949 when KNDO forces reoccupied Namkham, and Ne Win indicated to embassy officials that he had evidence that Seagrave had been supplying the rebels with weapons, as well as allegedly giving Naw Seng medical supplies. These charges led embassy officials, with approval from the State Department, to attempt, once again, to persuade

Seagrave to come to Rangoon to meet with Burmese authorities. Although they did not think the government wanted to detain him, they feared that if he failed to cooperate it would have "no alternative but arrest and remove him."[15]

About the same time as the embassy was again trying to get Seagrave to come to Rangoon, the surgeon was writing a letter to US officials. In his letter, dated 15 February 1950 (but not received until mid-March), Seagrave acknowledged that during the rebel occupation he had given Naw Seng medical supplies, because, he stated, the rebel leader was in a position to take the supplies by force if necessary. Seagrave also acknowledged that several hospital nurses had joined Naw Seng, although he had tried to dissuade them. Seagrave's letter, together with information that the Burmese authorities had gathered from nurses and other hospital personnel when government forces reoccupied the hospital in January 1950, led the embassy to conclude that the government was now in a position to "present a considerable body of evidence to support its contention that Dr. Seagrave had given unwarranted assistance to Naw Seng"; Seagrave's situation appeared "to be an extremely difficult if not hopeless one."[16]

Despite Burmese anger, however, the embassy still did not think that the government wanted to arrest Seagrave. Fully aware that such action would complicate relations with the United States, the Burmese preferred to handle the matter quietly, and tried to force him out of Namkham by cutting off subsidies and ordering nurses and trainees to leave the hospital. Several planeloads of students were flown out.[17]

Seagrave, however, refused to leave and for the time being managed to hold on in Namkham. Indeed, as the year 1950 progressed conditions for Seagrave improved, mostly likely due to generally improved relations between the United States and Burma, the result of discussions then underway about possible American military and economic assistance.

Seagrave's recalcitrance about coming to Rangoon was a significant irritant in the slowly improving US-Burma relationship, and the State Department wanted to resolve the matter quickly and quietly, if possible. But the improving relations with the United States, plus the fact that for the moment the military seemed to be doing well in its war with the KNDO forces, led the Burmese authorities to let the Seagrave matter "rest quietly" for the time being, rather than give additional fuel for anti-American elements.[18]

By June 1950 Seagrave reported that the Burmese government, whose forces had captured the Karen "capital" of Toungoo, was releasing Karens "all over Burma" and allowing them to return to their homes. But the improvement proved to be only temporary. As relations between the United States and Burma deteriorated after the onset of the Korean War, and as the Burmese became more aware of the growing number of KMT troops entering Burma from China, relations with the United States steadily deteriorated—particularly when it became apparent that the KMT presence in Burma enjoyed covert American support.[19]

The Arrest of the "Burma Surgeon"

In the context of the quickly deteriorating relations, American officials reported that the Burmese government was again looking for a pretext to remove Seagrave from northern Burma, partly because he was "a hard man to deal with and is most uncompromising in his determination to run the hospital in his own way," partly because he had alienated several high-ranking officials, but perhaps most important of all because the Burmese government was "deeply suspicious of all Americans, especially missionaries, for alleged sympathy with the Karens, and probably consider Dr. Seagrave an agent of the American government."[20] It was an astute assessment of Burmese attitudes.

Thus it was not all that surprising that on 15 August 1950 Burmese officials suddenly arrested Seagrave, using a notorious statute that allowed the authorities to hold anyone without charge who was suspected of having taken actions against the state, flew him to the capital, and incarcerated him in the Rangoon Central Jail. Although the general public in the United States was shocked at the arrest, the American embassy, having been involved in situation for nearly a year, was not entirely surprised. Ambassador Key reported that the Burmese believed they had an "iron-clad case against him" and added ominously that Seagrave's "sympathy if not actual assistance insurgents made him enemy General Ne Win." Seagrave had also irked official Burmese because, despite government financial assistance to keep the hospital running, Seagrave insisted on "personal control his hospital." Finally, Key reported, Seagrave had angered Foreign Minister Sao Hkun Hkio by dismissing his sister from the nursing school.[21]

The State Department did, however, attempt to prevent a trial, ordering embassy officials to intervene unless there was clear evidence that Seagrave had voluntarily cooperated with the insurgents. Initial embassy representations, however, were less than vigorous, doubtless due in part to a new piece of evidence. Recently a Foreign Office official had shown Key an incriminating letter supposedly written by Seagrave on 16 September 1949 to a student nurse, Nang Leng (the wife of Dr. George N. Tu, who worked with Seagrave), that appeared to show his support for the rebel leader.[22] The letter, which would become a vital piece of evidence at any trial, doubtless reinforced earlier doubts about Seagrave's innocence.

The embassy was, nevertheless, solicitous in its treatment of Seagrave personally and did all it could to make him comfortable and to provide for his legal defense. Seagrave requested American cigarettes (he was a chain smoker), coffee, butter, and news magazines and other light-reading materials, which the embassy provided. He said he was being treated well but vigorously protested the charges against him. He insisted that "he had never at any time been disloyal to the Government or people of Burma." Two days later the embassy proposed as defense counsel U Kyaw Myint, an eminent lawyer and former justice of the Supreme Court. Seagrave immediately agreed.[23] U Kyaw Myint was the lead attorney (with four or five others who assisted), all working on a pro bono basis.

Meanwhile, Seagrave's supporters in the United States mounted a campaign seeking forceful American intervention. Seagrave's wife wrote to Representative Charles B. Deane (D-NC) and to President Truman requesting vigorous intervention from Washington. Deane, who had followed events in Burma closely, promised to do all he could and wrote a lengthy letter to Truman, urging him to make strong efforts to have Seagrave released. The "Christian honesty" of the Karen leadership, he added, contrasted with the "worthless" Burmese government.[24]

The US government responded. The day after Marion Seagrave wrote to Truman, Acheson asked Key whether it would be advisable to send out an American lawyer to assist with the case. "In view widespread public interest in case in this country," he wrote, "DEPT wishes exhaust every possibility assisting Seagrave and assuring fair trial." Key, however, advised against sending an American counsel, as this would be regarded as an unfriendly act, an interference in the legal processes of the country. In any event, Kyaw Myint was "the best counsel Seagrave could have."[25]

On 31 August 1950 the government formally charged Seagrave with high treason. Seagrave's attorney requested bail on grounds that Seagrave's health was poor and was deteriorating in jail. The government opposed bail and prevailed, much to the distress of the American ambassador.[26] The decision also led to considerable outrage in the United States and led to the first significant American intervention when Key asked the prime minister to reconsider the denial of bail. Keeping Seagrave in jail would create a very unfavorable impression in the United States, he stated, and he also mentioned Seagrave's deteriorating physical condition, something that Burmese officials acknowledged. Key also challenged the government's case itself. When the prime minister brought up the incriminating letter, Key pointed out that Kyaw Myint considered it a fake. The prime minister responded that handwriting experts believed it to be genuine.[27] This forceful intervention had no immediate effect. Bail continued to be denied, and trial was set for 9 October 1950.

Meanwhile friends of Seagrave in the United States continued to call attention to his plight. A letter from Storer B. Lunt, the president of W. W. Norton, the publisher of Seagrave's books and a committed supporter of his work, appeared in the *New York Times*,[28] which along with other newspapers and news magazines was covering the Seagrave story. Lunt and others mounted a campaign to raise a defense fund that within a few weeks amounted to over ten thousand dollars. A well-known screenwriter, Ben Markson, asked Seagrave if he could make a motion picture about him. The State Department agreed to try to "stimulate press interest in the case," something the embassy had recommended.[29]

Although previous interventions had not been successful, embassy officials continued to contact Burmese officials about the case. Key called on the foreign minister and emphasized Seagrave's health. (Among other problems, Seagrave had recently had seven teeth pulled.) A few days later the embassy suggested transferring Seagrave to the Seventh-day Adventist hospital (considered the best in Rangoon) or to another health care facility.[30]

These interventions proved partially successful. The Burmese refused to transfer Seagrave to the Adventist hospital (they were suspicion also of the Adventists), and they would not allow bail. But a few days before the trial began they transferred him to a "comfortable house in the suburbs" where he remained under police supervision. His new residence was, in fact, a bungalow owned by the American embassy that had been temporarily transferred to the Burmese for this purpose. Seagrave had a cook and could walk outside and even converse with people (at a safe distance across the street). In return, Seagrave promised not to press the issue of bail further.[31] His health improved noticeably.

The Trial

The trial got underway on 12 October 1950 before a Special Tribunal of three jurists: U Ba Swe, Bo Gyi, and U Tun Tin. There were three specific charges:

1. That Seagrave, by entertaining Naw Seng, offering him tea, allowing his followers free access to the hospital compound, and allowing them to play football and to take up defensive positions in the hospital compound, had "aided and comforted Naw Seng and his followers" at a time when he should reasonably have known that Naw Seng was committing high treason.
2. That Seagrave by sending his incriminating letter to Nang Leng had "encouraged, aided and comforted" Naw Seng.
3. That Seagrave had given medicines and surgical instruments to Naw Seng during the rebel leader's second occupation of the hospital.[32]

The first phase of the trial was to determine if there was a sufficient case to go forward. Government witnesses testified that they had come under heavy fire as they approached the hospital (thus contradicting Seagrave's account that the Karens were firing blanks) and that Seagrave showed a pronounced preference for the rebels and a strong distaste for the government forces. They disputed most allegations (though not all) of improper behavior by the troops, and they charged the doctor with calling the Burmese armed forces (the *tatmadaw*) a "dog army" (*khway-tat-madaw*). In addition to testifying to the official charges, they accused Seagrave of expelling and threatening nurses and student nurses who expressed sympathy for the government, and giving preferential treatment to non-Burman student nurses. One student nurse also made the potentially inflammatory insinuation that Seagrave had behaved improperly toward the students. "He flirted with some of them," Ma E Mya testified. He also "teased" her and allegedly made "passes" at her which, she said, together with the Karen revolt, delayed her graduation. He also told her that she "would be expelled if I told anyone what was happening in the hospital."[33]

But the most damning evidence against Seagrave was the letter he allegedly wrote to Nang Leng on 6 September 1949—a few days after Naw Seng had occupied the hospital compound for the first time. This was the letter shown to Ambassador Key in August 1950, and it addresses the issue of Naw Seng's apparent impending arrest of the local hereditary leader, the sawbwa of the region of Hsenwi who sided with the government against the rebels:

My Dear Nang Leng,

> If you say one single word about Peggy's statement to you (about the Hsenwi Sawbwa's arrest by Naw Seng) to *anybody* I will turn you over to Naw Seng as a spy immediately. This is an ultimatum *order*. I mean what I say. Give Dr. Ba Saw a list of people you have already told. I will handle Peggy myself.
>
> Gordon S. Seagrave[34]

This central piece of evidence suggested that Seagrave had close relations with Naw Seng and was working to keep secret Naw Seng's impending arrest of the sawbwa, while also threatening those who might take the government's side. Seagrave had insisted adamantly that the letter was a forgery (and had told this to his attorney), but before the trial began his sister informed the embassy that the letter was authentic, and soon Seagrave himself acknowledged his authorship. As expected, after hearing the prosecution witnesses the tribunal determined that there was sufficient evidence to proceed. Seagrave pleaded not guilty.[35]

Seagrave was the first witness in the second phase of the trial. In extensive testimony over a period of three days he systematically disputed, or attempted to explain and put in context, the actions that had led to the charges against him.

Seagrave denied having ever served Naw Seng or his men tea. He denied making any negative references to the army and said he had never used or even heard the term "dog army." As for the insurgents' football game, about which there was much testimony, Seagrave stated that the football field had been built with government funds and was open to anyone to use without his permission. In any event he was personally unaware of game. "I knew nothing until the match was over," he said.[36]

Seagrave spent considerable time explaining the apparently incriminating letter that he had written to Nang Leng. Seagrave said that when he wrote the letter he was not attempting to assist Naw Seng by stifling rumors of the impending arrest of the Hsenwi Sawbwa from reaching the sawbwa and thus warning him. On the contrary, he thought (incorrectly as it turned out) that the sawbwa had already been arrested, and he wanted to keep that information from spreading among the students. News of the sawbwa's arrest would have created panic, he said, particularly among the many Shan students who had "intense respect" for the sawbwa. Seagrave's letter was direct and strong, he said, because Nang Leng was not very fluent in English, and he wanted to make his intentions absolutely clear. He wanted to frighten her so that she would not spread rumors that would result in mass panic. Thus he used words like "order" and "ultimatum," words that he would not have used with a person more fluent in English. In any event, the letter needed to be understood in the context of a situation, which he described as "a keg of gunpowder." "I was frantic with anxiety at the time," Seagrave told the court. All in all, when he wrote the letter he had no "intention of aiding, encouraging or comforting the insurgents. My intention was exactly the opposite." Also, he "had no intention of carrying out the threats mentioned" in the letter, a reference to turning Nang Leng over to Naw Seng as a "spy." That, he said, was a "wild threat" and he certainly did not mean that Nang Leng was really a spy. Seagrave acknowledged giving Naw Seng supplies, but only because Naw Seng's men had him surrounded by armed men "guns at the ready." He bitterly resented, he said, that Naw Seng had caused so much harm by entering the hospital compound.[37]

In sum, Seagrave's testimony intended to demonstrate that he had no sympathy for the rebellion, that his sole concern was to protect the hospital and the nurses' training program, and to the extent he aided Naw Seng it was under severe duress. "It is not true that my sympathies were with Naw Seng," he stated.[38]

Witnesses for the defense supported Seagrave's contentions, including about the use of the football field and his dealings with Naw Seng. Several witnesses testified that Seagrave did not discriminate among nurses and students of different ethnic groups, and also refuted allegations that Seagrave had made disparaging comments about the government army. Perhaps the most effective witness was a captain in the Kachin Emergency Corps, a part of the government forces, who had known Seagrave since January 1949. "The accused extended whatever help was needed by the military forces," he testified, noting that he and his wife had both benefited from Seagrave's attention while patients at the hospital.[39]

On 12 January 1951 the two sides made their summations before the court. Seagrave's attorneys argued that even if the actions alleged had taken place, there was clearly no criminal intent. All actions had been taken under duress to protect the hospital and its staff. The prosecution, however, argued that intent was irrelevant under the law, and that in fact Seagrave was guilty of "conspiring to wage war against the union" and deserved the death penalty. The prosecution summation rattled Seagrave, but he and his attorney remained optimistic. It all depended, they felt, on whether intent was a defense. If so, Seagrave would be acquitted. The prevailing opinion, according to the US embassy, was that an acquittal was likely. Journalists in Rangoon estimated the odds at a hundred to one for acquittal.[40]

But the optimists were wrong. On 17 January 1951 the Special Tribunal rendered its decision. To be sure, in a well-reasoned opinion, with references to legal opinions drawn from British and American jurisprudence, the court rejected several of the prosecution's allegations. It found reason for Seagrave to be angry when government forces and insurgents fought at the hospital compound. "We do not think it fair in these circumstances to attach undue weight to some unfortunate expressions that escaped him while in a temper," the court concluded.[41]

Much to the defense's satisfaction, the court accepted the importance of intention. Acts in themselves did not rise to the level of high treason without intent. There was insufficient evidence to conclude that Seagrave had intended to assist Naw Seng to wage war against the state, and no real evidence that Seagrave had allowed the rebels free access to the hospital. Likewise, the justices believed Seagrave's contention that the football field was a public one and that he did not even know about the game until after it was over. They were also doubtful about the testimony of some of the prosecution witnesses who potentially held grudges against Seagrave. All in all, the court concluded that the prosecution had failed to prove that Seagrave was guilty of high treason as defined Section 3(1) of the high treason act, a provision that required the death penalty, and it acquitted him of these charges.

However, the judges were much more skeptical about Seagrave's testimony on other matters. They were not persuaded by his explanation of how and why he wrote the letter to Nang Leng, something they analyzed at length. "We do not accept the accused's contention that he has merely used empty threats to frighten the young woman into silence," the jurists wrote. Threatening to turn her over to Naw Seng as a spy showed "clearly that the accused was definitely pro–Naw Seng."

The letter demonstrated that Seagrave intended to, and did, facilitate Naw Seng's arrest of the sawbwa and thus gave comfort to the insurgents. He was thus found guilty under a different provision of the act, Section 4(1), which involved the crime of assisting another person guilty of high treason. For this Seagrave received a six-year prison sentence.

As for providing Naw Seng with medical supplies, the justices thought that since the government had withdrawn its protection from Namkham at the time Seagrave did not deserve severe punishment, but they did not exonerate him. Seagrave's argument that he was surrounded by armed men was not tested on the prosecution witnesses at the trial and "appears to be an afterthought," but even if true this would not be a defense. The court did, however, take into consideration Seagrave's "distinguished medical and military service" to the country and sentenced him to one year on this charge, to run concurrently with the six-year sentence received on the other charge.[42]

In conclusion the court found that at a time that the country was in a state of near anarchy as the result of various rebellions, Seagrave "acted in a manner prejudicial to the State" and behaved, as a Burmese proverb put it, like someone who "presses down with a pole a drowning man." That Seagrave was a resident alien made the matter more egregious: the court cited as a precedent a decision by the British Privy Council. *Time* magazine reported that Seagrave "did not flinch," when he heard the verdict, "but suddenly he looked older than his fifty-three years."[43]

Given the optimism that had preceded the court's decision, the reaction in the United States was one of disbelief. The *Boston Herald* called the conviction "a tragic miscarriage of justice." The *New York Times* commented a little later that "no one who knew Dr. Seagrave could possibly suspect that he could plot against the Government. He could not plot against anybody." Few Americans were willing to credit Burmese justice. Even more than that, however, there was a sense that Seagrave's trial was evidence of a deeper conspiracy. In 1954 journalist Peter Kalischer wrote that people felt that the trial was "rigged." Cold War fears were paramount, and to many it seemed that the verdict demonstrated that Burma was going communist. "The rigged trial, the American missionary defendant beloved by thousands—the pattern was all too familiar," his article stated. "In the battle of ideologies there is no room for a debt of gratitude."[44] Kalischer's piece nicely encapsulated Cold War thinking in the United States, but it vastly oversimplified the actual situation; the attacks constituted undeserved criticisms of the Burmese judicial system.

The court's decision was thoughtful and well reasoned, particularly in the case of the incriminating letter to Nang Leng. While Seagrave's initial denial seems not to have come up at the trial, it certainly suggests that he understood how damaging the letter was, and furthermore, his explanations were strained. It was not unreasonable to find that the letter constituted assistance to Naw Seng. The court's second guilty decision, on the charge of assisting Naw Seng with medicines, was less persuasive, and the court itself understood that. Its sentence of one year to run concurrently suggests some ambivalence. Based on Seagrave's own account written at the time of the first rebel occupation of Namkham and the hospital, it is evident that Seagrave did sympathize with the Karen rebels and disliked the government, both military and civilian. He did his best to hide this during the trial. But his primary intent was to preserve the hospital and his own position there, not to support the rebellion.

The Appeals

Lost in the outpouring of criticism was the fact that, in sentencing Seagrave to six years, the court had astutely left open the possibility of appeal. Under the statute, no appeal was allowed for a sentence of five years or less, and this Seagrave and his attorneys determined to pursue.

While awaiting appeal, Seagrave was housed in the Rangoon Central Jail but was placed in a small house of his own with a separate bathroom and cooking facilities, and with another prisoner serving as his cook. He was not visible to the other prisoners, who in his previous incarceration had stared at him, causing him much anxiety. The US embassy provided reading material and cigarettes, and it urged the government of Burma to expedite the appeals process, though it actually considered a reversal of the charges "remote."[45]

On 23 January 1951 U Kyaw Myint appealed the verdict to the High Court of Rangoon, raising a number of points where he believed the Special Tribunal had erred, including its interpretation of the Nang Leng letter and the hospital supplies given to Naw Seng. Oral arguments began on 13 February 1951, with the defense presenting its case. An embassy official thought that the three judges hearing the case (Chief Justice Tun Byu, and Justices On Fe and Aung Tha Gyaw) appeared "receptive" to the defense case. But at the same time the prosecution indicated that it planned to try to raise the charge to actually committing high treason (something the Special Tribunal had rejected), instead of merely encouraging it.[46]

In the meantime there was considerable protest emerging in the United States and elsewhere, especially in Britain. Mrs. Seagrave wrote several letters to the State Department, which attempted to be as accommodating as possible, even seeing whether it could send supplies to Seagrave if they were not available in Rangoon. Several Congressional representatives protested the verdict, and there continued

FIGURE 3. Gordon S. Seagrave in Rangoon, March 1951, after the first appeal of his conviction for assisting a person committing high treason. Howard Sochurek/Time & Life/Getty Images.

to be much discussion in the newspapers and news magazines, including a story in *Time* magazine on 29 January 1951. Even Averell Harriman entered the fray by forwarding to Dean Rusk a letter from his friend Owen D. Young, the prominent industrialist and businessman, appealing for more action. Burma's ambassador to the United States stated that if the verdict were upheld there would be "serious repercussions," and he reportedly recommended to his government that that in that event Seagrave receive a full pardon and be allowed to continue to work in Burma.[47] Much depended, then, on what the court would decide.

On 9 March 1951 the court issued its verdict. It reversed the conviction based on the Nang Leng letter and, while it upheld the verdict based on Seagrave's contribution of supplies to Naw Seng, it reduced the sentence to time already served. Seagrave's jailers heartily congratulated him, and an embassy official brought out a bottle of champagne.

Seagrave was now a free man again, and he praised his lawyers. All of them had been "swell," he wrote, "and none of them will take a cent for defending me." He also thanked those who had organized his defense fund, and thought seriously of writing another book that would, he hoped, "improve Burmese American relations." Reflecting on the months since his arrest, Seagrave wrote that it was "good medicine for a man to be imprisoned without bail for at least two months once in his life." But he added that "you feel as if you are stripped naked on top of a pedestal with atomic gamma rays showing through you. I'd rather go through another war." All he now wanted to do was to "get off the front pages and hide behind a huge banyan tree somewhere and get back into surgical work for the thousands that need me still."[48] But whether he would be allowed to stay in Burma or resume his work in Namkham was uncertain. Prime Minister Nu reportedly overruled those who wanted to force Seagrave out of Burma altogether, but Namkham was in a sensitive military zone, and it was not at all clear that the military would allow Seagrave back.

A more pressing issue was whether to appeal the remaining guilty verdict. Seagrave initially preferred not to do so, provided he could return to his work. The State Department opposed an appeal, fearing it would antagonize those officials who might otherwise compromise.[49] Burma's ambassador to Washington proposed a compromise: Seagrave could return to the hospital, but a Burmese doctor trusted by the government would be assigned to work with him. This would reduce suspicion and, as the embassy put it, "tend to give the hospital a Burmese tone, which heretofore had been somewhat lacking." The State Department found this to be a constructive idea and urged the embassy to "make every effort" to discourage an appeal. Seagrave thought, at least in retrospect, that the State Department wanted him to leave Burma because his presence there was interfering with US-Burma relations.[50] Ultimately Seagrave rejected the compromise offer and decided to appeal to the Supreme Court.

While the appeal was pending, Seagrave lived in a flat owned by U Kyaw Myint's wife (because the attorney did not want his client to receive any favors from the embassy, the Baptist Mission, or the Karens). He formally applied for permission to return to Namkham, and many in the government, particularly the civilians, said they favored this. But there was opposition, most notably from General Ne Win, a man who, as the home minister later told Ambassador Key, was "not the type of man who, once his mind was made up, would readily change his opinion."[51] On 9 August 1951 the government rejected his application.

The next day Key spoke confidentially with U Nu about the prospects of Seagrave returning permanently to Namkham. Nu said that Seagrave should continue with his appeal to the Supreme Court. He acknowledged his own belief that Seagrave had not been disloyal to Burma, and he recalled how before World War II Seagrave had defended the Burmese against British charges that they were "shiftless and lazy." U Nu had attacked the British strongly on that occasion, and Seagrave was one of the few foreigners who had shaken hands with him afterward. There were, however, Burmese officials who were still convinced of Seagrave's guilt, he said, and it would take some time to overcome their views.[52]

The Supreme Court heard Seagrave's appeal on 31 October 1951. Two weeks later Seagrave was fully vindicated, the court deciding that his actions were intended to save his property and not to give succor to the insurgents. Though the court ruled in Seagrave's favor, it did chastise him for bringing "all this trouble on himself."

> His attitude towards the Karen nurses and Naw Seng and his men during their first occupation of Namkham . . . would make some people suspect that his sympathies were with the Karens. Once this suspicion was engendered, whatever he did or said would appear, not only to a lay mind but even to some trained minds as an act to help and encourage the Karen rebels. This is exactly what has happened in this case. Therefore, what we like to urge is that those who come to our country and enjoy our hospitality should not give grounds for suspicion, either by words or deeds, that they are taking sides in our internal affairs. We are a small country and we desire, as is the policy of our Government to live on terms of friendship with everybody. We like to settle our affairs and promote the welfare of our people in our own way. If anybody is found interfering in our internal affairs in disregard of our laws, he will be punished irrespective of whoever and whatever he may be.[53]

It was not an inaccurate summation. If anything it was generous to Seagrave who had unquestionably sympathized with the Karens. Nor was its admonition unfair. It was also true, however, that Seagrave's primary interest was to protect his hospital; he had not plotted to subvert the state. To the extent that he had assisted Naw Seng, it was because of circumstances beyond his control.

Soon thereafter Seagrave's attorney again applied for permission to have him return to Namkham. Burma's military continued to resist. The American embassy was probably ambivalent at best about his return in any case, given the fact that Seagrave was an irritant in a Burmese-American relationship that was already a challenging one. Seagrave's son, Sterling, later wrote that "behind the scenes the American Embassy worked hard to get him out of Burma, virtually promising the Burmese government that the old man would be no more nuisance."[54] Nevertheless, in December 1951 the government of Burma granted Seagrave permission to return to Namkham, with the stipulation that in the future he would leave if ordered to do so. He was back at his hospital before Christmas and remained there until his death in 1965, never once traveling to the United States.

What, then, accounted for the government's decision to prosecute Seagrave in the first place? After the initial verdict the American embassy concluded that the government had yielded to the "vindictiveness" of the Shan sawbwas ("probably including Foreign Minister") who needed a scapegoat for their own failure to resist Naw Seng. None of the local officials had "lifted a finger to stop Naw Seng," yet none of them had been arrested. Seagrave's sister, Grace (who died during the trial) pointedly accused the sawbwa of Hsenwi of trying to conceal his own treasonous activities by blaming Seagrave. Seagrave's wife also blamed the Shan and Kachin ministers and other Burmese politicians who were "jealous of Gordon's prestige among the hill peoples."[55]

A related argument was that the government wanted to gain control of the hospital and hoped to do this by deporting Seagrave. The embassy had agreed with the second point: "locally powerful interests are determined that Seagrave leave Burma," Day had reported in January 1951.[56]

There may well be some truth in these assertions; perhaps this was a case of selective prosecution. It also seems likely that Seagrave's own brusqueness, his unwillingness to comply with bureaucratic niceties, and his propensity to criticize local and national officials made it easier for the government to move against him. The timing of the arrest was very likely related to the general deterioration in Burmese-American relations at the time.

Still, the case against Seagrave was not a frivolous one. Even the American embassy initially reported that the Burmese had a good case. Seagrave was clearly a defender of the rights of the Burmese minorities, even in times of insurrection. He found the resistance justified, at least early on, and the government could reasonably have believed that he might be assisting the insurgents. He had, in fact, assisted them, though under duress.

The trial itself was fair, something the American embassy acknowledged,[57] and which, given the civil wars going on in the country, was quite remarkable. Seagrave had the very best counsel he could have hoped for. Furthermore, it appears that the courts were genuinely independent. The Special Tribunal rejected the harshest prosecution claims and credited a number of the points made by Seagrave and the defense witnesses. The appeals court threw out the most incriminating evidence (the Nang Leng letter), and the Supreme Court dismissed the last remaining charge. At the same time it issued a temperate admonition and warned the defendant to be careful in his actions. The popular response in the United States to Seagrave's detention reflected Cold War America and suggested a not uncommon disdain for the judicial systems and capabilities of nonwhite colonial peoples.[58]

Gordon Seagrave and the Cold War

Particularly significant was the US government's ambivalent response to Seagrave's arrest and trial. It might have viewed Seagrave as an asset in the developing Cold War in Southeast Asia. He was a Christian anticommunist and a war hero, devoting his life to helping the hill peoples of Burma. Seagrave could help win "hearts and minds" in the struggle with international communism. He might have been seen as someone roughly comparable to the fictional character Homer Atkins in *The Ugly American* (1958). Atkins, unlike the superficial and ignorant diplomats portrayed in the novel, understood Southeast Asia and worked quietly to better the lives of the people, thus winning them over to the American way. Lederer and Burdick wrote their novel because they thought that the United States was losing the struggle with communism in Southeast Asia because of its ignorant approach.

But the "Burma Surgeon" was too unreliable as a Cold War asset. Seagrave represented the ambiguous relationship that experienced American missionaries and humanitarian workers often had with their own government. In general supportive of Western ways, often (in earlier years) including the need for imperial rule, these moral reformers (to use Ian Tyrrell's phrase) sometimes found themselves at odds with particular policies and practices. They were, with some notable exceptions, too independent to be reliable "assets" in advancing American policies.[59]

As with other moral reformers, Seagrave's life was ultimately not about serving American cultural or political objectives. He was too independent, too cantankerous, and above all too committed to the people he served; furthermore, his career was fully formed before the Cold War; and in any event, he had spent almost all of his life in Burma. His antipathy for the Burmese government, and his very positive views of the Karens and other minorities, ran counter to current American Cold War policy, which was to support the government against the insurgents so that it could devote its full attention to fighting the communists. He also considered the KMT aggressive intruders, and he refused to give them asylum at his hospital—this at a time when the United States was covertly supporting them. "Dr. SEAGRAVE was especially outspoken in condemning the wanton destruction of villages by these troops," reported an American Foreign Service officer in 1954.[60] Given Seagrave's popularity in the United States, the long-time presence of the American Baptist Mission in Burma, and the embassy's obligation to protect American citizens abroad, the government could hardly disown him, and in fairness American diplomats worked very hard on his behalf. (Retrospectively Seagrave told an American official in 1954 that he had "acted like a fool in Rangoon" and that "the Embassy was wonderful in doing what it had for him.")[61] But it was not surprising that American diplomats preferred to avoid a trial, supported a compromise solution, and advised against appeals. In a sense, then, Seagrave's was a cautionary tale in Cold War politics. Later the US government would develop and support the "hearts and minds" approach with less complicated people like Dr. Tom Dooley, who knew much less about Southeast Asia than Seagrave did and whose actions and attitudes were more clearly in line with what the United States wanted to achieve.

The trial did no damage to Seagrave's reputation in the United States; he continued to be revered for the selfless ways in which he served the people of northern Burma. But the trial did bring out the surgeon's less admirable qualities as well, including his quick temper, his near dictatorial approach to running the hospital, his tendency to bully subordinates, and his reluctance to "indigenize" the hospital.

After the appeals Seagrave took the court's admonition to heart, going out of his way in future years to avoid offending the government. There was even a rapprochement of sorts. In October 1952 Seagrave informed the American embassy that ever since his return to Namkham Burmese and Shan officials had "been most kind and courteous to me and most cooperative in our mutual efforts for the welfare of the people." In 1954 when Ambassador William J. Sebald and his wife visited Seagrave in Namkham, they were impressed with his work and asked the Burmese government if it could provide the surgeon with some financial support. U Nu quickly agreed, and, despite its own severe budgetary problems, for the next three years the government gave Seagrave the equivalent of fourteen thousand dollars per year, with no restrictions on how the funds were to be spent.[62]

THE KUOMINTANG EMBARRASSMENT

The Seagrave trial was a great distraction that complicated the bilateral relationship. Furthermore, it tended to poison American popular opinion about Burma. However more important in the long term was the presence of Nationalist Chinese (Kuomintang or KMT) forces in northern Burma. Forced out of China by the advancing Communist army, they created enormous difficulties for Burma in its relations with the PRC. Although the American embassy in Rangoon and some State Department officials condemned the KMT activities and wanted strong American intervention to end them, the US government, despite its great leverage over the Republic of China on Formosa (Taiwan), seemed unable to force a troop withdrawal. This was because the CIA, with approval at the very highest level, covertly supported the KMT.

Just as the Seagrave trial revealed the unusual importance of the missionary presence in Burma in particular, so too the KMT affair was largely confined to that country. But the decision to support the KMT also demonstrated that containment of communism and resistance to the PRC were at the center of American goals across the region. Doubts quickly emerged, however, about whether that decision advanced these larger goals.

The KMT Enters Burma

In some respects the situation in Burma looked brighter in 1951 from the American perspective than in earlier years. The government moved away from its strongly leftist orientation. The procommunist elements withdrew from official positions, and the government was having some success in bringing the ethnic insurgencies under control. There was some economic improvement, and the United States had more influence. With Burma's permission, the Voice of America began broadcasting to Burma, and exchange programs, such as the Fulbright Program, led to better relations. Also, American technical and economic aid contributed to Burma's rehabilitation, including assistance with repairing several of Burma's ports that had been badly damaged during World War II.[1] In addition, at the end of the year Gordon Seagrave was back in Namkham.

But there were also some negative factors, most of them the result of outside influences. Reports of Chinese support for Burmese communists and some ethnic insurgencies troubled the Americans. Naw Seng had retreated into China with about fifteen hundred troops, where he received support. In addition, the Chinese Communists had as many as fifty thousand troops in the border area. The Burmese could not possibly stop them from invading, should they choose to do so. Finally, there were the KMT forces. Their presence became a major headache for Burma and a genuine security concern. If the KMT remained in Burma, the Chinese would always be tempted to cross the border and capture or eliminate them.

As early as 1948 refugees had fled the civil war in China and entered Burma. The following year, with the Communist victory in sight, "army deserters" joined the exodus. Some "organized KMT units" passed through Burma on their way to Laos, where the French turned them back. Remnants of the 93d KMT Division reportedly moved into Burma's Kengtung Province early in 1949. According to initial reports there were between thirty-five hundred and five thousand KMT troops there.[2]

Whatever the number, the PRC threatened to invade Kengtung unless the sawbwa of that region immediately disarmed them and returned them to China. (By some accounts Communist troops were already across the border, and the British reported a short-lived incursion in January 1950.) The sawbwa did not have the forces to even begin such an operation, nor did the central government, particularly since its army was deeply engaged with the various insurgencies. As historian Matthew Foley writes, "the main effect of their [the KMT's] presence was to destabilize the Burmese government, and expose Burma to possible Chinese reprisals."[3]

The United States also feared a possible Chinese invasion and made worried inquiries to the British—who, however, found the situation much less frightening. A Chinese move into Burma would jeopardize their position all across Southeast Asia, the British Foreign Office felt. Furthermore the Chinese government would want to consolidate internal control after its recent victory.[4] The British attitude appears to have persuaded the United States that no immediate action was called for, and for several months discussion of KMT forces in the border region, and a possible Communist Chinese response, appeared less frequently in the diplomatic correspondence.

Perhaps the Americans were unaware that in March 1950 an additional fifteen hundred KMT troops, along with five hundred dependents, had moved into Burma. By June they were "increasingly truculent" and demanded that Burma release those KMT troops it had captured and interned (only about thirty). At the same time the PRC demanded that Burma disarm and intern the KMTs. An invasion seemed increasing likely,[5] and the Burmese sent more troops to the border.

American Connections with the KMT

A new factor now entered the picture. Just after the outbreak of the Korean War on 25 June 1950, Burma claimed that KMT intransigence was "due to American backing." Key told the Burmese that such reports were "absolutely baseless," but the next day U Hla Muang, Burma's ambassador to Thailand, told Key that he "not only believed the rumors . . . but . . . had evidence which proved that two unidentified Americans were working with the Nationalists in Kengtung." Key thought this important, for U Hla Muang was a leading figure, a close associate of Ne Win and one whose influence on Burma's policy "should not be underestimated."[6]

The extent of American involvement with the KMT at this point is not entirely clear. Six months later there would be no question, but as the Burmese suspected, some American intelligence agents may already have been working with the KMTs. The PRC victory the previous October had produced a sense of urgency within the US administration, and in April 1950 the Joint Chiefs of Staff, looking for ways to "reduce the pressure from Communist China," noted with interest the "renewed vitality and apparent increased effectiveness of the Chinese Nationalist forces." This led them to propose that covert actions be undertaken "to interfere with Communist activities in Southeast Asia."[7] Reports similar to U Hla Muang's continued to surface. In fact, in the spring and summer of 1950, the major commander of the KMT troops, General Li Mi (to whom the United States had awarded the Legion of Merit in 1946 for his services in World War II against the Japanese) met with sympathetic American agents in Hong Kong.[8]

If American covert agents were involved with the KMTs at this early date, the State Department seemed unaware of it. On 7 July 1950, responding to Burmese requests, Assistant Secretary of State for Far Eastern Affairs Dean Rusk summoned Nationalist China's ambassador, Wellington Koo, and told him that the United States wanted the KMT troops to disband and be interned by Burma. Rusk reacted negatively to Koo's suggestion that the KMTs return to Yunnan.[9]

Two weeks later Rusk told Koo that the Burmese considered the KMT presence a provocation to the PRC. The KMT troops posed little threat to China, and he again discouraged thoughts of their invading Yunnan. Two days later Rusk summoned Koo back. The United States wanted Chiang Kai-shek's government "to take steps at once to order these troops to accept disarming by the Burmese authorities," partly to forestall a Burmese appeal to the UN. Acheson also told Taiwan that the presence of the KMT troops played "into hands of Commies." He wanted "immed[iate] action." In August he stated that the United States was not interested in getting involved with Li Mi's "ventures."[10]

In spite of the State Department's seeming ignorance, reports of American involvement continued to surface. Ne Win complained that officials from the American embassy in Bangkok, including the army attaché, had been seen in Kengtung. If he were seen there again he would be arrested. The Burmese were "highly suspicious our true attitude re Kengtung problem which has become politically acute," reported Key.[11]

Even more embarrassing, potentially, the US Army Liaison Group in Hong Kong had issued letters to various American military attachés introducing them to Li Mi. Later, it would become known that Americans in Hong Kong constituted an important part of the CIA's efforts to support the KMT. At the time, however, Key could only say that if the letters' existence became known to the Burmese, this would convince them that previous American denials of US involvement with the KMT could not be believed, a serious embarrassment.[12]

In September 1950 the Nationalist embassy in Washington made a startling claim: "all nationalist forces were withdrawn from Burma at the end of August." It is possible that there was a drawdown of troops, for in November Key referred in the past tense to "the period of time that KMT troops were in Kengtung." But it may also be that the KMT remained dispersed in remote areas, and that the Nationalists were deliberately misleading Washington. A CIA report later stated that an evacuation order had been "ignored." In any event by December 1950 the KMT troops had again established themselves at their new headquarters in Mong Hsat in eastern Burma near the Thai border, were allying with Mon and Karen rebels, and had placed an agent in the nearby town of Tachilek who supplied them "with arms, ammunition, and other assistance." Two weeks later a missionary reported that there were approximately three thousand KMT personnel in the Mong Hsat area. The troops claimed that they were "being paid and supplied by US." The missionary was probably Paul Lewis, who was named as reporting that the KMT troops acknowledged receiving supplies from Americans, and that another missionary, Vincent Young, was very friendly with the KMTs and outspokenly critical of the Burmese government.[13]

In any event, unbeknownst to American diplomats in Burma, by the end of 1950 the United States government was certainly involved with the KMT. The Korean War had significantly altered American involvement in Burma, as it did so many other aspects of American foreign policy. Although the Joint Chiefs of Staff had proposed covert action before the war, it appears that only after the war began did the United States begin systematically to support the KMTs. After PRC troops entered Korea in November 1950, aid was accelerated as President Truman approved expanding American covert capabilities. Among the actions he approved was Operation Paper, supporting a KMT invasion into southern China.[14] But just how this came about and who supported it remains controversial. According to Scott Kaufman and Alfred McCoy, the CIA's Office of Policy Coordination thought that the KMT remnants in Burma could be used to divert Beijing's attention away from Korea. CIA Director Walter Bedell Smith opposed the plan as too risky, but the OPC wanted it, and Truman approved it probably in December 1950. The most recent study, by former foreign service officer Richard M. Gibson, agrees that Bedell Smith firmly opposed Operation Paper, as did Desmond Fitzgerald, the chief of the OPC's Far Eastern Division (despite the division's being heavily invested in regional covert activities). According to Gibson, it was top-level State and Defense Department officials who supported the action. Coordinating the whole operation were Alfred Cox, head of the OPC in Hong Kong, and Sherman B. Joost, a former OSS officer in Burma now stationed in Bangkok. Key was deliberately not informed[15] and consistently told the Burmese that there was no American involvement. It seems likely that Ambassador Stanton in Bangkok was also bypassed.

At the end of February 1951 Foreign Minister Sao Hkun Hkio said that the KMTs were "no longer merely a group of bandits but a well-organized, well-disciplined, and well-supplied small army" that received outside support.[16] This the embassy knew, but it did not know precisely how the KMT was supplied, except that the supplies appeared to come from Thailand.

Actually, Li Mi had been talking to American agents about support for several weeks. In addition to his earlier discussions in Hong Kong, he met on 8 September 1950 for five hours with General Graves B. Erskine in Bangkok, who promised to try and secure assistance. Once Operation Paper was approved, the Thais quickly agreed to funnel American supplies to the KMT. This was easily arranged, for the CIA already had a large covert program in Thailand to equip the police. The Americans most directly involved in Thailand were two former military and OSS officers, Willis Bird and Paul Helliwell, who worked through a CIA dummy company, the Southeast Asia Supply Corporation, referred to variously as the Sea Supply, Sea Supply Corporation, or Sea Supply Company, with Thailand's police chief Phao Siyanon their most prominent collaborator. The first supplies under Operation Paper were shipped from Taiwan in February 1951.[17]

By April 1951 there were possibly as many at fifteen thousand KMT troops in Burma, with perhaps half of them planning to cross into Yunnan, and their increased numbers provoked a PRC response. The CIA reported that there was "a large concentration" of troops on the Chinese side of the border. The next month Burma complained again to the United States, pointing out that the KMT forces now had "modern weapons" that made it impossible for the government to drive them out. This time, they said, they would have no choice but to take the matter to the UN. The American chargé, Henry B. Day, convinced the foreign minister to hold off until he could get the views of the State Department,[18] which, of course, wanted to discourage such a move.

Now a potentially explosive factor entered the picture. The British, who were belatedly becoming very concerned about the KMT presence, suspected by at least late February 1951 that the United States was involved. Some surmised that General Douglas MacArthur's headquarters in Tokyo (which, one official wrote, "pay little or no attention to what is said or done in Washington") was instrumental. When the British discovered that Thai Prime Minister Plaek Phibunsongkhram (Phibun) thought his country ought to support Li Mi, they objected strongly. It was would be "most ill-advised" to help the KMT "in any way whatsoever," the Thais were told. The British also suspected that some clandestine American agencies were behind Thai connections with the KMTs, perhaps without the State Department's knowledge. They therefore tried to persuade the American ambassador in Bangkok to protest Thai involvement with the KMT. Ambassador Stanton agreed with the British position and urged the Thais to eliminate their support for the Nationalists. However, he doubted if Phao (who was, as Richard Gibson puts it nicely, "intelligent, ruthless, and arguably, the most corrupt man in Thailand") would comply because of his lucrative involvement in the KMT opium trade. Nor was Phibun much interested in cutting ties with the KMT.[19]

About the same time, at an OPC meeting in London an informant (whose name has been redacted in the available document) reported that the Americans "tacitly admitted that they knew operations were going on," despite pro forma denials. The informant suspected that Americans working with the KMTs were military intelligence (G2) people under MacArthur's command. The British ambassador in Rangoon, Richard Speaight, telegraphed that "certain agencies of the United States Government must be actively involved." Speaight deplored this and saw only disaster ahead. He feared a "general revulsion of feeling against the Americans."[20] The British antennae were generally accurate. Operation Paper was now going in earnest, with supplies coming to Thailand from Taiwan and

Okinawa by ship and by plane, including planes of the CIA's recently acquired airline, Civil Air Transport (CAT).

Although the British did not know all of the details regarding American involvement, they knew enough to object. They feared the consequences of an American-supported KMT invasion of China, and the Foreign Office was determined "to take all possible action to restrain the Americans."[21] As they told the American embassy in Rangoon, the result of the KMT presence would be a "Commie Govt in Burma." The Burmese were "fearful almost to the point of hysteria" that PRC troops would invade at any moment. Early in May 1951 the foreign minister told Key that the United States had three days to come up with a solution. Otherwise Burma was going to go to the UN.[22]

Key was not personally informed about the CIA connection, but Americans who lived in northern Burma had no doubts. Baptist missionaries Don and Jean Crider commented about the "very evident American support of Chinese Nationalists still in Burma's western border areas, who are openly giving aid to the rebel movement," and they fully understood why Burma suspected that they were themselves "undercover agents involved in the whole operation!"[23]

By now Key had come to detest the KMT. The KMT was "poisoning our relations with the Burmese," he wrote, and their presence would not have the "slightest effect" on the Chinese Communists' military capabilities. "In other words the game is simply not worth the candle even from a strictly military viewpoint." He asked that Acheson or Rusk send a personal message to Burma "unequivocally stating presence KMT troops" was "contrary to our policy" and that the United States would do all that it could resolve the situation.[24]

It is unlikely that Acheson's response, which came quickly, reassured the ambassador. He was instructed to assure the British that he had "no knowledge" of American involvement, and to tell the Burmese that an appeal to the UN would give the Chinese Communists an excuse to be aggressive. It was hardly worth responding to the British representative who, as the American embassy in Bangkok put it, "thinks he smells rats" when hearing American denials.[25] However, Acheson also asked Taiwan for an estimated KMT withdrawal date—which raises the question of how much Acheson knew about CIA involvement with the KMTs. Most likely Acheson did know and intended only to gain some time. Key told the Burmese that the United States was giving "no support" to the KMTs and wanted to see them withdrawn, and the Burmese agreed to postpone an approach to the UN. (One British official commented that it was surprising that the Burmese had expressed appreciation to the Americans on this occasion since they "might well have regarded" the American statement "as obvious duplicity.")[26]

Karl Rankin, US chargé d'affaires in Taipei, acted almost as an advocate for the Nationalists and could scarcely conceal his contempt for Key's appeal for pressure on Taipei. Still, Key refused to give in. If Taiwan could not control all KMT activities, he responded, at least it could stop Li. Furthermore, it could stop a possible invasion of Yunnan, which would likely provoke a Chinese counterattack into Burma. The State Department concurred with Key. It did not want the Burmese to take the issue to the UN, and instructed Rankin to get the Nationalist government to order Li to stop the invasion. Rankin complied, and the Taiwan government issued the order—"but without real expectation troop's compliance." According to Burma's prime minister, there were now six American advisers and six French nurses with the KMT forces.[27]

On 12 May 1951 Key reported that the well-armed KMT forces would likely attack PRC forces in Yunnan; if they were unsuccessful, Key feared they would retreat to Burma with the Chinese Communist troops in pursuit. This would provoke an all-out war, something that the KMT wanted, Key suggested with disgust.[28]

Meanwhile the British, convinced that American diplomats in Southeast Asia did not know about American covert support for the KMTs, decided that the situation was so serious that they had to approach the American government in Washington at a high level. "I am anxious to take all possible action to restrain the Americans," wrote Foreign Secretary Ernest Bevin. British suspicions about MacArthur's involvement gained further support when they learned from a British informant that CAT aircraft were flying supplies to the KMT twice a week. The supplies came from Okinawa and were transported via Bangkok.[29]

Suspecting MacArthur's involvement, the British embassy decided that Chairman of the British Joint Services Mission in Washington William Elliot would make the first approach to the US government. He spoke with CIA director Smith and came away convinced (certainly mistakenly) that Smith knew nothing of the operation. British diplomats then spoke with William S. B. Lacy, Director of the State Department's Office of Philippine and Southeast Asian Affairs. Lacy said (unhelpfully) that it was American policy to encourage the withdrawal of the KMT troops. Deciding that these approaches were not sufficiently forceful, the Foreign Office instructed Ambassador Oliver Franks to inform the State Department that there were six Americans working with the KMT troops, that the troops had modern American equipment supplied by CAT, and that the KMT troops were now moving toward China. Franks was to ask the State Department to press the Taiwan authorities to stop this and "to exert pressure on the appropriate United States agency to bring about the withdrawal of these Kuomintang troops."[30]

This was a powerful démarche, and according to the British the State Department promised "immediate and drastic action." But when Acheson informed Key about the British approach, he offered no advice beyond noting that Lacy had denied knowing anything about the British allegations. KMT troops were ready to invade Yunnan. Operation Paper was under way. "We have failed in our object of getting these troops to disperse," noted a British official.[31]

Aside from denying involvement, the United States had also been assuring Burma that the KMT forces were not under Taipei's control. This became increasingly difficult as more and more evidence emerged that supplies from Taiwan were arriving regularly, and Key became unwilling to convey such assurances. A few days later the British informed Key that a Major Stewart and an unnamed captain were working with the KMT. The British later speculated that "Major Stewart" was possibly Jim Stewart, a former USIS official. The speculation was correct. The two Americans with the KMT when they invaded Yunnan were James Stewart and a Lieutenant Marks.[32]

This increased Key's disillusionment. He had assured Burma that the KMT had no American or Taiwanese support. Both assurances were incorrect, and he was "increasingly embarrassed" by this. "Let us at least clear ourselves of Burmese suspicions of covert connection Stewart by taking action against him and . . . take positive measures designed to put end smuggling from Thailand," he wrote. A State Department official replied that he and his colleagues were "eager" to implement Key's recommendations, "but there are complications here that make it difficult for us." Key would later resign because he had unwittingly given the Burmese false assurances.[33]

On 24 May Li sent some six thousand troops into Yunnan. Unbeknownst to Key, one of Li's reasons for entering Yunnan was to get promised American aid. The Americans delivered, parachuting in some three thousand rifles and 160,000 rounds of ammunition and other supplies in late May and early June 1951. The incursion soon failed, as the PRC troops (as Key had predicted) drove the KMTs back into Burma. They had been "effectively routed."[34] Back in Burma they were reportedly "pillaging Burmese villages." This, the CIA reported, was causing "intense resentment among the local people." The KMT had also lost much of its "heavy arms and radio equipment," presumably American-supplied, to the Chinese Communists who also now had another pretext to invade. The Burmese responded by sending an additional six hundred troops to the border areas, a move that the CIA predicted would "weaken the government's efforts to contain the Burmese Communist insurrection."[35] The same agency that was helping the KMT was now saying, in effect, that it was a wrongheaded thing to do, a fiasco.

The Yunnan adventure led to further charges of American involvement. The Taipei authorities contended (at least partially correctly, as it turned out) that the forays into Yunnan had been undertaken "at the urging of American officials." The sawbwa of Kokang State reported that four Americans were working with the KMT forces in his region; they had the latest American weapons, he said.

Such reports continued to frustrate Key, who wrote that the "inability explain reports presence American citizens with KMT troops" put the embassy in an "awkward position. . . . These suspicions," he wrote, were "detrimental to US policies in Burma" and gave an opening for the communists to criticize the United States.[36]

Meanwhile, although the British had failed to stop the invasion, they still hoped to end American support for the KMT and planned to compile a dossier about KMT activities and "United States complicity in them."[37] However, they now had to acknowledge that their previous premise—that the State Department had been unaware of the covert activities and, once made aware, was working to stop them—might not be correct. It was probable, they now correctly concluded, that support for the KMT was part of the larger American policy toward China that "could not be reversed without a major effort by us." This they were unwilling to make, but they did make it clear in direct conversation with the Americans that they were convinced that the United States was involved with the KMT.[38] The Americans certainly got the word. "It was inescapably clear that the British Government like the Burmese Government is convinced that the United States Government is involved in equipping the Kuomintang contingents," the American record of a conversation at the State Department read.[39]

When the State Department again denied involvement, the Foreign Office expressed astonishment and provided the ambassador in Washington with a "large volume of information available to us [several words redacted] which indicates that the United States had been responsible for supplying arms to the Kuomintang . . . and is continuing to do so and that American Officers are serving with these troops." A few days later the British decided to lay their cards on the table. and gave the State Department a memorandum that presumably provided detailed evidence of American involvement. They did this, they said, because of the "'near hysterical' frame of mind of the Burmese Government on this matter." If nothing were done, the Burmese would take the matter to the UN, which would result in "difficulty and embarrassment for all concerned."[40]

When Ambassador Franks presented this additional information to the State Department, the American response was not much more forthcoming than before. American officials continued to deny any official involvement, though there was a tacit admission that "freelance Americans," including General Chennault and the CAT, might be involved.[41]

The public, meanwhile, was mostly unaware of developments along the Burma-China border. It was only at the end of July 1951 that much of the world learned about the KMT penetration of Yunnan when Associated Press correspondent Seymour Topping reported that Li had moved troops into China where they were fighting Chinese Communist forces. He hinted at CIA assistance to Li when he reported that the Burmese believed that the Americans were involved.[42]

By this time suspicion amounting to near certainty that the CIA was involved was apparent. In addition to British representations, there were persistent reports in newspapers in Burma, China, and Indonesia, for example, some of them giving specific numbers of Americans who were directing the forces and sending supplies to them. One even identified a specific "U.S. Intelligence Unit" (No. 101). But the State Department told Key to deny categorically that there was any "official or unofficial US GOVT connection whatsoever" with the KMT troops.[43]

Ambassador Key had now had enough. "This adventure has cost us heavily in terms of Burmese good will and trust," he wrote. It was also clear to him that, despite the denials, the United States was involved, and there was not much point in continuing to deny this:

> Participation by Americans in these KMT operations well known to GOB [Government of Burma] and constitutes serious impediment to our relations with them, a fact which has become only too apparent to all of us here. Denial of official US connection with these operations meaningless to GOB in face of reports they constantly receiving from their officials in border areas that KMT troops are accompanied by Americans and receiving steady supply American equipment, some of which dropped from American planes, and of reports from their Bangkok Embassy of American support activities going on in Siam, which is an open secret there. Thus American participation in KMT operations, which have brought chaos to eastern Shan states and have been conducted in flagrant disregard Burmese sovereignty, cannot but make a mockery in Burmese eyes of our officially expressed desire to aid in restoration of internal stability and to strengthen Burmese independence. This situation is prejudicing everything which we are striving to accomplish here and threatens all our future prospects.

Rusk responded unconvincingly that an "exhaustive investigation" had failed to turn up any American involvement. Key could tell the Burmese government that the United States had not had, nor would it have, any official or unofficial connection with Li's forces.[44]

A few days later Key met with Nu and received a report summarizing the KMT situation. Nu stated that he now had no choice but to appeal to the UN. He was under enormous pressure from Ne Win and others to do so, even though personally, he said, he would not want to take this course. With the KMT situation now "so urgent," there was no point in trying to resolve the matter along previously attempted lines, all of which had failed. American embassy officials agreed that Nu's political standing was now so precarious that he had to do something about the KMT.[45]

Key's impassioned telegrams finally had an impact. After careful consideration, the State Department responded, the United States would no longer attempt to restrain the Burmese from taking the matter to the UN.[46] But in the end, cautionary advice from the British and Indians persuaded Burma again to postpone its UN appeal. Probably the embarrassment that the country would face in acknowledging its inability to control its northern territories figured into the decision.

Key's telegrams may also have been responsible for a joint meeting in August 1951 of State and Defense Department officials on the KMT issue. They proposed a way forward along lines that Key would have approved: Li's forces would have to leave Burma, lest they become "a festering sore" in US-Burma relations and provide a pretext for PRC incursions. The United States would tell Burma that it did not support, officially or unofficially, Li's troops, and Key would ask the Burmese to propose as a solution preferably repatriation to Taiwan through Thailand.[47]

The meeting indicated growing criticism of American support for the KMT, even at high levels of the government. Whether it meant that the Americans were now committed to ending support for Li Mi is open to question. It certainly did not result in an immediate cessation of assistance. In September, for example, a "reliable witness" told an Australian official that a four-engine plane delivered supplies to the KMT forces once or twice a week and that "two Americans operating an American radio were supposed to be in contact with the plane." The Burmese also reported that two helicopters also brought in supplies and that others came overland from Thailand.[48]

The State Department continued to deny any official American involvement. Acly did acknowledge to the Australians the probable involvement of two unofficial Americans—"adventurers or gun runners" (one was named Stewart)—who perhaps had connections with Chennault. There was also some evidence, Acly stated, that Chennault's airline, CAT, was involved in supplying the KMT troops. The Bangkok embassy was instructed to investigate and to impound the passports of any Americans found to be involved, including Stewart.[49] Acly did not reveal that the CIA had begun subsidizing CAT in November 1949 and had purchased the airline outright in July 1950. A British diplomat once described the airline as "a chameleon organization which can conveniently turn Chinese or American at will, and which is not bothered by an uneasy conscience."[50]

The State Department did approach the Nationalists about cutting off supplies, but it is not clear that this was a serious intervention. The Nationalists were unlikely to be more receptive to such proposals now than they had been in the past, indeed they were defiant. As a British official wrote, "the real trouble is, apparently, that Chiang Kai Shek will not pay any attention to United States advice—he thinks the Americans are so committed to him that he can do as he pleases."[51] More fundamentally, at the highest levels it still remained American policy to support the KMT.

In addition to approaching Taiwan, the United States accepted a British proposal that the two countries jointly approach the Thai government about cutting off supplies to the KMT. Both the United States and Great Britain pointed out that if Burma took the issue to the UN, this would embarrass Thailand. Part of the State Department's motivation, however, was that failure to join with the British "might be interpreted as evidence of complicity" with Thailand in supplying the KMT.[52]

The British had initiated the proposal for a joint approach because they thought that the United States might have changed its policy and was now committed to cutting off supplies and preventing "private" Americans from assisting them. Perhaps the initiative was intended to test this hypothesis. They were therefore distressed to learn that the CIA's Sea Supply Company was continuing its operations. Prior to an approach to the Thais, the Foreign Office wrote, the United States must either restrict the company or, at the time of the joint approach it must tell the Thais that the United States did not approve the company's activities and would "prevent further American association with them."[53]

Given continued covert American support for the KMTs, the British ambassador in Bangkok, G. A. Wallinger, was distressed about a joint appeal. He shared his misgivings with the American chargé, William T. Turner, who reported them in detail. When the ambassador also informally mentioned the forthcoming US-UK appeal to Phibun, the prime minister responded that the matter was "really up to Americans as everything was being done in conjunction Americans." Wallinger himself was embarrassed at having to "participate in such a disingenuous approach" primarily because it would put the American representative in an "absurd position." He had "sufficient information," he said, "to prevent any illusions about the real source of supply of KMT troops in Burma," including the use of "four-motored planes," helicopters, Major Stewart, and "huge profits" made by General Phao and "probably" by Phibun himself on the opium that came out of Burma on the supply planes' return trips.[54]

To his own government Wallinger was even more direct. Phibun had told him that "a representative of the American Intelligence Agency" had asked him to support General Li, and that he had quickly agreed. "Why are you surprised?" he asked the startled ambassador. "Aren't you just as interested in killing Communists as I am, or as the Americans are?"[55] Willis Bird and the Sea Supply Company were central to the problem. They were supplying the KMT, General Phao and Prime Minister Phibun were involved, and the only way to "stop this nonsense" was to get the "highest levels" of the United States government to change course.

It was "useless" to speak to the American embassy in Bangkok, Wallinger stated. Embassy officers bitterly resented Bird and his company but were "obviously powerless to intervene." All of this, he suggested, put the American representative in a terrible situation. How could he complain to the Thais and yet be powerless to rein in the Americans who were supporting the Thais? Wallinger would make a démarche if ordered to do so, but he clearly found it distasteful.[56]

Foreign Office officials were sympathetic, but they were in a difficult position because the British themselves had proposed the joint approach. To be sure, they had done so under the false assumptions, but now that the United States had agreed to the British proposal, it was difficult to change course. Wallinger gave Turner every opportunity to refer the matter back to Washington, but Turner, though tacitly acknowledging that Bird's company was an embarrassment and that the request that he was about to make to the Thais was "somewhat disingenuous," decided not to contest his instructions.[57]

On 1 October 1951 the British ambassador and the American chargé d'affaires jointly requested that Thailand investigate the supply of American-made munitions to the KMT forces and do everything possible to prevent it. In response Foreign Minister Nai Worakan Bancha remarked to Turner that he "must be aware that there are Amers involved and that Amer arms were being delivered." Turner made no response.[58]

It may be that the démarche to the Thai government and the circumstances surrounding it led embassy officials in Bangkok to draft a letter to Rusk complaining about the Sea Supply Company's operations. Rusk was then away, but John Allison, who was about to replace him, read the protest and praised the writers for taking the initiative.[59] Pressure was mounting in Washington for a policy change.

A Possible Change of Course

Two possible ways to resolve the KMT issue were now considered. One was to allow the KMT troops to be sent to Taiwan, exiting Burma through Thailand or perhaps Indochina. A serious drawback to this plan was that the Burmese would probably insist on a token military expulsion of the KMT troops and might also be reluctant to accede to a voluntary move to Taiwan because China would probably complain that this was a violation of international law. Rusk raised another possibility: What if Burma allowed the KMT troops to remain in the Shan states, settle down as farmers, and relinquish their weapons? The Burmese responded that probable objections from China would not allow this. Although nothing came of these plans immediately, it was indicative of new thinking in Washington.

As for stopping the flow of munitions to the KMT through Thailand, the British kept up the pressure. British officials in Washington repeatedly discussed this with State Department officials, and British diplomats in Rangoon did the same with their American counterparts in Burma. They concluded that four-engine CAT planes, supposedly flying from Saigon to Rangoon, never landed in Rangoon but instead dropped off supplies in Kengtung. The British suggested that the American legation in Saigon pass along to Rangoon "any information concerning the reported CAT flights in Kengtung." (Significantly, Donald Heath, the American minister in Saigon who supported KMT involvement in Burma, passed the buck to the State Department, causing the military attaché in Rangoon to write on the telegram, "looks like Saigon doesn't want to 'play.'")[60]

Perhaps the Americans did eventually attempt to stop or minimize the flow of supplies to the KMT. A retrospective report stated that when the Nationalists asked CAT to undertake supply flights from Taiwan to Burma in February 1952, they were told that the US government had instructed them not to do so.[61] Thailand also may have modified its position, and Burma decided once again to defer an appeal to the UN.

But if aid through Thailand actually ended, it was only temporarily and against Phibun's wishes. He told the British ambassador that "he could not understand why there should be a move to put a stop to these Kuomintang operations," as they were part of an effort to contain communist expansion from the Himalayas to Korea. As a British official put it, "it is clear that Pibul [Phibun] had not been influenced by the joint approach and will not change his attitude until the Americans have firmly disowned ... Bird's activities." By the end of October the Foreign Office believed that the supplies were continuing to flow and perhaps were even increasing. Li continued to enjoy "close and profitable connections with the Thai police chief." Key, then in Paris, certainly did not think the supply of arms had stopped, for he wrote that one of the best ways to assist the Nu government was to "end the smuggling of arms to the KMT" and to stop the "unauthorized activities of Americans allegedly involved in the smuggling." The Thais and Americans should let the Burmese know that we were "doing something about this scandalous situation."[62]

Key's views received an important endorsement from Malcolm MacDonald, the well-regarded British commissioner general for Southeast Asia. MacDonald told Phibun that the KMT's presence was "far more of a present danger than it could be useful," and that it required the Burmese to divert attention away from the suppression of communist insurgents. It was the most dangerous problem the Burmese government faced, he said. Phibun was noncommittal, but MacDonald came away with the impression that he now realized that Thailand would have to end its KMT support.[63]

Why, then, did the CIA continue to support the KMT forces when there was such strong opposition from the embassies in Rangoon, Bangkok, and elsewhere? Probably, with American troops tied down in Korea and none to spare for other theaters, and the administration was looking for cheap ways to keep the Soviet Union (and its supposed client Mao Zedong) off balance and prevent Stalin from expanding his control over South and Southeast Asia. In January 1951 former OSS Director William J. Donovan had written to CIA Director Smith, urging him to build up "secret armies within those countries occupied by the enemy" and to "encourage the resistance groups in various countries to so engage Stalin and threaten his rear as to make it impossible for him to consolidate his present position in the Far East." Though Donovan did not specifically refer to support of the KMT (at least within those parts of the document that have been declassified), such support was consistent with his recommendation.[64]

Another probable reason that the CIA did not end its support of the KMT was its assessment that the PRC would not invade Burma under almost any circumstance, regardless of how provocative the KMT was. The CIA surmised that while China planned a hot war in Indochina and a "war of nerves" against Thailand, only "intensive political activity in Burma" was expected. Such reasoning, of course, undercut a major rationale for ending support of the KMT adventure: that its presence in Burma might cause the Chinese to intervene and perhaps take over Burma altogether. As it turned out, the CIA's judgment was probably correct, although neither the United States nor Burma could have been certain of this at the time.[65]

In any event, despite criticism, the United States continued to support the KMT. A British official concluded in January 1952 that it certainly looked as if the United States "had not stopped backing of Kuomintang operations in Burma." And a few days later in a conversation with the British ambassador, Phibun implied that "he was still receiving American support for these operations."[66]

Meanwhile Li Mi had returned to Taiwan, where he was met at the airport "by a few Chinese friends and Chennault. The Americans," reported a British consul, "were obviously nervous lest he should 'talk.'" Li was reportedly seeking additional funds and assistance. He may have succeeded, for soon thereafter the London *Observer* reported that Chiang Kai-shek had "recently reinforced Kuomintang General Li Mi's 93rd Division in Burma" with one of his "best battalions from Formosa." The newspaper added that American assistance to Li was "indisputable." This report, picked up by Soviet UN delegate Andrei Vyshinsky, caused a real stir, and the State Department felt obligated to dispute it. On 23 January Acheson personally issued a strong denial, and a few days later in Rangoon the American chargé asserted that "these rumors are completely without foundation. . . . The United States has never aided nor supported these troops in any way." Such charges were "absurd." Soon thereafter the State Department complained that the BBC "had given currency to the 'Observer' story."[67]

But the report was accurate. The British ambassador in Rangoon commented that it "tallies entirely with my own information." Also attesting to its validity was that the *Observer*'s sources were "certain members of the United States Embassy in Rangoon who appeared to be very frank and bitter about the operation being conducted through Siam, in which it was suggested General Chennault was involved." This demonstrated, one official minuted, that "the Americans do know that reinforcements have recently arrived from Formosa—in spite of their denials." The British also received another "hint" from the American embassy in London that as many as eight hundred new troops had arrived from Taiwan, flown in by CAT. About the same time the Burmese embassy in Bangkok reported that on 29 January 1952 Li had returned to Thailand in the American military attaché's airplane, though the report could not be confirmed.[68]

Supporters and Critics

Criticism of American support for the KMT did not let up. In Bangkok Stanton urged the Thai government to take strong measures to prevent more supplies from reaching the Nationalists. In London Ambassador Walter S. Gifford argued that any more raids into Yunnan would endanger the "whole western position in SEA." The KMT presence made it difficult for such countries as India to support American aims in the region. The French were embarrassed at unscheduled CAT flights carrying Chinese passengers refueling in Tourane (Danang) on their way to Bangkok, flights they pledged to block (although according to Richard Gibson the French cooperated with the Americans and simply destroyed the paperwork).[69]

Still, the KMT had its supporters. In addition to Rankin on Taiwan, Donald Heath, the American minister in Saigon, urged continuing American support for the Nationalist troops. "If US not engaged in supporting guerilla action against Commie Chi," he wrote, "it ought to be."[70] The American consul in Hong Kong also supported assistance to the KMT.

Henry B. Day, the American chargé in Rangoon, objected at length to Heath's views. The KMT troops in Burma were little better than "bandits" who preyed "upon an agricultural countryside which can ill afford to support them." Should there be direct communist aggression in the region, he wrote, the KMT would likely be a hindrance, rather than a help. Similarly, in New Delhi Ambassador Chester Bowles was "profoundly disturbed" at Heath's suggestion that the United States should be supporting the KMT forces. The different recommendations caused Ambassador Gifford to request a clarification, and Acheson came down strongly against Heath's position. While the United States was certainly not opposed to actions intended to weaken or embarrass the communists, the KMT presence in Burma threatened to stir up anticolonial feelings that would in turn hinder the larger American objective of retaining the support and friendship of Asian people, he wrote to Heath.[71]

Still, of course the CIA continued its support of the KMT. Acheson's strong response to Heath's dispatch suggests that he no longer favored American support, but the opponents of such support had to deal with the toxic atmosphere of McCarthyism then enveloping Washington. A particular focus of McCarthy's antagonism was the State Department, which he alleged was infiltrated by communists. In addition, the "fall" of China in 1949 had been traumatic for many Americans, and the China Lobby joined with the McCarthyites to assert that the Truman administration, particularly the pusillanimous State Department, was responsible. Although none of this appeared in American diplomatic reports, the British were well aware of it. As Oliver Franks put it, "if Chennault (or Bird) were to complain to the right Senators and Congressmen that potentially valuable help to anti-communist forces was being withdrawn because of weak-kneed policy of the State Department, they might well be able to stir up trouble in the press. If that were to happen we and the State Department would be the losers since the position is not one in which the rights and wrongs are easily comprehensible to the uninformed."[72]

Reports continued to surface about American involvement with the KMT. The Indians reported that "several" Americans were with the KMT troops. With remarkable specificity, the report also stated that there were "six or seven" Americans living in the Nhai Narong Hotel in Chiang Mai engaged, with General Phao's support, in supplying the KMT. These reports also produced some dissent at home. After the *St. Louis Post-Dispatch*'s military analyst, Brigadier General Thomas R. Phillips, concluded that American arms were being sent to the KMT forces, for example, the newspaper editorialized that this contradicted the "heated denials" coming from American officials; there appeared to be two policies, one public and one secret. This, the paper concluded, denied the public its right to know what was going on. The influential *New York Herald Tribune* reprinted the *Post-Dispatch*'s editorial.[73]

Only a few days later one of the most persuasive accounts of what was happening in Kengtung and other border areas appeared in a series of articles in the leading English-language newspaper in Rangoon, *The Nation*. The newspaper's sober, restrained account indicated that there were between twelve and thirteen thousand KMT troops in Kengtung with American arms and ammunition, that there were Americans with them, and that the Thais were clearly supporting them. American Foreign Service officers in Rangoon, when queried by the State Department about the reports, gave "full support" to *The Nation*'s accounts.[74]

It is possible that the growing opposition caused a change in Washington's policy at this point. According to Richard Gibson, on 3 March 1952 Acheson persuaded Truman to reverse. The evidence for this is not entirely conclusive, however, for over the next several weeks reports continued to surface about continuing American support. The American air attaché in Rangoon, Colonel J.S. Coward, told his British counterpart that he believed "that quite a large measure of support is given by America and that it reaches the K.M.T. by drops from Chinese [*sic*] Air Transport Aircraft." Coward had recently seen CAT Dakotas being loaded in Bangkok, presumably for just such a mission. Furthermore, small units of KMT troops entered Yunnan on more than sixty occasions during the first half of 1952.[75]

On the other hand, the United States expressed renewed willingness to try and assist Burma in repatriating the KMT troops. Some weeks before, Ne Win had floated a plan to remove them through Rangoon and had inquired about the American reaction. The United States responded that if a formal request were made it would attempt to find commercial aircraft to assist and would use its good offices to gain acceptance from Taiwan. However, nothing came of this, perhaps because Ne Win was not able to persuade his colleagues in the government to make an official request.

For the rest of the year the KMT affair festered. The British decided the time was not ripe for additional approaches to the Americans. The year 1952 was an election year and, as a British official put it, the American government had to deal with "powerful and ignorant pressure in any matter where Communist China was concerned." Additional Burmese troops were sent to Kengtung, but there was little hope that they could defeat the KMT. For a time there were fears that the KMT would unite with the Karens to oppose the government. This was a matter of grave concern to the United States, and Taiwan promised to try and control Li Mi. In the end no significant cooperation between the Karens and the KMT emerged. Still, as the new ambassador, William J. Sebald, reported in August 1952, there was "no doubt" that the Burmese public was greatly concerned about the KMT presence. When Sebald denied American involvement with the KMT, Ne Win responded, "Mr. Ambassador, I have it cold. If I were you, I'd just keep quiet."[76]

Meanwhile Sebald was preparing his first full-length report on the KMT problem. By this point (September 1952) the American estimate was that there were between six and eight thousand KMT troops under Li's control and another two to five thousand who did not follow him. Whatever the exact tally, it was a substantial number. Like his predecessor, Sebald clearly believed reports of American involvement, which he thought was asinine. The KMT presence was undermining American programs in Burma and constituted a "serious liability" for American objectives across Southeast Asia. A "complete liquidation" of the problem was the only solution, he argued. If in fact the administration had changed course in March, six months later this was still not apparent on the ground. When a State Department official wrote to Sebald that the department had consistently followed a policy of "maximum cooperation" with the government of Burma "involving the promotion, in so far as possible, of the principle of international law applicable in this case," the ambassador scribbled, "incomplete."[77]

Sebald's irritation with American policy was also evident in his response to a request from Rankin to assist in obtaining the release of KMT prisoners in Burma. Could the Burmese authorities simply allow small groups of prisoners to "escape" to Thailand, Rankin suggested, where Nationalist authorities could assist them? In reply Sebald observed that the root problem was the KMT presence in Burma, and in any case the last time the embassy had prevailed on the Burmese to release a Nationalist prisoner, Dr. Ting Tao-shao, Ting had rejoined the KMT troops in Burma, despite promises that he would return to Taiwan. Sebald would not approach the Burmese government. Many (probably most) American Foreign Service officers were opposed to the United States supporting the KMT. "It seems . . . that State Department thinking on this subject is substantially the same as our own," minuted one British official.[78]

The State Department now attempted (perhaps not coincidentally, now that the US presidential elections were about over), for really the first time, to find a solution. At the end of October 1952 it dispatched Assistant Secretary Allison to Taipei to meet with Chiang Kai-shek. Allison bluntly told him that the KMT presence in Burma was now hindering the anticommunist effort in Southeast Asia. When Chiang "emphatically disagreed,"[79] Allison wrote a memorandum condemning the KMT and its impact on Burmese-American relations, and then drafted a plan to withdraw KMT troops from Burma (via Rangoon) and ship them to Taiwan.[80]

Before Sebald received Allison's proposal he suggested that he and a State Department representative meet personally in Bangkok with Rankin and Stanton late in December to discuss the matter. The State Department liked Sebald's suggestion but wanted first to arrive at an agreement with "other interested agencies" in Washington. Stanton was more skeptical. Though willing to meet with Sebald, he questioned the meeting's utility and argued that the only way to evacuate the KMT troops, many of whom had now settled down in the Shan states, was to offer them individually a substantial financial inducement. "If some agency of US Govt" could do this, he argued, it might work, and given the serious problems that the KMT was causing, the expenditure would be justified. Most resistant was Rankin. He replied to Sebald, deliberately not sending a copy of his telegram to the State Department, that a meeting would accomplish nothing since policy was decided in Washington, and they should await the views of the incoming administration (which, he no doubt thought, would be friendlier to Taiwan than Truman and Acheson).[81]

Rankin's telegram angered Sebald. He immediately asked him to send a copy of his telegram to the State Department because he (Sebald) wanted to comment on it officially. Rankin refused on the grounds that it contained nothing new and might be "embarrassing to someone in Washington" (Allison?). So Sebald sent a "personal and top secret" four-page, single-spaced letter to Philip Bonsal, the director of the State Department's Office of Philippine and Southeast Asian Affairs, summarizing Rankin's telegram and stating that he and his colleagues in Burma thought it necessary to refute Rankin's views. He then copied verbatim a telegram he had drafted to the State Department (but had not sent) in which he stated that even to consider giving Li Mi support was "unmoral, unrealistic, and contrary to U.S. record of support of international law." The KMT forces, he wrote, were "ill-organized, semi-bandits and smugglers" who lived off the countryside at the "expense innocent villagers." He considered the KMT to be agents provocateurs who wanted to provoke another world war (as Key had once suggested). "Are we not in a position to stop this sort of thing?" he wrote.[82]

State Department officials disagreed with Rankin's analysis on most points, but they did agree that no further action should be taken until the Eisenhower administration took office on 20 January 1953. If the new administration did decide to support the KMT evacuation, the Taiwan government might well co-operate since it would want to "get off to a good start in its relations with the Eisenhower Administration."[83]

CHINA, COMMUNISTS, AND OTHER INSURGENTS

If the KMT issue was the most important problem in Burma's relations with the United States, the larger question for American policymakers all across Asia remained how best to resist the expansion of "international communism." American policy was formalized in May 1951 with NSC 48/5 ("United States Objectives, Policies and Course of Action in Asia") and in a more detailed way in February 1952 with NSC 124 ("United States Objectives and Courses of Action with respect to Southeast Asia"). The authors of both documents hoped "to prevent the countries of Southeast Asia from passing into the communist orbit, and to assist them to develop the will and ability to resist communism from within and without and to contribute to the strengthening of the free world," because communist domination of Southeast Asia "would seriously endanger in the short term, and critically endanger in the longer term, United States security interests." These included the vital rubber and tin reserves of Indonesia and Malaya and the need to prevent Japan having to accommodate to communism if Southeast Asia were not available to it as a market and a source for vital raw materials. Burma was important because, among other considerations, its rice exports were critical to Malaya, as well as to Ceylon and Hong Kong.

The American policy in Burma was similar to that in other Southeast Asian countries. The United States attempted to provide economic and technical assistance, enhanced propaganda and cultural activities, encouraged increased trade with the "free world," mounted covert operations, and supported anticommunist activities in the country's Chinese communities. The United States was also open to providing some military assistance (as it did to most of the other countries in the region) and contemplated working with nongovernmental groups that would resist communism. Should there be overt Chinese Communist aggression against Burma, the United States envisaged a military response, which could include employing Chinese Nationalist forces.[1] Thus American policy in Burma was part of a regional and worldwide effort to contain the spread of communism. Failure to do so in Southeast Asia would result in a series of falling dominoes.

U Nu and Communism

Aside from the KMT presence, the Americans continued be concerned with the perceived instability of the Nu government, the possibility of a Chinese Communist occupation of Burma, widespread PRC subversion and assistance to Burmese communists, Burmese communist political strength, and the ongoing noncommunist insurgencies.

By 1951 the United States had become much more supportive of U Nu because he had demonstrated discreet but clear anticommunist attitudes. By this point Nu's efforts to achieve leftist unity in the AFPFL had failed. The communists had left, many were in armed opposition, and many PVOs followed them. In December 1950 the AFPFL expelled left-wing socialists, with the result that moderate socialists now controlled the party. One sign of this was that early in January 1951 the government released from jail U Ba Sein, described by the American embassy as one of the "most anti-communist and pro-Western" Burmese politicians; the Americans thought that his release was part of a deliberate effort to confront the communists. About the same time Nu told a youth rally in Rangoon that the Soviet Union was using international communism to promote its own interests and that the Burmese should look to their own nationalism to guide their future. He "set himself against communism without directly condemning it," reported chargé d'affaires Henry Day.[2]

Some Americans felt that the government was demonstrating real ability in suppressing communist and other dissident groups. The CIA commented that Burma might actually be able to "destroy organized rebel resistance by the end of 1951." In March the embassy reported that military operations against the insurgents were "successful in the main." The embassy remained concerned about PRC support for the Burmese communists and the possibility that the government could not stop them.[3] But on this occasion Washington officials actually took a less alarmist view, telling the embassy that they doubted the embassy's fear of communist success. They thought American programs in Burma were achieving their objectives.

Still, there were mixed signals and conflicting and changing assessments of Nu's government. In April insurgents cut off Rangoon's water supply; it took ten days to repair the damage. (By July 1952 they had cut off the water supply on at least nine occasions.) Furthermore, in May 1951 the CIA reported that there was "increasing evidence" of PRC assistance to the BCP, including training in Yunnan; of Chinese military forays into disputed areas along the border; and of efforts to foster a separatist movement among the Kachins. Burma's inability to control the border meant that "most of Burma north of Mandalay is vulnerable to Communist operations." The establishment of a Soviet embassy and the arrival of more Viet Minh representatives in Rangoon were also troubling. All in all, the communist movement in Burma, which had been divided and uncoordinated, was now thought to be more unified and dangerous. A CIA informant even predicted the "imminent overthrow" of the government. The embassy and the CIA itself considered this assessment "overly pessimistic," but the agency did foresee a "long range threat" to the government and increased "instability in the country." Still, Acheson was wary of involving the United States too directly. He put on hold an embassy suggestion to "adopt covert measures to create public pressure on the Government to take effective action against the Chinese."[4]

One potential way to resist communism in Burma, it was thought, was for the United States to support Buddhism. As Ambassador Key put it, "Buddhism unquestionably strong force against spread communism." Nu, a very devout Buddhist, was doubtless sincere in his desire to emphasize the importance of Buddhism in Burmese life, but he may also have wanted to replace leftist unity with Buddhist unity. In any event, Nu had urged the United States to provide one to two million dollars to support all religious groups in Burma, the funds to be apportioned in accordance with the number of adherents of each religion. Key liked Nu's idea but understood US constraints against appropriations for religious purposes and proposed instead that the State Department see if a private foundation might fund the effort. The embassy also concluded that American aid should be limited to help only the Buddhists, since they were so overwhelmingly important in Burma. Interestingly, the embassy also wanted the State Department to see if there were any "secret funds" from the CIA for this purpose.[5]

Key discussed the matter with a CIA official ("GAC"). Together they agreed that a CIA front organization, the Far Eastern Foundation, should be created to channel funds to support Buddhism in Burma. They then went to Nu, where GAC posed as a representative of the foundation and stated that it "would be receptive" to providing funds. Nu responded positively, and it was agreed that a representative of the foundation would return to Rangoon in two or three months to work out details with the Buddha Sasana Organization (whose mission was to spread the teachings of Buddha), which was just then being formed.

The next day Nu summoned Key to his office and said he wanted one to two million dollars to found a proposed Buddhist University, as well as to restore two important pagodas, one of which contained a hair from the Buddha. Although Key remonstrated that GAC had told Nu's attorney general that the foundation could not undertake such an ambitious project, Nu persisted. In the end, Key recommended that at least some funds be provided. Perhaps the pagodas, one of which had been destroyed by Allied bombing, might be restored.[6]

It may well be that some secret CIA funds were transferred to Burma, for in August Key reported that the Buddha Sasana Organization would hold its first meeting on 28 August 1951, and that Nu was pleased that a "representative of American private organization" would probably arrive in Rangoon in the near future.[7] Whether such a representative arrived, and what eventuated, is not clear from the available records. In September 1951, however, the State Department recommended that Burma approach the Ford Foundation directly for assistance to support Rangoon University. If the funds were granted, the State Department indicated, Burma could then redirect the funds it currently spent in support of the university toward a religion department or a religious institution. In October Brad Connors (perhaps W. Bradley Connors, a State Department public affairs officer) did arrive in Rangoon, and the State Department agreed to discuss using counterpart funds to somehow support Nu's Buddhist projects.

Attorney General U Chan Htoon finally put Nu's proposal in writing, and Key strongly urged the department to approve it. It had the potential to "deal Communism in Burma a heavy blow" and, if it were not approved, this would "bitterly disappoint" the prime minister. It was about the last recommendation to the State Department that Key would make. A few days later he left for Paris to attend a UN General Assembly meeting. He never returned to Burma in an official capacity, having resigned in protest over the KMT issue. Albert Low Moffat, who was in charge of American economic assistance to Burma, supported Key's recommendations with an impassioned plea to the Economic Cooperation Administration. By late November 1951 the proposal to use counterpart funds had gained "almost universal approval" at the ECA. The State Department endorsed the idea, and Burma's ambassador expressed his appreciation. But in the end the Mutual Security Administration, which had just replaced the ECA as the agency that administered foreign aid, disapproved the plan.[8]

The Eisenhower administration elevated the importance of the religious factor in foreign affairs, however, feeling that it was a potent anticommunist weapon. The Operations Coordinating Board, established in 1953 to coordinate and implement national security policies, established a working group to investigate how the religion factor could be exploited to enhance American foreign policy objectives. Whether this resulted in Burma's requests being revisited is not certain, but CIA initiatives were not publicized, and it may be that there were covert sources of funds.[9]

Meanwhile the communists had suffered a "crushing defeat" in the elections in June 1951, with the AFPFL winning a good majority of the seats (though fewer than before). But over the summer there were many worrisome signs, including probable PRC support for the BCP. The government denied this, which to Key revealed its naiveté, a "refusal believe Mao Govt wld do such a thing"[10] (although in fact Nu remained suspicious of Chinese intentions, including support for the BCP).

Tensions between Ne Win and socialist leaders added to the uncertainty and the ability of the army to take on the insurgents forcefully, and in July Ne Win took a leave of absence from the government. (The scuttlebutt was that he was enamored of a married woman; several years later one of his American advisers commented that his home life was "very 'unhappy.'")[11] Finally in July the embassy reported that Mandalay was "virtually surrounded" by communist insurgents; the situation was so dangerous that many trains had ceased to operate because they were so often attacked. Some missionaries were considering evacuation as Chinese communist forces approached the border. Since missionaries were always most reluctant to abandon their posts, the situation must have been "truly alarming."[12]

Fears of the Collapse of the Government

These pessimistic assessments were more formally expressed on 1 August 1951 in a National Intelligence Estimate (NIE 36) entitled "Prospects for the Survival of a non-Communist Regime in Burma." The prospects were not bright. Given PRC assistance to the BCP, it would "probably be able within the next year or two to achieve *de facto* control over a considerable area of northern Burma." This in turn would produce "an effective Communist-dominated coalition of insurgent groups." China itself had the capability to overrun Burma altogether—a frightening prospect that, if accomplished, would be "a great strategic advantage to both the Chinese Communists and the USSR." It would "drive a wedge" between South and Southeast Asia, result in increased communist penetration of Indochina and other areas of Southeast Asia, and create a psychological sense that communism was "an irresistible force." It would give China control over Asia's rice bowl which, aside from feeding the Chinese, would be used as a political weapon to intimidate other countries in the region. Fortunately, China was unlikely to move militarily against Burma since it probably believed that the BCP would eventually triumph. The communists were apparently in the ascendant.[13]

The insurgent situation grew worse as insurgent activity broke out in new areas of central Burma. Furthermore, as NIE 36 had predicted, the BCP made more headway in uniting with other communist and noncommunist insurgent groups. The communist movement, which a year ago was in disarray, "is being transformed into a vigorous force with a clearly-defined strategy for obtaining control of Burma," reported the CIA. Acts of sabotage and attacks on railroads, highways, and riverboats continued at a high level. Ne Win (who still commanded the armed forces) acknowledged by October 1951that "the initiative had passed into the hands of the insurgents." There were even predictions that a communist offensive in November would attempt to win control of Burma from Mandalay northward.[14]

Not surprisingly the British attitude had changed from "cautious optimism to sober pessimism." When Nu announced that conditions were improving daily and that the rebellions were no longer serious, the CIA commented that this was "a deliberate distortion of the facts." The British ambassador agreed, informing his government that the situation was disintegrating. There were even fears that Ne Win, a man of "doubtful loyalty," might defect to the communists.[15]

The State Department now feared that communist insurgents would seize power, perhaps in two years. Given the apparently precarious situation, the Americans thought the time had come for the government to make peace with the minorities. This was, however, a complicated and difficult proposition. Despite the Karens' cooperation with the Allies during World War II, the Christian faith of many of them (especially among the leadership), their anticommunist posture, and their generally positive attitude toward the West, the United States had lined up with their enemy, the Burmese government (even as the government suspected that American sympathies were with the Karens). The Americans had refused to give arms to the Karens, and over time the Karens became increasingly bitter toward the United States; there were persistent reports that they were cooperating with communist insurgents. Furthermore, a culture of guerrilla life had emerged among some Karen youth. But Ne Win's intransigent attitude toward the Karens was perhaps the most difficult obstacle to peace, the Americans thought.[16]

As the situation worsened, Burma became more tempted to request American assistance, provided it came without strings. Burma's ambassador to the United States inquired about obtaining American arms. Despite the increasing threat from the insurgents, however, military assistance to Burma was problematic. The British refused to supply all the arms that the Burmese requested because, they said, Burma already had enough, and surplus arms would be sold or end up in the hands of the insurgents. The State Department's Philippine and Southeast Asian Affairs Office concurred, adding that the army was "demoralized, corrupt and inefficient" and therefore more assistance would not be useful. But fundamentally the problem was that the Burmese government was "not yet prepared to depart sufficiently from its policy of neutrality in the 'Cold War' to become an active ally against Soviet imperialism." Or, as the CIA concluded, high-level civilian and military officials continued to be indifferent "to the threat of international Communism." This was due to a combination of fatalism, a belief that the Burmese communists were not real communists, and a "blind reliance on Buddhism to save Burma from an alien faith."[17] More likely, neutralism reflected the importance of Burmese nationalism, the legacy of colonialism, and the need to concentrate on domestic development. Key had more faith in Nu and his anticommunist credentials, but he did not control official thinking.

Still, there was some American support for approving a limited supply of arms to Burma. Burma had entered into a contract for ammunition from Olin Industries, and the State Department was willing, for political reasons, to allow some, but not all, of the ammunition to be shipped.[18]

The Americans became more open to armed assistance when reports in October 1951 indicated that the Karens were cooperating with the communists. These reports led to near panic. The earlier prediction of communist control in two years suddenly seemed optimistic. The communists were now likely to control northern Burma "within the next few months," and, even more alarming, would "have control over the whole of Burma within the next year." Malcolm MacDonald commented that Burma was "the weakest spot in Southeast Asia," and predicted that its government would not survive without outside assistance. The CIA now similarly concluded starkly that the "progressive disintegration of the Rangoon regime's position" was "leading to Communist control of Burma." In a review of NIE 36, intelligence officials made the alarming prediction that within six to eight months much of northern Burma would be under communist control, and a "pro-Communist regime" could well replace the present government "within the next few months."[19]

The State Department's highest officials shared this pessimism and called for a reexamination of American policy, including exploring a joint or coordinated approach with the British. Dean Rusk ordered Ambassador to the Philippines Myron Cowen to discuss this with Malcolm MacDonald in Singapore, whose knowledge and judgment the State Department respected. Though Rusk ostensibly selected Cowen rather than Key because Key was then in Paris, it is more likely that the State Department had lost confidence in Key. Not only did Key strongly object to American support for the KMT in Burma, but he did not share the pessimism expressed by the CIA or the State Department. In fact, such pessimism infuriated him: there was "no particular reason for alarm." He also found MacDonald's judgments ill informed and ignorant. MacDonald had, for example, contended that U Nu was little more than a monk without political insights. On the contrary, thought Key, Nu was astute and "covertly anti-communist." He was a devout Buddhist, but MacDonald failed to understand the political strength of Buddhism in Burma. What the United States ought to do, he argued (as he had often done in the past) was to find a way to support religion in Burma. "Buddhism is a vital force in Burma," he wrote, and "the Prime Minister knows his people."[20]

Not surprisingly Key made no immediate impression. The CIA's Board of National Estimates approved the alarmist revision of NIE 36,[21] and MacDonald continued to believe that the "Burmese situation has never been so bad." A little later the CIA predicted a Burmese communist attack early in 1952, joined by Naw Seng's Karen forces. The CIA also reported that U Ba Swe, "an extreme leftist," was plotting to replace U Nu in January 1952 and that he would "be hostile to the US and would probably seek much closer relations with the Chinese Communists." Finally, US military intelligence concluded that the situation in Burma was "chaotic" and that the communists were growing in strength and might well attempt to overthrow the government.[22]

The Americans deemed the situation in Burma so serious that the State Department prepared a position paper for President Truman to use in forthcoming discussions with British Prime Minister Winston Churchill. Truman was to review with Churchill ways to "improve the seriously deteriorating situation in Burma." Perhaps more military matériel could be provided, and perhaps British and American information services could be made more effective. If the communists did in fact take over northern Burma, perhaps there could be coordinated or joint Anglo-American action. The Joint Chiefs of Staff generally concurred with the draft, noting that the fall of Burma would endanger not just all of Southeast Asia but also Pakistan, India, and Ceylon.[23] Thus, the less alarmist views of Ambassador Key were overridden.

It is important to recall that in the early 1950s, the United States considered Burma to be nearly as important to the security of Southeast Asia as Indochina. Indeed, a CIA memo in January 1952 noted that although Indochina was often referred to as the "key" to Southeast Asia, it was in fact "extremely difficult to distinguish the relative importance to the security of Southeast Asia" of the two countries. Extremely serious consequences would result throughout the region if either country came under communist sway. And in both countries there was "a wasting away of anti-Communist assets," primarily due to the success of communist insurgencies. In sum, American policymakers considered the situation in both countries critical.[24]

Burmese officials, however, despite their continuing problems with China, did not consider their situation desperate, as was evidenced in their reluctance to renew the American assistance agreement scheduled to expire in January 1952. They feared that the required language would tie them to one side in the Cold War, and restrictions under the Mutual Defense Assistance Act of 1951 (more commonly known as the Battle Act) that prohibited aid to any country supplying strategic materials to communist countries also concerned them. It did not help that further revelations about American involvement with the KMT surfaced at this very moment. When the agreement lapsed, all aid was temporarily suspended. In February, however, the two countries did arrive at mutually acceptable language, and the Americans convinced the Burmese that the Battle Act's restrictions did not apply. Thus, despite strong domestic opposition, the Burmese agreed to accept some American assistance.[25]

When it was learned in January 1952 that negotiations between the Karens and the communists had collapsed, the Americans could breathe a sigh of relief. But the United States did not like the appointment of U Ba Swe as the new minister of defense, replacing the weak but pro-Western U Win. Ba Swe also had higher ambitions, and it was feared that his presence in the cabinet would in general reduce U Nu's authority. Furthermore the possibility of a Karen-communist alliance continued to surface. According to the CIA in April the two rebel groups agreed on joint operations and administration of certain areas. But a formal alliance had not yet been concluded, as the Karens hoped to acquire arms from noncommunist sources if possible.[26]

Ambassador Key Vindicated

Over time the pessimistic projections proved to be largely inaccurate, thus vindicating Ambassador Key. Burmese forces made significant headway against the communists, forcing them to mount a "peace offensive." Ba Swe surprised the Americans, turning out to be a pragmatic nationalist who as minister of defense took strong action against the communist underground. "We are all delighted by the vast improvement in the situation in Burma," wrote a State Department official, noting also Ba Swe's "renaissance," which indicated "a genuine change of heart."[27]

At the same time the government was making considerable progress against the Karen insurgency. The American military attaché was reportedly "astonished" at these successes, and the CIA concluded that the KNDO resistance was "getting weaker." Due to the death of the Karen leader Ba U Gyi, the KNDO was "increasingly desperate." When the new American ambassador, William Sebald, arrived in July he was "definitely encouraged with the situation here."[28] He attributed the negative assessments regarding Burma to a bad press.

To be sure there remained some skeptics, including the CIA which, while admiring the hardline attitude of the government toward the communist insurgents, noted that government forces had not yet inflicted a decisive defeat on them or reduced their overall capabilities. Furthermore, the communists' determination to move toward political methods of achieving their goals might well prove a more serious long-run "threat to Western interests." The *New York Times* correspondent, Hanson Baldwin, thought Sebald's positive assessments of Burma and particularly of its leaders was naive. Baldwin believed that virtually all "oriental politicians" sought power for their personal advantage. Even Sebald sometimes felt frustrated; he resumed smoking.[29] But all in all the alarmist views seemed increasingly foolish. Although Burma still faced serious problems, there had either been a remarkable turnaround or the earlier pessimistic assessments had been incorrect. With Western support for its economy, Burma stood a good chance of surviving as a strongly neutral, yet generally anticommunist country. The United States was again looking seriously at providing military aid. But, as Australian ambassador to the United States P. C. Spender astutely observed, it was foolish to expect (as he feared many Americans did) that countries like Burma were likely to "be brought into line with our policies."[30]

Meanwhile American economic and technical assistance continued at a modest level. Knappen, Tippets, and Abbott Engineering Company of New York provided consultants to survey Burma's economy. Economic assistance increased from $10.8 million in FY 1951 to $14 million in FY 1952.[31] The program, directed by Moffat and administered by a significant number of American officials in Burma (twenty-two in public health alone), included development and technical assistance in finance and trade, public administration, agriculture (aimed primarily at increasing rice production), public health (especially malaria abatement—almost 30 percent of the Burmese population was infected), industry, transportation, and education. Also, increasing numbers of Burmese were being sent to the United States for technical training. The program got off to a slow start, due to Burmese suspicions: only three trainees were sent in FY 1951, but the following year sixty-nine went. They did very well, in part because most were fluent in English.[32]

A flap occurred in July 1952 when Stanley Andrews, the administrator of American aid programs, reportedly said that the program in Burma was expensive and had little impact on communism. Asked about the $2 million in mutual security funds awarded to Robert Nathan Associates "to survey Burma's economic needs," Andrews commented, "that sounds awful damn high to me." These remarks angered Ambassador Sebald. Andrews regretted that his comments "caused embarrassment," but it was not clear that his remarks were really taken out of context as he contended. Technically Nathan was hired directly by

Burma to provide economic planning, although the United States paid Burma for his services. Conservatives disliked Nathan, an unreconstructed New Deal liberal, but their criticisms commended him to U Nu. A critical editorial in the conservative *Chicago Tribune* was "the best recommendation," Nathan wrote.[33]

The prospect of significantly decreasing assistance for FY 1953 troubled American officials in Burma because American aid was just beginning to show some positive results, and Burmese officials liked the programs. To reduce aid at this moment seemed foolish. Among other things, the Americans had restored the port of Rangoon, begun construction of a hospital and medical college, funded flood control projects, and decreased the incidence of malaria in the Shan States from 50 percent of the population to 10 percent. In addition, in view of the "great improvement" in Burma's stability and its increasingly anticommunist stance, the State Department wanted to "give all possible encouragement" to the country's desire to strengthen its armed forces, including the provision of American military assistance. The Burmese again seemed to want this: Nu had specifically requested small arms for the police and village militias. The British found the situation in Burma sufficiently improved that they were now willing to provide most of the armaments requested, though they had no objection to Burma receiving some from the United States.[34]

Perhaps not surprisingly, communist governments now began to speak critically of Burma. Beijing launched vicious attacks on "Traitor" Nu. When a broadcast critical of Burma came from Albania the Americans passed it along to U Thant, the future UN secretary general and at the time the secretary of information. Thant planted the report in the *New Times of Burma*, which responded critically to the Albanian broadcast.[35]

By September 1952 both Sebald and the CIA concluded that the situation in Burma was much improved. The country had subtly shifted its foreign policy toward the West and had made significant headway against all insurgent groups in the country, including the communists, as Ne Win's efforts to expand the armed forces and improve its capabilities began to show. These developments, concluded the CIA's Office of National Estimates, were "considerably more favorable" than those projected in earlier national estimates, and the office called for a new estimate. The title of NIE 36, "Prospects for the Survival of a Non-Communist Regime in Burma," was out of date. Reflecting the new assessment, the State Department's desk officer for Burma commented that the situation was as favorable as "at any time since its independence," and when Assistant Secretary Allison visited several Asian countries in October 1952 he came away very much impressed. "I was more encouraged about Burma than about any other particular place," he wrote. Former Ambassador Key's more measured views were proved correct, if unacknowledged.[36]

The improving relations allowed the reopening the USIS Library in Mandalay in October 1952, an occasion at which Ambassador Sebald delivered his first public address in Burma. The new situation also inhibited the CIA from implementing that part of NSC 124 that called for development of anticommunist guerrillas to be activated if Burma fell to the communists.[37]

To keep relations moving in a positive direction, Sebald lobbied hard to invite Ne Win to the United States. This would be the highest-ranking military mission yet that Burma had sent abroad (that it would go to the United States irritated the British), and Sebald urged that the proposed ten-person mission be accorded "red carpet treatment." He encountered some resistance from military officials in Washington. ("Washington can be very stupid at times," he confided to his diary.) But Sebald ultimately succeeded in having the trip approved, and Ne Win demonstrated his appreciation by inviting the ambassador to join him at the local horseraces. It was the first time Sebald had ever been to a horserace.[38]

Sebald regarded the visit, scheduled for October and November 1952, as "the biggest break we have had in our relations with Burma in recent years." Although arranging the visit was a "colossal headache," he predicted that the trip would result in improved bilateral relations. Despite what Sebald regarded as gross mismanagement by the Department of Defense (the military's handling of the trip was "stupid and demonstrating a complete lack of imagination"), Ne Win was reportedly pleased with his visit, during which he discussed the possible purchase of arms. He also told American officials that his government was making progress against the various insurgencies, particularly the communists. More and more rebels were surrendering—three to five hundred each month, he claimed. The government "knew the Communist mentality very well" and was able to induce many to surrender. Defence Minister Ba Swe told a visiting American delegation that "the backbone of the insurrections had been broken." Soon thereafter Ne Win indicated that he wanted a significant increase in the size of the British military mission in Burma, indicating a further move toward the West.[39] Prime Minister U Nu even wanted a large US naval vessel to call at Rangoon. Sebald bragged that he personally had "made more progress in Burma in four months than was made in the previous four years."[40]

Continuing Sources of Tension

Although Ne Win's visit highlighted the improved relationship, not all was sweetness and light. One problem concerned racial segregation in the United States and its impact on relations with nonwhite countries. As labor leader and civil rights advocate A. Philip Randolph wrote after a visit to Burma in 1952, "racism in the United States . . . tends to undermine the faith in moral leadership of this country."[41] That same year a Burmese judge visiting the United States was refused service in a Washington restaurant (Washington being still a racially segregated city). Even more embarrassing, shortly after Ne Win's return to Burma another Washington restaurant refused to serve Burma's minister of housing and labor, while another official was roughly treated by an FBI agent. Burma's Foreign Office told American diplomats that his sort of thing would "undo much of good will created by U.S. in Burma" and would make future accommodation between the two countries difficult. The State Department complained about "the unfortunate effects of thoughtless discrimination of this kind" but did not want the incidents publicized, lest the communists take advantage of it in UN meetings then discussing discrimination.[42]

Also, the Burmese remained suspicious of American motives. U Kyaw Nyein, an important AFPFL leader, for example, criticized the Marshall Plan and feared that if American capitalism dominated the world "it will mean the end of Socialism." Burma would remain strongly neutralist. The KMT issue, of course, remained to rile relationships. Finally there were some problems regarding the overbearing behavior of official Americans in Burma. Reports of such behavior seldom made their way into official American dispatches, but Australian observers could be more frank. Thus late in 1951 a high-ranking Australian mentioned that "the Americans may have provoked some of their unpopularity by thoughtless behaviour offensive to Burmese susceptibilities." A year later the Australians judged the new ambassador, Sebald, to be "well suited to mitigate the American reputation for aggressiveness and over-assertion." They were especially impressed with Sebald's references to the spiritual strengths of Buddhism, something that Key had also emphasized. Sebald's Japanese wife also made a good impression and cultivated contacts with Burmese women. On the other hand some members of the Technical Cooperation Administration offended their Burmese counterparts. "Particularly unsuitable" was the acting head of the mission, Frank Trager, who was reportedly "forceful and well informed but remarkably tactless." He would, for example, lecture Buddhists about Buddhism, "instruct the Chief Justice in the weaknesses and deficiencies of the Burmese legal system," and tell newspaper editors how to run their businesses. The result, the Australians stated, was that the Burmese refused to take the technical program seriously. The Australian report appears to have been accurate. In January 1953 a source told the CIA that many American engineers working in Burma exhibited "tactlessness" and might well "imperil future relationships." The Americans, the source went on, also enjoyed upscale housing and had much more household help than they would have had in the United States, which caused "some resentment."[43] Their salaries were also many times higher than those of their Burmese counterparts.

If Sebald needed educating about the attitudes of these Americans, the Burmese were quick to inform him. U Hla Maung, who chaired Burma's Economic Aid Committee, complained to Sebald personally that the technical advisers talked down to the Burmese. The ambassador also found himself critical of Sidney Browne, the embassy's counselor, who believed that it was not good for the Burmese to try to raise their living standards. Browne was clearly a problem. He advised Sebald not to go to the airport to see off a Burmese mission to the United States because it would appear he was "coddling the Burmese!" Sebald, clearly outraged, went to the airport. Although Sebald did consider reducing technical assistance while increasing economic assistance, he did not recommend any overall changes in American aid to Burma, which he regarded as essential to the country's "defense against communist subversion."[44]

The year 1952 was thus a year of significant change. It began with fears that Burma was about to be taken over by the communists. It ended with a growing sense of confidence that this would not happen. The leadership—even those most identified as leftists—were determined nationalists who went after the communists and other insurgent groups vigorously. By the end of the year the alarmist views of earlier months were out of date, and there was a growing sense of optimism that Burma, though a decidedly neutral country, would resist communism and would be informally on the side of the West—despite anger over American covert support for the KMT, irritations over racial discrimination, and overbearing behavior of some Americans.

Indeed, in January 1953 U Nu himself publicly expressed deep appreciation for the American aid and attacked those who had objected as "fools or blockheads." The aid, he said, was absolutely essential to Burma's reconstruction needs, and the agreements were not in any way detrimental to Burma's interests nor (as some had asserted) did they provide the United States with military bases. He would "have my throat cut off" if anyone could prove otherwise, and he thanked the United States for its "sincere motives in giving us most needed assistance." It was a remarkable speech, and the incoming secretary of state, John Foster Dulles, expressed his appreciation.[45]

Soon, however, Burma began to reassess its needs for assistance, especially technical assistance. This probably was the result of irritation at the condescending attitudes of some of the advisers, but it also reflected concerns that the cost of the advisers consumed a large portion of the aid and also that they were not always of the best quality.

Nu's recent praise of the assistance also produced some backlash within his own administration.[46] Burma's unease also reflected fears that the incoming Dwight Eisenhower administration would demand more conditions for aid. Finally, Burma was frustrated about the apparent inability or unwillingness of the

United States to rein in KMT activity. Sebald told Ne Win that, if anything, the new Republican administration would pay more attention to Asia than the outgoing Democratic one, but the Burmese wanted to be certain before they asked formally for more assistance.

For the moment, however, questions about American military and economic assistance would have to wait. A crisis was developing over the continuing presence of KMT troops.

CHANGING COURSE ON THE KUOMINTANG

On 10 January 1953 Ambassador Sebald sent his quarterly security report to Washington. He pulled no punches. Repeating what had become a consistent litany of complaints, the ambassador wrote that the KMT was "a constant threat to security, since it disrupts the economy of the area, forms a standing pretext for invasion by Communist China and detracts from the efforts of the Burmese Army to defeat the communist insurgents." On the same day a Burmese military commander, Douglas Blake, told the Americans that the KMT forces had now reached seventeen thousand, with additional troops arriving regularly by air. The CIA commented that Blake had "a reputation for integrity." If his estimate was anywhere near the mark, the number of KMT troops in Burma was astounding. By March 1953 some 80 percent of Burma's armed forces were engaged with the KMTs rather than with the communists.[1]

In Thailand, Ambassador Stanton was equally forceful in his condemnation of the KMTs. He confronted Nationalist Chinese officials and accused them of cooperating with Karen insurgents, of overthrowing local Shan officials, and engaging in such hostile actions against the government that they were "playing straight into the hands of Communists." Indeed, their forces in Burma were not "interested in fighting Communists but in extending their area influence in territory which did not belong to them." The results, he stated, would be "disastrous"; the only solution was to recall the troops to Taipei.[2]

This flurry of angry telegrams forced the issue to the highest levels of the government. On 19 January 1953 (the last day of the Truman administration), it was discussed at the CIA. Two days later the CIA complained that a plan to remove the KMT forces from Burma "was stalled in State Department."[3]

Quite possibly Karl Rankin's reports were responsible for any State Department stalling. Rankin did not want to rein in the KMT, hoping that the new administration would take to his point of view. He was to be disappointed. On the administration's first full day the State Department (in John Foster Dulles's name) authorized Sebald to tell the Burmese government that it was "more concerned than ever." More significantly, Rankin was ordered to make vigorous representations to Chiang Kai-shek himself to "terminate activities Chi Natl troops on Burma soil and permit troops return Taiwan." "Interested agencies" concurred, he was brusquely informed, and his opinions were not requested. The new administration had decided to address the KMT problem vigorously.[4] It may be that, with negotiations to end the Korean War ongoing, American interest in supporting the KMT in Burma eroded over time. In the end the United States ended its support for the Nationalists and helped forge a partial withdrawal.

Seeking a Solution

On 4 February 1953 Burma formally requested American assistance in finding a solution. After waiting some time for a response from Washington, Sebald wrote, "I hope Department appreciates that continued delay in proposing solution . . . is fraught with serious danger our relations with Burma. . . . I can not in good conscience follow delaying tactics much longer without undermining good faith not only myself and Embassy but also Department and U.S. Government. . . . I cannot (rpt not) stress too strongly the danger which KMT problem poses to U.S.-Burma relations," he concluded.[5]

The delay was mostly the result of Rankin's inability to secure Chiang's approval. Dulles, who despite his rhetorical support of the Nationalists actually disliked and distrusted them, ordered him to try harder. Instead of accepting the American position, however, Chiang insisted that he must consult with General Li, whom he had recalled from Burma. This angered the State Department. The situation in northern Burma was "deteriorating so rapidly that it does not admit of further delay," Dulles advised Rankin. He ordered Rankin to see Chiang, even if it meant traveling to the southern town of Kaohsiung where the generalissimo was thought to be. The Nationalist Chinese government, Dulles stated, was to arrange shipping to bring the KMT troops back to Taiwan.[6]

Rankin did run Chiang down in Kaohsiung and, according to his report, conveyed his instructions directly and forcefully, but Chiang still refused. Rankin appealed to him to yield, arguing that this was the first request from the new administration. Even if Chiang disagreed, Rankin argued, it would be best to go along with American wishes, but Chiang insisted on seeing Li first. Rankin may have followed his instructions, but he thought them asinine.[7]

The State Department did not back down. In a lengthy response Dulles told Rankin that the KMT troops in Burma were little better than marauders and, in fact, hurt the anticommunist cause. Rankin was to continue to "press matter urgently." Chiang must take action. "When can such an official statement be made?" he asked a few days later. The KMT presence in Burma, he added the next day, "increases rather than otherwise Commie threat to Burma."[8]

KMT activity had definitely increased. By one British account, in the entire period from October to December 1952 only two airplanes had landed at Mong Hsat. Beginning in January 1953 two airplanes per week landed, and by March supply planes were reportedly landing in northern Burma daily and "sometimes two and three daily."[9]

As KMT activity increased, criticism of American support for it also became more vocal. Ne Win "showed considerable disturbance of mind over the K.M.T. and over the fact that they are still being supplied by air."[10] Burma suspected that this increased activity was due to the new administration's stronger support of Taiwan, as was evidenced in the administration's reported decision to withdraw the Seventh Fleet from the island, thus "unleashing" Chiang. This, the Burmese feared, had emboldened the KMT and signaled renewed American support for it as part of a more aggressive plan to harass the PRC.

Having heard nothing from the State Department in response to Burma's request for assistance in solving the KMT problem, with Ambassador Key's resignation and disillusionment now a matter of public record, and now also confronted with the published report by widely read columnists Stewart and Joseph Alsop that the KMT enjoyed CIA support, Sebald again urged "speedy action." The KMT problem was "seriously endangering U.S.-Burma relations," he wrote in his diary, and he feared a downward spiral that would be difficult to counteract.[11] Sebald was able to tell the Burmese only that the United States had approached the Nationalist government about the KMT problem but there was no solution yet.

When nothing had happened by March, Nu took the matter to the Chamber of Deputies. In a long speech he weighed various options that had been considered ever since 1950: appealing to the UN, negotiating with the Nationalist government through the good offices of the United States, and attacking the KMT marauders. Nothing had worked. Therefore the Burmese armed forces would now turn their full weight against the KMT and drive them out.[12]

The failure to obtain Chiang's consent to a withdrawal of KMT forces had clearly caused Burma to up the ante and, as Sebald had predicted, threatened the improvement in the bilateral relationship with the United States. This was evident almost immediately when the Burmese War Office failed to invite the American military attaché to join British, French, and Indian military personnel to observe an operation against the KMT forces.[13] Furthermore, Burma recalled its ambassador in Washington to prepare for a presentation to the United Nations. Following up on his speech, U Nu wrote personally to Paul G. Hoffman, director of the Ford Foundation, explaining his decision to go to the UN. The Burmese public, he informed Hoffman, believed that the KMT forces were "the proteges of the United States and that the United States has been actively supporting them." He asked Hoffman to support Burma's case with American policymakers. Sebald, for his part, confided to his diary that he was "boiling over" about the KMT issue and could not understand why Washington had not yet found a solution.[14]

A good part of the reason for delay was Rankin, who continued his campaign of subtle support for the KMT. On 2 March 1953 he met with Li, who claimed to have twenty-six thousand troops in Burma (far more than the CIA and the Burmese thought he had) and was receiving substantial financial support from Taiwan. He said that his last payment from "other sources" (presumably the CIA) had been received the previous July. He denied reports that his army had committed depredations against the Burmese but considered the government hopeless and U Nu a "Communist sympathizer." Furthermore, Li stated flat out that his forces would not obey orders to withdraw from Burma and that he "would not transmit orders to evacuate." Nor, he said, would Chiang agree to US demands that he withdraw from Burma. Rankin commented that Li's presentation was "substantially factual" and urged the State Department to reconsider its instructions.[15]

By this time the United States government was apparently genuinely determined to remove the KMT. "All agencies of the United States administration were agreed that every effort should be made to get them out," reported the British ambassador in Washington. Taiwan's continued foot dragging angered the Americans. A high-level State Department official told the British ambassador "in the strictest confidence that the reaction of the Chinese Nationalists had so far been extremely unsatisfactory." The State Department ordered Rankin to carry out his instructions.[16]

Deciding that it could not rely on Rankin, the State Department summoned the Chinese Nationalist ambassador Wellington Koo for a long discussion with former CIA Director Walter Bedell Smith (recently appointed under secretary of state). The United States wanted Li to withdraw his troops, Smith told Koo. They were militarily insignificant, were involved in smuggling arms and opium, made alliances with the Karens and Kachins, and generally angered Burma's government. Their presence provided a pretext for a PRC invasion of Burma which, if it occurred, would be a devastating blow to American interests in Southeast Asia.

Anticommunist interests would be better served if Li's troops withdrew to Taiwan where, together with KMT troops currently interned in French Indochina, they could form the basis of additional army divisions for possible future use against the mainland.

The State Department Compromises

Significantly, however, Smith did not ask for an immediate withdrawal. Rather, he wanted a commitment in principle to withdraw, which, he hoped, would forestall a Burmese appeal to the UN. It would take months to work out the details, he pointed out. Equally significant, he did not envisage a total withdrawal. He thought "about 5–6000 men could be withdrawn." Since he put the number of KMT troops in Burma at about fifteen thousand, a very large number would remain. Despite the tough language, then, this represented a significant weakening of the American position and suggested that the China Lobby had an impact on administration thinking.[17] The United States did want a withdrawal, but for the time being, at least, it would be only a withdrawal "in principle" and would not include all KMT troops.

The same day that Smith talked with Koo, Rankin was again ordered to take "speedy action" in Taiwan to arrange a troop withdrawal. Rankin did as he was instructed, but the Nationalist government's response suggests that his approach was not forceful—partly due to the new policy of a withdrawal in principle. In his report Rankin included an extended discussion of the Nationalist perspective, which was that all of this fuss was the result of communist agitation.[18]

Shortly thereafter the Nationalist government refused to sign an agreement in principle to withdraw. It was willing to agree to form an international body to investigate conditions and the practicality of a withdrawal which, Rankin thought, was a "substantial concession" to Burma's position; he implied that it ought to be accepted. Once the investigation was completed, then an agreement for withdrawal would be appropriate. Sebald correctly determined that Rankin was "being led by the nose by the Chinese and that his heart is not in it for finding a speedy solution."[19]

Although the American position had softened, the State Department would have none of Rankin's stalling. It chastised him for telling the Taipei government that he was presenting the "State Department's" position, when it fact it was the US government's position. On 9 March President Eisenhower himself had impressed this on Madame Chiang, who was then in the United States. But Dulles cut to the chase when he pointed out the obvious: the KMT had no right to be on Burmese territory, and the Burmese were "completely within their rights in demanding expulsion these troops." If Chiang's government remained intransigent, Dulles stated, the United States might have to review its entire policy toward Formosa. It was a very tough cable. A few days later Dulles ordered Rankin to "leave no stone unturned" in getting an "immediate favorable decision" from Chiang Kai-shek to agree in principle to withdraw the KMT forces from Burma. He then personally asked Koo, "when are you going to get your troops out of Burma?"[20]

With no agreement in sight, Burma had run out of patience. It decided to terminate the American aid program, something explained explicitly as the result of the lack of movement on the KMT problem. Correspondent Homer Bigart wrote that Sebald's courageous dispatches about the issue were "apparently ignored in Washington." An angry Dulles stated that American "aid cannot be turned on and off like faucet"; if the Burmese decision held, American efforts to assist Burma with the KMT problem would end.[21] Sebald tried to remind his colleagues that, irritating as the Burmese action was, it was largely the result of domestic political pressures, aggravated by the failure to solve the KMT problem. But in the emotional climate of the moment, Sebald's explanation was not persuasive. American officials had only a limited amount of time to spend on Burma, and they could not devote the time needed to acquire a full understanding of the subtleties of Burmese politics.[22]

On 25 March 1953 Burma filed a complaint with the UN without even informing the United States. Sebald blamed his own government for this development. "It is unbelievable how little the Department appeared to have appreciated that time was of the essence," he wrote, and he predicted a quick unraveling of the relationship. The United States had apparently decided that Taiwan was more important to American foreign policy objectives than Burma, particularly since the Korean War had not yet been ended, and the Burma issue had made Taiwan less cooperative on other issues.[23]

There is also tantalizing evidence that CIA opinion weighed heavily. Under Secretary Allison, who after his trip to Taiwan the previous January had been very critical of Chiang, directly handled the correspondence with Taipei—but, as Day wrote, "sometimes under direct instruction and guidance" of Bedell Smith who had just resigned as CIA director.[24] Perhaps Allison had been reeled in by the CIA.

It is also possible, as historian George Kahin has argued, that after the Korean War armistice in July 1953, the American rationale for assisting the KMT forces in Burma shifted. Previously it had been to divert Chinese attention and resources away from Korea. Now that the fighting in Korea had stopped, the new rationale was to provoke the PRC into invading Burma, which would drive Burma into the Western camp. Kahin himself, writing in 1979, said that was "highly skeptical of this interpretation" until he read about it in a Rand Corporation study. Kahin may have been right. Six years earlier Robert H. Taylor had written that some in the CIA actually hoped that the KMT's presence in Burma would provoke a Chinese invasion, forcing Burma to turn toward the West for assistance.[25] Both Key and Sebald had occasionally made similar observations.

Perhaps. Still, the United States did want an agreement in principle to withdraw the KMTs, which Rankin tried to water down even further, proposing an agreement that read, "in view of the practical difficulties the Chinese Government envisage in the implementation of the above agreement, it can not be held responsible for not accomplishing more than is feasible and reasonable under the circumstances." This of course was no commitment at all. It did not meet even what the United States' softened position was demanding. After Dulles rejected Rankin's proposal, the latter tried to persuade the Nationalists to accept the American demand, arguing that agreements in principle did not bind anyone to anything. (Rankin's actions disgusted Sebald. Recalling that Rankin once proposed that the United States should "give all-out support to Li Mi," he confided to his diary, "I bristle." If that were to happen, he wrote, he would resign from the Foreign Service "in five minutes.")[26]

Initially the State Department fought back. It rejected most of Rankin's assertions and saw no reason why an "unqualified" Nationalist agreement in principle could not be arranged.[27] But within a day the State Department capitulated and stated that it found acceptable a Nationalist note agreeing in principle to working with the United States to remove the KMT troops, but with a number of caveats that Rankin had previously endorsed. For example, the "feasible or reasonable" proviso was included on the grounds of Taiwan's claim not to have full control over the KMT troops. In addition, Taiwan would not exercise any influence on Li unless Burmese attacks on KMT forces were ended. As Sebald astutely put it, Taipei's "agreement was so hedged with provisos that it meant nothing."[28]

As the CIA had foreseen, there was soon evidence that the Taiwan authorities had little intention of settling the KMT issue. The American relationship with Burma grew more tense. On 26 March the *New Times of Burma* asserted that the United States was "primarily responsible" for the "growing strength" of the KMT forces. Dulles then ordered Rankin to stop any use of CAT or other American planes to supply the KMT. Everything that Sebald and the CIA had predicted had come true within a matter of days: the Nationalists were more intransigent than ever, a possible American link with the KMT forces was now a matter of public discussion, and, as the American ambassador in London noted, American-Burmese relations over the past month had deteriorated to an "extraordinary" degree.[29]

With everything unraveling Sebald thought the time had come for the United States to hunker down and limit its involvement in Burmese affairs. "It will be a miracle if we can pull the chestnuts out of the fire in time to salvage something of the previously growing friendliness of this country for the United states in particular and the Free World in general," he wrote. The ambassador was depressed. On 8 April he spent much of the morning going over the KMT file in his office. "The more I read, the more discouraged I become because of the dilatory tactics of Taipei, bolstered by downright untruths in some cases, and the apparent inability of the Department to find a policy for the solution of this problem."[30]

Still, despite its irritation with Burma and its partial capitulation to Chiang, the State Department wanted discussions among Burma, Thailand, Taiwan, and the United States to review the practical problems involved in a withdrawal of at least some of the KMT troops. This would require Burmese agreement to suspend military actions in return for Taiwan's public acknowledgment that it agreed in principle to the removal of the KMT forces. Sebald was not impressed. "I have the impression that the Department does not mind putting all the heat and pressure on Burma to do its bidding, but supinely accepts whatever Taipei wishes it to accept." He was particularly scathing in his comments about the China Lobby which, he believed, unduly influenced American policy. He drafted a letter of resignation, though in the end he did not send it.[31]

Despite Sebald's skepticism, after some back-and-forth discussion Burma agreed to the Nationalist proposal, with the added conditions that Taiwan would take immediate steps "to implement withdrawal of these troops." As a first step the KMT forces would move into specific zones.[32] Burma ended most military operations against the KMT and accepted an American proposal to establish a "Joint Military Committee for the Evacuation of Foreign Forces from Burma" composed of representatives from Burma, Thailand, Taiwan, and the United States.

In the meantime, on 23 April 1953 the UN General Assembly adopted almost unanimously (Burma and Nationalist China abstained) a resolution that condemned "foreign forces" in Burma, and declared that they "must be disarmed and either agree to internment or leave the Union of Burma forthwith." The resolution, introduced by Mexico, was much watered down from Burma's original proposal; it did not condemn the Chinese Nationalists by name, for example. Nevertheless, the Burmese were not unhappy with the Mexican compromise. The Indians and Yugoslavs told them that it was "more than they ever expected." The American vote in favor of it discomforted Taiwan. Retrospectively the British ambassador in Bangkok thought the American vote was critical: it finally caused Taiwan to take seriously demands for evacuation of the KMT troops.[33]

Following the UN vote Chiang Kai-shek agreed to participate in the Joint Military Committee and appointed Colonel I Fu-de to represent his government. "The Nationalists now appear to be making a genuine effort to tidy up their affairs in S. E. Asia," reported a British intelligence officer in Hong Kong.[34] On 22 May 1953 the committee met for the first time in Bangkok.

Operation Heaven

Almost immediately, however, problems emerged, as some Nationalist military officials objected to the whole process. The United States complained, and Taiwan got the message. Secretly, however, the Nationalists were engaged in a deliberate subterfuge, Operation Heaven. They would evacuate up to two thousand troops, but these would be unreliable, poorly trained personnel disguised as a professional KMT force. The real troops would remain in Burma, and Taiwan would continue to supply them.[35]

By mid July Stanton was "alarmed at the turn of events," as Taiwan stalled. Privately Sebald thought that the Nationalists were "being very stupid," but he feared that they would "win out" and probably never leave Burma. He flew to Bangkok to investigate.[36]

Sebald's cynicism was understandable. CAT planes had apparently continued to supply KMT forces in May and June 1953, possibly from the Philippines.[37] The State Department soon ordered Rankin to complain about the continuing "dilatory and inconclusive Chinese government action."[38] The Americans concluded that Chiang genuinely wanted to resolve the issue but was faced with a real problem of insubordination. Thanks to profits from the opium trade, Li was not as dependent as before on Taiwan for support and might be able to defy Chiang. "Evacuation of Chinese Nationalists from Burma appears doubtful," concluded the CIA late in August 1953. The Burmese soon concluded that the Chinese intended to block a settlement; they had lost faith in the Joint Military Committee.[39]

In an act of desperation, on 12 September U Nu wrote an eloquent letter to President Eisenhower, appealing for his personal intervention. If he would please use his "good influence" and "make these unwanted people leave our country," he stated, Eisenhower would "gain the gratitude of a long suffering people."[40]

While awaiting a response from Eisenhower, the Burmese presented a final four-point proposal (sometimes described as an ultimatum): all foreign forces must leave, no fewer than five thousand must evacuate within twenty-one days of signing the agreement which must be signed no later than 23 September, and if the Nationalists refused to sign, Burma would withdraw from the talks. They wanted, they said, to "prevent Bangkok from becoming a Panmunjom" (a reference to the endless negotiations in Korea). When the Nationalists found the proposal entirely unacceptable, the Thais got the Burmese to agree to extend the time for withdrawal to thirty-five days, and the Americans, though believing that the five thousand figure was unrealistic, generally supported Burma.[41]

What the Americans now wanted was a reasonable counterproposal from the Nationalists, and they wanted it soon. Specifically, the Americans wanted the Nationalists to (1) sign an evacuation agreement; (2) issue orders for all troops to leave; (3) evacuate about two thousand troops by 31 October with more to follow; (4) evacuate the six KMT bases in Burma; (5) declare any troops who remained in Burma deserters. Should the Nationalists not agree, the United States would no longer actively support them.[42]

On 22 September the Nationalists replied that they would sign the evacuation plan but that it was beyond their power to issue a blanket order for evacuation. They expected fifteen hundred to two thousand KMT troops to be evacuated and would abandon their six bases in Burma, provided the Burmese did not occupy them until the withdrawal was complete. Then Li would dissolve his army, and any KMT personnel who remained behind would do so at their own risk. The Americans tried to get the number of evacuees raised, urged a public order for evacuation, and complained that the Nationalist response did not specifically disown those KMT troops who remained.[43]

Shortly thereafter Eisenhower's response to Nu arrived; it could not have given Nu much hope. The president focused on the real limitations facing Chiang, but he said he would write to Chiang stating again his sense of urgency about having this problem solved.[44]

If the president's letter to Nu was doubtless a disappointment, the letter to Chiang was stronger than might have been expected. While recognizing limitations on Chinese control over the KMT forces, Eisenhower wanted Chiang to use his influence "to the maximum to bring about immediately the evacuation of as many of the irregular forces as possible and to make clear that those who remain will not have your sympathy or support." He was sure, he concluded, that he could "count on your full cooperation."[45] In a personal meeting the following day with Chiang's son, Chiang Ching-kuo, Eisenhower reiterated his desire for an early removal of the KMT troops. Chiang Ching-kuo reaffirmed Taiwan's decision to withdraw two thousand troops, and the president responded that "he was glad to hear that." The next day Assistant Secretary Walter Robertson told Koo that the KMT troops in Burma "could serve no useful purpose." Koo disagreed, but under the circumstances he said that Taiwan would withdraw two thousand troops and had already suspended sending supplies to them.[46]

Sebald gave the Nationalist proposal to Foreign Minister Sao Hkun Hkio on 5 October 1953 (since Burma had withdrawn from the Joint Military Committee, the United States had to pass along Nationalist communications), telling him that it was the best offer attainable. But Sebald also indicated that the United

States considered this only a first step. Hkio responded that if the Nationalists had agreed to evacuate five thousand instead of only two thousand troops, the Burmese would have immediately accepted it. As it was, the proposal would require some reflection. On 10 October Burma's president told Sebald that Burma would probably "give passive co-operation for the evacuation plan." On 12 October the remaining members of the committee—the United States, Nationalist China, and Thailand—signed the plan. The Burmese officially stated that they would not interfere with any evacuation and would not take any military action against the KMT before 15 November.[47] The Burmese suspended air attacks on KMT positions, appointed liaison officers, and were prepared to admit evacuation teams to Tachilek where the movement to Thailand was to commence. The evacuees would cross into Thailand and be flown from Lampang airfield directly to Formosa. By 24 October both sides appeared to have "reached a full understanding"; the first evacuations were finally to begin on 8 November.[48]

Evacuation Begins

Although there were many Nationalist resentments (they threatened to make public the CIA connection), the evacuation began on schedule, the first troops crossing into Thailand on 7 November. The United States had estimated that about two hundred KMT soldiers could be evacuated daily. But the evacuations then stalled for a few days (one reason was that the KMT had tried to evacuate several Shans who "had apparently been hired as 'evacuees' 4 days previously"), and "Burmese temperatures boiled."[49] When the evacuations resumed on 13 November they were so limited that Sebald thought "the whole business is a fraud." A week later he still felt that they were likely a "smokescreen for continuing KMT operations in Burma" to keep control of a lucrative opium trade. No arms were surrendered, as they were supposed to be. The Burmese were certain this was a charade. Assertions that Chiang had little or no control over KMT forces in Burma were "patently transparent," Sebald wrote, and it was time for the United States to take strong measures against Chiang's government if it persisted in the "present halfway measures."[50]

The common view in Burma was that the "hard core" KMT elements supposedly being evacuated consisted of "old people, disabled, and women and children," and, as the Australian chargé d'affaires put it, "this view is supported by the facts." Indeed the "jungle generals" and Li were "organizing 'phoney' operations" and "completely discrediting themselves."[51] Particularly frustrating was the failure to turn in working weapons. By 23 November the 976 evacuees had handed in only forty rifles and carbines, only eleven of which "were at all serviceable."

The bulk of the weapons, Robertson asserted, were left behind to train new KMT recruits. This was, of course, a deliberate part of Operation Heaven, which specified that only inoperable or out-of-date weaponry would be surrendered.[52]

On 24 November Dulles summoned Koo to the State Department where Assistant Secretary Robertson complained that the limited withdrawal of troops and the few weapons surrendered were disappointing and embarrassing. He hinted darkly that this situation could even affect Nationalist China's seat in the United Nations.[53]

There was no immediate improvement. On 8 December the CIA reported that "scarcely any arms have been brought out by the evacuees." Clearly distressed at the limited nature of the evacuation, U Nu sent another letter to President Eisenhower, urging him to intervene more forcefully.[54]

In the midst of this heated environment in Burma, Vice President Richard M. Nixon arrived in Rangoon for a short visit. (When he learned that Nixon was coming, Sebald stated that it might have been nice if he "had asked the Burmese" if it was all right to come.) Nixon received a nineteen-gun salute, an honor

FIGURE 4. Vice President Nixon and Patricia Nixon with President U Ba U and his daughter during the Nixons' visit to Rangoon in August 1953. Bilal M. Raschid/TN Ahujas Co., 66 Phayre St, Rangoon. Courtesy of the Richard Nixon Presidential Library and Museum, catalog number A10-024.17.9.1.

guard, and a Burmese Navy band salute; but he quickly found the Burmese "completely obsessed with the KMT issue,"[55] for which they blamed the United States. Whether the visit was successful or not is a matter of dispute. The Australian chargé d'affaires reported that it was "a failure." To be sure, the "Go Home Nixon" placards and signs had been removed, and the government prevented large-scale demonstrations. Still, Nixon did not receive the enthusiastic receptions he was accustomed to, due in part, the chargé suggested, to the Americans' failure to understand Burmese anger at the KMT issue. The Australian almost mocked Nixon's campaign-style activities, including shaking hands with numerous ordinary Burmese, among them the "drink waiters . . . and the police guard" (though many people refused to shake his hand). Nor did he give a press conference; instead he distributed some written information to the press which, the chargé reported, "served to make more obvious his unwillingness to answer questions." In sum, if Nixon's objective was to "gain goodwill," it was a "failure."[56]

The American ambassador, by contrast, termed the visit an "extraordinary success." There was some initial suspicion, and Nixon caused something of a stir by breaking away from his entourage to greet a group of monks who were startled by his campaign-style actions, but he dealt very successfully with a small group of anti-American demonstrators in Pegu. In direct contrast with the Australian assessment, Sebald characterized the vice president's "handling of the press and public" as "masterful." It was the Burmese government, he reported, that feared close contact between Nixon and the press. In the end "smiling pressmen, including some who had been most critical, pressed gifts on Vice President at departure."[57]

Although the two accounts cannot be entirely squared, the Australian acknowledged that he did not have information about what went on in private discussions. Contrary to what he reported, of course, the American embassy was very well aware of Burmese feelings about the KMT forces, and indeed shared much of their anger. During Nixon's visit, therefore, Sebald made certain that he heard the Burmese side of the KMT story at length—and Nixon was open to listening. He had received a fairly thorough briefing before he arrived, in which he was told that because of the KMT problem the Burmese government had virtually suspended operations against the insurgencies (including the communist ones) so that it could concentrate its limited military resources against the KMT. Once the KMT issue was resolved, the vice president was informed, the government would "almost certainly resume its determined efforts to suppress insurrection in Burma." However, the failure to resolve the KMT issue would "cause a serious deterioration in Burmese-US relations."[58]

The American account was the more accurate one. In the end the visit turned out to be unexpectedly successful, and Sebald went so far as to say that it had "momentarily at least reversed trend of deteriorating US-Burma relations and waning US prestige."[59] Nixon had, at least, raised hopes. As one Burmese newspaper editorialized, cautiously but hopefully:

> Mr. Nixon will, of course, tell his chief that the KMT problem is the major subject in Burma. Burmese feelings are strong in this connection and as long as the US continues supporting Chiang Kai-shek by endorsing his actions in Burma, openly or otherwise, the Burmese people should not be blamed if they are a little suspicious of American policy in Asia in general and Burma in particular and inclined to treat with more than the wonted reserve what the US says. This also we hope Mr. Nixon will tell Ike.[60]

It was therefore not totally surprising that Nixon was effective in his discussions with Burmese officials. "We are fully in accord that these irregular troops have no business in Burma," he stated. ". . . Let there be no mistake about the position of the United states in this matter. The Government of the United States is far from giving tacit approval to the presence of these foreign troops."[61] As he was on board his plane about to leave, furthermore, Nixon told Nu and Sebald that he would recommend "in the strongest terms" that the United States pressure the Taipei authorities. Nixon emerged from the plane arm in arm with Nu.[62]

In the end the Americans pressured both sides to keep the process going. They kept urging the Burmese to extend the ceasefire, while also pressing the Nationalists to enlarge the limited evacuation and conform to agreements about arms. In December the UN General Assembly formally noted the limited evacuation taking place and urged that it be continued.

Chiang Changes Course

What neither Washington nor Rangoon knew was that late in October 1953 Chiang Kai-shek had decided to abandon Operation Heaven and pursue a meaningful withdrawal. For this to succeed, he could not share his decision with Li, for then Li would not have proceeded even with Operation Heaven.[63]

In keeping with Chiang's new view, the Nationalists announced that, in return for an extended and expanded ceasefire to last for three months, they would evacuate 150 KMT soldiers per day, beginning in January 1954, resulting in three to four thousand, maybe even five thousand, troops leaving Burma rather than the two thousand previously anticipated. The British thought that this change might have been due to Nixon's visit in November,[64] though it was more directly related to Chiang's secret change of heart. One can speculate that the American warning about possible questions about Nationalist China's UN seat might have prompted Chiang's revised view.

Sebald, unaware of Chiang's decision, was immediately skeptical of Nationalist assurances. They had not carried out previous agreements, and therefore the
commitments in the new proposal were "worthless." His assessment was scathing.[65] Nevertheless, by the end of the year, some 2,250 KMT personnel had been
evacuated, for which U Nu expressed his appreciation to Eisenhower. Only a few
weapons had been collected, however.

The Burmese then agreed to continue a ceasefire as long as the evacuations
continued. The "jungle generals" raised obstacles, mostly, it would appear, to try
and extract money from the Americans (who thought their demands "nothing
short of blackmail"), though the United States was apparently willing to pay
them something for their cooperation. When Li Mi learned of Chiang's determination to have a real evacuation, he did his best to undermine and sabotage it,
but the United States made it crystal clear to the "jungle generals" that they would
receive no more foreign assistance if they continued to object.[66]

A lot of frustration remained, but, after many fits and starts, the Burmese
extended the ceasefire to 28 February 1954, and the evacuation began again on
14 February, the target being again to withdraw 150 persons each day for an
indefinite period of time. When the ceasefire expired, Burma agreed to extend it
only in selected areas, and beginning on 2 March the army launched a concerted
offensive against KMT forces in areas that were not in those zones. The advance
was very successful, resulting in only one Burmese soldier killed and another
wounded, but the military actions irritated the United States and Taiwan. The
Thais were also "furious" because of Burmese air attacks on KMT villages in
Thailand.[67] In addition, the Burmese backed away from their former agreement
to have the collected arms flown out of Kengtung. They maintained control of
the weapons, and no one knew where they were. The planes that had been sent,
at considerable expense, to pick up the weapons remained stranded in Thailand.

Although Burma was within its rights (except for attacks across the border),
the Americans complained that its actions made it difficult for the United States
to help the country attain its aim: the withdrawal of the KMT forces. Sebald, on
instructions, complained to the Burmese. Privately, however, he was more forgiving, reporting to Washington that the military pressure had indeed hastened the
withdrawal of KMT forces, as the Burmese had contended.[68]

The Burmese adamantly refused to back down, believing that military force
was the only way to speed up the evacuation. Besides, their successes were very
popular at home and helped the government consolidate its position with the
people. When on 15 March the ceasefire expired around certain important
towns, Burma granted only a very limited safe area for KMT personnel to gather.
The matter became so serious that U Nu wrote another lengthy letter to Eisenhower defending Burma's successful military actions. He asked for Eisenhower's

understanding, reminding him that for four years the KMT forces had "been living on the land and committing atrocities."[69]

A few days later the Burmese captured the KMT headquarters at Mong Hsat. In an apparent response to American complaints about Burmese military action, an article in the *New Times of Burma*, thought to have been written by U Thant, warned the United States not to sacrifice its "silent ally" in its crusade against communism by supporting the KMT. Probably as a result of Burma's negative response to American pressure, the president's reply to U Nu was muted, though he did reiterate American concern at Burmese actions and commented on Chiang Kai-shek's important role in helping arrange for the evacuation of nearly five thousand KMT personnel and his assurances that any KMT who remained would receive absolutely no support from Taiwan.[70]

Ironically, the very day that Eisenhower responded to Nu, the American embassy in Taipei reported that Burmese suspicions about Nationalist intentions were in fact correct: embassy officials had learned about Operation Heaven. As he read this report Sebald felt "a sense of depression brought on by the realization that the United States Government could be so thoroughly hoodwinked by a friendly government." All the while the United States had been vouching for the bona fides of the Taiwan regime the Nationalists had been scheming to undermine the evacuation plans that they had agreed to. "We in the field were called upon again and again to nurse along, in strong language and with soothing promises, the Burmese and others, and to explain away the Chinese delays and frustrations," he wrote. For unexplained reasons (perhaps, he thought, because of Burmese military pressure, perhaps because of Eisenhower's intervention) the Nationalists had reversed course and decided upon a fuller withdrawal, but Sebald assumed that eventually the whole truth would out. "In the Orient, there are no secrets," he wrote, and in time someone would inform the Burmese government of the truth, at which time the United States would be placed in a most unenviable position.[71]

Meanwhile creditable reports of KMT brutality continued to embarrass the United States. One American Foreign Service officer, for example, who traveled in northern Burma reported that there was "a great amount of bitterness" at KMT depredations. Doctor Seagrave was particularly outspoken about KMT's "wanton destruction." In Seagrave's hospital, the official saw "several old villagers in his wards who had been shot up." Particularly troubling, Burmese army officers blamed the United States for this situation. "The prestige of the United States had suffered greatly among this important elite group and . . . it will take years to restore it," the officer reported.[72]

Having been successful in operations against the KMT in the Shan States, the Burmese army now turned its attention to Tenasserim, where it successfully took on

KMT and KNDO forces. Consequently the government agreed to a new ceasefire in that area, to extend until mid-May. When this third phase of the evacuation was concluded on 9 May, an additional 817 KMT troops and twenty dependents were evacuated, less than the one thousand to fifteen hundred originally anticipated.[73]

The evacuations of 1953 and 1954 eventually extracted an impressive number of KMT personnel—far more than was originally expected. By mid May sixty-nine hundred had left, including about fifty-five hundred combatants. At the end of May, Li announced that he was dissolving his army. However, several thousand KMTs remained scattered across the Shan States and other areas of Burma. One estimate was that up to four thousand remained in the Shan states, with another three thousand in southern areas of Burma.[74] The Joint Military Committee's estimate was 4,350, but this did not include KMT forces in some parts of Burma where the evidence was unreliable. Nevertheless, it was a substantial withdrawal, and Burma was "reasonably satisfied" with the result. The Burmese acknowledged that a "fair amount of arms and ammunition" had been surrendered, some of which "were in good condition," and they proceeded to repatriate 179 KMT prisoners of war and 175 Chinese civilians to Taiwan.[75]

The United States pressured the Taiwan government to continue evacuating any other KMT personnel that it could. Taiwan wanted an immediate end to the evacuations, but the United States wanted to keep facilities open to remove stragglers. The number of those who might be evacuated was of course unknown, but American officials wanted to plan for a movement of at least two thousand more KMT personnel. One official wrote that they wanted to try to move "several thousand" more. The main issue was the cost. The State Department wanted $645,000 to fund this final evacuation. In the end the CIA's Operations Coordinating Board agreed to find funds only for those whose evacuation in Phase III had been anticipated but had not happened, a total of 674 persons. The operation was to be completed no later than 1 September 1954.[76] On 1 September there still remained about $75,000 in unexpended funds. The American embassy in Rangoon recommended that these funds remain available to help repatriate any KMT stragglers who presented themselves, and the OCB concurred. On 15 December those funds still remaining were released for other purposes.

Shortly before Sebald left for a home leave in July 1954 he called on U Nu. The prime minister did not blame the United States for the KMT problem and expressed his appreciation for American help in partially resolving it. Even Chiang Kai-shek could not compel all of the KMTs to leave Burma, he told the ambassador. "They simply will not go." Shortly thereafter, Sebald stopped smoking—again. Perhaps the easing of the KMT problem relieved a lot of stress. Or perhaps he was relieved at leaving Burma altogether, for at this very time the new Australian minister in Rangoon found Sebald "rather punch drunk after all the battering he has had, both from Washington and Rangoon, over the K.M.T. troops issue."[77]

U Nu may privately have expressed his appreciation to Sebald, and the ambassador may have stopped smoking, but whether U Nu's comments represented his true thoughts is doubtful. Two months later Nu met with two British officials and "launched out on a tirade about the K.M.T. Troops issue." It had "shaken his faith in friends and alliances." By contrast he praised the Communist Chinese for not intervening. Later that year the Australian minister reported that the KMT issue had "poisoned" Burma's relations with the United States, "fed their traditional distrust of the Siamese and increased their reluctance to co-operate with the rest of us."[78]

If U Nu still resented American involvement with the KMTs, generally the Americans felt the Burmese were insufficiently grateful for their assistance. The issue continued to fester. On 29 October 1954 the UN General Assembly passed resolution 815 (XX) by a vote of fifty-six to zero, with no abstentions (the Nationalist Chinese representative was not present), which noted with approval that nearly seven thousand KMT personnel had been evacuated from Burma, but also deplored the fact that many remained in the country. Over the next several years the KMT continued to cause problems. They appeared to subsist on the narcotics trade, Sebald wrote in the late 1960s.[79]

Many years later, as published reports began to appear about a CIA connection to the KMT forces (including in 1964 David Wise and Thomas B. Ross's book, *The Invisible Government*, and an article by Selig Harrison in the *Washington Post* in 1966), Sebald wrote that no "responsible" Burmese official had ever made such a charge to him.[80] But his own diary entries and reports to Washington indicate that he was well aware of creditable allegations of American covert involvement with the KMTs, including contemporary articles by the Alsops, even if he was not briefed explicitly about it.

In the final analysis American support for the KMT was, as historian Matthew Foley concludes, "an unmitigated political and military disaster."[81] The KMT posed no threat to China, had little if any value in diverting China's attention away from Korea, endangered the noncommunist government of Burma, and gravely disrupted United States–Burma relations. The United States ultimately exerted considerable pressure on Chiang Kai-shek—even at a time that the China Lobby was a powerful force supporting the Taiwan government—to remove a substantial number of KMT forces from Burma, for which the Eisenhower administration deserves more credit than it sometimes receives. That does not, however, excuse the United States for having embarked on an ill-conceived, covert policy to build up and support the KMT troops early on, thus taking on considerable responsibility for the damage that the KMT wreaked in Burma. Despite U Nu's private expressions of appreciation to Sebald, Burma did not forget.

THE NEUTRALITY CONUNDRUM

Although the United States had assisted in the withdrawal of the KMT troops, the larger American objective of preventing communist domination of Burma remained fully intact. This applied, of course, to all of Southeast Asia. Indeed, as with other regional countries, the United States was interested in providing economic and military aid to bolster the government's ability to take on the communist rebels, and to maintain its independence from China. In December 1954 President Eisenhower explained to his brother that the administration's interest in Asia was to stop the "Communist menace." If that menace should recede, he stated, "we would consider ourselves still friends, but we would feel largely relieved of any obligation to help them economically or militarily."[1] During his time as president, however, the "menace" remained, so the United States continued to be involved in Asia, including Burma. This was not always easy. Because of Burma's determined adherence to nonalignment, it insisted that whatever aid was provided had to come without strings. Since US law and policy often did require conditions, the bargaining could be very difficult. Something of the same situation applied to Cambodia, another neutral country; but there the United States gradually took over much of the responsibility for training and supplying Cambodia's army, something that could not have happened in Burma.

Burma's ethnic rebellions also posed unique challenges for the United States. The Burmese government often suspected that the United States supported the rebels, despite its denials. Such support was, in fact, allowed under certain conditions, and there may have been some assistance at times, though probably nothing very significant. But Burmese suspicions added to the "delicate dance" that characterized the bilateral relationship.

The United States and the Ethnic Rebellions

In addition to charges that the United States was helping the KMT, the Burmese sometimes asserted that the Americans were also supporting the rebellions of the ethnic minorities, particularly the Karens. That many Americans were sympathetic to the Karens and other minority peoples in Burma is certain. Since Burma's independence, the American government had concluded that its anticommunist objectives were best served by supporting the government. Still, it appears that, beginning early in 1952, "certain American circles were in favour of direct support for the Karens in the setting up of their separate state." The British had attempted to dissuade these Americans, with apparent success, probably because the Burmese government had in 1952 made a genuine effort to conciliate the Karens. U Nu appointed Mrs. Ba Maung Chien, a highly respected Karen, as minister for Karen State. No settlement was reached, however, and in March 1953 Ba Maung Chien resigned, perhaps because the government was no longer interested in a negotiated settlement, perhaps because of reports of cooperation between the Karens and the KMT. This led the British to surmise that the Americans were covertly supporting the Karens to gain another ally in the struggle against Communist China and perhaps also to broaden "the base for K.M.T. operations."[2]

Perhaps there was some assistance to the Karens and other noncommunist groups in Burma. Karen delegations called regularly at the American embassy in Bangkok to request support. The official line was that they were always rebuffed; reports that Americans or Europeans had been seen with KNDO forces were also dismissed. If there were any, they had no connection with the American government. Assertions of American noncooperation with the Karens may have been accurate, but the explanations sounded very much like those dismissive reports of Americans working with the KMT forces.

Any American connection with the Karens would have derived from NSC 5405, approved in January 1954. As with previous NSC documents, NSC 5405's objective was to prevent Communist domination of Southeast Asia. In the section on Burma the document called for fostering "united action and cooperation among indigenous anti-communist groups." More worrisome, it made it American policy to prepare to establish "guerrilla forces among suitable ethnic groups for possible use against the Communists."[3]

When Ambassador Sebald read the document, he was appalled. It was now official American policy to work "through minority groups (Karens, Kachins, and possibly Shans and others)" to influence the center. Implementing it would "not only be fruitless, but dangerous." Instead of this "entirely unrealistic" approach, the US government needed to recognize that the Burmese government was "a going concern, is anti-communist, and above all else has wide popular support." The core of American policy should be one of "sympathetic understanding" and be "designed to strengthen rather that [sic] weaken the central government."[4] But NSC 5405 certainly laid the groundwork for possible covert connections with the minority groups in Burma that the government was fighting. Sebald could only plead for reconsideration.

Sebald's objections made no immediate impact. In April 1954 (about the time Dienbienphu was falling to Ho Chi Minh's Viet Minh forces in Vietnam and the Geneva Conference was getting under way) a high-level committee recommended longer-range policy options and "courses of action for possible future contingencies in Southeast Asia and not covered by NSC 5405." The committee's recommendations were very hard line. The CIA, Defense Department, and State Department should organize "guerrillas and para-military organizations, as well as anti-subversion police forces" in Thailand and, "if possible," in Indonesia and Burma. Also, the committee recommended promoting and supporting, largely through covert methods, "able and honest indigenous anti-Communist leaders" and strengthening anticommunist parties "and other influential indigenous groups in Southeast Asia."[5]

Evidence of possible American involvement with the insurgents came from an Operations Coordinating Board progress report at the end of July 1954 on the implementation of NSC 5405. Regarding those sections of the document that called for developing "united action and cooperation among indigenous, anti-communist groups in Burma to resist communist encroachments," establishing guerrilla forces among "suitable ethnic groups," and activating the guerrillas in the event that the communists attempted to take over Burma, the OCB reported only that whatever was done "would be separately reported,"[6] which certainly suggests that something was done or at least attempted.

Even as there were allegations of US assistance to the Karens, there also continued to be sporadic reports of Karen cooperation with Burmese communists. This was moderately worrisome, from the American perspective. The embassy took comfort in the fact that "most Karen leaders" were "ardent Christians," thus making an agreement with atheistic communists unlikely. But the Karen dalliance with the communists also reflected the desperation of some of the Karen military forces at a time when neither the British nor the Americans were willing to assist them.[7] Similarly, the Karens sometimes cooperated with the KMT forces but came to resent overbearing Chinese behavior. As the British Embassy put it, "neither alliance was happy." (The failure of the various insurgents to cooperate wholeheartedly was one of their long-term weaknesses.) By the end of the year the American assessment was that the Karen rebellion had withered during 1953, although the end was not yet in sight. In 1954 the government made steady gains, a tribute to Ne Win's gradual improvement of the Burmese armed forces. Organized KNDO resistance was reportedly broken.[8]

Contacts between Karens and American officials in Thailand continued, and they confirmed that the Karens had many American weapons bought, the Americans said, from the KMT and Thai firms. The Americans also reported a number of Europeans working with the Karens, including a French priest and the infamous British Captain Vivian, wanted for involvement with the murder of Aung San and his Cabinet. The officials belatedly acknowledged that late in April 1955 a USIS employee, Daniel Moore, and an associate, had had a "chance contact" with Vivian. Supposedly they had only gathered information about Vivian and the Karens, but it is suggestive that, though they were urged to make a report on the information they had obtained, the report was forthcoming only eight or nine months later—supposedly because other USIS work took priority. Later, beginning in August 1955 and continuing about every six weeks for the rest of the year, Moore had several meetings with rebels who visited him at his home in Bangkok. These visits were ostensibly purely social, and he reportedly told the Karens not to expect any American support, though he acknowledged his personal sympathy for them. Finally, in February 1956 Moore ended the contacts, apparently on instructions from the State Department.[9]

On 10 November 1955 an assistant American military attaché in Thailand, Captain Harlan Koch, crossed the border into Burma and spent the night with Karen rebels. In response to Burmese complaints, the Americans replied that Koch had acted on his own initiative and had been "reprimanded severely." Although American policy forbade contact with the insurgents, the temptations "to individuals at least to disregard them [these instructions] prove sometimes too strong." Furthermore, despite the policy, Ambassador to Thailand Max Bishop thought that contacts with the Karens and others should be maintained to gather intelligence.[10]

Containing Communism

More generally, of course, the United States was concerned about Burma's attitude toward communism internally and internationally. When on 22 October 1953 the government of Burma outlawed the BCP and the Peoples Comrades

Party (which grew out of the former PVO), the Americans were encouraged. The government had come to "a belated realization . . . that no peace with the Communists is possible." Also the government made slow but steady progress against the communist insurgencies, so that by 1956 they no longer represented a "serious threat." By that time, in fact, there were only about twelve thousand insurgents in the country of all stripes.[11]

But if there was some reason for guarded optimism in Burma, that was not necessarily the case in the other areas of Southeast Asia. With the conclusion of the Geneva Conference in July 1954, the northern part of Vietnam was at least temporarily (and in all likelihood permanently) under the control of Ho Chi Minh's Viet Minh forces, with a possible unification of all of Vietnam under communist control as a result of elections scheduled for 1956. The American response was to try and establish an alliance of Southeast Asian nations to combat communism. This ultimately resulted in the Southeast Asia Treaty Organization (SEATO), which came into existence in February 1955.

Burma reacted cautiously to the alliance proposal. Though a rapprochement with China was just beginning, Burma's relationship with its northern neighbor remained fraught with suspicion. Very high-level Burmese officials told Western diplomats that, while they could not join an alliance, they understood the threat of communism, viewed the Viet Minh as primarily communist, and would therefore not oppose a defensive organization of other regional countries. Army Chief of Staff Ne Win said that he was "in substantial accord with the developments of S.E.A.T.O." and would be "resolute in a crisis." Similarly, U Nu stated bluntly at a Martyrs' Day event on 19 July 1954 (an annual national holiday remembering the death of Aung San and other leaders assassinated in 1947), "we do not like communism; we do not want to see the spread of this creed into our territories."[12] Sebald believed that Nu's speech, coming only three weeks after Zhou Enlai had visited Rangoon, reaffirmed "Burma's determination resist Communist encroachment." The new Australian minister thought the American interpretation was optimistic. "The Americans expect so little from Burma nowadays," he reported, "that American-like, they may be too much affected by a few kind words." Still, a few kind words were better than none; but in September 1954 U Nu said in no uncertain terms that he was not sympathetic to SEATO.[13]

By the fall 1954 the bilateral relationship had improved, but Burma's neutrality and its need to conciliate China kept its relationship with the United States somewhat distant. Thus, when in October 1954 U Nu indicated to a *New York Times* correspondent that he would like to visit the United States, the American response was decidedly cool. All of the available slots for 1954 were already booked, the State Department responded, and there were no plans to invite him in 1955. It would not serve American interests.[14]

The State Department softened after U Nu visited Beijing in December 1954, was impressed with what he saw, received assurances of China's intentions toward Burma, including Zhou Enlai's and Mao Zedong's promises that China would not invade Burma or export its revolution there, and that Chinese nationals there would be told to obey Burmese laws. Nu returned hoping he could mediate the conflict between China and the United States, and sent out feelers that he would like to be invited to the United States. Dulles was sympathetic, provided (as one official put it) that U Nu "was not going to plaster his US-CPR mission all over the press." It was a delicate matter. A Nu visit "could be very much worth while if handled well, but very dangerous if not."[15]

Nu's visit to Beijing marked an important turning point in Burma's relations with China. Beijing no longer saw the world in black-and-white terms and had decided to court neutral powers and treat them favorably.[16] No doubt because they sensed this, there was a remarkable change in the Americans' attitude at the highest levels. Previously wanting to discourage a Nu visit, not only were they now ready to issue a specific invitation, but John Foster Dulles himself was designated to visit Rangoon and extend the invitation in person.

Adding to the pressure to take a more active interest in Burma was the influential conservative *Washington Post* columnist Joseph Alsop, who visited Burma in January 1955. "We have even virtually ceased communication with Rangoon," he wrote. The United States had had no ambassador in Burma since the previous July, and, while the hard-working junior diplomats serving in Rangoon impressed Alsop, he concluded that "American representation in Rangoon today has the approximate dynamic effectiveness of an old wet washrag." China was now ascendant.[17]

A month later Dulles was in Rangoon (the first secretary of state to visit Burma, and the last until Secretary Hillary Clinton arrived in 2011). He had a friendly visit with U Nu, detailed American views of China, and heard Nu advocate China's entry into the United Nations. Dulles did not try to get Burma to join SEATO, and he extended an invitation to visit the United States. Dulles told a Cabinet meeting, with Eisenhower present, that he had come away from his meeting with U Nu convinced that "the Chinese Communists have a fanatical determination to obliterate any U.S. influence in that part of the world." This was not, perhaps, the impression Nu wished to leave, but as a neutralist he could, especially in private, be strongly critical of Chinese actions. The Americans hoped that the visit might reverse declining American prestige and influence. Foreign Secretary U Tun Shein thought that "the meeting had gone off well." And Dulles reported personally to Eisenhower that U Nu was "very appreciative" of the invitation.[18]

Robert R. Nathan, who held the contract with Burma's government for economic advice, thought U Nu's forthcoming visit very important. But he knew that something could easily go wrong, including possible U Nu remarks that might be misunderstood. He wanted the Burmese to hire an American public relations specialist, Tom Wilson, to offer advice. Wilson was hired. In addition, Nathan urged Barrington to secure the services of Burma's "best publication relations man," and he even suggested a candidate, Kyaw Htun, then serving on Burma's Economic and Social Board. Kyaw Htun, temporarily assigned to the Washington embassy, would work with Wilson and thus ensure a successful visit, suggested Nathan.[19]

Nathan was particularly hopeful that an American university might offer U Nu an honorary degree, and when it appeared that the University of Michigan was interested, he enlisted his employee in Rangoon, Louis Walinsky, to encourage Nu to accept. Nu had always refused to accept honorary degrees. Walinsky tried, but Nu declined the offer.

American Assistance

In this confusing and complex context—American involvement with the KMT, possible connections with the Karens and other insurgents, Burmese neutrality in the Cold War but with an anticommunist focus at home, failure of the American-supported French military campaign in Vietnam, and in 1954 the beginnings of a Burma-China rapprochement—whether the United States should assist Burma with economic and military aid was hotly debated. For several years the United States had had a limited program of economic assistance intended to encourage Burma to become more resistant to communist subversion. Should the program be reduced, contended Ambassador Sebald in January 1953, this would put "a considerable strain upon the incipient friendship and understanding between the United States and South East Asia."[20]

Burma was apprehensive that the new Eisenhower administration might be less tolerant of the country's neutralism than its predecessor. In return for assistance it might demand commitments that Rangoon could not make, and if so, Burma would have to end the assistance. Furthermore, Burmese complaints about the quality and attitude of some of the technical advisers persisted. Most of the "so-called experts sent here were of the type that could not land a job anywhere else," complained a respected newspaper. There was surely some truth in this assessment, for in 1955 the British chargé reported that the American technical personnel in earlier years had been of "poor quality. . . . Too many proved technically incompetent or morally unscrupulous, seeking either personal advantage or commercial benefits for parent companies."[21] As Walinsky later wrote:

> some [American advisers], on the verge of retirement, were interested primarily in the money. Some were maladjusted persons who could not function satisfactorily at home. Still others were adventurers, innocent "do-gooders," impractical academicians, hypochondriacs, egotists, "milktoasts" overeager to please, or cynical sophisticates scornful of the environment in which they found themselves and of the Burmese. Professional competence, integrity and sense of workmanship, ingenuity, adaptability, imagination, patience, health, energy, realistic optimism, sense of values and tactics, some teaching instinct and pinch of missionary zeal—all highly desirable in foreign specialists—were rarely combined. And matters were not helped by the highly disparate and ... even ostentatious, living standards of the foreigners, which tended to make them a cultural enclave within the broader community.[22]

Burma itself cut off aid in March 1953 because of the KMT issue. Work on ongoing projects continued into 1954, but by this point the program was so small that it no longer represented "either an important continuing factor in the Burmese economic situation or a major instrument for the achievement of United States policy objectives in this country."[23]

Although official American assistance was about ended, an American presence involving the country's economic development continued, for the government of Burma independently hired two American firms to provide economic and technical advice. Tippetts, Abbott, McCarthy, and Stratton (always referred to as TAMS) had been in Burma since 1951, originally as part of the official American aid program (the firm was then known as Knappen, Tippets, and Abbott). When the aid program ended, the government engaged TAMS on its own. According to the British ambassador, the firm was well regarded by the Burmese. In 1957 TAMS had a staff of twenty-six persons.[24] Burma also extended the contract of Robert R. Nathan Associates to provide economic advice, and for the next five years Walinsky headed up the team of seven Nathan advisers in Rangoon. Among other things they devised an economic development plan for Burma to last from 1953 to 1960 at a cost of $790 million. U Nu was particularly fond of Nathan himself, though he also got along well with Walinsky who, it was said, had few social skills, but whose expertise and hard work were admired.

As for military assistance, the United States had provided a minimal amount in 1950–51, and none thereafter. In February 1953, however, soon after Ne Win had visited Washington, Burmese authorities asked about renewing military aid, and the State Department responded positively. The talks ended when Burma

FIGURE 5.   Robert R. Nathan with U Ba Swe, Burma's prime minister (to Nathan's left) from 12 June 1956 to 25 February 1957, and an unidentified man. Ba Swe is presenting Nathan with a traditional Burmese figurine, possibly a Lawkanat, a symbol of world peace that is often given to foreign dignitaries. Nathan, a strong New Dealer, traveled often to Burma, and his economic consulting firm worked with the Burmese government during the 1950s. Louis J. Walinsky Papers, box 6, file 6-1, Cornell University Library. Photo by Government of the Union of Burma, Ministry of Information, Executive Director's Office, Photography Unit.

cut off all aid in March 1953, but late in April 1953 Ne Win and other Burmese officials indicated that they wanted to resume discussions.[25]

Discussions proceeded apace. The American insistence on including the British in the negotiations angered the Burmese, but they still wanted American arms. In June terms were agreed upon, and lengthy and frustrating negotiations then began on developing a list of needed supplies, and by July Burma had submitted a preliminary list of its military needs. The Americans considered the list much too ambitious, and late in August a revised informal list was transmitted to the Americans for assorted arms, seventy-eight aircraft of various types, two destroyers, seventy-two torpedo boats, and many other naval craft. The

Americans found the Burmese new request "not unreasonable," but disputes with the British over the proposed package created confusion and delay. As with most matters affecting American views of Burma, Cold War considerations were first and foremost. As far as the State Department was concerned, Burma's objective need for additional military assistance was not in itself a determining factor. The question was whether extending aid would further American Cold War policy objectives. The State Department thought that it would. Strengthening Burma's armed forces would "encourage a pro-western orientation" and "minimize risks that Burma will turn to the Communist bloc," wrote Sebald. He wanted to move quickly since previous delays had resulted in bad feeling.[26] American aid became even more critical when Burma's agreement with the British to provide military aid and training lapsed in January 1954. Burma's need for military equipment, the CIA concluded, was "becoming acute," and the country's ability to fight communist and other insurgents was deteriorating.[27]

The Burmese, however, found the long delays required for Anglo-American consultations about armaments obnoxious and unsettling, and it was only in March 1954 that the Americans, with British approval, finally gave the Burmese a list of available munitions for purchase. The Burmese were "appalled at the prices," but the State Department was strongly in favor of finding an acceptable formula.[28]

Sebald thought that the United States had already bungled the matter. It had been self-defeating to work closely with the British on arms supplies to Burma, he argued, since the British perspective was too narrow. If the United States wanted to make any real impression on the Burmese it would have to offer Burma far more than what the British would approve and, in effect, break the British monopoly. Instead, however, the Americans had offered Burma a restricted list of armaments at high prices, including some that were of only marginal use in the country. All in all, Sebald wrote, the Burmese regarded the American response as "a polite brush-off."[29]

Desultory discussions continued over the next several months. In September 1954 a proposed policy of selling arms and military supplies to Burma went to the OCB Working Group. Thanks largely to Sebald's arguments, the United States had by now determined that it would not be bound by a British veto. A variety of ways of financing the sale of these supplies was put forward. If Burma expressed interest, a purchasing mission could come to the United States to negotiate.[30]

Burmese authorities were still interested, but skittish. The United States was willing to provide up to $20 million in military aid, but Burma insisted that any transaction be concluded without publicity. The matter again drifted for months with no conclusion, and only in March 1956 did Ne Win again inquire about possible military assistance. He was interested, he said, as long as American aid would be provided on a continuing basis. In light of the improving Burma-China relationship, Ne Win's interest was significant. The United States remained interested, if for no other reason than that there would be "grave consequences if we turn Ne Win down." Even though Burma was unlikely to enter into the usual, formal agreement for military supplies, State wanted to provide the equipment.[31] Just how to provide assistance without entering into a normal military agreement produced immense bureaucratic headaches, which only became worse when it became clear that the Joint Chiefs of Staff opposed military aid. They objected to Burma's neutral status and questioned the need for assistance.

The matter of military aid came to something of a head when Ne Win visited Washington in June 1956. The Defense Department refused to engage in discussions of possible American assistance, and Ne Win unquestionably felt that he was getting the runaround. This upset the State Department. Douglas MacArthur II, the department's counselor, in an impassioned two page memorandum to Dulles argued starkly, "*we are now faced with no problem in the field of Foreign Affairs which is any more important*" than aid to Burma. The country had been sliding toward the communist bloc, he asserted, but had now recognized the dangers and had asked the United States for assistance to help it become less dependent on the communist countries. "If we can *rapidly* exploit this situation, the effect on all the uncommitted and neutralist Arab-Asian States will be tremendous. . . . Burma, in a sense, is the key to the prevention of Communist domination of Southeast Asia." If we cannot act on Burma's request for military aid, he stated, "I do not think we should be in business."[32]

It was now up to the president to decide, and he wanted to provide the assistance. The Defense Department was not happy but had little choice but to cooperate, though there were disagreements over the funding source. State and Defense agreed in September that Ambassador Joseph C. Satterthwaite should discuss military assistance on a "loan or technically reimbursable basis" with the Burmese. If they were interested, the United States would send out a small military mission, headed by General Graves B. Erskine. Satterthwaite was "very pleased." He hoped that a military assistance program would help keep Burma "out of the clutches of the Soviet bloc." The Burmese also were pleased, but the two countries were still not close to a deal.[33]

Even as desultory discussions of possible military assistance proceeded, there were parallel discussions about resuming economic aid. These turned out to be equally byzantine. Burma was experiencing difficult economic times and needed assistance. Nathan Associates thought an American loan would be very useful to the country's economy and actively pushed for it. The American government was interested, Walinsky writing late in April 1955 that the loan question "has become quite hot." The Americans, reported Walinsky (who took credit for pushing the embassy to recommend a loan), were "thinking in terms of fifty to sixty million dollars." In May 1955 the Burmese Cabinet authorized U Nu to pursue an American loan. It was the start of long and frustrating discussions. In fact nothing happened at first because U Nu decided not to pursue the matter, ostensibly because he feared corruption at lower levels.[34]

U Nu Visits Washington

Shortly thereafter Nu came to Washington for a visit that was pleasant and generally successful. He made a very favorable impression with an unexpected decision to hand over a check for five thousand dollars to be used for the children of deceased or wounded veterans of World War II who had served in the Burma campaign, an act of generosity that was even mentioned at an NSC meeting. As the British ambassador reported, the charitable gesture was "in marked contrast to the demands normally put forward by visitors to the United States, and was very well received."[35] The president in turn gave Nu a painting, one of his own works. Nathan arranged a breakfast at his house for Nu, where he met important liberals. Secretary Dulles presided over a formal dinner, and U Nu spoke at the National Press Club.

FIGURE 6.   U Nu gives a check to President Eisenhower for five thousand dollars on 3 July 1955 in appreciation for those Americans who served in Burma in World War II. The gesture was much appreciated. From Wikimedia Commons.

Nu received widespread, and positive, attention in the American press, and his appearance on Edward R. Murrow's popular television show, "Person to Person," was particularly helpful in this regard. All in all Nu "made a very good impression on those with whom he came into contact." He felt the visit provided an opportunity to explain Burma to Americans, including its policy of neutrality. According to the American ambassador to Burma, he was "very happy indeed over the cordial reception which he received" and had a great admiration for President Eisenhower. He also thanked Vice President Nixon for his "warm and generous hospitality." Upon his return to Burma Nu "eulogized Americans at length" for a variety of accomplishments and values and stated that, if Burma felt free to criticize the United States when criticism was due, it should not hesitate to express praise when warranted.[36]

During his visit Nu said that he did not want a loan from the United States, but after further reflection he changed his mind and asked for $100 million. In the embassy's view, Burma's request proceeded directly from the warm reception Nu had received in Washington. Intensive informal discussions took place in Washington in August 1955 about a loan in the $50 million range. As usual were several problems, but the State Department attempted to overcome them. Indeed, moving at almost unprecedented speed, at the end of August the Far Eastern Bureau in the State Department (then headed by former ambassador to Burma William Sebald) urged Dulles to enter into discussions with Burma to determine the minimum loan needed. If the United States failed to act, Sebald said, Burma would probably turn to Russia for assistance.[37] Dulles quickly signed off, and serious negotiations began.

Barrington appreciated the energy now being devoted to the loan matter but remained concerned that the negotiations might not be concluded in time to avert an emergency situation in Burma. The first secretary of the Burmese embassy, U Ohn Khin, told a State Department official in impassioned language that if the United States wanted to "win the friendship of Burma and pull Burma farther over on the free world side, now was the time for a dramatic gesture." If the United States could offer a loan without strings, this would "have a tremendous effect upon the attitude of the Burmese people toward the United States," he stated. A "clean-cut, generous offer of assistance" would be invaluable."[38]

Meanwhile Nu wrote a long letter to Dulles reflecting on his recent visit. Nu professed to admire several aspects of American economic development and wondered if there was any possibility of sending a team of American experts to assess whether similar developments could assist Burma to advance economically. The Tennessee Valley Authority particularly interested the prime minister, who observed that nothing had been done to harness the energy of Burma's rivers. Nu also expressed admiration for American agriculture and commented

FIGURE 7. Burma's ambassador to the United States James Barrington (left) and US official Robert Blum with a film reel of Prime Minister U Nu's appearance on Edward R. Murrow's television program, 1 July 1955. Barrington served in several important diplomatic capacities, including ambassador to the United States from 1950 to 1955. In 1965, during Ne Win's dictatorship, Barrington, then ambassador to the UN and Canada and fearful of what would happen to him if he returned to Burma, sought political asylum in the United States but ultimately was allowed to retire from Burma's Foreign Service and settled in Canada. National Archives II, RG 84, US Department of State Post Files, Burma, US Embassy, Classified General Records, 1945–1961.

favorably on how American farmers diversified their crops. He also thought American experts should survey Burma's uranium deposits, while other Americans could advise him about new agricultural techniques and governmental administration. Finally, he sought American assistance for one of his pet projects: the building of a Union Central Medical Centre, where specialized treatments for diseases would be available. He requested "sympathetic and urgent consideration" of these requests.[39]

Given the recent bad relations, including the ending of American aid only two years earlier, this was a remarkable request, and negotiations continued into the fall. The requirements of the Battle Act were, as always, worrisome since by contract Burma was obligated to sell rubber and minerals to various communist countries. Barrington thought the Battle Act issue could be finessed, provided Burma was willing to negotiate, particularly over export of rubber to China which was in contravention of a United Nations embargo.[40]

The Battle Act itself was one of those pieces of legislation that State Department professionals found obnoxious because it made the crafting of an intelligent policy toward countries like Burma so difficult. But that was the political reality, and it reflected the influence of the China Lobby. A good example of the attitudes with which the State Department had to contend were those of Walter Judd (R-MN), an influential congressman who had spent many years in pre-communist China as a medical missionary. Judd was emotionally supportive of Chiang Kai-shek and vehemently opposed to Mao Zedong and the admission of the Beijing government to the UN. In November 1955, just as the United States was considering extending both military and financial assistance to Burma, the congressman visited Rangoon with a delegation of the House Foreign Affairs Committee. Judd's delegation spent fifteen minutes with U Nu and later had dinner with him and several members of his Cabinet. Judd was not impressed. Nu was "either a clever one who has given in to the Reds and thinks he may as well get all he can out of it, or he is a starry-eyed naive simpleton. Probably the former," he wrote. "I fear he has delivered the country into the Kremlin's hands."[41]

A major complication had to do with Burma's surplus rice. Burma had few markets for its major export, and the problem was exacerbated by American disposal of its own surpluses in Asian markets, thus undercutting Burmese sales. The United States would not buy any Burmese rice, so Burma was left with little choice but to turn to the communist countries, which were willing to take the rice using barter transactions. (China, like the United States, exported rice but unlike the United States was willing to purchase Burmese rice in emergency situations.) When Nikita Khrushchev visited Rangoon in November 1955 he loudly promised he would take "every grain of rice you like to let me have."[42]

Further complicating the situation, following his visit to the Soviet Union in October 1955, U Nu accepted a Russian agricultural mission, which apparently embarrassed Ne Win and other Burmese leaders. This ended discussions with the International Bank for Reconstruction and Development which was just then in Burma doing an assessment of Burma's agricultural needs, and IBRD representative Antonin Basch informed U Nu that acceptance of the Soviet mission made it impossible for the IBRD to fund an agricultural project. In any event, the prospects of American economic assistance now looked bleak. It was becoming "increasingly difficult as Burma's economic orientation shifts toward communist countries," wrote Kenneth P. Landon, a Southeast Asian specialist in the State Department.[43]

What Landon may not have known, however, was that at almost the same time the Burmese minister of trade concluded that Burma should stop quibbling and sign a financial agreement worth about $21 million with the United States. It took some weeks to work out the details, but finally an agreement was reached at the end of January 1956 and signed on 8 February. It provided for the purchase of $20.8 million of American surplus products, notably cotton, under the new PL 480 program that allowed developing countries to purchase American surplus agricultural products on favorable terms using their own currencies.[44]

It was in actuality a small agreement that did not come close to addressing the issues that Nu had raised in his letter to Dulles the previous September, and even then it had taken an enormous effort over several months. Initially Burma had wanted $50 million or even $100 million in an emergency loan to tide it over, and the agreement with the United States was not what got Burma through this difficult financial period. A loan from India and above all the willingness of the Soviet Union and other communist countries to purchase Burmese rice and to provide aid and technicians, were more important. Burma had reason to feel discouraged at the difficulty of negotiating with the United States. Also, there had not been any more movement on an arms deal or on Nu's request for technicians and for help in building a medical center. All in all, Ambassador Satterthwaite suggested, the American proposal was too little and too late to blunt Russian efforts to woo Burma. Mississippi writer David L. Cohn, visiting Burma in January 1956, put it this way in a letter to his friend Sam Rayburn, the powerful speaker of the US House of Representatives: "Instead of moving quickly when the opportunity offers, and with some of the Yankee ingenuity that we like to boast of, we seem to move slowly, heavily and without imagination or ingenuity."[45]

However, discussions did continue on a large loan and a deal that would involve sending American technicians to Burma. The State Department also wanted the IBRD to rethink its opposition to involvement in Burma, given Burma's temptation to increase its economic ties to the communist world. Burma sent a well-prepared team to Washington to resume discussions with the IBRD. It received help from the State Department, and surprisingly from Antonin Basch, "the Burmese Beté Noir [*sic*]" who had canceled the IBRD mission to Burma. Basch did "a complete flip-flop" and gave the Burmese "a great deal of help and encouragement over and beyond the call of duty." Satterthwaite believed that there needed to be a decision on the loan and support for the medical center by early April 1956 if the United States hoped to counter the Soviet aspirations for more economic influence in Burma. "In our opinion importance this problem cannot be over-emphasized," wrote the ambassador in hyperbolic language, "if Burma is to be saved for free world."[46]

Agreement Reached

Now the Americans moved quickly. Not only was a rice-for-technicians deal in the works but Dulles wanted to certify that Burma's cooperation was adequate to meet the Battle Act's requirement (needed to complete the PL 480 loan), to provide $3.4 million to help fund the medical center so much wanted by U Nu, to tentatively earmark $20 million from the President's Emergency Fund to provide "military and police aid," and finally to agree in principle that the US embassy in Rangoon could enter into negotiations for a development loan. "I sure hope the deal goes through," wrote Robert Nathan.[47]

There were, as usual, glitches along the way. A major problem developed early in April when Soviet Deputy Prime Minister Anastas Mikoyan and U Nu signed a barter agreement whereby the Soviet Union agreed to accept 400,000 tons of Burmese rice every year for four years in return for development aid and consumer goods. It was a generous deal, due in part, embassy officials felt, to the American rice policy. A week later Kyaw Nyein complained to the departing Australian minister that, while Burma did not especially like the barter agreements signed with communist countries, "the West had not been prepared to help in the way Burma wanted."[48]

In April the Burmese submitted a list of technicians that it intended to hire under the technicians-for-rice program, once it was finally approved. But then a major roadblock appeared. On 7 May 1956 Kyaw Nyein told the American chargé that Burma would not agree to any aid conditioned by the Battle Act. The United States had tried every way it could to finesse the act, but Burma was not satisfied.

Then U Nu sent a lengthy personal letter to Eisenhower, laying out Burma's position. Burma, he frankly admitted, needed American economic assistance. His government had already signed the PL 480 loan, had used Japanese reparations, had tapped World Bank and IMF funds, and yet it needed more to stay afloat.

Burma could not accept grants, but it would accept loans and would be glad to have reduced prices on goods. It needed to repay some of the loans with rice, and Nu pleaded with the president to accept even a token amount of rice in partial repayment, which the United States could then distribute to famine-stricken countries. However, Burma simply could not accept the restrictions of the Battle Act, even tacitly. To do so, he wrote, would "place my Government in an untenable position," especially since the Russians were now "making economic assistance available unconditionally." The tragedy of this, he went on, was that the volume of Burma's exports that were covered by the Battle Act was "so small as to be almost negligible." Was there any possibility, he asked, of waiving the Battle Act's requirements in Burma's case?[49]

The American embassy in Rangoon sympathized with Nu's point of view. So did Douglas MacArthur II, who, after reading Nu's letter to the president, wrote a personal memorandum to Dulles. The United States was now at "a crossroad in our relations with Burma," he stated, and it should "move heaven and earth to act" to respond positively to Nu's pleas. Dulles himself urged the president to reply to Nu that a response would come soon. Before Eisenhower could write, however, Burma rejected both the already signed loan provided under the PL 480 program and the proposed $25 million economic development loan, due to the Battle Act requirements.[50]

Nevertheless, the United States did not immediately throw in the towel. Even when Burma unexpectedly refused to sign the rice-for-technicians deal, on the grounds that the United States would have to "clear" the technicians that the Burmese would hire, Dulles decided to move ahead, as a matter of foreign policy, and on 30 June 1956 the United States and Burma finally concluded that agreement. One British official thought that the agreement "required boldness on the part of the U.S. administration to negotiate this agreement" (in view of its own rice surplus). "I think they are to be congratulated," he added.[51]

Then, on 28 June 1956 the State Department reoffered Burma the two loans previously discussed: the PL 480 loan of $17.8 million in local currency and another $25 million in dollar assistance. In a letter to the new prime minister (Nu having resigned temporarily in favor of Ba Swe), Dulles wrote that the United States was now prepared to "renew economic assistance to Burma in accordance with the spirit of U Nu's letter." What this really meant was that, while the United States was bound to obey the Battle Act, Burma was not. Therefore, the agreement did not have to refer explicitly to the act, but it would be understood that if in the future Burma took actions that were contrary to the act, the United States might have to suspend the aid. Barrington, then permanent secretary in Burma's Foreign Office, understood this, pointing out that this was what U Nu himself had suggested.[52]

The response to the offer, which soon leaked to the Burmese press, was mostly favorable, but the Burmese continued to worry that the Americans had too much control over the projects selected. The Americans tried to accommodate Burmese concerns. As Sebald told Burma's ambassador in Washington, "we would go as far as we possibly could in bending our procedures" to take account of Burmese apprehensions. A British diplomat in Rangoon reported that the loan negotiation "seems to have been temperately and skilfully carried out." Indeed, he complimented the American diplomats in Rangoon for pursuing a "very gentle" policy, of "scrupulously" not intervening in day-to-day Burmese affairs, and for having refrained from giving advice—"not always an American characteristic."[53]

Finally, after several delays, on 12 December 1956 the American embassy gave the Burmese the draft text of a revised Economic Cooperation Agreement. It was very similar to the previous economic agreement of 1950, but it spoke only of loans, not grants. The embassy expected Burmese acceptance soon, but by the end of 1956, no agreement had yet been signed. It was not until 21 March 1957, shortly after U Nu had once again taken over as prime minister, that the United States and the Union of Burma finally signed the agreement. It was twenty-two months since the Burmese Cabinet had authorized discussions with the Americans about an economic development loan. It would be another year before a small military assistance deal was completed.

The process had been a long and tortuous one, and it revealed much about Burma and its international and domestic situations. Burma had chosen neutrality in the Cold War, the result of its colonial past, its long border with China, and its intense sense of nationalism. Consequently it was wary of anything that might conceivably draw it toward one side or the other. It was inevitably very concerned about China to the north, a neighbor that did not want Burma doing business with the United States. Domestically there was a strong leftist opposition ready to criticize closer relations with the West. All of this led to careful scrutiny of agreements with the United States and made the process of concluding them agonizingly slow.

But the process also made it clear that Dulles and Eisenhower were not reflexively opposed to neutralism, as they are sometimes portrayed. Although Dulles had made some unfortunate remarks about the immorality of neutralism, both he and the president understood that, in the Cold War context, it was in the national interest to placate and woo neutral countries. With the domino theory firmly entrenched in American strategic thinking about Southeast Asia, the fall of a neutral country like Burma or Cambodia to communism was just as much to be feared as the fall of Vietnam. This led to the almost panicked reaction when Burma made economic deals with the Soviet Union and China that, the Americans were quite certain, threatened its independence over time.

THE CHINA BORDER, A "POLITE COUP," AND RETURN TO DEMOCRATIC GOVERNMENT

By the time U Nu resumed his prime ministership in March 1957 the United States was reasonably satisfied with its relationship with Burma. The American position "seems as favorable at present as at any time since independence," wrote Ambassador Satterthwaite. The Burmese had praised American opposition to the recent British, French, and Israeli attacks on Egypt during the Suez crisis and applauded American condemnation of the Soviet invasion of Hungary. The just signed Economic Cooperation Agreement made a "favorable impression," and if implemented intelligently would reestablish "confidence in our intentions and goodwill which were damaged by grievances over previous aid frictions and Chinese nationalist affair." The United States should not "expect immediate results in terms of foreign policy orientation," but Satterthwaite was optimistic for the long term.[1] Considering earlier fears that Burma was on the edge of communist domination, the change in American perception was remarkable.

But the Cold War was still in high gear. The United States was attempting to build an anticommunist nation in South Vietnam, was distressed with Sukarno's efforts in Indonesia to create a nonaligned movement that was not friendly toward the West, worried about rural discontent in the Philippines and the success of the Hukbalahap rebellion, and fretted over Norodom Sihanouk's efforts in Cambodia to court the PRC. In all of these the United States engaged in covert actions designed either to destabilize the existing governments (Indonesia and Cambodia), or reduce perceived communist threats to friendly governments (South Vietnam and the Philippines). In Burma, although relations had improved, the United States remained nervous about U Nu's administration, which it considered inept and insufficiently concerned about the communist menace. It would probably not object if there was a change of government.

One concern was the apparently growing ties between Burma and communist bloc countries. The opening of a Chinese economic exhibition in March 1957 which attracted over 400,000 visitors, for example, led to worried inquiries from Washington. While the Chinese exhibition was in progress, chargé d'affaires ad interim Daniel M. Braddock (characterized by the British as a man of "timid appearance" but nevertheless "most friendly and co-operative")[2] complained to Barrington about the apparently closer ties between Burma and communist countries. When asked to provide evidence, Braddock pointed to the growing sympathy among the Chinese community in Burma for the PRC, the number of Russian technicians in the country, and the "lavish attention" that the government tended to pay to visitors from communist countries while Americans were "losing ground." Government officials accepted social invitations from communist embassies "with alacrity." Braddock thought that his conversation with Barrington might "have done a little good," but more likely Barrington found it both amusing and irritating. It was precisely the kind of reproachful, heavy-handed interaction with Burmese officials that American diplomats were supposed to avoid, and Barrington responded to each of Braddock's observations, noting, among other things, that government officials flocked to the PRC embassy when invited because the Chinese always offered a "free show."[3]

Braddock's actions suggest that there were quite different lines of thinking in the State Department. As Lewis Purnell put it in a conversation with a British diplomat, "there were those who saw no future for Burma but the rake's progress on the road to ruin and who interpreted every event in Burma as further evidence this." Others "interpreted every event as evidence of the opposite." It had been that way every year since 1948, he said. He himself was in the optimistic camp.[4]

Insensitive American behavior was again reemerging. The Americans' "use of Cadillacs, many servants, and frequent visits to the cocktail lounges" had "definitely alienated the feelings of the Burmese people toward Americans," one person wrote to Assistant Secretary of State Christian H. Herter. U Thet Tun, for example, thought Walinsky behaved imperiously.[5] Others, on the other hand, praised his work.

Often U Nu attempted to bring American and Soviet leaders together. His efforts were regularly belittled as naive, even by some Burmese, and they came to nothing. Still, U Nu had his supporters. In April 1958 he told Ambassador Walter P. McConaughy that the United States should maintain "a strong military posture in the Far East," that he feared China, welcomed American military equipment and training for Burma's armed forces, and preferred American policy toward

China to that of the United Kingdom. America's policy was "clear, firm, and well understood." Significantly, Dulles passed along Nu's comments to Eisenhower.[6]

American Aid

One issue still outstanding when Nu returned was that, despite months of talk, no military aid agreement had been reached. General Erskine, who arrived to assess Burma's military needs, was impressed with the officers he met. Shortly thereafter Satterthwaite assured Nu that the United States "would do everything we could to give them needed assistance." Satterthwaite's assurance came in the context of what the Americans thought was a Soviet offer of military assistance. If Burma did accept Soviet aid, he reminded the prime minister, this would result in the need for Soviet military experts to come to Burma. Nu, having just returned to office, professed ignorance of any Soviet offers but did not think that this would interfere with the American offer. Erskine returned to the United States and appears to have recommended in excess of $10 million in assistance.[7]

Over the next several weeks Burma continued to express interest in a military aid agreement, and in August 1957 the American embassy urged the State Department to make "every effort" to provide the aid and not allow the current "favorable atmosphere" to dissipate.[8] It was not to be, however. The State Department has not yet secured the necessary intragovernmental clearances.

In addition to military assistance, the Burmese wanted help with internal security and police equipment. According to an Australian report, "there seemed to be new and real determination on the part of the Government to establish internal order." The Americans were pleased that U Nu was turning his attention to internal security, but at the same time they were dismayed that the Burmese parliament had not yet ratified the original $25 million economic assistance package, and they therefore could not yet promise more.[9] On 9 October 1957 the parliament finally approved the loan agreement.

The Americans liked Burma's focus on internal security matters, but they were even more impressed when the foreign minister affirmed Burma's anticommunist perspective. Perhaps there was a major policy shift taking place. Consequently, the inability of the American government to respond quickly to Burmese requests for assistance frustrated embassy officials. The embassy had "been scanning the incoming telegrams with frenzied eagerness each morning for the hoped-for telegram announcing that we can say something definite to the Burmese in response to their various requests," wrote Herbert Spivack. The Burmese were serious this time about the need to do more with internal security, were growing disillusioned with China because of delays in settling a border

dispute, and were willing to move discreetly toward the West. A quick and positive decision "could open to us a great many doors which we have been seeking
to enter," he wrote. "Conversely, I feel that if we allow the Burmese to become discouraged at this time we may miss a golden opportunity which may not soon be
repeated." Soon thereafter the JCS approved military aid, and the State Department informed Burma that the United States would offer up to $10 million for
military assistance. In the end, the United States offered up to $20 million worth,
to be repaid with a token payment of up to $2 million in Burmese currency. The
reaction of Ba Swe was one of "quiet elation."[10]

Although the Americans thought that providing aid to Burma would help
keep Burma out of communist hands, some officials (very privately) were not
banking on the current civilian government to do that. The "future of the AFPFL
and of U Nu in particular" was "unpredictable," wrote Kenneth T. Young, director of the State Department's Office of Southeast Asian Affairs. It was therefore
important to insinuate American influence into the army, which was more reliably anticommunist. This was similar to how the Americans forged close ties with
the armed forces in such countries as Cambodia and Indonesia, despite strained
relations with their governments. Thus in Burma Young wrote that providing
assistance to the army would hopefully "assure that continued non-Communist
alignment of Burma regardless of what happens to the AFPFL." In sum, the State
Department was already hedging its bets and hoping that, over the long run, Burma's armed forces would be a reliably anticommunist force, regardless of which
civilian leaders were in charge of the country.[11]

Although Young may not have been aware of it at the time, two days earlier commander of the armed forces Ne Win told a Time-Life correspondent in a rare on
the record interview that he did not want arms from communist countries, that he
hoped to build up the army so that it could be a "delaying force" against an invasion
from the north, and that the army's purpose was "to fight Reds tooth and nail inside
country." Ne Win's comments were deliberately planned, McConaughy reported,
either to get his voice heard "over heads of Burmese political figures," or to counter
negotiations then in progress with communist bloc countries for assistance.[12] This
must have cheered Young and other officials when they learned of it.

Soon the Burmese indicated their willingness to accept an American survey
team to examine Burma's need for police equipment, and they also requested a
new loan to cover these internal security requests. The police survey team arrived early in November 1957 and issued its report in December. Early in February 1958 the United States offered a $10 million loan to Burma for policing needs
to be spread over three years.[13]

Further evidence of Burma's desire for military assistance was its request, early
in March 1958, to have twelve air force officers trained in the United States. The

State Department recommended approval. The same month a Burmese mission arrived in the United States to discuss military assistance. It went out of its way to assure the Americans that despite Burma's neutralist stance internationally it had "no illusions whatever as to the nature of Communism."[14] Still, there was yet no final agreement on supplying military assistance.

Even as discussions about police and military assistance moved forward, Burma also requested additional economic aid. The first discussions about assistance under the PL 480 program began in May 1957, but they soon bogged down, a development that Nathan blamed mostly on the United States and the byzantine processes by which such aid was approved. "We sure do tie our hands behind our backs for many important fights," he confided to his diary. When late in 1957 negotiations were transferred to Burma they soon deadlocked, due, thought Nathan, "to stubborn behavior on both sides."[15]

This time, however, there was, in fact, a relatively quick response, though it still took several weeks to complete the deal. The case for making the agreement was largely political, and that was useful but problematic. "In doing so," wrote Eric Kocher, ". . . we have . . . unquestionably approached the limits of the intent and letter of the law" and had to "muster sizeable artillery to override the objections of other areas and other parts of the Department." But on 27 May 1958 the United States and Burma signed an agreement for $18 million in surplus agricultural commodities and a loan of $14.5 million in Burmese currency.[16] All in all, American assistance to Burma had increased significantly, even as Soviet and Eastern European aid was declining.

With regard to military assistance, on 4 June 1958 President Eisenhower finally issued a required finding allowing the assistance under Section 401 of the Mutual Security Act. On 25 July Burma signed the long-delayed agreement. Despite the inordinate length of time it took to negotiate, the "agreement" was not really very clear. The State Department found the whole matter in a "shocking state of dishevelment." Given the "lamentable confusion," it would take more time to determine exactly what would be shipped and under what conditions. The records of discussions, which had taken place in December 1957, were embarrassingly sketchy. Still, the Americans did want to send an advance shipment of armaments with delivery in January 1959. But it was Ne Win's soft coup in September 1958 that really shook the matter lose. The American military, reported a State Department official, was so pleased with the coup that they wanted to hand-carry howitzers to Burma.[17] It moved the first partial shipment date up to mid-November.

The fundamental problem was that while the United States was committed to sending up to $20 million worth of equipment, the agreed list would now cost perhaps $40 million. A bit later the cost estimate was revised upward to

$45 million and then to $45.5 million. Herter, who was dismayed that the Defense Department had made an error of 125 percent, thought the funds ought to come out of the Defense budget. Since all agreed that the United States had a commitment to Burma, in the expectation that the funds would be found somewhere the partial shipment of supplies was loaded onto a ship in San Francisco—which did not sail, pending a resolution. The Burmese, meanwhile, were upset at the delays. The Americans acknowledged the frustrating holdup but denied any bad faith and said that Burma would be fully satisfied with the final list of supplies.[18] After further discussions, there seemed no recourse but to go to the president for a resolution.[19]

Before Eisenhower was approached, however, a bureaucratic solution had emerged, and Ambassador Satterthwaite was instructed to tell the Burmese government that the United States would send the materials on the agreed-upon list, with only minor exceptions. The ship with the initial installment of supplies was now allowed to sail. The Americans also expedited the shipment of several helicopters that the Burmese urgently wanted to fight insurgents. Burma would pay for all of the supplies with $2 million in local currency. Embassy officials were delighted with the outcome. "Although inclined to despair at times," one diplomat wrote, "our faith persisted that such a solution would be forthcoming."[20]

The Burma-China Border Issue

Another ongoing issue was a border dispute with China, which flared up in 1956. Parts of the border had never been entirely agreed, and as early as 1951 there were Chinese incursions into areas that the Burmese, and the British before them, had claimed as Burmese territory. Initially these had been in areas of Wa State. Although China was reluctant to negotiate talks began in 1954, but in November 1955 there was an armed clash with Burmese forces, with casualties on both sides, and Chinese troops had entered Kachin State as well. Burma's government had concealed these matters, but at the end of July 1956 the news leaked out, and there were sensationalistic reports of a Chinese "invasion" with comparisons to Korea.

In August 1956 the Burmese claimed there were approximately three thousand Chinese troops in Wa State, occupying an area of 750 square miles. This led to a public uproar in Burma, with right-wing politicians calling for severing relations with China.[21] U Nu disputed reports that the Chinese had invaded Burma, but Deputy Prime Minister Kyaw Nyein admitted that "we are more perturbed than we will admit."[22] In fact, the government quietly ordered American

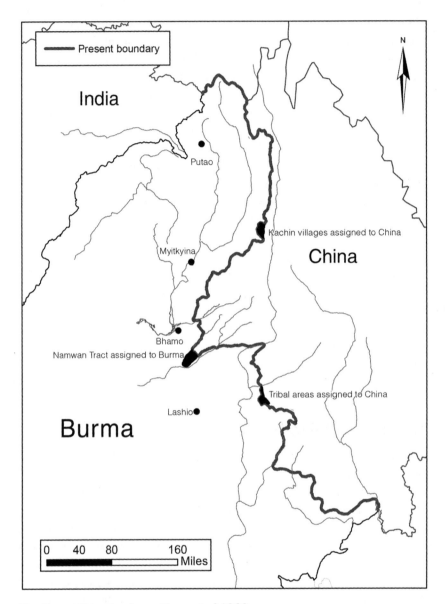

The Burma-China border settlement of 1960

missionaries in Kachin State to withdraw to Putao town because of "Red Chinese" encroachment.[23]

The Burmese insisted that a treaty signed in 1941 between the British government of Burma and China made it clear where the boundary in the Wa area lay. They were willing to negotiate and even perhaps revise the treaty, but they insisted that China first remove its troops. The Kachin area posed more difficulties from a legal standpoint, for unlike in the Wa area, there had never been a firm agreement between Burma and China there. Given the disparities in strength, the American embassy in Rangoon concluded that Burma would be unlikely to achieve "a fully satisfactory settlement without outside assistance." What the Americans did not then quite grasp was that Burma has already won. By putting China on the defensive in terms of international opinion, Rangoon had, as David Steinberg and Hongwei Fan write, "won an overwhelming victory in the boundary dispute in 1956," and for a time the Burma-China relationship was strained.[24]

The United States watched carefully for signs that the Chinese might have aggressive designs on Burma. Some Americans urged an aggressive responsive, but American diplomats in Rangoon, as well as the British and Australians, were more cautious. Former Ambassador Sebald, now deputy assistant secretary of state for Far Eastern affairs, saw no crisis and thought it best to allow Burma to deal with the situation without interference.[25] Dulles did bring up the border matter at a meeting of the National Security Council on 9 August 1956 but did not recommend taking any action. The United States had opted for caution.

Actually, the United States saw some advantages in having the border unsettled. As Satterthwaite put it, it was "undoubtedly in our interest" to have Burma and China "quarrel over issue." Leaving the border unresolved would demonstrate how untrustworthy and dangerous the Chinese really were, thus serving the larger American policy of keeping Burma wary of Chinese designs. By the middle of September Young concluded presciently that China would not soon give up its claims to Burmese territory. If pushed, it would retreat diplomatically and "possibly even remove troops," but it would then engage Burma "in endless and fruitless negotiations." This would redound to American interest.[26]

Late in September 1956, however, China suddenly became "friendly and conciliatory." Both the Chinese and the Burmese had concluded "that any further deterioration in mutual relations" was not in their interest. By one account the PRC army's incursion annoyed Zhou Enlai because "this gave offense to the Burmese, who are good friends of People's China."[27] Therefore, China decided to accept the boundary agreement of 1941 as the basis for negotiations on Wa State. There was not yet agreement on Kachin State, but most Chinese troops had withdrawn.

Late in October U Nu went to China, where he downplayed expectations but made considerable progress. China agreed to accept all Burmese claims to Wa State. With respect to Kachin, China was also willing to accept Burmese claims, with the exception of three Kachin villages, to which it had a good claim, and an area known as the Namwan Tract that the British had leased from China. Burma acknowledged the strength of China's claim to the three villages and quickly conceded that the Namwan Tract belonged to China; but it hoped China would give or lease the Namwan Tract back to Burma. If China agreed, it would "win much goodwill" in Burma.[28] Perhaps the matter would be quickly settled, particularly in light of the very recent Soviet invasion of Hungary.

The American embassy, however, noted accurately that China would be receiving territory that, despite the strength of its legal claims, it had not actually been administering.[29] This did indeed cause trouble. In December 1956 Zhou Enlai visited Burma for ten days, but the border issue was not finally resolved, largely because resistance had emerged in Burma to giving up the three Kachin villages. Zhou was greeted with signs that read, "We Welcome Chou With Tears," and "Great Chinaman, Spare Our Tiny Land." *The Nation* newspaper deplored the proposal (though it later favored the agreement because it was the best Burma was likely to get).[30] With Burmese nationalism aroused, the matter was not settled. During the negotiations, however, Zhou generously offered to give Burma the Namwan Tract, and while he said he had to retain the three Kachin villages, he would not quibble about the size of the area around the villages. The Burmese, therefore, felt that they must find some way to transfer the three villages to China.[31]

The Kachins were not thrilled about giving up three of their villages. The major political figure in the state, Sama Duwa Sinwa Nawng (known as the Duwagyi—Great Chieftain) said that "if the Kachin Ministers were to agree they would be hanged as traitors." At a meeting on 26 December 1956 196 of 200 Kachin leaders rejected the proposal. (The other four abstained.) "This posed a "serious problem" for the government. It is possible that China, and particularly Zhou Enlai, was willing to give up the three villages, a prospect that actually worried the State Department, which feared that, if the Chinese really did so, they "could turn what started out as aggression into almost complete psychological success throughout area."[32]

But if China had any serious thoughts about giving up the villages, this was never communicated to the Burmese or the Kachins, and soon thereafter Kachin opposition appeared to crumble. Despite the Duwagyi's previous threat to hang the ministers, he was close to U Nu, and when the prime minister made him minister of solidarity in the Union government (a post he had previously held and liked very much), he changed his tune. "My dear boys," he told Kachin students at Rangoon University, "they wanted to make me a Minister; how could I refuse?" Not surprisingly, his political party then came out in favor of the agreement. This showed, the British ambassador wrote, "how easily the Burmese can control the Kachins."[33] The Kachin State Council was scheduled to give its agreement at a meeting in February 1957. Zhou Enlai, it was reported, would soon return to Rangoon to sign the agreement.

But the matter stalled, perhaps because the Burmese wanted to reduce the area to be ceded to China. Furthermore, the Kachin Council did not take up the border matter after all, nor was the issue resolved when U Nu again traveled to China. *The Nation* blamed China. "We can only conclude that unlike ourselves, she is not interested in a lasting peace, and prefers to keep the border question . . . open indefinitely." Perhaps China was reacting to Burma's recently signed economic agreement with the United States. It was hard to explain because China was then engaged in what would later be called a charm offensive designed to show Burma that it was a friendly, nonthreatening neighbor.[34] It was all quite embarrassing to U Nu, who had led the country to expect a quick resolution.

In August China asked for some territorial adjustments in the Wa State region, involving about sixty square miles. It also wanted to enlarge the Kachin area to be incorporated into China. Westerners believed that these retreats from previous offers suggested that the Chinese wanted lengthy and detailed negotiations, though it was more likely the result of some internal resistance.[35] In October 1957 Chief Justice Myint Thein (known as "Uncle Monty") spoke several times with Zhou Enlai in Beijing, but little new emerged, and there was a growing consensus that a settlement would not come soon.

The United States was careful not to say anything publicly about the border dispute, but privately there was some acknowledgment that, as Lewis Purnell told an Australian diplomat, the "Chinese demands were not unreasonable" because "they had a good case," and it would be in Burma's interest to settle the matter quickly.[36]

Nu agreed that Burma should settle, but the issue was not quickly resolved. After Ne Win's coup in September 1958 Burma concluded that China wanted more of Kachin State than it had previously indicated, so that a settlement was not in sight. Burma wanted to reopen the talks in 1959, and Ne Win told McConaughy that he "would insist on showdown." He apparently gave the Chinese a "take it or leave it" proposal and insisted on a decision by December 1959. He did not anticipate a successful negotiation, doubting that China would give him the prestige of concluding an agreement, given his anticommunist attitude.[37] The Americans considered an agreement unlikely as well.

No negotiations took place again until January 1960 when Ne Win himself went to Beijing, a trip that surprised the Americans. Despite having the stronger case, China reached a tentative, and generous, agreement with Ne Win that accepted the Burmese plan, including the important principle that the watershed around the Kachin villages would serve as the boundary. Only two relatively small issues were set aside for future discussions: the extent of the territory around the villages that were ceded to China, and a very small amount of territory in Wa State.

The American response was one of grudging acceptance—grudging because it called into question American characterizations of communist perfidy. The secretary of state stated that the United States found it hard to express satisfaction with any agreement that brought about an "apparent atmosphere of understanding between any member of free world and CPR" and therefore should not express "hypocritical pleasure" at the outcome. At the same time the Americans did not want to be branded "poor sports," and so it was necessary to look upon the boundary agreement with a "certain amount of sympathy." There was also a silver lining: with a firm border in place, it would be easier to accuse China of aggression should there be future incidents.[38]

The Americans correctly speculated that the Chinese had settled the border issue because they wanted to demonstrate to India, Burma, and Indonesia that they could settle disputes in a friendly way, thus contradicting Western stereotypes of China's aggressiveness. In any event, in May 1960, shortly after U Nu resumed the prime ministership, Burma's legislature approved the settlement and an accompanying nonaggression pact almost unanimously. The final papers were signed on 1 October 1960. To the Americans this was all discomforting, and they in essence accused China of dissembling. "By pose of peaceful country willing to compromise differences with smaller neighbor," wrote Ambassador William P. Snow, "CHICOMS have been able to make substantial step in direction of restoring prestige in Southeast Asia at small cost to themselves." Although Burma thought the agreement would make Chinese aggression less likely, Snow was skeptical. It depended on "which fish has been hooked."[39] Perhaps the United States would have preferred no border settlement at all. It could then claim that the Chinese were stalling and holding the border matter over the heads of the Burmese, thereby giving themselves more control over Burmese policy.

Government Collapse and the "Polite Coup"

Meanwhile, a political crisis had engulfed Burma. In the spring of 1958 tensions between two factions of the ruling AFPFL party threatened to bring down the government. With the ouster of the more extreme elements some years before, the party had found much support for its moderate positions, but as the insurgencies had been brought under control, factionalism again emerged. The disputes were mostly personal with little ideological content. Kyaw Nyein and Ba Swe headed the Stable Faction, while U Nu led the Clean Faction. A temporary truce was reached in April 1958, and U Nu assured the public that differences would be settled by democratic means. The army, he stated emphatically, "would not take sides." Ne Win said that the army would remain neutral, but he also said he would not tolerate a resort to violence by either side. A week later the split degenerated into a "mud-slinging contest with each side washing dirty AFPFL linen in public."[40]

American policy was to continue normal relations with the government, while assuming that each faction was "sincerely patriotic, friendly to U.S., and determined resist internal Communists." There were rumors that the United States, generally unhappy with U Nu's administration, actually supported the Stable Faction, one of them being that Kyaw Nyein had received $600,000 from the US embassy to support his bid for power. The rumors were further stoked because McConaughy had just returned from a two-week trip around Burma with Ba Swe. There was a small demonstration at the American embassy, probably organized by U Nu's supporters, and the ambassador tried to counter speculation about American partiality by arranging a meeting with U Nu, whom he found self-assured and confident. This reassured the State Department, but there was concern that, regardless of which faction triumphed, leftist influence would increase because both sides would court the National United Front (NUF) party, which included some above-ground communists.[41]

In May the NUF threw its support to U Nu, so that if Nu won he would be closer to the NUF than before. When it began to look as if Nu would win a narrow, but clear-cut, victory, McConaughy was concerned lest it appear that the United States was disappointed. Nu would certainly be on the lookout for "any indication we regret his victory or no longer trust him." He suggested that, if Nu won, the State Department send Nu a warm message of "felicitation," in which Eisenhower would concur.[42] The department, however, demurred.

In the end, when a no-confidence vote was held in the parliament on 9 June, Nu prevailed by eight votes (127 to 119). Almost two-thirds of the AFPFL voted with the opposition, however, and Nu won because he received 44 NUF votes as well as a majority of votes from the Shans and other minority peoples. This did not promise long-term stability.

McConaughy soon told Nu that the United States would watch closely for possible communist exploitation of the situation. He believed that the PRC wanted to bring Burma "within its sphere of influence."[43] Nu said that would not happen, that the NUF was actually a diverse group with some anticommunists and many neutralists, and the NUF delegates would vote in favor of the assistance agreements with the United States. If he was wrong about this, he said, he would dissolve parliament and call for new elections.

Nu did not entirely convince the State Department. "We have entered a new period of greater uncertainty in our relations with Burma," Dulles wrote on 24 July 1958, "and . . . the heartening developments of the past year may be in jeopardy." He also implied that the United States might have to throw its limited influence to someone other than Nu. About the same time the BCP, which had previously more or less agreed to terms for a surrender, suddenly hardened its terms, perhaps as a result of the elections. Then the AFPFL expelled Nu.

J. Graham Parsons, the deputy assistant secretary for Far Eastern affairs, commented that Nu might well "become dependent on the Communists." The army, he added, "remained a hopeful element."[44]

Another worrisome development was that the Burmese press intensified its anti-American tone. There was much commentary about American complicity with the KMT troops, and a plethora of allegations: that the United States was involved with the Shan separatists with the intention of placing an intercontinental ballistic missile base in Shan State, that it was interfering in Burmese politics by supporting the Stable Faction, manipulating the Burmese economy through the PL 480 loan program, and engaging in subversion through the Asia Foundation, Nathan Associates, TAMS, and the American embassy. McConaughy attributed this "smear campaign" to "a concerted effort by Communist elements in Burma to take advantage of the recent political development, notably the AFPFL split and the support given by the NUF . . . to the Prime Minister." U Nu, however, then made a speech that was one of his "sharpest attacks" ever on communism. McConaughy surmised this was to reassure the West. U Nu himself later told the American ambassador that his wife "could not believe her ears" when she heard his speech. "She almost fainted from shock and surprise," he said.[45]

Rumors now began to emerge of military restlessness. Ne Win, it was said, was the only military person who could mount a creditable coup. To do so would go against his oft-expressed unwillingness to be the first military official to undertake a coup, but as the Australian military attaché put it early in August, "his fear of Communist domination may lead him to accept such a movement if he is convinced there is no alternative." The Americans also heard similar reports, including Ne Win's comments to a small group of officers late in July that the army would not tolerate a government dominated by communists. U Nu's rule, he felt, "seemed to be tending toward allowing Communists into power."[46]

The following week Nu forcefully repeated his lack of communist sympathies. McConaughy did not disagree but repeated American concerns that communists might now have the "balance of power." Nu in turn indicated that he had heard rumors that the United States "might be considering extending covert financial assistance to the Ba Swe–Kyaw Nyein group." McConaughy emphatically denied that, arguing unconvincingly that it was "entirely foreign to our principles and practice to participate in the internal political campaigns of any foreign country." Three weeks later the embassy recommended that the United States encourage divisive tendencies within the NUF—hardly a hands-off approach. The State Department found this suggestion "most interesting" and asked for specific proposals. McConaughy advised against involvement in the AFPFL quarrel, but it was clear that the embassy admired Ne Win and the military, which was now professional and deeply anticommunist; the Americans would probably not object if there were a coup.[47]

By September a coup looked more and more likely. U Nu was being "soft" on the insurgents and, from the American perspective, was being outmaneuvered by the communists. Ne Win likely agreed but was perhaps even more immediately troubled by U Nu's decision to dissolve the village militias, the Pyusawhti (named after an ancient warrior prince) that Ne Win and others had organized. According to the American embassy the Pyusawhti had been effective "in warding off insurgent raids and in preventing communist infiltration of loyal villages."[48]

On 25 September 1958 McConaughy reported that Rangoon was "rife with rumors imminent coup d'etat by Army elements." The air force had taken over Mingaladon Airport, though the US embassy did not think a coup was in progress. That same evening, however, Ne Win forced U Nu to resign and took over, although U Nu announced publicly that he had invited the general to take over for a period of six months, to be followed by free elections. According to the embassy the army moved to prevent the removal of top officers. "Failure by military to move promptly and effectively would almost certainly have led to widespread disorders and bloodshed," reported McConaughy. He termed it a "polite coup d'etat."[49]

There was no panicked response among the Americans, either in Rangoon or Washington. "Reactions at high levels were fairly calm and happily lacking in apoplexy," reported one official. This was partly because an army move had long been a possibility, and partly because it appeared to be aimed largely at containing communist influence in the country. Walter Robertson considered the coup "an anti-communist move" because, although U Nu was not a communist, the communists were supporting him. The Acting Secretary of State was informed that the army's control undoubtedly "presages a sterner policy in dealing with the communist insurgents and stricter controls over leftist activities," and would limit leftist gains in the next election. A few days later McConaughy predicted slightly better relations between the United States and Burma as a result of the change in government, and on 2 October CIA chief Allen Dulles told the National Security Council that what had happened in Burma was "probably a step in the right direction."[50]

In making this assessment American officials overlooked (and had doubtless forgotten) Ambassador Key's warning in 1950 that Ne Win was irresponsible, that he employed an "opportunistic and emotionally unstable approach to most issues." His seizure of power would "be a definite blow to Burmese-US relations."[51]

By prearrangement, on 28 October 1958 Ne Win officially took over as prime minister. The United States sent its congratulations. The new prime minister promised to improve internal security, organize fair elections, and reduce the cost of living. Fair elections did not apply to communists or those who were deemed to sympathize with them, for the new government soon arrested several prominent NUF officials. The State Department viewed Ne Win's takeover with a complacency similar to the way it reacted to almost simultaneous coups in Thailand and Pakistan: "without disturbed feelings," as Dulles put it. Still, there was a certain sense of unease. The United States supposedly favored democracy, yet it seldom objected to anticommunist military takeovers. A few weeks after the coup Herter expressed concern about the military insinuating itself into civilian departments to fight corruption and inefficiency. The army intended to "remain powerful and probably determinative force in Burma for some time to come."[52]

The United States and the Military Government

The first item that the Americans took up with Ne Win personally was the military assistance program. He said he appreciated the American aid, and that the military could completely crush the insurgencies in the coming months—his overriding priority. Much to McConaughy's liking, he also expressed his "uncompromising stand against domestic Communist menace." Among other things, Ne Win had withdrawn U Nu's generous terms to communist rebels who laid down their arms. He also planned to return the government to civilian rule just as soon as possible, a commitment that McConaughy thought was completely sincere.[53]

Ne Win also reassured the United States by indicating that there would be no change in economic policy. He would obtain Burmese ratification of the PL 480 loan and the police supplies agreement (both of which were subsequently approved). Walinsky spoke positively about the new government. He noted that one of U Nu's greatest failings was his inability to delegate authority, whereas Ne Win had no problem in this regard. Walinsky professed to see "a new and improved attitude on the part of most of the Permanent Secretaries dealing with economic matters."[54]

It therefore came as something of a shock when, shortly thereafter, the Burmese government announced that the contracts with Nathan Associates and with TAMS would not be renewed, effective 1 March 1959. The Johns Hopkins program at Rangoon University also began to close down, though it was not formally ended until 1962. (Burma also gave notice to Soviet agricultural experts.) The State Department hoped that the American accounting firms would accept the decision with a good grace and leave Burma without any recriminations. Walinsky was certainly inclined to do so. He did not suspect that anti-American attitudes contributed to the decision and even thought that a reduced American presence would benefit the bilateral relationship.[55] The State Department speculated that perhaps the contract termination was because of the need to balance Ne Win's current arrests of left-wing politicians, but more likely it was due to high salaries of the American advisers and the fact that the Burmese had to give them full diplomatic privileges.[56] The British were privately pleased with the failure to renew the contract. One diplomat euphorically stated that this foreshadowed a return of British influence.[57]

There appears to have been more to the termination of the agreements with the American firms than met the eye, however. Issues of fraud, corruption, personal misconduct, and extravagant life styles of some Americans contributed to the Burmese decision. One unofficial American adviser to Ne Win, Julian Licht, later told McConaughy that TAMS had "obviously . . . done a bad job and in effect . . . robbed the Burmese Government." Nathan Associates, on the other hand, had good people in Burma and had given "much good and sound advice to the Government."[58]

The Americans especially liked Ne Win's efforts to remove political influence from decision making, provide orderly and efficient government, and bring about a law-abiding society. Taxi drivers now found that they had to have licenses and keep their car lights in working order. Smoking was banned in theaters. Women government employees were to use less makeup and dress modestly. Broken sidewalks were repaired. Juvenile delinquents were rounded up, and the crime rate dropped. Pariah dogs were removed—fifty thousand were killed with poisoned meat (which supposedly did not violate Buddhist sensibilities since the dogs had the "choice" about whether to eat the meat or not).[59]

CIA operative Edward Lansdale applauded the Burmese military's new emphasis on civic action aimed at capturing the hearts and minds of the people in the struggle against communism. In a lengthy memorandum for the Dillon Anderson Subcommittee of the important Draper Commission, established to study American military assistance programs, Lansdale included photographs of the army installing refuse boxes and cleaning up drains and sewers in Rangoon and undertaking similar efforts in the countryside which, he thought, had been very successful in blunting the insurgencies. Lansdale's assessment of the success of counterinsurgency techniques in the rural areas may have been accurate, at least in the short term. Villagers were now reportedly "denying food to insurgents and passing information about their movements to army posts."[60]

Lansdale said nothing about the downside of Ne Win's arbitrary rule, however. American diplomats were more cautious. Ne Win had suspended the "democratic system," and if this continued for many years it would have profoundly negative effects, including probable divisions within the military itself. As time passed there was unease that Ne Win would not transfer power back to the civilians after six months, as he had pledged to do—and indeed, in

January 1959 he said it would be necessary to extend military rule for another six months. Aside from being contrary to his pledge, this also raised serious constitutional questions. The State Department, however, concluded that "on balance, the military takeover was a good thing," primarily because of its anti-communist posture.[61]

Although the Americans generally viewed Ne Win's takeover in positive terms, a jarring note was heard in January 1959 when intelligence reports suggested that Ne Win was disillusioned with the United States because of the difficulties negotiating military assistance. Admitting that the United States was partly at fault, the State Department thought that when he stepped down as prime minister he should be invited to come to Washington on an official visit.[62]

By late February 1959 "vague feelings of increasing uneasiness" were increasingly apparent among American diplomats. The campaign against the insurgents seemed to have stalled, and the military was beginning to act imperiously. Civil liberties were "largely in abeyance." The press was "being terrorized." Business was paralyzed "because of fear of what the Army will do next." Minority groups were under great pressure to support an extension of military rule. The generals appeared "to be very headstrong, very willful." Civilian officials were strongly encouraged to attend Marxist lectures. All in all, this painted a troubling picture of the government, much at odds with the previous positive portraits.[63]

Two weeks later, in a briefing paper for a regional meeting of American ambassadors, the US embassy in Rangoon wrote that the Ne Win administration had "given no indication that it possesses the insight, the aptitude or the administrative skills required to achieve long-term improvement in Burmese political life." Ne Win's government also knew little about economics, which was likely to result in financial crises "within weeks or months." Indeed, in its review of Burma's economy for the last quarter of 1958, the embassy reported that the government had given the economy "a series of shocks and jolts which had the effect of paralyzing both public and private enterprise."[64]

Confidence in Ne Win deteriorated further when in mid-March 1959 he conducted himself poorly at his first news conference since becoming prime minister. *New York Times* correspondent Tillman Durdin, who had had lengthy interviews with other military figures but had been unable to arrange an interview with Ne Win, was "perturbed and annoyed" at his arrogant behavior. The embassy concluded that the press conference demonstrated that Ne Win took counsel from no one but himself in deciding policy.[65]

Still, the same month Ne Win took the unusual step of sending U Law-Yone, the publisher of the *Nation* newspaper, to the United States with a request that he speak directly to President Eisenhower about cooperation and aid. Law-Yone held no position in the government but during the war had worked for the OSS and over the years had been close to the Americans. Ne Win wrote that he had his complete confidence. At the State Department U Law-Yone reiterated Ne Win's anticommunist views and his interest in American grants in aid. He particularly wanted the United States to fund and construct a four-lane highway from Rangoon to Mandalay, and then on to Myitkyina. Ne Win's attitude encouraged the United States, and Acting Secretary Herter arranged for Law-Yone to see Eisenhower.[66] The president responded politely that negotiations should be conducted through the American embassy.

Meanwhile U Nu was increasingly unhappy with Ne Win's government. Many more of his followers had been arrested than those of the rival faction. In February 1959 he urged passive resistance, and in April he spoke of the need to engage in the "moral battle to protect democracy," urging his followers to go to jail, if necessary. On 8 April 1959 he left for the United States.[67] Ne Win was not pleased. After Burma's ambassador to the United States, U Win, sponsored a visit by U Nu to Washington, Ne Win replaced him with U On Sein.

China's brutal crackdown on Tibetans in April 1959 helped Ne Win restore his reputation in the West. He privately denounced China's actions, while his army organized Buddhist demonstrations. The newspaper closest to the Army, the *Guardian*, published an editorial entitled "The Rape of Lhasa" and suggested that Burma's neutral policy be reconsidered. There were even some suggestions that Burma should join SEATO. The result was that the bilateral relationship between the United States and Burma was now "more satisfactory than hitherto has been the case in during the history of post-war Burma."[68]

All of this encouraged the United States to increase its assistance to Burma. Ne Win requested a grant of a hundred million dollars to fund the highway. The case for a new one was strong. The existing highway was fifty years old and had deteriorated badly, and the lack of an adequate road connecting the capital and major seaport of Rangoon with the second most important city, Mandalay, in central Burma and continuing northward to Myitkyina, had hindered Burma's economic development, internal security and defense, and national unity. The road would complement existing rail and water transport systems and serve as a "backbone" for "a critically needed new highway network."[69]

Given that such a project would be very provocative to China, it was significant that Ne Win wanted the United States to finance and build it. McConaughy suggested to Ne Win that the road would serve "as a warning and deterrent to Communist China." Ne Win agreed entirely. CINCPAC Admiral Harry D. Felt believed that it was "essential that the US take advantage of this unprecedented opportunity to move while the welcome mat is in evidence. We may never have another opportunity as favorable to the attainment of US objectives in Burma as that which presents itself now."[70]

Ne Win made several other observations that must have pleased the ambassador. He promised to go after the Burmese communists once a border agreement
with China was finalized. He wanted more foreign private investment. He did
not want state ownership of companies; the people who ran them became lazy
and complaisant. He thought that in an election the Stable AFPFL would prevail
and that, if so, his policies would continue. If U Nu won, all bets were off; he
would probably revert to the older, corrupt practices. McConaughy then, at his
own request, returned to Washington for consultation, telling Ne Win before he
left that he was "planning to present the Burmese case as effectively as I could."
He also offered to bring back with him a copy of Harry and Bonaro Overstreet's
new book, *What We Must Know About Communism*. Ne Win said he would like
to have a copy.[71]

In June 1959 the State Department informed President Eisenhower that Ne
Win planned to move Burma away from neutralism "toward closer political and
economic relations with the United States." Therefore the department recommended that Eisenhower approve up to $30 million for the highway to Man-
dalay (it was not thought prudent to include an extension to Myitkyina at this
time) and some buildings at Rangoon University, pending final negotiations of
the details with Burma. Eisenhower quickly signed off, and the Burmese felt that
McConaughy had "achieved the near-impossible." The final agreement provided
for $37 million in grant aid over a period of four years. Both U Nu and Ba Swe
supported the project, and the ambassador wrote that "We are off to a good start."
The public announcement of the agreement referred only to the economic value
of the proposed highway and an improved atmosphere for learning at the university, but it was presented to Eisenhower as valuable in Cold War political terms: the
projects would convince Burmese leaders that they could "plan their international
relations on the basis of a continuing close association with the United States."[72]

All in all, then, developments in Burma in the summer of 1959 encouraged
the United States. The Ne Win government had introduced "stability and vigor"
into Burma's policies. Its armed forces were now engaging the insurgents, with
American military assistance being helpful. Communist influence in Burma
had declined, due in part to China's brutal policy in Tibet and the defection of
two Russian embassy employees. Ne Win had privately made it clear that he was
aligned with the West, and a US Corps of Engineers team was already in Burma to
examine the feasibility of the new highway. Only occasional allegations of American connections to the KMT and suggestions that Americans at the consulate at
Chiang Mai were involved with the Shan dissidents clouded the generally good
relationship.[73]

U Nu and the Clean AFPFL, on the other hand, suspected that the United
States was covertly assisting their opponents, which McConaughy vehemently

denied. Nu had no direct evidence but complained that the Stable AFPFL was getting enormous amounts of money from somewhere, and many believed that the United States was the only possible source of funds. That the Americans preferred the Stable faction was certainly correct, although no evidence has come to light that they were covertly funding it. It is, however, suggestive that Nu's allegations were not included in the original American memorandum of his conversation with McConaughy. "Because of the sensitive nature of the subject," they were instead the subject of a subsequent memorandum.[74] U Nu's suspicions were certainly not allayed.

In the meantime Ne Win's government appeared to be moving ever closer to the West. In October Burma requested two American military advisers and one civilian for its National Defence College. This was a "fine opportunity" to gain American influence over "future policy and thinking of Burmese officials," wrote the American ambassador, recommending that the request be approved. There were also some contrary signals, however. The Burmese told the Americans that they could no longer afford to pay allowances and living expenses for the thirty-four advisers in the country who were training the military how to operate and maintain the new American equipment, and they asked the United States to assume the costs. Also the government now wanted a Burmese firm to design and build the new university buildings for which the United States was paying. "If they wanted replicas of outmoded buildings, we would do our best to live with the decision and to make it work," the ambassador responded. He clearly thought this was ill advised.[75]

Nascent Troubles

There was also some backtracking on the highway project. Although Ne Win still favored it, he complained that there always seemed to be scandals when projects of this sort were contracted out to private firms. If the US Army did the work, that would be fine, but involving private firms ran risks. McConaughy pushed back forcefully, arguing that American private firms were "in general honorable and dependable." McConaughy could only surmise that some powerful persons or interests had been influencing Ne Win.[76]

Questions of trust, so often a problem in the past, were beginning to reemerge. Foreign Minister U Chan Tun Aung complained that the United States "seemed to have a preponderant voice in everything. The lender was always looking into things, asking questions and making checks, but despite this the Burmese were not being consulted." The disagreements came to a head when McConaughy had a difficult conversation with Maung Maung, director of military training and one of the most influential men in the government, about the American assistance programs. "We are seriously threatened with a breakdown of understanding," he reported. The Burmese had reverted, it appeared, to earlier excessively suspicious attitudes, questioning the good faith of the United States, believing that all American aid programs were filled with fraud and scandal. They were not signing anything.[77]

One possible culprit was the elusive Julian Licht. An American, Licht was an unofficial adviser to Ne Win, with whom he had established a close personal relationship, taking his breakfast and dinner at Ne Win's house. He had advised Ne Win to cancel a contract with a British firm involved in the Rangoon Water Supply project that had been let by the US International Cooperation Administration. According to Licht, there were obvious conflicts of interest with the contract, and the Water Supply affair was apparently an important factor in Ne Win's growing suspicions of all private contractors.

Ne Win's other American personal adviser, Thomas J. Davis, later told an American diplomat that Licht's influence on Ne Win was "not a healthy one." Licht had apparently urged Ne Win to reject a contract for oil exploration by a company that Davis had recommended to the general. Also, according to Davis, Licht also used "extremely vulgar language during 'family' gatherings in the Prime Minister's house," to which Mrs. Davis, who was "far from being a squeamish person," objected.[78] After Davis left Burma he spoke with Southeast Asian specialists at the State Department "for several hours." The officers were sufficiently impressed with him that they recommended that Assistant Secretary Parsons speak with him. Among the topics recommended for discussion: "the influence of Julian Licht." When they met, Davis told Parsons that Licht was "a terrible influence" on Ne Win.[79]

McConaughy thought there was little the United States could do to alleviate Burma's suspicions. All foreigners, particularly those from big and powerful countries, were distrusted in Burma, and suspicions were almost inevitable.

Just before he left Rangoon in November 1959 McConaughy reflected on his time in Burma. His final interviews with U Nu, Ne Win, and U Ohn Khin had influenced him. He commented on the general movement of Burma toward the West, for which he credited Ne Win's takeover, but he also contended that if Army rule were prolonged, it would not necessarily be good for Burma or for the United States. In addition, Ne Win's "irritability and irrational behavior" of late was a problem, which McConaughy blamed largely on the general's small group of advisers. The ambassador appears to have had Licht in mind, noting that Ne Win had developed an "almost paranoiac obsession that all foreign firms (especially engineering) are corrupt and seek to defraud innocent Burmese, and anyone recommending their use must be five-percenter."[80]

Despite emerging problems, McConaughy and other embassy officials continued to believe that, overall, the relationship had never been better. Ne Win, however, was probably more aggravated at the United States than the Americans understood. Davis told Parsons that relations between the embassy and the Burmese government were "poor" because of several alleged American lapses. These included a second-hand dredge passed off as a new model, faulty and double-priced airport construction, the Rangoon Water Supply contract issue, cost-plus contracts that invited graft and fraud, and Ne Win's sense that the United States did not really approve of his takeover in 1958. Davis had good things to say about Ne Win, who was "completely dedicated and honest." In a very insightful characterization of the Burmese leader, however, he called attention to Ne Win's "long background of secret activities" reaching back before World War II and continuing during the Japanese occupation, which had made him "a victim of the 'clandestine mind' which influences him to see events and personalities in terms of tricks, secret motives, dissimulation, etc."[81]

Still, the two major American aid projects—the university buildings and the Mandalay highway—seemed to be on track. The US Army Corps of Engineers was investigating the road project and planned to give the Burmese a variety of choices. The State Department wanted to move ahead quickly, persuaded by the embassy's analysis that delays would raise Burmese suspicions.[82] A potential problem loomed, however: if the projected costs exceeded $37 million, the United States expected Burma to pay the difference.

Meanwhile the government announced that elections would be held in January or February 1960, after which the country would return to civilian rule. Ne Win was reasonably confident that the Stable faction, which he clearly favored, would win, but there was some uncertainty. Some restiveness over the constraints of military rule was evident, and this restiveness tended to rub off negatively on the Stable faction because of its identification with the military government.[83] U Nu, by contrast, predicted a clear victory for the Clean faction. By this point the American embassy, which had previously thought a Stable faction victory likely, was noncommittal. The British thought U Nu would win.

If the municipal elections in Mandalay in December 1959 were any indication, the British were right. U Nu's party won all thirty-five seats that were contested. This led Ba Swe to make a strong effort to win in Moulmein, but there too the Clean faction took all twenty-five contested seats while the Stable faction won only two uncontested seats. It was beginning to look bad for the Stable faction. By January 1960 embassy officials had concluded that a U Nu victory was now probable, and they were not heartened by the prospect. Nu was likely to appease China and would be "less susceptible to US influence than Ne Win Govt." The best course for the United States, the new ambassador William P. Snow suggested, was to continue to keep channels open to the army. "This group has shown realistic appraisal of danger which strong Communist China poses for Burma," he explained, "and willingness to take anti-Communist position."[84]

On 6 February U Nu emerged with a great victory. His party won 159 of 250 seats in the legislature, including all nine seats in Rangoon, while the Stable faction won only 41 seats. U Nu's party won 57.2 percent of the vote versus 30.7 percent for the Stable faction. Even the army voted two to one in favor of U Nu, Ne Win confided to Law-Yone. The NUF received a humiliating 4.8 percent of the vote, capturing a single seat. U Nu's victory troubled the Americans: immediately after the election the President's Committee on Information Activities Abroad (the Sprague Committee) reported that "the Communists can be expected to enjoy somewhat greater freedom of action under a successor government." U Nu was reportedly very bitter at the West for allegedly supporting his rivals. The future, which had so recently appeared bright, was no longer quite so appealing.[85]

Nor was the Burmese Army's leadership happy with the results. The CIA concluded that the army was keeping a close eye on U Nu and intended "to take over again should it appear necessary." The agency did, however, predict that U Nu would likely remain in office for the next two years. The Australian military services attaché was doubtful, predicting that "the Army will be back within eighteen months."[86]

THE U NU INTERREGNUM

Racial problems at home posed a particular challenge to the United States as it waged the Cold War. American law had long banned virtually all immigration from Asian countries (the Philippines excepted). This was moderated slightly during and after World War II, but few immigrants from Asia were allowed. Furthermore, it was difficult to persuade nonwhite countries of the benefits of the American way of life when segregation, discrimination, and disfranchisement were common realities in much of the United States. It was particularly embarrassing when diplomats from African and Asian countries found themselves mistreated at US Customs and Immigration checkpoints and in restaurants in Washington. Burmese diplomats were among those who suffered such indignities. The most serious of these events occurred in 1960 when Ne Win visited Washington, where his wife was racially insulted. This contributed to a dramatic change in Ne Win's attitude toward the United States when he again took over the government in 1962.

Before Ne Win's takeover, the United States faced other issues with Burma. Some of these were similar to those of the past: questions about U Nu's ability to govern effectively, fears of Chinese gains in Burma, the usual difficulties in reaching economic and military aid agreements acceptable to both sides. The most important issue in these years, however, was a resurgence of KMT activities. Unlike in the early 1950s, this time the United States moved quickly to restrain Taiwan and get KMT forces out of Burma. Chinese military intervention against the KMT, at the secret request of U Nu, encouraged American action.

Ne Win's successful border settlement with China, followed almost immediately by U Nu's impressive electoral victory, set off alarm bells in Washington and discussions of possible policy changes. But in the end Secretary of State Christian A. Herter concluded that, on balance, the outcome was "probably good" for the bilateral relationship. He pointed to how free the elections were, that Nu was certainly "Mr. Burma" who had "soundly trounced" his opponents, including the procommunists whose support he would no longer need. Not that U Nu was pleased with the Americans. After the election he told Ambassador Snow that the United States "favored Stable faction."[1] This was in fact true. Whether it went beyond sentiment remains unproven. President Eisenhower sent the new prime minister a congratulatory telegram.

U Nu's Cabinet appointments generally encouraged the United States, as did his promises of a more democratic, efficient government that would cut through red tape. He changed his Clean faction into a new party, the Pyidaungsu (Union) Party. He promised to retain Ne Win's appointments at the secretarial level. But the Americans were well aware that Ne Win was still "the dominant political figure in Burma" and had little respect for U Nu. The Americans kept in touch with Ne Win. "It is just a matter of time" until the internal political situation unraveled, Ne Win told Snow. "It will not explode soon—maybe in about a year."[2]

The General Visits Washington: Race and Foreign Policy

Following his resignation as prime minister, Ne Win prepared for a trip to the United Kingdom and the United States. Part of the reason was medical: he had sinus and prostate problems. Ne Win and his party arrived in New York in June 1960 where Julian Licht met and entertained him. The former prime minister played golf and went sightseeing, then flew to Minnesota for a medical checkup and then on to Washington for further medical tests.

It turned out to be a disastrous visit. Ne Win was not interested in having business meetings in Washington, yet the Americans had arranged some. When he went to them, the first three officials he was supposed to meet were not there. "He was so angry," reported an American military officer, "that he refused to adhere to any schedule the American prepared for him." He was also upset that customs officials had examined his luggage.[3] By some accounts he was also upset that during the Washington visit, Maung Maung, whom he distrusted, was received in a friendly way by Pentagon officials.[4]

But the most troubling incident occurred while Ne Win was hospitalized at Walter Reed Medical Center, where his wife was racially insulted—perhaps by the president's wife herself. By one account, when Ne Win's wife, Daw Khin May Than (known as "Kitty"), and her friends were walking up and down the hall while waiting for a nurse, "a piercing voice through the open doorway in one of the neighboring rooms screamed, 'Get those damned niggers out of here.' The voice allegedly belonged to Mamie Eisenhower."[5]

Such an inflammatory allegation requires a careful assessment, particularly in view of Mrs. Eisenhower's reputation as being relatively progressive on racial issues.[6] The information came from an Englishman, Dick Leach, who was at one time head of the Burma Corporation, formerly directed by Herbert Hoover, a private firm that ran the Bawdwin Namtu Mines. Leach's Australian wife Elsa was a close friend of Kitty (Elsa "was generally regarded as Kitty's confidante and lady-in-waiting"), and Kitty apparently relayed the story to Elsa, who presumably told her husband. He in turn told it to Lewis Purnell, the first secretary of the American embassy in London, who had previous Burma experience. Purnell then included the story in a letter to John B. Dexter, the Burma desk officer in the State Department. Purnell himself professed to doubt the story, noting, however, that what was important was that Ne Win did believe it.[7]

Despite Purnell's apparent skepticism, the story could have been true. Mamie Eisenhower was in Walter Reed at the time, hospitalized for bronchitis,[8] and would presumably have been in a section of the hospital for VIPs, where Ne Win would also have been. Two months after Purnell's report Dr. Tun Thin, the assistant director of the IMF's Asian Department, partially corroborated the story in a conversation with Dexter, his long-time acquaintance:

> One day, when his wife Katie [Kitty] was waiting in a reception room in the hospital, she was rudely asked to leave because Mrs. Eisenhower was in the room. This so offended the General that he immediately left the hospital despite warnings from the doctors that his treatment was incomplete and there would be troubles as a result. Subsequently, Ne Win had, in fact, suffered the predicted difficulties and had to have emergency treatment.[9]

Then in 1966, when Ne Win again visited the United States, a State Department paper listed several incidents that had upset him and his wife in 1960, including: "Mrs. Ne Win overheard an insulting reference to herself by a high official's wife (allegedly Mrs. Eisenhower) while she was in a private waiting room at Walter Reed Hospital."[10] Thus three creditable sources—one British, one Burmese, one American—related similar stories. There seems little doubt that Ne Win's wife suffered some kind of racist insult and that there was some connection to Mamie Eisenhower.

Although Under Secretary of State C. Douglas Dillon wrote that the Ne Win visit was "carried out with courtesy appropriate to his position and in accordance his clearly expressed desire to hold both official and social commitments to a minimum," and that Ne Win himself seemed generally to be in a good mood, Ne Win was not pleased. When Snow met with him in Rangoon a few weeks after his return to Burma, he paused ten seconds before responding to a question as to how his trip had gone, and then said, "perhaps we can say that it was all right on the whole."[11]

Ne Win's treatment in Washington was a major factor in changing his attitude to the United States. Before his mistreatment he had generally favored the United States, having once even offered to align Burma openly with the West, but no longer. In June 1961 Australian ambassador A. H. Loomes reported that the slights Ne Win had suffered had changed his mind. In 1962 Tun Thin confirmed this, telling Dexter that Ne Win had developed a "genuine 'hatred' for everything American. He commented that this feeling was so intense and unreasoning that 'Ne Win refuses even to eat American corn.'"[12] At a dinner party in 1964 for Frank Trager and his wife, Ne Win and Kitty indicated that they were still bitter over the treatment they had received. In 1966 an American embassy official informed the secretary of state that Ne Win's visit to Washington in 1960 had been "unbelievably badly . . . mishandled."[13]

Ne Win also disliked the appointment of Snow as ambassador. Ne Win was on close terms with his predecessor, Walter P. McConaughy, a career diplomat with considerable experience in Asia. Snow, although also a career officer, had never served in Asia and, according to Loomes, had "little interest in or knowledge of the area." To Ne Win this further indicated American disregard for Burma.[14]

Meanwhile, the embassy in Rangoon reported that, despite Nu's efforts for reform, signs of "administrative stagnation" were again evident.[15] The Americans were also troubled by small, but perhaps significant, moves by U Nu that seemed to benefit the communists. For example, an enthusiastic celebration of the border settlement with China was planned; East Germany's diplomatic appointment at Rangoon was elevated to a consulate general (up from a mere trade representative); the Czechoslovak national airline received permission to fly into Burma; communist activists were released from detention. None of these matters in themselves was cause for great alarm, but the United States feared that taken together, they signified a pulling away from the Westward orientation of the previous government.

Even the course of discussions about the Rangoon-Mandalay highway fed into the view of U Nu as weak and naive about communists. In January 1960 (while Ne Win was still in control) a survey indicated that the highway might cost over $100 million—far higher than had been previously thought. This led to much frenzied internal correspondence about whether there were ways to reduce the cost and even whether, given the incoming Nu administration, it was in the long-run interests of the United States to proceed.[16] The Americans, therefore, required the Burmese to explain more convincingly the overall importance of the highway, particularly in terms of its economic benefits, before deciding to proceed with construction.

Financing Burma's portion of the expense was a vexing problem. At one point Burma suggested that the United States pay for the entire road, or that part of the road be constructed until American funds were exhausted; but the Americans' response was unequivocally negative, although they were willing to consider ways to make the road less costly and pay for additional surveys. Nor was the United States interested in funding many more projects until there was more progress on those for which funds were already committed.[17] This was in marked contrast to the rush to make assistance agreements to Burma, largely on political grounds, when Ne Win came to power.

British attitudes regarding Burma reinforced the growing American concerns about the country under U Nu's government. The head of the Southeast Asia Department, Frederick Warner, told the CIA that the British attitude was "definitely one of gloom." Under U Nu Burma was "again beginning to deteriorate." The government was again becoming inefficient; Rangoon, which had been scrubbed clean during Ne Win's tenure, "was reverting to its previous unsightly and odoriferous state"; banditry was on the rise; "apathy, sloth, and the desire to be left alone" were once again reasserting themselves. Then there was U Nu's "sloppy love affair" with the Chinese Communists.[18]

Even as skepticism of U Nu grew, the United States wanted to provide additional military assistance because, as Parsons put it, "the Burma Army is the strongest organized anti-communist element and force for stability in Burma."[19] By the end of December 1960 the United States was ready to propose a program of military assistance worth $43 million to be spread over four years with deliveries of supplies over five years.

By the end of the year the ambassador was less critical about U Nu's government. However, the Americans were alarmed when Zhou Enlai came to Rangoon in January 1961 to ratify the border treaty and brought with him a non–interest-bearing loan agreement worth $84 million, the largest aid package ever from a communist country. Perhaps as a direct swipe at previous American advisers, the agreement specified that Chinese advisers would live like Burmese people of the same rank. For the moment, the Chinese had scored a major coup.[20]

Ne Win and the military had disliked the elaborate reception for Zhou Enlai, but they had reversed their opposition to Chinese assistance while their desire for American military aid had cooled. According to U Law-Yone, the border settlement with China and the red carpet treatment that Ne Win had received during his visit to Beijing in October 1960 (a nice contrast to the disrespect he had felt in Washington) had caused the general to change his attitude. He had not suddenly developed an affinity for communism, thought Law-Yone, but had been impressed with China's power and the geographical realities of a strong China sharing a long border with a weak Burma. When, therefore, the Chinese complained directly about the attitude of Ne Win's colleague, Brigadier Maung Maung, Ne Win listened. He told Maung Maung that he should resign because of his strong advocacy of American military assistance. When some Army officers who disliked the rapprochement with China objected, and talked of sidelining or even killing Ne Win, the general moved first. He forced Maung Maung out, then reassigned or dismissed other officers thought to be planning a coup. Ne Win had reestablished his leadership which, according to the American ambassador, was "not likely to be pleasing to us." Ne Win was "in a towering mood of xenophobia" and wanted to rid the army of foreign influences, including America's. Snow's replacement as ambassador, John Scott Everton, later wrote that this purge had "decimated" the army's "Western oriented–anti-Communist leadership."[21] It was a dramatic change, apparently precipitated by the poor treatment Ne Win had received in Washington and the red carpet treatment in Beijing.

KMT Redux

Another reason for Burma's (and Ne Win's) noticeably cooler attitude toward the United States was a revival of concern over the KMT forces. After the partial withdrawal in 1954 the KMT issue had subsided from public view.[22] The KMT forces that remained in Burma were unable to undertake sustained military actions and broke up into several private armies. However, they all remained in contact with their headquarters at Kenglap on the Mekong River, where they received supplies by air from Taiwan; according to an Australian report, they were also "still in touch with American agencies." In January 1955, in fact, Law-Yone's *Nation* reported that "white men," whom the local people reported were Americans, had been observed with KMT escorts. Perhaps, thought the embassy's reporting officer, they were French or British, but the fact that the Burmese invariably assumed that they were Americans "further exacerbates already bitter feelings."[23]

In March 1955 the Burmese army moved against the remaining KMT forces in Burma and drove some of them into Thailand and Laos, but the main body remained in Burma. The campaign ended in May 1955 by which time the Burmese claimed that the offensive had been so successful that the KMT remnants were "more or less inactive during the two following years."[24]

The KMTs who remained were increasingly involved with the opium trade, and, while they were less of a threat now, the Burmese government was convinced that Taiwan continued to support them. It also suspected that the Americans continued to have some contact. If the Burmese were correct, the American embassy warned in January 1956, this would undermine the anticommunist coalition in Asia. It urged that "all feasible pressure be exerted on the Chinese [Nationalist] government to sever these connections." The Burmese ambassador in Bangkok was "disturbed to find out that irresponsible American clandestine activities seem to be continuing."[25]

The State Department, in conjunction with the Defense Department and other agencies, sent out a strong warning for all official Americans to scrupulously refrain from any contacts with anyone who had connections to the KMTs, but this may not have ended all contact. The British planned to approach Washington about continuing American involvement. What came of this démarche is not known, but it is significant that the Foreign Office forbade the British ambassador in Rangoon to tell the American ambassador "anything about the Washington operation, which will be a delicate one involving the use of top secret material."[26]

By 1958 Taiwan had increased the amount of supplies and reinforcements to the KMTs, in violation of the United Nations resolution and pledges made in 1954, and clashes increased.[27] Although it was official American policy to "discourage further foreign assistance to Chinese Nationalist irregulars," accusations were once again heard that the Americans were providing supplies.[28] In September 1958 a correspondent for the *Nation* reported that two Americans were working with the KMTs. In the late summer and fall of 1958 the KMT, whose numbers had increased in part due to the enlistment of Yunnanese escaping into Burma during China's Great Leap Forward, began renewed military operations, including cross-border raids. The KMT action reinforced Burmese bitterness about the Taiwan government. It was "deplorable" that the KMT remnants "still plague us at time when [Ne Win's] strongly anti-Communist government has come to power in Burma which recognizes Communist China as principal threat," wrote Ambassador McConaughy. After KMT clashes with Burmese army troops in June 1959, the Burmese informally requested the United States to use its influence with Taiwan to stop these actions, and the Americans complied.[29]

Rumors of American connections continued to surface, however. In October 1959 Maung Maung alleged that three Americans from Chiang Mai, Thailand were engaged in subversive activities with the Shan insurgency and the KMT forces. He named names: "Mr Young, an American resident of Chiang Mai and the son of a Baptist missionary"; "Mr Jones, allegedly a member of the American Consul's staff in Chiagrai [sic]"; and "the American Consul himself." The missionary's son, he said, was "alleged to be passing arms to the Shan dissidents and to be having clandestine meeting with their leaders and with KMT leaders." He made a similar allegation against Jones, and said that the American consul had expressed sympathy with the Shans and had urged the Burmese to make concessions to them.[30]

Maung Maung's allegations were probably true. The missionary's son was William Young who, though born in California, spent his childhood and youth in Shan State, where he learned a number of local languages. His father, Harold Young, had worked closely with the OSS and later with the CIA, and sometime in the mid-1950s William Young also joined the CIA. According to Bertil Lintner, Young helped "organize the 'secret war' in Laos."[31] It is quite conceivable, then, that the Burmese reports were correct: that William Young, as a CIA agent, was indeed in touch with both the Shan rebels and the KMT troops. And since there had been previous reports of contacts between members of the American consulate in Chiang Mai and the KMT (and other insurgent groups), Jones may well have had the contacts alleged. Indeed, the next summer it became official American policy to "implement as appropriate covert operations designed to assist in the achievements of U.S. objectives in Southeast Asia."[32]

In any event, the KMT continued to export opium and receive supplies from abroad. Their airstrip could accommodate DC-3s and a little later four-engine aircraft, and the KMT reportedly received supplies twice weekly. KMT troops had "new equipment of United States origin." In November 1960 President Eisenhower was personally informed that the "Nationalist Air Force makes an average of two flights a month to resupply Nationalist irregulars."[33]

The situation was dramatically (if secretly) altered when, after the conclusion of the border agreement with China in October 1960, U Nu invited China's People's Liberation Army troops to enter Burma and, working with Burma's army, drive the KMTs out once and for all. The KMT forces were soon in retreat, though apparently with significant casualties to Burmese forces.[34] U Nu vigorously denied reports that PLA troops were in Burma but President Eisenhower was also personally informed that American intelligence had confirmed the existence of the Sino-Burmese agreement permitting Chinese troops to enter Burma.[35]

In January 1961 military operations against the KMTs increased in intensity, this time involving primarily Burmese troops. Ne Win himself visited Kengtung to see the action first-hand.[36] With the battle underway U Ohn, a personal adviser to U Nu, told Snow that the KMTs had modern American weapons. The charges of American involvement were once again becoming a serious irritant in the bilateral relationship. As the Burmese army achieved important victories, including the capture of Kenglap and two airfields, suspicions of an American connection with the KMTs only increased. Large quantity of American arms and ammunition were discovered at the air bases. Pictures of American cannons with massive amounts of ammunition appeared in the newspapers. An Australian diplomat reported that "astonishing quantities of brand-new, modern U.S. ammunition and equipment had been abandoned." The victorious troops were drinking liberated cans of Pabst Blue Ribbon beer. Later, Burma's representative to the UN, U Thant, told Australian diplomats that the "American C.I.A. was clearly involved." He was less certain about the State Department. This threatened "to damage severely our position here at a critical period," reported the American ambassador. Several American military advisers had to depart early from Burma.[37]

Not surprisingly the news of the captured American supplies sparked a small demonstration at the American embassy, allegedly consisting of procommunist NUF supporters. The demonstrators threw tomatoes at, and into, the embassy building. There was relatively little damage, but the embassy formally objected to the inadequate police response. The following day there was an NUF demonstration at the American consulate in Mandalay, and several windows were broken at the American library there. Soon the situation got even worse. The Burmese air force shot down a B-24 bomber that was attempting to deliver supplies to the KMT. The plane crashed in Thailand, as did a Burmese plane, and the Burmese pilot died. This led to strong condemnations in the press (an "explosion of anger," as a British journalist put it), including in newspapers that were usually friendly to the United States. The supply plane was a Nationalist government aircraft that the United States had provided to Taiwan. (Shortly after the plane crashed, Burma's military attaché in Bangkok attempted to book a seat on a flight to Chiang Rai so that he could inspect the downed supply plane and found that all seats had been booked by the Nationalist Chinese embassy.)[38]

News of the crash brought the KMT issue to the attention of the new president, John F. Kennedy, who requested a memorandum from Secretary of State Dean Rusk outlining the issue's history. In contrast to his opinion expressed in the early 1950s, Rusk wrote that "all available information indicates that President Chiang personally is the driving force behind the whole irregulars operation." For two years, he went on, Taipei had been resupplying and reinforcing the KMT troops, despite repeated American requests to desist. The KMT posed no threat to China, yet its existence was a provocation that had finally resulted in a Burmese invitation to China to interfere militarily. The result had been a joint Burmese-PLA military operation that succeeded in overrunning the KMT headquarters and airfield. American remonstrations with Taiwan were ignored, as the shooting down of the American-supplied Nationalist Chinese airplane with American weapons on board demonstrated. "This flight was undertaken clearly in disregard" of American representations made to Chiang, Rusk wrote.[39]

Since the first reports of Taiwan's renewed support for the KMTs, the United States had strongly complained to Chiang's government. As had happened a decade earlier, Chiang Kai-shek had initially resisted American pressure, making acerbic responses when Ambassador Everett F. Drumwright presented the first protest early in February 1961. Given Taipei's consistent disregard of American demands, what, Rusk asked, should the United States do? Taiwan was important to the United States in contexts other than Burma, and dramatic action, such as cutting off the supply of armaments, would have strongly negative impacts on these American-supported programs. But Rusk did suggest "a limited, selective cessation of military aid," such as ending the training of special forces personnel.[40]

While Kennedy was absorbing Rusk's memo, on the afternoon of 21 February the American embassy in Rangoon found itself besieged. There were reportedly twenty-one busloads of demonstrators, who burned an effigy of Uncle Sam and threw rocks and bricks, breaking embassy windows. The 150 police protecting the embassy responded with tear gas, fire hoses, and smoke bombs and soon gained control of the situation. Though pushed back from the embassy (sometimes brutally), the demonstrators continued to protest well into the night. They also attacked the Pan American Airways office, where windows, furnishings, and an automobile were destroyed. According to a police source, these riots were the "worst in Burma since communal conflicts before Independence."[41] By midnight the army had to be called in to restore order. Two people were killed, and about fifty were admitted to hospitals.

Just how Kennedy reacted is not known for sure, but he must have been angry with Chiang Kai-shek. Although the cable itself remains classified, Assistant Secretary Parsons stated that he could "not recall any language of comparable severity being used with President Chiang on any subject in recent years."[42]

Anti-American sentiment remained strong for many days, and the embassy urged Americans to stay off the streets. Although the Americans had every right to object to damage to the embassy and other property, their denials of US association with the KMT were not persuasive. Such denials had been made a decade earlier and had turned out to be wholly inaccurate. The KMT presence in Burma was no more justified in 1961 than it had been in 1951. As the *New York Times* put it, the issue had "poisoned U.S. relations with Burma for the last ten years. . . . If there is indeed United States involvement with the Burma Chinese it ought to be terminated, and the United States should do whatever it can to see that the Nationalists on Taiwan likewise cease their support of these trouble-making vagabonds."[43]

Getting the KMT issue resolved was essential if there was to be any improvement in the bilateral relationship, and the United States protested vigorously to Taipei. Snow told Barrington that if the Burmese government "had drafted our instructions, they would not have been sterner or more vigorous." Snow's characterization was correct. Nonetheless, U Nu thought it was important to appeal directly to President Kennedy, and wrote an eloquent and frank letter to the president complaining about the KMT forces and expressing his belief that the United States could stop supplies from reaching these illegal intruders. "If the United States could prevent the Formosa regime from raiding the mainland of China," he wrote, "our people cannot understand why she is unable to prevent that regime from sending supplies to its adherents in the far more remote region of the Burma border." He was, he said, "unable to give our people any satisfactory explanation on this point." Snow commented that the letter was a "relatively temperate exposition of Burmese point of view."[44]

In an effort to end the crisis, Kennedy responded almost immediately and with considerable sympathy for U Nu's position. He shared U Nu's "deep concern" over the presence of the KMT forces in Burma. It was "tragic" that their presence there had "marred the traditional friendship" between the two countries. He insisted that the United States did not condone the KMT troop presence and had "repeatedly made clear to" Taiwan officials "its opposition to their activities." Kennedy requested full information about any captured arms to see if they were provided in violation of American agreements with Taiwan. Once the investigation was completed, Kennedy promised to "give its results my personal attention." He reported that the Taiwan government had already agreed to "withdraw to Taiwan all irregular troops responsive to its influence" and would not send supplies to any that remained in Burma. "I assure you," he concluded, "that this matter will receive my close personal attention."[45]

Kennedy's letter was remarkable on several counts. For one thing, in contrast with Eisenhower's communications with U Nu, the response was almost immediate. For another, it was much more forthcoming and hit hard against the KMT presence in Burma. A new spirit of cooperation, it appeared, was now emerging.[46]

In the meantime, the military pressure on the KMT forces was having its effect. KMT troops had been pushed into Thailand and Laos—perhaps as many as eight thousand into Laos alone, including dependents. The Nationalist government was arranging an airlift from Thailand and Laos: the United States wanted the KMTs out of Laos in particular at the earliest possible date, lest their presence provoke Chinese intervention into that country at a particularly delicate time. The United States pressed Chiang to publicize the withdrawal, something the generalissimo was loath to do. If there was "further footdragging" the United States would tell the Burmese about Taiwan's assurances and allow them to publicize these. Taiwan soon complied.[47]

In contrast to 1953, an evacuation was planned with extraordinary speed and began in mid March 1961 with one thousand expected to be moved in the first wave. The Burmese appreciated the stance of the new American government. As U Thant put it, its "position had greatly improved after the new administration came into office."[48] By 26 March 1961 2,108 KMTs had been evacuated to Taiwan. Furthermore, whereas the earlier withdrawal had consisted mostly of poorly trained militia members and dependents, now many hard core troops were among those evacuated.

Kennedy's firm policy toward Taiwan was a welcome change, and the Burmese, too, despite their public criticism of Washington, seemed interested in reestablishing better relations. But distrust did not disappear. On 18 March 1961 Barrington, acting on instructions from U Nu, asked if he could have an hour with Dean Rusk when he came to Bangkok for a SEATO conference, and a meeting was scheduled for 29 March. Whether the meeting actually cleared the air and improved the relationship is doubtful. Barrington complained about the several hundred KMTs who had returned to Burma, many linking up with Karen or Shan rebels. He also feared that the evacuation would end prematurely and that the Thai military would again assist the KMTs.[49]

Rusk, who had once commanded KMT troops himself during World War II, assured Barrington that the United States would continue to help resolve the crisis. But he emphasized that the United States was "not involved" in any way and at any level. Coming from Rusk, who had regularly denied any American involvement with the KMT in the early 1950s, this could hardly have reassured Barrington. Kennedy, Rusk stated, was much concerned about American "good faith" and did not like to have it questioned. For example, said Rusk, citing a particularly unfortunate example, there had been many anti-American demonstrations around the world accusing the United States of being responsible for the recent death of Congolese leader Patrice Lumumba. The United States government, Rusk stated incorrectly, "had had no part whatsoever in his death." Barrington was completely unpersuaded that the United States could not compel Taiwan to end completely the KMT presence in Burma, and he complained about various other American lapses. Thus the meeting does not appear to have improved the relationship and may even have exacerbated it.[50]

Ne Win expressed similar views about the relationship of the United States with the KMT. In a lengthy conversation with Malcolm MacDonald he expressed such strongly negative opinions about American actions that MacDonald provided the Americans with an incomplete record of the conversation, leaving out the most the critical comments. In the unexpurgated version, Ne Win was said to be "extremely critical of the Americans," suggesting that they had encouraged the KMT forces within Burma, and that after these had been driven out, the Americans had worked to station them in Thailand on the Burmese border.[51]

Nevertheless, by early April some forty-two hundred KMTs (including about seven hundred dependents) had been evacuated. The Americans believed that this was about all who would voluntarily be repatriated. Although a significant number, this still left between one thousand and thirty-five hundred KMTs in the region. The Burmese estimated that two thousand of these were in Burma; of these five hundred had joined forces with the KNDO, while the remainder were said to be in league with the Shan resistance. To the Americans this was all very frustrating. They had exerted much pressure on Chiang to withdraw the KMTs, Kennedy had responded quickly and sympathetically to U Nu, a substantial number of KMTs had been rapidly withdrawn. Yet the United States was now being blamed for those who had not evacuated and who were making common cause with the rebels. Thus, even the destruction of a train by the Karen rebels was somehow traced to the United States, and there were rumors that Americans were secretly training the Shan and Karen insurgents at Thai military bases.[52]

Harold Young, the American Baptist missionary in Thailand, was often directly accused of aiding the Shans. Although the Americans had previously denied any connection with Young, Snow reported allegations of Young's involvement in "gun running and aiding Shans." He was allegedly in contact with the Mahadevi of Yanghwe (the sawbwa of Yanghwe's royal consort), who had strong Shan nationalist tendencies. Previous American denials, thought Snow, lacked credibility.[53] The KMT crisis only made such reports more believable in Burmese eyes.

An Australian report nicely summarized the legacy of the KMTs in Burma:

> The KMT venture in Burma has done no harm to the security of the Communist regime in China and has done no good to the Nationalist regime in Formosa: it has strengthened the Communist cause by encouraging the spirit of co-operation between Burma and Communist China; it has weakened the Western position by exposing the United States to criticism; it has added yet a further ingredient to the witch's brew in Laos; it has inflicted years of exactions and terrorization on the people of the Shan State, first at the hands of the KMT themselves and then at the hands of the disorderly Burma Army; and the only beneficiaries apart from the Communists have been the KMT officers and certain personages in Thailand who have profited handsomely from the opium trade.[54]

Anti-Americanism Increases

One consequence of the deteriorating relationship was that, except for construction of the American-funded buildings at Rangoon University, American aid programs slowed down. The Burmese had not recently drawn on their

$25 million credit for economic development, nor had they requested more assistance. Similarly, there was little progress on the Rangoon-Mandalay highway project, and Burma was now less interested in paying a large amount for the highway. One possibility that emerged early in 1961 to reduce costs was not to build a new highway but to improve the existing road. Both governments were open to this, but the Americans insisted that Burma pay 25 percent of the cost, regardless of the total, and there was little prospect, under the present circumstances, that any agreement could be reached.

In addition to problems with the road, military cooperation had been reduced. Some American supplies did arrive, but the number of American technicians who were to instruct the Burmese in how to use and maintain the equipment was reduced from thirty-four to only five. No discussions were contemplated about a new military assistance agreement, and when Ne Win announced that the new National Defence College would not be opened for a year, the three American advisers assigned to the college were no longer needed. The future of Burmese-American relations did not look promising.[55] American fears that Burma was moving closer to the communist bloc were not alleviated.

Not that all was negative. U Nu stated that the United States and Thailand had played a useful role in the evacuation of the KMT forces.[56] He wrote a personal note to President Kennedy thanking him for "all the assistance which the United States Government have rendered" in this matter.[57] Kennedy responded by dedicating the Burmese edition of his book, *Profiles in Courage*, to the memory of Aung San. Burma also published a series of documents that showed close cooperation between the KNDO forces and the BCP since May 1959 and an apparent end to KNDO contacts with the KMT in 1958. By implication, the communists were now seen once again as the major threat to Burmese unity, not the KMT. Burma's interest in having Peace Corps volunteers also suggested a warming relationship. Peace Corps Director Sargent Shriver received a warm welcome when he visited Burma. Perhaps the crisis was ending faster than anyone had expected. As U Thant put it in the middle of May, "the differences between the United States and Burma over the K.M.T. now seem to be a thing of the past."[58]

Although the Burmese had ratcheted down the rhetoric, their suspicions of American involvement with the KMT had not disappeared, and indeed the KMT issue continued to fester. Most serious of all, the CIA reported that the KMT forces remaining in Burma were still in contact with agents from the Republic of China's minister of national defense. This was potentially very dangerous. The Burmese continued to accuse the KMTs of teaming up with the ethnic insurgencies, and an American Baptist missionary, Robert Morse, who lived in Kachin State, reported hearing that the KMTs had trained the Kachins. Interestingly, he reported that Naw Seng, the Kachin leader who had once led the Karen insurgency and who had gone over to the communist side, had defected and had then received training in Taiwan, along with assurances that he would receive "planeloads of American equipment." Whether this was true, and if so, whether Naw Seng was back in Kachin State, was not clear. Still, Morse's report showed clearly that the Burmese continued to be suspicious of American involvement with both the KMTs and the ethnic resistance forces; the possibility of a dramatic deterioration in the bilateral relationship was always possible. Late in August 1961 the Burmese stated—for the first time officially—that the Kachin rebel leadership had been trained in Taiwan.[59]

Further complicating the American attempts to improve relations was former Ambassador Key's statement in the New Leader magazine that the CIA had supported the KMTs in the past. "The CIA gave supplies to the Nationalist Chinese in Burma and didn't inform me," Key told reporter Ronald May. "Before 1952, we had a pretty good reputation in that region," Key added. "Now we are put on the level of the Communists." Then in October creditable reports appeared that six hundred KMTs, under the command of General Tuan Hsi-wen, had moved back into Burma from Thailand. This created a dangerous situation, reported the American embassy in Rangoon, for it provided an excuse for Chinese troops to enter Burma, and it also would likely touch off a new anti-American campaign in the Burmese press.[60]

Still, there did seem to be some interest among the Burmese in reestablishing a stronger relationship. Although they postponed signing a Peace Corps agreement, they did not seem opposed in principle. Brigadier Aung Gyi, second only to Ne Win in the military hierarchy, wanted to resume military aid talks, and discussions about the Rangoon-Mandalay highway restarted in the summer of 1961. In August Under Secretary of State Chester Bowles visited Rangoon and had extensive conversations with U Nu, which pleased the prime minister. While there were no specific agreements reached, "US stock" with U Nu was "probably higher now than anytime since the KMT issue erupted again early this year."[61]

The Bowles trip was a positive development, but there still remained problems in the relationship. Burma declined to accept Peace Corps volunteers after all. The minister of education commented that the volunteers were "not well qualified, young and inexperienced men." Actually, this was completely inaccurate so far as the first volunteers selected were concerned. One was an experienced chemist with an advanced degree, his wife an occupational therapist with six years' practice who was currently employed "directing occupational therapy for cerebral palsied children"; she was also a board member of a training center for physically challenged people.[62] Probably the government had concluded that accepting them would call into question Burma' neutral posture and would cause problems with China, with which its relationship had improved notably following the border agreement.

In addition the Burmese had not yet approved a visa for Dr. M. Donald Olmanson who was going to assist Gordon Seagrave in Namkham and whose visa application had been pending since February 1961, and getting the business cleared up required a personal request to U Nu. More significant were differences over American military assistance. Within days of Bowles's departure the Burmese complained strongly about the way the United States had conducted new talks about military aid. The current American proposals were very "unsatisfactory" on several counts, including the proposed delivery dates, the amount of equipment that was included (or, more accurately, excluded), and the payment terms. "I would be glad to know," wrote Brigadier Aung Gyi, "whether present administration still entertain friendly attitude towards our defense forces adopted by previous administration." If the Kennedy administration could not provide aid on the same terms, Aung Gyi stated, then "I regret to say it would not be in interest of our two nations to pursue matter any further." Ambassador Everton, like his predecessors, argued that military aid was justified on political grounds alone, and he wanted the amount increased from $10 million to $15 million. Nor was the ambassador at all happy when CINCPAC recommended not sending Caribou aircraft and V-107 helicopters to Burma. That, replied Everton, would be "tantamount to scuttling" the proposed military aid program.[63] Washington was not persuaded, however.

The discussion about military assistance continued into 1962. In January Kennedy's air force aide, Godfrey T. McHugh (who had once dated Jacqueline Bouvier who later married Kennedy) in a formal memo to the president acknowledged the obsolescent state of the Burmese air force but thought that Burma's requests were "unrealistic in terms of cost and technical sophistication." He did recommend including F-86F tactical fighter planes (Sabre jets), along with C-47 transports but demurred on a number of other requested aircraft, including the Caribou.[64]

Meanwhile, involved discussions about the Mandalay highway continued. Over the summer the Americans had presented the Burmese with three options, to cost between $38.4 and $42.5 million. The new proposals envisioned a new highway between Rangoon and Pegu, with a reconstructed highway along the existing route from Pegu to Mandalay. Both the United States and the Burmese thought the third option at $42.5 million was the best choice, and Burma was committed to pay $9.5 million, while the United States was committed to $28.5 million. That left about $4.5 million, and the only remaining question, it seemed, was how to come up with the additional funds. Agreement seemed in sight. Haggling over a few million dollars seemed silly. Everton sent a long letter urging that an agreement be quickly concluded. But a "long haggle" ensured, and Everton, who considered the highway "one of the most important efforts in Burma," concluded in November 1961 that some American agencies were out to sabotage it. He specifically accused USAID of undermining the project, and he asked for a "definitive Department decision" on whether to continue the negotiations. Washington, however, did not share Everton's sense of urgency. A confidential "background paper" on the project concluded that a delay would not result in serious political damage.[65]

Discussions for economic assistance also took place. Bowles had suggested long-term loans at low interest—transparently in response to the Chinese loan of $84 million. U Nu was interested and said he would also like the Americans to fund a hospital then under construction. This also, the ambassador noted, would balance off some Soviet gifts, including a technological institute, a hospital, and a hotel. Those in favor of more aid argued that the Americans should not allow the Chinese to gain more influence in Burma without resistance. There were also hopeful reports that U Nu had become disillusioned with Soviet and Chinese aid programs and was now looking "more to the West for assistance."[66]

By 1961 Vietnam was beginning to emerge as another potentially divisive issue. In October General Maxwell Taylor made his famous recommendation to insert quietly eight thousand American ground troops into Vietnam, and U Nu, who had seen press reports of the recommendation, urged Kennedy not to do so. He expressed his sympathies with South Vietnamese President Ngo Dinh Diem but stated that there was no military solution. What Diem needed was more popular support. Whether U Nu influenced Kennedy's view may be doubted, but the president did not send the troops. As he told Nu (in a letter that included a full-throated attack on North Vietnam and a disingenuous discussion of the Geneva Accords), "we are not sending U.S. Combat forces to Viet-Nam." Still, there was great concern that, if Vietnam fell to the communists, this would "mean the eventual communist domination of all of the Southeast Asian mainland," and a "'pink' Burma," as Lyman Lemnitzer, chairman of the JCS, put it, would certainly not be much of a barrier to the communists.[67]

Even as the Americans confronted these matters, another issue emerged: Burma's representative to the UN, U Thant, was being considered for secretary general. Important Americans thought his appointment would be a bad idea. In September 1961, for example, former ambassador to Burma (and now Assistant Secretary of State) McConaughy wrote to Rusk urging him not to support U Thant's candidacy. Thant had many strengths, thought McConaughy, but he was "naive in regard to Communist Bloc (especially Communist China)." Were he to be elected, "the scales would be dangerously tilted against our interests on many important UN issues and operation." McConaughy's recommendation did not prevail. The United States and the Soviet Union agreed to support U Thant. This represented the Kennedy administration's effort to be more sensitive to Third World interests than its predecessor had been. The United States was also seriously considered inviting U Nu to visit the United States in June 1962.[68]

There were some positive signs by this point. For example, U Nu agreed to be honorary co-chair, with President Kennedy, of a committee that was organizing a celebration of the fortieth anniversary of the Burma Surgeon's work; and he accepted the invitation to visit the United States "with the greatest of pleasure." However, the Americans, or at least those in the United States embassy in Rangoon, had concluded that Nu has failed. "His government can only be described as a disappointment," the embassy reported in a lengthy review in January 1962. The administrative efficiency achieved under Ne Win's government had "been largely dissipated." The government lacked direction, was not firm in the face of pressure, and could not even make decisions. The embassy laid this failure squarely on U Nu's shoulders. He had come to power with great popular support but had failed to provide "firm and consistent leadership." He had made little progress in solving the country's many problems and opened the door to unrest and communist advance. The embassy did not foresee a military takeover again, unless the army's own interests were threatened or internal security collapsed. But one White House official suggested that the military might indeed be getting ready to take over. "This is one of those situations where it is not evident that the U.S. has any immediate role to play," he concluded.[69]

The KMT issue continued to fester under the surface. Most of the KMTs were out of Burma, but they remained capable of causing political complications in the region, and Ambassador Everton wanted them evacuated and/or dispersed. Kennedy himself continued to follow the KMT issue.[70] But all of these concerns—the invitation to U Nu, the renewed concerns about the KMT, possible increased military assistance, the Mandalay road—faded instantly on 2 March 1962 when Ne Win, acting on his own and apparently having informed only a very small number of associates, announced that the military was taking over the government. He arrested about fifty persons, including U Nu and various government officials. There was only one fatality, the son of a former president who had resisted the arrest of his father and was shot. A Revolutionary Council would now run the country.

NE WIN'S WAY TO SOCIALISM

The year 1962 marked the end of democracy in Burma and the beginning of Ne Win's dictatorial rule. The economy gradually declined, the result of Ne Win's "Burmese Way to Socialism." Ne Win also began to isolate his country from the rest of the world. Foreigners and their institutions were expelled, and even tourism was discouraged. For the most part, then, Burma was different from the other Southeast Asian countries. However, despite Ne Win's deep dislike of the United States, Burma maintained a strict nonalignment policy and was not about to allow any foreign power to gain ascendancy; eventually the United States accommodated itself to this reality. As long as Burma was determined to maintain its independence, the United States could live with it, despite the deplorable character of the new regime.

American Reaction to the Coup

The initial American explanation of Ne Win's coup was that it was inspired by domestic concerns, perhaps involving the relationships between the central government and the ethnic minorities. U Nu was reportedly on the verge of offering concessions to the Shans, whose leaders were in Rangoon to discuss redress of their grievances; they wanted more autonomy or even independence (which in theory was an option for them under the constitution). U Nu's alleged administrative laxness may have contributed, along with anger at corruption and his

FIGURE 8.   General Ne Win, Burma's prime minister from 1958 to 1960 and from 1962 to 1988.

decision to make Buddhism the state religion (which had sparked a rebellion by the largely Christian Kachins). Then there were "emotional and subjective factors operating upon Ne Win himself." U Nu's attempts to give the ethnic minorities more autonomy was perhaps the most fundamental reason—or at least a

convenient excuse for the military to act. To Ne Win the idea of a federal constitution was, in historian Michael Charney's words, "a sign of unforgivable weak-
ness," and he moved to stop it.[1]

Whatever the causes, US embassy officials were not yet prepared to say if the
new Revolutionary Council would be more beneficial to the United States than
the ousted U Nu administration, and they cautioned against simplistic assessments of Ne Win. He could behave as a statesman and was "probably" still basically anticommunist. But he was also "suspicious, erratic, and capable of acting in
highly emotional and irrational fashion." He had also recently stated that neither
the United States nor the USSR was to be trusted, and he had helped engineer
a rapprochement with China.[2] In any event the United States quickly accommodated itself to the new development and five days after the coup in effect
recognized the new government and invited Ne Win to Washington (although
he declined to come).

Whatever his views of the United States, Ne Win now wanted to conclude the
long-delayed military assistance agreement. Following a by now familiar pattern,
the ambassador urged prompt action to supply equipment needed to suppress
the insurgencies. A specific list of equipment was approved, and Ne Win seemed
pleased.[3] An exchange of notes on 10 July 1962 formally concluded the agreement.

Ne Win also hoped to conclude an agreement on the Rangoon-Mandalay
highway project. Without resolving all of the issues, the Americans had offered to
begin construction on the first section of the highway. This was, in effect, a final
offer, and if Burma accepted it, the United States would proceed. But Ne Win
wanted the entire highway built, despite its expense (estimated to be between
$60 and $85 million) and he also resisted American suggestions that Burma seek
additional funding for the highway, such as from the IBRD or Japan.[4]

Despite these setbacks, the Burmese (or at least some Burmese) were willing
to make concessions to the Americans. Apparently Aung Gyi, Ne Win's second in
command, took the initiative when the general was away.[5] As the Americans had
suggested, the Burmese now agreed to draw on some of their substantial reserves in
Japanese reparation payments. The Americans would contribute $28 million and
an additional $3.76 million in kyats (the Burmese currency) that they had already
agreed to. They would build the road along the alignment originally preferred by
both the United States and Burma—that is, an entirely new road that would bypass
the cities and towns connected by the old road. Although this road would be much
more expensive, the Burmese would cover all of the costs beyond the American
commitment. They would employ the Corps of Engineers during the planning
phase and allow it to assist with supervision of the actual work, which would be
undertaken by a Burmese company.[6] This was a very reasonable proposal.

Ambassador Everton privately agreed and thought that building the road was
very much in American interest. However, he was forced to say that the road as

proposed was not justified economically because most of the traffic would still use the old road that connected the towns. U Soe Tin, the permanent secretary at Burma's Foreign Office, remonstrated that since the Burmese were paying for most of the road, and the United States was not being asked to pay any more than it had already agreed to, the United States should defer to Burmese opinion on this point. Everton replied that Congress would insist that the road be economically justified, even if the United States was only paying for a portion of it. American quibbling seemed "incomprehensible" to the Burmese. The United States had given the Burmese a choice of approaches to building the road, they had settled on one and had agreed to provide "all the additional funds required," and now the Americans were raising questions about the economic justification for building the highway.[7]

The real stumbling block was that USAID did not want to spend any money on the highway, regardless of the route. It found no economic justification for the new highway preferred by the Burmese, and it was not persuaded that the current road could be modernized. The American government's position caused "considerable damage," stated IMF official Tun Thin (no fan of Ne Win). Everton surely agreed.[8]

One final Burmese effort to get American funding occurred late in September when Foreign Minister U Thi Han visited Washington. He reiterated arguments made in previous weeks: the Burmese had agreed to pay most of the costs using Japanese reparations, the road as proposed was important for a variety of reasons (including the need to avoid flood-prone areas and to speed up communication by bypassing urban zones, and advantages for military movements), the Berger consulting firm had recommended the route, and the Americans had agreed with that recommendation. It seemed perverse that the Americans would now raise objections.

The American response was weak. Although the Berger firm had recommended the new road alignment, the United States claimed that it had never formally agreed with the company's assessment, so that when Burma itself had initially rejected it because it was too costly, there had been no need for the United States to enter its objections. The Burmese understanding was that the both countries had accepted the Berger recommendations. The United States also lectured U Thi Han that the proper way to construct a highway system was to upgrade existing roads first and only construct new roads when traffic growth justified it—this at a time when the United States had undertaken its vast interstate highway network that bypassed cities and towns, in part for military reasons—very much the same justification that the Burmese were using for their own highway. The Americans had not made a final decision, Thi Han was informed, but it was apparent that a positive response was unlikely.[9] So much had things changed since the first enthusiastic American responses to the idea of funding the highway.

Thi Han's meeting with American officials came after several months of deteriorating relations. Originally they had been cautious in their assessment of the coup, but by mid-April some of Ne Win's actions were beginning to elicit strongly negative responses. It was now evident that, unlike in 1958, he had overthrown a constitutional government, scrapped the judicial system, and established a "virtual military dictatorship." He was xenophobic and particularly suspicious of Westerners. He ordered the Ford and Asia foundations to close up shop: no new programs were to begin, and current specialists had to leave Burma by October 1962. The Johns Hopkins program was ended altogether. No doubt this was part of Ne Win's intention to drastically limit foreign influences. Furthermore, although Ne Win did not say so explicitly at the time, he believed that Americans connected to the foundations were involved with the Shan and Karen dissidents, as were CIA and American embassy personnel based in Bangkok.[10] He was actually correct on at least one point: the CIA was involved with the Shans. Requiring listening posts near the China border, the CIA provided arms to the Shans in return for their protecting the posts.[11]

The Relationship Deteriorates

More troubling officially to the Americans was the Burmese decision to suspend the Fulbright Educational Exchange Program without even consulting with the United States. The Fulbright program had existed in Burma on a continuous basis longer than in any other country. No Fulbrighters could come to Burma during the coming year while the program was under review, causing considerable personal hardship for the fourteen grantees who had been appointed and had made arrangements to come. Everton formally protested the decision, particularly Burma's failure to consult with the Americans ahead of time, but without success. Soon thereafter Ne Win commented that American teachers sent to Burma had been unsatisfactory ones, with degrees from "inferior American universities." They had maintained lax standards and were responsible, he inferred, for the poor discipline in Burma's universities.[12] At the same time twenty-eight Chinese technicians were on their way to Burma, the first of three hundred expected to arrive under the recent loan agreement.

There were additional disquieting signs as well. On 28 April 1962 the Revolutionary Council approved what would become Ne Win's infamous "Burmese Way to Socialism." Everton characterized it as "vague and superficial," though vaguely communist. But he urged a cautious response until it was clear how it would be implemented. Interestingly, the Chinese disparaged it as well, though they chose to support Ne Win because of his neutralism and his administration's friendly relations with China.[13]

Indicative of the deteriorating relationship, on 10 May Ne Win definitely decided not to accept the invitation to visit Washington. He recalled the unpleasant way he had been treated on his previous visit, the objectionable American response to the cancellation of Ford and Asia Foundation activities and the suspension of the Fulbright program, and the generally bad state of US-Burma relations. He expressed no appreciation for the invitation, nor did he suggest that a future visit might be explored. The climate for investment also changed. It was now "Heavily Overcast and Unsettled." In addition, Ne Win's government revoked the visas of three student tourists, including one American.[14]

In reflecting on developments, Everton concluded that in 1960 Ne Win had decided that establishing a good relationship with China was his foremost goal. If this was the case, it represented an about-face from his previous anticommunist and anti-Chinese positions. He harbored resentments over the shabby treatment he had received on his previous visit to Washington and American involvement with the KMTs. According to Ne Win's father-in-law, Ba Than, then the dean of the Mandalay Medical School, American support of the KMTs "completely changed the General's attitude toward the United States. . . . It had a great effect on the new government's policies."[15]

Whatever one's assessment of the coup and of Ne Win, the basic validity of American policy objectives remained: to keep Burma independent and out of communist control. The developments in Burma raised serious questions about Burma's ability to attain the objectives for which the Americans thought it should strive, while at the same time severely limiting the ability of the United States to influence Burma's direction. While a policy of restraint seemed reasonable under the circumstances, the embassy did not want to suggest an attitude of indifference. Given the current Burmese decision to have as little contact as possible with American diplomats, this was challenging. As Lewis M. Purnell put it, "it would appear we are in for trouble."[16]

The one area where there was still some significant contact between American and Burmese officials related to the military, and supplying the military thus remained a high priority. Burma continued to want previously contracted American military supplies, and the United States intended to honor those contracts. It hoped to provide 9,000 carbines by the end of the year, with another 9,792 to be delivered in the third quarter of 1963, along with a considerable amount of ammunition. Another sign that all was not lost was what Ne Win told Malcolm MacDonald in a series of conversations from 28 April to 2 May. Ne Win's attitude toward the United States was "one of almost unqualified criticism, resentment and suspicion." But in MacDonald's view Ne Win was not ideological, certainly not procommunist, and, while he admired China and appreciated its treatment of him, he would not let China or any other power dominate Burma. His foreign policy would be strictly neutral.[17]

Meanwhile Ne Win was gradually ending democratic freedoms and other institutions that were said to come from "western imperialism." The process was gradual. At first Ne Win moved slowly, trying to "co-opt and cajole, rather than dictate." Political parties continued to exist, and the press, though restrained, retained some freedom. Gradually, however, the press was brought under state control, first by ending access to foreign news sources, then by gradually eliminating private news publications. The *Nation*'s editor, Edward Law-Yone, with whom Ne Win had previously had cordial relations, was arrested and remained imprisoned until 1968, where he used copies of "The Burmese Way to Socialism" as kindling for his cooking stove. When he was released, Ne Win gave him and his family passports to leave the country.[18] The film industry faced a similar fate, first with the establishment of a Film Censor Board, and finally with the nationalization of all cinemas.

One of the first institutions to feel Ne Win's heavy hand were the universities. In May 1962 he "dissolved the university councils," and in July 1962 he moved against students at Rangoon University. The students were protesting new dormitory rules that required men to be in the dorms by 8:00 p.m. The army was called in, and fifteen people, mostly students, were reportedly killed and forty-seven wounded. Eyewitnesses put the numbers much higher. The army also destroyed the Rangoon University Student Union (on the grounds that it was a gathering place for radical students, including those belonging to the White Flag communists), and closed the university. The American embassy concluded that this response had "destroyed any impression of concern for attracting favorable public opinion and has increased resentment at army rule." The attack on the student union was "gratuitous and unnecessary," an act that turned public opinion "against the government."[19] Shortly thereafter, in a private conversation with Averell Harriman in Vienna, Ne Win defended the use of violence against the students. Communists dominated the universities, he told Harriman; the Student Union had become a fortress that even the police could not storm. In the future, he said, such students would not be allowed to enroll, and he said that over time the public would approve what he had done.[20]

Harriman's discussion with Ne Win was very wide ranging, and he thought it "unusually useful." Ne Win strongly criticized American actions, especially past CIA operations in Burma, but he also expressed his appreciation for Kennedy's diplomacy. All in all, while Ne Win still harbored resentments and suspicions about the United States and was determined to remain steadfastly neutral in foreign policy, the conversation seemed to clear the air. On the basis of Harriman's account, the State Department's Southeast Asia Task Force concluded that the government's "leftist, anti-western tendency . . . may be moderating."[21]

Or perhaps not. When Tun Thin stopped over in Vienna to see Ne Win shortly after Harriman's visit, he found that the visit had not changed the general's mind about the United States. In fact, Ne Win spoke "'derisively' of various things the Governor had said to him." By this point American relations with Burma were "friendly and correct, but not cordial."[22]

Ne Win also reversed U Nu's efforts to establish close ties between the state and Buddhism—which did not mean, however, that the Revolutionary Council would not interfere in Buddhist affairs if the monks acted contrary to government wishes. In March 1965 monks led a violent demonstration in Mandalay against the regime, and over the next year several hundred were arrested. About the same time Ne Win ended Christian missionary activity in the country, further isolating the country from corrupting Western influences.

As for the Mandalay highway, it was not quite dead yet. Everton had continued to push for a political determination rather than a purely economic assessment, and in August the State Department responded with skepticism but did not close the door. To proceed on political grounds would require a finding that "US immediate and long-term interests in Burma would be seriously jeopardized by continued insistence upon economic criteria," and a decision to move forward would require "high level" approval. The embassy was invited to submit a proposal on the matter.[23]

Soon thereafter the Burmese made it clear that they wanted to revive discussion of the highway, with the United States providing $30 million, and Burma the remaining cost. "If this one goes sour," Everton wrote, "then the future is going to be very difficult indeed and we are in for a long, cold winter." In October 1962 the United States offered a compromise: the United States would pay the entire cost of the first part of the highway, northward from Rangoon "as far as we could mutually agree on alignment and specifications." The farthest north the road could be built with American funds would be Pyu. Burma could use its own funds to build the highway farther north toward Mandalay along any alignment it chose.[24] This position was close to Burma's.

The United States wanted immediately to begin the process of designing and building the first part of the road, from Rangoon to Pegu (today's Bago—a distance of about 137 kilometers), while a study of the road from Pegu to Pyu (about 159 kilometers) was undertaken. If the Burmese and Americans agreed on the design and construction of the road to Pegu, then American funds would be used to build the extension to Pyu as well. If there was no agreement, the Burmese would have to fund that section of the road. The Burmese wanted agreement on a new alignment for the road from Pegu to Pyu, and the Americans had not agreed to that. Still, the Americans hoped that the road could at least be begun, with a decision on the next section deferred.[25]

The Burmese then presented two counterproposals to Harriman. The first was for the United States simply to give Burma $28 million to be used to purchase highway equipment in the United States. This was not possible, but the other proposal was quite close to the American plan: the Americans could use their funds to build the road from Rangoon to Pyu, but the Burmese wanted the United States to build the entire section along the new alignment recommended by Berger. Harriman appeared to agree with this, but in fact his "agreement" hinged on the completion of a survey that would support a new alignment. This was, in fact, what the United States had previously offered. The issue separating the two sides was whether either the United States or the government of Burma would be able to accept the other's proposed route for the section from Pegu to Pyu.[26]

The American position caused much bitterness in the Burmese government. In March 1963 U Soe Tin let loose when Ambassador Everton came calling. The Burmese had originally thought they were getting a road from Rangoon to Mandalay, he told Everton. "Now all they were getting was to be a road from Rangoon to Pyu, at most." The US "Government simply did things the way they wished to do them and usually dictated the terms of reference," he complained. The United States, he concluded, "always wants things on its own terms."[27]

Despite Soe Tin's righteous indignation, it appears that soon thereafter an agreement was reached, and construction was scheduled to begin on the first section of the highway. The two government had agreed on the design for that part of the road, and the United States was prepared to provide the needed funds for construction.[28] Ne Win was reportedly pleased.

Continuity in Foreign Policy

In the meantime there was much discussion in American government circles about what the United States might do to influence Burmese developments in a positive way. President Kennedy personally inquired about this. The State Department concluded that there was little to be done. Burma did not want to be under China's domination any more than under American domination. It was neutral in its foreign policy, and even Ne Win's "Burmese Way to Socialism" did not have Chinese roots. At present there was little the United States could do.[29]

If the State Department thought little could be done, Edward Lansdale had some ideas. Despite Ne Win's efforts to reduce American influence, Lansdale

wrote, the people were inherently friendly toward Americans. The most immediate way to gain influence, he thought, was to work with the 120 Burmese military
still being trained in the United States. He urged Adam Yarmolinsky in the Department of Defense to "do some constructive work" with them.[30]

Ambassador Everton agreed that the people were much more favorably dis-
posed to Western ideas and institutions than the government, and he hoped
that the United States could help sustain these positive attitudes. He had little
specific to offer, however, on how the United States might engage in "preven-
tive diplomacy" or nourish residual pro-Western attitudes. Everton was by then
on his way out. The circumstances of his departure are not clear (his correspondence with Rusk about this remains classified), but it probably related to
his inability to have a close relationship with Ne Win. A former president of
Kalamazoo College, Everton was not a career officer and resigned entirely from
government service. He suggested to Kennedy that his successor "have enough
in common with General Ne Win to assure a closer relationship than most of
us in the Diplomatic Corps now enjoy. In Burma, personal relationships are
all-important, and this is particularly true in the case of the General." Everton
did not think Burma was "beyond the point of no return yet," but it would take
"all of our best efforts to avoid this happening. The room for maneuverability
is steadily diminishing."[31]

About the same time Allen S. Whiting, head of the State Department's Far
Eastern Division of the Bureau of Intelligence and Research, summarized the
situation in Burma for Harriman. Whiting's analysis paralleled what Everton had
reported, but it is of particular significance because Michael Forrestal, a senior
staff member of President Kennedy's National Security Council, immediately
passed it on the president with a note that this was "as good an assessment of
the situation as I have seen." Like Everton, Whiting did not think that Burma
was moving into the Sino-Soviet orbit. The government's fundamental characteristic was that of "a uniquely xenophobic system of state socialism in which *all*
foreign influences, Sino-Soviet, neutralist or western, will be held to an irreduc-
ible minimum." Ne Win was in absolute control, and his personality was what
was causing difficulty. He had little formal education, little experience outside
of the military, and, as "the product of a clandestine revolutionary movement,"
was suspicious of everyone, including his close associates. On the other hand,
both his domestic objectives and his foreign policy differed little from those of
his predecessors. Whiting postulated that under Ne Win there was little hope
that Burma would "support Free World interests," but it would also remain free
from communist control. Like Everton, too, Whiting had nothing to offer in
terms of changes in American policy.[32] In sum, despite the White House's desire
to do something about Burma, no one had much to suggest in terms of what

specifically the United States might do, beyond Edward Lansdale's idea of attempting to influence Burmese sent to the United States for military training.

The United States became more concerned in the summer of 1963 when Ne Win's government arrested numerous persons, including many leaders of the AFPFL who had spoken out in favor of a return to parliamentary democracy. This indicated that the Revolutionary Council had decided that the Burmese Way to Socialism Party (later the Burma Socialist Programme Party) would be the only legal political party, although that decision was not made final until 1964. It was initially a small cadre party, and only slowly made a transition to a mass-based party early in the 1970s. The transformation was an intelligent way for Ne Win to gain wider support. He concentrated on getting military personnel into the party, who as a result far outnumbered those with no military background.[33] The Revolutionary Council also replaced local administrative structures with ones run by the military.

Ne Win now made it his top priority to reach an accord with the communists. This troubled the US embassy more than the political repression and led it to conclude that Ne Win was "flirting with exceedingly great danger." There was much speculation about why Ne Win was doing this, ranging from allegations of advanced syphilis to fears of a possible Chinese occupation of certain areas of Burma in the event of a Sino-Indian war.[34] The embassy recommended that there be no immediate change of policy, however, until the situation was clearer.

In light of Ne Win's move closer to China and the communists the embassy weighed the advantages and disadvantages of continuing the military assistance program. There were strong arguments on both sides, and in the end the embassy declined to make a recommendation. The Americans realized that they wielded little influence in Burma, but for the time being they would continue their modest military and economic assistance programs. They would try, over time, to increase their contacts with Ne Win in the hopes that "we may eventually be able to develop a more understanding and fruitful relationship him." To this end the State Department wanted the new ambassador, Henry A. Byroade, who departed for Burma on 11 September 1963, to express Kennedy's hope to meet Ne Win personally. The State Department also wanted Byroade to assure Ne Win that the United States would "not stay idly by" if China attacked. Nor was the United States about to make an issue of Burma's lack of democracy or its human rights violations.[35]

Kennedy's instructions to Byroade followed the State Department's suggestions. When the new ambassador met with Ne Win in October, he indicated that the United States wanted to see Burma retain its independence and that, while it could not make specific military commitments, it was determined "to take all feasible measures to support Burmese resistance against foreign aggression,

direct or indirect." Burma's neutrality and its internal arrangements did not affect this commitment. Hoping to lessen Ne Win's antagonism, the ambassador
extended Kennedy's hope to visit personally with the general. Byroade explicitly
mentioned that he hoped to overcome the legacy of disappointment that resulted
from Ne Win's previous visit during the Eisenhower administration. Ne Win appreciated these remarks, but it was evident that the slights he had encountered
still bothered him, for he recounted them to Byroade "in some detail."[36]

Ne Win also repeated his anger about alleged CIA actions, including the sub-
verting of Maung Maung, who, he said, had become an American agent, as a
result of which Maung Maung had been sent off to Israel as ambassador. He was
pleased, however, to note that Kennedy "was making progress" in bringing even
the "most difficult agency" in the American government under control, though
he had not fully succeeded in this. Byroade informed him that "the President had
already succeeded" in doing so.[37]

Byroade appreciated Ne Win's frankness but felt that it would be a long slog
to overcome the general's suspicions of the United States. American policy would
therefore continue to maintain a low profile, persist with the limited economic
and military assistance programs still in place, and work, as opportunity presented itself, to lessen Ne Win's antagonism and to reassure him that the United
States considered Burma a very important country in Southeast Asia whose independence it valued. No doubt also this was related to the administration's growing concern about developments in Vietnam. With the Buddhist crisis in South
Vietnam reaching a peak at just this time, and with consideration being given to
encouraging the overthrow of President Ngo Dinh Diem, the United States did
not want to antagonize needlessly an important country in the region, despite its
dubious domestic policies.

A possible chance to improve relations came earlier than expected. Ne Win's
government had failed to reach an accommodation with the Burmese communists, perhaps opening the door for conciliation with the ethnic insurgents and
better relations with the United States.[38] When Byroade returned to the United
States for medical treatment, the State Department urged the White House to
find time to see him, given Burma's sensitivities. It was important, the department pointed out, for Byroade to return to Burma with evidence of Lyndon
Johnson, the new president's, confidence in him. Johnson did meet with Byroade,
and when the ambassador returned to Rangoon, he requested an appointment
with Ne Win, commenting on "my recent conversation with President Johnson
which revealed his keen interest in your own aspirations and impressions."[39]

Unfortunately, Byroade's hope that Ne Win might be able to conciliate the
ethnic rebels and then turn his full attention to the communists did not come
to pass. Talks with the Shans, which had been going on since August 1963, broke

down on 8 December, and most other rebel groups also broke off talks. Soon fighting resumed, this time resulting in KMT assistance to the Shans, developments which were not likely to reduce Ne Win's suspicions about the United States. The government curtailed the distribution of the publications of foreign embassies and limited contact with them. More restrictions were also placed on foreigners traveling within Burma, and transit visas were reduced from ten days to twenty-four hours.[40]

Burmese Dissidents Request US Assistance

Various antigovernment plots, real and imagined, added to Ne Win's suspicions. Up to a point these had some basis—not that the United States was deeply engaged in plots to overthrow Ne Win, but that, as his rule became increasingly autocratic, dissidents within Burma, and those who had defected or fled the country, often did seek American assistance. In January 1964, for example, two Buddhist monks from Arakan Province came to the American embassy to seek support.[41] More troubling were the activities of an American, Baird V. Helfrich, and of Ne Win's former confidant, Bo Setkya. Helfrich was a former OSS agent in Burma during World War II who had returned to Burma with his family in 1952 and had settled there. He had worked with the AFPFL in its early years, was in touch with the rebels, and supported the overthrow of the Ne Win government. In April 1963 he sought American support to depose Ne Win, and though he had been warned that this was contrary to American policy, the embassy believed that Helfrich would "maintain his interest in subversive activities in Burma."[42] It was an accurate prediction. He tried to persuade embassy officers to back the dissidents and wrote at least two letters to the State Department along similar lines. From the embassy's perspective, this was very dangerous, for if the Burmese were to discover the letters, it would only confirm their suspicions. This time the embassy warned Helfrich that, if he continued to engage in political activities in Burma, his passport might be restricted.[43] Helfrich kept up his activities, and after several months the State Department was prepared to move against him. There were objections, however: if Helfrich chose to appeal a ruling restricting his passport, for example, the Americans might have to reveal to the Burmese that not only had Helfrich been engaged in subversive activities for some time but American officials had known about it. This would only feed Burmese suspicions of official American involvement in subversive efforts.[44]

My mid-1965 Helfrich finally seemed resigned to returning to the United States. He felt "washed up," was a "defeated man, and a somewhat desperate one." On the other hand, the Americans feared that he would not leave "until he is sure that he can do nothing more to harm" Ne Win's government." He told an American official that he wanted to blow up a Burmese supply depot, which he had been casing. This was probably a fantasy, but it indicated the depths of his disgust with Ne Win. Because the embassy thought that it was urgent that he leave Burma—both for his own sake and for that of the United States—the embassy recommended flying Helfrich and his entire family to the United States on a military aircraft, free of charge. In the end Helfrich left Burma as an indigent on a coal steamer to New York by way of India and Aden. His daughter and son had previously been deported.[45]

The Burmese were even more concerned about Bo Setkya, who had organized a plot against the government. Ne Win almost certainly thought he was working with the CIA. He told Mountbatten that Setkya wanted to kill him, and he may have believed rumors that American submarines had earlier been patrolling off Burma's Tenasserim coast to contact Setkya and other revolutionaries.[46]

In Washington State Department officials told Burmese embassy officers that they would not meet with Setkya, except to inform him clearly of the American position regarding Burma (which they did). Louis Walinsky, who would increasingly be something of a thorn in the administration's side because of his activities opposing Ne Win, tried to persuade State Department officials to receive Setkya, but he was rebuffed.[47] Shortly thereafter Walinsky delivered a stinging speech at the Asia Society in New York, blasting American policy as "tired, timid and superficial analysis, soiled and shopworn." The United States, he suggested, ought to stand up for democratic principles; it should protest the overthrow of a democratically elected government and the imprisonment of U Nu.[48]

An interesting side note was the unannounced call that Setkya's estranged wife, Daw Win Min Than, made on embassy official Alexander Schnee and his wife in mid March 1964. Daw Win Min Than, who had once appeared with Gregory Peck in the movie *The Purple Plain*, complained that her husband had left her and the children bereft. She wanted Mrs. Schnee to hold her jewels for safe keeping and inquired about possible asylum for the children. The Americans suspected that she was an agent provocateur, in part because she had never been arrested, whereas one of Bo Setkya's former mistresses had been.[49]

Hunkering Down

With Ne Win's suspicions about the United States at a peak, it was not surprising that only a very few Burmese military officials attended a farewell reception for the outgoing Military Equipment Delivery Team chief—"the smallest it has ever been at any of the MEDT receptions"—despite a large invitation list.[50] Ne Win's opinions about the United States did not soon improve, and Burma began to censor foreign library holdings.

On the more positive side, the Burmese government accepted an American invitation to send three Burmese engineers for USAID-sponsored instruction in highway engineering. Since Burma almost routinely declined invitations of this sort, this acceptance indicated its continuing interest in the highway project. Shortly thereafter, however, Ne Win was reportedly furious over a recent article about Burma in *Life* magazine that referred to him as a "dictator" whose forced nationalization of the economy had resulted in an economic disaster. Ne Win's failures were "spectacular," and he was so paranoid that "anti-aircraft guns are mounted on the roof [of his house] and manned around the clock." Ne Win believed that the *Life* article reflected official American policy. "Such a reaction is typical of the General, who resents the Anglo-Saxon attitude of superiority which he thinks he sees in all Americans and Englishmen, and who seems to be especially sensitive to the tone of criticism in *Time* and *Life*," the embassy reported. "Ne Win's tendency to confuse Luce editorial policy with US foreign policy is common among Burmans."[51]

Ne Win's reaction to the *Life* article reflected Ne Win's xenophobia, which the article doubtless reinforced. The government severely restricted the movement of foreigners who resided in Burma. "Tourists and visitors of all kinds are unwanted," reported the American embassy.[52] Foreigners leaving Burma could not leave with their wedding rings. Missionaries were especially suspect, and their residence permits were seldom renewed once they expired. By December 1965 they were receiving direct orders to depart, and in March 1966 most of those who still remained in the country were ordered out.

By this time Byroade was discouraged about Burma's future and the future of American relations with Burma. Ne Win was "a far different man than we estimated him to be in 1958 and again in 1960 when he voluntarily returned power to civilian government," he wrote. Every move he took was designed only to enhance his own power. A particular danger, thought Byroade, was that he had isolated himself, speaking only with a few unsophisticated military cronies. Even letters from heads of state went unanswered. To be sure his motives were probably pure, and he would not be pushed around by the Chinese, but his xenophobia and self-imposed isolation reduced Western influence.[53]

Immediately after Byroade sent this lengthy, secret analysis of current developments in Burma, he drafted another telegram to the State Department and sent it at an even more highly classified level. In this telegram the ambassador gave his truly unvarnished opinion of Ne Win. The general, he reported, was genuinely afraid of the United States, convinced that it was out to "do him in, possibly violently." After Kennedy's assassination he had doubled his personal guard, fearing that the "CIA might act in conjunction with Bo Setkya" and that US pilots might target him from the air. He seemed to have a positive impression of Byroade (based on their one and only meeting), but in Ne Win's view that was of no importance since the ambassador had no control over Washington or the CIA; he recalled Ambassador Key's resignation over CIA support to the KMT forces. In response to Ne Win's paranoia it was tempting, Byroade thought, to bring things to a head, to cut off what limited aid programs existed, for example, but in the end he advised against that. The best thing to do was to continue a policy of restraint and to complete projects already begun, including the highway. The administration agreed. Despite temptations to confront Burma, the administration decided to maintain the relationship. The United States had connections with the Burmese military, and more importantly Ne Win had been "damn good" at resisting communist influence. It was perhaps not the time to alienate a neutral country.[54]

The relationship nonetheless continued to deteriorate. USIS activities were "enfeebled," its films and publications "all but eliminated," its libraries closed. U Hla Taw, the president of the Burma-American Institute, was arrested. The previous American ambassador, John Everton, was accused of "anti–Ne Win plottings." The government was establishing "totalitarian control," and an "intensive wave of xenophobic nationalism combined with overtones of Marxist class warfare" was "driving out foreigners and foreign influence." The Buddhists were preparing for "all-out resistance."[55]

In this context, then, it was not all that surprising that on 15 May 1964 the government informed F. William Small, the USAID representative in Burma, that it wished to terminate the agreement to build the Rangoon-Mandalay highway. The Burmese contended that they had to weigh the "importance of highway project against continued irritations affecting Burmese-American relations" and had determined that it was best to avoid the inevitable complications that would arise if the project went forward.[56]

The embassy surmised that the real reason for the termination was to reduce even further the American presence in Burma, virtually precluding any future aid projects that involved any level of American oversight. Furthermore, in the embassy's view, the longer-range implications were ominous, because Burma would henceforth be reliant on assistance from communist countries. Soon thereafter Burma retracted its decision to send Burmese engineers to the United States for training in highway engineering.[57] It also decided not to purchase American military jets in favor of Soviet MiGs.

Throughout this period Ne Win refused to meet with Byroade. The only Americans who had any relationship with the general were academics Frank Trager, who had been in charge of American foreign assistance to Burma during the Truman administration, and Helen Trager. In June 1964 Ne Win and Kitty threw a party for the Tragers, at which Kitty in particular expressed "bitterly anti-American" views and recalled their ill-treatment in the United States. Because the Tragers appeared to be the only Americans that Ne Win trusted, James C. Thomson Jr., then on the NSC staff, suggested that he be considered for ambassador to Burma. Thomson's assessment may, however, have been in error. A Burmese official and intellectual who resented the government's leftward tilt told an American diplomat that, when Frank Trager left the dinner, Ne Win had said, "there goes a little CIA."[58]

The internal situation resulted in an exodus, or an attempted exodus, of people—and not just foreigners. Among these seeking to leave was Dr. Kyaw Than, the brother of Ne Win's wife. Kyaw Than, a urologist trained at the University of Minnesota, was married to an American woman and wanted accept a position in the United States. He told an American officer that there was no chance for professional advancement in Burma, that his wife wanted to leave, and that his children needed a better education than they could get in Burma.[59] Perhaps partly to stem the exodus, the government made it increasingly difficult for officials to socialize, or in any way to interact, with Americans.

Then in July 1964 there were hopes that the pendulum was beginning to swing back. Maxwell Taylor's appointment as ambassador to Vietnam, with U. Alexis Johnson as his deputy, seems somehow to have reassured the Burmese. There was also much optimistic talk about calling a new Geneva Conference on Southeast Asian affairs. The Burmese press modulated its harsh anti-Americanism, and the USIS was once again permitted to publish its monthly magazine. Soe Tin hinted to Byroade that a meeting with Foreign Minister Thi Han and perhaps with Ne Win himself was possible. Byroade did meet with U Thi Han and U Ohn Khin, the Secretary of the Ministry of National Planning, and discussed a recent visit by Zhou Enlai; in addition, both thought a meeting with Ne Win was possible and perhaps useful. But U Ohn Khin also pointed out that Ne Win was easily irritated, was particularly angry at CIA activities in Southeast Asia, and doubted that the American ambassador in Burma could exert any control over the agency. The three previous ambassadors had assured him that they could, and all had been proven wrong. Byroade assured the foreign minister that he was in control of all American activities in Burma, and that if Ne Win did not accept that, there was no reason for a meeting. Privately, however, he hoped that his forthright line would result in an appointment, and he received strong support from Assistant Secretary William Bundy who hoped that Byroade could "disabuse him of his obsession about CIA."[60]

Ne Win's current suspicions were at least partly inspired by creditable reports that Taiwan was once again supporting KMT troops in Thailand and Burma, with the intention of mounting raids into Yunnan. Although such reports were not yet confirmed, the United States wanted to head off a replay of 1959–60 and instructed its ambassadors in Bangkok and Taipei to discuss KMT paramilitary operations with the governments to which they were accredited. The United States was not, however, objecting to "clandestine intelligence operations."[61]

Finally, Ambassador Byroade got his appointment with Ne Win and spoke with him for ninety minutes on 30 July 1964. He characterized the meeting as "rather disappointing" and "perplexing," with Ne Win being "ill at ease and not very communicative." Byroade attempted to dispel Burmese suspicions that the United States was working covertly with dissident forces in Burma, particularly the KMT. It is doubtful if he convinced Ne Win, but the general did say that he would let bygones be bygones. He was also critical of foreign libraries and said they could not reopen, that Burma had to develop its own knowledge base. Byroade came away from the interview with the impression that the United States could live quite easily with Burma's approach to external relations, which would not allow domination by China (or anyone else). The more pressing problem was Ne Win's inability to govern the country in a realistic way, and there was little the United States could do about that. The State Department concurred. As long as Ne Win pursued a genuinely neutral policy of noninvolvement, "we cannot be too dissatisfied." He was likely to run the country into the ground, however, and a rebellion was a possible outcome, though not in the short term.[62]

Despite a number of irritations on both sides, the relationship was beginning to stabilize. From the American perspective the Ne Win government, which had appeared to be moving closer to the communist countries, had in July veered back toward a more neutral position. Among other things Burma rejected a Chinese request to condemn American policy in Vietnam. Ne Win had destroyed democracy, imprisoned his opponents, and might well be destroying the country's economy. He distrusted the Americans, severely restricted American information programs, and limited contacts between Burmese and American officials. Still, he was determined to keep Burma independent, so that his foreign policy was not one that particularly alarmed the United States. As the American embassy put it in a paper prepared for other American embassies in the region: "In general we find the present degree of Burmese involvement with the communist world tolerable, we see little prospect of changing it much, and we are content to set for ourselves the objective of keeping it from growing or at best reducing it a bit. In the short run, thanks largely to Burma's determination to remain independent, the prospects seem fairly good."[63]

Thus, for some time to come the United States maintained a very low profile in Burma. The Americans were well aware that if they overreached, there would be a backlash. The United States continued its cultural programs whenever possible, including visits by sports figures and celebrities. In April 1965 golfer Gene Sarazen offered instruction for three days and later sent over a new set of clubs for the best caddy. In February 1966 USIS put on an exhibition, "U.S. Progress in Space and Science," and invited astronaut John Glenn and the US Davis Cup tennis team to come to Burma as part of the occasion. When Glenn arrived to open the exhibition he received an enthusiastic reception—"one of the biggest press plays a non-official personality has received in years." The tennis team played three exhibition matches, with an audience response described as "the largest and most enthusiastic of their trip," leading the embassy to conclude that sports were perhaps the best way to show American interest in Burma.[64]

The most significant of the remaining American programs in Burma, however, was the modest military assistance program. The Burmese military liked American arms and equipment. Aside from its actual utility, the Burmese accepted American military aid as a kind of balance to its close relationships with China and the USSR. The United States welcomed this tenuous connection with official Burma and justified its continuation on political grounds.

There still remained points of tension. On 1 April 1965, Burma announced that all private schools would be nationalized, thus implementing a policy that had been announced the previous year. Baptists owned the lion's share of American schools with property values amounting to several million dollars. Soon thereafter the government also began to nationalize private hospitals, beginning with Seagrave's hospital in Namkham shortly after the surgeon's death. A Baptist institution in Moulmein was also taken over. The respected Seventh Day Adventist hospital in Rangoon and the Okkalapa Catholic hospital, the largest private hospital in the country, soon suffered the same fate. Embassy centers for teaching English were forced to close as well, affecting about four hundred students, and foreigners were kept under surveillance. The government announced even tighter regulations restricting interaction between Burmese officials and foreign diplomats. Burmese were now even scarcer at diplomatic receptions, and even nonofficial Burmese felt impelled to reduce their contacts with foreigners. The Burma-American Foundation could not elect new officers and had to cancel its annual Boat Race Day. "Those concerned prefer not so stick their necks out," reported an embassy official. Burma had become "a police state."[65]

The war in Vietnam was potentially a problem. Ne Win was not an enthusiastic supporter of American involvement there, but he did not want China or North Vietnam to dominate the region either. Most of all he wanted to stay out of the conflict. As the war heated up in 1965 Zhou Enlai tried repeatedly to enlist Ne Win to support North Vietnam. Ne Win resented Zhou's pressure—the Chinese leader came to Rangoon three times in April 1965 alone, and North Vietnamese Prime Minister Pham Van Dong came once. By one account Ne Win had referred to Zhou as "that bastard. He thinks he can drop in here every two weeks and that I should be at his beck and call."[66] But the communists' visits motivated Dean Rusk to plan to stop over in Rangoon for a low-key visit later in the year (although the visit did not take place). Burma also facilitated American contacts with North Vietnam, and Byroade remained in contact with his North Vietnamese counterpart, exchanging notes about possible peace negotiations—until renewed American bombing of North Vietnam in February 1966 blocked that channel.

The KMT issue also remained a problem. There were troublesome reports early in 1965 that Taipei had resumed its support for the KMT forces in Burma to harass China. In May correspondent Seymour Topping made the renewed KMT activity public with a front-page story in the *New York Times* that mentioned previous CIA support.[67]

Like all other American ambassadors to Burma, Byroade thought the KMT presence was dangerous, almost inviting China to intervene. "Continued calm on Burma front is far more important to Free World position in SEA than anything Chinats [Chinese Nationalists] could hope to achieve from harassing operations," he wrote. He wanted strong representations made in Bangkok and Taipei. Instead, however, the State Department asked Byroade to try to "quiet Burmese fears over KMT activities." It asked for more evidence, not just the "distorted" Topping report.[68]

The State Department response angered Byroade. He was "deeply disappointed," he said, that objections from the American embassies in Bangkok and Taipei had reversed the department's initial intention to approach Thailand and Taiwan about the continuing KMT problem. He was "particularly disturbed" at the suggestion that he ought to try to soothe Burmese opinion. He had no interest in misleading the Burmese. "Up to the present at least I have, unlike my predecessors, not had to make untrue statement on this subject and I plan to keep it that way."[69]

Meanwhile the domestic situation became tenser, as Ne Win ordered the arrest of 130 monks and 150 political party leaders. The monks, who, according to a CIA informant, referred to Ne Win as a "communist military dog," had been sparring with the government for several months over issues of political and religious freedom. Some dissidents, led by Bo Yan Naing, one of the Thirty Comrades (the famous nationalist leaders of the independence movement) and a former military hero, fled to Thailand to join a group of armed resisters already there. The United States followed this development with interest but did not think that the resistance groups would be very effective. This was particularly so after Ne Win arrested his former comrade Aung Gyi in 1965, who had been Ne Win's number two man until two years earlier. The Americans had thought that

Aung Gyi was the only military person who might conceivably be able to mount a creditable effort to overthrow the general. Apparently Ne Win thought so too. Several of Aung Gyi's close associates were also jailed.[70]

United States diplomats listened, at least, to those who wanted to overthrow Ne Win. For example, on 1 May 1965 Thida Sturdevant, the daughter of former Prime Minister Ba Maw, approached Alexander Schnee in Washington. Acting on behalf of dissidents Ba Maw and Bo Yan Naing, she requested about one million dollars worth of American arms. If victorious, they would take the country in a more pro-American direction. Schnee said he would make inquiries at the State Department (he was no longer directly involved in Burmese affairs). The conversation ended with Schnee agreeing to "get in touch with Mrs. Sturtevant again."[71] The Americans probably welcomed news of dissident activity, but they almost certainly concluded that the Ba Maw–Bo Yan Naing plot, like others that they knew about, was not likely to succeed, and they did not assist it.

The revolution was beginning to turn on its own. Rangoon University professor of political science Dr. Kyaw Thet told Americans that he wanted out, that the university was under the control of hardline leftists, as was the army. All moderate elements had been purged. More significantly James Barrington, Burma's ambassador to the United Nations and Canada (and formerly ambassador to the United States), requested political asylum in the United States. He was reported "profoundly frightened and shaken to the core." Ambassador to Canada W. Walton Butterworth assured him "again and again that the U.S." would "not hand him and his family over to anyone's tender mercies." But in the end Barrington remained in Canada, where he became professor of history at the University of Alberta, apparently having been permitted to resign from Burma's foreign service, effective 28 August 1965. He remained in Edmonton until his death in 1992.[72]

The year ended on a more positive note when Senator Mike Mansfield (D-MT)), a trained Asian expert, brought a delegation of senators to Rangoon in November 1965. They had an informative discussion with Foreign Minister U Thi Han and Ne Win, primarily about Vietnam. The visit went off "extremely well."[73] Still, a close relationship was hard to imagine.

THE RELATIONSHIP STABILIZES

Although by the mid-1960s the United States had accommodated itself to Ne Win's rule, he remained bitter about his visit to Washington in 1960, and the Americans hoped to at least reduce his antagonism. The Cold War was still on, and China remained a major antagonist whose efforts to conciliate Burma were a matter of concern. Furthermore, the United States was now engaged in a full-scale war in Vietnam and wanted Asian support. There was no chance that Burma would provide troops under Johnson's "More Flags" campaign, but the Americans did hope that Burma would not join the chorus of critics and certainly would not agree to China's request that it condemn American actions.

Ne Win's visit to Washington was successful in this regard, and furthermore, for a time Burma's relations with China soured dramatically. However, Ne Win's determination to remain nonaligned and uninvolved internationally, his continued repression at home, and his poor management of the economy did not presage a close relationship. In addition, as the United States began to change its policy toward China at the end of the decade, Burma became less important in Cold War terms. By the end of the decade, Burmese-American relations had stabilized. They were civil but not close.

In September 1966 Ne Win came to Washington. Previous invitations to visit the United States, first extended in 1962 and periodically reiterated, had been declined. Given that relations between the United States and Burma had not been exactly cordial in recent times it "took a bit of persuading" to convince the White House that a Ne Win visit was a good idea. However, by 1966 there had been "a slight warming in United States–Burmese relations," begun with the Mansfield delegation's visit. The United States, now deeply involved in Vietnam, wanted to reinforce Burma's neutrality and hoped to make amends for the disastrous visit in 1960. This time Ne Win accepted the invitation, though he initially seemed to view the trip as a vacation rather than a serious business trip. He expressed interest in playing golf with an American pro and filming his own golf swings ("in strict privacy"). He wanted to see some tobacco fields in Virginia, visit Denison University because of its long-time interest in Burma, watch an American football game, a swimming meet, and a rodeo, and visit his wife's brother in California.[1]

Much effort went into planning the trip. As usual Ne Win wanted to minimize the pomp and circumstance, whereas the Americans feared that if the visit were too informal it would appear that he was being slighted. Foreign Office official U Ohn Khin reminded the Americans, however, that the problems with the previous visit had involved "certain disagreeable incidents," not protocol questions. Byroade concurred, commenting that an important objective of the visit was to "submerge in friendly and genuine hospitality remaining vestiges of ill will from the slights and oversights of Ne Win's last American visit in 1960."[2]

Controversy

Not everyone thought Ne Win should be welcomed to the United States. Louis Walinsky wrote to the Asia Society that Ne Win had destroyed democracy in Burma and that to honor him would help perpetuate his rule. On the other hand, the Asia Society's Burma Council (which included former ambassador Everton), recalling his earlier shabby treatment, voted unanimously to "extend some sort of hospitality" to the general.[3]

Ne Win also received a generally favorable review from Harrison Salisbury in the *New York Times*. Salisbury's portrait of Ne Win, based on a recent visit to Burma, was more positive than many other accounts. Ne Win had frankly acknowledged economic problems caused in part by his determination to put the economy in the hands of Burmese. This had meant the expulsion of thousands of Chinese and Indian merchants and traders, but "unless we Burmans can learn to run our own country we will lose it," he told Salisbury. The general's puritanical streak had resulted in closing down the racetrack and the nightclubs, but it had also produced a corruption-free government, at least at the top levels. None of the leading officials were millionaires, Salisbury wrote. "There are no transfers of funds to Swiss banks, no flashy cars, no high living, no lush trips to Paris or Hong Kong." Ne Win also insisted that he had no sympathy for communism ("there is no stauncher anti-Communist in Asia"), that China posed a real threat to Burma, and that he had "the warmest regard and respect for the United States." Salisbury's portrait looked almost like the Ne Win of the early 1950s. "It seems absolutely certain that the Chicoms are unhappy," wrote an embassy official. The "honeymoon" period in Burma-China relations was indeed coming to an end, as China's policy was veering toward an ideologically based one.[4]

Ne Win's wife Kitty also appeared to have changed her views about the United States. She and her husband were tired of being connected to leftist leaders and were looking forward to the forthcoming visit. "Kitty was certainly no friend of ours a year or two ago," the ambassador wrote; ". . . she has softened up considerably."[5]

Demonstrations by those opposed to Ne Win, including some dissident Burmese like Bo Setkya who had made it to the United States, worried American officials. Setkya had recently entered the United States (on 8 August 1966) with a valid visa but one obtained under false pretenses: his Burmese passport had been revoked, a fact that the US authorities in Paris, who issued the visa, did not know. The United States feared that Setkya's presence might even cause Ne Win to cancel his visit, which led to a frantic search (the *Washington Post* called it "a paroxysm of official concern")[6] to find Setkya.

Ne Win was informed about Bo Setkya's presence in the United States even before Setkya had been located. He probably already knew of Setkya's whereabouts anyway but said little except to chide the Americans for slipping up and issuing the visa in the first place. He did not seem overly perturbed.[7]

After three weeks Bo Setkya was apprehended in the Selton Towers Hotel in New York, and friends and acquaintances in the State Department attempted without success to get him to leave the country quickly and voluntarily.[8] Instead, he moved into Walinsky's residence near Washington, which resulted in a high-level discussion at the State Department involving Walinsky, William P. Bundy, and two knowledgeable Foreign Service officers. (The fact that Walinsky's son was on Senator Robert F. Kennedy's staff added to the government's caution.) Walinsky did not back down from his anti–Ne Win views and hoped to get some critical press reporting about him. He added, however, that if the issue was Ne Win's personal safety, there was no need for concern because he would keep the department informed about Setkya's whereabouts. This was insufficient assurance from the department's point of view, and Bundy suggested that perhaps Setkya could seek needed medical attention in New York during Ne Win's visit.[9]

In the meantime government agents were camped out near Walinsky's house in Chevy Chase. "Six strange cars. Different ones every day, with changing out-of-state license plates. Furtive G-man types sitting at their steering wheels from dawn until midnight eyeing every arrival and departure at the big gray stucco house.

An occasional mysterious message barked into radio sets." Curious children were shooed away. As Selig S. Harrison put it in a *Washington Post* front-page story with a banner headline, it "could have come straight out of Ian Fleming."[10]

In the end an agreement was reached: the government would not immediately attempt to deport Bo Setkya, and he would enter a New York hospital for treatment of hypertension (the aftermath of a minor stroke suffered in Paris). He would remain there while Ne Win was in the country, and because he was indigent, the United States would pay for his medical care. The matter was considered sufficiently important that President Johnson himself was briefed.[11]

The Bo Setkya incident did remind Americans about Ne Win's record: the coup d'état that brought him to power; the abrogation of the constitution; the abolishing of the parliament and the courts; the arrest and incarceration of former Prime Minister U Nu and his entire Cabinet, along with the chief justice of the Supreme Court and thousands of lesser-known opponents; the ouster of tens of thousands of Indians; the nationalization of mission schools and hospitals; and the adoption of the "Burmese Way to Socialism," which had virtually destroyed the country's economy. As the distinguished columnist Marquis Childs put it the day before Ne Win's arrival in Washington, his visit "makes a sad mockery of that much-abused phrase, 'the free world.'"[12]

The Burmese government, however, appreciated the American effort to sideline Setkya. All was now ready for Ne Win's visit to Washington on 8–10 September. Dean Rusk briefed the president, noting how Ne Win and his wife still resented the treatment they had received in 1960. There were few substantive issues to discuss. The main point was to treat Ne Win well and assure him that the United States supported Burmese neutrality.

A Lavish Welcome Produces Dividends

The United States pulled out all the stops in welcoming Ne Win. He received a full twenty-one-gun salute and a parade complete with bands and banners. He met President Johnson at the White House for substantive talks, after which the two leaders issued a communiqué in which Johnson expressed understanding and support for Burma's neutralism and both expressed hope for an early peace in Vietnam. Johnson described the meeting as "one of the most successful and 'stimulating' visits he had had." That evening there was an informal dinner at the White House, attended by thirty people. There was an exchange of gifts: Ne Win received a set of custom-made golf clubs, and Johnson a teak table. Johnson commented that both countries wanted peaceful relations with their neighbors, "provided they stay on their side of the fence, and out of our melon patch." It was a sentiment Ne Win could agree with.[13] Presidential adviser Walt Rostow characterized the dinner as "a remarkably pleasant and lively affair; truly a family affair." The following day Ne Win met with Acting Secretary of State George Ball (Secretary Rusk being ill), where they discussed the Bo Setkya case and Vietnam (neither saw any hope of a quick settlement). Ball told the ailing Rusk that "Ne Win was very well pleased" with his visit. The Burmese leader then played golf at Burning Tree, visited Williamsburg, flew in Johnson's plane to New York to attend the UN session, and departed for Hawaii for an eight-day vacation.[14]

It was a very successful visit. Press coverage in Burma was "excellent, substantially exceeding our expectations," the embassy reported, and the visit "should go far to counteract chronic Burmese suspicion of our motives." It "could not be more heartening," Rostow wrote to President Johnson. Byroade, who was with Ne Win in Hawaii, was euphoric. Writing to the president and the secretary of state on the day that Ne Win departed, he concluded that Johnson "apparently did more in two hours to accomplish our modest objectives re Burma that we could have done in two years at lesser levels."[15] Ne Win even invited Admiral U. S. Grant Sharp Jr., the commander of US forces in the Pacific, to visit Burma. The wounds of 1960 appeared to have been healed.

An immediate positive consequence of Ne Win's Washington visit was the release in October of U Nu and U Ba Swe. Other detainees, it was thought, would be released soon (although in fact none were, the next significant release of political prisoners occurring a year later). As Byroade put it, "one could almost feel that with time" the Washington visit would result in "visible dividends."[16]

After the visit Burma's relations with China deteriorated, though primarily because of China's Cultural Revolution. When local procommunist Chinese in Rangoon (allegedly encouraged by the Chinese embassy) defied a government ban on schoolchildren wearing Mao buttons, there were anti-Chinese riots. China responded with strong criticism, suspension of Chinese aid projects with all technicians ordered to leave, vilification of Ne Win, and open endorsement of the White Flag communist rebellion. Diplomatic connections were reduced to the level of chargé d'affaires.[17] "There are now reasons to believe, for the first time in several years, that U.S.–Burmese relationships can develop into mutually satisfactory and beneficial accord," Byroade wrote.[18]

The military supply connection continued, allowing some US interaction with Burma's ruling elite as, to a lesser extent, did the small economic assistance program. The program was scheduled to end in 1968, though there were already indications that Burma would request an extension.[19]

The KMT issue briefly raised its head in January 1967. KMT activity was not a figment of Burmese imagination, for during the previous year Taiwan had strengthened its forces significantly and clashed with the *tatmadaw* (the

Burmese army). The newspapers did not charge the United States with complicity, but Byroade apparently feared that there might be an American connection, for he replied to a message from William P. Bundy that "he had been slowly burning over this issue and probably would have blown my top." Bundy had apparently assured him that the United States was not involved and had protested strongly to Taiwan. "How nice to be headed off!" Byroade concluded.[20] For the moment, the KMT issue did not interrupt the improving relations between the two countries.

Furthermore, in June 1967 there were more clashes with procommunist Chinese students who again demonstrated against the government order prohibiting them from wearing Mao buttons. Over thirty people died in the subsequent riots, including one Chinese embassy officer who was stabbed to death. "With almost incredible obtuseness," as the American embassy reported, the Chinese embassy had incited the students to defy the government. Later that month there were serious anti-Chinese riots in Rangoon, where "roving bands of Burmese have been . . . systematically wrecking Chinese shops, restaurants, offices, and in some cases homes, smashing and burning furnishings in middle of street." The response from police and firefighters was half-hearted and ineffective, and Stanley Karnow characterized the disorders as an "anti-Chinese pogrom." In response China's news agency described Burma's government as "fascist reactionary." (The American consul in Hong Kong termed China's Burmese-language broadcasts "vituperative," whereas its English-language commentaries were only "strident.") Red Guards burned Ne Win's effigy in front of the Burmese embassy in Beijing. Furthermore, China began to openly urge the White Flag communists to "step up their rebellion against the Rangoon regime." Byroade admitted to taking "some satisfaction in witnessing ordinarily passive Burmese become so spontaneously excited to action over an issue involving Red China," although he also regretted the violence and its impact on ordinary, long-term, nonpolitical Chinese residents.[21]

These events led the State Department to take more interest in Burma. Its Bureau of Intelligence and Research prepared several reports about Burmese developments, one of which noted China's strange allegation that Ne Win was working with the KMT, the United States, and the Soviet Union. Probably reflecting the intensity of the Cultural Revolution, China's levels of attacks against Burma now equaled "in intensity those made against any of its most hated enemies." There were continuous demonstrations at the Burmese embassy in Beijing; embassy officials could not leave the building and survived on food brought in by other embassies. Though heartened by the Sino-Burmese tensions, however, Byroade did not anticipate dramatic changes in US-Burma relations.[22] Still, for the first time in years seven Burmese were sent to the United States (by the UN) for training in operating drilling machinery and in compiling agricultural statistics. Soon

Boeing representatives were in Rangoon discussing the sale of Boeing 727s to Burma's national airline.

Chinese-Burmese relations continued to deteriorate over the next several weeks. Chinese radio repeatedly broadcast slashing attacks on Ne Win personally—he was "a dog, a lackey, a murderer." Burma again expelled Chinese technicians, and by November 1967 the Chinese aid program was ended altogether. A CIA analysis completed in April 1968 concluded that Ne Win might actually break diplomatic relations with China.[23]

Although Burma's anger at China encouraged the United States, there were some bumps, notably the brief emergence of the KMT issue and demonstrations at the American embassy against the war in Vietnam. On the other hand a renewed American aid program was now thought probable, especially in view of the termination of Chinese aid. After review, however, the United States did not encourage a Burmese aid request, and Burma did not make one. American cultural influence in Burma, like that of other countries, remained rigidly controlled, and the sending of students to American colleges and universities ceased almost entirely. But the United States did enjoy an advantage in sports—particularly in golf and tennis—with important personalities continuing to visit, perform, and give clinics. In March 1968, for example, golfer Paul Harney played golf with Ne Win, after which the prime minister hosted a small dinner that included Byroade and his wife. The following January the Davis Cup team again visited Burma, held clinics, and played exhibition matches "before capacity crowds."[24] Also in 1968 Burma relaxed its restrictions on American foreign correspondents, granting two-week visas to four well-known journalists.

In sum, American relations with Burma, while not close, had improved. An internal State Department overview concluded that "it was a major achievement for US diplomacy that General Ne Win had greater confidence in US intentions toward Burma in 1968 than he had in 1963." The State Department attributed this improvement to careful American diplomacy, in which the United States was the "friendly but disinterested bystander, willing to be helpful if called upon but not interested in imposing our aid or our advice."[25] But China's Cultural Revolution also helped.

However, Burma's internal economic situation remained "a horror story." While the country's economy was an internal matter, it had implications for American interests in the region, for if the economy collapsed, it could only benefit the communists. Accordingly, Byroade departed from the general low-key American posture to try to stir Burmese interest in economic reform. This was dangerous, for Burma was extremely sensitive about any foreign pressure or advice. Nonetheless, Byroade, who was returning to the United States after more than four years as ambassador, decided to stop over in London and speak with Ne Win, who was vacationing there. He described the conversation as "a long frank discussion" with a focus on the crumbling economy. But he doubted he had made much of an impact.[26]

Meanwhile, by mid-1968 China and Burma were slowly trying to repair their damaged relationship. The first evidence of this came when China invited Burma's chargé in Beijing to attend May Day festivities. The next month China made a small donation forty-five hundred dollars) to help victims of a cyclone that had ravaged Arakan, leaving hundreds dead. To be sure, in August Radio Peking viciously attacked the Soviet Union for supporting the "Ne Win fascist military clique": perhaps Radio Peking had not gotten the memo, or perhaps China had turned away from conciliation. In addition, Chinese-supported and equipped communist insurgents in the northern part of the country engaged in "unprecedentedly large and effective . . . raids,"[27] and in March 1969 China criticized Ne Win in the strongest terms yet. But underneath both sides were working to restore the relationship, particularly after Zhou Enlai regained control of China's Foreign Office from Cultural Revolution radicals.

Meanwhile U Nu, having been released from prison and emerging from a five months stint as a monk, developed new political ambitions. Encouraged by the release of many political prisoners late in 1967 and early in 1968, as well as by some ambiguous comments by Ne Win that he wanted to work with civilians, U Nu hoped to run for president. A State Department Intelligence Note considered this delusional thinking. Ne Win had no intention of diluting his own power, and U Nu and others might be rearrested or, as U Ba Swe had threatened, go into "illegal opposition" to the government, with unforeseen results. Still, in late November 1968 Ne Win did meet with former political and ethnic minority leaders to discuss the country's future, and the group formed the Internal Unity Advisory Board to advise the Revolutionary Council about a possible new constitution for Burma.[28] The board met several times in December, and U Nu presented a proposal, which gained wide support within the board, to return to parliamentary rule, reassemble the 1963 parliament, and then install Ne Win as president, thus giving him legitimacy.

The new American ambassador, Arthur Hummel, was not sanguine about the Advisory's Board's chances for success. In contrast to other Americans, Hummel believed that Burmese society had considerable sympathy with certain aspects of Ne Win's rule, though it had strong objections to others. However, U Nu was "still far and away the most popular and respected Burman alive." Because of Ne Win's determination to carry on with the "Burmese Way to Socialism" while also protecting the army's place in society, however, Hummel saw little prospect of meaningful change.[29]

Hummel turned out to be correct. In February 1969 the Advisory Board made proposals to civilianize the government, but Ne Win ignored them, and U Nu then gave up attempts at reform. The tentative movement toward cooperation with the military regime had collapsed, and the government began attacking U Nu personally in the controlled press.[30]

About the same time Burma requested additional American military assistance. In particular it wanted fragmentation bombs and rockets for T-33 aircraft that the United States had previously supplied. Hummel, like his predecessors, favored providing the requested aid, arguing that the military assistance had kept Burma independent and neutral and had been the one program that allowed the United States to retain some influence. Furthermore, if the United States did not supply the armaments, the Soviet Union was likely to do so.[31]

U Nu's Rebellion

That summer, U Nu, then in India, inquired about getting a visa to visit the United States, a request that the State Department was inclined to grant. The department clearly did not relish having him in the country but thought that, on balance, it would be counterproductive to refuse him entry. Hummel, however, objected strongly to U Nu's efforts to overthrow Ne Win. The "near collapse of Burma in 1958 and 1962," he asserted, was due to U Nu's poor leadership.[32]

In Thailand Nu formed the Parliamentary Democracy Party to replace Ne Win, preferably by peaceful means. It was something of an open secret that Nu had at least the tacit support of the Thai government. American journalists had all heard this but did not immediately file stories about it because they were not certain about the reliability of their sources (Edward Law-Yone and Sterling Seagrave, the son of the late Gordon Seagrave, who had recently married Law-Yone's daughter, Wendy).[33]

Meanwhile U Nu applied for his visa, causing a hostile Burmese reaction, but the Americans determined that U Nu was now a political refugee. He had burned his bridges with the government of Burma and would lead a campaign outside the country to try to bring Ne Win down. The State Department issued the visa but warned U Nu to refrain from political activities, telling him that if he did not do so, future visa applications might be denied and also warning his friends in the United States to the same effect. In the end, Burma made no official protest.

Burma was nonetheless increasingly nervous about Nu's efforts to recruit army personnel for what would presumably be an armed insurrection against Ne Win. U Nu's press conference in London on 29 August 1969 would have not soothed Ne Win's nerves, for after criticizing the government Nu would neither confirm nor deny reports that he was intending to try to remove Ne Win by armed force. Burma's newspapers printed U Nu's statements verbatim. Just why the government decided "to publish these damning indictments by widely re-vered leader" was not immediately clear. But perhaps Ne Win intended to show his "utter contempt" for U Nu's efforts and also make it more dangerous for people in Burma to identify with the former prime minister. Antiregime politi-cians were "crawling into their shells," and rumors soon circulated that U Nu enjoyed CIA backing.[34]

U Nu arrived in New York on 5 September 1969. He hoped to bring about a peaceful transition, he said upon his arrival. He received almost no attention in American media, but this changed abruptly when four days later he announced that by the end of the year he would have a guerrilla force fighting in Burma. He abhorred violence, he said, but there was now no choice. It was either his forces or the communists, and he feared he might already be too late to prevent a com-munist takeover. The same day he appeared on the NBC "Today" show (arranged by Walinsky) and appealed for support. He also asked for an end to the "quite substantial" American military assistance to the Ne Win regime. He cleverly ap-pealed to American sensibilities by noting that the Kachins, then in an armed conflict with the government, were mostly Baptists. Some of U Nu's American supporters regretted that his "Today" appearance overemphasized the need for force, but they organized a number of events, including meetings with Congres-sional representatives as well as talks at the Overseas Writers group, the Johns Hopkins School of Advanced International Studies, and the Council on Foreign Relations. While in Washington, U Nu told reporters that Ne Win was "more ter-rible than Ivan the Terrible."[35]

Nu's activities in the United States, which clearly ignored the State Depart-ment's admonition to avoid political activity, threatened to strain official relations between the United States and Burma. Stories were now regularly ap-pearing in Burmese publications questioning where U Nu was getting his money, with much suspicion centering on the CIA. Burma had been moving toward al-lowing its citizens to once again come to the United States for training, but that was now in doubt. In response the State Department forbade American officials from meeting with Nu. It had battened down the hatches "so tightly that no of-ficial was permitted to stray into any Washington dinner party where U Nu might be a guest."[36]

By this time American officials thought it possible, though not likely, that Burma could disintegrate. A more immediate possibility was that the Thais might try to reassert control over parts of the Shan areas, just as they had under the Japanese, while the most likely scenario was that Burma would drift leftward and move closer to the communist countries. There was little that the United States could reasonably do to stop any of these from happening. It soon appeared that the last prediction was the correct one: the regime was committing itself to "authoritarian socialism," with the "deliberate destruction of private enterprise." Political moderates lost any hope of negotiating with Ne Win, and although U Nu's prospects remained "poor," military defections to him had increased, and the possibility always existed of spiraling domestic disturbances.[37] In fact, there were major student demonstrations in Rangoon and Mandalay, aimed at Ne Win and his government, and indicative of Ne Win's lack of support, the counselor of the Burmese embassy in Washington, U Ba Thaung, inquired about applying for political asylum.

Meanwhile, Thailand had granted U Nu asylum. He resided in a section of Bangkok known as the "American Ghetto," next door to an American family,[38] and established a training camp near Sangkhlaburi, close to the Burma border, where he was joined by defectors who had arrived in October and November 1969. Burma objected to U Nu's presence and activities there, and because of historic Burmese fears of American connections with insurgents, the United States wanted Thailand to enforce its stated policy of not allowing U Nu to engage in actions against Ne Win. Thai officials made such pledges, but they seem to have been honored more in the breach than otherwise.

Although a Burmese intelligence officer had told Ambassador Hummel that he believed there was no CIA support for U Nu, the allegations continued to appear in Burmese publications. The time had come, Hummel suggested, for a formal protest. The State Department concurred, adding, however, that at least two former American military personnel were working with U Nu and that Hummel should report this to the Burmese government at the same time that he made his protest. The United States disclaimed any connection with these Americans and asked Burma to inform the embassy whenever it discovered Americans working with U Nu.[39]

There were in fact at least three Americans working with U Nu's group in Thailand: William Young, James Wesley Hamerle, and Harry Farmer. Ambassador Leonard Unger in Bangkok had apparently asked Marshal Dawee Chullasaspyra, Thailand's deputy minister of defense and chief of staff of the Supreme Command, to revoke, or restrict, their visas. But Dawee had refused, and Unger had then advised that the United States should no longer attempt to interfere with their activities. Hummel objected. This would set the "stage for long-term friction and misunderstanding with Burmese," he wrote. Could not something more be done? Two of the men (Farmer and Hamerle) were former military servicemen (Hamerle was a lieutenant colonel, Farmer "an irascible US Army tech sergeant"). Perhaps the government could put their pensions in jeopardy if they continued to assist "an armed dissident group operating to overthrow a friendly government." At least, they could be asked to desist. The Americans supporting U Nu clearly troubled the ambassador, for a week later he complained that

American representations to the Thais about U Nu were not forceful. "From here it seems possible that Thais may have attributed to USG [United States Government] only a desire to keep our own hands clean, believing that we don't much care if RTG [Royal Thai Government] does the dirth [*sic*] work," he wrote.[40]

The State Department's response was cautious. It agreed with Hummel that the activities of the three Americans were inimical to US-Burma relations, and it suggested that diplomats in Thailand inform them about American policy. There was little more that could be done, however, particularly if Thailand was unwilling to be helpful. Unger did send out a notice to American consulates in Thailand telling them to report any requests for passport services by these three individuals and to defer action on the requests until they received instructions. But the department's response was tepid and suggests that there may have been a covert American connection with U Nu. William Young had a long history of links with the CIA. He came from a long line of Baptist missionaries who had served in Burma until they were forced to move to Thailand. The CIA had recruited his father, Harold Young, to make forays into Yunnan, and William had helped organize the secret war in Laos. On the other hand William reportedly had a falling out with the CIA in 1968, so by 1970 he may not have been on the agency's payroll when working with U Nu. According to Wendy Law-Yone, however, he had "half a dozen ethnic minority armies at his beck and call," which he had recruited to Nu's cause.[41] The American government may have reluctant go after Young, lest his former relationship with the CIA come to light.

In April 1970 American officials did contact Farmer and Young, though apparently without results. As before, however, the instructions were not particularly forceful. The department realized, for example, that "there are reasons why it might be inadvisable to press Dawee directly for specific action at this time." Marshal Dawee, a former OSS officer, was in fact one of Nu's most important contacts in the Thai government.[42]

On paper, at least, Nu posed a threat to Ne Win. Although the ethnic minorities were not initially attracted to Nu, eventually he formed an alliance with the Karen, Mon, Chin, and Shan rebels, who had formed the United National Liberation Front (UNLF) and together had 50,000 troops. This was less than the government's 150,000 troops, but they felt confident that they could mount a strong guerrilla campaign against the regime and predicted victory within a year. U Nu also had the advantage of still being a respected figure within Burma, he had some support from the Thai government, and Ne Win was thought to be in poor health, having recently suffered a mild heart attack. Should Ne Win die, or if there were internal strife, U Nu might emerge once again.[43]

In mid-April U Nu's group began broadcasts from its clandestine radio station in Thailand (though they claimed it to be in Burma), but whether this would prove advantageous seemed doubtful to the American embassy. He had not yet made much headway with the ethnic minorities (the UNLF soon disintegrated), and significant defections later in April weakened his movement. Still, in June 1970 when Hummel took an extensive trip across Burma (shadowed at all times by Burmese military intelligence officers), he reported that U Nu's "clandestine broadcasts are widely listened to." On the other hand the people, though alienated from Ne Win, gave U Nu little chance of success.[44]

The Burmese government staged an "elaborate press conference" on 25 April in which it exonerated the US government from connections with U Nu, though Deputy Director of Military Intelligence Tin Oo did point to a recent critical article in the *Atlantic Monthly* by Sterling Seagrave, and also to the involvement of William Young with U Nu. His remarks were probably intended subtly to warn the United States and Thailand not to become involved with the dissidents and their supporters.[45]

By this time even the limited official American connections with Burma were winding down. The military assistance program had ended in 1968, though deliveries of equipment continued into 1971. The embassy included two officers who coordinated the small USAID program, which continued to help with three previously approved construction projects: a teak mill, a natural science college, and a water supply system. The Burmese expressed interest in additional assistance for the college and teak mill projects and were informed that the United States would consider requests to fund them with American-owned local currency but not with dollars. As of June 1970 the Burmese had not responded with any requests.

More significant now were cultural connections, for Burma had relaxed restrictions on American presentations. Late in January 1970 Duke Ellington and his orchestra performed in Rangoon ("a great success" the State Department reported). In March three Apollo 12 astronauts visited Rangoon. They had an unusually successful visit, including a motorcade which the Burmese themselves had suggested—a very unusual event since the government discouraged large assemblies of people. "Huge crowds" lined the streets, despite scant advance publicity, and the astronauts presented to the Burmese government a moon rock and a Burmese flag that they had taken with them to the moon.[46] Golfer Paul Harney returned for his third visit, staying this time for sixteen days and visiting several cities. Basketball stars from the Boston Celtics came through, and there were a number of educational exhibits as well.

Meanwhile, the U Nu situation continued to fester. Though the United States continued to give the former prime minister poor odds of success, Ne Win's government was nervous. In June 1970 radio broadcasts resumed, and the government organized an anti–U Nu rally in Moulmein consisting (the government claimed) of sixty thousand people. (A local embassy employee insisted that no more that five or six thousand had attended.) Speakers denounced Nu, and the embassy predicted more such rallies in response to his continuing broadcasts, which had become more effective. To the Americans the most disturbing aspect of the demonstration was that, for the first time since the previous winter, speakers linked U Nu with the CIA, allegations about which the embassy complained to the Foreign Ministry.[47] Meanwhile, Sterling Seagrave's *Standard Bangkok Magazine* published favorable stories about U Nu and negative ones about Ne Win. More significant, the Thai government now appeared even more sympathetic to U Nu than before.

Perhaps U Nu's fortunes were looking up after all, a possibility that seemed all the stronger because Louis Walinsky, U Nu's erstwhile economic adviser when he worked for Nathan Associates, had negotiated a contract for U Nu with Asamera Oil Company of Indonesia. In exchange for the right to explore for oil in Burma once U Nu returned, the company gave U Nu $2 million with another $2 million promised for later. Asamera was later identified as a Canadian company, and there may have been several Canadian firms involved, though Mobil Oil was probably the major actor behind this deal. It is worth quoting Hummel's summary of Mobil's involvement at length:

> It appears that Mobil has found some legal and contractual formula that perhaps makes it technically correct to tell USG [United States Government] "that reports of Mobil involvement with U Nu were untrue". At same time they admit that they have paid a middleman $300,000 to put together a deal that does in fact supply funds for U Nu's insurrection, and that they are also working through Asamera Oil and perhaps other companies as further middlemen. Whether Mobil has already supplied funds for Asamera to pass on to U Nu we may never know, but it does seem likely in view of Asamera's statement to U Nu group nearly a year ago that Asamera did not itself have enough funds to finance deal.

Mobil worked through middlemen to disguise the company's involvement, but Hummel's unidentified informant asserted "that Mobil was the major contributor of funds in this deal" and that "at least half of $2 mill now available to U Nu group must have come from Mobil."[48]

American intelligence sources also believed Mobil was behind the deal, concluding that "the money involved was largely contributed by Mobil with the Canadian firms serving as a channel." Mobil's vice president for governmental relations, Robert Barnes (a former American ambassador), acknowledged to a CIA agent that there was a contingent deal with U Nu but denied that Mobil had actually paid Nu any money. The CIA felt certain that Mobil's involvement went considerably beyond what Barnes would acknowledge, and the deputy assistant secretary of state cautioned Mobil about its actions. The Mobil issue was the most important item about U Nu contained in a three-page memorandum to National Security Adviser Henry Kissinger. In any event, two million dollars were "laundered through a Swiss bank and deposited in the Bangkok Bank," where U Nu had access to the money.[49]

In any case, the US government thought that Walinsky might have violated American laws in helping to put together the deal, though the State Department's legal adviser was less certain of this. However, the Americans were more immediately concerned that Ne Win would blame the United States when he learned of the oil companies' support.[50] Indeed, Burma's military intelligence was soon alleging that the CIA was definitely supporting U Nu.[51]

Whatever the Burmese may have felt about American connections with U Nu, it did not stop Ne Win from making a secret but potentially very significant request to the United States through intermediaries in Manila for thirty F-4 jet fighters. The Americans tried to discourage this while trying to identify aircraft that were more suitable for Burma's needs, and the Burmese later denied making any such request.[52]

In November 1970 the Burmese indicated that they were thinking of acquiring thirty OV-10 and twelve A-27 light attack aircraft. These were more appropriate to the country's needs, from the American perspective, but the aircraft would cost about $25 million, and Burma had limited foreign exchange. Could they get concessional pricing and appropriate credit arrangements, or possibly even some kind of barter agreement, the Burmese asked. Concessional pricing was doubtful, replied Hummel, and a barter arrangement involving rice was almost impossible, so a straight credit deal seemed the most likely solution. Hummel said he would take it up with Washington.

The military suggested that Burma consider purchasing instead reconditioned T-33 aircraft costing about $129,500 each, or look at certain commercial aircraft. In the end, Burma made no formal request and a few months later asked that all military assistance, which had flowed from the agreement in 1958, be ended by 30 June 1971. Though the ambassador found this "regrettable," there was no choice to but terminate the agreement.[53] Future cash or credit sales were still possible.

Meanwhile relations between China and Burma were finally improving. For three years following the anti-Chinese riots in Burma and Chinese support for the Burmese communists, neither country had assigned an ambassador to the other's capital. As late as March 1969 Radio Peking had referred to Ne Win's regime as a "bloody fascist clique," and to Ne Win himself as a "ruthless hangman," a "traitor," a "cunning and despicable swindler." Hummel could not recall such vituperative characterizations since the anti-Chinese riots of 1967. In 1970, however, there was some improvement, and finally in November Burma appointed an ambassador to Beijing. China did not immediately reciprocate, but in January 1971 Zhou Enlai sent a congratulatory message on Burma's Independence Day, the first such message since 1967, high-level Chinese officials called at the Burmese embassy to offer congratulations as well, and finally in February China appointed an ambassador.[54]

Although a warming in the Chinese relationship might be expected to cause Burma to distance itself from the United States, the Americans now favored an improvement between Burma and China as a way of stabilizing Burma's internal political situation. In fact, the United States itself was already talking secretly with China about a rapprochement.

In sum, Ne Win's visit to the United States in 1966 had stabilized the bilateral relationship. The United States and Burma were not close friends, but their relationship was civil—as Ambassador Hummel put it a little later, "friendly but not cordial."[55] The United States refrained from offering Burma advice, carried out its remaining minimal obligations, and looked disapprovingly on U Nu's efforts to overthrow the government, though it made no overt efforts to stop him or his supporters in the United States. Americans certainly deplored Ne Win's domestic rule. As Ambassador Hummel reported in 1970, a Burmese citizen stated that "if there were an election in Thaton, the votes cast for the Revolutionary Government would not fill a condensed milk can, while a rain barrel would not be big enough to hold the votes of the opposition."[56] But Ne Win's despotism was a secondary concern. There were few issues of importance in terms of foreign relations between the two countries, and diplomats had little to do except manage day-to-day affairs and hope that the relationship did not deteriorate.

THE NARCOTICS ERA

By the early 1970s, American relations with Southeast Asia had changed significantly. The United States and China had begun a historic rapprochement, thus reducing American Cold War fears. The US military presence in Vietnam was first reduced and then ended entirely after the peace agreement in January 1973. In Indonesia, which had been a major headache for the United States, Sukarno had been ousted, the Communist Party was decimated in the massacres that followed, and the United States supported the new Suharto regime. Likewise, the Americans were not displeased by the overthrow of Cambodia's Norodom Sihanouk in 1970, who had periodically irritated them, and the United States fully supported the more pro-American successor regime of Lon Nol. Indicative of the new situation in Southeast Asia, Indonesia's Suharto now supplied weapons to Lon Nol, albeit very secretly. The United States continued to be active in Cambodia even after the withdrawal from Vietnam, but in April 1975, shortly before the North Vietnamese defeated the South Vietnamese, the murderous Khmer Rouge won the Cambodian civil war. With the defeats in Vietnam and Cambodia, most Americans wanted nothing to do with Southeast Asia. American relations with Burma during this period reflected these changes. With the rapprochement with China, Burma became less important in the Cold War context. There was some residual American concern about Chinese support for the Burmese communists, but overall Burma's strategic significance diminished. By now, however, another issue had pushed to the forefront: narcotics control. Cheap narcotics were reaching American troops in Vietnam, American cities were inundated with a flood of drugs, and in 1971 President Nixon declared his War on Drugs. Narcotics control was suddenly a matter of great interest to the United States. Increasingly the drugs were coming from the Golden Triangle, a region that encompassed parts of Burma, Laos, and Thailand. Thus control of narcotics became the major American policy concern in Burma. It remained that way until the Burmese revolution of 1988.

Early in 1971 Ambassador Hummel, then six weeks into his new position, wrote that Rangoon presented "a picture of a nineteenth-century city under heavy sedation rather than the twentieth-century capital of a country of almost thirty million people. The soporific and indeed deadening effect of nine years of an authoritarian military regime is evident everywhere." Most people seemed "to take even their limited pleasures sadly." The economic situation in downtown Rangoon was "more suited to the bullock cart age than to the automotive era." Whether Rangoon would "remain under anesthetics for the indefinite future" or would "rouse . . . from its torpor" was uncertain. The situation was discouraging and dangerous.[1]

But no one could say how the danger would manifest itself. Perhaps U Nu would be able to rally the populace to his side. The Americans continued to be skeptical but kept watch on his activities. Although the Burmese, with Soviet help, had successfully jammed Nu's radio broadcasts in January 1971, he soon established a second station. The government was also successful in jamming this station, at least in the Rangoon area, but U Nu's continued ability to establish and operate radio stations remained an irritant.

The oil companies' support for U Nu remained an issue. Since at least one Canadian company was involved, Hummel raised the question with the Canadian ambassador, who "was considerably shocked" to learn of Asamera's involvement. Hummel urged him to see that additional funds for U Nu were cut off. Though support for U Nu was contrary to Canadian policy, the ambassador was not certain what could be done, and Hummel urged the State Department to have the CIA brief him. "Question of whether and how we should deal with Canadians on this delicate subject is now under consideration," Secretary of State William Rogers informed the American embassies in Singapore and Kuala Lumpur, cautioning them not to discuss it with the Canadian ambassadors "or anyone else." The next day, however, Hummel urged the State Department not to intervene. If the Canadians chose to act, they would handle it as a "delicate internal matter."[2] There was apparently no follow-up from the Canadians.

The U Nu matter remained potentially a serious problem in the bilateral relationship. At a news conference Tin Oo commented that U Nu was getting aid from "Cosmopolitan Intelligence Agencies." In addition Tin Oo noted that U Law-Yone had also left Bangkok, presumably to seek more aid, but very soon he and Nu had a falling out and he left, much to Nu's relief. The embassy subsequently concluded that Tin Oo's news conference had been a psychological blunder because it gave the impression that U Nu was more of a threat than he actually was. He was really only an annoyance (Sterling Seagrave wrote that the United States considered U Nu "a backyard nuisance"),[3] but if he did manage to establish himself in a significant portion of the country there could be dramatic changes in the public attitude.

The War on Drugs

By this time, however, narcotics had come to the forefront of American concerns. Growing numbers of American troops in Vietnam had been using heroin and other narcotics at disturbing rates, while American cities were experiencing a drug epidemic. Previously most of the narcotics had originated in Turkey and had reached the United States through France. In 1969 Turkey was still the source of 80 percent of opium derivatives reaching the United States, while Burma, Laos, Thailand, and China's Yunnan Province together accounted for only 5 percent. That was now changing, however, as Turkey began to restrict production, and by 1971 the Golden Triangle had become an important source. As a CIA Intelligence Memorandum put it: "The Golden Triangle has become the source of heroin for the US troops in Southeast Asia, and there is evidence that increasing amounts of opium derivatives from Southeast Asia are finding their way to the US domestic market."[4] The United States wanted this stopped.

President Richard Nixon took a personal interest in the drug issue. As early as 1969 he had demanded a report on the extent of the problem and what had been done to address it, and by 1971 the drug problem had become a "national emergency" that required a vigorous response. In June Nixon told representatives of several agencies that interdepartmental cooperation would be required. In one of his periodic displays of masculinity he added that he would be "tough with our allies," that "diplomatic niceties" would no longer be employed, that he would "not temporize anymore," and that interstate drug pushers would suffer harsh penalties, including death.[5]

As a part of the newly declared War on Drugs the director of the Bureau of Narcotics and Dangerous Drugs, John E. Ingersoll, held discussions with Burmese officials in June 1971. The talks went well, and the Americans believed that although Burma "was a tough nut to crack on this whole subject," it would now seriously attempt to deal with the problem. This included working to strengthen the UN's Single Convention on Narcotic Drugs, an important document adopted in 1961 to codify existing multilateral treaties and allow the production of narcotics exclusively for scientific and medical purposes. Over time, too, perhaps Burma could be persuaded to join the UN's Commission on Narcotic Drugs and have representation on the UN's International Narcotics Control Board.[6]

Actually, for some time Ne Win had been interested in the narcotics issue for reasons of his own. Unlike in some other countries, no high government official in Rangoon profited personally from the traffic, and Ne Win was increasing concerned about the growing addiction problem in his country. He was more concerned about the communist insurgency, however, and in 1967 he had deputized some fifty "warlord armies" (the Ka Kwei Yei or Ka Kwe Ye, more commonly referred to simply as the KKY) as official militias to fight the insurgents. In return he allowed them to engage in opium smuggling. In the early 1970s, realizing that the KKY were essentially bandits whom he could not control, Ne Win outlawed them, and the so-called Chinese Irregular Forces (CIF—descendants of the KMT), and the Shan United Army (SUA) became the predominant narcotics players.[7]

As a result, interactions with the Burmese about narcotics were "increasingly frank and cooperative." Still, working closely proved difficult. In September Henry Kissinger informed Nixon that Burma was resisting "our efforts to stimulate action." Burma welcomed American intelligence reports, but otherwise it was not working cooperatively with the United States. Egil Krogh Jr., the executive director of the Cabinet Committee on International Narcotics Control, commented that "the Burmese problem was the toughest in Southeast Asia."[8]

When the new American ambassador, Edwin W. Martin, made his initial call on Ne Win in October 1971, narcotics control was the main subject of conversation. Ne Win blamed the British and Chinese for causing the problem in the first place but made it clear that he was determined to take action against it. He needed no prodding, he said, probably having sensed American efforts indirectly to pressure him.[9]

Meanwhile, the United States was considering another approach to the Burma opium issue: purchasing the entire crop. In September 1971 Burma proposed that the United States buy some fifty tons of opium that the government had purchased over the last four years at "one third the illicit price," which it was willing to sell for what it had cost. Nelson G. Gross, the Nixon administration's official in charge of international narcotics (who later went to prison for campaign finance irregularities), urged that the proposal be considered.[10] Gross was determined to sound out Ne Win—in person if possible. Ne Win was then in England for a medical checkup and holiday, and Gross flew to Germany where, in the Steigenberger Hotel in Bad Godesberg he spoke with Dr. Rudolph Meyer, a German businessman and long-time friend of Ne Win. If the proceeds from the opium sale would go toward narcotics control, the Americans were willing to consider a purchase.

Meyer said that he could bring the narcotics issue up with Ne Win in London, but Ne Win did not make decisions quickly and would have to be convinced that no political conditions were involved. Meyer's meeting with Ne Win indeed went very well: the prime minister declined to see Gross in London but said that he would respond favorably to a letter from President Nixon asking him to speak with a presidential emissary. The American embassy in Bonn recommended a quick and positive response, the bureaucracy worked with unusual speed, and Nixon sent the requisite letter.[11]

On 21 December 1971 Ne Win invited Nelson Gross to visit him in Rangoon in January. Nixon expressed his personal appreciation, and the meeting took place on 18 January 1972. Despite Gross's having arrived at a particularly difficult time (Ne Win had reportedly just divorced Kitty after a particularly violent quarrel, the divorce to be effective on 19 January), the meeting was cordial and constructive. Ne Win appeared to be devoted to curtailing opium production and commerce and remarked on how in the past he had dealt severely with military units involved in smuggling. Gross urged him to seize some eighty tons of opium that he said was stockpiled at Tachilek. As for the fifty tons that Ne Win had previously offered to sell to the United States, Gross replied, not knowing that Ne Win had repudiated the KKY, that perhaps the money paid for it could be used to hire KKY officers to block the smuggling. The KKYs "lie, cheat and steal," Ne Win responded. To "crack down on them" was the only solution. Most significantly, Gross offered to supply helicopters on favorable terms, along with photographic equipment and even arms. Ne Win indicated that he would be happy with all of these. He could not promise that he could solve the entire problem, he told Gross as he was departing, "but he would do his best."[12] The question of the United States purchasing Burma's seized fifty tons of illicit opium appeared no longer of interest, however.

Gross left the meeting very pleased, even euphoric. He discussed the meeting with ambassadors in the region, CIA station chiefs, and military representatives, and then sent a lengthy telegram to Secretary of State William P. Rogers in which he urged immediate follow-up action before any doubts emerged in Burma. In Rangoon, Ambassador Martin was cautious. Given the previous experiences with supplying military aid to Burma, he did not think that any US assistance would affect Burma's "policies or attitudes." In addition, it was not clear that Burma would be able to utilize the aid effectively. For example, all of Burma's fourteen H-43 helicopters were currently grounded because of lack of spare parts. Nevertheless, Martin generally supported Gross's recommendations and urged that a list of available equipment be provided quickly.[13]

The State Department responded promptly, indicating that narcotics control was indeed an important priority for Nixon and that Gross had the ear of the president. The department wished to dispatch a technical team to consult with the Burmese within two weeks, but they wanted a list of available equipment prior to having a technical team sent out. Perhaps in an effort to assure Burmese cooperation, Nixon sent Ne Win a personal letter thanking him for speaking with Gross and expressing his appreciation for all that Burma was doing to address the illicit narcotics problem.[14]

The American government now moved with unusual speed. Funding for the program ($3 million) would come from USAID, and by mid-February 1972 a detailed list of possible equipment, including helicopters and fixed-wing aircraft, went to Burma. The Burmese invited the American technical team to come to Rangoon in April, and seemed committed to working diligently to reduce the production and export of drugs. Nixon sent Gross a personal note thanking him for the "splendid job" he had been doing.[15]

By the time the technical team arrived in Burma, however, there were (as so often happened) some signs of difficulties. The State Department was taken aback when the Burmese "simply requested everything that has been even tentatively suggested." The Burmese also seemed to think that a final agreement might emerge from the technical talks. The United States, on the other hand, viewed the talks as exploratory, to discuss issues such as operation and maintenance of various aircraft and training of personnel. In earlier periods, discussion of the types of equipment needed, reviews of activity, accountability, costs, and funding mechanisms had led to tortuous negotiations. The same pattern now emerged. For example, the Americans thought that the first priority should be an assessment of equipment that Burma currently possessed, whereas the Burmese insisted that they needed new planes and helicopters. Similarly, the Americans wanted to visit "operational areas," but the Burmese refused, citing safety reasons. The final meeting on 7 April made clear that the different priorities of the two sides had not changed. Though the talks ended cordially, there was no agreement.[16]

With the talks concluded, Martin reflected on the matter in a lengthy telegram that he asked be passed along to the White House. Most of the opium in Burma was grown in areas controlled by the insurgents, Martin pointed out, so that any really effective control of the opium traffic was inextricably linked with the insurgencies. Unfortunately, the situation was not improving and, if anything, was deteriorating, and therefore the Burmese desire for new equipment made considerable sense. Furthermore, the recent discussions were "unprecedented for Ne Win regime" and hopefully presaged Burmese "cooperation almost unthinkable a few months ago." Martin seemed to be pleading for acceptance of the Burmese position, and he got what he wanted. In May the State Department decided that it would provide new equipment for narcotics control and would do all it could to expedite delivery. To begin, the United States would provide three aircraft on a trial basis to determine which ones would be most useful in this effort.[17] When its proposal was finalized in May, the United States offered to provide equipment intended for the suppression of narcotics, but would allow Burma to also use it in anti-insurgency efforts that were connected to the antinarcotics efforts, or occasionally when the equipment was not being employed in antinarcotics operations at all. In other words, Burma could use the equipment almost as it wanted.

But in the end Burma decided not to proceed with the agreement. It would focus its attention on crop replacement efforts, would still appreciate receiving American intelligence reports, and would undertake some suppression efforts of its own. This disappointed the Americans, but they responded that the offer of equipment was still open. A month later, when Rogers met Ne Win in Rome the Burmese leader explained that he had decided not to accept planes or helicopters because Burma could not afford such equipment and also because Burma's military would become too dependent on them. More likely, however the Burmese refusal came because the United States wanted the equipment used primarily for narcotics suppression, rather than in anti-insurgency operations. In spite of the provisions in the proposed agreement that allowed for incidental use against insurgencies, the Burmese probably felt that the conditions were still too restrictive. Indeed in April 1973 Foreign Minister U Kyaw Soe told a high-level American delegation that Burma resented the stipulation that the equipment could only be used for narcotics suppression. "You should not say that," he stated.[18]

Another reason that Burma rejected the American aid offer was that its government benefited from the narcotics trade. To be sure, it was the remnant KMTs and Shan rebels who produced much of the opium, but the overall economy also benefited to some extent from narcotics; the opium trade had become Burma's most profitable export. "Without it," writes Al McCoy, "the consumer economy would have collapsed." It was not that the government officials, least of all Ne Win, wanted to support the narcotics trade or personally benefited from it, but if they wanted to retain a government presence in rebel areas, and with the economy dependent on opium profits, they had to tolerate it.[19]

American embassy personnel were nonetheless generally optimistic that Burma was reducing the traffic, but in September 1972 the US Cabinet Committee on International Narcotics Control accused Burma's government of obstructing efforts to control the trade. As a result Assistant Secretary Marshall Green and Arthur Hummel pressed U Lwin, the important minister of planning and finance, to increase cooperation with the United States. The "narcotics flow out of Burma," they told him, "has serious effects not only on U.S. but on other countries as well, including Burma." U Lwin was sympathetic, but it was doubtful that there would be any immediate change.[20]

Complicating the situation was the passage on 25 September of an amendment to the foreign military assistance bill, introduced by Senator Vance Hartke (D-IN), that would cut off all assistance to Burma unless the president certified that the country was taking adequate steps to control the narcotics traffic. If the Hartke amendment became law, and the president was unable to certify Burmese cooperation, the limited assistance the United States was providing to Burma, and possible future assistance, would be affected. However, the Senate rejected the amendment, doubtless to the relief of American diplomats.

The Insurgency Intervenes

In September 1972 Ne Win's wife Kitty died in London. Despite their tumultuous marriage, her death deeply affected the general, but it did not change his governing style. The government soon arrested several hundred more Burmese politicians, and others remained under surveillance.[21]

The crackdown resulted in part from fear of U Nu's movement. In the midst of the negotiations about narcotics control, for example, a plane managed to drop leaflets over Rangoon urging citizens to join the insurgency. The regime was embarrassed that it had not been able to prevent the leaflet drop, and there was much speculation about who had piloted the airplane. The pilot must have had a good knowledge of the Rangoon area, like, for instance, Brigadier Tommy Clift, the former head of the Burmese air force who now resided in Bangkok. Aside from security doubts, the main question seemed to be whether this was a one-time event or whether U Nu's insurgency would be able to drop more than leaflets.[22] This matter actually delayed the ongoing discussions about narcotics.

The matter soon became more complicated when it turned out that the pilot was an American, Stanley L. Booker, who had taken off from Bangkok. According to the State Department, Booker owned a number of airlines in Southeast Asia, including International Air (Singapore), Transna Airways (Indonesia), and Khmara Air Transport (Cambodia). Booker's actions angered the American government. The State Department looked into possible legal action against him and encouraged Burma to complain to Singapore where Booker was currently a resident: the United States was even willing to endorse Burma's complaint if the Burmese wished. American diplomats in Thailand interviewed Booker and concluded that he had had "some degree of official Thai collusion." The United States complained to the Thais, and. Ambassador Martin turned over much information about the incident to U Tin Oo who responded that he did not blame the US government. "Men of this stripe were for sale all over the world," he told Martin.[23]

It was therefore embarrassing when it was discovered that just a few days earlier the embassy had requested permission for Booker to fly an International Air plane over Burma on 8 May. Consular officials, it turned out, had not been informed about Booker and had simply filed the request in a routine manner. When Martin found out about it he immediately urged Burmese officials not to grant the request. He angrily declared that Booker had "not only willfully and flagrantly violated Burmese air space but in so doing has carried out warlike acts against Burmese Govt." He wanted no American agency to have anything to do with Booker or his airlines in the future.[24]

Another embarrassment for the United States government was Burma's arrest of Justin R. Morse, the seventy-four-year-old patriarch of the famous Morse "dynasty" of missionaries, and his extended family. The Morses, from Tulsa, Oklahoma but sponsored by nondenominational churches in California, had been in Burma for fifty-one years working with the Lisu people in Kachin State. They had managed to elude orders dating from 1965 expelling missionaries, but in March 1972 they were taken into custody and taken to Khamti, the provincial capital, where they were sentenced to eighteen months of hard labor for ignoring the expulsion order. They were then sent to the Mandalay Central Jail, where they lived in a separate enclosure and were treated well. Three younger children were allowed to live with the American consul, Carl Taylor, who also arranged for a lawyer to represent them.[25]

The Burmese wanted to settle this matter without getting into a serious dispute with the United States, and the agreed solution, apparently, was to reduce the Morses' sentence to three months and deport them without allowing them to have further contact with American officials. As the American consul reported, the "eloquent arguments" of the Morses' distinguished lawyer (who had had only the most limited contact with his clients in any case) "were probably in vain; he probably could just as well have read the dictionary out loud." Taylor concluded that the Morses were fortunate to have gotten off with a light sentence. Eugene Morse agreed: "It was probably as much as we could hope for." But he also found it "depressing" that Burma's proud judiciary had been so degraded to the point that the military treated the judges as "puppets."[26]

Meanwhile, insurgents made their presence known in the capital. On 16 October 1972 four hand grenades exploded in Rangoon, apparently detonated by U Nu supporters. This led to another crackdown on alleged Nu sympathizers. Rangoon was edgy; the insurgents had demonstrated new capabilities.[27]

Possible additional support for U Nu from Canadian oil companies surfaced again in November 1972. Hummel, now Deputy Assistant Secretary of State, told the Canadians that U Nu did not pose a serious threat to the Burmese government and that therefore any outside assistance would have "only mischievous consequences." The Canadians did inquire but found no complaints about the oil companies from the Burmese or the Thais and further concluded that the companies were wholly owned subsidiaries of American oil corporations. A few months later the United States had to inform Burma that an American citizen, Ahmed Kamal, was involved in transferring funds from Asamera to U Nu's group in Thailand. Ambassador Martin told the Burmese that Asamera's initial payment was for $2 million and that the total amount promised over five years was $14 million.[28]

Suspicions and Cooperation

The Further complicating the security situation was the growth of a new Taiwanese military presence: forces controlled by the Intelligence Bureau of the Ministry of National Defense (IBMND). They operated in Burma and Thailand and in the 1960s had made raids into Yunnan. Burma's government had largely ignored them, but by the late 1960s it "could no longer ignore the growing IBMND presence as it enmeshed itself in the web of anti-Rangoon insurgents." Like the remnants of the KMTs, they were deeply involved in the drug trade. As the Nixon administration made the War on Drugs a priority, the United States once again tangled with Taiwan, confronting Taipei with evidence of its direct involvement in the traffic. The Americans wanted IBMND chief Yeh Hsiang-chih to investigate. Not surprisingly, Yeh found no evidence of IBMND involvement, a report that ambassador to Taiwan Walter P. McConaughy termed "even more of a whitewash that we had expected." Needless to say, "the IBMND's drug trafficking in Burma continued unabated."[29]

At the same time, however, the United States thought Burmese enforcement activities had improved and had "really begun to hurt" the drug smugglers. They had also stepped up publicity about their internal narcotics problems, were admitting UN specialists, were going after rogue KKY units, and were attacking drug caravans.[30] The Americans were pleased.

The relationship threatened to deteriorate, however, when on 1 February 1973 the Burmese military downed a Thai helicopter over Burmese air space near Mong Hsat and took into custody three Americans, along with five Thais who were apparently narcotics officers. One Thai was seriously injured and one American slightly wounded. This was the kind of incident that in the past had disrupted Burmese-American relations, but initially, the Burmese handled it in a way that encouraged both the Thais and Americans. They transported the men to Rangoon, gave them immediate medical attention, put them up in a government guest house, and allowed embassy officials to speak with them. They even allowed them to leave the guest house if accompanied by a Burmese official. Perhaps, thought the Americans, the Burmese had determined that it was mainly important to nurture the improving relations with both Thailand and the United States; perhaps Burma was even embarrassed that it had shot down an unarmed helicopter.

The situation became more complicated, however, when the Burmese discovered, or claimed to have discovered, inconsistencies in the accounts of the Americans. They suspected that one of them "had another mission than that stated," and furthermore, the helicopter had flown previous missions into Burma. Consequently, the Americans were removed to an army camp, where, at least for the moment, embassy officials could not visit them. Martin stated that this "unhappy and entirely unexpected development" was "ominous," indicating that the Burmese now considered this "a serious case."[31] It would inevitably fuel suspicions that the United States was covertly assisting the insurgents. The best course, the Americans decided, was to act cautiously and hope that the detainees would soon be released. When nothing had changed after several days, however, Hummel called in the Burmese ambassador, expressed his regrets that the helicopter had inadvertently entered Burma's airspace, assured him that the Americans on board had no connection with the CIA (as the Burmese clearly suspected) and were, in truth, antinarcotics agents, and asked that Burma complete its investigation soon and release the men.

A few days later Lloyd Hand, former chief of protocol under Lyndon Johnson, fortuitously arrived in Rangoon on a private trip. A friend of Ne Win, Hand played golf with the prime minister, and took the opportunity to ask that American embassy officials be allowed to speak with the detainees. By the time Hand joined Ne Win at dinner the next day, the detainees had been released and flown to Bangkok (the Thais left a few days later). The United States was grateful that the matter had not dragged on longer.

There had, then, been a few modest improvements in the bilateral relationship. There was some cooperation on narcotics, and Burma was pleased with the end of the war in Vietnam and had given some indications that it might be willing to play a larger role in regional affairs. The United States continued to have success in bringing in cultural programs. Among them was American pianist Jeannette Haien, who was very well received at concerts in Mandalay. According to the American consul, Haien "coped gamely with the unexpected mishaps which inevitably occur in a place like Mandalay—chief among them being a snake which, under the influence of Schumann's etudes, made its way to the center-front during the first concert, causing some havoc in the 'VIP' section."[32]

The improvements, however, were marginal. The embassy reported in February 1973 that Burma's leaders were ideologically "strongly pro-Communist and anti-United States." They believed that the United States was "a capitalistic and imperialistic super-power." Relations with midlevel officials were good, but "almost every promising start toward closer US/GUB relations is stopped 'by higher authority.'" The embassy advocated continuing to maintain a low profile, refraining from pressing any kind of aid on Burma, and avoiding "any clandestine involvement in Burma's internal affairs."[33]

There was some movement on the narcotics issue, however. Burma had rejected the previous offer of aircraft, but in the spring of 1973 officials hinted that a new offer might have a different reception, probably because they had stepped up their interdiction efforts and were in general more concerned about the problem. Indeed in May the Burmese army occupied Tachilek, drove out some fifteen thousand CIF/KMT (and other) residents who fled to Thailand and Laos, and burned three heroin plants run by drug kingpin Lo Hsing Min, reportedly after having captured Lo's wife and spirited her to Rangoon. Nevertheless, Burma turned to the UN rather than the United States, perhaps concerned in part with China's objections to Burma acquiring American aircraft or other military assistance.[34] No US assistance was currently needed, Ambassador Martin learned in May.

Another issue in the drug war concerned the continuing IBMND forces. The State Department began to investigate the possibility of getting "their mischievous activities" out of Burma altogether. This was not unlike previous American efforts to dislodge the KMT, and the State Department feared that the IBMND forces would stir up unpleasant memories. The department seriously considered a strong approach to both Taiwan and Thailand to try to end IBMND activities in Burma, something the embassy in Rangoon heartily endorsed. Little happened, however: much as the KMT issue had dragged out over many years, the IBMND matter was not quickly resolved. In January 1975 Burma's army defeated a CIF/KMT force after a "pitched battle" that resulted in 39 KMT deaths. In subsequent encounters another 59 were killed and 90 captured. "Badly beaten and demoralised, another 109 surrendered." Thereafter the SUA was left alone as the leading narcotics-trafficking organization.[35]

Soon the Burmese decided that they now wanted helicopters and other aircraft, but there were several problems and objections. With the Vietnam War having just ended, Congress was in no mood to fund military assistance programs anywhere in Southeast Asia. There were also worries about how Burma would use the aircraft, including to suppress the ethnic minorities. Lester Wolff, however, a member of the House Committee on Foreign Affairs and chair of a special study mission to examine the narcotics situation in Southeast Asia, concluded that Burma could not increase its suppression efforts without more helicopters, and thought it possible that Burma would agree to limit their use to antinarcotics missions. Despite some disagreement within the government, the United States proposed sending eighteen aircraft to Burma, about six to be delivered in each of the next three years. "No stone" would "be left unturned in the president's effort to fight this horrifying menace to our youth," explained one official.[36]

The Shan State Army (SSA), not to be confused with the SUA (though both were involved in drug trafficking) was also an important actor, forced into the business to support its rebellion against the central government. The SSA opposed the CIF/KMT because the latter's narcotic activities cut into its funding base. In May 1973 the SSA made a proposal that could potentially have altered the entire dynamic of the narcotics business: it offered to sell up to four hundred tons of opium annually to the United States and to help control the trafficking. It would allow US Drug Enforcement Administration (DEA) agents to gather intelligence so that drug caravans that were not part of the agreement could be intercepted, and it also offered to attack these caravans. What the SSA required in return was American intervention to negotiate a truce with Ne Win's government and work toward a permanent solution of the conflict. Ultimately what it wanted was an independent Shan state. The SSA lined up several warlords and former KKY leaders and then on 17 July presented the proposal to the American embassy in Bangkok.[37]

The Americans were skeptical of purchasing opium as a control mechanism, particularly after the infamous "27th ton" incident in 1972. At that time the United States and Thailand had agreed to purchase the CIF/KMT's annual production of twenty-six tons of opium, which they then burned. Soon thereafter the CIF/KMT allegedly offered a twenty-seventh ton, leading the Americans to conclude that purchases would only stimulate production.[38] More fundamentally, however, the Shan offer came at a time of growing cooperation between the United States and Burma on drug control, and it therefore had no chance of being accepted.

In 1975 the SSA again approached the United States with a similar plan, this time with the support of Representative Wolff. When Wolff held a hearing on the matter, however, the State Department and DEA opposed the plan, which Wolff thought was a lost opportunity to control the production at its source. A similar offer emerged in 1977, this time from drug lord Khun Sa and the SUA. Wolff again supported it, but the Jimmy Carter administration was no more open to the proposal than its Republican predecessors.[39]

Even as the United States focused much of its attention on narcotics, it also watched Burma's relations with China. While these were now quite cordial, Burma knew that China had stepped up its support of BCP rebels in Shan State who were "trained, equipped, directed and partly manned by Communist Chinese." This was part of China's "Dual Track Diplomacy" of seeking friendly relations with Burma's government while continuing to supply the BCP clandestinely. By April 1974 there may have been as many as nine thousand PRC troops in northern Burma,[40] and the *Christian Science Monitor* reported that "without the direction and support of the Chinese, the BCP insurgents would be getting nowhere." The next year American intelligence reported that for the first time the BCP had built a "military training installation" at Pang Shan near the Chinese border, specifically as "as a staging base for Chinese-provided military equipment."[41]

The policy question for the United States was whether this unpublicized Chinese presence might make the Burmese more open to US military assistance. Ne Win remained deeply suspicious of all of the great powers, but Burma did indeed modify its isolationist policy, though this was more likely the simple result of economic desperation—there was serious labor unrest in 1974. The country welcomed international organizations like the World Bank; it relaxed its prohibition on domestic and foreign investment and invited three American oil firms to explore for offshore oil; it released over 1200 political prisoners; but for the time being there was no request for military assistance.

Burma did request some commodity assistance (including cotton and wheat flour), and loans to purchase consumer goods as well as for irrigation projects. Had these requests been granted, it would have meant the resumption of economic assistance, the last projects having been funded in 1969. The United States declined to come to Burma's aid, however, feeling that Burma's problems were self-inflicted and that assistance, without important internal economic policy changes, would have only short-term palliative effects. The Americans did, however, provide the small sum of twenty-five thousand dollars in emergency assistance to help alleviate flood damage in August 1974, which was initially used to purchase snake antivenom.

Finally, however, in 1974 there came a breakthrough in the relationship when Burma accepted eighteen American aircraft primarily for narcotics suppression. Burma sent several technicians for helicopter training in the United States, and the first two helicopters were delivered late in June 1975; two more arrived in August. Soon thereafter the Burmese government produced a wonderful propaganda film featuring scores of farmers who, now recognizing the error of their ways, assisted the army in destroying their crops in return for compensation. The film also featured American-supplied aircraft attacking traffickers.[42]

Older patterns of suspicion of the United States were momentarily revived in December 1974 soon after U Thant, UN secretary general, died on 25 November in New York. His body was returned to Rangoon, which "provided a catalyst for the release of frustrations with all the economic problems the Burmese faced." The government, which disliked U Thant's former association with U Nu, refused to arrange a state funeral, but fifty thousand people attended a ceremony in his honor, after which students from Rangoon University and elsewhere took his coffin and buried it near the site of the Rangoon University Student Union, which Ne Win's forces had destroyed in 1962. This action infuriated the government, which then forcefully removed the coffin and reburied it near the Shwedagon Pagoda. Several students were killed, more than forty-five hundred persons were arrested, and riots swept Rangoon.[43] As often happened in times of chaos or disturbance, rumors soon circulated that the American Embassy or the CIA was involved. "Ludicrous as these stories may seem," wrote an American official, "they illustrate the kind of thought pattern which characterizes some senior members of the regime." After all, U Thant, a friend of U Nu, had lived in the United States, and an American plane had brought his body back to Burma. For some, this was evidence enough.[44]

Mike Mansfield's Visit

In August 1975 Senator Mike Mansfield arrived in Rangoon for a visit lasting several days, as part of a trip through several Southeast Asian countries to gauge sentiment in the wake of the defeats in Vietnam and Cambodia. Upon his return to the United States Mansfield sent President Gerald Ford a twenty-six-page report. The first eight pages dealt with Burma.[45]

Mansfield, who had visited Burma six years earlier, found that nothing had changed. "It had simply aged," as he put it. He spent several hours with Ne Win and found that his sentiments about Burma's foreign relations remained the same. The prime minister was suspicious of all of the great international and regional powers, including China, India, Japan, and the United States. He would therefore continue to keep contacts with all outside powers limited.

Mansfield considered the various ethnic and communist rebellions to be traditional and irritating but not particularly important in a political sense. The communists were the more formidable, but none of the rebellions threatened the government. This was in part because Ne Win's policy of economic nationalism appealed to anti-Chinese, anti-Indian, and antiminority sentiment among the Burmans. Despite widespread poverty, there was little flaunting by those who were wealthy. Ne Win's residence on Rangoon's Inya Lake, for example, though far from modest, was a far cry from the mansion where the British governors-general had resided.

As for American relations with Burma, Mansfield saw little hope for much change. Burma was still "chagrined by past relations with the United States," stemming particularly from the aid programs. Ne Win "found the U.S. administrators over-bearing" and basically uninterested in developing Burma's resources for Burma's advantage. He singled out his own work with Nathan Associates as particularly "disillusioning" (though this retrospective opinion perhaps derived from Walinsky's support of U Nu after the coup in 1962). He also felt that the Americans had in the past pressured Burma to accept military assistance. Mansfield himself thought that Burma could benefit from technical assistance in various areas, but he thought it improbable that Burma would accept such help from anyone, "unless it is proffered in a most understanding fashion."

On the slightly more positive side, Mansfield noted that there was now some cooperation on suppressing the narcotics trade. Interestingly, however, Ne Win indicated that he had accepted the American helicopters "after much reluctance" and was still not certain that using them to suppress narcotics was the way to go. Some younger officers supported the program, so he was going ahead with it but only on an experimental basis. Therefore, Mansfield advised, if the United States wanted to continue this program it has to excise "the greatest sensitivity" in dealing with the Burmese, to employ what historian Andrew Rotter refers to as the "gestures of diplomacy."[46]

Despite oppressive military rule and widespread, though not extreme, poverty, Mansfield pointed out, unlike Indochina Burma had at least not "suffered millions of casualties and enormous physical damage." Thus, unlike Ne Win's domestic policy, there was almost no objection to his nonaligned, isolationist foreign policy. There was little likelihood that this would change, even if he were to step down. Mansfield concluded that the current limited cooperation on narcotics, if well handled, might lead to additional positive connections, but the United States should scrupulously avoid any interference in Burma's internal affairs. Mansfield clearly felt that the United States should keep a very low profile in Burma and indeed should lower its profile everywhere in Southeast Asia.

In Mansfield's view, even now the United States failed to understand the "gestures of diplomacy." When the US government denied a request that both he and the US embassy had made for a small donation to help repair the earthquake-damaged Pagan monuments, Mansfield's published reaction was scathing. "The request was denied, apparently on some semantic or obscure basis and the matter was buffeted from pillar to post in the bureaucracy," he wrote. "It is amazing to find that . . . an Executive Branch which frequently finds ways unknown even to Congress to rush tens of millions in aid to shore up a sinking regime as in the closing days of the Cambodian debacle, is unable to find a basis for a modest human gesture in the face of a natural disaster such as occurred in Burma last summer." Perhaps shamed by Mansfield's report, in January 1977 the United States found ten thousand dollars to help repair the damaged pagodas.[47]

Soon the United States was expressing much appreciation for Burmese efforts at narcotics suppression. When President Gerald R. Ford accepted the credentials of Burma's ambassador to the United States in September 1975, he commended the country's efforts. The following May Secretary of State Henry Kissinger's senior advisor, Sheldon Vance, was even more effusive. Burma had done "more than 18 times what the US could do in the entire year 1975 with all the efforts, manpower and technology available here," he stated. Eighteen months later a State/CIA working paper commended the Burmese for strict enforcement of antinarcotics laws, crop substitution efforts, poppy eradication campaigns (eighteen thousand acres of poppies were destroyed in 1976), interdiction of drug caravans and destruction of opium refineries, and serious interference with drug traffickers. The Americans were especially pleased that the American-supplied helicopters, as well a fixed-wing aircraft and related supplies, were being used effectively. Burma also continued to acted upon American intelligence reports.[48]

In April 1977 President Carter's aide in charge of antinarcotics programs, Peter Bourne, traveled to Burma and came back convinced that there was "a total commitment from the top to deal with the narcotics problem." He asked Carter to write to Ne Win, which the president quickly agreed to do, and urged sending more fixed-wing aircraft to Burma. With American relations with Burma "on a reasonable footing after many years," Bourne also urged the White House to arrange a brief meeting for Carter with a Burmese delegation then visiting the United States, arguing that the president had "a special interest in our efforts to improve relations with the Burmese government." The meeting did not take place, vetoed by National Security Adviser Zbigniew Brzezinski on the grounds that the Burmese delegation was not sufficiently high-level, but the bilateral relationship was now as good as it had been for some time. In August 1977 the DEA reported that Burma had seized "the second-largest or third largest haul ever made anywhere," and Carter informed Congress that Ne Win had "shown a resolute determination to control drug cultivation and trafficking."[49]

However, the ethnic minority peoples complained that the helicopters were being used against them rather than the drug traffickers. "We are against the communists. We are against drugs. We are for democracy. Why doesn't the free world want to help us?" asked a Karen official in December 1977. But such pleas did not change American policy, and the helicopters continued the spray the opium poppies. The Americans professed to believe that the Burmese used the aircraft in accordance with "their designated purpose," but of course, that purpose was always vague. Burma certainly took the diplomatic risk of accepting the aircraft from the United States because of the close connection between the insurgencies and the narcotics trade, as well as ever present sensitivities about China.[50]

In July 1976 there was an coup conspiracy against Ne Win. The government became aware of the "Captains' Coup Plot" as it came to be called (since eleven of the plotters were captains), and arrested the fourteen military officers who were allegedly involved. Among the plotters' motivations was anger at corruption within the governing Burma Socialist Programme Party, something that Ne Win implicitly recognized when he soon ordered party officials to live more modestly. One of the alleged plotters sought political asylum at US Ambassador David L. Osborn's residence. Unable to contact Washington without alerting the Burmese authorities, Osborn, who spoke fluent Burmese, gave the fugitive two choices: he could stay in the embassy, but if the government requested, he would be turned over, or he would drive him to any point in Rangoon that he wished and leave him there. The fugitive chose to be dropped off near the Sule Pagoda and managed to remain free for a few weeks until he was arrested, imprisoned, and probably executed.[51] Six of the plotters were ultimately brought to court in September, along with two other military leaders, including General Tin Oo, the former army chief and defense minister, who had been dismissed the previous March. Though not one of the coup plotters, he was accused of knowing about the coup plan and failing to report it. Tin Oo was convicted and sentenced to seven years in prison but was released in 1980. Eight years later he became vice chairman of the newly founded National League for Democracy (NLD).

Osborn acted to dispel the inevitable rumors that the United States was behind the plot, and whether the Americans were privately sympathetic with the coup attempt or not, they appreciated Ne Win's cooperation on drug issues. In January 1977 the influential *Far Eastern Economic Review* characterized relations between the United States and Burma as "good." The term was relative, however. In a lengthy analysis of Burma's political and economic situation from late 1976 to May 1977, Ambassador Osborn was skeptical of the occasional reports of economic liberalization. If "effective reforms" did occur, they would be "visible to the naked eye." Meanwhile, the United States should keep a low profile: "Our waiting posture is not going to push the GUB over any otherwise avoidable brinks." Osborn's caution was well grounded. As a *New York Times* story put it in October 1977, "hopes that were raised last year about impending liberalization of General Ne Win's rigidly doctrinaire 'Burmese way to socialism' and an opening toward the world beyond Burma's borders have been dashed."[52]

The Burmese people may have been repressed, and the economy was awful, but cooperation on narcotics had resulted in a good, if still somewhat distant, official relationship. Perhaps, some thought, the United States could now develop closer ties to Burma. In the fall of 1977, Burma's chief of psychiatric services suggesting sending Peace Corps volunteers to Burma.[53] The new ambassador, Maurice Bean, himself a Peace Corps alumnus, regretted that he saw no likelihood that the government would consent.

Economic and Military Assistance Resume

For the next few years there was little change in American relations with Burma. Ne Win accepted some assistance from international organizations like the World Bank, and China remained a major donor, despite its continuing assistance to communist rebels (which, however, lessened considerably in the 1980s), while Japan was the largest donor of all. Some in the State Department wanted to reopen the question of US economic assistance. After the Burmese made an informal request in 1978, an American aid mission, headed by David I. Steinberg, recommended a positive response, arguing that the United States "could not afford not to be involved" in Burmese developments. It recommended a modest package of $5 million per year for several years, to initially fund public health initiatives and to increase over time if conditions warranted. As so often happened, the two sides could not quickly come to a final agreement. "No one is guessing how long it will take for the AID representative in Rangoon finally to have money to disburse and projects to handle," stated a *Far Eastern Economic Review* article. Still the discussions indicated, as the American consul at Mandalay, David Harr, recalled, that the United States was now attempting to "establish better relations with the Burmese government."[54]

An agreement actually came more quickly that the skeptics predicted. In 1980 the United States provided a small grant for health care, and the next year the two countries signed a formal agreement on the first significant aid in over fifteen years, providing $30 million for agricultural projects. Though small compared with what Japan, China, and international organizations provided, it was nevertheless an important milestone, signaling a closer relationship. For this Ambassador Patricia M. Byrne was substantially responsible. As Byrne's successor Daniel O'Donohue recalled, the Burmese came to see Byrne "as someone who was sympathetic to Burma. And so there was certainly some improvement in the atmosphere."[55]

In 1979 the United States and Burma also agreed to reinstate the International Military Education and Training program that brought Burmese military officers to the United States and which had lapsed twelve years earlier. The program resumed the following year. Part of a worldwide effort to suppress communist insurgencies and promote American strategic and economic interests, in Burma the program had the added goal of helping with the ongoing efforts to suppress narcotics trafficking. It was, to be sure, a small program at first, costing only $31,000. Within a few years this had risen to $1 million, and forty to fifty Burmese military officers were studying in the United States annually.[56] The program provided one of the very few avenues of contact at high levels with the Burmese government.

The United States also reported numerous impressive seizures of drugs in Burma and Thailand. In 1978, for example, Mathea Falco, senior adviser to the secretary of state for international narcotics matters, wrote that Burma had been "conducting an increasingly aggressive anti-narcotics program." The Burmese also destroyed poppy fields with chemical spraying, including American-supplied 2, 4-D herbicide, one of the chemicals that made up the infamous Agent Orange used in Vietnam. The Thais had rejected its use because of its toxicity, but Burma went ahead with it, and many of the Burmese military personnel who conducted the spraying were trained in the United States.[57]

The use of the chemical would become an increasingly controversial part of the opium eradication program, but the continuing suppression initiatives and the new economic aid agreement reflected a positive change in Burma's over-all relations with Washington. These, the *Far Eastern Economic Review* reported, "have shown a remarkable shift from the cool cordiality of the 1960s and early 1970s to increasing trust and goodwill in recent years."[58]

Still, narcotics control continued to be a vexing problem. In 1982 President Ronald Reagan called for stopping the "the flow of illegal drugs into this country," and despite the alleged successes, Burma remained "the largest producer of illicit opium and heroin in East Asia." This was partly because the SUA, characterized by the CIA as "a private army of brigands and narcotics traffickers," had now been joined by the BCP as the two most important traffickers.[59]

It was actually intensified CIA antinarcotics activities along the Thai border and in Burma that had probably increased the BCP's involvement in the narcotics business. Under its new director, William J. Casey, the CIA ran commando raids along the border and into Burma itself, and in so doing alienated the State Department and many in the DEA, who were sometimes not informed of CIA raids. Beginning in 1982 the CIA also sponsored raids into Burma by the Thai military to disrupt the SUA, then headed by the notorious Khun Sa. These raids were successful in the short term, but they pushed Khun Sa deeper into Burma so that he actually controlled more territory than ever before. In addition they had the unintended effect of strengthening the BCP, which entered the narcotics business to raise funds for arms. As a senior US official put it, "we may have a Pyrrhic victory."[60]

Soon thereafter the United States did suspend funds (for FY 1983–84) for narcotics suppression, the reason being that apparently for the first time, involvement in the narcotics trade by senior Burmese officials had surfaced. The matter came to light in June 1983. Brigadier Tin Oo (not to be confused with General Tin Oo, the NLD leader), thought to be a possible successor to Ne Win, re-signed from the powerful Council of State and from the People's Assembly. Also forced out was Bo Ni, the home and religious affairs minister. Tin Oo's fall was ostensibly because of his "extravagant lifestyle and undisguised ambitions," which irritated Ne Win, and Bo Ni was allegedly ousted because of the corrupt activities of his wife.[61] More likely, however, both men had used "the security services to facilitate drug trafficking." Both men were tried for corruption and received life sentences.[62]

The suspension did not last long, and soon the United States was again supporting Burma's aerial efforts to eradicate opium poppies. It seemed, however, a nearly hopeless task. In 1984 the Burmese government "eradicated more acres of opium poppy this year than at any other time in it history," yet because the government did not control large areas of the country, the American embassy expected a record crop. After more than fourteen years of active antinarcotics activities, Burma still accounted for about 90 percent of the opium produced in Southeast Asia. In 1984 an estimated 20 percent of the heroin reaching the United States originated in the Golden Triangle, double what it had been only a year before. As a CIA report put it in August 1985, the intensified efforts by both Thailand and Burma to disrupt the production and transportation of narcotics "had not yet significantly reduced opium cultivation." Still, Ambassador O'Donohue considered the American antinarcotics program in Burma of some utility. "We had a military committed to do something in narcotics control instead of nothing," he recalled. "Though the Burmese military did not like to engage in armed conflict with the traffickers, they did undertake limited operations."[63]

However, American efforts to control narcotics was not entirely based on the harm that the drugs did to people at home. The Cold War was still on, and keeping Burma nonaligned remained important. As a State Department official said, "if Burma went the wrong way, it could be a real problem." Also the antinarcotics program continued to provide one of the few avenues of contact with Burmese intelligence officials. The DEA agents in Burma in that period (whose work O'Donohue praised) had direct access to their Burmese military/police counterparts without needing special permission.[64]

In September 1985 former President Richard Nixon arrived in Burma. Accompanied by Treasury Secretary John B. Connally, he met with Ne Win and Burma's President U San Yu. The visit was primarily a sentimental one: Nixon was retracing his visit to Southeast Asia in 1953. It was not widely reported and probably had no immediate political significance. However, the fact that it took place at all, and that a high-level Reagan administration official accompanied Nixon, suggests that the administration appreciated Ne Win's quiet anticommunist posture. American appreciation was also apparent when, about the same time as Nixon's visit, the United States prepared to install a new mainframe computer in Burma's Planning and Finance Ministry, which would revolutionize computing in Burma. At that time the only mainframe computer in Burma was an ancient

International Computers and Tabulators 1902S model that dated from the 1960s. It was thought to be the last such computer in the world still operating.[65]

Soon after Nixon's visit, the United States invited U San Yu, Ne Win's heir apparent, for an unofficial visit for a medical examination. Reagan sent him a warm letter of welcome. San Yu stayed for several weeks and upon his departure expressed his "deep appreciation" for the assistance and hospitality extended to him. Clearly the relationship between the two countries, while not close, was relatively friendly. As a *New York Times* correspondent put it in November 1985, "Burma has been on increasingly cordial terms with a number of countries, including the United States."[66] The United States provided modest economic and military assistance programs and continued its support of Burma's antinarcotics program.

The antinarcotics program was controversial, however. The newly founded human rights organization, Project Maje, and its activist leader, Edith T. Mirante, carried on a vocal protest against the use of herbicides in Burma, claiming that the chemicals were being used primarily "to wage a campaign of chemical terror" against the Shans and other minorities. The United States was deeply implicated. Not only did it supply the chemicals, as well as the helicopters, and later fast armored fixed-wing aircraft to carry out the spraying, but it trained Burmese involved in the program, including pilots. Mirante wrote to several persons in the State Department, complained personally to at least one knowledgeable official, and wrote a lengthy letter to Kenneth Barun, who headed up Nancy Reagan's drug abuse program. Mirante's actions were noticed. Dr. Carlton E. Turner, a deputy assistant to the president and the official in charge of drug abuse policy, requested an aide to draft a "strong, hard-hitting response." He got it. It included the incredible assertion that 2, 4-D was not harmful to animals or humans and was "both safe and effective." The aerial spraying program in Burma, he asserted, was "one of the most successful narcotics control initiatives anywhere in the world."[67]

Turner's provocative response accurately reflected the Reagan administration's position, despite the doubts of its own Environmental Protection Agency. The use of the chemical did, however, attract negative opinion. The Shans, insisting that the chemical was very harmful, characterized its use as genocidal; the National Cancer Institute and other organizations feared the carcinogenic effects of 2, 4-D; and Project Maje continued its activities. In 1987 the organization published Mirante's exposé about the dangers that the chemical spraying caused. The criticism did not disturb the Reagan administration. In March 1987 a State Department official commented on the "excellent cooperation between our two countries in the area of narcotics control."[68]

The State Department's comment came in the context of a proposed visit by Ne Win to the United States, his first since 1966. During President San Yu's recent visit, Reagan had invited Ne Win to come, and the Burmese leader decided to make a private trip to the United States on 10–15 April 1987. The visit attracted no attention. For the month of April the *New York Times* published four stories with references to Burma, none of which mentioned Ne Win. Nor, apparently, did stories in other newspapers and magazines. Indeed, the visit seems to have been deliberately kept secret. Only in June did the *Far Eastern Economic Review* reveal that Ne Win had gone to Oklahoma City to visit Ardith Delese, "the widow of an American friend," to seek medical treatment, and perhaps to seek assistance in revitalizing Burma's oil industry.[69] A clandestine broadcast by a Burmese opposition group stated that Ne Win had been in the United States to negotiate a lease of one of Burma's Coco Islands for a military base—an unlikely claim.[70] The Reagan administration was, of course, well aware of the visit, and Reagan sent Ne Win a gold golf putter, as well as a warm welcoming letter expressing his appreciation for Burma's "strong steps . . . in the fight against narcotics," and followed up with a telephone call, in which he repeated his appreciation for Burma's cooperation in narcotics control. Although the visit had little political importance, it did give Reagan a chance to reiterate the American concern with narcotics, as well as the "growing interest in Burma among Americans," signified by the establishment at Northern Illinois University of the Center for Burma Studies.[71]

If Ne Win's visit did not make an impression on the Americans, news of Burma's sorry internal condition did. The *Far Eastern Economic Review* ran a series of critical accounts in 1987, and Bertil Linter published several articles about the ethnic insurgencies that still ravaged parts of the country. Symbolic of Burma's decline, the Burmese government even petitioned the UN to lower its status to the "poorest nation" category so that it might receive more economic assistance. Ne Win also continued to keep his country isolated—so much so that journalist Rodney Tasker wrote in 1983 that Burma was "the Albania of Asia." The future did not look bright. Newly appointed American ambassador Burton Levin wrote in a personal letter about the "serious economic problems" the country was facing. Inflation was "beginning to gallop," there was little foreign exchange, fuel shortages hampered transportation, and few if any people really believed in Ne Win's disastrous ideology.[72] However, worse was still to come: Ambassador Levin was soon to witness the regime's nadir.

REVOLT

The situation the United States faced in Burma in August 1988 was unprecedented in Southeast Asia. The people rose up the challenge the ruling military junta, and quite by accident Aung San Suu Kyi, daughter of Burma's martyred independence hero, emerged to lead the opposition. Some thought she approached sainthood. The closest comparison was with the Philippine People Power Revolution of 1986, which ended the Ferdinand Marcos administration. Corazón "Cory" Aquino, widow of the martyred Benigno "Ninoy" Aquino Jr., killed by Marcos's goons when he disembarked at Manila's airport, emerged to lead the revolution. Like Suu Kyi, Cory had saintly qualities, and both situations evoked questions about human rights.

There were also similarities in the American responses. The Reagan administration was reluctant to withdraw support from Marcos, although in the end it helped facilitate the transition. In Burma the administration was also cautious and indeed not only the Reagan, but also the George H. W. Bush and Bill Clinton administrations were all hesitant to impose sanctions.

There were also differences, however. The dramatic People Power Revolution succeeded very quickly, and there was little bloodshed. Marcos and his entourage went into exile, and Cory Aquino became the president. In Burma, the revolution failed, thousands died at the hands of the regime, and Aung San Suu Kyi was put under house arrest, where she remained for much of the next two decades.

After 1990 the United States did not have an ambassador in Rangoon (Yangon) for more than two decades, and there were calls for sanctions and other strong measures against the ruling junta. Human rights, which had seldom been at the top of the American diplomatic agenda in Southeast Asia, was suddenly the focus of American policy debates. The brutal response of the junta brought this about, but Aung San Suu Kyi was enormously important in keeping the international community focused on human rights. She wielded enormous indirect influence on American policy, far more than any other Southeast Asian leader has ever done. No one liked the junta, and the debate in the US government was mostly about means and tactics. For perhaps the first time Burma received more attention in the United States than any other Southeast Asian country, except in the early 1990s when efforts to settle the complicated Cambodian imbroglio and prevent a return of the Khmer Rouge received at least equal attention.

Geopolitical and economic concerns did not, of course, disappear entirely. Burma was situated strategically between two rising Asian powers, China and India, and it had valuable natural resources as well as a potential market for American goods. But there were relatively few concrete American interests in Myanmar, there were serious human rights violations there—and there was the charisma of Aung San Suu Kyi. Human rights was what drove American policy, by and large, in good part because of Congressional and public pressure.

8888

By the mid-1980s Burma's economy was near collapse. In 1985, in an effort to fight the black market, the government suddenly declared high-denomination kyat bills without value and replaced the hundred-kyat bill with a new seventy-five-kyat one, a move that created economic chaos. In August 1987 Ne Win, who had stepped down as Burma's president but retained his position as head of the ruling BSPP and thus remained the most powerful figure in the country, complained that "he had been misled" about the true state of affairs in Burma. "It's the first promising sign here in years," American Ambassador Burton Levin wrote in August 1987. Actions soon followed. On 1 September the government liberalized the grain trade, allowing a free market in rice and other grains. There was optimism that other reforms would follow. However, Ne Win undercut whatever good was accomplished with this liberalization by once again changing the currency. It was "perhaps the most sweeping demonetization in the contemporary world." As before this was ostensibly to punish the black marketers, though it may also have been intended to cut inflation. Another possible factor was what Steinberg terms "abstruse astrological calculations that would enable Ne Win to live to be ninety."[1] The demonetization, which overnight wiped out people's savings, led to a short-lived student protest that closed the universities for a month but did not result in further disturbances or a long-term protest movement. By the end of the year Burma's economy had "hit rock bottom."[2]

There had been some resistance to the military's rule in the past, but things finally began to fall apart in March 1988. Aung Gyi, Ne Win's heir apparent many years earlier, wrote several lengthy letters to Ne Win that became public, including one on 7 March that criticized the regime. On 12 March there was a non-political dispute between students from the Rangoon Institute of Technology and the owner of a tea shop that led to widespread rioting and a brutal police response. Among the dead were forty-one students who suffocated in a closed police van.[3] On 9 May Aung Gyi wrote another long letter to Ne Win, after which he was imprisoned.

During the summer the BSPP responded by liberalizing the economic system. Ne Win admitted that many people now distrusted the government; he proposed a national referendum to decide whether to allow a multiparty system and then resigned as party chairman. In the end, however, nothing significant was conceded. The BSPP rejected the referendum idea and replaced Ne Win with General Sein Lwin—a particularly unfortunate choice because Sein Lwin had been in command of the troops that had suppressed the previous uprising and was largely responsible for the student casualties. Students and others were outraged and began to demonstrate. On 5 August the government declared martial law, and three days later the pent-up anger exploded across the nation, on what is now known as 8888. Over the next several days, at least three thousand people died in Rangoon alone. Four days later Sein Lwin was out, replaced by Maung Maung, the only civilian close to Ne Win, which ended the demonstrations for the time being. The demonstrators did not much like Maung Maung, but he did make numerous concessions and announced that a special congress would convene to consider holding a national referendum on allowing a multiparty state. The opposition, however, rejected a referendum as unnecessary and called for his resignation by 7 September. Maung Maung did not resign, but the special congress he had called met on 10 September and voted not to have a referendum but instead to hold general multiparty elections within three months for a new parliament.[4] Maung Maung supported the decision and criticized the BSPP for its many failings, but he did not support the protesters either, whom he saw as anarchists.

From this protest, Aung San Suu Kyi, who was in Rangoon quite by accident to care for her ailing mother, emerged to bring organization and leadership to the movement. As Ambassador Levin later wrote, "Aung San Suu Kyi gave voice and provided organization to what might have otherwise been an inchoate eruption. She stood and continues to stand as a symbol of the resistance and aspirations of the Burmese people: it is no wonder that the regime so fears her."[5] In the weeks that followed she spoke eloquently to huge crowds who came to hear her. Suu Kyi,

FIGURE 9. The 8888 Uprising in Rangoon (caption courtesy of Radio Diaries). A main goal of the August and September demonstrations was to convince soldiers to leave their posts and join the uprising. Photo courtesy of Gaye Paterson.

FIGURE 10. The 8888 Uprising in Rangoon (caption courtesy of Radio Diaries). Democracy demonstrators wave the Burmese flag in August 1988, when millions of Burmese took to the streets. Students led the protests, but were soon joined by civil servants, police, soldiers and ordinary citizens. Photo courtesy of Gaye Paterson.

FIGURE 11. The 8888 Uprising in Rangoon (caption courtesy of Radio Diaries). Demonstrators piled on buses in downtown Rangoon. "The Buddhist monks, the housewives' union—they were all joining in the street," recalls student activist Khin Ohmar. Photo courtesy of Gaye Paterson.

along with U Tin Oo and U Aung Gyi, who would soon found the NLD, objected to the proposed elections and insisted that despite the many concessions and the establishment of a multiparty election commission to run the election, the BSPP government was not to be trusted. What was needed before an election was the establishment of a neutral government, which Suu Kyi said would not be possible unless Ne Win went into exile.

When the election commission accepted some of the protesters' demands, the army became nervous, fearing a complete breakdown of governmental control. The army itself was on the brink of disintegration, as numerous soldiers were joining the opposition. On 18 September the army mounted a coup, replacing Maung Maung with military officers. General Saw Maung, who had led the coup, announced that once law and order had been restored the army would hold multiparty elections, in which it would not interfere. On 26 September the army leaders announced the formation of the State Law and Order Restoration Council (SLORC), the junta that would run the country, and the very next day it promulgated the rules for taking part in the elections. The coup did not bring an end to the protests, which the military suppressed violently: though the total number of people who died is unknown estimates run as high as ten thousand.[6]

The Burmese government's actions deeply shocked Ambassador Levin. He later recalled the "horrific casualness with which army units killed their demonstrating compatriots," something that he and other embassy officials personally witnessed. The army's actions were "little short of murder,"[7] and he opened the American embassy's outside water taps and distributed food packages to demonstrating monks. He even smuggled medicine to wounded demonstrators. "I am stunned to the point of disbelief at the Government's continuing effort to hold on in the face of a massive popular uprising which has divested it of control of all major urban centers, deprived it of any semblance of credibility and brought all services to a halt," he wrote on 8 September. The best solution, Levin thought, was for a new leader to come to power, probably someone from the military's middle ranks, who would turn the government over to civilian rule. That, however, was unlikely. Only the "unpredictable, eccentric Ne Win," who still called "the shots from behind the scenes," could bring about a government capitulation. "These are the times for heros [sic]," Levin wrote. But there were few fresh faces, although Levin thought Tin Oo, who was "attractive and sincere," might fill the bill. Tin Oo was working closely with a possible hero, Aung San Suu Kyi, whom Levin thought "very impressive."[8]

Despite what must have been Levin's impassioned dispatches to the State Department, the US government had not taken a strong position. As the protests continued, the State Department drew up plans to evacuate dependents, but it was cool to cutting off American assistance, in part because Reagan was strongly committed to the cooperative antinarcotics initiatives in Burma. But pressure to do something was growing. In the Senate Daniel Moynihan (D-NY) introduced a resolution condemning the actions of the Burmese army. Despite opposition from the administration (it "did not welcome it at all," Moynihan said)[9] the resolution passed unanimously on 11 August 1988.

The Burmese demonstrators welcomed the resolution and Levin's sympathy. "It is no accident that our Embassy has been the focal point for anti-Government demonstrators," Levin wrote. The "thousands upon thousands" who marched past the embassy demanding democracy exhilarated him. "Now if only that small band of willful fools can be convinced to give up the ghost," he concluded, Burma could recover from "a quarter of a century of irrelevant, malicious rule."[10]

The revolution caused difficulties for the American embassy. On one occasion, shortly after 8888 when the military government had imposed a rigid curfew, American embassy officials sought permission to leave for home after the curfew had begun. Eventually the regime agreed, but the word was not communicated to the soldiers manning the checkpoints. When embassy vehicles approached a checkpoint they were challenged, with soldiers pointing rifles at them. After a tense standoff, Colonel John Haseman, who spoke Burmese, persuaded the officer in command to call Intelligence Chief Khin Nyunt. He complied, and the soldiers lowered their weapons and allowed the cars to pass.[11]

The administration's position began to change when Representative Stephen J. Solarz (D-NY), Congress's leading authority on Southeast Asia, introduced a resolution similar to the one that the Senate had adopted. Solarz wanted the United States to stand "strongly on the side of democracy" in Burma. This time the administration decided not to oppose his resolution, which passed without opposition on 7 September. The administration had not committed to cutting off financial aid, however, and Moynihan urged Reagan to act because, he charged, the Burmese army had "murdered peaceful demonstrators" and had sprayed American-supplied carcinogenic chemicals intended for narcotics control on ethnic minority peoples.[12]

The desire to do something to protest Burmese developments increased following the military coup on 18 September. "Hundreds and perhaps thousands have been killed," stated Moynihan. "We cannot wait any longer. We must cut off aid now." This new violence, along with Congressional opinion, brought about a change of mind. Levin was ordered to protest the government's resort to violence and ask that it carry out promised reforms. On 22 September 1988 the United States suspended all arms sales and ended economic assistance. It recalled its technical assistance advisers, cut off all commodity shipments (even diverting one shipment of fertilizer to Bangladesh), and stopped a program training Burmese, including military officers, in the United States. Between 1980 and 1989, 255 Burmese officers had graduated from American military schools. Now that too was ended.[13]

The Burmese military belatedly justified its takeover on grounds of "blatant [American] interference in the internal affairs of Burma." On 12 September 1988 an American fleet, including an aircraft carrier, had entered Burma's territorial waters some 190 miles south of Rangoon. The fleet was there only to evacuate embassy staff, if needed, but the Burmese government deeply resented the American deployment because it implied a lack of confidence in the regime. In fact, the Burmese insisted that the US fleet's movement was part of a conspiracy. "It was a time when traitors at home were conspiring with their masters abroad to enslave the country again," a government-owned newspaper wrote a few months after the coup. Actually, no American official, civilian or military, wanted to use the American military for anything other than a possible emergency evacuation. Former Prime Minister U Nu did request American military intervention against the regime, but he was politely rebuffed.[14]

In the end American forces were not needed for evacuation as the embassy managed to persuade Thai Airways to send in a large plane to carry out those who wished to leave. No Burmese officials were at the airport when the plane arrived, and the gangway available at the airport would not reach to the plane's door. Eventually the Americans found a ladder that reached to the door when placed on top of the gangway, and an orderly process of boarding ensued. Americans had the first priority, but nationals of several other countries were also evacuated. All who wanted to board were able to, and the plane departed without incident.[15]

There was no invasion, but the cut-off of assistance rankled with the junta and cheered the opposition, and the area around the American embassy, then in the center of Rangoon, became a favorite gathering place. As Levin recalled, "for veterans of the Foreign Service, it was a rare and comforting experience to witness admiring, rather than hostile, crowds gathered before an American Embassy." Levin himself, reported the *Bangkok Post*, had "become an inspiration" to the antigovernment demonstrators, who particularly welcomed his participation in a memorial tribute to the dead. Several times Aung San Suu Kyi met with him, though they tacitly agreed not to meet too often lest the government accuse her of being an American stooge.[16]

Levin believed that the Reagan administration supported a forceful policy toward Burma, writing in December 1988 that recent consultations with administration officials in Washington had "left me pleased. There was full agreement on maintaining a tough attitude toward the regime," and even those in charge of the antinarcotics program, whom he feared would object, were "on board." But the administration's moves against the government came primarily in response to Congressional and public opinion and were at heart cautious. Moreover, while Reagan (and then Bush) asserted that it was in the American interest to encourage a democratizing process in Burma, one suspects that the administration was less enthusiastic than Levin. Reagan seemed to believe that significant political change was just around the corner. Best to encourage that process gently, he thought.[17]

In fact, the human rights situation was worsening. Reports emerged that student refugees who had been promised safe passage back to Rangoon had been arrested, tortured, and killed. Still, the administration seemed reluctant to take a hardline position toward Burma. In Congressional testimony, Deputy Assistant Secretary of State David Lambertson disparaged the ethnic insurgencies, commenting that they were "no more than narcotics syndicates with private armies," and stated that he hoped the United States would soon be able to reactivate cooperative relations with Burma on the narcotics issue.[18]

On the other hand, the Americans viewed the junta's decision to proceed with multiparty elections favorably. In January 1989 Levin met with the Burmese elections commission to inquire about the rules and procedures. No date had yet been set, but political parties were registering, he was told. Levin was concerned that the rules would prevent Aung San Suu Kyi from running. Soon thereafter the

FIGURE 12. A poster of Aung San Suu Kyi that was popular in the United States. Her great influence with the American public and lawmakers was a crucial factor in the policy debate in the years after 8888. Courtesy of Shepard Fairey/ObeyGiant.com and Thomson Reuters.

junta announced that elections would be held in May 1990. On 1 March 1989 the Burmese government released a draft election law, which the United States hoped would result in free and fair elections early in 1990.

But the United States was clearly still upset with what had been happening in Burma. A few weeks later the new president, George H. W. Bush, made it more difficult for Burma to trade with the United States by suspending it indefinitely from the Generalized System of Preferences, based on Burma's violations of worker rights. At the end of June Aung Lwin, a founding member of the NLD, was arrested; in the following weeks many more people were jailed. After an unauthorized rally in Mergui on 19 July, the anniversary of Aung San's assassination, Aung San Suu Kyi herself was placed under house arrest, and Amnesty International soon listed her as a prisoner of conscience. Somewhere between two thousand and six thousand NLD members were arrested.[19] A fair and free election seemed unlikely.

The US Congress, meanwhile, directed $2 million in humanitarian aid to student exiles living on the Thai-Burmese border, and in August Levin confirmed that dissidents had been beaten and tortured, and sometimes killed. The next month Khin Nyunt, Burma's intelligence chief, named Levin as part of a "rightist conspiracy" to overthrow the government. Meanwhile a groundswell of opinion rose in Western countries in support of Aung San Suu Kyi, who was still under house arrest. "She is Burma's best hope for democracy," Elie Wiesel telegraphed President Bush, asking him to intervene on her behalf.[20]

A New Ambassador?

There is a popular myth that after Ambassador Levin left Burma in 1990, he was not replaced because the administration downgraded diplomatic relations to protest the government's repression. There was, in fact, no American ambassador in Burma until 2012, but it was not for want of trying. In October or early November 1989 President Bush decided to nominate Frederick "Freck" Vreeland to replace Levin. Vreeland was a long-time friend of Bush. Both had belonged to Skull and Bones at Yale, both had served in the CIA—Bush as its director for a time and Vreeland as a career operations officer from 1951 to 1985. Vreeland had worked on Bush's presidential campaign, raising over $100,000 for him, and desperately wanted an ambassadorial appointment. Bush wrote that embassy appointments were "tricky" but that Vreeland was on his list, and Vreeland was "thrilled." He preferred an appointment in the Mediterranean area, but Burma was among the countries he listed.[21]

In nominating Vreeland, Bush was most likely simply rewarding a long-time friend and supporter at a time when Levin's normal rotation was at hand. Levin had already served for nearly three years and would likely remain another year, a three-year stint being about average for American ambassadors in Rangoon. There was also some uneasiness with Levin's identification with the opposition, however. The junta listed Levin in a book entitled *Who's Who in the CIA*.[22] Given Burma's hostility toward Levin, perhaps his usefulness as an official representative was at an end. Still, Levin had extensive experience in Asia, and at a time of crisis the thought of sending an ambassador who had no Asian experience deserves criticism.

On 16 January 1990 the Burmese government ruled that Aung San Suu Kyi, who was still under house arrest, could not be a candidate for election, allegedly because she had consorted with insurgents. Khin Nyunt commented that women should never be allowed to become leaders in Burma, lest the country be ruined. The government also barred U Nu from running and arrested many opposition figures. It was now widely assumed that the government's National Union Party (the successor to the BSPP) would win the election now scheduled for 27 May 1990. The United States criticized these actions, and the White House urged the Burmese government to release Suu Kyi and allow her to be a candidate. Further raising tension was the Burmese rejection of American election observers. There was no need for them, a government spokesman told reporters, because the election would be free and fair. In February the United States decertified Burma as a cooperating country on narcotics control. Drug Enforcement Administration officials objected, and Senator Moynihan, characterizing the government of Burma as "contemptible," accused the DEA of "running its own foreign policy."[23] The DEA lost the battle—for the time being.

Moynihan soon introduced legislation to ban imports from Burma, which passed the Senate unanimously on 27 April 1990. Opposition figures in Burma cheered, and SLORC accused Moynihan of "false accusations." About the same time Asia Watch, founded in 1985 and one of the predecessors of Human Rights Watch, issued a detailed, scorching condemnation of Burma, alleging a "consistent pattern of gross human rights abuses." A free and fair election, the report concluded, was impossible. Asia Watch also supported Moynihan's legislation to ban all imports from Burma, a bill then in a conference committee with the House. But despite the unanimous vote in the Senate, the Bush administration formally opposed the Moynihan legislation, arguing that sanctions would not be effective, would "severely complicate the possibility of constructive dialogue with the Burmese government," and would in general interfere with the flexibility that the administration wanted.[24]

Meanwhile, by 11 May 1990 all of the paperwork was ready for Vreeland's nomination. Burma's government had agreed to the appointment, and a draft press release was ready to go. On 6 June 1990 Bush made the official announcement: he was nominating Vreeland to succeed Levin.

There was only one problem: Vreeland's biography submitted to the Senate Foreign Relations Committee was phony. It included no mention of his long-term employment as a covert operative in the CIA. The Senators would only know that Vreeland was a Foreign Service officer in training in 1951 and 1952, joined the Foreign Service in 1952, and served in various posts until his retirement in 1985.[25]

Vreeland's paperwork made its way from the State Department to the Asia and Pacific Subcommittee of the Senate Foreign Relations Committee, then chaired by Alan Cranston (D-CA). Richard Kessler, the majority subcommittee staff director, reviewed the file and was suspicious; it looked like a "cover bio," something the CIA would prepare. The State Department told Kessler that the bio was real, but Kessler asked Marvin Ott, then on the staff of the Senate Intelligence Committee, to check it out. Ott went to John Stolz, the new head of the CIA's Operations Division, brought in to clean house in the wake of the Central American death squad scandals, and Stolz immediately confirmed Vreeland's former association with the agency. This revelation embarrassed State Department officials, who had not conducted a thorough review of Vreeland's background because this was an appointment that the president himself was pushing. Had the president not been involved, at this point the State Department would have pulled the nomination. Cranston privately accused Vreeland of lying about his past,[26] but instead a compromise was reached: there would be the usual public confirmation hearing, followed by a closed executive hearing at which Vreeland would apologize profusely for the misleading information. The committee would then recommend confirmation.[27]

At the public hearing on 1 October 1990, only Senators Cranston and Claiborne Pell (D-RI) were present. A couple of reporters and State Department officers, and Ott, along with Vreeland and his family, made up the audience. Surprisingly, no one was there from the Burmese embassy. In his opening remarks Vreeland introduced his family and his fiancée. He reviewed his long career in public service, his more recent service as director of the Aspen Institute's branch in Italy, and his current position as vice president of John Cabot University and American College in Rome. He spoke of Myanmar's "valiant people," and of the "tragic and fateful days in Rangoon and Mandalay" and elsewhere in "this beautiful country." He said little that might have seriously offended the Burmese government, beyond noting that human rights were "of universal importance." In response to Cranston's question about the administration's view of sanctions,

Vreeland commented that no decision had yet been made, though when pressed, he acknowledged that he thought sanctions were "inescapable." When asked about US efforts to prevent other countries from providing weapons to Burma, Vreeland replied that the administration was privately urging countries to join the American arms embargo. There was, in sum, nothing inflammatory or exceptional in Vreeland's remarks, certainly nothing that went beyond stated American policy toward Burma.[28]

On the other hand Senator Cranston denounced Burma's government in scathing terms. It was a "renegade government" that had "massacred 3,000 or more pro-democracy demonstrators" in 1988, and it was "in cahoots with narco-terrorist drug lords." After Senator Pell spoke briefly in support of Vreeland's nomination, the hearing ended.[29]

Three days later the Burmese government withdrew its acceptance of Vreeland as ambassador. Ott believes that the Burmese government mistakenly attributed Cranston's highly critical remarks to Vreeland. The ambassador designate himself wrote that Burmese officials were influenced by a BBC broadcast that had taken several of his comments out of context. The White House stated that Burma objected to Vreeland's comments on "arms sales, possible economic sanctions, narcotics and internal Burmese political developments." A Burmese spokesman explained that Vreeland had "changed his professed desire to promote friendly relations with Burma" and was now "advocating an economic blockade."[30] Since Vreeland's comments in the hearing bore little resemblance to those attributed to him in these criticisms, it seems likely the Burmese, who did not have their own representatives at the hearing, misconstrued what he had said.[31]

With Vreeland out, the administration turned to Parker W. Borg, a career Foreign Service officer with considerable Asian experience who at one point had been the youngest ambassador-qualified officer in the Foreign Service. Bush approved Borg's nomination on 8 January 1991 and formally nominated him on 19 July. Borg prepared seriously for his new post, including taking intensive language training. By this point, however, Senator Moynihan was the leading authority on Burma in the Senate, and he opposed appointing a new ambassador. Staffers Marvin Ott and Robin Cleveland, both friends of Borg, tried to find a way to overcome Moynihan's resistance, arguing that it was very important to have an ambassador in Rangoon, in part because of the importance of a rising China in the region. Eventually they struck a deal: the Foreign Relations Committee would go forward with the nomination, provided it was not presented in such a way as to be interpreted as approval of the Burmese regime. The would be signaled by the ostentatious withdrawal of two of the three defense attachés from the embassy in Rangoon. Finally, Moynihan insisted that Secretary of State Lawrence Eagleburger must personally ask him to go ahead with the confirmation. But how could they get Eagleburger to make the call? Shortly thereafter Ott was on the same plane to Tokyo with Eagleburger to attend a Cambodia donors' conference, and on the trip he spoke with Eagleburger about the Borg nomination. Eagleburger refused to make the call, however, stating that he did not like the precedent of the Senate conditioning appointments in this way. If it was the Paris embassy at stake, he said, he would nevertheless call, but Burma was not important enough.[32] Borg had much support, and Steinberg told a Senate committee that he was impressed with Borg's "understanding and competence," and he "would make an excellent representative of the United States."[33] Eagleberger never called, however, so Borg waited in limbo for two years but never got his hearing.

"Phooey to 80%"

Meanwhile in Burma there was an election to hold—one that no one thought would be free and fair. As a *Christian Science Monitor* story put it, the arrest of even more NLD candidates in April 1990 reduced "to zero the chances of the party winning the election." But much to everyone's surprise, on 27 May 1990 the NLD won an overwhelming victory, with nearly 80 percent of the seats (392 out of 492), and about 57 percent of the votes. SLORC's party won ten seats—only 2 percent. At least the counting of the ballots had been fair, even if the ground rules and the campaigning had not been. It was a staggering defeat for the military.[34]

There has been some contentious disagreement about what the election was actually for. Was it for a new government, or was it essentially for a constituent assembly to draft a new constitution, during which time the military government would remain in power? At first the military said it planned to turn power over "to whomever won the election," but in mid-1989 it announced that it intended to remain in power until a new constitution was drafted. In other words, if there was to be a transfer of power, it would be slow and deliberate rather than immediate. The military apparently feared that its decades-long fight against Burma's communists would be for naught and that retribution and a possible war crimes tribunal were real possibilities if there was a quick transfer, despite NLD assurances to the contrary. Apparently before the election Aung San Suu Kyi and the NLD were not insistent on an immediate transfer of power and understood that a new constitution would be the first order of business. If this was their view, however, it changed soon after the surprising election results were in. Neither side would compromise, and the NLD now expected a quick transfer.[35]

Those who voted surely thought they were voting for a new government. As former British diplomat Derek Tonkin put it, "over 99 percent of those eligible to vote really thought they were electing a new parliament and a new government."

That was also the view of the US and other Western governments, and if the military junta had allowed the election results to stand, its relationship with the West would have improved dramatically. The Bush administration urged a quick transfer of power and the release of political prisoners. When nothing had happened by August, Secretary of State James Baker wrote to SLORC chairman Saw Maung urging the military to step down.[36] In the end, the junta simply ignored the results of the election. The military had decided not to give up its power. As the *Economist* magazine put it, the junta had said "phooey to 80%."[37]

With the military now remaining in control, the DEA, the Bush administration, and some elements in the State Department wanted to resume an antinarcotics program that would presumably include aerial spraying and interdiction. Some Congress members, including Charles Rangel (D-NY), who was concerned about the heroin epidemic in the United States, agreed. But with the postelection military crackdown, there was little likelihood of a consensus developing; those most concerned with Burma affairs in the Congress, including Moynihan and Solarz, along with human rights officers in the State Department, opposed resuming cooperation.[38]

As it became clear that the Burmese military was not about to relinquish power, pressure grew from the Congress and the interested general public to respond. On 1 October eleven prominent senators wrote to President Bush urging him to impose sanctions under authority of the Customs and Trade Act of 1990, which authorized presidential action. The administration agreed with the senators that Burma/Myanmar had not met the conditions of the trade act. (The United States continued officially to use Burma in spite of the military government's change of the country's name in 1989.) Soon thereafter, when the military raided 133 monasteries, the United States protested its "total disregard for human rights."[39]

Still, the administration held off on imposing sanctions. Letters of protest continued to arrive at the White House, however, and on 21 May 1991 several members of Congress urged Bush to make a public statement about the human rights situation on the anniversary of the 1990 election. Finally, on 18 July 1991 Bush took his first step toward new sanctions: he decided not to renew a bilateral textile agreement that had expired at the end of 1990. This made the importation of Burmese textiles into the United States difficult, and Moynihan, who praised the president's action, said he intended to see to it that no textiles were allowed to arrive.[40]

Pressure continued to mount on the Bush administration to do more. On 11 October 1991, for example, forty-eight members of Congress signed a letter to Bush to urge that Aung San Suu Kyi be released and that the duly elected candidates be allowed to take office.[41] Three days later the Norwegian Nobel Committee awarded the Peace Prize to Aung San Suu Kyi and asked Saw Maung to pass the news to her.

The prize brought worldwide attention to the repression in Burma. It was the subject of editorials in major US newspapers, including the *New York Times* and the *Washington Post*. More calls for American action flowed in, and the administration's rhetoric became stronger. Bush applauded the Nobel Prize Committee, praised Suu Kyi's courage, condemned the Burmese military's actions, and urged the junta to "transfer power to the duly elected civilian government and to release all political prisoners, including . . . Aung San Suu Kyi."[42] The Congress joined in congratulating Suu Kyi and condemned the Burmese government for its continuing human rights violations. In one of the strongest condemnations of Burma yet, a State Department official testified that the Burmese military's human rights abuses "are among the most flagrant in the world." Not only had thousands been killed in 1988, but 500,000 people had been forcibly relocated. Others had been forced to be porters for the military, used as human mine detectors, and "otherwise treated as expendable beasts of burden." While there were other repressive governments in the world, many of them had at least some support among the populace, but decidedly not in Burma.[43] Burma's response to Suu Kyi's Nobel Prize, in contrast, was a massive purge of its civil service and a warning to the public not to confront the authorities.

The administration's strong rhetoric did not translate into significant policy shifts. Bush resisted further sanctions and resumed engagement with Burma on narcotics. Nor did the administration encourage the opposition's provisional government, the National Coalition Government of the Union of Burma, which claimed to be the true government. When U Sein Win, the Coalition Government's prime minister, came to Washington in November 1991 he was unable to get an appointment with any White House official, though members of Congress gladly met with him. A few weeks later, in fact, the Coalition's ambassador to the United Nations, Bilal Raschid (son of U Raschid, one of independent Burma's founders and a Cabinet minister during U Nu's administration) was invited to testify before the Subcommittee on East Asian and Pacific Affairs.

These events symbolized the divergent approach to Burma. Congress, deeply impressed with Aung San Suu Kyi and angered at Burma's military for its atrocious behavior, wanted a forceful American posture, including encouragement of the opposition, the imposition of sanctions, and keeping American diplomatic relations with Burma at the chargé d'affaires level, if not breaking them off entirely. The administration was willing to criticize the Burmese regime in strong language, but its actual policy was cautious, arguably even timid. It wanted to have an ambassador in Burma, resumed cooperation on narcotics control, had no real interest in encouraging the Coalition provisional government, and accepted limited sanctions only in response to Congressional and public pressure. In April 1992 Senators Moynihan, Paul Simon (D-IL) and Jesse Helms (R-SC) accused the administration of timidity. "This President is too comfortable dealing with dictators," Simon stated. "We seem to have forgotten how to stand up for human rights."[44]

Pressure for stronger action also grew from the public. Many letters arrived at the White House urging the administration to take action. Newspapers and magazines published stories about the horrific conditions in Burma; editorials urged action. Michele Bohana, a well-known human rights activist on Burma, compared the situation there to the Cambodian killing fields. She urged breaking diplomatic relations, a worldwide arms embargo, banning all American trade with Burma, and exposing SLORC's involvement in the heroin trade. Morton Abramowitz (president of the Carnegie Endowment for International Peace), Richard Holbrooke (managing director of Lehman Brothers in New York and a former diplomat), and Peter Tarnoff (president of the Council on Foreign Relations) characterized Burma's government as "among the worst in the world," and urged the United States to take strong action at the United Nations. Thant Myint-U, the grandson of U Thant, urged sanctions, an arms embargo, and stronger UN action. Former ambassador Burton Levin spoke out against any investments in Burma. "Anything than brings investment into the country is just siphoned off to buttress the regime," he told the *Wall Street Journal*.[45]

The Bush administration's response to the new waves of criticism was to contribute generously to help the unfortunate Rohingya people in Arakan (Rakhine) State, a Muslim group not recognized by the government as an official minority, then being subjected to a brutal military offensive which ultimately drove over 200,000 Rohingyas out of Arakan.

The Rohingyas

Because the Rohingyas remain today a matter of great concern, it is worth digressing here to say something about their history. There have been Muslims in Burma since the ninth century. They were particularly significant in the Kingdom of Arakan, which Burma conquered in 1785. When the British took over Burma in the nineteenth century and administered it as a part of British India, more Muslims from Bengal emigrated to Arakan, particularly after 1870, and were integrated into the local Muslim (or Rohingya) population. Generally speaking they lived peacefully with the Buddhist Burmese; but Muslim expansion to southern Arakan displaced Buddhist villages, and there was some animosity and violence. In the 1930s there were anti-Indian and anti-Muslim riots. By the start of World War II, perhaps 215,000 of the 700,000 people in Arakan were Muslims, most of whom lived in the north, regarded themselves as Burmese citizens, and had little interest in maintaining any ties with India. Burmese Buddhists seldom distinguished between Burmese and Indian Muslims, however, and this put the Rohingyas, many of whom had lived there for generations, "in a most difficult strait."[46]

During the Japanese occupation of Arakan in World War II there was cruel violence against the Muslims, particularly against those who lived in the southern part of Arakan, who fled to northern Arakan or to Bengal. The Muslims then retaliated against the Buddhists who lived in northern Arakan and drove them out, so that Arakan became divided between a Muslim north and a Buddhist south. Most Muslims supported the British and hoped that Britain would grant them independence after the war. With Burma's independence, however, the situation of the Rohingyas deteriorated as Buddhist officials replaced Muslim ones. The result was an armed rebellion, not so dissimilar from those of the other ethnic minorities, against the central government, that ended in 1961.

U Nu, having just been reelected after Ne Win's interim administration, promised that Arakan would become a state within the Union of Burma. Some Muslims insisted on having an autonomous area outside of the new state, while others, particularly in Akyab (now Sittwe), only wanted guarantees that protected them in Arakan and gave them political representation. As a result of consultations, much progress was made in resolving this complicated issue, but Ne Win's coup in 1962 ended any discussion of autonomy for minority groups. Muslim rebel activity then resumed, though at a low level. In 1974 a new constitution made Arakan a state within the Union of Burma, but this did not enhance minority rights. As David Steinberg wrote, the new constitution "effectively codified the dominance of the Burman majority throughout all organs of state power, and the effects of this shift can only exacerbate the tensions that have been built up between the Burmans and the minorities."[47]

In 1962 Burmese citizens received identity cards, but the Rohingyas were offered only Foreigner Registration Cards, which they refused to accept. As a result they were not only not considered citizens but had no legal status at all. The few Rohingyas who had received National Registration Cards (issued to citizens) were forced to return them in 1977. The following year Burmese forces drove tens of thousands of Rohingyas into Bangladesh, where they lived in refugee camps where some died in the unhealthy conditions. The following year many were allowed to return to Burma but often not to their original villages, which had been taken over by Buddhist Burmese. No services were provided for them, and following their return, in 1982 the Burmese government enacted an immigration statute that made the Rohingyas "de facto foreigners," which greatly angered them, especially those who had lived in Burma for generations. To this day the Burmans generally refer to the Rohingyas as "Bengalis" and deny the existence of a separate Rohingya ethnic group.

Muslims participated in the revolutionary events of 1988, and in 1989 SLORC began to drive them out by settling Buddhists in Muslim areas. The army also arrested many, burned mosques, and engaged in acts of violence and terror against the Rohingyas. In 1991 the government began a more widespread movement against them, creating a new wave of refugees; something over 200,000 people fled to Bangladesh. The United Nations condemned SLORC's actions. Over the next few years some refugees returned to Burma, though under difficult circumstances. In 2002 the Israeli diplomat and scholar Moshe Yegar wrote that the Rohingya issue would continue and that "new crises will break out periodically. . . . There is no reason to suppose that there will be a change in the situation of the Muslim population in Arakan."[48] Unfortunately his prediction has turned out to be correct, as there has been significant anti-Rohingya and anti-Muslim violence since then. In Arakan (now Rakine State) there was very serious anti-Rohingya violence in 2012 and again in 2014 and 2015.

The Debate over Sanctions

While the Bush administration deplored SLORC's actions and provided humanitarian assistance to Rohingyas, it continued to resist calls for strong political or economic sanctions. As the *New Republic* later put it, "under President Bush, the U.S. Embassy in Rangoon condemned SLORC atrocities, but Bush himself did little to counteract them."[49]

On the other hand international criticism may have had some momentary effect on Burma after Saw Maung retired unexpectedly on 23 April 1992. General Than Shwe replaced him, and the government then freed a few prisoners, including U Nu, and allowed Aung San Suu Kyi's family to visit her. There was, as the *Christian Science Monitor* put it, "A Glimmer in Burma."[50] Later in the year Burma reopened the universities, ended a curfew, released more prisoners, relaxed restrictions on foreigners and journalists, made some economic reforms, and promised a constitutional convention for January 1993. There were no indications that SLORC was about to transfer power to the victors of the election of 1990, however, and in December 1992 the United Nations approved a strongly worded condemnation of Burma's refusal to release Aung San Suu Kyi and transfer power.

Whether the new Bill Clinton administration would make any changes in American policy toward Burma was uncertain. Clinton's campaign had been mostly about domestic issues, and the new secretary of state designate, Warren Christopher, had a reputation for discreet, cautious diplomacy. At his confirmation hearing before the Senate Foreign Relations Committee, foreign policy challenges in China, Eastern Europe, and the Balkans occupied his attention. When he did get to Asia (outside of China), Burma was far from first on his list. The new administration would encourage free elections and promote human rights there, he said.

A month after Christopher's testimony, five Nobel Peace Prize laureates, including Desmond Tutu, went to Thailand, where they met with Burmese refugees on the border and demanded the unconditional release of their fellow laureate Aung San Suu Kyi. The Peace Prize winners' travels to Burma's border did not move the Clinton administration to action. Initially, it was as cautious as its predecessor. "Burma's horrors seem to have moved this administration no more than the last," wrote Susan Blaustein in April 1993. One frustrated administration official told her that the United States had "no Burma policy. . . . We're drifting." Much like the Bush administration, the Clinton administration countered that it had to balance pressure on Burma with incentives to bring about change. It also had to take into account the views of Burma's neighbors, including Thailand, which did not support aggressive sanctions. If there was going to be a more forceful American response, it would have to come from Congress. As Catherine Dalpino, then Deputy Assistant Secretary of State for Democracy, recalled, "Congress owned the issue."[51]

In May 1993 Congress urged the president and other US officials to "seek the immediate release of Daw Aung San Suu Kyi from arrest and then transfer power to the winners of the 1990 elections in Burma." The resolution also urged the adoption of a UN arms embargo and the enactment of sanctions against Burma.[52] Perhaps in response, Clinton ordered the State Department to conduct an interagency review of US Burma policy. The review stalled, however, and by late summer 1993 the Clinton administration had begun to speak out more strongly in favor of democracy in Burma; it also reassessed cooperation on narcotics that the Bush administration had quietly reinstated. By late in the year the administration had determined to go against the views of many Asian countries, and co-sponsored a UN resolution calling for a special envoy to be appointed to Burma and also for limiting UN work in the country. By resisting pressures to water down the UN resolution, the *New York Times* editorialized, "the Clinton Administration honors American and United Nations principles."[53]

The Burmese government claimed that it paid no attention to criticism, but in fact it did. In recent months it had made some gestures of reform, and on 1 February 1993 it hired former Democratic congressman Lester Wolff to burnish its credentials in the United States. Wolff, who was reportedly paid $10,000 per month, sponsored trips to Burma for Congressional representatives such as Bill Archer (R-TX) and Nancy Johnson (R-CT)), who returned and defended the SLORC in Congress.[54]

In its most significant response to outside pressure, in February 1994 the SLORC allowed Representative Bill Richardson (D-NM), along with a UN representative, an American diplomat, and a *New York Times* reporter to visit Aung San Suu Kyi. "The Junta Blinks," wrote the *Far Eastern Economic Review*. It was a remarkable occasion, one that made the front page of the *Times*—the first delegation of foreigners allowed to speak with Suu Kyi since her arrest. Richardson said that he thought the Clinton administration's policies lay behind SLORC's decision to allow the meeting. Suu Kyi appreciated Clinton's repeated calls for her release, but in an implicit criticism of American timidity she commented that "she hoped to see a 'more clear-cut policy in favor of the movement for democracy'"; she hinted that economic sanctions would be appropriate. Without sanctions in place, major American firms continued to do business in Burma.[55]

Richardson came away cautiously optimistic that a dialogue might now take place between the military and Aung San Suu Kyi. Burma watcher Michele Bohana, however, suspicious of SLORC and not optimistic, commented dismissively that "they're certainly not doing this because they had a religious epiphany," and noted that the very day after Richardson left Rangoon, the SLORC extended Suu Kyi's house arrest for an additional six months.[56]

The skeptics were right. As the chairman of the House Subcommitteee on Asia and the Pacific put it, "alas, our hopes that these developments represented something more than mere cosmetic changes seem to have been illusory."[57] In March 1994 the junta ruled out early talks with Suu Kyi. Khin Nyunt commented that she lacked legitimacy: she was married to a foreigner and had spent nearly three decades abroad.

More US Pressure—But Not Sanctions

The Clinton administration responded angrily to Khin Nyunt's remarks, and suggested that it might now expand the limited existing sanctions. At the very least, one official commented, referring to the long-delayed interagency review of American policy, the remarks would affect the ongoing policy deliberations in negative ways.[58] Indeed, only four days later the administration decided to take a tougher stance on Burma, specifically in response to Khin Nyunt's refusal to open talks with Suu Kyi. After some hesitation, sending a new ambassador was ruled out, while pushing for an international arms embargo was now under serious consideration. In addition, Clinton wanted a UN special envoy for Burma appointed. Suu Kyi's husband Michael Aris, Bill Richardson, and Madeleine Albright (then the US representative to the UN) also wanted a special envoy appointed. Secretary General Boutros Boutros-Ghali responded by sending Under

Secretary General Rafeeuddin Ahmed to an upcoming meeting of the Association of Southeast Asian Nations (ASEAN), where he could meet discreetly with the Burmese representative. After that Boutros-Ghali would decide if he could appoint a special envoy for Burma. Perhaps there was still some hope for stronger action after all.

As far as the United States was concerned, Burma had a limited amount of time to decide to engage with the opposition. If it did not, the United States would adopt tougher measures, even if it resulted in tensions with its ASEAN friends. John Finney, director of the State Department's Office of Thai and Burmese Affairs, was designated to go to Rangoon and inform SLORC of the new American position. Those in the Congress who had long urged a stronger stance applauded the new initiative. "It's heartening that they're going to get tough," said one important staffer, "although I can't see why it took them so long."[59]

Little change was apparent in Burma by the summer, however, and at the end of June the House subcommittee held hearings to consider a resolution urging the Burmese government to release Aung San Suu Kyi, transfer power to the opposition, and end its human rights abuses. It also called on the US government to apply pressure in various ways. It did not specifically call for a general trade embargo or prohibition on investments in Burma, but it urged making the American arms embargo an international one.[60] The hearing was really the result of frustration at the lack of change in Burma and the apparent lack of direction in American policy, or even the existence of a coherent policy.

Among the questions was whether there was any prospect of significant change over time. Bill Richardson, freshly back from his visit with Suu Kyi, still held out hope that the government's recent policy modifications might signal real change. He believed that Khin Nyunt wanted to move forward but was held back by more conservative junta members. As for the American response, he wanted the administration to clearly define its Burma policy and soon, since Aung San Suu Kyi was about to complete five years' detention under house arrest. He suggested that American policy ought to be tougher. He hoped for international sanctions, but if that proved impossible he would accept unilateral sanctions. He warned American companies that if they did not voluntarily refrain from doing business in Burma they would face a trade embargo. He also thought that it was better to have an ambassador in Rangoon who could hammer away on human rights issues more effectively than a lower-level officer, though this was admittedly a close call.

The State Department was represented at the hearing by two officials: Thomas C. Hubbard, deputy assistant secretary of state for East Asian and Pacific affairs, and Catharin Dalpino, the deputy assistant secretary of state for democracy. Hubbard announced a change in the administration's attitude toward narcotics control: no longer would cooperation on narcotics trump human rights and democracy concerns. This was an important shift in emphasis from the that of the previous administration which had tacitly put antinarcotics interests first.[61] In contrast to Richardson, Hubbard saw little in SLORC's policies to indicate that there had been any "fundamental change in the government's repressive rule." Also the administration had decided not to appoint a new ambassador to Burma. "Such an appointment must be evaluated with great caution, lest it be taken by the SLORC as a sign of U.S. approval," stated Hubbard. This seemed to presage a tougher policy, but the long-expected policy review was still underway—much to the frustration of some Congressional leaders. Hubbard concluded with a strong reaffirmation of the administration's intent to support democratic forces in Burma, including its "unflagging support for Aung San Suu Kyi and other political prisoners."[62]

Burma united Democrats and Republicans, particularly when it came to human rights and the detention of Aung San Suu Kyi and other dissidents. Similarly, while there was divided opinion on whether to impose strong sanctions, the division was by no means partisan. Dana Rohrabacher (R-CA) was the most outspoken supporter of sanctions on the subcommittee. Rohrabacher argued against engagement, asserting that this only empowered the regime and would never change's SLORC's character. To think otherwise, he stated, was "absolute nonsense." One did not engage constructively with despots. Mike Jendrzejczyk, director of Asia Watch's Washington office, generally agreed, though his view was more nuanced. He did want the United States to oppose "new or expanded investments by private U.S. companies in Burma" and urge other countries to do likewise.[63]

The administration was still not interested in unilateral sanctions, however, nor was it about to advise American firms not to invest. It found some support for this position on the committee. Matthew G. Martinez (D-CA) thought sanctions were ineffective and pointed to Cuba as the best example of this (for which Rohrabacher questioned his patriotism). None of Burma's neighbors was much interested in sanctions, so it was difficult to see how they would be very effective. Also opposed to sanctions, though from an entirely different perspective, was Miriam Marshall Segal, chairperson of Peregrine Capital Myanmar Limited, an investment banking firm that had secured fishing rights in Burma, ironically in 1990. Segal was an outspoken defender of the regime, perhaps even more than that, and strongly objected to actions that might inconvenience it.

Although Segal was hardly persuasive, the issue of sanctions had a good airing. However, the passage of resolutions in both the House and the Senate condemning Burma's human rights violations and calling attention to Aung San Suu Kyi's continuing detention indicated growing impatience. If nothing changed and if

SLORC continued to restrict Aung San Suu Kyi, some form of sanctions was likely to pass the Congress.

In November 1994 Burma received a high-level American delegation, led by Thomas Hubbard, the highest-ranking American to visit Burma since 8888. Before Hubbard's arrival the top-level SLORC figures, General Than Shwe and Khin Nyunt, had twice spoken with Aung San Suu Kyi, their first meetings in six years. The Hubbard visit resulted in Burma's agreement to allow the United States to conduct an opium survey and the International Committee of the Red Cross to visit political prisoners in jail. But the American visitors were not allowed to see Suu Kyi, and there was no progress on human rights and democracy.

Nevertheless, the Clinton administration concluded that the regime's moves, including agreeing to meet with Hubbard, amounted to something more than just window dressing and approved engagement. There were few political results, although Burma continued to privatize significant parts of its economy and invited foreign firms to invest. In February 1995 there were 110 American firms with Burma connections, the largest investors being oil company Unocal (now Chevron) and Pepsico. Burma was growing economically (at about 6 percent annually), and new building projects, including hotels and shopping centers were sprouting up.[64]

As money became to pour into Burma, the generals became cocky. "They said, 'Screw you. We don't need you. If you drop your investments we'll get them from someone else," Richardson said. Senator John McCain (R-AZ)), who visited Burma in April 1995 and met with Khin Nyunt, found the atmosphere frightening and could not wait to get out. "They are very bad people," he commented.[65] There was a growing sense in Washington that the administration was entirely too timid; the world's only superpower should lead on this issue, the critics thought. In September the administration did increase its interest in Burma when UN representative Madeleine Albright visited Yangon and criticized the junta in a press conference without bothering about "diplomatic niceties." She was very tough on the junta and expressed great admiration for Suu Kyi.[66] Some of the American diplomats "looked pained." The "highest ranking member of our embassy" (presumably chargé d'affaires ad interim Marilyn Meyers) told her resentfully, "now we will have to clear up the mess you have left." Albright was unapologetic.[67]

Some important American firms had already withdrawn from Burma: Levi Strauss in 1992, Liz Claiborne in October 1994, Eddie Bauer in February 1995. And there was now new energy in the Congress to craft restrictions on American connections with Burma. Mitch McConnell (R-KY) who visited Burma in May 1995 and, after listening to what he considered to be lies from SLORC reportedly asked to be photographed wearing an NLD hat, was the sanctions leader.

He subsequently stated that "constructive engagement" had failed in Burma and determined to introduce legislation requiring economic sanctions.[68] On 1 June sixty-one members of Congress wrote to Clinton urging him to discourage new investments in Burma.

SLORC responded with some political gestures in 1995, including in March the release of U Tin Oo, a former army chief and leader of the NLD, after six years in Insein Prison. At the same time it released U Kyi Maung, who had succeeded Aung San Suu Kyi as NLD leader following her detention. The most spectacular concession, however, was the release of Aung San Suu Kyi herself on 10 July 1995 after six years of house arrest. The release was front-page news in newspapers around the world. Nicholas Burns gave the official American response: "We welcome very, very much the announcement," he stated, while noting cautiously that the United States was still concerned about the general human rights situation in the country. Aung San Suu Kyi's release was good news, the *New York Times* editorialized, but "it is too soon to welcome Yangon back into the democratic community."[69]

Threats of American sanctions may have contributed to the junta's decision to free Suu Kyi. Just days before she was released Senator McConnell put forward the "Free Burma Act of 1995" which ended all US assistance and investment and banned Burmese imports, among other provisions. On 21 September the sanctions passed as part of the foreign aid bill with an overwhelming bipartisan majority 91to 9. Still, no sanctions legislation became law at this time. McConnell himself ultimately withdrew his legislation, apparently because it complicated the larger foreign aid bill, but he seemed determined to find another vehicle to pass it, and he did succeed in getting the so-called "Burma earmark" inserted into foreign assistance legislation in 1995. For two years both the House and the Senate had directed USAID "to provide meaningful assistance to refugees and exiles supporting a restoration of democracy in Burma," but the agency had ignored this. The new earmark provided $2 million "to support the restoration of democracy and free market activities in Burma." The funds could assist "Burmese students and groups both inside and outside Burma," and the State Department and USAID had until 15 December 1995 to draft a plan for spending the funds. The following year the legislation provided $2.5 million, and similar earmarks were included for the next several year. The State Department programmed the funds through the National Endowment for Democracy to support its work on Burma issues.[70]

The sanctions issue did not disappear. For one thing the Burma junta members rarely talked with Aung San Suu Kyi. "I've been released, that's all," she said; ". . . the situation hasn't changed."[71] Early in December a House subcommittee introduced a resolution calling on Burma's government to enter into a dialogue with Suu Kyi, release all political prisoners, and control the narcotics trade. And at the end of the year McConnell and others introduced Senate Bill 1511, "The Burma Freedom and Democracy Act of 1995," which ended American investment in Burma and gave the president authority to prohibit Burmese imports. It even banned most travel to Burma by American citizens (perhaps a response to Burma's "Visit Myanmar Year" in 1996), and it urged the president to keep diplomatic relations at a low level.

Matters drifted until May 1996 when the SLORC arrested 46 NLD members to prevent them from attending a parliamentary conference that Aung San Suu Kyi had called for 26 May. (By the time of the conference 250 persons had been detained, including most of the delegates. Later the junta accused the US embassy of collaborating with the NLD to organize the occasion.) This led McConnell to testify before the Senate Banking Committee that Burma was "now in free fall"; he urged the imposition of sanctions. Sanctions were in the interest of the United States, as well as those of ordinary Burmese. He cited the report of Dr. Yozo Yokota, the UN's special envoy on Burmese affairs. It was a "catalogue of crimes. . . . Rape, detentions, killings, forced labor, relocations are just a few of the tools" that the SLORC used routinely to retain power. And private American investment was helping the regime.[72]

Deputy Assistant Secretary of State Kent Wiedeman agreed that the SLORC retained "its iron grip on the country and rules by fear." Wiedeman's language was strong, but the administration was unwilling to endorse Senate Bill 1511 because it was too inflexible. The administration was willing to discuss discretionary sanctions but it disliked having its hands tied. For her part, Aung San Suu Kyi was clear about foreign investors: they should "jolly well wait" until a democratic government was installed."[73]

At almost exactly the same time Roger Truitt, president of the Atlantic-Richfield oil company, was in Rangoon signing a contract for exploration, and the signing was featured in the government newspaper, *The New Light of Myanmar*. SLORC intended this as a rebuke to the NLD conference, as well as to the United States. It was actions like this, however, with oilmen dining with the junta leaders and signing contracts, that enraged prodemocracy advocates. Such brazen displays of defiance ultimately improved the chances of sanctions being enacted and weakened the administration's resistance. In September, Massachusetts passed a bill making firms that did business in Burma ineligible to do business in the state (though this was later overturned in court). The pressure to do something was increasing.

The same month Senators William Cohen (R-ME) and Dianne Feinstein (D-CA) introduced an amendment to the McConnell bill that included some sanctions but left implementation of the strongest sanctions up to the president.

It reflected the views of the business lobby and provided an alternative to the original Bill 1511.[74]

Moving Toward Sanctions

The Clinton administration was divided on the sanctions issue. Those who focused on human rights were inclined to support them. "If we weren't prepared to stand up and speak very very strongly, then nobody would," recalled Eric P. Schwartz, special assistant to the president for multilateral and humanitarian affairs. There was no likelihood that the administration would support the McConnell bill, but its introduction enabled Schwartz to recruit support within the administration for the Cohen-Feinstein amendment as an alternative. While not as strong or automatic as McConnell's proposal, it offered the prospect of real sanctions; it was a foot in the door.[75] Congress approved the amendment, and it was passed as part of the Omnibus Consolidated Appropriation Act. It ended any nonhumanitarian assistance to Burma, banned entry of Burma's leaders into the United States, and instructed American delegates to international financial institutions to oppose assistance to Burma. The president was also authorized to block future American investments if repression in Burma worsened. The bill was passed on 30 September, and on 3 October President Clinton issued Presidential Proclamation 6925 that banned Burmese leaders indefinitely from entering the United States. "The regime has failed to enter into serious dialogue with the democratic opposition," Clinton stated. Madeleine Albright commented that "those who are directly responsible for the repression of the Burmese people must begin to understand that their actions have consequences for them personally."[76] Clinton's action was more symbolic than anything else, but it did represent a move toward stronger sanctions, the first since 1991.

Soon there was much debate about whether Clinton must apply deeper sanctions, since the law required that they be implemented if Burma's democratic opposition was subjected to "large scale repression." Whether such sanctions were required or not, there was concern within the administration that failure to invoke them would only encourage the junta. As one administration source defined the dilemma, "the law is designed as a deterrent, so ideally we don't want to use it. But if it is to be credible, we have to be willing to use it."[77]

The actions of Congress and the Clinton administration were important, but perhaps of more concern to the junta was that because of the its crackdown, ASEAN foreign ministers did not endorse the plan to give Burma full membership in the organization in 1997. The rejection, coming only two months after ASEAN had given Burma observer status, was galling. Given its isolated position, the junta had become increasingly dependent on China, the only country that could actually do serious harm to Burma if it chose to. Without full membership in ASEAN, this dependence would continue.[78]

In November a mob attacked Aung San Suu Kyi's supporters in Rangoon, apparently attempting to disrupt her weekly address to them. One person struck Suu Kyi's car with a knife. She charged government instigation, and the State Department expressed outrage. It was almost as if the Burmese government was deliberately attempting to bring on additional American sanctions. "Burma is a human rights disaster that demands a further response," said human rights activist Mike Jendrzejczyk. Five senators wrote to Clinton, who was about to leave for the Philippines to attend the Asia Pacific Economic Cooperation forum and make a state visit to Thailand, urging him to ban new investments in Myanmar. The signers spanned the political spectrum, from Jesse Helms to Patrick Leahy (D-VT). "It would be an enormous step forward if, before your departure for Southeast Asia, the administration were to announce the administration's decision to impose a ban on new US investment in Burma," they wrote.[79] Clinton did not immediately impose additional sanctions, but in Asia he spoke movingly about democracy and aligned the United States with Aung San Suu Kyi.

Even as the United States was moving toward stronger sanctions, one American company was expanding its connections with Burma. Pepsico had recently pulled out of the country, but Unocal signed an agreement to expand considerably its rights to explore for offshore gas fields. Unocal paid the Burmese government several million dollars at the signing. The agreement was signed the same day that the State Department issued its annual human rights report on Burma, which detailed the many violations taking place.

Unocal's action highlighted the debate that was still going on in the Clinton administration and beyond. Some in Congress were almost apoplectic, a spokesman for Jesse Helms stating, "it's simply mind-boggling. . . . Does she [Aung San Suu Kyi] have to be assassinated before they will impose sanctions?" In the administration Bill Richardson, who had replaced Madeleine Albright as UN representative, believed that sanctions should now be implemented, that the conditions of the Cohen-Feinstein amendment had been met. Cohen himself, now Clinton's secretary of defense, favored continued diplomatic pressure. The competing positions circled around two major considerations: whether the sanctions would have any impact, with European or Asian companies simply rushing in as American companies left; and the rationale for cracking down on Burma when there were other countries with equally questionable human rights records, like China. The argument for not imposing serious sanctions on China boiled down to the obvious points that that country was much more important than Burma and that the American relationship with China was complex. With relatively few interests in Burma, the United States was free to allow its human rights concerns to take precedence. In the end, Clinton's most senior advisers did not reach consensus, and a memo prepared for the president reflected a split recommendation about whether to impose sanctions.[80]

It was now up to President Clinton. Perhaps influenced by his new national security adviser, Sandy Berger,[81] on 20 May 1997 he decided to approve new sanctions, in particular a ban on new investment. Existing contracts were not affected. There was some speculation that Clinton acted when he did because McConnell and Moynihan were about to introduce a bill that was more restrictive and would have had an impact on Unocal's current investments. When the sanctions went into effect, however, Unocal announced that it would no longer explore the potential gas fields.[82]

The reaction in much of Asia was defensive. Indeed, ASEAN defied the United States the next month by allowing Burma to join the organization after all—this due to Malaysian Prime Minister Mohammed Mahathir's wish to have all Southeast Asian countries in the organization for its thirtieth anniversary celebration, as well as his desire to express his pique at the United States and his conspiratorial view that George Soros's involvement with currency manipulations had brought on the region's economic collapse. All the same, the American position carried considerable symbolic significance. The dissidents had not forgotten that the American embassy had been a focal point for demonstrators during the revolution of 1988. Zarni, a Burmese graduate student at the University of Wisconsin who in 1995 founded the Free Burma Coalition, an umbrella organization for groups working for change in Burma, wrote to Secretary of State Albright expressing his deep gratitude and inviting her to come to Los Angeles ("the home of Unocal and Arco") to give the keynote address to a Burma conference. He also sent her a framed photo of Aung San Suu Kyi.[83]

That Clinton decided to approve sanctions was also a sign of the growing power of the newly arisen internet, a vital factor in publicizing what was going on in Burma and organizing citizen involvement. It was much easier now to get information about the country: freeburma.org had it all available. "Cyberspace spawned the movement to restore human rights in Burma," said Mike Jendrzejczyk of Human Rights Watch. "The proliferation of information has put Burma higher on the U.S. policy agenda than it ever would have been otherwise." Central to the internet effort was Zarni, who spent fifteen hours each day at his computer running the Free Burma Coalition website, putting out information and calls for action. Over a hundred campuses had Free Burma clubs, and there was pressure for Boards of Trustees to divest their stock holdings of companies that did business in Burma. Shortly before Clinton's sanctions decision the regents of Zarni's own University of Wisconsin announced that they had sold their shares in Texaco which had a stake in an off short natural gas project.[84] One can make a good case, in fact, that the internet, more than any other single factor, produced the sanctions.

A "quiet coup" in November 1997 brought to power younger, apparently more cosmopolitan military leaders, headed by military intelligence chief Kyin Nyunt, though Senior General and Prime Minister Than Shwe remained in control at the top. For a time there appeared to be more openness to the outside world, and some hope that there would be some meaningful political changes in Burma. The regime changed its name from SLORC to the more neutral-sounding SPDC (State Peace and Development Council). But the changes were fleeting. Within a few months the harder-line elements had regained at least a measure of influence. In April 1998 the junta refused to give Richardson a visa, retaliating for American sanctions against the Burmese leadership, and later in the year the regime arrested scores of NLD members. None of this boded well for improved relations between the junta and the United States. Furthermore, a new high-level champion of Aung San Suu Kyi had emerged: Madeleine Albright, Clinton's secretary of state as of January 1997. Albright had met Aung San Suu Kyi in 1995 and considered her one of her heroes. As Priscilla Clapp, chargé d'affaires in Rangoon from 1999 to 2002, recalled, Albright "took a personal interest in her fortunes and was extremely outspoken in public against the military."[85]

The Burmese reacted negatively to Albright. A writer in the official newspaper, *New Light of Myanmar*, referred to her as "that old lady," as well as describing White House official Tom Malinowski as a "Polish-American half-caste" who thought he was "a great Myanmar expert." Malinowski, the writer thought, was much too influenced by his Burmese wife, a corrupt "mud-plugged cow." Such comments amply support Steinberg's comment about the Burmese regime's extreme xenophobia—"among the world's most vitriolic."[86]

In any event, behind the scenes (and working with diplomats from other countries) American diplomats in Yangon saw it as one of their responsibilities to try and get communication going between Suu Kyi and the junta. However, efforts to encourage dialogue ran afoul of the government's determination to impose restrictions on Suu Kyi's movements. On at least four occasions from 1998 to 2000 military authorities prevented her from traveling. Once in 1998 she spent thirteen days in her small white Toyota when soldiers prevented her from proceeding to meet her supporters in Bassein. Her efforts to take the train to Mandalay were thwarted on at least two occasions, and in August 2000 military authorities again stopped her car in a town close to Rangoon and refused to allow her to proceed. This led to international criticism. The United States officially condemned interference with her "right to freedom of movement and her right to visit whomever she chooses."[87]

No more sanctions were enacted during Clinton's final years as president, but the position of the American government was made clear. In 1999 and 2000 the administration refused to allow Myanmar's foreign minister to come to the United States to attend academic forums,[88] and on 6 December 2000, President Clinton awarded the Presidential Medal of Freedom to Aung San Suu Kyi in absentia.

THE THAW

Burma was not the only Southeast Asian country subjected to American sanctions. The Eisenhower administration restricted trade with North Vietnam in 1954, and sanctions on that country, including a very strict trade embargo, were not lifted until 1994. Cambodia was subjected to similar measures, also including a trade embargo, beginning in 1975 when the Khmer Rouge took over, and ending only in 1992. As with Burma, human rights violations accounted in part for these measures, particularly in the Khmer Rouge case, and in addition, Congress often pushed for the sanctions. Critics of all these sanctions used similar arguments: they were ineffective and hurt ordinary people; it would be better for the United States to be involved in these countries rather to isolate them. However, each situation was different. The moves against Burma had nothing to do with anticommunist sentiments, whereas those against Vietnam and Cambodia were heavily influenced by such feelings, particularly directed against the Soviet Union. Furthermore, no one in the other sanctioned countries had anything like the appeal and influence of Aung San Suu Kyi.

Under the George W. Bush administration, sanctions were expanded, but there was increasing frustration that, however justified they were, they were not achieving their objective of regime change. The NLD was no nearer to taking office in 2008 than it was in 1990, when the junta disregarded the results of the election, and for most of that time Aung San Suu Kyi remained under house arrest. Then, after a policy review, the Barack Obama administration decided to change course. Instead of regime change, it would work toward regime modification.

This proved to be more successful: eventually there were remarkable changes in Burma, to which American policy contributed.

George W. Bush Ignores Burma

In 2000, for the first time in nearly five years, the Myanmar regime agreed meet with Suu Kyi; in January 2001 she met with intelligence chief Khin Nyunt himself. Many observers believed that the pressure of sanctions and international criticism led to this development, although there were undoubtedly internal factors that figured in as well. Some military officials, for example, perhaps including Khin Nyunt, understood the need for reform. United Nations representative Razali Ismail called the talks "extremely significant" and dismissed arguments that they were only a military publicity stunt.[1] Still, whether the military would negotiate seriously, particularly if this involved giving up power, seemed unlikely.

By May 2001 the talks were on the brink of failure, and some suggested more American pressure, but the new George W. Bush administration was not listening. It had "almost no interest in what was going on there," recalled Priscilla Clapp, the American chargé in Rangoon.[2] No one high in the new administration shared Madeleine Albright's passion about Burmese affairs.

To be sure, more important developments concerned the administration, notably the 9/11 attacks.[3] However, pressure was growing to take action against the junta. Senators Tom Harkin (D-IA), Jesse Helms, and Mitch McConnell, for example, urged action against Burma. And journalist Joshua Kurlantzick asked in an important article, "Why Isn't Burma on Bush's 'Axis of Evil' List?" The generals had recently decided to build a nuclear reactor, he noted, and had been accused of amassing chemical weapons. They "would do virtually anything, including . . . producing fissile materials, to remain in power." Kurlantzick was probably mistaken about Burma's nuclear ambitions; in addition he wrongly asserted that "Burma has always been a lefty cause" and that Republicans had opposed Clinton's sanctions because of their support of the oil lobby. With the likes of conservatives Jesse Helms and particularly Mitch McConnell in the forefront of the sanctions debate, this was unfair. Still, his article was one of a growing number to call for more attention to Burma.[4]

Perhaps in response to growing international condemnation, the junta invited Razali Ismail to return, and talks resumed. There was much hope that they would finally succeed. Ismail himself stated that he expected a breakthrough soon, which might include the release of political prisoners. On 6 May 2002

Aung San Suu Kyi was again freed from house arrest (after nineteen months), and allowed to resume her political activities. Professor Josef Silverstein, a leading Burma expert, commented that if Suu Kyi was allowed true freedom, this would be "a monumental change." The State Department applauded the move but insisted that Aung San Suu Kyi "be afforded full freedom of movement and association." A euphoric Suu Kyi appeared on the front page of the *New York Times* (and other newspapers) and spoke of "a new dawn for the country." David I. Steinberg thought that the twelve-year-old stalemate in Burma "seems now to be in the process of breaking, and that's progress." A new day appeared to be at hand; perhaps the international sanctions had helped.[5]

The government allowed Suu Kyi to travel freely to Mandalay and elsewhere, and over the next several months she opened over sixty-five NLD offices, while more than 350 NLD members were released from prison and the small NLD headquarters in Yangon provided health screenings and free lunches for indigent mothers and their children. Hundreds of political prisoners remained behind bars, however, such as the student leader Paw U Thun, known as Min Ko Naing, who had been imprisoned since 1988, much of the time in solitary confinement. Or U Hla Min, a sixty-three-year-old activist imprisoned in 1996 for distributing cassettes of a friend's political music. Would they too be released? "Keep the champagne on ice and the sanctions on the table," said Senator McConnell.[6]

In November 2002 the junta leaders spoke with Ismail for only fifteen minutes. "The meeting was hardly long enough to sit down and pick up a cup of tea," commented Silverstein. The United States government found creditable reports by several NGOs that the Burmese military had raped hundreds of women and girls in Shan State,[7] though there was disagreement as to whether this was the result of military policy. Doubts about the junta's intentions grew.

For the moment, Aung San Suu Kyi continued to travel freely. Early in 2003 she spoke to twenty-five thousand people in Arakan State, standing on a fire engine that had been sent to intimidate the crowd. She expressed her views in popular American publications, such as *Parade* magazine, where she appeared on the cover. However, she was not convinced that the military was actually interested in a democratic transition, and she urged Western countries to keep their sanctions in place. Activists began once again to insist that investment firms that held stock in companies that did business in Burma divest. A leading financial institution, TIAA-CREF (Teachers Insurance and Annuity Association–College Retirement Equities Fund), for example, was urged to dump its shares of Unocal.[8] But what really spurred the Bush administration and the Congress to action was the junta's brutal crackdown on Suu Kyi and the NLD at the end of May 2003.

The Depayin Incident and Bush's Engagement

Worried about the large number of Burmese who flocked to hear Suu Kyi, and perhaps concerned at possible NLD links with the ethnic minorities, the military determined to regain control. On 30 May 2003, as Suu Kyi and her party were approaching the town of Depayin near Mandalay, a group of perhaps five thousand soldiers and convicts released for the task attacked their motorcade. Initial reports were that four or five persons died (although it was much higher), and many others, including NLD vice chairman U Tin Oo, were wounded. A report on the incident by the ASEAN interparliamentary group concluded that it was "essentially an assassination attempt on Aung San Suu Kyi and members of the NLD." Aung San Suu Kyi's car was "riddled with bullets." Though not seriously injured, she was arrested and held in "protective custody" in an undisclosed location, later determined to be the Yemon military camp near Yangon. Whether it was really an assassination attempt is a question. It does seem doubtful that the military would have wanted to make Suu Kyi a martyr. Nonetheless it was a very violent incident. Radio Free Asia reported that up to 282 persons died in Depayin that night (although it was probably fewer—the station now claims "at least 70" deaths). "The Depayin Massacre and the ensuing crackdown have been the most ruthless and bloodiest attack on the democracy movement in Burma since the 1988 crackdown," concluded the ASEAN interparliamentary report.[9] The junta then closed all NLD offices, cut phone lines to Suu Kyi's house, and again closed the universities.

Depayin resulted in immediate condemnation in much of the world. The US government was reportedly "mad as hell and isn't going to put up with the outrages perpetuated by Burma's military rulers any more." Secretary of State Colin Powell denounced the "contemptible" actions and demanded Aung San Suu Kyi's release.[10] Most important of all, however, Senator McConnell introduced the Burmese Freedom and Democracy Act, co-sponsored by senators across the political spectrum from Edward Kennedy (D-MA) to Sam Brownback (R-KS). The bill ended imports from Burma, placed further visa restrictions on Burma's leaders, and required the United States to oppose loans to Burma by international financial institutions. Introduced initially on 4 June, then in final form on 11 June, this time with fifty-six co-sponsors, the bill reflected the sense of outrage in the country. Editorials in the *Baltimore Sun*, the *Washington Post*, and the *New York Times*, among others, all supported the bill. Moving with unusual speed, the Senate passed the bill 94 to 1 (only Mike Enzi [R-WY] voted no). On 15 July the House followed suit with a 418 to 2 vote. President Bush signed the bill on 28 July and immediately implemented the act's provisions.

Albeit responding to pressure, the Bush administration was now actively engaged in the Myanmar issue. The United States took the lead in demanding that Aung San Suu Kyi be released, and Bush even quoted her sentiments about democracy during his speech to the UN General Assembly. For the time being she remained incarcerated, however, returning to her home only on 26 September where she was again placed under house arrest. "The military seems more firmly entrenched in power today than at any time since it first seized power in 1962," wrote Burma watcher Bertil Lintner.[11]

Not everyone thought that sanctioning Myanmar was wise policy. From the beginning the leading American scholar of modern Burma, David I. Steinberg, had opposed sanctions on the grounds that they would not change the junta members' minds or actions and that quiet, careful diplomacy was more effective. If "regime change" was the goal of the sanctions, they were doomed to fail. In the spring of 2004 a group of similarly minded Burma scholars, including Steinberg and Robert Taylor, collaborated on a volume edited by John H. Badgley and published by the National Bureau of Asian Research (NBR), a Seattle think tank. The executive summary made their conclusions clear: "Sanctions Have Not Worked in Myanmar," "Sanctions Have Been Counter-Productive in the Short Term," and "Sanctions Will Not Work in the Long Run." A confrontational policy, the authors believed, was wrong headed. As Taylor wrote, it was "unseemly" for Colin Powell to refer to the Burmese government as a "bunch of thugs."[12]

The sanctions issue and how best to respond to developments in Myanmar since 1988 deeply divided both the scholarly and the practitioner communities, and the response to the NBR report was swift. Australians Adam McCarty and Paul Burke issued a point-by-point rebuttal, and in any case the antisanctions advocates were in the minority, or at least did not succeed in persuading the US government to adopt their approach. As the *Far Eastern Economic Review*'s correspondent Murray Hiebert observed, "this pro-engagement argument seems to have had little influence in Washington." Powell stated that the United States would continue with its policy of pressure, and Bush again praised Aung San Suu Kyi, calling her "a courageous reformer."[13] In July Bush renewed the sanctions for another year, and in the same month Powell rebuked the Burmese regime for failing to move toward democracy.

In contrast to the disinterest it had shown in the early years, the Bush administration now became actively involved in working with other governments and international organizations to bring about pressure on Burma. It tried to persuade ASEAN to convince Burma not to chair the organization's meeting scheduled for 2006. It coordinated sanctions policy with the European Union. It tried to work with China, India, and other countries. In addition it moved at the UN. In December 2005 the United States, prompted in part by democracy advocates like the US Campaign for Burma, persuaded the Security Council to receive a briefing about Burma for the first time, an important precedent that presaged possible UN intervention. The UN also appointed Ibrahim Gambari, the UN's under secretary general for political affairs, to visit Burma and report back to the Security Council. In May Gambari met with Senior General Than Shwe as well as with Aung San Suu Kyi, after which he briefed the Security Council.[14] In September, over the objections of China, the council held its first formal discussion of the situation in Burma. It was not lost on some that this resembled the way the Bush administration had maneuvered in the UN prior to moving aggressively against Iraq's Saddam Hussein. Perhaps forced regime change applied to Burma as well. The Burmese military had always feared US intervention, possibly using its Thai ally. However irrational such fears were, it was apparently believed, and accounted in part for the junta's closer ties to China as something of a security guarantee against American threats.[15] Perhaps not coincidentally, Burma hastily transferred its government to a new capital, Naypyitaw, located well inland from Rangoon. The naval and air commands were also relocated inland.

The Bush administration was standing firm on the side of sanctions, and its more aggressive stance enjoyed bipartisan support. In February 2006 Congressional representatives pointed to numerous egregious examples of human rights infringements, including Suu Kyi's current plight. The administration fully agreed. As Assistant Secretary of State Christopher Hill put it, "there are few places in the world where democracy has been suppressed and with human rights violations as brutally and systematically as in Burma."[16]

Laura Bush, the Saffron Revolution, and Sanctions

In 2007 the Burmese junta encountered a new adversary: first lady Laura Bush. Particularly after the regime crushed new demonstrations in August 2007, she became involved, telephoning UN Secretary General Ban Ki-moon and asking him to denounce the government's actions. "I wanted the U.N. to be on record saying, at least, that we know what's happened in this recent crackdown," she told a journalist. Like many Americans, Laura Bush was drawn to the heroism of Aung San Suu Kyi, and she joined with the sixteen women senators to make a public appeal for her release. "It's important for governments to put as much pressure [as possible] on the military regime to listen to the people," she stated. She stated publicly that she hoped that the Security Council would again put Burma on its agenda. (The previous effort to act against Burma had encountered Russian and Chinese vetoes.) Aung Din, director of the U.S. Campaign for Burma, a veteran of the student revolt of 1988 and former political prisoner, recalled that she "helped us a lot."[17]

The Bush administration had found its Madeleine Albright. As ABC News commentator Cokie Roberts recalled in 2013, "one of the things I can't get over is that people think of her as some sort of a prim librarian—and she hates that of course—but she's the only first lady to come to the White House press room, come grab the microphone, and use it to call for the overthrow of the Burmese government."[18]

What had aroused Laura Bush's wrath turned out to be the opening of the so-called Saffron Revolution, a demonstration by thousands of Buddhist monks against the regime. It was the strongest challenge to the junta since 8888. The uprising began in mid-August 2007 when protesters rallied against a sudden increase in fuel prices. After a subsequent incident on 5 September between soldiers and monks (hence the term "Saffron Revolution," a reference to the color of the monks' robes), the cause was transformed into a general protest against repression. Since the junta had touted itself as a defender of Buddhist values, the presence of so many monks complicated the government's response, but on 25 September the government decided that it must crack down. Estimates of those killed in the brutal response vary widely. Among the dead was Kenji Nagai, a Japanese news photographer killed in cold blood by a Burmese soldier. Thousands were arrested and jailed. Even more were detained once the revolution was suppressed.[19]

The response in the United States was one of outrage. Shari Villarosa, the American chargé d'affaires in Rangoon, said, "I think they just are arresting anybody that they have the least bit of suspicion about. This is a military that rules by fear and intimidation." Laura Bush stated that it was "time for General Than Shwe and the junta to step aside and to make way for a unified Burma governed by legitimate leaders." Demonstrations and teach-ins occurred across the United States, and reports about those who had taken part in these events found their way back to the junta. Sometimes those who had participated were later denied entry into Burma.[20]

On 25 September President Bush spoke to the UN General Assembly and stated that Americans were "outraged by the situation in Burma." He promised to "tighten economic sanctions" on the regime's leaders and "their financial backers," along with introducing an expanded visa ban on those Burmese leaders responsible for egregious human rights violations. Finally, he urged the United Nations and "all nations" to pressure the Burmese government to change its ways.[21]

The Senate's Subcommittee on East Asian and Pacific Affairs quickly convened a hearing, chaired by Senator Barbara Boxer (D-CA), who set the tone of the hearing: "The people demanded freedom from a government that restricts the basic freedoms of speech and assembly, engages in human trafficking, discriminates against women and ethnic minorities, uses children as soldiers and laborers, imprisons arbitrarily, abuses prisoners and detainees, and rapes and tortures. . . . The time for the Burmese people to prevail is now. Brutal response of the military has captured the attention of the international community, and shame on us if we take our eyes off this." Senator John Kerry (D-MA) referred to the regime's "deception and . . . lies. . . . There are zero redeeming qualities about this regime," he added, statements with which Deputy Assistant Secretary of State Scot Marciel agreed.[22]

While there was little disagreement about the nature of the Burmese regime and the reprehensible actions it had recently taken, the Senate hearings were unusually frank and intelligent. The administration spelled out what it was doing but welcomed suggestions. "I'm the first to admit that they [American policy initiatives], by themselves, have not solved the problem, nor, frankly, has any other approach, which is why I said we're so open to new ideas," Marciel stated.[23] Sanctions were explored in depth, but most agreed that without support from Thailand, India, and especially China, they would not change the situation in Burma. Much of the discussion therefore focused on how the United States might be able to get more cooperation from these frontline states. Some witnesses and committee members thought that additional sanctions might prove effective, such as closing one major loophole: while imports were banned, American companies could still operate in Burma. The most notorious of these was Chevron which had taken over Unocal and was involved with the Yadana offshore natural gas field. The company had been grandfathered in by the legislation in 1997 and was still doing business in Burma. Getting Chevron out of the country would not bring down the regime but would enhance the moral position of the United States. The State Department was noncommittal, only indicating that this was one possibility that was being considered. Another sanction that should be enacted, stated Tom Malinowski of Human Rights Watch, was to target Burmese jade and gems that were used in other countries for jewelry. Malinowski also suggested pursuing strong banking sanctions against the regime and its leaders who, he said, were getting rich, largely from the drug trade. If the United States could freeze the junta's offshore accounts by instructing American banks not to have relationships with banks that did business with the regime, that would be very effective. Aung Din agreed, as did Michael J. Green, senior adviser at the Center for Strategic and International Studies.

Aung Din also suggested introducing a binding resolution in the Security Council ordering the Burmese government to stop the killing and release all political prisoners, including Suu Kyi. China and Russia might, of course, veto such a resolution, but at the very least they would have to go on the record. Senator Boxer was particularly taken with this suggestion. In her view it was not always necessary to be certain that there would be no veto before introducing a UN resolution.

In sum, the hearings were a productive, thoughtful, and meaningful review of policy options. As Senator Boxer put it when the subcommittee had concluded its work, "This panel was terrific."[24] In the end Bush took the following executive actions: he froze the assets of senior officials in the Burmese government, as well as of other individuals and corporations who had engaged in serious human rights abuses and who provided support to the Burmese government. No American citizen could help any of the proscribed persons evade these restrictions. Among the specific entities mentioned were the Htoo Trading Company and Air Bagan, an important domestic airline, both controlled by businessman Tay Za.[25] If Bush's actions did not go as far as those testifying before the committee had suggested, they did nevertheless indicate the administration's anger at Burma. In February 2008 Bush added some additional companies to the list, all controlled by Tay Za.

Behind the scenes China urged the junta to speak with Aung San Suu Kyi and to moderate its behavior. China was immediately concerned because of the upcoming Olympic games to be held in Beijing in 2008, and it did not want things in Myanmar to get out of hand. More generally its own strategic interests were not advanced when Burma was unstable, in particular when ethnic minorities remained at odds with the central government. Armed factions could, after all, interfere with Chinese plans to construct an oil pipeline across Myanmar from the Indian Ocean to Yunnan, for example. China even helped arrange a meeting in Beijing between Burmese ministers and a US assistant secretary of state. None of this resulted in change, however. Some ASEAN members condemned Burma during the Saffron Revolution, but ASEAN itself backtracked, rejecting American calls to suspend Burma or at least censure it at its November meeting.[26]

In April 2008 Bush added three additional state-owned companies to the list of those with which Americans could not conduct business. The order, it was thought, would effectively prevent "even indirect dealings with these companies ... on international markets." All told, Bush's order applied to 38 individuals and 13 companies (as compared, it might be noted, with the European Union's designation of over 400 individuals and nearly 1,300 companies). Finally, the United States began to fund assistance for many internally displaced persons in Burma. Funneled through the International Rescue Committee to the Thailand-Burma Border Consortium, the funds provided supplies for brave activists to carry supplies into Burma. Begun with an appropriation of $2 million, the funding increased annually to about $5 million in 2012.[27]

Nargis

Then came Nargis, a major cyclone that devastated Burma's delta region on 2 May 2008, killing tens of thousands of people. The military government was soon criticized for its ineffective response, and Laura Bush accused the regime of failing to warn its citizens of the impending storm. The American embassy promised $250,000 immediately for emergency assistance, but Mrs. Bush feared that the junta would not accept American aid. Soon the United States offered $3 million in assistance through USAID, but Myanmar would not admit AID officials. American warships and aircraft were also prepared to assist, including airdropping food and supplies, but the junta, fearing an American invasion, refused. Even if the Americans just brought in supplies, they might not leave, the junta feared. "They are very suspicious," stated Shari Villarosa regarding Myanmar's distrust of foreigners. "They think they're up to no good."[28] After a crucial delay of several days, the Burmese government did allow foreign assistance—but not from the United States.

Eventually, the junta relented and approved delivery of some US aid: deliveries by three military aircraft were allowed, the first arriving on 12 May. This was soon increased, and by 16 May seventeen flights had landed. Even so this was a limited amount, given the scope of the disaster. By this point it was thought that 100,000 people had perished. "There is absolutely more we could do, if only the Burmese government would permit us to do it," said the Pentagon press secretary. Ultimately the United States was able to send in ninety-five planeloads, but the regime never allowed American naval vessels to bring in supplies, which the secretary of defense thought amounted to "criminal neglect." Also, during this period the government-controlled newspaper's rhetoric "suggested a consistent antipathy toward the United States." In the end, as many as 200,000 people may have perished, many of them needlessly because the government had hindered the receipt and distribution of aid. Adding insult to injury, the junta extended Suu Kyi's house arrest for a sixth year. "The reality is that nothing substantive has changed since 1988," wrote Bertil Lintner in October 2007. Laura Bush expressed similar sentiments in August 2008. "Everything is still the same, or maybe worse, in Burma," she said.[29]

Aside from fear of a possible invasion, Burma's refusal to allow foreigners, particularly Americans, into the country at this time was probably due to a referendum on a new constitution that was unfortunately scheduled for 10 May. The proposed constitution guaranteed the military 25 percent of the seats in the legislature; one provision appeared to make it impossible for Aung San Suu Kyi to become president. Not surprising the NLD opposed the constitution but had great difficulty publicizing its position due to government interference. The government did not want foreign visitors, particularly Americans, to observe the voting. On 6 May the US Congress voted almost unanimously to condemn the constitution and the upcoming referendum. The flawed referendum nevertheless took place as scheduled in much of the country but was delayed until 24 May in

Nargis-affected areas. Foreigners were not allowed in until after the vote. The government contended that nearly 94 percent of those voting approved the new constitution.

Congress responded in frustration to these developments by passing Tom Lantos's Burmese JADE (Junta's Anti-Democratic Efforts) Act. Originally introduced in October 2007, the bill was not finally enacted into law until 24 July 2008—after the Nargis debacle and the referendum. It extended the ban on imports to include jadeite, rubies, and other gems of Burmese origin. It also incorporated the presidential executive orders placing financial and travel restrictions on certain Burmese individuals and included other provisions, among them one that urged Chevron to leave Burma. It was the last sanctions bill passed by Congress.[30]

For the rest of the Bush administration there was no change in American policy. Thanks to preoccupation with a disintegrating economy at home, attention was elsewhere. Stories about Myanmar continued to appear prominently in the press, however, under such titles as "Aftermath of a Revolt: Myanmar's Lost Year." Nor did the NGO community forget. The National Democratic Institute honored Desmond Tutu, in part for his "advocacy for democracy in Burma and the release of Aung San Suu Kyi, the world's only imprisoned Nobel Laureate." Upon receiving the award, Tutu said of Aung San Suu Kyi, "we are coming one day to your inauguration, and Burma will be free." The other awardee was the Women's League of Burma. Former Secretary of State Madeleine Albright presided and presented the awards. In addition, as one of the last acts of his administration, shortly before his term ended Bush extended sanctions to several organizations, including more that were related to Tay Za, and ten Singaporean firms. He also froze the assets of businessman Zaw Zaw and others who had close ties to the junta.[31]

The Barack Obama Reset

After a period of initial indifference, the Bush administration had adopted the cause of restoring democracy in Myanmar, but there was little to show for it. Perhaps sanctions simply did not work in this situation, or perhaps Bush's foreign policy had alienated much of the world on grounds unrelated to Burma, and getting the needed international consensus proved difficult. "President George W. Bush tried to help Burmese dissidents, but he had zero international capital," wrote *New York Times* columnist Nicholas Kristof.[32] By contrast, the new president, Barack Obama was highly thought of abroad. Perhaps there could be a better result in Burma.

Obama's secretary of state, Hillary Clinton, ordered a policy review. She was frustrated. Sanctions had not worked, she said, but then neither had engagement.

Michael Green and future Ambassador to Burma Derek Mitchell, both then associated with the Center for Strategic and International Studies, had reached a similar conclusion, and their article in *Foreign Affairs*, "Asia's Forgotten Crisis," suggested a new approach. "Sanctions policies will need to coexist with various forms of engagement," they wrote.[33] The Obama administration ultimately adopted this approach.

It may be that the junta initiated a process of dialogue with the United States in February 2009; so indicates a Wikileaks cable. Presumably attempting to judge the seriousness of the junta, Clinton responded by sending a midlevel diplomat, Stephen Blake, to call on Naypyitaw. Blake met Myanmar's foreign minister, a meeting quite unprecedented in protocol terms. He also met with senior NLD leaders, though not with Aung San Suu Kyi, and the state-controlled newspaper reported that there was a "cordial discussion" of issues. Secretary Clinton then offered to considering signing a Treaty of Amity and Cooperation with ASEAN, something the previous administration had resisted because it "would constrain . . . its ability to penalize Burma."[34] These were possible straws in the wind hinting at a better relationship.

An unexpected complication occurred in May when one John William Yettaw swam across Inya Lake in Rangoon to Suu Kyi's lakeside home. When he first heard of this incident, American chargé d'affaires Larry Dinger recalled that he hoped that Yettaw was of any nationality but American—but American he was. Yettaw apparently had a vision that he must get the Book of Mormon to Suu Kyi and also warn her of an assassination plot. The junta realized that Yettaw was mentally unbalanced and released him to Senator Jim Webb (D-VA) in August. But the regime used his escapade as an excuse to arrest Suu Kyi for sheltering Yettaw, which further strained Myanmar's relations with the United States. Carl Gershman, president of the National Endowment for Democracy, stated that Suu Kyi's trial made it crystal clear that the junta "has no interest whatsoever in a new relationship, either with the United States or with its own people."[35] He may have been wrong about that, but it was a common perception.

In July 2009 Congress reauthorized existing sanctions, and President Obama signed the legislation. But the same month Clinton attended the ASEAN Regional Forum and signed the ASEAN amity treaty on 22 July. Despite the anger at Burma and the Yettaw distraction, the administration was already moving toward its as yet unannounced policy of "pragmatic engagement." Indeed the Obama administration was paying more attention to Asia in general than its predecessor, a policy move later described as a "pivot" to Asia. "The United States is back," Secretary Clinton told the forum. On 11 August Aung San Suu Kyi had her house arrest extended for an additional eighteen months, ensuring that she would not be able to participate in elections scheduled for 2010. President Obama personally condemned the sentence.

Soon thereafter, however, Senator Webb, who was in Burma to collect Yettaw, spoke with Than Shwe. He was the first high-level American ever to meet with the Burmese leader. Significantly, Webb was allowed to visit with Suu Kyi, a month after UN Secretary General Ban Ki-moon was forbidden from seeing her. Perhaps the Burmese were shifting gears after all. Webb returned opposed to continuing the sanctions, particularly if there was some reciprocity from Myanmar. Though the reasons for imposing sanctions were laudable, he wrote, "the result has been overwhelmingly counterproductive." He suggested talking with the government and ultimately restoring trade. He noted that when the United States finally dropped its sanctions against Vietnam, the results had been very good, both for Vietnam and the United States. Perhaps the same thing could happen with Burma.[36]

Indeed, shortly before Webb held a hearing on 30 September 2009 to examine the effectiveness of US policy, the Obama administration, having finally completed its policy review, announced its new approach. Perhaps intending to retain control over policy and not cede it to Congress, the administration announced that the sanctions would remain in place for the time being, but that it would engage with the regime and consider moderating or removing sanctions, depending on progress made. As Assistant Secretary of State Kurt Campbell told the Senate Subcommittee on East Asian and Pacific Affairs, the policy now would be one of "of pragmatic engagement with the Burmese authorities."[37] In effect, the administration was now calling for regime modification rather than regime change.

Seth Mydans of the *New York Times* characterized the shift as "the most significant modification of administration policy toward Myanmar in decades." Then, after Suu Kyi had written to Than Shwe indicating her willingness to cooperate in getting the sanctions lifted, the junta allowed Western diplomats to meet with her. Thomas Fuller, another *Times* correspondent, surmised that this was "part of what appear to be early but tentative signs of détente between the Junta and western governments." The meeting itself also raised the question of whether the sanctions had been effective. Though Webb and others had maintained that they were not, they may well have contributed to the Burmese decision to seek détente. As Fuller wrote, "the Myanmar government has long been eager for the removal of the sanctions, which bar certain senior members of the government from carrying out financial transactions through Western banks and from traveling to the United States, European Union countries or Australia." The ban on exports, including the recent ban on gems, also affected them.[38]

China and the Sanctions

The sanctions may also have worked in an unanticipated way: they drove Burma closer to China. That China's economic involvement with Myanmar soared during the sanctions era is amply demonstrated in David I. Steinberg and Hong-wei Fan's recent study, *Modern China-Myanmar Relations: Dilemmas of Mutual Dependence.*[39] In its ever increasing search for energy resources, China secured new concessions in Myanmar to search for oil and natural gas. More important, it began to build a pipeline to transport oil from a port on the Indian Ocean to China, thus mitigating the need to send most of its purchased oil through the Malacca Straits where it had to depend on the United States for security (although Steinberg and Fan argue that the pipeline would not really solve China's "Malacca dilemma"). China has also invested heavily in developing hydroelectric power on Burmese rivers. Seven dams have been or are being constructed, in Kachin State alone. Finally, Chinese mining operations in Myanmar have increased significantly. China has been able to do these things because it seldom takes into consideration the internal policies and practices of those countries with which it engages. Western sanctions, therefore, gave Chinese interests a great advantage.

As developmental assistance from Western countries dried up because of the sanctions, China stepped in to replace what was lost. In 1998, for example, China helped Myanmar cope with the Asian financial crisis by providing a preferential loan of $150 million. It may have provided the Burmese military with some $3 billion in assistance. In 2011, furthermore, China became the largest foreign investor in Myanmar, with much of it coming from Chinese state-owned enterprises.

But perhaps the most obvious change was in the volume of trade. In 1988 the value of China's imports from and exports to Myanmar was $255.62 million, but by 2009 this had increased to $2,907.36 million. The trade has been particularly important to China's Yunnan Province, and cross-border trade—an unknown amount of which is illegal—has rapidly expanded. This was in part due to the junta's decision to scrap Ne Win's "Burmese Way to Socialism" and liberalize the economy, but Western sanctions that discouraged or forbade trade also helped Chinese merchants. As Fan Hongwei discovered, "Chinese traders and entrepreneurs interviewed [in 2005] unanimously recognized the significance of the 1988 tipping point for their lives and economy. They remarked that 'All the current successful big Chinese entrepreneurs in Myanmar started their businesses in 1989.'"[40] The new opportunities made many Chinese businesspeople wealthy.

The Chinese quickly came to dominate the major markets in the country. They controlled the cross-border trade, owned the major supermarket chains in Yangon, and ran many of the big restaurants. By 2000 "there were about 25,000 Chinese enterprises selling groceries and other sundry goods. . . . Half of the private banks belonged to the Chinese." Some cities have become almost Chinese, and the northern part of Myanmar is now "economically dependent on China."[41]

The antisanctions advocates pointed to this increased Chinese influence to demonstrate that the sanctions were counterproductive. As the Western powers

FIGURE 13.   U Tin Oo, former general and commander in chief of Burma's armed forces, has since 1988 been vice chairman of the National League for Democracy. Photo by Marlee Clymer, 2012.

pulled back, China moved in to fill the gap. To be sure, the sanctions were not the only reasons for Chinese expansion into Myanmar, but "the catalyst function of economic sanctions against Myanmar and its major allies in China-Myanmar trade and economic nexus should not be ignored," Steinberg and Fan conclude.[42]

However, Burma has never liked being overly dependent on anyone, including China. As Ernest Z. Bower, director of the Center for Strategic and International Studies' Southeast Asia Program, wrote on the eve of Secretary Clinton's visit to Myanmar in 2011, "Myanmar's leaders privately describe tacit Chinese control of their economy as suffocating and encroaching on sovereignty," or as U Tin Oo stated in 2012, the regime now realized "that all of their valuable resources are gone" to China.[43] Though we do not know with certainty all of the factors that led Myanmar's government to alter course, the nationalistic desire to distance the country from China contributed to the change. The sanctions thus had an important impact, although in a way quite unintended by their sponsors. China provoked a nationalist backlash.

"Pragmatic Engagement" and the Burmese Elections

However, the new Obama policy of "pragmatic engagement" seemed to produce few immediate results. When Kurt Campbell went to Burma in November 2009 he met only with Prime Minister Thein Sein, a former general then thought to have little power. He did not see Than Shwe, which was generally interpreted as a snub. However, this did not stop President Obama from attending a meeting of all ASEAN leaders, including Thein Sein, in Singapore later in the month—the first time in over four decades that an American president had been in a joint meeting with Burmese officials. It was still unclear whether the new American policy would be successful, however, and Burmese dissidents and human rights activists remained skeptical, suspicious, and fearful that the administration would give too much away. As Aung Din wrote, the administration needed to be careful that its "policy of 'pragmatic engagement' . . . does not legitimize a fundamentally corrupt regime."[44]

By January 2010 progress was still minimal. The United States was pleased that there had been high-level interaction between the regime and Suu Kyi, but ethnic minorities were still persecuted, about two thousand political prisoners remained incarcerated (including thirty-seven students who were part of the "88 generation"),[45] and Suu Kyi remained under house arrest. Furthermore, rumors of North Korean nuclear assistance abounded. Myanmar also reportedly was repressing Christianity.[46] Relations were not improved when in February 2010 a Burmese court sentenced an American citizen of Burmese descent to five years hard labor. The charges, said an American embassy spokesman, were "politically motivated," the sentence unjust. Burma's Supreme Court also reaffirmed Aung San Suu Kyi's sentence of continuing house arrest, and reports of serious human rights violations appeared periodically.[47]

Then came what were anticipated to be sham elections, the result of the sham constitution approved in 2008 during the Nargis debacle. The State Department's assessment was that the election law "makes a mockery of the democratic process and ensures that the upcoming elections with be devoid of credibility." Regardless of the vote, the military would still be in charge. After visiting with Aung San Suu Kyi, Kurt Campbell stated, "it is simply tragic that Burma's generals have rebuffed her countless appeals to work together to find a peaceable solution for a more prosperous future."[48] The new policy of conditional engagement did not seem to be producing any better results than the sanctions regime. The Senate, meanwhile, condemned the Myanmar government and called on it, once again, to free Aung San Suu Kyi.

Nothing changed over the summer of 2010 to modify these assessments. In August the National Democratic Institute concluded that the election, now scheduled for 7 November, "offers no prospect of establishing a government based on the will of the Burmese people."[49] Because of the lack of progress the United States supported a UN inquiry into Burma's war crimes and crimes against humanity.

Some, however, thought that the United States should not prejudge the elections and instead see how they played out before imposing more restrictions. Expressing moral outrage would salve American consciences but would prove counterproductive in terms of bringing change. The electoral process was indeed seriously flawed and would, as the critics pointed out, keep the military in control, but now there would be at least some opposition legislators, political prisoners were likely to be released, and economic reforms would probably be enacted.[50] This analysis did not commend itself to the American government, however. When the elections were over, the result would be a civilianized government but one still dominated by the military, and President Obama condemned them as "neither free nor fair" and not meeting international standards. Aung San Suu Kyi was still in detention, as were some twenty-one hundred other political prisoners. "Ultimately," he concluded, "elections cannot be credible when the regime rejects dialogue with opponents and represses the most basic freedoms of expression, speech, and assembly."[51]

Activists and analysts also dismissed the elections. Aung Din, for example, writing after the elections, asserted that they and the new constitution would change the forms but not the substance. "The political game will continue to be monopolized by the same old figures and played with the same destructive attitude," he wrote. This was a common perception, although arguably the elections were part of the military's plan for very gradually moving toward more democracy.[52]

After the elections the junta released Aung San Suu Kyi. There was much skepticism that she would be allowed to organize politically; if she went too far the military would simply rearrest her. Overseas groups of Burmese refugees and activists were particularly unimpressed. Suu Kyi's release, they felt, was "a hoax to hoodwink the world." Indeed, within a few weeks the junta threatened to discipline Suu Kyi and the NLD for not supporting an end to sanctions (suggesting, incidentally, that the sanctions had some bite), and even threatening "tragic ends."[53]

However, despite strong criticism, the elections did not fundamentally alter American policy. Thus in December 2010 Deputy Assistant Secretary Joseph Yun traveled to Burma, where he met with government officials as well as with Suu Kyi. Nothing specific apparently emerged from these discussions, but the fact that Yun was allowed to come and meet with both regime figures and Suu Kyi signaled that at least the government was still interested in dialogue and perhaps in gradual movement toward better relations with the United States. By late April 2011, however, Yun stated that engagement with sanctions had resulted in "no or very limited success."[54] When Yun visited Burma the next month he found little reason to be more optimistic, seeing little change in the human rights situation and a continuing Burmese relationship with North Korea. Obama extended the Clinton-era sanctions on new American investment in Burma for another year.

Though the US policy of engagement with sanctions still remained in place, it was coming under increasing criticism, particularly from those who thought engagement would never work. Criticisms emerged at a House Congressional hearing on 2 June 2011 and continued on 22 June before the Subcommittee on Asian and Pacific Affairs. Committee chair Donald Manzullo (R-IL) rejected the argument that despite the fraudulent nature of the elections, they might ultimately bring about changes. Nor had the policy of constructive engagement been successful: "if proponents of pragmatic engagement are correct, then Burmese leaders should recognize this unprecedented opportunity being offered by the Obama administration and seek to improve relations with the U.S. by demonstrating tangible change," he stated. "Unfortunately, this is not the case. The State Department's visit to Burma in May is further proof that change in Burma is extremely difficult to achieve." Witness Aung Din also expressed his frustration. Although he had supported pragmatic engagement with sanctions, he disliked the open-ended quality of the engagement and complained that not all sanctions had been employed. "Mr. Chairman, please help us to end the 'open-ended engagement policy and this is not a right time attitude' of the U.S. Government," he testified. "The world has given the regime plenty of time, and so many opportunities to survive to this day. Now is the time to support and strengthen the democracy movement by weakening the regime stronger and harsher."[55]

The Manzullo hearing was the first US Congressional hearing to have Aung San Suu Kyi as a witness; she testified on videotape. She did not address the sanctions issue or American policy directly, but made it clear that there had been very little progress in resolving human rights abuses. She urged the committee to do whatever it could to see that the Burmese government implemented the demands contained in a UN Human Rights Council Resolution, approved the previous March, that called for the release of political prisoners and the establishment of an independent judiciary. She also supported the proposal of Professor Tomás Ojea Quintana, the UN's human rights rapporteur, for a UN inquiry into human rights abuses in Burma.[56]

Whatever momentum had existed in improving US-Myanmar relations appeared to have stalled. There were at least two reasons for some optimism, however. For one thing, Myanmar very much wanted to host the annual ASEAN meeting in 2014, but ASEAN had so far refused to accept Burma's bid. Making changes in Myanmar would help, particularly freeing political prisoners. Furthermore, change was then sweeping the Arab world—the so-called Arab spring. Junta leaders may have feared that a similar uprising could occur in Burma unless there was change.

Flickers of Progress

An early indicator of change came in President Thein Sein's inaugural address on 30 March 2011. He bemoaned internal ethnic strife that, he said, had brought a "hell of untold miseries," and called for national unity and rebuilding of the deteriorating infrastructure and health services. He wanted the country's educational system "to meet the international level and encourage human resource development." He hoped to increase the living standards of workers and farmers and pledged partially to deregulate the economy while welcoming foreign investment. In terms of political rights, Thein Sein stated that all citizens had to obey the constitution, but he pointed out that there were ways to amend it. Quite remarkably, he appeared to welcome the opposition into the electoral process: "If an individual or organization stands for election in accordance with the democratic practice to come to power in a justice [sic] way, that will be acceptable to everyone. Therefore, I would say our government will keep peace door open to welcome such individuals and organizations." He also wanted to "amend and revoke the existing laws and adopt new laws as necessary to implement the provisions on fundamental rights of citizens or human rights," and he pledged to work for democracy and respect the rights of minorities. It was a remarkable speech in terms of substance and tone. Perhaps the elections of 2010 were unexpectedly ushering in a "new era."[57]

Then in August 2011 Aung San Suu Kyi met for the first time with the labor minister, Aung Kyi. Furthermore, the government did not make good on its earlier threat to move against her if she undertook political trips: she encountered no problems traveling outside of Yangon for an overtly political purpose, addressing thousands of people. In October she received the University of Michigan's Raoul Wallenberg Medal and delivered a videotaped public lecture, with no objections from the new government. These were among the indications that the government might be serious about dialogue and change.

Many were still doubtful,[58] but an indication that major changes might be in the wind came on 30 September when Thein Sein suspended the construction of the China-sponsored Mytisone Dam in Kachin State. The dam, which would have been the first one on the Irrawaddy River, was unpopular with many Burmese, especially the Kachins, thousands of whom had to be relocated. Aung San Suu Kyi was among those asking that the dam, which was already under construction, be reviewed. In making his announcement, Thein Sein made it clear that he was responding to popular feelings, though there may have been other reasons why he acted, including distancing himself from China. Thant Myint-U wrote that suspension of the dam project was a "previously unimaginable development. . . . This was a victory of Myanmar's nascent environmental movement and the area's minority Kachin people. That the president would stop a Chinese-backed project of this magnitude was the clearest sign yet that the country was at a turning point. . . . What we're seeing today," he concluded, "is Myanmar's best chance in half a century for a better future."[59]

The United States responded to Myanmar's gestures. In August 2011 it had appointed a high-ranking special envoy to Burma, Derek Mitchell, who had spent years involved with Burma issues. (The position had been mandated by Congress under the JADE Act and required Senate confirmation, thus allowing the Senate to influence executive branch policy.)[60] Mitchell's entire responsibility was to focus on Burma. "We are going to meet their action with action," he said. "If they take steps, we will take steps to demonstrate that we are supportive of the path to reform." Only the previous week the United States had modified travel restrictions and welcomed to Washington Burma's foreign minister, U Wunna Maung Lwin, who had been attending the UN General Assembly meeting in New York—the country's first foreign minister to visit the United States since the military took power. Furthermore, the entire sanctions regime was under review.[61] Mitchell was back in Myanmar late in October, speaking with government officials and Aung San Suu Kyi. Speculation was that Mitchell was there to talk about possibly easing sanctions. A week later Thein Sein invited Suu Kyi to attend an international forum on green energy. "Things are changing very rapidly," observed former American chargé d'affaires Priscilla Clapp.[62]

Signs of high-level American interest in a renewed relationship with Burma were even more evident in the final two months of 2011. In November President

Obama, en route to Indonesia to attend a conference of Asian leaders, telephoned Aung San Suu Kyi from Air Force One. In this, their first conversation, Suu Kyi endorsed Obama's intention to send Secretary Clinton to Burma for an historic visit, and her blessing allowed the White House to outflank possible Congressional opposition. Sending Clinton was, nevertheless, a risky endeavor, given the numerous false starts in the past. But Obama was determined to test "flickers of progress," as he put it, that had already occurred and to encourage additional reforms, including the release of all political prisoners.[63]

By the time Clinton arrived, the pace of change had accelerated, which encouraged many, both in Burma and abroad. As one opposition leader told a reporter, "what has happened in these last few months is a miracle for us. . . . To be frank, in the very beginning I didn't believe a word of what they were saying. . . . Now I believe that what is happening is for the good of the people."[64]

Clinton's visit was the first by an American secretary of state in over half a century since February 1955, when John Foster Dulles had been in Rangoon. The issues behind the two visits were different, but they were both unexpected (a year before each of them neither could have been envisioned), and both responded to recent changes in Burma. Clinton's visit occurred against a background of apparent relaxation of Burma's harsh military rule and that country's desire to distance itself from China. Dulles's visit had come at a time of Cold War fears of growing Chinese influence and alarm that Burma was about the take the communist side in the Cold War. As a result of his visit, the United States had looked at the country with new eyes and was soon negotiating economic and military assistance programs. Clinton went at a time of positive change, this time hoping to encourage Myanmar's government to release more political prisoners and move toward a democratic political system.

Unlike with the Dulles visit, it is doubtful that US concerns about China motivated Clinton's trip. To be sure, American involvement in Asia ever since the late eighteenth century has often centered on China, and during the Cold War the United States sought to contain China. After the Cold War China pursued an adept and (until recently) very successful effort to woo Southeast Asian nations, setting forth an agenda of peace and mutually useful trade and investment relationships, which are enshrined in several treaties with the individual countries of the region, and when Obama "pivoted" toward Asia, it set off alarm bells in Beijing that the United States was challenging its relationships with Southeast Asia and a new policy of containment was beginning, which it deeply resented. As the respected Chinese international relations scholar Jin Canrong put it, containing China's ambitions in Burma was "a very stupid choice. . . . China cannot be contained." Not surprisingly, therefore, Clinton's visit to Myanmar "clearly rattled Beijing." China's *Global Times* asserted that her trip was "undermining the [Chinese] wall in Myanmar."[65]

FIGURE 14.   Secretary of State Hillary Clinton meeting Daw Aung San Suu Kyi for dinner on 1 December 2011 in Yangon. Her visit marked the beginning of the thaw in relations between the United States and Myanmar. Department of State photo by William Ng.

Before the thaw the Burmese military had also asserted that American efforts at regime change, seen in the imposition of sanctions, were directly related to the US policy of containing China. Burma under the junta was closely tied to China, so that if the government were removed or changed, it would be a victory for the US containment policy.[66]

Those who contend that concern with China underlies American policy in Burma are most probably wrong. In February 2012 chargé d'affaires Michael Thurston stated:

> I think China is much less a factor in this than is commonly believed. We have not once gone to them [the Burmese] and said you need to do this because of the Chinese. They have tried to tell us that we should be worried about the Chinese. We told them that we are only worried about you and what you need to do. We have been very consistent in this message. This is not about them and their relationship with China. We hope that they have a good relationship with China. They share a long border. That's a reality that doesn't change. They should be able to get along with one of their neighbors. . . . It's not about China for us.[67]

FIGURE 15.   Aung San Suu Kyi gives a speech to supporters at Hlaing Thar Yar Township in Yangon on 17 November 2011. Photo by Htoo Tay Zar, Open Myanmar Photo Project.

Ambassador Mitchell fully agrees. China figures "not at all" in the Burma policy of the United States, he stated. Contentions that it is "all about China" are simply "absurd." While the general "pivot" toward Asia certainly included a desire to balance growing Chinese influence in the region, in Myanmar moral outrage at the actions of the military regime was the most important factor. The charisma of Aung San Suu Kyi is considerably more important than China, and her influence on American policy has been unprecedented. As Steinberg wrote, "no living foreigner has shaped contemporary United States policy toward a single country more than Aung San Suu Kyi."[68] Those who looked to Suu Kyi to guide American policy were not thinking of China.

Changes and Sanctions

Secretary Clinton's visit, though historic, was relatively low-key. The official Burmese newspaper gave considerably more attention to an upcoming visit by the prime minister of Belarus, Mikhail V. Myasnikovich, than it did to the American secretary of state. All the same, Clinton met with Thein Sein, delivered a letter from President Obama, announced that the United States would extend $1.2 million to Burma mostly for educational and health projects, and would no longer block funding from international financial institutions. She also discussed upgrading diplomatic relations. Clinton met twice with Aung San Suu Kyi, who urged the United States to appoint an ambassador.

All in all, the changes were impressive. "It's Burma rebooted," said U Tin Oo, the NLD's second in command. "Everything is happening with a speed we couldn't even foresee." As Human Rights Watch's David Mathieson (who was not quite sure whether to jump on board or not) put it, a "near pandemic [of] optimism" had developed.[69] By 2012 foreign businesspeople, not wanting to be left behind when Myanmar was fully open, flocked to Yangon, along with NGO representatives and tourists of all kinds. Three months after Clinton's visit, Microsoft's Bill Gates arrived to see the country for himself. Hotel prices tripled, and reservations were at times difficult to obtain. Gone were the days when one could make internal airplane reservations on the spur of the moment.

The government continued to move in the direction favored by the United States. In January 2012 it released 651 prisoners, most prominently Min Ko Naing. About the same time it signed a ceasefire agreement with Shan and Karen rebels, the latter of whom had been fighting the central government since 1949. "We have never been more confident in our talks," stated the deputy director of the Karen National Union.[70] The United States responded to the changes by announcing that it would now send an ambassador to Burma, the first since Burton Levin left in 1990. Burma was also preparing for by-elections, in which Aung San Suu Kyi and the NLD would compete for those seats being contested.

The big questions were whether the United States would lift the remaining sanctions, and if so when. Aside from the complexity of the sanctions regime (the removal of some sanctions required legislative approval, for example), would the forthcoming by-elections be free and fair? Assuming that the NLD won many of the contested seats, would its representatives be able to serve and be listened to? Though many political prisoners had been freed, others were still in jail. Until they were all released, it would be difficult for the United States to have completely normal relations with Myanmar. The United States also insisted that Myanmar end its military connections with North Korea, as well as any nuclear ambitions that it might have. Finally—and perhaps the most difficult, if not the most central to the bilateral relationship—was the issue of the ethnic conflicts and associated charges of continuing, widespread human rights violations by Burma's military forces, particularly in Kachin State.

In contrast to 2010, Burma invited foreign observers, including Americans, to be present at the elections held on 1 April 2012. Forty-five seats in the parliament were up for grabs, the incumbents having died or resigned to enter the Cabinet—only a small portion of the 664 seats in total. Nevertheless, the elections were extremely important in a symbolic sense because of the NLD's participation. In the end, the NLD won an overwhelming victory, claiming forty-three of the forty-five seats, including those in regions dominated by the military. "I feel like I want to dance," said one sixty-five-year-old voter. "I'm so happy that they beat the military. We need a party that stands for the people." Aung San Suu Kyi rejoiced. It was "Suu Kyi's moment."[71] Soon thereafter she felt confident enough to apply for a passport—her first in twenty-four years—so that she could travel to Thailand and Europe, her first foreign trip since the uprising of 1988.

The elections impressed the American government, and in response it lifted the travel ban on Burmese leaders and eased other sanctions, with the promise of more easing to come, including those affecting US investment. Clinton praised President Thein Sein for having "helped launch the country on a historic new path. . . . We applaud the president and his colleagues for their leadership and courage."[72] Within a few weeks the White House nominated Derek Mitchell to be ambassador to Burma. Mitchell, having devoted much of his attention to Burma for several years while working at the National Democratic Institute and then serving as the US special representative, was well acquainted with the issues at hand. It was another step toward resolving differences with Burma. The European Union, meanwhile, suspended most of its sanctions, while the United States relaxed restrictions on American NGOs. In the summer of 2012 Coca Cola and Pepsi were legally back in Burma. (People there had, of course, previously been able to purchase Coke and Pepsi products, smuggled in from Thailand and Singapore.)

Although there seemed to be a rush to remove all sanctions as quickly as possible, the remaining issues slowed the momentum. The most persistent of these was the continuing violence in some of the ethnic minority regions. The most serious at the moment was in Kachin State where, as one observer put it, "bullets, not ballots are the currency." Thein Sein had promised to pull back troops from the region in December 2011, but this did not happen. Instead, the Kachins were subjected to brutal military rule, forced into makeshift camps with poor sanitation and insufficient food.[73]

Thein Sein appeared to want to end the bloodshed in Kachin, and from time to time announced that a ceasefire was in place, but the fighting continued, perhaps because he could not completely control military operations. A little later concern shifted to the oppression of the Rohingya people in Rakhine State. In the summer of 2012 this would boil over into anti-Muslim violence (as it had occasionally at other times in the past) and close the province to tourism. By late August at least eighty-eight persons had perished in violent clashes.

The ethnic conflicts continued to form an obstacle to normalizing relations completely. In February 2012 the American chargé, Michael Thurston, said, "unless they address this issue regarding the ethnic groups, they have not met our expectations."[74] Some of the rebellions had been in existence for over sixty years, and it was unlikely that they could all be ended permanently in a short time, but, as Thurston said, the United States wanted to see movement toward settlements. It was unlikely that, in the final analysis, the United States would insist on final settlements of all of the conflicts prior to lifting sanctions. Progress in resolving the conflicts was reasonable to expect, but demanding complete peace immediately as a condition of fully normalizing relations was unrealistic. Indeed, less than a week after Ambassador Mitchell raised concern about violence against the Rohingyas, the administration waived the visa requirements for Thein Sein to travel to the United States where he planned to attend the General Assembly. More significantly, the United States lifted its long-term ban on new US investments in Burma.

More likely to delay the lifting of all sanctions was the issue of political prisoners. Though the government had released many, including 514 prisoners in September (of whom an undetermined number were political), it was thought that over 200 remained incarcerated. Most of these were released by the end of 2013.[75] Even when released, former political prisoners sometimes encountered difficulties. Thus even as Aung San Suu Kyi was in the United States in September 2012, Min Ko Naing refused to travel to Washington to receive an award from the National Endowment for Democracy at which she would deliver the keynote address. He valued the award, but he would not make the trip because over twenty prodemocracy activists had been denied passports (though the next year he did travel to Washington for the award).

Meanwhile, Suu Kyi was taking the United States by storm. On 19 September she received the Congressional Gold Medal (Congress's highest award, which Congress had conferred on her four years earlier) in the Capitol rotunda. Laura

Bush and Secretary Clinton attended, and the next day President Obama received her in the Oval Office, where he praised her courage. She also received the Atlantic Council's "Global Citizen Award" in New York, where she met with President Thein Sein. More substantively, she urged the United States to end the sanctions. "I do not think we should depend on the U.S. sanctions to keep up the momentum of our new democracy," she said at one appearance. "We have got to work at it ourselves."[76]

Soon thereafter Secretary Clinton also met with Thein Sein in New York and announced that the United States would ease sanctions on imports from Burma. Tellingly, the *New York Times*' story about this decision featured a four-column colored photograph of Aung San Suu Kyi at Queens College in New York. There was no photograph of Myanmar's president,[77] but Thein Sein did get the sanctions lifted.

The North Korean Connection

Burma's military relationship with North Korea and alleged nuclear ambitions were potentially major impediments to ending sanctions and establishing a close relationship with the United States. The country's interest in nuclear power actually dated from 1956, when it established the Burma Atomic Energy Center for peaceful use. This ended with Ne Win's takeover in 1962. Only in 2000 did Myanmar consider revitalizing its nuclear program, possibly because it wanted a nuclear deterrent against the United States and other powers, and the next year it signed an agreement with Russia to purchase a small research reactor. A number of Burmese technicians received training in Russia, but only in 2007 did the two countries sign a cooperation agreement, the delay probably because Myanmar lacked the funds to pay for the reactor. Apparently no construction had taken place by the time Senator Webb visited Myanmar that year; Burmese officials denied having nuclear ambitions.[78]

That Burma had a military relationship with North Korea was clear. North Korea had assisted Burma with defense fortifications and provided small arms and perhaps some missiles.[79] In 2004 the United States had intercepted a shipment of North Korean ballistic missiles bound for Burma. Perhaps Burma had intended the missiles to target US bases in Thailand in case of a feared American invasion.

However, the evidence for North Korean involvement in Burma's nuclear program was always shadowy and unconfirmed. The Wikileaks cables included dispatches from the American embassy in Rangoon in 2004 which, by one account suggested, though it did not definitely state, that the North Koreans were helping the Burmese build a nuclear facility.[80] The United States was also concerned about a secret month-long trip that Thura Shwe Mann, head of Myanmar's military, made to North Korea in 2008.[81] However, the United States never officially accused North Korea of helping Burma with its nuclear program, always referring to "reports" of such activity. Perhaps the best judgment on the Burmese nuclear issue is that of Bertil Linter in March 2011: "The progress of Myanmar's nuclear research is not known, but it is believed to be in its infancy and widely regarded as a pipedream that is unlikely to succeed in developing nuclear weapons."[82] The United States appeared to agree with Lintner. The Burmese regime had nuclear ambitions but was not at all close to producing a bomb.

In any event, in December 2011 Secretary Clinton asked Burma to end its "illicit ties to North Korea." A few months later Burma apparently informed South Korea that it would no longer purchase weapons from the north, something it admitted having done for the previous twenty years. In November 2012 Burma announced that it was abiding by a UN resolution banning the purchase of military goods or training from North Korea. The Americans wanted Burma to cut all military ties to the country and seem to have gotten their wish, although in July 2013 they accused one high-ranking military official of continuing to do business with North Korea. In December 2013 Ambassador Mitchell commented that there were still some questions about Burma's military connections with North Korea that concerned the United States, and in December, in fact, as in July, the United States sanctioned an individual for the continuing relationship. Those sanctioned are prohibited from entering the United States, and Americans are not allowed to do any business with them.[83] But the North Korean nexus, while potentially serious, has so far not been an impediment to easing the general sanctions regime.

In sum, the existence of the remaining political prisoners and the regime's general human rights record were the two most significant reasons that all sanctions were not removed. The ethnic minorities question, which also involved human rights abuses, was important but would probably not ultimately stand in the way of fully normalizing relations. The North Korean connection was potentially a major stumbling block, but the issue of Burma's nuclear interests faded away, and the Burmese government appeared willing to cut its military relationship with Pyongyang.

The reforms continued apace, Burma welcomed more American influence, including allowing the Voice of America's English-language teaching program; USAID once again began work in September 2012, focusing primarily on health care, rural development, democracy, and human rights, and humanitarian assistance; agreement was reached to send a Peace Corps contingent to Myanmar in 2015; and the prospects of military engagement was also under active examination.

There has even been recent agreement for some US technical assistance to improve the Rangoon-Mandalay highway.[84]

A Presidential Visit

In November 2012, a safely reelected Barack Obama visited Yangon, the first sitting American president ever to visit Burma. Some observers thought this was premature: it would only reward "Burma for what they've already been rewarded for, and it wastes enormous political capital which could have been saved up and used to reward future events." There was also the possible embarrassment if, after the visit, there was retrogression. On the other hand, Aung San Suu Kyi herself had encouraged Obama to make the visit. Steinberg agreed, writing that while Myanmar had much to do before full democracy was reached, the president had "the opportunity to move the reforms forward" while at the same time reassuring Beijing that the American interest in transforming the Burmese economy and societal institutions was also in China's interest.[85]

In the end Obama's visit to Yangon was an unexcelled triumph, marked by his stirring speech at the hurriedly refurbished Yangon University auditorium. Obama pushed a democratic agenda while praising the courage of Aung San Suu Kyi and other dissidents. He forthrightly recalled the transgressions of the regime, while noting the significant changes that had occurred. Even the normally hostile *Wall Street Journal* termed the speech "among the best of his Presidency. . . . His call for greater freedom left no doubt where America stands." Concrete results of the trip included the release of more political prisoners, the admission of the Red Cross to Burma's prisons, approval for USAID to work again in Burma, and Burma's signature on the nuclear nonproliferation treaty. Relations between the United States and Burma had never been better, and there was praise from all sides for how the Obama administration had approached Burma. As the National Endowment for Democracy's Brian Joseph put it in January 2012, "we don't take a position, but I think they've handled it very, very well."[86]

There were significant developments in Burma in 2013. The military continued to fight in Kachin State, and there was major religious violence elsewhere. In March troops had to be dispatched to the city of Meiktila to end three days of vicious anti-Muslim violence in which at least thirty-two people died. "I can't handle what I saw there," said one Burmese human rights activist.[87] Then the anti-Muslim riots spread to other cities in Burma. There was also a major protest over the Chinese-owned Letpadaung open pit copper mine in central Myanmar, and Aung San Suu Kyi was now tested as a political leader rather than an icon.

The conflict in Kachin State and particularly the anti-Muslim riots troubled the United States, concerned that the violence might sidetrack or even subvert the country's progress toward reform, but at least for the time being it did not affect the overall bilateral relationship. USAID announced new projects in Burma, the Fulbright Program was reinstituted, and Johns Hopkins and other American universities were again present at Yangon University. In April more political prisoners were released.

Then in May Thein Sein received a warm welcome at the White House. It was a symbolically significant visit. Obama had been the first American president ever to visit Burma, and it had been nearly half a century since a Burmese leader had come to Washington. The American business community welcomed Thein Sein with enthusiasm, while some human rights activists and refugees from ethnic minorities objected. Obama urged continued political and economic reform, as well as an end to the anti-Muslim violence then still under way in the country. "The displacement of people, the violence directed towards them, needs to stop," he said.[88] In this way, the visit marked the maturation of the US-Burma rapprochement. "'That initial euphoria, that honeymoon period, is starting to wear off,' a senior Obama administration official said before Thein Sein's arrival. 'This is a check-in meeting,' to cement democratic advances that Thein Sein has made . . . and to apply gentle pressure for more changes."[89]

FIGURE 16.   Myanmar's President Thein Sein is pictured here with Barack Obama at the White House on 20 May 2013. White House video, https://www.youtube.com/watch?v=aILkTGb4NYM.

A Delicate Relationship

The changes in Myanmar were truly remarkable, as was the transformation in the bilateral relationship, due in part to the deft diplomacy of the Obama administration. Secretary Clinton considered the transformation to be the administration's greatest foreign policy triumph. It was also one of the few issues, domestic or foreign, that had almost complete bipartisan support, both because the disgust with the Burmese junta extended all across the American political spectrum and also because Aung San Suu Kyi was such a compelling figure to people of all political persuasions. By the time Obama engaged with the issue, there was a realization that new thinking about Burma was needed. Obama decided to forgo regime change in favor of regime modification and accommodation between the opposition and the government, nonetheless retaining the sanctions while engaging with the junta. Certainly the Americans were not entirely responsible for what developed, and it is easy to overlook internal Burmese dynamics, as well as other external factors. In a commencement speech at West Point in May 2014 Obama noted the importance of "the enormous courage of the people in that country," but also credited American "diplomatic initiative, American leadership" for the reforms needed to open "a once closed society" and for turning Burma away from North Korea to a new engagement with the United States.[90] Perhaps, as Obama's Burmese critics said, he was guilty of boasting a bit. Still, the United States was not insignificant in the process of change.

The role that the sanctions played in altering Burmese behavior is hotly contested. The opponents of sanctions have criticized them on a number of grounds, but at heart is a belief that they were enacted emotionally. A careful, rationally calculated foreign policy, à la George F. Kennan, based on what was truly in the national interest, would have achieved better results. This view may be right, but the emotional response was predictable and understandable, and the junta itself was responsible for this reaction. Ne Win had driven the economy of Burma into the ground. He had ended democracy and any semblance of civil liberties, and had imprisoned possible opponents. The junta killed several thousand of its own citizens in 1988, ignored the results of its own election in 1990, and continued to brutalize its own people thereafter. It refused to allow Suu Kyi's dying husband to visit her in his final days. To respond unemotionally to such things was difficult, and besides, Aung San Suu Kyi captured the world's imagination—someone who seemed to encompass the feelings and ambitious of a repressed people. The election results of both 1990 and 2012 bear this out.

Even supporters of the sanctions concluded eventually that by themselves they would not force the junta from power, but on the other hand, those opposed to the sanctions sometimes dismiss too quickly their importance. If they could not in themselves bring down the junta, the regime clearly wanted them ended. As U Tin Oo put it in February 2012, if they had been ineffective, then "why do they [the government] ask to lift the sanctions?" The late U Thet Tun, an eminent economist, agreed that the sanctions bit hard, stating that it was especially difficult for pensioners, who had trouble withdrawing funds from their pensions, presumably because of the banking sanctions. The Burmese did not like having the reputation of a pariah state, and the targeted sanctions that the Americans imposed may have been particularly effective.[91] Finally, and paradoxically, the sanctions' role in pushing Myanmar ever closer to China actually created a nationalistic backlash that contributed to the changes.

Although the changes that have taken place in Myanmar have been received with much fanfare and favor in the United States (and elsewhere), it would be a mistake to assume that Myanmar will pursue policies in the future that will align it with the West. For most of its history as an independent nation Burma sought complete nonalignment and neutrality. Though this was a Cold War construct, it is unlikely that Myanmar will want to be identified as an ally of any power. Even if Aung San Suu Kyi should become the country's president, Myanmar will pursue its own course. Its relationship with China is a case in point. Myanmar may from time to time take positions at odds with those of China, as it did with the Mytisone dam project, but in the long run it will surely be try to be friendly with its powerful northern neighbor with which it shares a very long border. There is still truth in the old Burmese saying, "When China spits, we swim."[92] Nor will China be passive. In November 2014 China pledged $7.8 billion to improve Myanmar's crumbling infrastructure and to "increase energy production"; the United States pledged $150 million.[93] Furthermore, there will doubtless be tensions with the United States. The relationship will continue to be delicate.

In any event, Myanmar is today a changed country. American chargé d'affaires Michael Thurston put it this way in February 2012: "this country is trying to pull off a transformation that's almost unheard of. If they can do it, it's really going to be something to see." There are still problems, and not all issues are settled. "Several difficulties and potential pitfalls lie ahead," Ambassador Mitchell noted in December 2013. However, the relationship with the Burmese authorities had become "very constructive, essentially 180 degrees from what it was perhaps two and a half years ago."[94]

In 2014 there were concerns that Burma was backsliding. The military resisted any further diminution of its power, and efforts to amend the constitution so that Aung San Suu Kyi could run for president in 2015 had not been successful. In May President Obama extended some economic sanctions against persons who had repressed the democratic movement, and in October the United States froze the assets of U Aung Thaung, minister of industry from 1997 to 2011.

"By intentionally undermining the positive political and economic transition in Burma, Aung Thaung is perpetuating violence, oppression, and corruption," explained Adam Szubin, the director of the Treasury's Office of Foreign Assets Control. There remains considerable concern about the continuing plight of the Rohingyas, many of whom have been forced into camps with few if any services. Myanmar ordered Médecins Sans Frontières, one of the few organizations providing medical help to the Rohingyas, to leave the country. In November 2014, on his second visit in Myanmar, President Obama commented that "discrimination toward the Rohingya or any other religious minority, I think, does not express the kind of country, over the long term, that Burma wants to be."[95]

The delicacy that has historically characterized the bilateral relationship will continue, but for the moment there is a sense of cautious optimism that Myanmar is generally moving in the right direction. Let us hope that the changes in Burma will be long-lasting and that the people of Burma will find freedom and peace. If that is the final result, the United States can be proud of its role, even if a limited one, in helping to bring it about.

Appendix

US AMBASSADORS AND CHARGÉS D'AFFAIRES APPOINTED TO BURMA

Source: http://en.wikipedia.org/wiki/United_States_Ambassador_to_Burma.

All ambassadors were career Foreign Service Officers and had the title of Ambassador Extraordinary and Plenipotentiary.

- J. Klahr Huddle
  - Appointed: 17 October 1947
  - Presented credentials: 3 March 1948
  - Terminated mission: 28 November 1949
- David McKendree Key
  - Appointed: 17 March 1950
  - Presented credentials: 26 April 1950
  - Terminated mission: 28 October 1951
- William J. Sebald
  - Appointed: 25 April 1952
  - Presented credentials: 18 July 1952
  - Terminated mission: 15 July 1954
- Joseph C. Satterthwaite
  - Appointed: 4 April 1955
  - Presented credentials: 10 May 1955
  - Terminated mission: 1 April 1957

- Walter P. McConaughy
  - Appointed: 20 May 1957
  - Presented credentials: 20 August 1957
  - Terminated mission: 2 November 1959
- William P. Snow
  - Appointed: 9 November 1959
  - Presented credentials: 1 December 1959
  - Terminated mission: 4 May 1961
- John Scott Everton
  - Appointed: 4 May 1961
  - Presented credentials: 10 June 1961
  - Terminated mission: 21 May 1963
- Henry A. Byroade
  - Appointed: 10 September 1963
  - Presented credentials: 7 October 1963
  - Terminated mission: 11 June 1968
- Arthur W. Hummel Jr.
  - Appointed: 26 September 1968
  - Presented credentials: October 1968
  - Terminated mission: 22 July 1971
- Edwin W. Martin
  - Appointed: 10 August 1971
  - Presented credentials: 1 October 1971
  - Terminated mission: 20 November 1973
- David L. Osborn
  - Appointed: 28 February 1974
  - Presented credentials: 22 March 1974
  - Terminated mission: 25 July 1977
- Maurice Darrow Bean
  - Appointed: 19 September 1977
  - Presented credentials: 8 November 1977
  - Terminated mission: 10 August 1979
- Patricia M. Byrne
  - Appointed: 27 November 1979
  - Presented credentials: 14 January 1980
  - Terminated mission: 14 September 1983
- Daniel Anthony O'Donohue
  - Appointed: 14 November 1983
  - Presented credentials: 26 December 1983
  - Terminated mission: 16 December 1986

- Burton Levin
  - Appointed: 7 April 1987
  - Presented credentials: 26 May 1987
  - Terminated mission: 30 September 1990
- *Note*: No ambassador was appointed to replace Levin until 2012. The U.S. was represented by a succession of chargés d'affaires (see below).
- Derek Mitchell
  - Appointed: 5 July 2012
  - Presented credentials: 6 July 2012

Chargés d'Affaires

- Franklin P. Huddle Jr. (September 1990–September 1994)
- Marilyn Meyers (September 1994–October 1996)
- Kent M. Wiedemann (October 1996–May 1999)
- Priscilla A. Clapp (July 1999–August 2002)
- Carmen Maria Martinez (August 2002–August 2005)
- Shari Villarosa (August 2005–September 2008)
- Larry M. Dinger (September 2008–August 2011)
- Michael Thurston (August 2011–July 2012)

Uncompleted appointments

- Frederick Vreeland was nominated to the ambassadorial post by President George H. W. Bush on 6 June 1990, but the government of Myanmar withdrew its agrément to his appointment before the Senate could vote on his nomination.
- Parker W. Borg was nominated by President George H. W. Bush on 22 July 1991, but the Senate declined to act on the nomination.
- Michael J. Green was nominated by President George W. Bush on 17 November 2008 to fulfill a special envoy position delegated by the Tom Lantos Block Burma JADE Act, but the nomination was not voted on by the end of the Bush administration.

Notes

The following archive abbreviations are used in the notes:

AMCB	American Medical Center for Burma records, manuscript division, Library of Congress
BNA	British National Archives, Kew, Surrey, UK
CDF	Central Decimal File
CFPC	Central Foreign Policy File
CREST documents	CIA Records Search Tool database
DDEL	Dwight D. Eisenhower Presidential Library
DF	Decimal File
EXAF	External Affairs Office (Australia)
FBIS	Foreign Broadcast Information Service
FO	Foreign Office (Burma, UK)
FRUS	*Foreign Relations of the United States*
GHWBL	George H. W. Bush Presidential Library
GRFL	Gerald R. Ford Presidential Library
HIA	Hoover Institution Archives
HSTL	Harry S. Truman Presidential Library
JCL	Jimmy Carter Presidential Library
LBJL	Lyndon B. Johnson Presidential Library
Memcon	Memorandum of Conversation
MNA	Myanmar National Archives
NA	(US) National Archives, Washington, DC
NAII	(US) National Archives II, College Park, MD
NAA	National Archives of Australia
NPM	Nixon Presidential Materials, RMNL
NSF	National Security Files
OF	Office Files
RMNL	Richard M. Nixon Presidential Library
RRL	Ronald Reagan Presidential Library
SNF	Subject-Numeric File
SS	Secretary of State
Transcript of Evidence	Testimony at trial of Gordon S. Seagrave
USDS	US Department of State
WHCF	White House Central Files
WHORM	White House Office of Records Management

INTRODUCTION

1. Steinberg, "Aung San Suu Kyi and U.S. Policy toward Burma/Myanmar," 45, 36.

2. Thant Myint-U, *River of Lost Footsteps*, 43–46, 56–57; Cady, *United States and Burma*, 23. I am grateful to Yangon University Professors Margaret Wong and Kyaw Win for information on the Sakiyans.

3. Steinberg, *Burma: A Socialist Nation*, 21. Thant Myint-U, *River of Lost Footsteps*, 63.

4. Cady, *United States and Burma*, 58–60.

5. Thant Myint-U, *River of Lost Footsteps*, 21–22.

6. Steinberg, *Burma: A Socialist Nation*, 28, 37–41; quotation on p. 39.

7. Thant Myint-U, *River of Lost Footsteps*, 215–16.

8. G. Bhagat, *Americans in India 1784–1860* (New York: New York University Press, 1970), ix, vi.

9. Darkow, "American Relations with Burma," 2–4.

10. Gerald H. Nash, *The Life of Herbert Hoover: The Engineer 1874–1914* (New York: Norton, 1983), 424; Darkow, "American Relations with Burma," 9–10. On Coca Cola in Burma, see the photograph at http://www.coca-colacompany.com/press-center/image-library/coca-cola-in-yangon-in-1927.

11. Knowles, *Memoir of Mrs. Ann H. Judson*, passim; Darkow, "American Relations with Burma," 19–21.

12. Trager, *Burma Through Alien Eyes*, 9–22.

13. Ibid., 57–80, 173–203.

14. Darkow, "American Relations with Burma," 41–42.

15. Ibid., 50–54. John Cady to George Kahin, 21 October 1953, George Kahin Papers, box 74, folder 74-9, Cornell University Library; Cady, *Contacts with Burma*, 1–39.

16. Walinsky, *Economic Development in Burma*, 552.

17. Darkow, "American Relations with Burma," 59–60.

18. Robert E. Sherwood, *Roosevelt and Hopkins: An Intimate History* (New York: Harper, 1948), 289–90, 404–5.

19. Darkow, "American Relations with Burma," 82.

20. Seagrave, *Burma Surgeon*, 151–295.

21. An excellent recent account is Sacquety, *The OSS in Burma, 1942–1945*.

22. "The Burma Campaign," in Frank Roberts Papers, box 1, folder "Burma Campaign, 1942," HSTL.

23. Thorne, *Allies of a Kind*, 6.

24. Ibid., 595.

1. BURMESE NATIONALISM AND THE PATH TO INDEPENDENCE

1. William O. Douglas, "Revolution in Burma," *Look*, 2 December 1952, 38.

2. Charney, *History of Modern Burma*, 7–13. Taylor, *The State in Burma*, 66–79. Callahan, *Making Enemies*, 21–24 (quotation on p. 23).

3. Charney, *History of Modern Burma*, 11–17, 32–45. Thant Myint-U, *River of Lost Footsteps*, 212–14.

4. Charney, *History of Modern Burma*, 46.

5. Cady, *United States and Burma*, 168–70.

6. Statement Presented to Parliament on 17th May," enclosed in W. Garnett (Official Secretary, Office of the High Commission for the United Kingdom, Canberra) to Secretary, Australian Prime Minister's Department, 18 May 1945, series A461, control symbol F350/1/1/7, NAA. Garnett to Secretary, Australian Prime Minister's Department, 18 May 1945, ibid.

7. Coulter D. Huyler Jr., "The Burma Communist Party and the Burma Patriotic Front," 28 June 1945, enclosed in Howard Donovan to SS, 13 July 1945, Despatch 2177, 845C.00/7-1345, RG59, DF 1945–1949, box 6117, NAII. Memcon, Cady and Mr. Richardson of *Life* and *Time* magazines, 19 November 1945, 845C.00/11-1945, ibid., box 6117, NAII. Office Memorandum, Cady to Abbott Low Moffat and Lampton Berry, 27 July 1945, 845C.01/7-2745, ibid., box 6123.

8. Office Memorandum, Cady to Moffat and Berry, 1 August 1945, 845C.01/7-2745, 27 July 1945, 845C.01/7-2745, RG59, DF 1945–1949, box 6123, NAII. Earl of Listowel, *Memoirs*, 13–15; Cady, *United States and Burma*, 172–77.

9. Memcon, Cady and Mr. Seligman, 6 November 1945, 845C.00/11-645, RG59, DF 1945–1949, box 6117, NAII.

10. John F. Cady, "The Burma Legislative Council," 2 February 1946, Despatch 8, RG 84, Burma: US Embassy, Classified General Records, 1945–1961, box 1, NAII. Office Memorandum, Berry to Loy W. Henderson and Mr. [?] Allen, 7 December 1945, 845C.00/12-745, RG59, DF 1945–1949, box 6117, NAII.

11. Dean Acheson to US consul, Rangoon, 25 January 1946, Tel. 15, 845C.00/1-2546, RG59, DF 1945–1949, box 6118, NAII.

12. Abbey to SS, 25 January 1946, Despatch 21, 845C.00/1-2546, ibid., box 6117.

13. Ibid.

14. Abbey to SS, 21 November 1945, Despatch 5, 845C.00/11-2145, ibid., box 6117, NAII.

15. Abbey to SS, 22 April 1946, *FRUS* 1946, 8:2.

16. Abbey to SS, 4 May 1946, Despatch 99, 845C.00/5-446, RG 59, DF 1945–1949, box 6118, NAII.

17. Abbey to SS, 23 May 1946, Airgram A-43, 845C.00/5-2346, ibid.

18. Abbey to SS, 5 July 1946, Despatch 157, 845C.00/7-546, ibid.

19. Earl L. Packer to SS, 20 September 1946, Tel. 296, 845C.00/9-2046, ibid. Packer to SS, 20 September 1946, Tel. 298, 845C.00/9-2046, ibid., box 6118.

20. Memcon, Hubert Elvin Rance and Packer, 5 November 1946, enclosed in Packer to USDS, 7 November 1946, Despatch 65, RG 84, Burma: US Embassy, Classified General Records, 1945–1961, box 1, NAII. Packer to SS, 3 October 1946, Despatch 37, 845C.00/10-345, RG 59, DF 1945–1949, box 6117, NAII. Packer provided Rance's government with a copy of the Philippine constitution as a possible model for Burma. Rance quoted in Waldemar J. Gallman to SS, 27 September 1946, Tel. 8467, RG 59, DF 1945–1949, box 6117, NAII.

21. Packer to SS, undated (received 1 October 1946), Tel. 327, 845C.00/10-146, RG 59, DF 1945–1949, box 6118, NAII. Clipping, "Burma 'Grown Up,'" *Times* (London), 10 October 1946, FO 643/25, BNA. Dorman-Smith quoted in Gallman to SS, 27 September 1946, Tel. 8467, RG 59, DF 1945–1949, box 6117, NAII.

22. Memcon, Aung San and Packer, 31 October 1945, enclosed in Packer to SS, 1 November 1946, Despatch 56, 845C.00/11-146, RG 59, DF 1945–1949, box 6117, NAII.

23. Memcon, Rance and Packer, 2 October 1946, enclosed in Packer to SS, 3 October 1946, Despatch 37, 845C.00/10-346, ibid. Memcon, Aung San and Packer, 31 October 1945, enclosed in Packer to SS, 1 November 1946, Despatch 56, 845C.00/11-146, ibid.

24. B.R. Pearn [?], "The Foreign Relations of Burma as an Independent State," 31 May 1948 [?], FO 435/1, BNA. R. Austin Acly to SS, 20 August 1948, Despatch 658, RG 84, Burma US Embassy, Classified General Records 1945–1961, box 4, NAII.

25. Press Release no. 259, USDS, 31 March 1948, series A1838, control symbol 3008/11/161 Part 1, NAA.

26. Office Memorandum, Berry to Mr. [Loy ?] Henderson and Mr. Allen, 7 December 1945, 845C.00/12-745, RG59, DF 1945–1949, box 6117, NAII. Memcon, Rance and Packer, 4 October 1946, ibid. Memcon, Aung San and Packer, 31 October 1945, enclosed in Packer to SS, 1 November 1946, ibid.

27. Acheson to US Embassy London, repeated to US consulate Rangoon, 4 May 1946, Tel. 101 (to Rangoon), RG 84, Burma: US Embassy, Classified General Records, 1945–1961, box 1, NAII.

28. Governor's Secretary's Office, Rangoon, to OFFBURLON-London, 9 March 1946, FO 643/35, BNA.

29. Douglas Flood to USDS, 25 July 1946, file no. 501, RG 84, Burma: US Embassy, Classified General Records, 1945–1961, box 1, NAII. Memorandum, Division of Foreign Reporting Services, USDS, 10 October 1946, 801-C, ibid.

30. Memcon, Aung San and Packer, 31 October 1945, enclosed in Packer to SS, 1 November 1946, Despatch 56, 845C.00/11-146, RG 59, DF 1945–1949, box 6117, NAII. Acheson to U.S. Embassy London, 8 November 1946, Tel. 7614, 845C.00/11-846, ibid.

31. Gallman to SS, 13 November 1946, Tel. 9463, 845C.00/11-1346, RG 59, DF 1945–1949, ibid. Packer to SS, 16 December 1946, Tel. 502, 845C.00/12-1646, ibid.

32. Acheson to US Embassy London, 10 December 1946, Tel. 8099, 845C.00/12-646, ibid. James Byrnes to US Embassy London, 20 December 1946, Tel. 8258, 845C.00/12-1646, ibid.

33. Gallman to SS, 20 December 1946, Tel. 10195, 845C.00/12-2046, ibid.

34. Packer to SS, 31 December 1946, Tel. 532, 845C.00/12-3146, ibid. Packer to SS, 2 January 1947, Tel. 4, 845C.00/1-247, ibid., box 6118. Packer to SS, 8 January 1947, Tel. 19, 845C.00/1-747, ibid.

35. Byrnes to US Consul Rangoon, 17 January 1947, Tel. 25, RG 84, Burma Embassy and Consulate, Classified General Records, box 1, NAII.

36. Gallman to SS, 28 January 1947, Tel. 606, 845C.00/1-2847, RG 59, DF 1945–1949, box 6118, NAII.

37. Packer to SS, 30 January 1947, Tel. 79, 845C.00/1-3047, ibid. Packer to SS, 13 February 1947, Tel. 116, RG 84, Burma US Embassy, Classified General Records 1945–1961, box 1, NAII. Packer to SS, 10 February 1947, Tel. 112, 845C.00/2-1047, RG 59, DF 1945-1949, box 6118, NAII.

38. Packer to SS, 30 November 1946, Airgram A-149, RG 84, Burma US Embassy, Classified General Records, 1945–1961, box 1, NAII. "News in English," 22 March 1947 and 5 April 1947, series A1838, control symbol 3008/11/161 Part 1, NAA. George C. Marshall, "Memorandum for the President," 28 May 1947, OF 48K, box 248, Truman Papers, HSTL.

39. Packer to SS, 19 July 1947, Tel. 603, 845C.00/7-1947, RG 59, DF 1945–1949, box 6119, NAII.

40. Packer to SS, 25 July 1947, Tel. 631, 845C.00/7-2547, ibid. Packer to SS, 29 July 1947, Tel. 645, 845C.00/7-2947, ibid.

41. Packer to SS, 6 August 1947, Tel. 676, 845C.00/8-647, ibid.

42. Packer to SS, 25 July 1947, Tel. 631, 845C.00/7-2547, ibid. Packer to SS, 29 July 1947, Tel. 645, 845C.00/7-2947, ibid.

43. Packer to SS, 25 July 1947, Tel. 631, 845C.00/7-2547, ibid. Packer to SS, 29 July 1947, Tel. 645, 845C.00/7-2947, ibid. Thant Myint-U, *River of Lost Footsteps*, 255. Earl of Listowel, *Memoirs*, 24–25. Allen, "'The Escape of Captain Vivian,'" 65–69.

44. Packer to SS, 6 August 1947, Tel. 667, 845C.00/8-647, RG 59, DF 1945–1949, box 6119, NAII. Charney, *History of Modern Burma*, 70.

45. Allen, "'The Escape of Captain Vivian,'" 65–69.

46. U Nu, *Saturday's Son*, 136.

47. Byrnes to US Consul, Rangoon, 8 March 1946, Tel. 51, 845C.00/3-846, RG59, DF 1945–1949, box 6118, NAII. Howard Donovan to SS, 13 July 1945, Despatch 2177, 845C.00/7-1345, ibid., box 6117.

48. Donovan to SS, 13 July 1945, Despatch 2177, 845C.00/7-1345, RG59, DF 1945–1949, box 6117, NAII.

49. Huyler, "The Burma Communist Party and the Burma Patriotic Front."

50. Abbey to SS, 13 August 1946, Despatch 187, 845C.00/8-1346, RG59, DF 1945–1949, box 6118, NAII.

51. Packer to SS, 30 October 1946, Tel. 390, 845C.00/10-3046, ibid., box 6117. Packer to SS, 5 November 1946, Tel. 413, 845C.00/11-546, ibid.

52. Packer to SS, 26 February 1947, Airgram A-47, 845C.00/2-2647, ibid., box 6118. Raymond E. Murphy to Henderson, 6 March 1947, RG 84, Burma US Embassy, Classified General Records 1945–1961, box 1, NAII.

53. Henderson to Packer, 7 March 1947, RG 84, Burma US Embassy, Classified General Records 1945–1961, box 1, NAII.

54. Packer to SS, 7 April 1947, Tel. 259, 845C.00/4-747, RG 59, DF 1945–1949, box 6118, NAII. For Aung San's radio address, see "A.F.P.F.L. Leaders at Cross-Roads," *New Times of Burma*, 6 April 1947, in Packer to SS, 8 April 1947, Despatch 268, 845C.00/4-847, ibid., box 6119.

55. Memcon, U Kyaw Nyein and Packer, 23 May 1947, enclosed in Packer to SS, 27 May 1947, Despatch 335, 845C.00/5-2747, box 6119, NAII. Memcon, U Aung San and Packer, 28 May 1947, enclosed in Packer to SS, 31 May 1947, Despatch 345, 845C.00/5-3147, ibid.

56. Memcon, Thakin Mya and Packer, 31 May 1947, enclosed in Packer to SS, 3 June 1947, Despatch 349, 845C.00/6-347, ibid.

57. George Marshall to Packer, 30 June 1947, Airgram A-78, 845C.00/6-3047, ibid. Packer to SS, 19 July 1947, Tel. 601, 845C.00/7-1947, ibid. Packer to SS, 4 August 1947, Despatch 442, RG 84, Burma US Embassy, Classified General Records 1945–1961, box 2, NAII.

58. Abbey to SS, 22 April 1946, *FRUS* 1946, 8:1. Packer to SS, 21 October 1947, Despatch 67, 845C.11/10-2147, RG 59, DF 1945–1949, box 6123, NAII.

59. W. Stratton Anderson Jr. to SS, 10 November 1947, Despatch 2532, 845C.01/11-1047, RG 59, DF 1945–1949, box 6123, NAII.

60. Edwin F. Stanton to SS, 8 January 1948, Despatch 6, 845C.01/1-848, ibid.

61. Ibid. For Truman's comments see Robert A. Lovett to US Embassy Rangoon, 29 December 1947, Tel. 134, 845C.01/12-2947, ibid.

62. Stanton to SS, 8 January 1948, Despatch 6, 845C.01/1-848, ibid.

2. THE LEAKY DERELICT

1. U Nu, *Saturday's Son*, 136.

2. Steinberg, "Burma-Myanmar: The U.S.-Burmese Relationship and Its Vicissitudes," 210. Hugh D. S. Greenway, "Which Is the Burma Road: Ne Win or U Nu?" *New York Times Magazine*, 3 May 1970, 41.

3. Acly to SS, 11 February 1948, Tel. 56, 845C.00/2-1148, RG 59, DF 1945–1949, box 6120, NAII. Acly to SS, 12 February 1948, 845C.00/2-1248, ibid.

4. J. Klahr Huddle to SS, 20 February 1948, 845C.00/2-2048, ibid.

5. Huddle to SS, 6 March 1948, Tel. 91, 845C.00/3-648, ibid.

6. Acly to SS, 7 September 1948, Despatch 192, 845C.00/2-748, ibid. Huddle to SS, 2 March 1948, Despatch 275, 845C.00/3-248, ibid. US Embassy Rangoon to SS, 2 March 1948, Despatch 279, 845C.00/2-348, ibid.

7. Huddle to SS, 20 March 1948, Tel. 107, 845C.00/3-2048, ibid. U Nu, *Saturday's Son*, 163.

8. Memcon, J. Russell Andrus and "a former alien employee of a United States Agency," 19 March 1948, enclosed in US Embassy Rangoon to USDS, 22 March 1948, Despatch 358, 845C.00/3-2248, RG 59, DF 1945–1949, box 6120, NAII.

9. Huddle to SS, 28 March 1948, Tel. 117, 845C.00/3-2848, RG 59, DF 1945–1949, box 6120, NAII.

10. On Law-Yone, see Wendy Law-Yone, *Golden Parasol*. [USDS] to US Embassy Rangoon, 28 April 1948, Tel. 43, 845C.00/3-2248, RG 59, DF 1945–1949, box 6120, NAII.

11. Acly to SS, 28 June 1948, Despatch 563, 845C.00/6-2848, 845C.00/6-2848, RG 59, DF 1945-1949, Box 6120, NAII. Albert B. Franklin to USDS, 20 February 1952, Despatch 715, RG 59, CDF 1950–1954, box 4137, NAII.

12. Huddle to SS, 31 March 1948, Tel. 124, 845C.00/3-3148, RG 59, DF 1945–1949, box 6120, NAII. Huddle to SS, 2 April 1948, Despatch 385, 845C.00/4-248, ibid.

13. Huddle to SS, 16 April 1948, Tel. 155, 845C.00/4-1648, ibid.

14. Memorandum of Telephone Conversation, James Barrington and Andrus, 14 April 1948, RG 84, Burma US Embassy, Classified General Records 1945–1961, box 5, NAII.

15. AAR, Office Memorandum, 26 April 1948, ibid. Huddle to SS, 25 May 1948, Despatch 514, 845C.00/5-2548, RG 59, DF 1945–1949, box 6120, NAII.

16. Huddle to SS, 26 May 1948, Tel. 213, 845C.00/5-2648, ibid. Huddle to SS, 27 May 1948, Tel. 214, 845C.00/2748, ibid. Huddle to SS, 4 May 1948, 845C.00/5-448, Despatch 471, ibid. Huddle to SS, 27 May 1948, Tel. 214, 845C.00/5-2748, ibid.

17. Huddle to SS, 3 June 1948, Tel. 236, 845C.00/6-348, ibid. Acly to SS, 19 June 1948, Tel. 260, 845C.00/6-1948, ibid.

18. Acly to SS, 28 June 1948, Despatch 564, 845C.00/6-2845, ibid. Grady, quoted in Memcon, U Tin Tut, Barrington, Acly, and Andrus, 1 July 1948, enclosed in Acly to SS, 2 July 1948, Despatch 570, 845C.00/7-248, ibid.

19. Memcon, U Tin Tut, Barrington, Acly, and Andrus, 1 July 1948, enclosed in Acly to SS, 2 July 1948, Despatch 570, 845C.00/7-248, ibid. Acly to SS, 6 August 1948, Tel. 333, 845C.00/8-648, ibid.

20. Acly to SS, 9 August 1948, Tel. 338, 845C.00/8-948, ibid. Acly to SS, 11 August 1948, Tel. 345, 845C.00/8-1148, ibid. Navy Department to SS, 12 August 1948, Navy Message 111726Z, 845C.000/8-1248, ibid.

21. Memcon, J.C. Tulloch and G. Lewis Jones, 14 July 1948, enclosed in Jones to SS, 15 July 1948, Despatch 1566, RG 84, Burma US Embassy, Classified General Records 1945–1961, box 5, NAII.

22. Acly to SS, 8 September 1948, Despatch 700, 845C.00/9-848, RG 59, DF 1945–1949, box 6120, NAII.

23. Thant Myint-U, *River of Lost Footsteps*, 261.

24. Lewis Douglas to SS, 8 September 1948, Tel. 4025, 845C.00/9-848, RG 59, DF 1945–1949, box 6120, NAII. Burma soon requested five thousand carbines, 2.5 million rounds of ammunition, and 150 jeeps. Barrington to Acly, 2 September 1948, RG 84: Burma US Embassy, Classified General Records 1945–1961, box 5, NAII. Andrus, "The Karen Problem," 2 February 1949, Despatch 8, RG 84: Burma US Embassy, Classified General Records 1945–1961, box 6, NAII. Acly to SS, 10 September 1948, Despatch 705, 845C.00/-9-1048, RG 59, DF 1945-1949, box 6120, NAII.

25. Acly to SS, 13 September 1948, Tel. 411, 845C.00/9-1348, RG 59, DF 1945–1949, box 6120, NAII. Acly to SS, 8 September 1948, Despatch 700, 845C.00/9-848, ibid.

26. Acly to SS, 8 September 1948, Despatch 700, 845C.00/9-848, ibid. Acly to SS, 21 September 1948, Tel. 426, 845C.00/9-2148, ibid. Gordon Seagrave agreed. Tin Tut, he wrote, was "the biggest man in Burma bar none. . . . He was the real Burmese closer to our type of democracy than any other. He was reputed to be the only man in Burma that really understood finance." Gordon S. Seagrave to "my dear friends," 28 October 1948, ABHS, BIM, box 12.

27. Memcon, U Kyaw Nyein, George Marshall, et al., 21 October 1948, 845C.00/10-2148, RG 59, DF 1945–1949, box 6120, NAII.

28. Andrus to Richard E. Usher, 10 November 1948, 845C.00/11-1048, ibid. US Embassy Rangoon to USDS, 17 November 1948, Despatch 855, 845C.00/11-1748, ibid. Acly to SS, 9 December 1948, Tel. 535, 845C.01/12-948, box 6123, NAII.

29. US Embassy Rangoon to USDS, 28 December 1948, Despatch 937, 845C.00/12-2848, box 6120, NAII. Edwin M. Martin to USDS, 14 April 1951, Despatch 706, 790B.00/4-1451, RG 59, CDF 1950–1954, box 4136, NAII.

30. Acly to SS, 7 December 1948, Tel. 534, 845C.00/12-748, RG 59, DF 1945–1949, box 6120, NAII. U. S. Embassy Rangoon to USDS, 24 November 1948, Despatch 872, 845C.00/11-2448, ibid. Lewis Douglas to SS, 10 December 1948, Airgram A-2292, 845C.00/12-1048, ibid.

31. CIA, Office of Reports and Estimates, "Intelligence Highlights No. 34," 5 January–11 January 1949, CREST documents, NAII.

32. US Embassy Rangoon to SS, 11 January 1949, Despatch 17, RG 84, Burma US Embassy, Classified General Records 1945–1961, box 5, NAII. Acly to SS, 27 January 1949, Tel. 23, 845C.00/1-2749, RG 59, DF 1945–1949, box 6121, NAII. Dean Acheson to US Embassy Rangoon, 4 February 1949, Tel. 24, 845C.00/2-149, ibid.

33. Memcon, Barrington and Acly, 24 January 1949, enclosed in Acly to SS, 10 February 1949, Despatch 73, 845C.00/2-1049, RG 59, DF 1945–1949, box 6121, NAII. Acly to SS. 1 February 1949, Tel. 33, 845C.00/2-149, ibid.

34. Steinberg, *Burma: A Socialist Nation*, 62.

35. Ibid., 12.

36. Ibid.; Thant Myint-U, *River of Lost Footsteps*, 294–95.

37. CIA, Office of Reports and Estimates, "Intelligence Highlights No. 38," 2 February–8 February, CREST documents, NAII. Memcon, Nu and Acly, 9 February 1949, enclosed in Acly to SS, 16 February 1949, Despatch 80, 845C.00/2-1649, RG 59, DF 1945–1949, box 6121, NAII. Acly to SS, 23 February 1949, Tel. 61, 845 C.00/2-2349, ibid. Acheson to US Embassy Rangoon, 5 March 1949, Tel. 43, ibid.

38. US Embassy Rangoon to USDS, 7 March 1949, 845C.00/3-749, Despatch 110, RG 59, DF 1945–1949, box 6121, NAII. Acly to SS, 3 March 1949, Tel. 73, 845C.00/3-349, ibid.

39. US Embassy to USDS, 23 April 1949, Despatch 161, 845C.00/4-2349, ibid. Far East/ Pacific Branch, Office of Reports and Estimates, CIA, "Intelligence Highlights No. 50," 4–10 May 1949, CREST documents, NAII. Far East/Pacific Branch, Office of Reports and Estimates, CIA, "Intelligence Highlights No. 51," 11–17 May 1949, CREST documents, NAII.

40. Huddle to SS, 18 May 1949, Despatch 206, and the enclosed "Office Memorandum," 14 May 1949, 845C.00/5-1449 RG 59, DF 1945–1949, box 6121, NAII. Memcon, M. E. Dening, G. C. McGhee, et al., 14 September 1949, 845C.00/9-1449, ibid.

41. J. Klahr Huddle to SS, 1 June 1949, Tel. 210, 845C.00/6-149 RG 59, DF 1945–1949, box 6121, NAII. Charney, *Modern Burma*, 81–82.

42. Huddle to SS, 1 June 1949, Tel. 210, 845C.00/6-149 RG 59, DF 1945–1949, box 6121, NAII. Huddle to Elbert G. Matthews, 3 June 1949, RG 84, Burma US Embassy, Classified General Records 1945–1961, box 6, NAII.

43. CIA, Far East/Pacific Branch, Office of Reports and Estimates, "Staff Study Project No. 6: Communist Influence in Burma," 23 August 1949, CREST documents, NAII. This study is a lengthy, insightful, and balanced analysis.

44. Teletype, "Ne Win in Washington," 24 July 1949; teletype, "News in English," 26 July 1949 [?]; newspaper clipping, "Burmese Talks," 28 July 1949; all in series A1838, control symbol 3008/11/161 Part 1, NAA. Memcon, U E Maung, Dean Acheson et al., 15 August 1949, Dean Acheson Papers, box 66, Memoranda of Conversations, file 1949–1953, HSTL. Huddle to SS, 5 October 1949, Despatch 395, 845C.00/10-549 RG 59, DF 1945–1949, box 6121, NAII.

45. British Embassy Washington to East Asia Department, FO, 28 July 1949, FO 371/75684, BNA. Herbert B. Spivack to USDS, 18 October 1949, "Monthly Political Report for September, 1949," Despatch 77, 845C.00/10-1849 RG 59, DF 1945–1949, box 6121, NAII.

46. Memorandum, George G. McGhee to Acheson, 21 October 1949, 845C.00/10-2149, RG 59, DF 1945–1949, box 6121, NAII.

47. Huddle to SS, 7 November 1949, Tel. 489, 845C.00/11-749, ibid.

48. Huddle to SS, 8 November 1949, Despatch 430, 845C.00/11-849, ibid.

49. Burmese Embassy Washington to FO, 24 January 1950, Tel. 169, folder "Question of Financial and Military Aid," series 15/3 (6), Acc. # 81, Year 1950, file 102 FMS 30, MNA.

50. Acheson to US Consulate Hong Kong (for Jessup), 20 January 1950, 790B.00/1-2050, RG 59, CDF 1950–1954, box 4135, NAII. Memorandum, George McGhee to Acheson, 20 January 1950, 790B.00/1-2050, ibid.

51. Memorandum, McGhee to Acheson, 25 January 1950, 790B.00/1-2550, ibid.

52. Steinberg and Fan, *Modern China-Myanmar Relations*, 14–18.

53. Memcon, U Nu, Philip C. Jessup, and William M. Gibson, 10 February 1950, *FRUS* 1950, 6:231. Day to SS, 10 February 1950, Tel. 74, RG 59, CDF 1950–1954, 790B.00 (W)/2-1050, box 4137, NAII.

54. Martin to SS, 14 February 1950, Tel. 85, 790B.00/2-1450, RG59, CDF 1950–1954, box 4135, NAII. Acheson to US Embassy Rangoon, 17 February 1950, 790B.00/2-1450, ibid.

55. Day to USDS, 6 March 1950, Despatch 99, 790B.00/3-650, ibid.

56. Raymond Hare to Livingston Merchant, 3 March 1950, 790B.5-MSP/3-350, ibid., box 4142. Day to USDS, 13 March 1950, Despatch 124, 770B.5MAP/3-1350, ibid., box 4141.

57. Oral history interview with Col. R. Allen Griffin, Pebble Beach, California, 15 February 1974, by James R. Fuchs, pp. 52–59, HSTL.

58. U Hla Maung, "Beginning of American Aid," in *The Beginning of American Aid to Southeast Asia: The Griffin Mission of 1950*, ed. Samuel P. Hayes (Lexington, MA: D. C. Heath, 1971), 209. Oral history Interview with Griffin. In his contemporary account, however, Griffin told the State Department that the Burmese were initially "a little reticent" to discuss assistance but soon became "quite cooperative." Memcon, Griffin et al., 4 May 1950, RG 84, Burma US Embassy, Classified General Records 1945–1961, box 12, NAII. "Visit to Rangoon of 3 Agricultural Experts of the United States Department of Agriculture from 31st March to April 4, 1950 and the Griffin Mission." Series 15/3 (2), Acc. # 15, Year 1950, file 422 FMG 49, MNA.

59. David McKendree Key (for Griffin) to SS, 30 March 1950, Tel. 164, RG 84, Burma US Embassy, Classified General Records 1945–1961, box 11, NAII. Acheson to US Embassy Rangoon, 31 March 1950, Tel. 131, file 501—Griffin Mission, ibid.

60. The Griffin Mission's detailed Burma report is printed in Hayes, *Beginning of American Aid to Southeast Asia*, 151–99.

61. "Oral Report by Ambassador-At-Large Philip C. Jessup Upon His Return from the Far East," 3 April 1950, *FRUS* 1950, 6:76. Sao Hkun Hkio to Jessup, 21 April 1950, in "Approach to the United States Government for a Loan," series 15/3 (6), Acc. #83, Year 1950, file 349 Nga Nya, MNA.

62. Herbert D. Spivack to USDS, 26 April 1950, Despatch 200, 790B.00/4-2650, RG 59, CDF 1950–1954, box 4135, NAII.

63. Jessup to Sao Hkun Hkio, 2 June 1950, "Question of Financial and Military Aid from the Emb. of the United States of America to the Union of Burma and other S. E. Asian Countries," series 15/3 (6), Acc. # 81, Year 1950, file 103 FMS 50, MNA.

64. Policy Statement Prepared in the Department of State, 16 June 1950, *FRUS* 1950, 6:233-44 (quotation on p. 235). The daily life of an American agricultural expert in Burma during this time can be explored in "Bill's Far East Letters" in the William J. Green Papers, box 22, HIA.

65. Key to SS, 28 April 1950, Tel. 238, 790B.00 (W)/4-2850, RG 59, CDF 1950–1954, box 4138, NAII. Memcon, 2 May 1950, General Lemnitzer et al., 2 May 1950,

790B.5-MAP/5-250, RG 59, CDF 1950–1954, box 4141, NAII. "Policy Statement Prepared in the Department of State: Burma," 16 June 1950, *FRUS* 1950, 6:235. Minute by F. Lemmering [?], 29 May 1950, on "Question of Financial and Military Aid from the Emb. of the United States of America to the Union of Burma and other S. E. Asian Countries," series 15/3 (6), Acc. # 81, Year 1950, file 103 FMS 50, MNA.

66. Key to SS, 30 June 1950, Tel. 370, 790B.00 (W)/6-3050, RG 59, CDF 1950–1954, box 4138, NAII.

67. Barrington to Win Pe, 22 August [1950], "Question of Financial and Military Aid from the Emb. of the United States of America to the Union of Burma and other S. E. Asian Countries," series 15/3 (6), Acc. # 81, Year 1950, file 103 FMS 50, MNA. Key to SS, 23 August 1950, Tel. 122, 790B.00/8-2350, RG 59, CDF 1950–1954, box 4135, NAII.

68. Day to USDS, 15 August 1950, Despatch 119, 790B.5 MAP/8-1850, RG 59, CDF 1950–1954, box 4141, NAII. See also "Burma Trip Dropped by U.S. Arms Mission," *New York Times*, 6 September 1950; Tillman Durdin, "Burma's Relations with U.S. Improve," ibid., 26 September 1950.

69. Key to SS, Tel. 184, 14 September 1950, 790B.5 MAP/9-1450, RG 59, CDF 1950–1954, box 4141, NAII. SS to US Embassy Rangoon, 20 August 1950, *FRUS* 1950, 6:252. "Military Assistance to Burma," *Department of State Bulletin*, 23, no. 595 (27 November 1950): 856.

70. Key to USDS, 18 September 1950, Despatch 190, 790B.00/9-1850, RG 59, CDF 1950–1954, box 4135, NAII. Fifield, *Americans in Southeast Asia*, 171.

71. "Burma Hails E. C. A. Grant," *New York Times*, 15 September 1950. Clipping, *New Times of Burma*, 13 October 1950, series A1838, control symbol 3008/11/161 Part 1, NAA.

72. Key to SS, 16 November 1950, Tel. 320, 790B.00/11-1650, RG 59, CDF 1950–1954, box 4135, NAII. Acheson to US Embassy Rangoon, 17 November 1950, Tel. 276, 790B.00/11-1650, ibid.

73. Key to SS, 22 November 1950, Tel. 336, 790B.00/11-2250, ibid. National Intelligence Estimate 20, 31 January 1951, p. 12, CREST documents, NAII. CIA, "Prospects for Survival of a Non-Communist Regime in Burma," National Intelligence Estimate no. 36, 1 August 1951, Truman Papers, President's Secretary's Files, Intelligence File, 1946–1953, box 213, HSTL.

3. THE TRIAL OF THE "BURMA SURGEON"

1. Sargent, *Twilight Over Burma*, 135. Regarding Seagrave's language competency, in his testimony at the trial he said he did not speak Karen, but he could speak Burmese and Shan. In *Burma Surgeon* (p. 27) he claimed he spoke Karen before he spoke English. Of course he might later have lost his fluency in Karen. But is may also have been a strategic decision at the trial to say he did not know Karen.

2. John F. Kennedy to Gordon S. Seagrave, 30 June 1961, Biographical Files—G. S. Seagrave, #3, ABHS. Clipping, "Dr. Gordon Seagrave, 68, Dies; 'Burma Surgeon' for 4 Decades," *New York Times*, 29 March 1965, in Gordon S. Seagrave Papers, Denison University Archives.

3. Clipping, Bob Considine, "On the Line," *Washington Times Herald*, November 1965, in Biographical Files—G. S. Seagrave, #1, ABHS. When Seagrave was mortally ill in 1965, President Lyndon Johnson personally intervened to allow Seagrave's son, Sterling, to fly to Burma in an Air Force plane. Clipping, "Johnson Cuts Red Tape for an Errand of Mercy," *Philadelphia Bulletin*, 6 March 1965, ibid.

4. Newhall, *The Devil in God's Old Man*, 61.

5. Information on Seagrave's career comes primarily from his own testimony on 12 December 1950 at his trial and from his book, *Burma Surgeon*. Seagrave's testimony is found in the unpublished "Transcript of Evidence of Witnesses in the Trial of Dr. Gordon

S. Seagrave Before the Special Tribunal," attached to Henry B. Day to Department of State, 9 March 1951, Despatch 633, 790B.00/3-951, RG 59, CDF 1950–54, Box 4136, NAII.

6. Gordon Seagrave to B.S. Joshi, 21 April 1946, Frontiers Areas Administration, Development II Branch, series 1/14, Accession #24, Year 1946, File 3FA (DD) 46 (microfilm), MNA.

7. Seagrave, *Burma Surgeon*, 58, 66–68; Newhall, *The Devil in God's Old Man*, 63; Seagrave, *Burma Surgeon Returns*, 254, 260–61.

8. Seagrave to Storer B. Lunt, Howard P. Wilson, and John F. Rich, 30 April 1949, Box 1, AMCB.

9. Seagrave to American Ambassador J. Klahr Huddle, Rangoon, 12 September 1949, ibid.

10. Ibid.

11. Ibid.

12. Ibid.

13. Huddle's letter is referred to in Day to Seagrave, [February 1950], RG59, CDF 1950–1954, Box 4135, NAII. Jack E. McFall to Marion Seagrave, 13 November 1950, ibid. Marion Seagrave to Howard P. Wilson, 31 October 1949, Box 1, AMCB. Mrs. Seagrave also apparently wrote that "any Karen who has had associations with white people is suspect." See John F. Rich to Wilson, 10 November 1949, Box 1, AMCB.

14. Memcon, "Outstanding Leader of the Karen National Union" and Andrus, 5 August 1948, enclosed in Acly to SS, 7 August 1948, Despatch 638, 845C.00/8-748, RG 59, DF 1945–1949, Box 6120, NAII. Acheson to US Embassy Rangoon, 7 December 1949, Tel. 343, 845C.00/12-749, ibid., Box 6121. Government of Burma Press Release, 21 August 1950, enclosure no. 5 in US Embassy Rangoon to SS, 25 August 1950, Tel. 129, RG59, CDF 1950–1954, Box 4135, NAII.

15. US Embassy Rangoon to SS, 14 February 1950, Tel. 84, 790B.00/2-1450, RG59, CDF 1950–1954, Box 4135, NAII. See also Day to SS, 10 February 1950, 790B.00 (W)/2-10-50, ibid., Box 4137, which reported that Ne Win told Jessup that the "only American in Burma now aiding KNDO is Seagrave." US Embassy Rangoon to SS, 14 February 1950, Tel. 84, 790B.00/2-1450, ibid., Box 4135.

16. Day to USDS, 18 March 1950, Despatch 116, 790B.00/3-1850, ibid. See also Marion Seagrave to Wilson, 2 March 1950, Box 2, AMCB.

17. Day to USDS, 18 March 1950, Despatch 116, 790B.00/3-1850, RG59, CDF 1950–1954, Box 4135, NAII. Marion Seagrave to Wilson, 2 March 1950, Box 2, AMCB.

18. Memcon, Bo Set Kya and L.M. Purnell, 19 April 1950, RG 59, CDF 1950–1954, Box 4135, NAII.

19. Seagrave to Rich, 19 June 1950, Box 2, AMCB. The most complete account of the KMT situation is now Gibson with Chen, *The Secret Army*.

20. Office Memorandum, Ely to Dean Rusk, 15 August 1950, 790B.00/8-1550, RG 59, CDF 1950–54, Box 4135, NAII.

21. Details about the arrest of Seagrave come from the testimony of Ali Husein, "Transcript of Evidence." Key to SS, 18 August 1950, Tel. 106, 790B.00 (W)/8-1850, RG 59, CDF 1950–54, Box 4138, NAII.

22. Acheson to US Embassy Rangoon, 16 August 1950, Tel. 103, 790B.00/8-1650, RG 59, CDF 1950–54, Box 4138, NAII. Box 4135. Day to USDS, 17 August 1950, Despatch 108, 790B.00/8-1750, ibid.

23. Memorandum, Herbert D. Spivack to Key, 19 August 1950, enclosed in US embassy Rangoon to USDS, 25 August 1950, Despatch 129; Key to SS, 19 August 1950, Tel. 111; Memorandum, Spivack to Key, 21 August 1950, enclosed in US embassy Rangoon to USDS, 25 August 1950, Despatch 129; all ibid. The Baptist mission in Rangoon offered to assist, but the State Department discouraged it, no doubt wise advice given the

government's suspicions of the Baptists. See Jesse R. Wilson to Herbert Anderson Jr., 27 February 1951, Biographical Files—G. S. Seagrave, #1, ABHS.

24. Marion M. Seagrave to Harry S. Truman, 21 August 1950, 790B.00/8-2150, RG 59, CDF 1950–54, Box 4135, NAII. Charles B. Deane to Truman, 15 September 1950, ibid.

25. Acheson to US Embassy Rangoon, 22 August 1950, Tel. 120, 790B.00/8-2250, ibid. Key to SS, 24 August 1950, Tel. 125, 790B.00/8-2450, ibid.

26. Key to SS, 14 September 1950, Tel. 153, 790B.00/9-1450, ibid.; testimony of Ali Husein, attached to Henry B. Day to Department of State, 9 March 1951, Despatch 633, 790B.00/3-951, ibid.

27. Key to SS, 16 September 1950, Tel. 188, 790B.00/9-1650, ibid.

28. *New York Times*, 6 October 1950.

29. Ben Markson to Seagrave, 12 January 1951, Box 2, AMCB. James E. Webb to US Embassy Rangoon, 19 September 1950, *FRUS* 1950, 6:253.

30. Key to SS, 26 September 1950, Tel. 207, 790B.00/9-2650, RG 59, CDF 1950–54, Box 4135, NAII.

31. Key to SS, 7 October 1950, Tel. 228, 790B.00/10-750, ibid. Roger Wilson to "Dear Pop" [Howard P. Wilson], 12 January 1951, Box 2, AMCB. Key to SS, 7 October 1950, Tel. 228, 790B.00/10-750, RG 59, CDF 1950–54, Box 4135, NAII.

32. "Press copy of charges of Special Tribunal against Dr. Seagrave," attachment #2 in Day to USDS, 19 January 1951, Despatch 487, 790B.00/1-1951, RG 59, CDF 1950–54, Box 4136.

33. Testimony of Ma E Mya, "Transcript of Evidence."

34. The letter is quoted in Day to USDS, 17 August 1950, Despatch 108, 790B.00/8-1750, RG 59, CDF 1950–54, Box 4135, NAII.

35. Key to SS, 7 October 1950, Tel. 228, 790B.00/10-750, ibid.; Key to SS, 6 November 1950, Tel. 295, 790B.00/11-650, ibid.

36. Testimony of Dr. Gordon S. Seagrave, "Transcript of Evidence."

37. Ibid.

38. Ibid.

39. Testimony of Captain Laraw, ibid.

40. Day to SS, 15 January 1951, Tel. 458, 790B.00/1-1551 RG 59, CDF 1950–54, Box 4136, NAII. Day to SS, 17 January 1951, Tel. 467, 790B.00/1-1751, ibid.

41. "Press Report of Text of Judgment of Special Tribunal in Seagrave Case," enclosed in Day to USDS, 19 January 1951, 790B.00/1-1951, Despatch 487, ibid.

42. Ibid.

43. Ibid.; *Time*, 29 January 1951.

44. Clipping, *Boston Herald*, 18 January 1951, in Biographical Files—G. S. Seagrave, #2, ABHS. "Dr. Seagrave Goes Free," *New York Times*, 11 March 1951; Peter Kalischer, "He's Still the Burma Surgeon," *Colliers*, 30 April 1954, 34.

45. Day to SS, 19 January 1951, Tel. 467, 790B.00/1-1951, RG 59, CDF 1950–54, Box 4136, NAII.

46. Day to SS, 16 February 1951, Tel. 550, ibid.

47. Memcon, Barrington, U San Lin, Lacy, and Acly, 21 February 1951, 790B.00/2-2151, ibid. Webb to US Embassy Rangoon, 2 March 1951, Tel. 547, 790B.00/3-251, ibid.

48. Seagrave to Lunt and Wilson, 30 March 1951 [misdated 1950], Box 2, AMCB.

49. Acheson to US Embassy Rangoon, 26 March 1951, Tel. 610, 790B.00/3-2651, RG 59, CDF 1950–54, Box 4136, NAII.

50. Memcon, Barrington, U San Lin, Lacy, and Acly, 21 February 1951, 790B.00/2-2151, ibid. Webb to US Embassy Rangoon, 2 March 1951, Tel. 547, 790B.00/3-251, ibid. Memcon, Key and Barrington, 19 March 1951, *FRUS* 1951, 6:270-71. Kalischer, "He's Still the Burma Surgeon," 37.

51. Memcon, U Win and Key, 3 September 1951, enclosed in Key to USDS, 5 September 1951, Despatch 212, 790B.00/9-551, RG 59, CDF 1950–54, Box 4137.

52. Memcon, U Nu and Key, 10 August 1951, enclosed in Key to USDS, 5 September 1951, Despatch 212, 790B.00/9-551, ibid.

53. "Burmese Supreme Court Decision in Seagrave Appeal," enclosed in Day to USDS, 16 November 1951, Despatch 453, 790B.00/11-1651, ibid.

54. Sterling Seagrave, "The Final Chapter in the Life of The Burma Surgeon," *Floridian*, 20 October 1974, 10. Copy in Biographical Files—G. S. Seagrave, #3, ABHS.

55. Day to SS, 23 January 1951, Tel. 484, RG 59, CDF 1950–54, Box 4136, NAII. Key to SS, 10 October 1950, Tel. 233, 790B.00/10-1050, ibid., Box 4135. Marion M. Seagrave to Rusk, 30 January 1951, 790B.00/1-3051, ibid., Box 4136.

56. Key to SS, 10 October 1950, Tel. 233, 790B.00/10-1050, ibid., Box 4135. Day to SS, 17 January 1951, Tel. 467, 790B.00/1-1751, ibid., Box 4136. Seagrave, "The Final Chapter in the Life of The Burma Surgeon," 10: "Politicians and Generals in Rangoon had decided that it was a rare opportunity to get rid of Dr. Seagrave and take possession of his $9 million hospital complex."

57. Day to SS, 17 January 1951, Tel. 467, 790B.00/1-1751, Box 4135, CDF 1950–1954, RG 59, NAII.

58. It is possible that the courts did not act quite so independently of the government as this analysis suggests. In November 1951 U Myint Thein, then chief of the Burmese delegation to the UN General Assembly, told an American official in Paris (perhaps Ambassador Key), that the Special Tribunal had acted on the incorrect assumption that U Nu wanted a conviction and then deportation. In fact, only Ne Win and his "small clique" wanted this. He further stated that the Supreme Court's decision to throw out the conviction "would convince the world of the impartiality and fairness of Burmese judicial proceedings." Spivack (for the ambassador) to USDS, Despatch 1355 (Paris), RG 84, Burma: Embassy and Consulate, Classified General Records, 1945–1961, Box 15, NAII.

59. For representative discussions of tensions the missionaries faced in terms of what William R. Hutchinson terms "God's Mission and America's," see William R. Hutchinson, *Errand to the World: American Protestant Thought and Foreign Missions* (Cambridge, MA: Harvard University Press, 1987), especially 1–14, and Kenton J. Clymer, *Protestant Missionaries in the Philippines, 1898–1916: An Inquiry into the American Colonial Mentality* (Urbana: University of Illinois Press, 1986), 153–90. A more recent account is Ian R. Tyrrell, *Reforming the World: The Creation of America's Moral Empire* (Princeton, NJ: Princeton University Press, 2010), especially part 4. Referring to the early twentieth century, for example, Tyrrell writes: "Friction . . . marked relations between reformers and imperial strategists as much as agreements did" (192)

60. Lewis M. Purnell, "Summary of Observations On Trip from Mandalay to Myitkyina," enclosed in Acly to USDS, 30 March 1954, Despatch 378, Box 25, RG 84, Burma US Embassy, Classified General Records 1945–1961, NAII. Seagrave, *My Hospital in the Hills*, 208, 215–17. See also Seagrave's comments about his trial and about KMT "aggression" in an interview that was part of an Edward R. Murrow "See it Now" television program on Burma, broadcast on 7 February 1957. Available on YouTube, "CIA Archives: Buddhism in Burma—History, Politics and Culture," https://www.youtube.com/watch?v=1Vajuce8nyU. I am grateful to Will Womack for calling this to my attention.

61. Purnell, "Summary of Observations On Trip from Mandalay to Myitkyina."

62. Seagrave to Sidney H. Browne, 17 October 1952, enclosed in Browne to USDS, October 31, 1952, 790B.00/10-3152, Box 4137, CDF 1950–1954, RG 59, NAII. William S. Sebald, diary extracts (unpublished), entries for May 14 and 16, 1954 and letter from Seagrave to Sebald, 23 November 1955 (included in diary entries), pp. 433–336, 457–458, HIA.

4. THE KUOMINTANG EMBARRASSMENT

1. *Burma* (Information bulletin of the Burmese Embassy, Washington, DC), 1:2, in Truman Papers, OF 3171, box 1571, HSTL.

2. Memorandum no. 694, T. K. Critchley to Secretary, EXAF, 11 September 1951, series A1838, control symbol TS383/2/1 Part 1, NAA. James Bowker to Ernest Bevin, 15 December 1949, "Situation in Burma," p. 45, FO 435/2, BNA.

3. Bowker to Bevin, 5 April 1950, "Situation in Burma," p. 19, FO 435/3, BNA. Foley, *The Cold War and National Assertion in Southeast Asia*, 98.

4. Acheson to US Embassy London, 21 January 1950, Tel. 327, 790B.00/1-2150, RG 59, CDF 1950–1954, box 4135, NAII. Julius C. Holmes to SS, 26 January 1950, Tel. 447, 790B.00/1-2650, ibid.

5. Taylor, *Foreign And Domestic Consequences*, 11–12. Key to SS, 15 June 1950, Tel. 340, 790B.54/6-1550, RG 59, CDF 1950–1954, box 4142, NAII. Key to SS, 29 June 1950, Tel. 369, 790B.00/6-2950, ibid., box 4135.

6. Key to SS, 29 June 1950, Tel. 369, 790B.00/6-2950, RG 59, CDF 1950–1954, box 4135, NAII. Key to SS, 30 June 1950, Tel. 397, 790B.00/6-3050, ibid.

7. McCoy, *The Politics of Heroin*, 165; Kaufman, "Trouble in the Gold Triangle," 441.

8. Gibson, *Secret Army*, 34–35, 39–40. Li Mi had escaped from Kunming just before the communists occupied the city, flying to Hong Kong. According to Bertil Lintner, "he was sent to the hills of Burma to rejoin his old regiment." Bertil Lintner, "REWRITING HISTORY—The CIA's First Secret War," *Far Eastern Economic Review*, 10 September 1993.

9. Notes of Conversation, Wellington Koo and Rusk, 7 July 1950, box 180, Koo Papers, Columbia University Library. See also Memorandum, Raymond A. Hare to Rusk, 1 July 1950, 790B.00/7-150, *FRUS* 1950, 6:244–45 and 245n. Acheson to American Embassy Rangoon, 7 July 1950, Tel. 16, file 360.01 Chi Nats—Surrender, RG 84, Burma US Embassy, Classified General Records 1945–1961, box 10, NAII. Key to SS, 25 July 1950, Tel. 41, folder 360.01 Chi Nats—Kengtung, RG 84, Burma US Embassy, Classified General Records 1945–1961, box 10, NAII.

10. Notes of Conversation, Koo and Rusk, 25 July and 27 July, 1950, box 180, Koo Papers, Columbia University Library. Acheson to US Embassy Taipei, 28 July 1950, *FRUS* 1950, 6:246. Gibson, *Secret Army*, 34–35, 39–40.

11. Key to SS, 10 August 1950, Tel. 76, 790B.00/8-1050, RG 59, CDF 1950–1954, box 4135, NAII.

12. Key to SS, 12 August 1950, Tel. 84-5-5-9, file 360.01 KMT Troops—Kengtung, RG 84, Burma US Embassy, Classified General Records, box 10, NAII.

13. Memcon, T. L. Tsai and Oliver E. Clubb, 19 September 1950, 793.00/9-1950, RG 59, CDF 1950–1954, box 4135, NAII. Key to SS, 22 November 1950, Tel. 336, 790B.00/11-2250, ibid. CIA, Office of Current Intelligence, *Current Intelligence Bulletin*, 5 April 1951, p.7, CREST documents, NAII. On Taiwan's posture, see Gibson, *Secret Army*, 49. Key, 28 December 1950, Tel. 426, 790B.00/12-2850, RG 59, CDF 1950–1954, box 4135, NAII. Henry B. Day to SS, 12 January 1951, Tel. 454, 790B.00 (W)/1-1251, ibid., box 4139. Conversation with Paul Lewis, 15 January 1951, enclosed in Day to Stanton, 18 January 1951, RG 84, Burma: Embassy and Consulate, Classified General Records, 1945–1961, box 15, NAII.

14. McCoy, *The Politics of Heroin*, 165–66.

15. Kaufman, "Trouble in the Gold Triangle," 441; McCoy, *The Politics of Heroin*, 167; Gibson, *Secret Army*, 60. John Prados contends that Fitzgerald was deeply involved in Operation Paper. Prados, *Safe for Democracy*, 134–37.

16. Memcon, Sao Hkun Hkio and Day, 28 February 1951, enclosed in Day to USDS, 3 March 1951, 790B.00/3-351, RG 59, CDF 1950–1954, box 4136, NAII.

17. Gibson, *Secret Army*, 59. 62; Kaufman, "Trouble in the Gold Triangle," 441–42. On Bird see Kurlantzick, *The Ideal Man*, passim.

18. Memorandum no. 694, T.K. Critchley to Secretary, EXAF, 11 September 1951, A1838, control symbol TS383/2/1 Part 1, NAA. Central Intelligence Agency, Office of Current Intelligence, "Daily Digest," 26 April 1951, p. 7, CREST documents, NAII. Day to SS, 2 May 1951, Tel. 763, 790B.00/2-551, RG 59, CDF 1950–1954, box 4136, NAII.

19. Minute by C.E. King, 2 March 1951, FO 371/92962, BNA. Minutes by Murray 27 March 1951, ibid. FO to British Embassy Bangkok, 30 March 1951, ibid. Gibson, *Secret Army*, 38. Richard Whittington to FO, 17 April 1951, Tel. 212, FO 371/92962, BNA.

20. Minute by Murray 5 April 1951, ibid. Richard Speaight to FO, 28 April 1951, Tel. 197, FO 371/92140, BNA.

21. FO to British Embassy Washington, n.d. [7 (?) May 1951], Saving Tel. 2316, ibid.

22. Walter M. Gifford to SS, 3 May 1951, Tel. 5725, 790B.00/5-351, RG 59, CDF 1950–1954, box 4136, NAII. Day to SS, 2 May 1951, Tel. 763, 790B.00/2-551, ibid. Key to SS, 5 May 1951, Tel. 779, 790B.00/5-551, ibid. Key to SS, 5 May 1951, Tel. 774, 790B.00 (W)/5-551, ibid., box 4139.

23. Don and Jean Crider to "Dear Friends," 6 June 1951, FM 429, ABHS. This portion of the Criders' letter was not included in the version that the Baptist mission board sent out to the couple's supporters.

24. Key to Acly, 2 May 1951, RG 84, Burma US Embassy, Classified General Records 1945–1961, box 7, NAII. Key to SS, 5 May 1951, Tel. 779, 790B.00/5-551, ibid., box 10. Day to SS, 2 May 1951, Tel. 763, 790B.00/2-551, RG 59, CDF 1950–1954, box 4136, NAII.

25. Acheson to US Embassy Rangoon, 6 May 1951, Tel. 714,790B.00/5-651, RG 59, CDF 1950–1954, box 4136, NAII. Dean Acheson to US Embassy Taiwan, 6 May 1951, Tel. 1202, 790B.00/5-651, ibid. William T. Turner to SS, 7 May 1951, Tel. 85, RG 84, Burma US Embassy, Classified General Records 1945–1961, box 10, NAII.

26. Speaight to FO, 8 May 1951, Tel. 213, FO 371/92140, BNA. Minute, 15 May [1951], ibid.

27. Karl Rankin to SS, 7 May 1951, Tel. 1547, 790B.00/5-751, RG 59, CDF 1950–1954, box 4136, NAII. Key to SS, 8 May 1951, 790B.00/5-851, ibid. Rankin to SS, 9 May 1951, Tel. 1558, 790B.00/5-951, ibid. Speaight to FO, 7 May 1951, Tel. 209, FO 371/92140, BNA.

28. Key to SS, 12 May 1951, Tel. 812, 690B.93/5-1251, RG 59, CDF 1950–1954, box 2993, NAII.

29. Bevin to British Embassy Washington, [7 May 1951], Saving Tel. 2316, FO 371/92140, BNA.S.O. (I) Hong Kong, to Admiralty (D[irector of] N[aval] I[ntelligence]), 6 May 1951, Tel. 051802 May, ibid.

30. Oliver Franks to FO, 10 May 1951, Tel. 1461, ibid. FO to British Embassy Washington, 11 May 1951, Tel. 1974, ibid.

31. Franks to FO, 14 May 1951, Tel. 1491, ibid. Acheson to Key, 12 May 1951, Tel. 738, 690B.93/5-1251, RG 59, CDF 1950–1954, box 2993, NAII. Minute by R.F. Stretton, 19 May 1951, FO 371/92140, BNA.

32. Key to SS, 14 May 1951, Tel. 815, 690B.93/5-1451, RG 59, CDF 1950–1954, box 2993, NAII. The British believed that he was the same Jim Stewart who had worked for the USIS in Korea and, before that, in China, and had reportedly left the USIS in about February 1951. G.L. Clutton to FO, 2 September 1951, Tel. 1200, FO 371/92142, BNA. Gibson, *Secret Army*, 62–63.

33. Key to SS, 31 May 1951, Tel. 863, 690B.93/5-3151, RG 59, CDF 1950–1954, box 2993, NAII. Acly to Key, 17 July 1951, RG 84, Burma US Embassy, Classified General Records 1945–1961, box 7, NAII. Taylor, *Foreign and Domestic Consequences*, 37.

34. Gibson, *Secret Army*, 74–75. William J. Sebald to USDS, 3 September 1952, Tel. 206, *FRUS* 1952–54, 12:29.

35. Key to SS, 15 August 1951, *FRUS* 1950, 6:288–89. CIA, Office of Current Intelligence, "Daily Briefing," 17 August 1951; CIA report (title redacted), 18 August 1951; both CREST documents, NAII.

36. Rankin to USDS, 3 October 1951, Despatch 134, RG 59, CDF 1950–1954, box 4137, NAII. Key to SS, 21 July 1951, Tel. 76, 790B.00 (W)/7-2151, ibid., box 4139. Key to SS, 30 July 1951, Tel. 124, 790B.001/7-3051, ibid., box 4140.

37. FO to British Embassy Bangkok, 21 June 1951, Tel. 236, FO 371/92140, BNA.

38. Minute by S.J.L. Olver, "Kuomintang Troops in Kengtung," 13 July 1951, FO 371/92141, BNA. FO to British Embassy Washington, 26 July 1951, Saving Tel. 3687, FO 371/92140, BNA. Memcon, William S.B. Lacy, Merchant, Christopher Steel, F.S. Tomlinson, 31 July 1951, 790B.00/7-3151, RG 59, CDF 1950–1954, box 4137, NAII. Oliver Franks to FO, 31 July 1951, Tel. 2357, FO 371/92141, BNA.

39. Memcon, Lacy, Merchant, Tomlinson, and Steel, 31 July 1951, *FRUS* 1951, 6:277–79.

40. FO to British Embassy Washington, 4 August 1951, Saving Tel. 3898, FO 371/92141, BNA. Memcon, Tomlinson and Merchant, 8 August 1951, 790B.00/8-851, RG 59, CDF 1950–1954, box 4137, NAII.

41. Franks to FO, 11 August 1951, Saving Tel. 808, FO 371/92141, BNA. FO to British Embassy Rangoon, 23 August 1951, Tel. 387, ibid.

42. Clipping, Seymour Topping, "KMT Troops Invade Yunnan Province?" *New Times of Burma*, 29 July 1951, series A1838, control symbol 3008/2/9 Part 1, NAA.

43. Memorandum, D.J. Horne to Secretary, EXAF, Canberra, Memo 177, series A1838, control symbol 3008/2/9 Part 1, NAA. Acheson to Key, 15 August 1951, Tel. 182, 790B.00/8-2251, RG 59, CDF 1950–1954, box 2993, NAII.

44. Key to SS, 15 August 1951, *FRUS* 1951, 6:288–89; Rusk to Key, 22 August 1951, ibid., 289–90.

45. Key to SS, 29 August 1951, ibid., 290–91.

46. James E. Webb to Key, 31 August 1951, ibid., 292.

47. Memorandum for the Record, Merchant et al., 23 August 1951, RG 59, CDF 1950–1954, box 4137, NAII.

48. Gibson, *Secret Army*, 91. T.K. Critchley to EXAF, 11 September 1951, series A1838, control symbol TS383/2/1 Part 1, NAA. Critchley was the acting Australian commissioner in Malaya.

49. D.W. McNicol to EXAF, 20 September 1951, Memorandum 1710/51, series A1838, control symbol 3008/2/9 Part 1, NAA. F.S. Tomlinson to Murray, 20 September 1951, FO 371/92142, BNA.

50. On the CIA's relationship with CAT, see Stuart Hedden (CIA), Memorandum for the Record, 2 January 1952, http://www.foia.cia.gov/sites/default/files/document_conversions/15/c05261065.pdf. The British characterization of CAT is found in E.H. Jacobs-Larkcom to C.H. Johnston, 14 February 1952, FO 371/101010, BNA. Jacobs-Larkcom was the British consul in Tamsui, Taiwan.

51. Rankin to SS, 3 October 1951, *FRUS* 1951, 6:300. Minute, Murray, "Kuomintang Troops in Burma," 20 September 1951, FO 371/92143, BNA.

52. Acheson to US Embassy Bangkok, 28 September 1951, Tel. 746, 790B.00/9-2851, RG 59, CDF 1950–1954, box 4137, NAII.

53. Minute, 26 September [1951], FO 371/92143, BNA. FO to British Embassy Washington, 27September 1951, FO 371/92142, BNA.

54. Turner to SS, 28 September 1951, *FRUS* 1951, 6:298.

55. Quoted in Memorandum, Merchant to John M. Allison, William S.B. Lacy, and Kenneth C. Krentz, 28 November 1951, *FRUS* 1951, 6:316–17.

56. G.A. Wallinger to R.H. Scott, 22 September 1951, 1031/115/510, FO 371/92143, BNA.

57. Wallinger to FO, 28 September 1951, Tel. 435, ibid.

58. Turner to SS, 1 October 1951, file 360.01 KMT 1951, RG 84, Burma US Embassy, Classified General Records 1945–1961, box 10, NAII.

59. Gibson, *Secret Army*, 114.

60. Day to SS, 2 November 1951, Tel. 406, RG 84, Burma US Embassy, Classified General Records 1945–1961, box 10, NAII. The comment about Heath is on Heath to US Embassy Rangoon, 10 December 1951, Tel. 8, file 360.01 KMT, ibid.

61. Robert W. Rinden to USDS, 9 December 1954, Despatch 287, file 360.01—KMT troops, supplies to, ibid., box 27. The flights were then undertaken by Foshing Airlines, a Taiwan carrier. But three American citizens of Chinese descent did participate: Chen Moon, director of the airline and its chief pilot; Chen Kuo-ming, a pilot; and Harvey Toy. Toy and Chen Moon were the principal shareholders in the country. The airline's founder was Ango Tai, the adopted son of Chiang Kai-shek.

62. Wallinger to FO, 12 October 1951, Tel. 449, FO 371/92143, BNA. Minute on this document, 16 October [1951]. Scott to Wallinger, 1 November 1951, 1019/94/G, ibid. CIA, Office of Current Intelligence, "Daily Digest," 5 November 1951, pp. 5–6, CREST documents, NAII. Key to Lucius D. Battle, 13 November 1951, *FRUS* 1951, 6:309–10.

63. "Foreign Office Report," 13 November 1951, series A1838, control symbol 3008/2/9 Part 1, NAA.

64. Memorandum, William J. Donovan to Walter Bedell Smith, 28 January 1951, CREST documents, NAII.

65. CIA, Office of Current Intelligence, "Daily Digest," 29 November 1951, CREST documents, NAII. Steinberg and Fan, *Modern China-Myanmar Relations*, 50.

66. Minute by Murray, 1 January 1952, FO 371/92143, BNA. Wallinger to FO, 7 January 1952, 1004/1/52, FO 371/101173, BNA.

67. E. H. Jacobs-Larkcom to Murray 11 January 1952, 100/S.1/52, FO371/101008, BNA. Clipping, Rawle Knox, "Chiang Stiffens Burma Force," *Observer*, 20 January 1952, ibid. Acheson to US Embassy Rangoon, 21 January 1952, Tel. 638, 790B.00/1-2152, RG59, CDF 1950-1954, box 4137, NAII. "United States Embassy Statement," 28 January 1952, FO 371/101009, BNA. Minute by R. H. Scott, 31 January 1952, FO 371/101010, BNA.

68. Speaight to FO, 29 January 1952, Tel. 45, FO 371/101008, BNA. UK high commissioner in India to Commonwealth Relations Office, 22 January 1952, Saving Tel. 19, and Minute on that document, 30 January [1952], ibid. FO to British Embassy Rangoon, 23 January 1952, Tel. 36, ibid. Entry for 5 February 1962, "Chronology," series 12/1, accession no. 240, MNA.

69. Gifford to SS, 1 February 1952, Tel. 3357, *FRUS* 1952–54, 12:5–6; Gibson, *Secret Army*, 100.

70. Donald Heath to SS, 4 February 1952, Tel. 1541, *FRUS* 1952–54, 12:7–8.

71. Day to SS, 15 February 1952, Tel. 679, 12–18, ibid. Chester Bowles to SS, Tel. 3382, 18 March 1952, RG 84, Burma—US Embassy, Top Secret Telegrams Received 1951–1954, Top Secret Telegrams Sent 1951–1953, box 1, NAII. Acheson to US Legation Saigon, 12 February 1952, Tel. 1142, *FRUS* 1952–54, 12:9–11.

72. Franks to FO, 17 October 1951, Saving Tel. 1055, FO 371/192143, BNA.

73. Bowles to SS, 19 March 1952, Tel. 3406, *FRUS* 1952–54, 12:22–23. Clipping, "Two Policies on Chiang?" *New York Herald Tribune*, 22 February 1952, reprinting an editorial from the *St. Louis Post-Dispatch*, FO371/101010, BNA.

74. British Embassy Rangoon to FO, 27 February 1952, 1091/39, FO371/101010, BNA.

75. Gibson, *Secret Army*, 113. M. Bunch, "American Support for K.M.T. Troops in Burma," 23 May 1952, FO 371/101012, BNA. A later British report, however, suggested that what Coward may have seen were preparations for a Thai Air Force Air Day parachute performance. British Embassy Bangkok to FO, 10 September 1952, 1024/149/52, ibid. Steinberg and Fan, *Modern China-Myanmar Relations*, 48.

76. Malcolm MacDonald to Anthony Eden, 9 June 1952, Despatch 34, FO 371/101012, BNA. Sebald to SS, 8 August 1952, Tel. 202, 790B.00 (W)/8-852, RG 59, CDF 1950–1954, box 4139, NAII. Prados, *Safe for Democracy*, 136.

77. Sebald to USDS, 3 September 1952, Tel. 206, *FRUS* 1952–54, 12:29–32. Philip W. Bonsal to Sebald, 7 August 1952, RG 84 Burma US Embassy, Top Secret General Records, 1951–1955, box 1, NAII.

78. Rankin to Sebald, 9 October 1952, RG 84 Burma US Embassy, Top Secret General Records, 1951–1955, box 7, NAII. Sebald to Rankin, 21 October 1952, ibid. Minute, 5 November [1952] on F. S. Tomlinson to J. G. Tahourdin, 21 October 1952, 1194/63/52G, FO 371/101012, BNA.

79. No memorandum of the conversation has come to light; the response to Allison was referred to in a dispatch dated 21 May 1953. See editorial note, *FRUS* 1952–54, 12:35.

80. Allison to David Bruce, 18 November 1952, ibid., 36–39. Allison's proposal, "Outline of Steps to be Taken to Transport to Formosa Chinese Nationalist Troops in Kengtung," dated 18 November 1952, is attached to Allison to Sebald, 24 November 1952, RG 84, Burma US Embassy, Top Secret General Records, 1951–1955, NAII.

81. Memorandum, Blancke to Bonsal, 28 November 1952, 690B.9321/11-2852, RG 59, CDF 1950–1954, box 2993, NAII. Stanton to SS, 29 November 1952, Tel. 980, 690B.9321/11-2952, ibid. Rankin to Sebald, 1 December 1952, Tel. 8, RG 84 Burma US Embassy, Top Secret Telegrams Received 1951–1954, Top Secret Telegrams Sent 1951–1953, box 1, NAII.

82. Rankin to Sebald, 3 December 1952, Tel. 9, RG 84 Burma US Embassy, Top Secret Telegrams Received 1951–1954, Top Secret Telegrams Sent 1951–1953, box 1, NAII. Sebald to Bonsal, 4 December 1952, ibid.

83. Memorandum, Walter P. McConaughy to Allison, 31 December 1952, 690B.9321/12-3152, RG 59, CDF 1950–1954, box 2993, NAII.

5. CHINA, COMMUNISTS, AND OTHER INSURGENTS

1. "A Report to the National Security Council by the Executive Secretary on United States Objectives and Courses of Actions with Respect to Southeast Asia," 25 June 1952, WHO, Office of the Special Assistant for National Security Affairs: Records 1950–61, Policy Papers Series, box 3, file NSC 124/2—Southeast Asia (2), Eisenhower Papers, DDEL.

2. Day to SS, 6 January 1951, Tel. 443, 790B.00 (W)/1-651, RG 59, CDF 1950–1954, box 4137, NAII. Day to USDS, Despatch 475, 16 January 1951, ibid., box 4136.

3. CIA, "OIR/DRF Contribution for NIE 20," 31 January 1951, CREST documents, NAII. Day to SS, 17 March 1951, Tel. 636, 790B.00 (W)/3-1751, RG 59, CDF 1950–1954, box 4139, NAII. Acheson to US Embassy Rangoon, 10 May 1951, Despatch A-284, 790B.001/4-651, ibid., box 4140.

4. Photocopies of letters of William J. Green in a bound volume, "Bill's Far East Letters, Series 1," 22 April 1951 and 19 July 1952, box 22, William J. Green Papers, HIA. Green was an agricultural officer with the American technical mission in Burma. CIA, Office of Current Intelligence, "Intelligence Memorandum," 7 May 1951; CIA, Office of Current Intelligence, "Daily Digest," 9 May 1951; both CREST documents, NAII. Acheson to US Embassy Rangoon, 10 May 1951, Despatch A-284, 790B.001/4-651, RG 59, CDF 1950–1954, box 4140, NAII.

5. Key to SS, 1 September 1951, Tel. 248, 790B.00 (W)/9-151, RG 59, CDF 1950–1954, box 4139, NAII. Charney, *History of Modern Burma*, 88–90. Key to Lacy, 14 June 1951, RG 84, Burma US Embassy, Classified General Records 1945–1961, box 12, NAII. Office Memorandum, Key, 15 June 1951, file 501-US-GOB Financial Aid, RG 84, Burma US Embassy, Classified General Records 1945–1961, NAII; Key to SS, 10 July 1951, RG 59, CDF 1950–1954, box 4137, NAII.

6. Key to Lacy, 14 June 1951, RG 84, Burma US Embassy, Classified General Records 1945–1961, box 12, NAII. Office Memorandum, Key, 15 June 1951, file 501-US-GOB Financial Aid, ibid. Key to SS, 10 July 1951, RG 59, CDF 1950–1954, box 4137, NAII.

7. Key to SS, 11 August 1951, Tel. 173, RG 84, Burma US Embassy, Classified General Records 1945–1961, box 12, NAII.

8. Key to Lacy, 24 October 1951, ibid. Moffat to Economic Cooperation Administration, 26 October 1951, Despatch TOECA D-687, ibid. Memcon, Barrington, Allison, R. Robert Acly, 29 December 1951, 790B.5-MSP/12–2951, RG 59, CDF 1950–1954, box 4142, NAII. MSA disapproval is mentioned in Lacy to Day, 8 February 1952, RG 84, Burma US Embassy, Classified General Records 1945–1961, box 12, NAII.

9. Memorandum, Edward P. Lilly to Elmer B. Staats, 3 March 1954, WHO, NSC Staff 1948–1961, OCB Central Files Series, file OCB 600.3, (1), box 2, Eisenhower Papers, DDEL. It is also suggestive that several documents remain classified in the "Financial Aid for Religious Purposes" file, box 12, RG 84: Classified General Records, 1945–1961, NAII.

10. Key to SS, 28 June 1951, *FRUS* 1951, 6:274–77.

11. Memcon, J. Graham Parsons, Thomas J. Davies, Richard Usher, Charles T. Greene, 17 November 1959, 790B.00/12–1759, RG 59, CDF 1955–1959, box 3852, NAII.

12. Key to SS, 27 July 1951, Tel. 115, 790B.00 (W)/7-2751, ibid., box 4139, NAII. Memcon, Edwin W. Martin, Eugene and LaVerne Morse, 27 July 1951, enclosed in US Embassy Rangoon to USDS, 24 August 1951, Despatch 178, ibid., box 4140. The Morses were Baptist missionaries.

13. CIA, "Prospects for Survival of a Non-Communist Regime in Burma," National Intelligence Estimate 36 (NIE 36), 1 August 1951, folder NIE 35–43, President's Secretary's Files: Intelligence File, 1946–1953, Truman Papers, HSTL.

14. Key to SS, 18 August 1951, Tel. 199, 790B.00 (W)/8-1551, RG 59, CDF 1950–1954, box 4139, NAII. CIA, Office of Current Intelligence, "Current Intelligence Review," 3 October 1951, 12; CIA, "Information Report," 22 October 1951; CIA, "Daily Digest," 23 October 1951, p. 5; all CREST documents, NAII.

15. Thomas Critchley to R. G. Casey, 12 October 1951, 12 October 1951, series A1838, control symbol 3008/2/9 Part 1, NAA. CIA, "Daily Digest," 29 October 1951, pp. 6–7, CREST documents, NAII. Speaight to Mr. Morrison, 13 October 1951, FO 435/4, BNA. Acly made this assessment of Ne Win; reported in Australian Embassy, "Internal Situation in Burma," 31 October 1951, series A1838, control symbol 3008/2/9 Part 1, NAA.

16. Aide Memoire, 14 November 1951, file 360.01 Internal Sit. Burma, RG 84, Burma US Embassy, Classified General Records 1945–1961, box 9, NAII. Webb to US Embassy Rangoon, 27 October 1951, *FRUS* 1951, 6:306–7. The embassy was not to make these suggestions unless the Burmese authorities invited advice, however. Day to USDS, 26 October 1951, Despatch 370, 790B.00/10–2651, RG 59, CDF 1950–1954, box 4137, NAII.

17. Clipping, "Thakin Nu Interview by New York 'Times' Correspondent," *New Times of Burma*, 7 August 1951, series A1838, control symbol 3008/7/1 Part 1, NAA. William M. Gibson to Livingston Merchant, 13 September 1951, *FRUS* 1951, 6:294–95. CIA, Office of Current Intelligence, "Current Intelligence Review," 3 October 1951, 13, CREST documents, NAII.

18. John C. Elliott to William B. Bennett, 9 October 1951, *FRUS* 1951, 6:302–3, 303n2. Acheson to US Embassy Rangoon, 16 October 1951, Tel. 352, ibid., 303.

19. Memorandum for Allan Evans et al., CIA, Board of National Estimates, 8 November 1951; CIA, Office of Current Intelligence, "Daily Digest," 9 November 1951, p. 4; CIA, Office of Current Intelligence, "Intelligence Memorandum," 9 November 1951, p. 2; CIA, "NIE-36/1: Prospects for the Survival of a Non-Communist Regime in Burma," 13 November 1951; all CREST documents, NAII.

20. Webb to US Embassy Manila ("For the Ambassador from Rusk"), 10 November 1951, Tel. 1450, 790B.001/11–1051, RG 59, CDF 1950–1954, box 4140, NAII. Key to Lucius D. Battle, 13 November 1951, *FRUS* 1951, 6:309–10.

21. CIA, Board of National Estimates, "Memorandum for the Intelligence Advisory Committee," 20 November 1951, CREST documents, NAII. The final version of NIE 36/1 suggested that a procommunist regime might come to power in Burma, but it eliminated suggested language that this would happen "within the next few months." See NIE 36/1, 26 November 1951, *FRUS* 1951, 6:312–13.

22. In John Goodyear to SS, 21 November 1951, Tel. 592, 790B.00/11–2151, RG 59, CDF 1950–1954, box 4137, NAII. CIA, "Information Report," 10 December 1951; CIA, "Daily Digest," 12 December 1951, p. 5; General Headquarters, United Nations and Far East Command, Military Intelligence Section, General Staff, "Political, Economic and Military Trends in the Far East," 18 December 1951, p. 11; all CREST documents. NAII.

23. "Draft Position Paper on Burma Prepared by the Department of State," 20 December 1951, *FRUS* 1951, 6:325–36; memorandum, Omar N. Bradley to Robert Lovett, 28 December 1951, ibid., 329–30.

24. Staff Memorandum 178, CIA, Office of National Estimates, 9 January 1952, WHO, NSC Staff, NSC Registry Series, box 5, Eisenhower Papers, DDEL.

25. CIA, "Daily Digest," 24 January 1952, pp. 2–3, CREST documents, NAII. Day to USDS, 11 February 1952, Despatch 693, 790B.5-MSP/2-1152, RG 59, CDF 1950–1954, box 4142, NAII.

26. CIA, "Daily Digest," 21 February 1952, pp. 3–4; CIA, "Current Intelligence Bulletin," 22 May 1952; both CREST documents, NAII.

27. CIA, "Current Intelligence Digest," 10 June 1952, p. 9, CREST documents, NAII. Acly to Albert B. Franklin, 22 May 1952, RG 84, Burma US Embassy, Classified General Records 1945–1961, box 7, NAII. Three years later, however, a Burmese military official informed the American army attaché that Ba Swe had directed him to deliver one thousand rifles to a communist leader. The official had refused to do so, but perhaps the earlier American assessment of Ba Swe was not so incorrect. See US Embassy Rangoon to SS, 19 May 1955, 790B.00/5-1955, RG 59, CDF 1955–1957, box 3849, NAII. CIA, "Current Intelligence Bulletin," 13 July1952, p. 4, CREST documents, NAII.

28. "Review of the Military Situation in Burma," E.B. Boothby to Anthony Eden, 31 May 1952, FO 435/5, BNA. CIA, "Current Intelligence Bulletin," 13 July1952, p. 4, CREST documents. NAII. William J. Sebald, "Burma Diary (1952–54): Some Unlearned Lessons in Southeast Asia," entry for 23 July 1952, HIA.

29. CIA, "Current Intelligence Digest," 15 August 1952, p. 6, CREST documents, NAII. Hanson Baldwin to Sebald, 20 August 1952, in Sebald, "Burma Diary (1952–54)," p. 30. In his reply, Sebald specifically disagreed with Baldwin's assessments of "Oriental politicians." See Sebald to Baldwin, entries for 4 September1952, ibid., p. 30, and 3 September 1952, p. 29.

30. US Embassy Rangoon to USDS, "Review of First Four Years of Burma's Independence," pp. 22–23, 20 June 1952, Despatch 1058, 790B.00/9-1652, RG 59, CDF 1950–54, box 4137, NAII. Office Memorandum, Foster to Acly, 7 July 1952, 790B.5-MSP/7-752, ibid., box 4142. P.C. Spender, Ministerial Despatch 12/52, 28 July 1952, series A1838, control symbol 3008/7/11 Part 1, NAA.

31. Office memorandum, Kenneth L. Mayall to Jack Bennett, 24 June 1952, in Andrews Papers, box 8, Government Service File, 1952 (Trip File), HSTL. By one account, KTA received the contract only "after being blackballed for the Indonesia assignment by U.S. Ambassador Cochrane." Memorandum for the File, Louis J. Walinsky, Interview with Homer Pettit, Walinsky Papers, Cornell University Library.

32. "Principle Issues and Problems in Present Conduct of Program—Burma (Briefing Paper for Mr. Andrews)," [June 1952], Andrews Papers, box 8, Government Service File, 1952 (Trip File), HSTL.

33. Clipping, "Point 4 'Awful Expensive' and Futile in Burma," *Chicago Daily Tribune*, 29 July 1952, in RG 84, Burma US Embassy, Classified General Records 1945–1961, box 11, NAII. Stanley Andrews to Sebald (David Bruce to US Embassy Rangoon), 21 August 1952, Tel. 249, ibid. Durr, *The Best Made Plans*, 99–100.

34. CIA, Office of Current Intelligence, "Briefing Notes for the Director," 5 February [1953], CREST documents, NAII. USDS to US Embassy London, 26 August 1952, Tel. 1386, RG 59, CDF 1950–54, box 4137, NAII. CIA, "Current Intelligence Digest," 12 August 1952, p. 7, CREST documents, NAII.

35. Steinberg and Fan, *Modern China-Myanmar Relations*, 24. Lionel Landry to USDS, 9 September 1952, Despatch 225, 790B.001/9-952, RG 59, CDF 1950–54, box 4140, NAII.

36. CIA, Office of National Assessments, Staff Memorandum 273, 23 September 1952, CREST documents, NAII. W. Wendell Blancke to John F. Rich, 29 September 1952, 790B.00/9-1852, RG 59, CDF 1950–54, box 4137, NAII. "Observations of John M. Allison on his Tour of U.S. Missions in the Far East," 26 September to 16 November 1952, Dulles Papers, box 8, DDEL. Allison thought Burma considerably more important to the United States than Thailand.

37. CIA, Working Paper, Policy Additions, 3 October 1952, CREST documents, NAII.

38. Sebald to SS, 11 September 1952, Tel. 415, 790B.5811/9-1152, RG 59, CDF 1950–54, box 4142, NAII. In the end the mission went first to London, thus assuaging British opinion. Sebald, "Burma Diary (1952–54)," entries for 23 September, 12 October, and 24 October, 1952, pp. 39, 53, 57.

39. Sebald to William M. Osborne, 13 October 1952, RG 84, Burma US Embassy, Classified General Records 1945–1961, box 11, NAII. Memcon, Ne Win, Alexis Johnson, et al., 31 October 1952, 790B.00/10–3152, RG 59, CDF 1950–54, box 4137, NAII. The Army considered the Ne Win visit a "great success." David Bruce to US Embassy Rangoon, 6 November 1952, *FRUS* 1952–54, 12:36. Sebald, "Burma Diary (1952–54)," entry for 1 November 1952, p. 60.

40. CIA, Office of Current Intelligence, "Current Intelligence Bulletin," 14 December 1952, 5, CREST documents, NAII. The CIA noted that Ne Win's actions indicated that efforts to obtain arms elsewhere had been unsuccessful. Sebald, "Burma Diary (1952–54)," entries for 16, 26, and 29 November 1952, pp. 68, 72, 74.

41. A. Philip Randolph, "My Trip to Asia," Microfilm Reel 31, Speeches and Writings File, A. Philip Randolph Papers (Bethesda, MD: University Publications of America, 1990). I am grateful to Eric Arneson for bringing Randolph's visit to my attention.

42. Sebald to SS, 5 September 1952, Tel. 369, 790B.00 (W)/9-552, RG 59, CDF 1950–54, box 4139, NAII. Sebald to SS, 28 November 1952, Tel. 895, 790B.13/11–2852, ibid. box 4140. William M. Gibson to Sebald, 26 September 1952, RG 84, Burma US Embassy, Classified General Records 1945–1961, box 11, NAII. On the way in which racism complicated American policy in the cold War, see Dudziak, *Cold War Civil Rights*.

43. U Kyaw Nyein, "How I Look at the Third Force," *Socialist Asia*, 16 November 1952, enclosed in Malcolm R. Booker, 21 November 1952, series A 1838, control symbol 3008/7/1, Part 1, NAA. Notes on Minister's Visit to Rangoon," [November 1951 ?], series A1838, control symbol 3008/2/9 Part 1, NAA. M. R. Booker to Secretary, EXAF, 9 October 1952, Memo. no. 192/52, series A1838, control symbol 3008/11/161 Part 1, NAA. CIA, "Burma: Attitude of Some US Engineers," January 1953, CREST documents, NAII.

44. Sebald, "Burma Diary (1952–54)," entry for 8 September 1952, p. 32; entries for 16 and 19 September 1952, p. 35–37; Sebald to USDS, 10 January 1953, Despatch 533, 790B.5-MSP/1-1053, RG 59, CDF 1950–54, box 4142, NAII.

45. Nu, quoted in Sebald to SS, 21 January 1953, Tel. 1316, 790B.13/1-2153, ibid., box 4140. Dulles to US Embassy Rangoon, 23 January 1953, Tel. 8280, 790B.13/1-2153, ibid.

46. CIA, "Briefing Notes for the Director, National Security Council," n.d. [probably 5 February 1953], CREST documents, NAII. Office Memorandum, W.W. Blancke to Bonsal, 4 February 1953, 790B.5-MSO/2-453, RG 59, CDF 1950–54, box 4142, NAII.

6. CHANGING COURSE ON THE KUOMINTANG

1. Sebald to USDS, 10 January 1953, Despatch 533, 790B.5-MSP/1-1053, RG59, CDF 1950–1954, box 4142, NAII. Office of Current Intelligence, CIA, "Current Intelligence Bulletin," 10 January 1953, 3, CREST documents, NAII. Steinberg and Fan, *Modern China-Myanmar Relations*, 23.

2. Stanton to SS, 13 January 1953, Tel. 1303, 690B.9321/1-1353, RG59, CDF 1950–1954, box 2993, NAII.

3. CIA, "Official Diary," 19 January and 21 January 1953, CREST documents, NAII.

4. Dulles to Sebald, 21 January 1953, Tel. 1110, RG 84, Burma US Embassy, Top Secret Telegrams Received 1951–1954, Top Secret Telegrams Sent 1951–1953, box 1, NAII. H. Freeman Matthews to US Embassy Taiwan, 30 January 1953, Tel. 524, *FRUS* 1952–1954, 12 part 2:48–49.

5. Sebald to SS, 13 February 1953, Tel. 1525, RG 84 Burma US Embassy, Top Secret Telegrams Received 1951–1954, Top Secret Telegrams Sent 1951–1953, box 1, NAII.

6. Tucker, "John Foster Dulles and the Taiwan Roots of the 'Two China' Policy," 235–62. Dulles to US Embassy Taipei, 19 February 1953, *FRUS* 1952–1954, 12 part 2:53.

7. Rankin to SS, 22 February 1953, Tel. 878, 690B.00/9321/2-2253, RG59, CDF 1950–1954, box 2993, NAII.

8. Dulles to US Embassy Taipei, 24 February 1953, Tel. 616, 690B.9321/2-2453; to US Embassy Taipei, 27 February 1953, Tel. 628, 690B.00/9321/2-2753; to US Embassy Taipei, 28 February 1953, Tel. 635, 690B.93212/2-2853; to US Embassy Taipei, 28 February 1953, Tel. 636, 690B.9321/2-2753; all ibid. For a more positive assessment of Rankin, see Gibson, *The Secret Army*.

9. Speaight to FO, 10 March 1953, Tel. 88, FO 371/106685, BNA. Ambassador to India Chester Bowles reported this, based on conversations with Burma's ambassador there. See Bowles to SS, 2 March 1953, Tel. 57, RG 84, Burma US Embassy, Top Secret Telegrams Received 1951–1954, Top Secret Telegrams Sent 1951–1953, box 1, NAII.

10. Extract from Tour Report by Air Commodore E.L.S. Ward, 26 January to 6 February 1953, quoted in Memorandum, Director of Military Intelligence, "K.M.T. Activity in Burma," 27 February 1953, FO 371/106685, BNA.

11. Key's "resignation in disgust" is mentioned in an editorial in the *Washington Post*, 27 January 1953. Memcon, Barrington and Day, 28 January 1953, 790B.5/1-2853, RG59, CDF 1950–1954, box 4141, NAII. Sebald, "Burma Diary (1952–54)," entries for 13 February and 21 February 1953, pp. 124, 130 Sebald to SS, 13 February 1953, Tel. 1525, *FRUS* 1952–1954, 12:52. The Alsops' column appeared on 11 February 1953 in the *Washington Post*.

12. "Translation of the Hon'ble Prime Minister's Speech in the Chamber of Deputies on Monday, 2nd March 1953," Paul Hoffman Papers, box 71, folder "Burma—withdrawal of KMT forces (Nationalist China) in 1953," HSTL.

13. CIA, "Current Intelligence Bulletin," 4 March 1953, CREST documents, NAII. The report of the British observer: "Report by Colonel H.C. Baker on His Visit to Areas in the Shan States Where Operations are being Conducted Against the K.M.T., 27th February–11th March, 1953," FO 371/106685, BNA.

14. EXAF to Australian Mission to the United Nations, 4 March 1953, Tel. 130, Series A816, control symbol 19/306/223, NAA. Nu to Paul G. Hoffman, 4 March 1953, Paul

G. Hoffman Papers, file "Burma—withdrawal of KMT forces (Nationalist China)–1953," HSTL. Sebald, "Burma Diary (1952–54)," entry for 6 March 1953, pp. 137–38.

15. Rankin to SS, 3 March 1953, Tel. 912, *FRUS* 1952–1954, 12 part 2:61–62. Rankin to SS, 4 March 1953, Tel. 913, ibid., 63n.

16. Roger M. Makins to FO, 6 March 1953, Tel. 482, FO 371/106685, BNA. Dulles to Rankin, 4 March 1953, Tel. 654, *FRUS* 1952–1954, 12 part 2:63–64.

17. Notes of a Conversation, Walter Bedell Smith and Koo, 6 March 1953, box 187, Koo Papers, Columbia University Library.

18. Dulles to Rankin, 6 March 1953, Tel. 671, *FRUS* 1952–1954, 12 part 2:64–65. Rankin to SS, 9 March 1953, Tel. 941, ibid., 65–67.

19. Rankin to SS, 12 March 1953, Tel. 956, ibid., 70–71; Sebald, "Burma Diary (1952–54)," entry for 12 March 1953, p. 141.

20. Dulles to Rankin, 13 March 1953, Tel. 700, *FRUS* 1952–1954, 12 part 2:71–72. Dulles to Sebald, 18 March 1953, Tel. 1470, ibid., 75–76; Dulles to Rankin, 18 March 1953, Tel. 713, ibid.,76 n. 2. Memcon, Koo, Dulles, Allison, 19 March 1953, ibid., 78.

21. Sebald to SS, 17 March 1953, Tel. 1773, ibid., 74 n. 2. Clipping, Homer Bigart, "Chiang Has Caused U.S. Setback in S. E. Asia," *Sydney Daily Telegraph*, 6 April 1951, Series A1838, control symbol 3008/11/161 Part 1, NAA. Dulles to Sebald, 18 March 1953, Tel. 1470, RG 84 Burma US Embassy, Top Secret Telegrams Received 1951–1954, Top Secret Telegrams Sent 1951–1953, box 1, NAII.

22. Henry B. Day to R. Austin Acly, 25 March 1953, RG 84 Burma US Embassy, Top Secret Telegrams Received 1951–1954, Top Secret Telegrams Sent 1951–1953, box 1, NAII. It seems likely that the decision, made the following September, to replace Sebald in Rangoon resulted from American irritation at Burma's action and Sebald's continuing defense of the Burmese government. The planned reassignment was explained as an attempt to accommodate Sebald's wife's poor health and because he had "already served at this hardship post for a considerable time." (John W. Hanes, Jr. to R. W. Scott McLeod, 28 September 1953, John Foster Dulles Papers, 1951–1959, Personnel Series, box 2, DDEL.) But Sebald had been in his post only a little more than one year, and there did appear to be some animosity toward the ambassador. Thus handwritten notes on Secretary Dulles' stationery commented that in his previous posting in Japan Sebald had been "competent but not outstanding," that he had no experience in Washington and "doesn't have the stature," that he was "personable but not impressive," and that he was "OK for #2," but not for the top spot. (See comments in Sebald, Ambassador file, Dulles Papers, 1951–1959, Personnel Series, box 2, DDEL.) In the end Sebald served until his two-year term expired in June 1954.

23. Sebald, "Burma Diary (1952–54)," entry for 25 March 1953, pp. 154–55. "Mr. Dulles, NSC Briefly, Wednesday, 18 March 1953." CREST documents, NAII.

24. Day to Acly, 25 March 1953, 360.00, RG 84 Burma US Embassy, Top Secret General Records, 1951–1955, box 1, NAII.

25. Kahin, "Burma," 5 March 1979, Kahin Papers, folder 74–13, box 74, Cornell University Library. Taylor, *Foreign and Domestic Consequences*, 45.

26. Rankin to SS, 22 March 1953, Tel. 989, *FRUS* 1952–1954, 12 part 2:82. Sebald, "Burma Diary (1952–54)," entry for 6 April 1953, p. 173.

27. Dulles to Rankin, 26 March 1953, Tel. 745, RG 84 Burma US Embassy, Top Secret Telegrams Received 1951–1954, Top Secret Telegrams Sent 1951–1953, box 1, NAII.

28. *FRUS* 1952–1954, 12 part 2:85n–86n. See also Dulles to Rankin, 27 March 1953, Tel. 1538, RG 84, Burma US Embassy, Top Secret Telegrams Received 1951–1954, Top Secret Telegrams Sent 1951–1953, box 1, NAII. Sebald, "Burma Diary (1952–54)," entry for 26 March 1953, p. 157.

29. CIA, Office of Current Intelligence, "Central Intelligence Bulletin," 28 March 1953, CREST documents, NAII. Dulles to Rankin, 4 April 1953, Tel. 778, *FRUS* 1952–1954, 12 part 2:92–93. Minute, R. W. Selby, 31 March 1953, FO 371/106683C, BNA.

30. Sebald to SS, 31 March 1953, *FRUS* 1952–1954, 12 part 2:87–88. Sebald to Stanton, 31 March 1953, RG 84 Burma US Embassy, Top Secret General Records 1951–1955, box 1, NAII. Sebald, "Burma Diary (1952–54)," entry for 8 April 1953, p. 174.

31. Sebald, "Burma Diary (1952–54)," entries for 15 and 16 April 1953, pp. 187–88.

32. Sebald to Dulles, 18 April 1953, Tel. 2014, *FRUS* 1952–1954, 12 part 2:97.

33. Ibid., 98–99. Taylor, *Foreign and Domestic Consequences*, 27–28. Gordon Whitteridge to the Marquess of Salisbury, 30 July 1953, Despatch 133, FO 371/106689, BNA.

34. Memcon, Rankin, Chiang Kai-shek, 1 May 1953, *FRUS* 1952–1954, 12 part 2:101–2. Hong Kong M. S. O. to Admiralty M. S. O., 12 May 1953, Tel. 120110Z, FO 371/106688, BNA.

35. Gibson, *The Secret Army*, 139–51. Office of Current Intelligence, "Current Intelligence Bulletin," 3 June 1953, CREST documents, NAII.

36. British Embassy Rangoon to FO, 15 July 1953, Saving Tel. 36, FO 371/106688, BNA. Sebald, "Burma Diary (1952–54)," entries for 5,16, and 20 July 1953, pp. 229, 236, 239.

37. Minute, C. C. Clemens, 16 July 1953, FB1041/172/G, FO 371/106689, BNA. M. N. F. Stewart to John G. Tahourdin, 21 July 1953, 1031/162/53G, ibid. P. E. Royal Air Force, "Air Supply from the Philippines of the K. M. T. In Burma," enclosed in P. E. Berryman to Under Secretary of State for Air, 8 September 1953, FO 371/106690, BNA.

38. Dulles to Rankin, 28 July 1953, Tel. 67, *FRUS* 1952–1954, 12 part 2:121–22. A British official wrote that the American representatives in Bangkok and Rangoon were "already on the side of the angels." Minute, R. W. Selby, 31 July 1953, FO 371/106689, BNA.

39. Roger Makins to FO, 13 August 1953, Tel. 1767, FO 371/106689, BNA. Office of Current Intelligence, CIA, "Current Intelligence Weekly," 28 August 1953, p. 10, CREST documents, NAII. Sebald, "Burma Diary (1952–54)," entries for 14 and September 1953, pp. 264–65. Speaight to FO, 7 September 1953, Tel. 340, FO 371/106689, BNA. NSC Briefing, "Developments in Southeast Asia," 9 September 1953, CREST documents, NAII.

40. U Nu to Dwight D. Eisenhower, 12 September 1953, *FRUS* 1952–1954, 12 part 2:135–38.

41. William J. Donovan to SS, 16 September 1953, Tel. 524, *FRUS* 1952–1954, 12 part 2:139–40. EXAF to Australian Legation Bangkok, 17 September 1953, Tel. 74, series A816, control symbol 19/306/223, NAA. Archibald R. K. Mackenzie to John G. Tahourdin, 22 September 1953, 10245/209/53, FO 371/106690, BNA.

42. Sebald, "Burma Diary (1952–54)," entry for 18 September 1953, pp. 267–68. Walter Bedell Smith to Rankin, 17 September 1953, Tel. 227, *FRUS* 1952–1954, 12 part 2:144–45. Roger Makins to FO, 24 September 1953, Tel. 2024, F) 371/106690, BNA.

43. Makins to FO, 24 September 1953, Tel. 2024, FO 371/106690, BNA.

44. Eisenhower to U Nu, 28 September 1953, *FRUS* 1952–1954, 12 part 2:151–52.

45. Eisenhower to Chiang Kai-shek, 28 September 1953, ibid.,152–53. The Nationalist foreign minister expressed his appreciation for the "tone and content" of Eisenhower's letter. Makins to FO, 5 October 1953, Tel. 2105, FO 371/106691, BNA.

46. Notes of a Conversation, Eisenhower and Chiang Ching-kuo, 29 September 1953, box 187, Koo Papers, Columbia University Library. Notes of a Conversation, Robertson and Koo, 30 September 1953, box 187, ibid.

47. Sebald, "Burma Diary (1952–54)," entry for 5 October 1953, pp. 277–78. Sebald to SS, 13 October 1953, Tel. 342, 1953, *FRUS* 1952–1954, 12 part 2:159–60. Memorandum, "Removal of Chinese Nationalist Troops from Burma," enclosed in Commonwealth Relations Office to UK High Commissioners, 15 October 1953, Tel. 295, FO 371/106691, BNA.

48. Annex "B," 26 October 1953, series A1838, control symbol 3008/11/87/1, NAA.

49. Australian Legation Rangoon to EXAF, 9 November 1953, Tel. 86, series A816, control symbol 19/306/223, NAA. Sebald to SS, 13 November 1953, Tel. 466, 790B.00(W)/11–1253, RG 59, CDF 1950–1954, box 4139, NAII.

50. Sebald, "Burma Diary (1952–54)," entries for 15 November 1953, p. 318. Sebald to SS, 23 November 1953, Tel. 504, *FRUS* 1952–1954, 12 part 2:173.

51. H.D. White to EXAF, 23 November 1953, Memorandum no. 461/53, series A1838, control symbol 3008/11/87/1, NAA. Wallinger to FO, 29 November 1953, Tel. 399, FO 371/106694, BNA. See also Office of Current Intelligence, CIA, "Current Intelligence Bulletin," 20 November 1953, p. 4, CREST documents, NAII.

52. Aide-Memoire, 24 November 1953, 790B.54/11–2453, RG 59, CDF 1950–1954, box 4142, NAII. Notes of a Conversation, Dulles and Koo, 24 November 1953, box 187, Koo Papers, Columbia University Library. Gibson, *The Secret Army*, 143.

53. Notes of a Conversation, Dulles and Koo, 24 November 1953, box 187, Koo Papers, Columbia University Library.

54. Office of Current Intelligence, CIA, "Current Intelligence Bulletin," 8 December 1953, p. 5, CREST documents, NAII. U Nu to Eisenhower, 26 November 1953, box 5, Eisenhower Papers (Ann Whitman File), DDEL.

55. Sebald, "Burma Diary (1952–54)," entry for 7 August 1953, p. 250. Department of State, "Vice President Nixon's Report to department Officers on his Trip to the Near and Far East," 8 January 1954, p. 21, WHO, NSC Staff Papers, 1948–61, OCB Central Files Series, box 69, folder OCB 091, Far East (file #1)(2) [November 1953–April 1954], Eisenhower Papers, DDEL.

56. H.D. White to E.C. Casey, Minister for External Affairs, 30 November 1953, Despatch 5/53, series A1838, control symbol 3008/11/161 Part 1, NAA. Not surprisingly one official minuted that "this should not be put in the Digest of Despatches." Minute, J. Plimsoll, 8 December 1953.

57. Sebald to SS, 28 November 1953, Tel. 522,), International Series, box 5, Eisenhower Papers (Ann Whitman File), DDEL. The account of Nixon's campaign-style greetings is from H.R. Oakshott (for Ambassador Gore-Booth) to Anthony Eden, 2 December 1953, Despatch 247, FO 371/106683C, BNA.

58. CIA, "Briefing for the Vice President," 28 September 1953, WHO, NSC Staff Papers 1948–61, Executive Secretary's Subject Files, box 19, Eisenhower Papers, DDEL.

59. Sebald to SS, 28 November 1953, Tel. 522, Eisenhower Papers (Ann Whitman File), International Series, box 5, DDEL. Sebald's telegram was forwarded to the White House.

60. Newspaper clipping, "Tell Ike," *The Burman*, 27 November 1953, in Paul Wyatt Caraway Papers, box 3, folder "Caraway Burma," HIA.

61. Reuters dispatch, 27 November 1953, included with Paul Gore-Booth to FO, 27 November 1953, Tel. 476, FO 371/106693, BNA. In private Nixon told Sebald that he would send a strong telegram to President Eisenhower recommending "that some further concrete action ought to be taken by the United States to bring Kuomintang business to an end." He could not say this in public because the final decision would be the president's. Paul Gore-Booth to FO, 30 November 1953, Tel. 483, FO 371/106694, BNA.

62. Sebald, "Burma Diary (1952–54), entry for 27 November 1953, p. 334.

63. Gibson, *The Secret Army*, 154.

64. Paul H. Gore-Booth to Anthony Eden, 26 January 1954, Despatch 28, "Burma: Annual Review of 1953," in "Further Correspondence Respecting Burma, Part 7, January to December 1954," FO 435/7, BNA.

65. H.D. White to EXAF, 7 December 1953, Memorandum 477/53, series A1838, control symbol 3008/11/87/1, NAA.

66. H.D. White to Secretary, EXAF, 11 January 1954, Memorandum no. 12/54, ibid. Gibson, *The Secret Army*, 156–57. Rufus Z. Smith to USDS, 4 January 1954, Despatch 31, RG 84, Burma US Embassy, Classified General Records 1945–1961, box 27, NAII.

67. British Embassy Rangoon to FO, 11 February 1954, 1091/11, FO 371/111967, BNA. Sebald to SS, 2 April 1954, Tel. 965, 790B.00(W)/4-254, RG59, CDF 1950–54, box 4139, NAII.

68. Sebald, "Burma Diary (1952–54)," entry for 6 March 1954, p. 382.

69. U Nu to Eisenhower, 15 March 1954, *FRUS* 1952–1954, 12:210–12. On the Burmese military success, see H.W. White to Secretary, EXAF, 15 March 1954, series A1838, control symbol 3008/11/87/3, NAA.

70. The *New Times* article is referred to in the US embassy's report for April 1954, Franklin Hawley to USDS, 17 June 1954, Despatch 524, 790B.00/6-1754, RG59, CDF 1950–54, box 4138, NAII. Eisenhower to U Nu, 6 April 1954, *FRUS* 1952–1954, 12:218–19.

71. Sebald to Bonsal, 29 April 1954, *FRUS* 1952–1954, 12:220–22.

72. Lewis M. Purnell, "Summary of Observations On Trip from Mandalay to Myitkyina," enclosed in R. Austin Acly to USDS, 30 March 1954, Despatch 378, RG59, CDF 1950–54, box 4138, NAII.

73. H.D. White to Secretary, EXAF, 3 May 1954, Memorandum 160/54, series A1838, control symbol 3008/11/87/3, NAA. Australian Legation Rangoon to Secretary, EXAF, 17 May 1954, Memo 181/54, NAA.

74. Berkeley E.F. Gage to FO, 18 May 1954, Saving Tel. 19, FO 371/11967, BNA. "Contingency Plans to Evacuate Possible Chinese Nationalist Stragglers from Burma After Phase III of Regulation Evacuation," 13 May 1954, WHO, NSC Staff: Papers 1948–1961, OCB Central Files Series, box 25, folder OCB 091, Burma (file #1) (1), Eisenhower Papers, DDEL. The Burmese newspaper *The Nation* estimated that only about two thousand KMTs remained in Burma. US Embassy Rangoon to SS, 14 May 1954, Tel. Joint Weeka 19, 790B.00(W)/5-1454, RG59, CDF 1950–54, box 4139, NAII.

75. Elmer B. Staats, "Memorandum for the [Operations Control] Board," 9 June 1954, CREST documents, NAII. Sebald to SS, 2 June 1954, Tel. 1166, *FRUS* 1952–1954, 12:224–25. "Situation Report on KMT Troops in Burma," n.d., pp. 4–5, series 1513 (29), Accession no. 26, MNA.

76. Rankin to SS, 11 June 1954, Tel. 674, *FRUS* 1952–1954, 12:227. Everett F. Drumright to Gerald Warner, 23 July 1954, RG 84, Burma US Embassy, Classified General Records 1945–1961, box 27, NAII. Elmer B. Staats, "Memorandum for the [Operations Control] Board," 9 June 1954, CREST documents, NAII. Sebald may not have supported keeping the Joint Military Committee functioning. See Gore-Booth to FO, 17 June 1954, 1091/80, FO 371/111967, BNA. SS to US Embassy Bangkok, 16 June 1954, Tel. 2508, *FRUS* 1952–1954, 12:227–28.

77. Sebald, "Burma Diary (1952–54)," entry for 27 June 1954, pp. 460–61. C.T. Moodie to EXAF, 28 June 1954, Despatch 3/54, series A1838, control symbol 3008/7/1, Part 1, NAA.

78. Moodie to EXAF, 30 August 1954, Despatch 11/54, series A1838, control symbol 3008/7/1, Part 1, NAA. The British ambassador, one of the officials who spoke with U Nu, did say that he thought the prime minister "was putting on something of an act" when talking about the KMT. Moodie to EXAF, 4 October 1954, Despatch 15/54, ibid.

79. British Embassy Bangkok to FO, 30 June 1954, 1024/59/54, FO 371/111967, BNA. Sebald, "Burma Diary (1952–54), note 35, pp. 519–20.

80. Ibid., note 16, pp. 509–10.

81. Foley, *Cold War and National Assertion*, 117.

7. THE NEUTRALITY CONUNDRUM

1. Eisenhower to Milton S. Eisenhower, 1 December 1954, DDE Diary Series, box 7, folder DDE: Diary December 1954 (2), Eisenhower Papers (Whitman File), DDEL.

2. South-East Asia Department, UK Foreign Office, "The Political Situation in Burma: June 1953," pp. 17–18, 5 August 1953, FO 435/6, BNA. Minute, S. J. Olver, 2 March 1953, on Speaight to R. H. Scott, 21 February 1953, FO 371/106684, BNA.

3. NSC 5405, 16 January 1954, *FRUS* 1952–1954, 12:375–76.

4. Sebald to Everett F. Drumwright, 5 March 1954, ibid., 204-5.

5. Draft (SC-P2-3), Special Committee Report On SOUTHEAST ASIA—PART II, 5 April 1954, WHO, NSC Staff Papers, 1948–1961, OCB Central Files, box 79, folder OCB 091, Southeast Asia (file #1) (4), Eisenhower Papers, DDEL.

6. Operations Coordinating Board, "Progress Report on NSC 5405 . . . ," 30 July 1954, WHO, Southeast Asia (file #2) (1), ibid.

7. Office of Current Intelligence, CIA, name of report redacted, 16 July 1953; CIA, "Information Report," 21 July 1953; both CREST documents, NAII.

8. P. H. Gore-Booth to Anthony Eden, 26 January 1954, "Burma: Annual Review for 1953," *Further Correspondence Respecting Burma, Part 7, January to December 1954,* p. 6, FO 436/7, BNA. Memorandum, W. Park Armstrong Jr. to the Acting SS, 28 January 1954, 790B.00/1-2854, RG 59, CDF 1950–1954, box 4138, NAII. Charney, *Modern Burma*, 76. Gore-Booth to Eden, 1 January 1955, "Further Correspondence Respect Burma," Part 8, January to December 1955, FO 435/8, BNA.

9. Bishop to SS, 21 February 1956, Tel. 2413, folder 360.01 kmt (illegal border crossing), RG 84, Burma US Embassy, Classified General Records 1945–1961, box 27, NAII.

10. Berkeley Gage to FO, 20 February 1956, Tel. 104; and FO to British Embassy Bangkok, 21 February 1956, Tel. 136; both in FO 371/123324, BNA. Hoover to US Embassy Rangoon, 22 February 1956, Tel. 838, *FRUS* 1955–1957, 22:43–44. Berkeley Gage to FO, 24 February 1956, Tel. 118, FO 371/123324, BNA.

11. CIA, NSC Briefing, "Burma," 3 November 1953, CREST documents, NAII. "General Discussion of Communist Threat in the Far East," n.d. (1956?), RG 84, Burma US Embassy, Classified General Records 1945–1961, box 25, NAII.

12. Steinberg and Fan, *Modern China-Myanmar Relations,* 28–40. Australian Legation Rangoon to EXAF, 13 August 1954, Tel. 125, series A1838, control symbol 3008/7/1, Part 1, NAA. Translation of U Nu's speech, 19 July 1954, series A1838, control symbol 3008/7/1, Part 1, NAA.

13. US Embassy Rangoon to SS, 20 July 1954, Tel. 54, 790B.00/7-2054, RG 59, CDF 1950–1954, box 4138, NAII. Moodie to EXAF, 24 July 1954, Despatch 7/54, series A1838, control symbol 3008/7/11, Part 1, NAA. OCB, "Daily Intelligence Abstracts No. 222," 14 September 1954, WHO, NSC Staff: Papers, 1948–1961, OCB Central Files Series, folder OCT 350.05 (file #1)(8), box 110, Eisenhower Papers, DDEL.

14. Herbert Hoover Jr. to US Embassy Rangoon, 17 October 1954, Tel. 263, 790B.13/1754, RG 59, CDF 1950–1954, box 4140, NAII.

15. Steinberg and Fan, *Modern China-Myanmar Relations,* 34–38. Office Memorandum, W. Wendell Blancke to Sebald, 11 January 1955, 790B.11/1-1155, RG 59, CDF 1955–1959, box 3855, NAII.

16. Steinberg and Fan, *Modern China-Myanmar Relations,* 31–38.

17. Joseph Alsop, "Burma Offers New Defense Line," *Washington Post and Times Herald,* 30 January 1955. The British ambassador in Rangoon privately defended the American embassy. Though an ambassador was indeed needed, the embassy had been right "in not trying to throw weight around and 'mobilize' Burma in a big way. They've tried this before and it didn't work. If they try it now, Gawdelpus. Sebald knows this. Alsop won't be told." Gore-Booth to Robert Scott, 23 February 1955, FO 371/117036, BNA.

18. Minutes of Cabinet Meeting, 11 March 1955, Cabinet Series, box 4, Eisenhower Papers (Whitman File), DDEL. Moodie to EXAF, 4 March 1955, Despatch 4/55, series

A1838, control symbol 3008/11/161, Part 1, NAA. Dulles to Eisenhower, in Dulles to USDS, 27 February 1955, *FRUS* 1955–1957, 12:3–4.

19. Robert R. Nathan to Louis J. Walinsky, 7 April 1955, file 3-13, box 3, Walinsky Papers, Cornell University Library. Nathan to Walinsky, 26 April 1953, ibid. Nathan to Barrington, 8 April 1955, file 3-13, box 8, ibid.

20. Sebald to USDS, 10 January 1953, Despatch 533, 790B.5-MSP/1-1053, RG 59, CDF 1950–1954, box 4142, NAII.

21. Newspaper clipping, "American Aid," *The Nation* (Rangoon), 15 October 1954, series 1838, control symbol 3008/11/161 Part 1, NAA. R. F. G. Sarell to Eden, 15 March 1955, Tel. 68, FO 435/8, BNA.

22. Walinsky, *Economic Development*, 552.

23. Sebald to USDS, 1 July 1954, Despatch 1, 790B.5 MSP/7-154, RG 59, CDF 1950–1954, box 4141, NAII.

24. "American Agencies Operating in Burma," attached to Richard H. Allen to Selwyn Lloyd, 26 June 1957, Despatch 163, FO 371/129419, BNA.

25. Sebald to SS, 28 April 1953, Tel. 2065, 790B.5/4-2853, RG 59, CDF 1950–1954, box 4141, NAII.

26. Stanton to SS, 22 June 1953, Tel. 2609, 790B.5/6-2253, ibid. Stanton to SS, 22 June 1953, Tel. 2609, 790B.5/6-2253, ibid. Dulles to US Embassies London and Rangoon, 28 September 1953, Tel. 2122, 790B.5/9-2853, ibid. Sebald's recommendations are discussed in Office Memorandum, Day to Mr. Beale, 18 January 1954, FW 790B.5/1-1054, ibid.

27. Operations Coordinating Board, "Daily Intelligence Abstracts No. 58," 22 January 1954, WHO, NSC Staff Papers, 1948–1961, OCB Central File Series, box 110, Eisenhower Papers, DDEL.

28. Memorandum for the OCB Working Group, n.d., file OCB 091. Burma (undated), box 79, ibid.

29. Sebald to Drumright, 29 April 1954, RG 59, CDF 1950–1954, box 4141, NAII.

30. Memorandum for the OCB Working Group, NSC 5405, 20 September 1954, WHO, NSC Staff: Papers, 1948–1961, OCB Central File, folder OCB 091. Burma, box 25, Eisenhower Papers, DDEL.

31. Daniel M. Braddock to SS, 3 April 1956, Tel. 1145, *FRUS* 1955–1957, 22:54–55. Sebald to Gordon Gray, 4 April 1956, 790B.5-MSP/3-856, RG 59, CDF 1955–1959, box 3855, NAII.

32. Memorandum, Graves B. Erskine to Reuben Robertson, 25 June 1956, RG 59, CDG 1955–1959, box 3855, NAII. Douglas MacArthur II to Dulles, 15 June 1955, *FRUS* 1955–1957, 22:71–72.

33. Herbert Hoover Jr. to Eisenhower, 24 August 1956, International Series, box 5, Eisenhower Papers (Whitman File), DDEL. Robertson to Joseph C. Satterthwaite, 17 September 1956, 790B.5-MSP/9-1756, RG 59, CDF 1955–1959, box 3855, NAII. Hoover to US Embassy Rangoon, 20 September 1956, Tel. 308, *FRUS* 1955–1957, 22:84–85. Satterthwaite to SS, 24 September 1956, Tel. 388, 790B.5 MSP/9-2456, RG 59, CDF 1955–1959, box 3855, NAII. Satterthwaite to Robertson, 25 October 1956, RG 59, CDF 1955–1959, box 3855, NAII.

34. Walinsky to Nathan, 29 April 1955, file 3-6, box 3, Walinsky Papers, Cornell University Library. Walinsky's associates questioned whether it was proper for him to urge such a loan on the Burmese government. See Memorandum, A. J. Creshkoff to Nathan, n.d., ibid. Satterthwaite to SS, 19 May 1955, Tel. 1146, *FRUS* 1955–1957, 12:8.

35. Roger Makins to Harold Macmillan, 11 July 1955, FO 435/8, BNA.

36. Nathan to Walinsky, 5 July 1955, file 3-13, box 3, Walinsky Papers, Cornell University Library; Nathan to Walinsky, 8 July 1955, ibid. Satterthwaite to USDS, 18 August 1955, Despatch 79, Dulles-Herter Series, box 5, Eisenhower Papers (Ann Whitman File), DDEL.

U Nu to Richard Nixon, 2 July 1955, Vice Presidential Collection, Country File [Cushman Files], PPS 320, box 2, folder Burma 1955–1960, Richard M. Nixon Library. Satterthwaite to SS, 27 July 1955, Tel. 79, RG 59, CDF 1955–1959, box 3855, NAII.

37. Barrington to Burma FO, 13 August 1955, Tel. C62; U Win Pe to Barrington, 15 August 1955, Tel. BW358/MA; both in "Loan from the United States," series 15/2, acc. #569, Year 1955, file B2, B5, Da, MNA. Daniel M. Braddock to USDS, 23 August 1955, Despatch 86, 350-BURMA pol trends, RG 84, Burma US Embassy, Classified General Records, box 20, NAII. Sebald to Dulles, 31 August 1955, 890B.10/8-2155, RG 59, CDF 1955–1957, box 5000, NAII.

38. Howard P. Jones to Robertson, 12 September 1955, 611.90B/9-1255, RG 59, CDF 1955–1957, box 5000, NAII.

39. Nu to Dulles, 7 September 1955, enclosed in Satterthwaite to USDS, 13 September 1955, Despatch 120, ibid., box 4998.

40. Barrington to FO, 17–18 September 1955, Tel C76, "Loan from the United States," series 15/2, Acc #569, Year 1955, file B2, B5, 1255, Da, MNA.

41. Copy, Walter Judd letter, Rangoon, 20 November 1955, folder "Congressional File, Trips, Middle East/General, box 83, Walter Judd Papers, HIA.

42. Gore-Booth to Lloyd, 31 December 1955, "Views of the Burmese President on the Current Situation in Burma," FO 435/8, BNA. Steinberg and Fan, *Modern China-Myanmar Relations*, 39.

43. Gore-Booth to Lloyd, 6 January 1956, in *Further Correspondence Respecting Burma, Part 9, January to December 1956*, p. 5, FO 435/9, BNA. Office Memorandum, Kenneth P. Landon to Elmer Staats, 29 November 1955, WHO, NSC Staff: Papers 1948–1961, file OCB.091.4 Southeast Asia (File #4)(4), OCB Central File Series, box 80, Eisenhower Papers, DDEL.

44. Memorandum, U Tun Shein, 28 November 1955, "Loan from the United States," series 15/2, Acc #569, Year 1955, file B2, B5, 1255, Da, MNA. Department of State Press Release no. 70, 8 February 1956, in Agricultural Commodities Agreement, FO371/123344, BNA.

45. Cohn to Rayburn, 11 January 1956, folder 5-2, box 5, Walinsky Papers, Cornell University Library. See also Walinsky to Nathan, 15 January 1956, file 3-8, box 3, ibid.

46. L. M. Purnell to Daniel M. Braddock, 23 April 1956, 890B.00/4-2356, RG 59, CDF 1955–1959, box 4998, NAII. Satterthwaite to SS, 18 February 1956, *FRUS* 1955–1957, 22:41–42.

47. Memorandum, Dulles to John B. Hollister, 28 February 1956, *FRUS* 1955–1957, 22:44–45. Nathan to Walinsky, 6 March 1956, file 3-15, box 3, Walinsky Papers, Cornell University Library.

48. Moodie to EXAF, 10 April 1956, Savingram 3, series A1838, control symbol 3008/2/2/2 Part 1, NAA.

49. U Nu to Eisenhower, 22 May 1956; suggested response, Eisenhower to U Nu, n.d.; both in International Series, box 5, Eisenhower Papers (Whitman File), DDEL.

50. Memorandum, Douglas MacArthur II to Dulles, 5 June 1956, 790B.5 MSP/5-556, RG 59, CDF 1955–1959, box 3855; also in *FRUS* 1955–1957, 22:65–66. "Summary of Current U.S. Action Regarding Aid to Burma," 1 June 1956; Memorandum, Landon to Staats, 27 June 1956; both in WHO, NSC Staff: Papers 1948–1961, OCB Series, box 25, folder OCB.091 Burma (File #1)(8), Eisenhower Papers, DDEL.

51. Minute on "Rice for technicians agreement," Peter Murray (for Gore-Booth) to FO, 2 July 1956, FO 371/123344, BNA.

52. Dulles to US Embassy Rangoon, 28 June 1956, Tel. 1305, *FRUS* 1955–1957, 22:75–76. Dulles to US Embassy Rangoon, 28 June 1956, Tel. 1306, ibid., 76–77. Dulles to US Embassy Rangoon, 28 June 1956, Tel. 1307, ibid., 77–78. Braddock to SS, 2 July 1956, Tel. 6, ibid., 78.

53. Richard E. Usher to USDS, 16 August 1956, Despatch 97, RG 59, CDF 1955–1959, box 3853, NAII. Peter Murray to F. S. Tomlinson, 3 October 1956, FO 371/123324, BNA.

8. THE CHINA BORDER, A "POLITE COUP," AND RETURN TO DEMOCRATIC GOVERNMENT

1. Satterthwaite to SS, 29 March 1957, Tel. 1248, RG 84, Burma US Embassy, Classified General Records, 1945–1961, box 20, NAII. This was apparently a draft telegram. When a telegram went off to Washington the next day, some of the more effusive comments were not included. See Satterthwaite to SS, 30 March 1957, Tel. 1248, 790B.00/3-3057, RG 59, CDF 1955–1959, box 3850, NAII.

2. Don W. Rogers to USDS, 2 May 1957, Airgram 744, 890B.191-RA/5-257, RG 59, CDF 1955–1959, box 5001, NAII. Comments about diplomats stationed in Rangoon, FO 435/10, BNA.

3. Memcon, Barrington and Daniel M. Braddock, 4 April 1957, RG 84, Burma US Embassy, Classified General Records, box 20, NAII. The comment about his conversation having "done a little good" is from Braddock to USDS, 10 April 1957, Despatch 676, ibid.

4. Arthur H. de la Mare to F. S. Tomlinson, 13 June 1957, FO 371/129409, BNA.

5. Memorandum, Herter to Dulles, 1 July 1957, box 2, Herter Papers, DDEL. Author's interview with U Thet Tun, Yangon, 6 February 2012.

6. Dulles to Eisenhower, 14 April 1958, White House Memoranda Series, box 6, Dulles Papers, DDEL.

7. Satterthwaite to SS, 21 March 1957, Tel. 1206, 790B.5 MSP/3-2157, RG 59, CDF 1955–1959, box 3855, NAII. *FRUS* 1955–1957, 22:107n.

8. Braddock to SS, 13 August 1957, Tel. 174, 790B.5-MSP/8-1357, RG 59, CDF 1955–1959, box 3855, NAII.

9. Australian Embassy Washington to EXAF, 24 October 1957, Savingram 424, series A1838, control symbol 3008/2/9 Part 4, NAA. McConaughy to SS, 21 August 1957, Tel. 252, *FRUS* 1955–1957, 22:115–16. Herter to SS, Tel. Secun.4, 6 September 1957, ibid., 116–17.

10. Spivack to Lewis M. Purnell, 17 September 1957, 790B.00/9-1757, RG 59, CDF 1955–1959, box 3850, NAII. Dulles to US Embassy Rangoon, 27 September 1957, Tel. 365, 790B.5-MSP/9-2757, ibid., box 3855. US Embassy Rangoon to SS, 2 October 1957, Tel. 381, 790B.5-MSP/10-257, ibid., box 3855. The figure of $20 million with repayment of $2 million in Burmese currency is in Operations Coordinating Board, "Weekly Activity Report," 7 April 1959, WHO, NSC Staff: Papers 1948–1961, OCB Secretariat Series, box 9, Eisenhower Papers, DDEL.

11. Young to McConaughy, 17 January 1958, folder 320—Burma-US Relations, box 19, RG 84 Burma US Embassy, Classified General Records 1945–1961, NAII.

12. McConaughy to SS, 21 January 1958, Tel. 717, ibid.

13. Operations Coordinating Board, "Weekly Activity Report," 16 December 1957, WHO, NSC Staff: Papers 1948–1961, OCB Secretariat Series, folder OCB 319.1 Activities Report (file #1)(7), box 8, Eisenhower Papers, DDEL. The United States informed the British of their plan to provide police assistance, but this was kept secret lest the Burmese become alarmed. Operations Coordinating Board, "Weekly Activities Report," 7April 1958, ibid., box 9.

14. Memcon, U Ba Aye, Rufus Z. Smith, 28 December 1957, RG 84, Burma US Embassy, Classified General Records 1945–1961, box 19, NAII.

15. Robert R. Nathan, "Eleventh Trip to Burma and Around the World," February–March 1958, entry for 18 February 1958, p. 23, folder 1-14, box 1, Walinsky Papers, Cornell University Library.

16. Eric Kocher to McConaughy, 30 April 1958, RG 84, Burma US Embassy, Classified General Records 1945–1961, box 19, NAII. *FRUS* 1955–1957, 22:124n3.

17. "Burma Desk Activity September 8–12, 1958," folder 350 Burma Desk Activity, RG 84, Burma US Embassy, Classified General Records 1945–1961, box 20, NAII. Office Memorandum, Kocher to Robertson, 11 September 1958, RG 59, CDF 1955–1959, box 3856, NAII. "Burma Desk Activity, September 15–19, 1958," folder 350 Burma Desk Activity, RG 84, Burma US Embassy, Classified General Records 1945–1961, box 20, NAII. "Burma Desk Activity, September 29—October 3, 1958," folder 350 Burma Desk Activity, RG 84, Burma US Embassy, Classified General Records 1948–1961, box 20, NAII.

18. McConaughy to SS, 16 October 1958, Tel. 357, 790B.56/10-1658, RG 59, CDF 1955–1959, box 3856, NAII.

19. McConaughy to SS, 16 October 1958, Tel. 357, 790B.56/10-1658, RG 59, CDF 1955–1959, box 3856, NAII. Kocher to McConaughy, 15 October 1958, 790B.56/10-1558, ibid.

20. Peyton A. Kerr to Kocher, 28 October 1958, 790B.5-MSP/10-2858, ibid.

21. Jovan Cavoski, "Neutralism in China's Shadow: Sino-Burmese Relations and the Cold War in Southeast Asia 1948–1962," unpublished paper presented at an international conference, "Mao's China, Non-Communist Asia, and the Global Setting," University of Hong Kong, 14–15 February 2012. A good recent account of the border dispute from both the Burmese and the Chinese perspectives is Steinberg and Fan, *Modern China-Myanmar Relations*, 55–68.

22. Peter Murray to Selwyn Lloyd, 24 September 1956, "Sino-Burmese Relations: The Frontier Dispute," Despatch 321, FO 435/9, BNA. Satterthwaite to SS, 24 August 1956, Tel. 253, RG 59, CDF 1955–1959, box 3853, NAII. Colin T. Moodie to EXAF, 14 September 1956, Tel. 297, series A1838, control symbol 2498/1, NAA.

23. Braddock to USDS, 2 October 1956, Despatch 199, RG 84, Burma US Embassy, Classified General Records 1945–1961, box 26, folder 360.01—CPR/Burma border missionaries, NAII.

24. Spivack to USDS, 3 October 1956, Despatch 202, folder 360.01—CPR/Burma border, ibid. Steinberg and Fan, *Modern China-Myanmar Relations*, 58.

25. Peter Murray to F.S. Tomlinson, 3 October 1956, 1065/6/56, FO 371/123324, BNA. Australian Embassy Washington to EXAF, 3 August 1956, Tel. 764, series A1838, control symbol 2498/1, NAA. Australian Embassy Manila to EXAF, 6 August 1956, Tel. 121, ibid.

26. Satterthwaite to SS, 1 August 1956, Tel. 132, RG 84, Burma US Embassy, Classified General Records, 1945–1961, box 26, folder 360.01 Red China/Burma, NAII. Young to Satterthwaite, 18 September 1956, ibid., box 20.

27. Young to Satterthwaite, 18 September 1956, ibid., box 20. Satterthwaite to SS, 12 October 1956, Tel. 496, RG 84, ibid., box 26, folder 360.01 CPR/Burma Border General Records, NAII. U Pe Kin, comments to an unnamed American correspondent, quoted in Satterthwaite to Kenneth T. Young, 30 October 1956, RG 84, Burma US Embassy, Classified General Records, 1945-61, box 19, NAII.

28. Satterthwaite to SS, 10 November 1956, Tel. 648, 790B.00(W)/11-1056, RG 59, CDF 1955–1959, box 3853, NAII. The Joint Sino-Burma Communiqué, dated 10 November 1956, is in RG 84, Burma US Embassy, Classified General Records 1945–1961, box 26, folder 360.01—China/Burma Border, NAII.

29. Spivack to USDS, 14 November 1956, Despatch 305, RG 84, Burma US Embassy, Classified General Records 1945–1961, box 26, folder 360.01—Border, NAII.

30. Quoted in Moodie to EXAF, 29 December 1956, Despatch 26/1956, series A1838, control symbol 3008/11/87/1, NAA. R.H. Allen to Lloyd, 27 December 1956, Despatch 404, "The Sino-Burmese Frontier," FO 435/9, BNA.

31. Sattherthwaite to SS, 22 December 1956, Tel. 866, RG 84, Burma US Embassy, Classified General Records 1945–1961, box 26, folder 360.01—China/Burma Border, NAII. The head of the Southeast Asia Division of the British Foreign Office told an American diplomat that the Chinese offer was "on balance as favorable as Burma could expect to get." Winthrop W. Aldrich to SS, 12 December 1956, Tel. 3263, ibid.

32. Allen to Lloyd, 30 July 1957, Despatch 191, "The Kachins," p. 47, FO 435/10, BNA. Satterthwaite to SS, 4 January 1957, Tel. 918, 790B.00(W)/1-457, RG 59, CDF 1955–1959, box 3853, NAII. Satterthwaite to USDS, 7 January 1957, Despatch 434, 790B.00/1-757, ibid. Dulles to US Embassy Rangoon, 4 February 1957, RG 84, Burma US Embassy, Classified General Records 1945–1861, folder 360.01—China/Burma Border, box 26, NAII.

33. Allen to Lloyd, 30 July 1957, Despatch 191, "The Kachins," pp. 46–47, FO 435/10, BNA.

34. Newspaper clipping, *The Nation*, 11 April 1957, series 1838, control symbol 3008/11/87/1, NAA. Spivack to USDS, 5 July 1957, Despatch 19, RG 84, Burma US Embassy, Classified General Records, folder 360.21 Burma Commies, box 26, NAII.

35. Moodie to EXAF, 13 August 1957, Tel. 214; Moodie to EXAF, 14 August 1957, Tel. 219; both in series A1838, control symbol 3008/11/87/1, NAA. Steinberg and Fan, *Modern China-Myanmar Relations*, 63.

36. Australian Embassy Washington, DC to EXAF, 6 November 1957, Savingram 454, series A1838, control symbol 3008/11/87/1, NAA.

37. McConaughy to SS, 7 April 1959, RG 84, Burma US Embassy, Classified General Records 1945–1961, box 36, NAII. Memcon, Ne Win, McConaughy, 18 May 1959, enclosed in William C. Hamilton to USDS, 22 May 1959, Despatch 588, ibid., box 35.

38. Herter to US Embassy Rangoon, 30 January 1960, Tel. 748, folder 320 Relations (Burma-China), RG 84, Burma US Embassy, Classified General Records 1945–1961, box 34. The Nationalist government on Taiwan declared that the border settlement was illegal.

39. Steinberg and Fan, *Modern China-Myanmar Relations*, 65–68. Snow to SS, 7 October 1960, Unnumbered Tel., 790B.00/10-760, RG 59, CDF 1960–1963, box 2103, NAII.

40. McConaughy to SS, 30 April 1958, Tel. 1008, 790B.00/4-3058, RG 59, CDF 1955–1959, box 3850, NAII. McConaughy to SS, 7 May 1958, Tel. 1048, RG 84, Burma US Embassy, Classified General Records 1945–1961, box 25, folder 350.1AFPFL, NAII.

41. R. Gordon Arneson to Dulles, [14 May 1958], 790B.00-5-1458, RG 59, CDF 1955–1959, box 3950, NAII. McConaughy to SS, 8 May 1958, Tel. 1057, 790B.00/5-858, ibid, box 3851. Office Memorandum, Eric Kocher to Walter S. Robertson, 9 May 1958, ibid.

42. McConaughy to SS, 4 June 1958, Tel. 1200, RG 84, Burma US Embassy, Classified General Records, 1945–1961, box 25, NAII.

43. McConaughy to USDS, 1 April 1958, Despatch 844, folder 320 Burma-China Relations, box 19, RG 84, Burma US Embassy, Classified General Records 1945–1961, NAII.

44. Dulles to US Embassy Rangoon, 24 July 1958, Tel. G-4, 790B.5-MSP/6-1858, RG 59, CDF 1955–1959, box 3856, NAII. Memcon, Malcolm Booker, J. Graham Parsons, 10 July 1958, folder 350 Burma, RG 84, Burma US Embassy, Classified General Records 1948–1961, box 20, NAII.

45. Spivack (for McConaughy) to USDS, 23 July 1958, Despatch 61, 990B.61/7-2358, RG 59, CDF 1955–1959, box 5384, NAII. McConaughy to SS, 24 July 1958, Tel. G-17, folder 350 Burma, RG 84, Burma US Embassy, Classified General Records 1948–1961, box 20, NAII. McConaughy to SS, 26 August 1958, Tel. G-37, ibid., box 24.

46. D.L.B. Goslett to Australian Ambassador Rangoon, 7 August 1958, series A1838, control symbol TS383/2/1 Part 1, NAA. Memorandum for the Files, "Views of General Ne Win," 12 August 1958, folder 350 Burma (Views of General Ne Win), RG 84, Burma US Embassy, Classified General Records 1948–1961, box 20, NAII.

47. McConaughy to SS, 26 August 1958, Tel. G-37, RG 84, Burma US Embassy, Classified General Records 1948–1961, box 24, NAII. Herter to US Embassy Rangoon, 15 September 1958, Airgram A-36, folder 350-Burma, ibid., box 20. McConaughy to USDS, 2 September 1958, Despatch 119, 790B.00/9-258, RG 59, CDF 1955–1959, box 3151, NAII.

48. Office Memorandum, Kocher to Robertson, 4 September 1958, ibid. For a critical account of the Pyusawhti, see Pho Thar Aung, "From Pyusawhti to the Present," *The Irrawaddy*, January 2003, http://www2.irrawaddy.org/article.php?art_id=2822&page=1.

49. McConaughy to SS, 25 September 1958, Tel. 277, 790B.00/9-2558, RG 59, CDF 1955–1959, box 3851, NAII. McConaughy to SS, 26 September 1958, Tel. 287RG 84, Burma US Embassy, Classified General Records 1948–1961, box 20, NAII.

50. "Burma Desk Activity, September 29—October 3, 1958," folder 350 Burma Desk Activity, RG 84, Burma US Embassy, Classified General Records 1948–1961, box 20, NAII. Memcon, H. J. van Roijen, Robertson et al., 26 September 1958, RG 59, CDF 1955–1959, box 3851, NAII. Hugh S. Cumming, Jr., to the Acting Secretary, 26 September 1958, RG 59, CDF 1955–1959, box 3851, NAII. 381st Meeting of the National Security Council, 2 October 1958, NSC Series, box 10, Eisenhower Papers (Whitman File), DDEL.

51. Key to SS, 22 November 1950, Tel. 336, 790B.00/11-2250, RG 59, CDF 1950–1954, box 4135, NAII.

52. Dulles to US Embassies Bangkok (Tel. 877) and Rangoon (Tel. 306), 31 October 1958, folder 350 Burma—Army Take-Over, RG 84, Burma US Embassy, Classified General Records 1948–1961, box 20, NAII. Herter to US Embassy Rangoon, 15 December 1958, Tel. 401, 790B.13/12-1558, RG 59, CDF 1955–1959, box 3855, NAII.

53. McConaughy to SS, 7 November 1958, Tel. 407, folder 350 Burma (Amb's first interview with Ne Win as Prime Min.), RG 84, Burma US Embassy, Classified General Records 1948–1961, box 35, NAII.

54. "Notes on a meeting with Mr. L. J. Walinsky on November 11, 1958," folder 500 Robert Nathan (Amb's Meeting with Walinsky), ibid.

55. McConaughy to SS, 2 December 1958, Tel. 413, ibid. The TAMS representative was less accepting of the decision and hoped to negotiate an agreement by which some TAMS representatives could remain in Burma. See Peyton Kerr to USDS, 16 December 1958, Despatch 254, ibid., box 28, folder 500 TAMS (Termination Contract).

56. A. H. Loomes to EXAF, 3 December 1958, Memo. 836, series A1838, control symbol 3008/2/9 Part 5, NAA.

57. Minute, H. M. B. Chevalier, 9 January 1959, on A. J. de la Mare to John O. McCormick, 5 January 1959; R. P. Heppel to de la Mare, 22 January 1959; both in FO371/143865, BNA.

58. Memcon, Julian Licht and McConaughy, 31 July 1959, 790B.13/MSP-7-3159, RG 59, CDF 1955–1959, box 3855, NAII. After TAMS and Nathan Associates left, it was difficult for their former local employees to find employment. Robert Kurlander to USDS, 11 March 1959 Despatch 452, 890B.00/3-1159, ibid., box 4998.

59. Stanley Karnow, "A Second Chance for U Nu," *The Reporter*, 30 March 1961, 32; Charney, *Modern Burma*, 98.

60. Edward G. Lansdale, Memorandum, "Civil Activities of the Military, Southeast Asia," WHO, Office of the Special Assistant for National Security Affairs: Records 1952–1961, OCB Series, Subject Subseries, box 6, Eisenhower Papers, DDEL. Australian Services Attaché, Australian Embassy, Rangoon, to DWI Canberra et al., 26 March 1959, series A1838, control symbol 3008/2/9 Part 5, NAA.

61. McConaughy to SS, 15 January 1959, Tel. 506, folder 350 Burma (Interim Govt.), RG 84, Burma US Embassy, Classified General Records 1948–1961, box 35, NAII. USDS to McConaughy, 14 January 1959, ibid.

62. Parsons to McConaughy, 19 January 1959, ibid., box 36.

63. Kerr to William H. Sullivan, 25 February 1959, folder 350 Burma, ibid., box 35.

64. US Embassy Rangoon to USDS, 4 March 1959, Despatch 442, 890B.00/3-459, RG 59, CDF 1955–1959, box 4992, NAII. US Embassy Rangoon to USDS, 19 March 1959, Despatch 474, 890B.00/3-1959, ibid., box 4998. "The Political Situation," enclosed in Herbert D. Spivack to USDS, 11 March 1959, Despatch 454, folder 310 CM Conference, RG 84, Burma US Embassy, Classified General Records 1948–1961, box 34, NAII.

65. Spivack (for the ambassador) to SS, 18 March 1959, Despatch 464, 790B.13/3-1859, ibid., box 3855.

66. Memcon, U Yone, Robertson, Kocher, William H. Sullivan, 24 March 1959, 790B.13/3-2459, ibid. Herter to Eisenhower, 1 April 1959, box 7, Herter Papers, DDEL.

67. McConaughy to SS, 8 April 1959, Tel. 868, folder 350 Burma (Nu's Comments on Political Situation), RG 84, Burma US Embassy, Classified General Records 1948–1961, box 35, NAII.

68. Memorandum, Spivack to McConaughy, "Reflections on Burma," enclosed in Peyton Kerr to USDS, 22 April 1959, RG 59, CDF 1955–1959, box 3851, NAII.

69. "Annex A" (manuscript), series 11/10, accession no. 64, MNA.

70. British Embassy Rangoon to FO, 14 May 1959, FO 371/143876, BNA. Memcon, Ne Win, McConaughy, 18 May 1959, folder 350 Ne Win, RG 84, Burma US Embassy, Classified General Records 1948–1961, box 36, NAII. CINCPAC to SS (for Robertson), 16 May 1959, Tel. DTG 162110Z MAY, 790B.00/5-1659, RG 59, CDF 1955–1959, box 3852, NAII.

71. Memcon, Ne Win, McConaughy, 18 May 1959, folder 350 Ne Win, RG 84, Burma US Embassy, Classified General Records 1948–1961, box 36, NAII.

72. Julian Licht, quoted in Memcon, Licht, McConaughy, 31 July 1959, 790B.12/7-3159, ibid., box 3855. McConaughy to SS, 23 June 1959, Tel. 1157, 790B.5-MSP/6-2359, ibid., box 3856. Memorandum, Dillon to Eisenhower, 10 June 1959, 790B.5-MSP/6-1059, ibid.

73. Operations Coordinating Board, "Report on Southeast Asia (NSC 5809)," 18 August 1959, WHO, Office of the Special Assistant for National Security Affairs: Records 1952–1961, NSC Series, Policy Papers Subseries, box 25, Eisenhower Papers, DDEL. On the changing climate, see Gilbert Jonas, "Burma Moves Toward the West," *The New Leader*, 21 September 1959, 16–17. On Burmese allegations of American connections with the Shans at this point, see McConaughy to SS, 24 April 1959, Tel. 909, RG 59, CDF 1955–1959, box 3856, NAII.

74. Richard T. Ewing to USDS, 21 August 1959, Despatch 135, 790B.00/8-2159, RG 59, CDF 1955–1959, box 3856, NAII.

75. McConaughy to SS, 7 October 1958, Tel. 336, 790B.553/10-759, ibid. Memcon, Ne Win and McConaughy, 25 September 1959, enclosed in Peyton Kerr to USDS, 28 September 1959, Despatch 211, 890B.2612/9-2859, ibid., box 5002.

76. Memcon, Maung Maung and McConaughy, 29 August 1959, enclosed in Kerr to USDS, 8 September 1959, folder 350 Burma (Memo of Conversation AMB-COL Maung Maung), RG 84, Burma US Embassy, Classified General Records 1948–1961, box 35, NAII.

77. Memcon, U Chan Tun Aung, Parsons, et al., 2 October 1959, 790B.5-MSP/10-259, RG 59, CDF 1955–1959, box 3856, NAII. Kerr (for McConaughy) to USDS, 9 October 1959, Despatch 224, 790B.5-MSP/10-959, ibid.

78. Memcon, Kerr and Thomas J. Davis, 20 November 1959, enclosed in Kerr to USDS, 24 November 1959, Despatch 297, 890B.00A/11-2459, ibid., box 4999.

79. Ibid. Office Memorandum, Anderson to Parsons, 17 December 1959, 890B.00/12-1759, ibid., box 4998. Memcon, Parsons, Davis, Richard Usher, Charles T. Greene, 17 November 1959, 790B.00/12-1759, ibid., box 3852.

80. McConaughy to SS, 3 November 1959, Tel. G-49, folder 320 Relations (Burma-China), RG 84, Burma US Embassy, Classified General Records 1948–1961, box 34, NAII.

81. Memcon, Parsons, Davis, Richard Usher, Charles T. Greene, 12 December 1959, 790B.00/12-1759, RG 59, CDF 1955–1959, box 3852, NAII.

82. Douglas Dillon to US Embassy Rangoon, 5 January 1960, Tel. 890B.2621/1-560, RG 59, CDF 1960–1963, box 2845, NAII.

83. Memcon, U Kyaw Nyien and McConaughy, 23 October 1959, RG 59, CDF 1955–1959, box 3852, NAII.

84. William P. Snow to SS, 8 January 1960, Tel. G-72, folder 310 Intl Conf (Chiefs of Mission), RG 84, Burma US Embassy, Classified General Records 1948–1961, box 34, NAII.

85. Memorandum, M.C. Debevoise to Executive Officer, Operations Coordinating Board, "Intelligence Material Pertinent to Agenda Items for Board Meeting of 10 February 1960," 9 February 1960, WHO, NSC Staff: Papers 1945–1961, OCB Secretariat Series, box 7, Eisenhower Papers, DDEL. Ne Win's comment to Law-Yone in Snow to SS, 10 February 1960, Tel. 800, 790B.00/2-1060, RG 59, CDF 1960–1963, box 2103, NAII. The Sprague Committee report is Office of Research and Analysis, United States Information Agency, "Communist Propaganda Activities in the Far East During 1959," US President's Committee on Information Activities Abroad (Sprague Committee), folder "Asia #30 (6)," box 9, Eisenhower Papers, DDEL.

86. Director of Central Intelligence, "National Intelligence Estimate Number 61–60," 12 April 1960, p. 4, CREST documents, NAII. Memcon, Colonel Gossett, D.O. Horen, C.O.F. Hogue, 22 April 1960, series A 1838, control symbol 3008/2/9 Part 5, NAA.

9. THE U NU INTERREGNUM

1. Herter to US Embassy Rangoon, 12 February 1960, RG 59, CDF 1960–1963, box 2105, NAII. Snow to SS, 13 February 1960, Tel. 809, folder 350 U Nu, RG 84, Burma US Embassy, Classified General Records 1948–1961, box 36, NAII.

2. Snow to SS, 10 May 1960, Tel. 1126, folder 350 Ne Win, RG 84, Burma US Embassy, Classified General Records 1948–1961, box 36, NAII.

3. Memorandum, F.R. Brickles to Snow, 9 August 1960, ibid. The customs issue is mentioned in Memcon, Alexander Schnee and U Soe Tin, 15 July 1965, in Schnee to USDS, 31 July 1964, Airgram A-40, RG 59, CFPF 1964–1966, box 1957, folder POL 8, NAII, and also in "Incidents During Ne Win's 1960 Trip," 6 September 1966, NSF—Country File, "Burma, Ne Win Visit 9/8-10/66," box 235, Johnson Papers, LBJL.

4. Memcon, John B. Dexter and Col. Kyi Han, 17 January 1964, RG59, Office of the Country Director, Bureau of Far Eastern Affairs, Office of the Country Director for Burma, 1964–11966. Lots 67D80–68D102, box 2, folder POL-POLITICAL AFF & REL, 15–1 Bo Setkya, NAII.

5. Lewis M. Purnell to John B. Dexter, 7 June 1962, RG 59, CDF 1960–1963, box 2104, NAII. According to Leach, Ne Win suffered a similar racist indignity while playing golf in England

6. Marilyn Irving Holt, *Mamie Doud Eisenhower: The General's First Lady* (Lawrence: University Press of Kansas, 2007), 40, 55,73,107; Carl Sferrazza Anthony, *First Ladies: The Saga of the Presidents' Wives and Their Power 1789–1961* (New York: William Morrow, 1990), 547, 580–82.

7. Purnell to Dexter, 7 June 1962, RG 59, CDF 1960–1963, box 2104, NAII.

8. Verification that Mamie Eisenhower was in the hospital comes from the president's schedule for June 1960 (http://web2.millercenter.org/dde/documents/presidential_papers/dde_diary_series/1960/dde_1960_06.pdf), and from a report in *Mr. Pop Culture*: http://www.mrpopculture.com/june-1-1960. I am indebted to Daniel Fong for the information about Mamie Eisenhower's hospitalization.

9. Memcon, Tun Thin and Dexter,16 August 1962, 790B.00/8-1662, RG 59, CDF 1960–1963, box 2104, NAII.

10. "Incidents During Ne Win's 1960 Trip" (note 3 above).

11. C. Douglas Dillon to US Embassy Rangoon, 18 August 1960, Tel. 118, folder 350 Ne Win, RG 84, Burma US Embassy, Classified General Records 1948–1961, box 36, NAII. Memcon, Ne Win and Snow, 21 September 1960, enclosed in Snow to USDS, 22 September 1960, Despatch 141, ibid.

12. A. H. Loomes to F. J. Blakenay, 1 June 1961, series A1938, control symbol TS383/2/1 Part 1, NAA. Memcon, Dr. Thin and Dexter, 16 August 1962, 790B.00/8-1662, NAII. Ambassador John Scott Everton thought Tun Thin's "hatred" characterization was too strong. Everton to Dexter, 5 September 1962, 790B.00/9-562, RG 59, CDF 1960–1963, box 2104, NAII.

13. Byroade to SS, 30 June 1964, Tel. 797, RG 59, CFPF1964–1966, box 1975, folder POL 15–1 Burma, NAII. US Embassy Rangoon to SS, 18 August 1966, Tel. 217, NSF, Name File, Jorden Memos, box 5, Johnson Papers, LBJL.

14. Loomes to Blakenay, 1 June 1961, series A1938, control symbol TS383/2/1 Part 1, NAA.

15. Briefing note to President Eisenhower, "Burma," 1 July 1960, WHO, Office of the Staff Secretary, 1952–1961, Subject Series; Alphabetical Subseries, folder Intelligence Briefing Notes, vol. 1 (2), box 14, Eisenhower Papers, DDEL.

16. Snow to SS, 22 January 1960, Tel. 715, 890B.2621/1-2250, RG 59, CDF 1960–1963, box 2845, NAII. Memcon, J. Graham Parsons, Leonard Saccio, Avery Peterson, 4 April 1960, 890B.2612/4-460, ibid.

17. Herter to US Embassy Rangoon, 26 July 1960, Tel. 67, 790B.5-MSP/7-2650, ibid., box 2106.

18. Robert J. Ballantyne to USDS, 17 October 1960, Despatch 717, 790B.00/10-1760, ibid., box 2103.

19. Parsons to Under Secretary, 29 October 1960, 790B.5-MSP/10-2960, ibid., box 2106.

20. Snow to SS, 12 January 1961, Tel. 491, folder 350 Relations (Burma-China), RG 84, Burma US Embassy, Classified General Records 1948–1961, box 34, NAII.

21. Snow to SS, 31 March 1961, Tel. G-204, folder 350 Burma—General, ibid., box 35. Snow to SS, 8 February 1961, Tel. 546, ibid. Snow to SS, 9 February 1969, Tel. 549, ibid. Everton to SS, 18 May 1962, Tel. 846, NSF—Countries File, box 16, Kennedy Papers, JFKL.

22. In 1955 the State Department discontinued using the term "KMT" for the Chinese Nationalist forces in Burma. Use of the term carried "an undesirable implication of affiliation with the Government of the Republic of China or the Kuomintang Party." Henceforth they were usually referred to as "Chinese irregulars" or "irregular Chinese forces" in official correspondence. Hoover to US Embassies Bangkok et al., 18 March 1955, Tel. CA-6170, RG 84, Burma US Embassy, Classified General Records 1945–1961, box 27, folder 360.1 "KMT'S—Burma Border Area—Use of TERM KMT," NAII.

23. Research Department Memorandum, "The KMT Troops in Burma and Neighbouring Countries," (unpublished), 9 March 1961, series A1838, control symbol 3008/2/5/1 Part 1, NAA. Acly to SS, 14 January 1955, Tel. 569, 790B.00(W)/1-1455, RG 59, CDF 1950–1955, box 3852, NAII.

24. Research Department Memorandum, "The KMT Troops in Burma and Neighbouring Countries," (unpublished), 9 March 1961, series A1838, control symbol 3008/2/5/1 Part 1, NAA.

25. Berkeley Gage to FO, 20 February 1956, Tel. 104, FO 371/123324, BNA.

26. Dulles to US Embassy Rangoon, Tel. 785, *FRUS* 1955–1957, 22:40. FO to British Embassy Rangoon, 22 February 1956, Tel. 77, FO 371/123324, BNA.

27. See, for example, William B. Hussey to USDS, 13 May 1958, 790B.00/5-1358, RG 59, CDF 1955–1959, box 3851, NAII.

28. NSC 5809, "U.S. Policy in Mainland Southeast Asia," 2 April 1958, p. 9, WHO, Office of the Special Assistant for National Security Affairs: Records 1953–1961, NSC Series,

Policy Papers Subseries, box 25, Eisenhower Papers, DDEL. William B. Hussey to USDS, 13 May 1958, 790B.00/5-1358, RG 59, CDF 1955–1959, box 3851, NAII. Spivack to USDS, 23 July 1958, 990B.61/7-2358, CDF 1955–1959, box 5324, NAII.

29. Memcon, 10 September 1958, Richard Myo Aung and William C. Hamilton, 10 September 1958, RG 84, Burma US Embassy, Classified General Records 1945–1961, box 25, NAII. McConaughy to SS, 22 January 1959, Tel. 629, box 34. For an account of Burma-China interaction over the KMT issue after 1954, see Steinberg and Fan, *Modern China-Myanmar Relations*, 50–55. Loomes to EXAF, 17 June 1959, Memo. no. 523, series A1838, control symbol 3008/2/9 Part 5, NAA.

30. Marvin A. Kreidberg to USARMA, Bangkok, 1 October 1959, Tel. C-106, RG 84, Burma US Embassy, Classified General Records 1945–1961, box 35, NAII.

31. Lintner, "Wise Man on the Hill," *Asia Times*, 8 April 2011, http://www.atimes.com/atimes/Southeast_Asia/MD08Ae01.html. William Young, suffering from serious illnesses, committed suicide in April 2011. According to Lintner "there was hardly a vacant seat in the Protestant church by the Ping River in . . . Chiang Mai for the funeral. American veterans of the Indochina war mixed with Thai and foreign residents, missionaries and intelligence officers, Lahu and Wa tribesmen, and even some wildlife conservationists."

32. NSC, "U.S. Policy in Mainland Southeast Asia," NSC 6012, 25 July 1960, WHO, Office of the Special Assistant for National Security Affairs: Records 1953–1961, NSC Series, Policy Papers Subseries, box 89, Eisenhower Papers, DDEL.

33. M. D. P. Hill to EXAF, 6 October 1960, Memo no. 645, series A1838, control symbol 3008/2/5/1 Part 1, NAA. Intelligence Briefing Notes, 7 November 1960, WHO, Office of the Staff Secretary, 1951–1961, Subject Series; Alphabetical Subseries, box 14, folder Intelligence Brief Notes, vol. 1 (2), Eisenhower Papers, DDEL.

34. South East Asia Section, Research Department Memorandum, EXAF, "The KMT Troops in Burma and Neighbouring Countries," 9 March 1961, series A1838, control symbol 3008/2/5/1 Part 1, NAA. Jovan Cavoski, "Neutralism in China's Shadow: Sino-Burmese Relations and the Cold War in Southeast Asia 1948–1962," unpublished paper presented at an international conference, "Mao's China, Non-Communist Asia, and the Global Setting," University of Hong Kong, 14–15 February 2012. Steinberg and Fan, *Modern China-Myanmar Relations*, 55. Later, in an interview with Malcolm MacDonald, Ne Win insisted that he was "extremely angry" when U Nu invited the Chinese to send troops into Burma to deal with the KMT forces. He "protested strongly at once," he told MacDonald, "and got U Nu's policy reversed." "Notes on Talks between General Ne Win and Mr. Malcolm MacDonald, April–May 1962," enclosed in Lewis M. Purnell to USDS, 5 July 1962, Airgram A-7, NSF—Countries File, box 16, Kennedy Papers, JFKL.

35. Snow to SS, 23 December 1960, Tel. 460, RG 84, Burma US Embassy, Classified General Records, 1959–1961, box 34, NAII. Intelligence Briefing Notes, 28 December 1960, WHO, Office of the Staff Secretary, 1951–1961, Subject Series; Alphabetical Subseries, box 14, folder Intelligence Brief Notes, vol. 1 (2) 28 December 1960, Eisenhower Papers, DDEL.

36. Snow to SS, 20 January 1961, Unnumbered Tel. (Joint Weeka no. 3 from SANA), 790B.00(W)/1-2061, RG 59, CDF 1960–1963, box 2105, NAII.

37. Snow to SS, 17 February 1961, Tel. unnumbered, Joint Weeka 7, 790B.00(W) 2–1761, RG 59, CDF 1960–1963, box 2105, NAII. M. D. F. Hill to EXAF, 22 February 1961, Despatch 106, series A1838, control symbol 3008/2/5/1 Part 1, NAA. Plimsoll to EXAF, 28 March 1961, Tel. UN 369, ibid. Snow to SS, 17 February 1961, Tel. unnumbered, Joint Weeka 7, 790B.00(W) 2–1761, RG 59, CDF 1960–1963, box 2105, NAII. "National Intelligence Estimate Number 50–61," 28 March 1961, p. 11, copy in NSF—National Intelligence Estimates, box 7, folder 50, Southeast Asia, Johnson Papers, LBJL.

38. Clipping, Dennis Bloodworth, "Burma Angry over Shot-down Bomber," London *Observer*, 19 February 1961, in series A1838, control symbol 3008/2/5/1 Part 1, NAA. Snow to SS, 17 February 1961, Joint Weeka 7, 790B.00(W) 2–1761, RG 59, CDF 1960–1963, box 2105, NAII. J. P. Stevenson to EXAF, 17 February 1961, Memo no. 316, series A1838, control symbol 3008/2/5/1 Part 1, NAA.

39. Memorandum, Rusk to John F. Kennedy, enclosed in Rusk to Kennedy, 20 February 1961, *FRUS* 1961–1963, 23:89–95.

40. *FRUS* 1961–1963, 23:87n4.

41. Snow to SS, 22 February 1961, Tel. NIACT 615, RG 84, Burma US Embassy, Classified General Records 1948–1961, box 34, NAII. The damage to American property was relatively minor. The damage to the American embassy on 16 and 21 February came to $1,195, which included replacing 515 window panes. See Snow to SS, 5 March 1961, Tel. 673, folder 320 Relations (Burma-US), box 34, RG 84, Classified General Records 1959–1961, NAII.

42. *FRUS* 1961–1963, 23:95n6.

43. "Burma's Chinese 'Irregulars,'" *New York Times*, 27 February 1961.

44. Snow to SS, 1 March 1961, Tel. NIACT 657, RG 84, Burma US Embassy, Classified General Records 1948–1961, box 34, NAII. U Nu to Kennedy, 2 March 1961, President's Office Files—Countries, folder Burma Security 1961–1963, box 112A, Kennedy Papers, JFKL. Snow to SS, 3 March 1961, Tel. 666, NSF—Countries File, box 16, ibid.

45. Kennedy to U Nu, 6 March 1961, enclosed in Rusk to US Embassy Rangoon, 6 March 1961, Tel. 663, NSF—Countries File, box 16, Kennedy Papers, JFKL.

46. Memorandum, Rusk to Kennedy, [6 March 1961], ibid.

47. Clipping, "Chinese Forces Have Left, Government Announces," *Bangkok World*, 7 March 1961, enclosed in M. R. Booker to EXAF, 7 March 1961, series A1838, control symbol 3008/2/5/1 Part I, NAA. Rusk to US Embassy Taipei, 4 March 1961, Tel. 434, President's Office Files—countries, box 112A, folder Burma Security 1961–1963, Kennedy Papers, JFKL. Australian Embassy Washington, DC to EXAF, 8 March 1961, Tel. 536, series A1838, control symbol 3008/2/5/1 Part 1, NAA. South East Asia Section, Research Department Memorandum, Australian Foreign Office, "The KMT Troops in Burma and Neighbouring Countries," 9 March 1961, ibid.

48. Plimsoll to EXAF, 28 March 1961, Tel. UN 369, series A1838, control symbol 3008/2/5/1 Part 1, NAA.

49. Snow to SS, 31 March 1961, Tel. 774, folder 320 Relations (Burma-US), RG 84, Burma US Embassy, Classified General Records 1948–1961, box 34, NAII.

50. Snow to SS, 31 March 1961, Tel. 774, folder 320 Relations (Burma-US), ibid. Loomes to EXAF, 7 April 1961, Memo 229, series A1838, control symbol 3008/2/5/1 Part 1, NAA.

51. "A Talk with General Ne Win," 27 April 1961, enclosed in K. C. O. Shann to Sir Arthur Tange, EXAF, n.d. [received 9 May 1961], series A1838, control symbol TS383/2/1 Part 1, NAA. In sending the unexpurgated record to Canberra, Shann (Australian high commissioner in London) warned against informing the Americans that two versions existed. The British Foreign Office "would of course be embarrassed if the Americans were ever to know that there are two versions of the record." An External Affairs official commented, "the Americans must not learn there are two versions of the record," and added that MacDonald tended to be critical of the Americans and have "optimistic interpretations of what Asian leaders whom he likes tell him." Minute by P. R. Hayden, 10 May 1961.

52. Richard T. Ewing to USDS, 21 April 1961, Despatch 487, 790B.00 (W)/4-2161, RG 59, CDF 1960–1963, box 2105, NAII. Loomes to EXAF, 7 April 1961, Memo 229, series A1838, control symbol 3008/2/5/1 Part 1, NAA. Loomes to EXAF, 7 April 1961, Memo 229, ibid.

53. Snow to US Embassy Bangkok, 2 March 1960, Tel. G-84, folder 350 Burma-Shan States, RG 84, Burma US Embassy, Classified General Records 1948–1961, box 36, NAII.

54. South East Asia Section, Research Department Memorandum, Australian Foreign Office, "The KMT Troops in Burma and Neighbouring Countries," 9 March 1961, series A1838, control symbol 3008/2/5/1 Part 1, NAA.

55. A. H. Loomes to EXAF, 7 April 1961, Memo 229, series A1838, control symbol 3008/2/5/1 Part 1, NAA.

56. Snow to SS, 28 April 1961, Tel. G-234, folder 320 Relations Burma CPR, RG 84, Burma US Embassy, Classified General Records 1959–1961, box. 34, NAII. Don D. Christiansen to USDS, 27 April 1961, Despatch 494, 790B.00(W)/4-2761, RG 59, CDF 1960–1963, box 2105, NAII.

57. U Nu to Kennedy, 29 April 1961, President's Office Files—Countries, box 112, folder Burma General 1961–1963, Kennedy Papers, JFKL. Though the letter is dated 29 April, Barrington handed it to Ambassador Snow only on 3 May 1961. Snow to SS, 3 May 1961, Tel. 838, NSF—Countries File, box 16, ibid.

58. Kennedy to "My Burmese Friends," n.d. (May 1961?), President's Office Files—Countries, box 112A, folder Burma General 1961–1963, ibid. Richard T. Ewing to USDS, 2 May 1961, Despatch 497, 790B.00/5-261, RG 59, CDF 1960–1963, box 2103, NAII. Plimsoll to EXAF, 15 May 1961, Tel. UN 620, series A1838, control symbol 3008/2/5/1 Part 1, NAA.

59. CIA, Office of Current Intelligence, "Chinese Nationalist Irregulars in Southeast Asia," 29 July 1961, NSF—Regional Security Folder, box 231, Kennedy Papers, JFKL. Memcon, Robert Morse and Marshall Hays Noble, 5 August 1961, enclosed in Noble to USDS, Despatch 8, 8 August 1961, RG 59, CDF 1960–1963, box 2013, NAII. Noble was the American consul in Mandalay. Everton to SS, 25 August 1961, Tel. 165, folder 350 Burma—Kachins, RG 84, Burma US Embassy, Classified General Records 1959–1961, box 35, NAII.

60. John M. Kane to USDS, 8 September 1961, Despatch 132, 790B.00(W)/9-861, RG 59, CDF 1960–1963, box 2105, NAII. Tristram Coffin, "Probing the CIA," *New Leader*, 15 May 1961, 4. (The story misnamed David M. Key as "Donald.") Kane to USDS, 20 October 1961, 790B.00(W)/10-2061, RG 59, CDF 1960–1963, box 2105, NAII.

61. Kane to USDS, 11 August 1961, Despatch 81, 790B.00(W)/8-1161, 90B.00(W)/8-1161, RG 59, CDF 1960–1963, box 2105, NAII.

62. Everton to SS, 7 July 1961, Airgram A-2, 890B.00-PC/7-761, RG 59, ibid., box 2845. Rusk to US Embassy Rangoon, 10 July 1961, Tel 03581, 890B.00-PC/7-1061, ibid., box 2842.

63. Everton to SS, 17 August 1961, Tel. 132, NSF—Countries File, box 16, Kennedy Papers, JFKL. Memorandum, Daniel V. Anderson to McConaughy, 29 September 1961, 790B.5-MSP/9-2961, RG 59, CDF 1960–1963, box 2106, NAII. Everton to SS, 29 September 1961, Tel. 287, 790B.56/9-2961, ibid.

64. Memorandum, Godfrey T. McHugh to Kennedy, 17 January 1962, President's Office Files—Countries, box 112A, folder Burma Security 1961–1963, Kennedy Papers, JFKL.

65. Memorandum, Everton to Bowles, 5 August 1961, 890B.2621/8-5-61, RG 59, CDF 1960–1963, box 2845, NAII. Everton to Andrew E. Rice, 7 September 1961, 890B.2612/9-761, ibid. Everton to SS (for McConaughy), 24 November 1961, Tel. 408, NSF—Countries File, box 16, Kennedy Papers, JFKL. "Background Paper: Rangoon-Mandalay Highway Project," 7 February 1962, 890B.2612/2-762, RG 59, CDF 1960–1963, box 2845, NAII.

66. Everton to SS, 25 August 1961, Tel. 164, folder 312 UNGA, RG 84, Burma US Embassy, Classified General Records 1959–1961, box 34, NAII. Schnee to SS, 5 November 1961, Airgram A-79, 790B.13/11-561, RG 59, box 2106, NAII.

67. U Nu to Kennedy, 13 November 1961, in Everton to SS, 14 November 1961, Tel. 380, NSF—Countries File, box 16, Kennedy Papers, JFKL. Kennedy to U Nu,

27 November 1961, President's Office Files—Countries, folder Burma Security 1961-1963, Kennedy Papers, JFKL. Lyman L. Lemnitzer to Robert McNamara, n.d. (January 1962), enclosed in McNamara to Kennedy, 27 January 1962, NSF—Regional Security Files, box 231A, Kennedy Papers, JFKL. McNamara did not endorse the Chiefs' views.

68. Bowles to SS ("For Secretary from McConaughy"), 22 September 1961, Tel. USUN 31, NSF—Countries File, box 16, Kennedy Papers, JFKL. Rusk to US Embassy London, 5 December 1961, Tel. 1084, ibid.

69. U Nu to Kennedy, 15 February 1962, ibid. Richard T. Ewing to USDS, 26 January 1962, Despatch 386, 790B.00/1-2662, RG 59, CDF 1960–1963, box 2103, NAII. Memorandum, Robert H. Johnson to Carl Kaysen, 11 January 1962, NSF—Regional Security Files, box 231A, Kennedy Papers, JFKL.

70. Everton to SS, 23 January 1962, NSF—Countries File, box 16, Kennedy Papers, JFKL. Memorandum, Kennedy to Rusk, 19 February 1962, President's Office Files—Countries, box 112, folder Burma General 1961–1963, ibid.

10. NE WIN'S WAY TO SOCIALISM

1. Memorandum, Roger Hilsman to Kennedy, n.d. [2 March 1962], NSF—Countries File, box 16, Kennedy Papers, JFKL. Steinberg, *Burma: A Socialist Nation*, 73–74. Richard T. Ewing to Dexter, 15 June 1962, 790B.00/6-1562, RG 59, CDF 1960–1963, box 2104, NAII. Charney, *Modern Burma*, 101.

2. Walworth Barbour to SS, 2 March 1962, Tel. 541, 790B.00/3-262, RG 59, CDF 1960–1963, box 2103, NAII. David Bruce to SS, 3 March 1962, Tel. 3236, 790B.00/3-262, ibid. Alexander Schnee to SS, 4 March 1962, Tel. 652, ibid.

3. Everton to SS, 30 March 1962, Tel. 749, 790B.00/3-3062, ibid., box 2106. Everton to SS, 22 May 1964, Tel. 856, NSF—Countries File, box 16, Kennedy Papers, JFKL.

4. The highway project's background is discussed in Everton to SS, 16 May 1962, Tel. 843, ibid. Memcon, U Soe Tin and Everton, 28 April 1962, enclosed in Everton to USDS, 17 May 1963, Despatch 526, 890B.2612/5-1762, RG 59, CDF 1960–1963, box 2845, NAII.

5. Memcon, U Tun Thin and Dexter, 16 August 1962, 790B.00/8-1662, RG 59, CDF 1960–1963, box 2104, NAII. Memcon, U Soe Tin and Everton, 6 August 1962, 890B.2612, 8–662, ibid., box 2845. Everton discounted the suggestion that Aung Gyi was acting on his own. Everton to SS, 22 August 1962, Tel. 134, NSF—Countries File, box 16, Kennedy Papers, JFKL.

6. Memcon, U Soe Tin and Everton, 6 August 1962, 890B.2612, 8–662, RG 59, CDF 1960–1963, box 2845, NAII.

7. Ibid. Memcon, Tun Thin and Dexter, 16 August 1962, 790B.00/8-1662, ibid., box 2104, NAII.

8. Task Force Southeast Asia, Department of State, "Status Report on Southeast Asia," 5 September 5, 1962, p. 13, NSF—Regional Security File, box 231A, Kennedy Papers, JFKL. "Everton to SS (for Harriman and Seymour Janow), 13 April 1962, Tel. 781, NSF—Countries File, box 16, ibid. Memcon, Tun Thin and Dexter, 16 August 1962, 790B.00/8-1662, RG 59, CDF 1960–1963, box 2104, NAII.

9. "Annex A," n.d., series 11/10, accession no. 64, MNA. Memcon, U Thi Han, Dexter et al., 29 September 1962, 890B.2612/9-2962, RG 59, CDF 1960–1963, box 2845, NAII.

10. Memcon, U Thi Han, John B. Dexter et al, 29 September 1962, 890B.2612/9-2962, RG 59, CDF 1960–1963, box 2845, NAII. In July Ne Win had told Averell Harriman that he thought the Ford Foundation was "not as bad as the Asia Foundation." Roger Tubby (from Averell Harriman) to SS, 18 July 1962, Tel. 72, President's Office Files—Countries, box 112A, folder Burma Security 1961–1963, Kennedy Papers, JFKL.

11. Weimer, *Seeing Drugs*, 142.

12. US Embassy Rangoon to SS, 13 April 1962, Tel. 781, 811.00/90B/4-1362, RG 59, CDF 1960–1963, box 2103, NAII. Everton to SS, 23 April 1962, Tel. 798, NSF—Countries File, box 16, Kennedy Papers, JFKL. Robert Trumbull, "Burma Banning Fulbright Men, Ford and Asia Fund Advisers," *New York Times*, 20 April 1962. Everton to USDS, 16 May 1962, Airgram A-25, RG 59, CDF 1960–1963, box 2845, NAII.

13. Everton to SS, 4 May 1962, Tel. 825, 790B.00/5-462, RG 59, CDF 1960–1963, box 2104, NAII. Steinberg and Fan, *Modern China-Myanmar Relations*, 79–80.

14. US Embassy Rangoon to SS, 10 May 1962, Tel. 833, NSF—Countries File, box 16, Kennedy Papers, JFKL. Arthur S. Abbott to USDS, 27 May 1962, Despatch 532, 890B.05111/5-2362, RG 59, CDF 1960–1963, box 2845, NAII. Ewing to USDS, 4 June 1962, Despatch 565, 890B.181/6-462, ibid., box 2844.

15. Everton to SS, 23 April 1962, Tel. 798, NSF—Countries File, box 16, Kennedy Papers, JFKL. Memcon, Ba Than and James E. Bradshaw, n.d., enclosed in Don. T. Christensen to USDS, 20 July 1962, Airgram A-1, 790B.00/7-2062, RG 59, CDF 1960–1963, box 2104, NAII.

16. "Analysis of the Current Situation and Implications for the Conduct of US Policy Towards Burma," enclosed in Everton to UDSD, 1 June 1962, Despatch 556, RG 59, CDF 1960–1963, box 2104, NAII. Significantly, this analysis was sent to the White House. Purnell to Dexter, 7 June 1962, RG 59, CDF 1960–1963, box 2104, NAII.

17. Rusk to US Embassy Rangoon, 29 June 1962, Tel. 712, NSF—Countries File, box 16, Kennedy Papers, JFKL. "Notes on Talks between General Ne Win and Mr. Malcolm MacDonald, April–May 1962," enclosed in Purnell to USDS, 5 July 1962, Airgram A-7, ibid.

18. Steinberg, *Burma: A Socialist Nation*, 75; Wendy Law-Yone, *Golden Parasol*, 140–41, 173–74.

19. Charney, *Modern Burma*, 115. Everton to SS, 13 July 1962, Tel. 38, 790B.00/7-1362, RG 59, CDF 1960–1963, box 2104, NAII. Steinberg, *Burma: A Socialist Nation*, 76.

20. Roger Tubby (from Averell Harriman) to SS, 18 July 1962, Tel. 72, President's Office Files—Countries, box 112A, folder Burma Security 1961–1963, Kennedy Papers, JFKL. At some point Ne Win seems to have understood the gravity of his actions against the students and tried to blame subordinates. Charney, *Modern Burma*, 116.

21. Tubby (from Harriman) to SS, 18 July 1962, Tel. 72, President's Office Files—Countries, box 112A, folder Burma Security 1961–1963, Kennedy Papers, JFKL. "Status Report of the Task Force Southeast Asia," enclosed in Memorandum, William H. Brubeck to McGeorge Bundy, 25 July 1962, NSF—Regional Security File, box 231A, ibid.

22. Memcon, Tun Thin and Dexter, 16 August 1962, 790B.00/8-1662, RG 59, CDF 1960–1963, box 2104, NAII. Everton to USDS, 14 August 1962, Airgram A-101, NSF—Countries File, box 16, Kennedy Papers, JFKL.

23. Rusk to US Embassy Rangoon, 18 August 1962, Tel. 83, NSF—Countries File, box 16, Kennedy Papers, JFKL.

24. Everton to Dexter, 5 September 1962, 790B.00/9-562, RG 59, CDF 1960–1963, box 2104, NAII. Rusk to US Embassy Rangoon, 18 October 1962, Tel. 194, ibid., box 2845.

25. Ibid.

26. Rusk (Joint State/AID message) to US Embassy Rangoon, 8 December 1962, ibid. Rusk to US Embassy Rangoon (Joint State/AID message), 28 December 1962, Tel. 237, President's Office Files—Countries, box 112A, folder Burma Security 1961–1963, Kennedy Papers, JFKL.

27. Memcon, U Soe Tin and Everton, 21 March 1963, enclosed in Everton to USDS, 22 March 1963, Airgram A-513, POL Burma—US, RG 59, CFPF 1963, box 3844, NAII.

28. Alexander Schnee to U Soe Tin, 22 January 1964, RG 84, Burma US Embassy Rangoon, Unclassified Central Subject Files 1964, folder AID, box 1, NAII.

29. Memorandum, George W. Ball to Kennedy, 4 May 1963, NSF—Countries File, box 16, Kennedy Papers, JFKL. Background Paper: The Burma Problem," n.d., enclosed ibid.

30. Memorandum, Edward Lansdale to Adam Yarmolinsky, 7 May 1963, Subject File—Burma, folder U.S. Department of Defense, Office of the Secretary of Defense, box 45, Lansdale Papers, HIA.

31. Everton to Kennedy, 9 May 1963, *FRUS* 1961–1963, 23:120–22.

32. Michael V. Forrestal to Kennedy, 18 May 1963, NSF—Countries File, box 16, Kennedy Papers, JFKL. [Allen Whiting] to Harriman, 16 May 1963, enclosed ibid.

33. Schnee to SS, 10 August 1963, Tel. 89, NSF—Countries File, box 16, Kennedy Papers, JFKL. Steinberg, *Burma: A Socialist Nation*, 79–82.

34. Schnee to SS, 13 August 1963, Tel. 96, NSF—Countries File, box 16, Kennedy Papers, JFKL. US Naval Attaché Rangoon to Defense Intelligence Agency, 17 August 1963, Tel. P 1707312, ibid.

35. Schnee to SS, 29 August 1963, Tel. 134, ibid. "Current Situation in Burma," n.d., enclosed in Benjamin H. Reed to McGeorge Bundy, 5 September 1963, President's Office Files—Countries, folder Burma Security 1961–1963, box 112A, Kennedy Papers, JFKL. Reed to McGeorge Bundy, 5 September 1963, ibid. "Assurances to General Ne Win," enclosed in Memorandum, Reed to McGeorge Bundy, 10 September 1963, *FRUS* 1961–1963, 23:131–32.

36. Byroade to SS, 7 October 1963, Tel. 245, NSF—Countries File, box 16, Kennedy Papers, JFKL.

37. Ibid.

38. Byroade to SS, 5 December 1963, Tel. 377, NSF—Country File, folder Burma vol. 1, cables 7/64–12/68, box 235, Johnson Papers, LBJL. Steinberger and Fan, *Modern China-Myanmar Relations*, 73–79.

39. Byroade to Ne Win, 7 January 1964, RG 84, Burma US Embassy Rangoon, Unclassified General Files, 1964, box 1, folder POL-Burma/US, NAII.

40. James V. Martin Jr. to USDS, 17 January 1964, Airgram A-282, POL 13-6 Burma, RG 59, CFPF 1964–1966, box 1957, NAII. Martin to USDS, 10 January 1964, Airgram A-295, POL 1-Burma, ibid., box 1955.

41. Martin to USDS, 17 January 1964, Airgram A-282, POL 13-6 Burma, ibid., box 1957.

42. Memcon, Baird Helfrich and L. O. Sanderhoff, 26–27 April 1963, RG 59, Office of the Country Director, Bureau of Far Eastern Affairs, Office of the Country Director for Burma and Cambodia, Records Relations to Burma, 1964–1966. Lots 67D80 and 68D102, box 3, folder Political Affairs & Relations, US—Baird Helfrich, NAII.

43. US Embassy Rangoon to SS, 14 January 1964, Tel. 466, POL 23-9 Burma, RG 59, CFPF 1964–1966, box 1958, NAII.

44. Unsigned confidential memorandum to Ritchie and John M. Kane, 5 October 1964, RG 59, Office of the Country Director, Bureau of Far Eastern Affairs, Office of the Country Director for Burma and Cambodia, Records Relations to Burma, 1964–1966. Lots 67D80 and 68D102, box 3, folder Political Affairs & Relations, US—Baird Helfrich, NAII.

45. Memorandum, Lee Reddy to Byroade and Kane, 30 July 1965; Memcon, Reddy and Helfrich, n.d.; both in RG 59, Office of the Country Director, Bureau of Far Eastern Affairs, Office of the Country Director for Burma and Cambodia, Records Relations to Burma, 1964–1966, ibid., box 2, folder POLITICAL AFF & REL, 6–1 Helfrich. E-mail correspondence from Paula Helfrich, 19 July 2013. I am grateful to Ms. Helfrich for this information about her father.

46. Martin to USDS, 7 February 1964, Airgram A-510, POL 2 Burma, RG 59, CFPF 1964–1966, box 1955, NAII. Byroade to SS, 21 January 1964, Tel. 486, POL Burma-US, ibid., box 1959. Byroade to SS, 1 February 1964, Tel. 508, POL Burma-US, ibid., box 1959.

Memcon, U Maung Maung Soe and Dexter, 16 January 1964, RG59, Office of the Country Director, Bureau of Far Eastern Affairs, Office of he Country Director for Burma, 1964–11966. Lots 67D80–68D102, box 2, folder POL-POLITICAL AFF & REL, 15-1 Bo Setkya, NAII.

47. Rusk to US Embassy Rangoon, 17 January 1964, Tel. 230, POL Burma-US, RG 59, CFPF 1964–1966, box 1959, NAII. The one meeting with Setkya lasted for an hour and a half—quite long, it would appear, if the only purpose was to inform Setkya about American policy. See "Summary of Bo Setkya's Contact with America Government officials," enclosed in James V. Martin Jr. to USDS, 24 January 1964, Airgram A-325, POL 12 Burma, RG 59, CFPF 1964–1966, box 1957, NAII. Setkya also spoke with Lewis Purnell, a State Department official then on leave at Harvard University who had known Setkya when he had served previously in Burma. The two men talked for several hours, and Purnell reported the conversation to the State Department.

48. Speech to the Asia Society, Louis J. Walinsky, "The Rise and Fall of U Nu," enclosed in Lionel Landry to John Dexter, 23 January 1964, RG59, Office of the Country Director, Bureau of Far Eastern Affairs, Office of the Country Director for Burma, 1964–11966. Lots 67D10–68D102, box 1, folder POL-POLITICAL AFF & REL, 15–1 U Nu, NAII. See also Walinsky's tribute to U Nu, "The Rise and Fall of U Nu."

49. US Embassy Rangoon to USDS, 13 March 1964, Airgram A-402, folder POL 30 Burma, RG 59, CFPF 1964–1966, box 1958, NAII.

50. Martin to USDS, 31 January 1964, Airgram A-332, folder POL 1-4 Burma-US, ibid.

51. Burma Foreign Office to US Embassy Rangoon, 20 March 1964, RG 84, Burma US Embassy Rangoon, Unclassified Central Subject Files 1964, box 1, folder AID, NAII. "A Time of Trial for Southeast Asia," *Life* (international edition), 27 January 1964, 29–30. US Embassy Rangoon to USDS,2 April 1964, Airgram A-425, RG 59, CFPF 1964–1966, box 1955, NAII.

52. Martin to USDS, 10 April 1964, Airgram A-433, RG 59, CFPF 1964–1966, box 1955, NAII.

53. Byroade to SS, 28 April 1964, Tel. 668, RG 59, ibid., folder POL 2-1 Burma.

54. Byroade to SS, 28 April 1964, Tel. 669, NSF—Country File, folder Burma vol. 1, Cables 7/64–12/68, Johnson Papers, LBJL. Byroade to SS, 28 April 1964, Tel. 668, RG 59, CFPF 1964–1966, box 1955, folder POL 2 Burma, NAII. Lyndon Johnson Telephone Conversation with McGeorge Bundy, May 13, 1964, Tape WH6405.06, Conversation 3446, Lyndon B. Johnson Presidential Recordings, Miller Center, University of Virginia. I am grateful to Rob Rakove for bringing this recording to my attention.

55. James V. Martin Jr. to USDS, 7 May 1964, Airgram 4–465, RG 59, CFPF 1964–1966, box 1955, folder POL 1 Burma, NAII. Martin to USDS, 7 May 1964, Airgram 459, ibid., folder POL 2 Burma. Martin to USDS, 8 May 1964, Airgram 468, RG 59, ibid., folder POL 2 Burma.

56. Byroade to SS, 16 May 1964, Tel. 702, ibid., box 1246, folder IT—Inland Transport Burma. The formal rejection is found in Foreign Office, Government of Burma, to US Embassy Rangoon, 21 May 1964, RG 84, Burma US Embassy Rangoon, Unclassified Central Subject Files 1964, box 1, folder AID, NAII.

57. Schnee to USDS, 5 June 1964, Airgram A-515, and Byroade to SS, 5 June 1964, Tel. 743, in RG 59, CFPF 1964–1966, box 1246, folder IT—Inland Transport Burma, NAII. Burma Foreign Office to US Embassy Rangoon, 13 June 1964, RG 84, Burma US Embassy Rangoon, Unclassified Central Subject Files 1964, box 1, folder AID, NAII.

58. Byroade to SS, 30 June 1964, Tel. 797, RG 59, CFPF 1964–1966, box 1957, folder POL 15–1 Burma, NAII. Memorandum, James C. Thomson, Jr. to William F. Bundy, 9 July 1964, Thomson Papers, box 21, folder Southeast Asia 1961–1965, Burma.

General 1961–1966, JFKL. Byroade to SS, 4 August 1964, Tel. 87, RG 59, CFPF 1964–1966, box 1957, folder POL 15-1 Burma, NAII.

59. Memcon, Kyaw Than and Ralph F.W. Eye, 24 June 1964, enclosed in Martin to USDS, 4 July 1964, RG 59, CFPF 1964–1966, box 1958, folder POL 23 Burma, NAII.

60. Byroade to SS (for William F. Bundy), 24 July 1964, Tel. 61, NSF—Country File, folder Burma vol. 1, Cables 7/64–12/68, Johnson Papers, LBJL. Rusk to US Embassy Rangoon (Bundy for Byroade), 25 July 1964, Tel. 33, RG 59, CFPF 1964–1966, box 1957, folder POL 15 Burma, NAII.

61. Rusk to US Embassies Bangkok and Taipei, 14 August 1964, Tels. 232 (Bangkok) and 137 (Taipei), Thomson Papers, box 21, folder Southeast Asia 1961–1965, Burma. General 1961–1966, JFKL.

62. Byroade to SS, 30 July 1964, Tel. 78, RG 59, CFPF 1964–1966, box 1959, folder POL 1, NAII. Byroade to SS. 31 July 1964, Tel. 81, ibid. Rusk to US Embassy Rangoon, 6 August 1964, Tel. 52, ibid.

63. "Country Paper for Chiefs of Mission Conference, Baguio—1965," 21 January 1965, RG 59, Office of the Country Director, Bureau of Far Eastern Affairs, Office of the Country Director for Burma and Cambodia, Records Relations to Burma, 1964–1966, Lots 67D80 and 68D102, box 1, folder EM Emergency Planning, 7 Emergency Relocation Program, NAII.

64. Byroade to USDS, 20 November 1965, Airgram A-144, RG 59, CFPF 1964–1966, box 1956, folder POL 2-3 Burma, NAII. Kingdon W. Swayne to USDS, 19 February 1966, Airgram A-222, ibid., folder POL 2-1 Burma. Swayne to USDS, 5 March 1966, Airgram A-232, ibid.

65. Swayne to USDS, 3 April 1965, Airgram 333, ibid., box 1957, folder POL 17-4 Burma. Draft CIA analysis, "Contingencies and Background Paper 1 August 1965–30 July 1966," 12 July 1965, enclosed in William E. Colby to Chester L. Cooper, 5 August 1965, Thomson Papers, box 21, folder Southeast Asia 1961–1965, Burma. General 1961–1966, JFKL.

66. Quoted in Byroade to SS, 19 April 1965, Tel. 562, NSC-CO File, box 235, Johnson Papers, LBJL. NSC staffer James C. Thomson, Jr. passed this "bit of gossip" along to National Security Adviser McGeorge Bundy, noting that it "should boost your spirits." Thomson to McGeorge Bundy, 19 April 1968, NSC-CO File, box 235 [?], folder Burma Memos & Misc., vol. 1, 7/64–12/68, Johnson Papers, LBJL. Foreign Minister Thi Han told Ambassador Byroade that Zhou's visits "always seemed to be difficult and annoying." Byroade to SS, 27 April 1965, Tel. 576, RG 59, CFPF 1964–1966, box 1957, folder POL 15-1 Burma, NAII.

67. Seymour Topping, "New Chiang Raids in China Reported," *New York Times*, 18 May 1965.

68. Byroade to SS, 1 July 1965, Tel. 1, Thomson Papers, box 21, folder Southeast Asia 1961–1965, Burma. General 1961–1966, JFKL. Rusk to US Embassies Rangoon, 13 July 1965, Tel. 19, Thomson Papers, box 21, folder Southeast Asia 1961–1965, Burma. General 1961–1966, JFKL.

69. Byroade to SS, 16 July 1965, Tel. 27, Thomson Papers, box 21, folder Southeast Asia 1961–1965, Burma. General 1961–1966, JFKL.

70. CIA, Central Intelligence Cable, 5 May 1965, ibid. Byroade to SS, 2 June 1965, Tel. 651, RG 59, CFPF 1964–1966, box 1958, folder POL 29 Burma, NAII.

71. Memcon, Thida Sturdevant and Schnee, 1 May 1965, ibid., box 1955.

72. W. Walton Butterworth to SS, 25 June 1965, Tel. 1591 (Ottawa), ibid., box 1958, folder POL 17 Burma-Can, NAII. Butterworth to SS, 2 July 1965, Tel. 1, W. Walton Butterworth to SS, 25 June 1965, Tel. 1591 (Ottawa), ibid. Swayne to USDS, 29 October 1965, Airgram A-121, ibid., box 1955, folder POL 2 Burma. "James Barrington, 80, Burmese Envoy to U.S.," *New York Times*, 4 April 1992.

73. Donald L. Ranard to Kane, 30 November 1965, RG59, Office of the Country Director, Bureau of Far Eastern Affairs, Office of the Country Director for Burma, 1964–1966, Lots 67D80-68D102, box 2, folder ORG—Organization & Administration, 12 Incoming Letters, NAII.

11. THE RELATIONSHIP STABILIZES

1. L. J. D. Wakely to D. F. Murray, 12 April 1966, FO 371/185948, BNA. Office Memorandum, Jim Grad to Swayne, 22 April 1966, RG 84, Unclassified Central Subject Files, box 5, folder POL 7 1966, NAII.

2. Byroade to SS (for William Bundy), 28 April 1966, Tel. 550, NSF—Country File, folder Burma, vol. 1, 7-64-68," box 235, Johnson Papers, LBJL. Byroade to USDS, 7 May 1966, Airgram A-290, RG 59, CFPF 1964–1966, box 1957, NAII.

3. Minutes of the Burma Council, Asia Society, 10 May 1966, Walinsky Papers, box 6, folder 6–15, Cornell University Library.

4. Harrison E. Salisbury, "Burma Chief Explains Neutrality," *New York Times*, 20 June 1966. Donald L. Ranard to USDS, 25 June 1966, Airgram A-338, RG 59, CFPF 1964–1966, box 1956, NAII. Steinberg and Fan, *Modern China-Myanmar Relations*, 91–92.

5. Byroade to SS, 16 July 1966, Tel. 75, RG 59, CFPF 1964–1966, box 1956, NAII.

6. Clipping, Selig S. Harrison, "Those Mystery Men in Chevy Chase Turn Out to Be Chasing a Burma Case," *Washington Post*, 2 September 1966. Copy in Walinsky Papers, box 6, folder 6-15, Cornell University Library.

7. Kaiser to SS, 19 August 1966, London Tel. 1388, RG 59, CFPF 1964–1966, box 1956, NAII. Rusk to US Embassy London, 19 August 1966, Tel. 31617, ibid.

8. Memorandum for the President, 23 August 1966, box 235, NSF—Country File, folder "Burma-Ne Win Visit 9/8–10/66," Johnson Papers, LBJL. The *Washington Post* identified the hotel as the Great Northern Hotel. Harrison, "Those Mystery Men."

9. Memcon, William P. Bundy, Walinsky, Schnee, Richard T. Ewing, 25 August 1966, RG 59, CFPF 1964–1966, box 1958, NAII.

10. Harrison, "Those Mystery Men."

11. "For the President's Evening Reading," n.d., box 235, NSF—Country File, folder "Burma-Ne Win Visit 9/8–10/66," Johnson Papers, LBJL.

12. Clipping, Marquis Childs, "Ne Win's Burma: Neutral Despotism," *Washington Post*, 7 September 1966, Walinsky Papers, Cornell University Library.

13. "For President's Diary—General Ne Win's visit with President Johnson," 9 September 1966, President's Appointment File, Johnson Papers, LBJL. Clipping, Dorothy McCardle, "LBJ Tells Gen. Ne Win to Mind the Melon Patch," *Washington Post*, 9 September 1966, Walinsky Papers, box 6, folder 6-15, Cornell University Library.

14. "News Conference at the White House with Bill Moyers and Walt Rostow," 9 September 1966, p. 5, NSF—Country File, folder "Burma-Ne Win Visit 9/8–10/66," box 235, Johnson Papers, LBJL. The United States Information Agency made a film about the visit, available at http://www.youtube.com/watch?v=LWY4YkBo3qo. Thanks to Nay Yan Oo for calling the film to my attention.

15. Ranard to USDS, 17 September 1966, Airgram A-54, RG 59, CFPF 1964–1966, box 1956, NAII. Rostow to Johnson, 10 September 1966, NSF—Country File, folder "Burma-Ne Win Visit 9/8–10/66, box 235, Johnson Papers, LBJL. CINCPAC to SS (Byroade to Johnson and Rusk), 18 September 1966, Tel. 015968, RG 59, CFPF 1964–1966, box 1956, NAII.

16. Byroade to USDS, 7 January 1967, Airgram A-130, RG 59, CFPF 1967–1969, box 1917, NAII. Byroade to USDS, 14 October 1967, Airgram A-63, ibid. Byroade to SS, 27 October 1966, Tel. 602, RG 59, CFPF 1964–1966, box 1958, NAII.

17. Steinberg and Fan, *Modern China-Myanmar Relations*, 106–9. Byroade to USDS, 4 January 1967, Airgram A-122, RG 59, CFPF 1967–1969, box 1920, NAII.

18. Byroade to USDS, 12 January 1967, Airgram A-140, RG 59, CFPF 1967–1969, box 1920, NAII.

19. Byroade to USDS, 12 January 1967, Airgram A-140, RG 59, CFPF 1967–1969, box 1920, NAII.

20. US Embassy Bangkok to SS, 13 February 1967, Tel. 10345, ibid., box 1919. Byroade to SS (for Bundy), 7 February 1967, Tel. 1028, NSF—Country File, Burma Cables, vol. 1, 7/64–12–68, Johnson Papers, LBJL.

21. Byroade to USDS, 1 July 1967, Airgram A-267, RG 59, CFPF 1967–1969, box 1917, NAII. Byroade to SS, 27 June 1967, Tel. 1585, ibid., box 1919. Edward E. Rice to SS, 30 June 1967, Tel. 9011, ibid. Stories filed by Stanley Karnow from Rangoon, 27 June, 29 June, and 4 July 1967, folder "China's relations with Burma," box 36, Stanley Karnow Papers, JFKL. Byroade to SS, 28 June 1967, Tel. 1587, RG 59, CFPF 1967–1969, box 1919, NAII. For a fuller discussion of the Chinese reaction to the "button" affair, see Taylor, *China and Southeast Asia*, 210–24, and Steinberg and Fan, *Modern China-Myanmar Relations*, 93–118.

22. Director of Intelligence and Research, "Intelligence Note," #545, 7 July 1967, RG 59, CFPF 1967–1969, box 1920, NAII. Rusk to US Embassy New Delhi, 5 July 1967, Tel. 1499, ibid. Byroade to SS, 10 July 1967, Tel. 103, ibid., box 1919.

23. Byroade to USDS, 16 September 1967, Airgram A-46, ibid., box 1917. CIA, Directorate of Intelligence, "Intelligence Report: Ten Years of Chinese Communist Foreign Policy, South and Southeast Asia," 4 April 1968, CREST documents, NAII.

24. "Burma," n.d. [1968], Administrative Histories, Department of State, vol. 1, chapter 7-9, folder "Chapter 7 (East Asia) Sections K.O.," box 3, Johnson Papers, LBJL. Hummel to SS, 25 January 1969, Airgram A-18, RG 59, CFPF 1967–1969, box 1918, NAII.

25. Department of State, "Burma," Administrative Histories, vol. 1, chapter 7-9, folder "Chapter 7 (East Asia), Sections K.O.," box 3, Johnson Papers, LBJL.

26. Marshall Wright to Rostow, 13 July 1968, NSF—Country File, Burma Cables, vol. 1, 7/64–12/68 folder, Johnson Papers, LBJL. Johnstone (American Consul Frankfurt) (for Byroade) to SS, 14 June 1968, Tel. 4209, RG 59, CFPF 1967–1969, box 1918, NAII.

27. Ranard to USDS, 10 August 1968, Airgram A-281, RG 59, CFPF 1967–1969, box 1917, NAII. Hummel to USDS, 23 November 1968, Airgram A-352, NSF—Country File, Burma vol. 1 Cables 7/64–12/68 folder, Johnson Papers, LBJL. See also Trager, "Burma: 1968," 113.

28. Intelligence Note 821, George C. Denney Jr. to Rusk, 18 October 1968, RG 59, CFPF 1967–1969, box 1917, NAII. Trager, "Burma: 1968," 108–9.

29. Hummel to William Bundy, 29 January 1969, RG 59, CFPF 1967–1969, box 1918, NAII.

30. Hummel to SS, 23 April 1969, Tel. 1308, ibid.

31. Hummel to SS, 24 April 1969, Tel. 2267, ibid., box 1919.

32. Hummel to SS, 4 July 1969, Tel. 2196, ibid., box 1920.

33. Charney, *Modern Burma*, 129. Norman B. Hannah to SS, 7 August 1969, Tel. 10798, RG 59, CFPF 1967–1969, box 1920, NAII. Hummel to USDS, 10 August 1969, Airgram A-228, ibid., box 1918.

34. Hummel to SS, 3 September 1969, Tel. 3004, ibid. The text of U Nu's prepared statement at the news conference is attached to Hummel to USDS, 6 September 1969, Airgram A-232, ibid. Hummel to SS, 9 September 1969, Tel. 3081, ibid.

35. Clipping, Andrew B. Malcolm, "U Nu, Here, Seeks Backing in Revolt," *New York Times*, 10 September 1969, folder 6-18, box 6, Walinsky Papers, Cornell University Library. USDS to US Embassy Rangoon, 10 September 1969, Tel. 153302, RG 59, CFPF 1967–1969,

box 1920, NAII. Clipping, "Burma Revolt Is Imminent, U Nu Says," *Washington Post*, 17 September 1969, folder 6-18, box 6, Walinsky Papers, Cornell University Library.

36. Clipping, Warren Unna, "Pacifist Whistling Up a Revolution," *Washington Post*, 21 September 1969, folder 6-18, box 6, Walinsky Papers, Cornell University Library.

37. Hummel to SS, 20 November 1969, Tel. 2823, RG 59, CFPF 1967–1969, box 1918, NAII.

38. Hugh D.S. Greenway, "Which Is the Burma Road: Ne Win or U Nu?" *New York Times Magazine*, 3 May 1970, 42.

39. William Rogers to US Embassy Rangoon, 7 January 1970, Tel. 2178, RG 59, SNF 1970–1973, box 2143, folder POL 33–5, NAII.

40. US Embassy Rangoon to SS, 5 March 1970, Tel. 631, ibid., box 2144, folder POL 23-9 Burma. The description of Farmer comes from Wendy Law-Yone, *Golden Parasol*, 208. Hummel to SS, 13 March 1970, Tel. 743, 13 March 2012, RG 59, SNF 1970–1973, box 2144, folder POL 33-5 Burma, NAII.

41. Wendy Law-Yone, *Golden Parasol*, 213.

42. Rogers to US Embassy Bangkok, 23 April 1970, Tel. 60765, RG 59, SNF 1970–1973, box 2143, folder POL 33-5, NAII. Wendy Law-Yone, *Golden Parasol*, 183–84.

43. U.S. Department of State, Bureau of Intelligence and Research, "Burma: U Nu's Campaign Against Ne Win: One Year Later," Intelligence Note, REAN-11, RG 59, SNF 1970–1973, box 2143, folder POL 33-5 Burma, NAII.

44. Hummel to USDS, 27 June 1970, Airgram A-140, ibid., box 3139, folder POL 2 Burma, NAII.

45. Hummel to SS, 27 April 1970, Tel. 1256, ibid., box 2143, folder POL 33-5 Burma.

46. Memorandum, Dexter to Paul Cleveland, 24 June 1970, ibid., box 2139, folder Political Affairs—Burma. Hummel to USDS, 20 March 1970, Airgram A-68, ibid., box 2140, folder POL 2-1 Burma, NAII. President Richard Nixon sent a personal note to Thaung Dan, Burma's minister of information, thanking him for the country's hospitality toward the astronauts. Nixon to Thaung Dan, 14 May 1970, WHCF, Subject Files, Country Files, box 13, folder CO24 Burma [1969–1970], NPM.

47. Fleck to USDS, 18 July 1970, Airgram A-157, RG 59, SNF 1970–1973, box 2140, folder POL 2-1 Burma, NAII.

48. USDS to U.S. Embassy Rangoon, 10 September 1970, Tel. 147732, ibid., box 2143, folder POL 30 Burma. Hummel to SS, 4 November 1970, Tel. 3139, ibid.

49. Memorandum, Theodore L. Eliot Jr. to Henry Kissinger, 11 December 1970, ibid., folder POL 23-9 Burma, NAII. Wendy Law-Yone, *Golden Parasol*, 204.

50. USDS to U.S. Embassy Rangoon, 10 September 1970, Tel. 147732, ibid., box 2143, folder POL 30 Burma, NAII.

51. For the possibility of legal action against Walinsky, see memorandum, Stanley N. Futterman to Dexter, 17 September 1970, ibid., box 2144, folder POL 33-5 Burma, NAII.

52. Byroade to SS, 22 September 1970, Tel. 8787, RG 59, SNF 1970–1973, box 1692, folder DEF Bul 1/1/70, NAII. The figure of thirty aircraft comes from Hummel to SS, 13 October 1970, Tel. 2989, ibid.

53. Hummel to SS, 27 March 1971, ibid., box 1852, folder DEF US-BURMA 1/1/70, NAII.

54. Hummel to SS, 26 March 1969, Tel. 969, ibid., box 1918, folder POL 12-Burma. On Burma-China reconciliation, see Steinberg and Fan, *Modern China-Myanmar Relations*, 119–30.

55. "Policy Analysis Resource Allocation Paper—Burma FY 1972," enclosed in US Embassy Rangoon to USDS, December 1971, Airgram A-165, RG 59, SNF 1970–1973, box 2144, folder POL Burma-US, NAII.

56. Quoted in Arthur L. Hummel to USDS, 18 March 1971, Airgram A-039, RG 59, SNF 1970-1973, box 2139, folder POL 2 Burma, NAII.

12. THE NARCOTICS ERA

1. Hummel to USDS, 27 February 1971, Airgram A-026, RG 59, SNF 1970–1973, box 2141, folder POL 15 Burma, NAII.

2. Hummel to SS, 9 March 1971, quoted in Rogers to US Embassies Kuala Lumpur and Singapore, 11 March 1971, ibid., box 2143, folder POL 30 Burma. Rogers to US Embassies Kuala Lumpur and Singapore, 11 March 1971, Tel. 40882, ibid. Hummel to SS, 12 March 1971, Tel. 668, RG 59, SNF 1970–1973, ibid. For an account of U Nu's activities at this time, including fundraising efforts, see Wendy Law-Yone, *Golden Parasol*, 183–99.

3. Hummel to SS, 29 May 1971, Tel. 1549, RG 59, SNF 1970–1973, box 2143, folder POL 30 Burma, NAII. Wendy Law-Yone, *Golden Parasol*, 213–15. Clipping, Sterling Seagrave, "U Nu Underground," *Far Eastern Economic Review*, 12 December 1970, in WHCF, Subject Files, CO Files, box 13, folder CO 24 Burma 1/1/71–, NPM.

4. Director of Intelligence, CIA, "Intelligence Memorandum: International Narcotics Series No. 5, Opium Poppy Cultivation in Northern Thailand," October 1971, p. 2, CREST documents, NAII.

5. McCoy, *Politics of Heroin*, 389–90. "Summary, Narcotics Meeting, State Dining Room, June 3, 1971," NSC Files, Subject Files, box 358, folder Narcotics vol. 4 [2 of 2], NPM.

6. Hummel to SS, 4 June 1971, Tel. 1601, RG 59, SNF 1970–1973, box 3055, folder SOC 11-5 Burma 1971, NAII. The Single Convention is available online at the International Narcotics Control Board website, http://www.incb.org/incb/en/narcotic-drugs/1961_Convention.html.

7. CIA, Directorate of Intelligence, "Thailand: Military Actions Against Narcotics Traffic," CREST documents, NAII.

8. Hummel to SS, 20 July 1971, Tel. 2145, RG 59, SNF 1970–1973, box 3055, folder SOC 11-5 Burma 1971, NAII. Memorandum, Kissinger to Nixon, 23 September 1971, NSC Files, Subject Files, box 358, folder Narcotics vol. 4 [1 of 1], NPM. Minutes of the Meeting of the Cabinet Committee on International Narcotics Control, 28 September 1971, & October 1971, enclosed in Memorandum, Egil Krogh Jr. to Cabinet Committee on International Narcotics Control, n.d., NSC Files, Subject Files, box 358, folder Narcotics vol. 4 [1 of 1], NPM.

9. Memcon, Ne Win, Colonel Ko Ko, U Saw Hlaing, and Edwin W. Martin, 1 October 1971, enclosed in Martin to USDS, 9 October 1971, Airgram A-155, RG 59, SNF 1970–1973, box 3055, folder SOC 11-5 Burma 1971, NAII.

10. Memcon, Nelson Gross, Armin H. Meyer, Dexter, Eugene Martin, 21 September 1971, ibid.

11. Frank Cash (DCM US Embassy Bonn) to U. Alexis Johnson, 12 November 1971, Tel. 811, ibid. Cash to U. Alexis Johnson, 16 November 1971, Tel. 820, ibid. Nixon to Ne Win, 23 November 1971, NSC Files, Presidential Correspondence 1967–1974, box 749, folder Burma Gen'l Ne Win Correspondence, Nixon Presidential Materials Staff, NPM.

12. Ne Win to Nixon, 21 December 1971, NSC Files, Presidential Correspondence 1967–1974, box 749, folder Burma Gen'l Ne Win Correspondence, Nixon Presidential Materials Staff, NPM. Nixon to Ne Win, 12 January 1972, ibid. Leonard Unger (for Gross and Martin) to SS, 19 January 1972, Tel. 874, NSC Files, Subject files, folder Narcotics vol. 5 [2 of 3], box 359, NPM.

13. Bunker (in Vietnam, for Gross) to Rogers, 21 January 1972, Tel. 957, RG 59, SNF 1970–1973, box 169, folder DEF BUL 1/1/70, NAII. Martin to Rogers, 24 January 1972, Tels. 230 and 239, ibid., box 3055, folder SOC 11-5 Burma 1971.

14. CINCPAC to CJCS, 29 January 1972, Tel. 12227, ibid. Nixon to Ne Win, in SS to US Embassy Rangoon, 4 February 1972, Tel. 20088, ibid., folder SOC 11-5 Burma 1-4-72, NAII.

15. Nixon to Gross, 3 March 1972, WHCF, CO Files, box 13, folder CO 34 Burma 1/1/71–, NPM.

16. Martin to SS, 5 April 1972, Tel. 857, RG 59, SNF 1970–1973, box 3055, folder SOC 11-5 Burma 1-4-72, NAII. Martin to SS, 7 April 1972, Tel. 878, RG 59, SNF 1970–1973, ibid.

17. Martin to SS, 12 April 1972, Tel. 919, RG 59, SNF 1970–1973, ibid. Rogers to US Embassy Rangoon, 1 May 1972, Tel. 075611, ibid.

18. Martin to SS, 20 June 1972, Tel. 1510, ibid., folder SOC 11-5 Burma 4-15-72. USDS to US Embassy Rangoon, 18 July 1972, Tel. 129502, ibid., box 2141, folder POL 15-1 Burma. Fleck to SS, 22 June 1972, Tel. 1540, ibid., box 3050, folder SOC 11-5 Burma 4-15-72. Memcon, U Kyaw Soe, G. McMurtrie Godley, et al., 4 April 1973, enclosed in Martin to USDS, 6 April 1973, Airgram A-044, ibid., box 2141, folder POL 15-1 Burma.

19. McCoy, *Politics of Heroin*, 367–70 (quotation on p. 369).

20. Martin to SS, 1 September 1972, Tel. 2619, RG 59, SNF 1970–1973, box 3055, folder SOC 11-5 Burma 4-15-72, NAII. "U.S. Panel Accuses Burma of Obstructing Drug War," *New York Times*, 21 September 1972. USDS to US Embassy Rangoon, 29 September 1972, Tel. 179058, RG 59, SNF 1970–1973, box 3055, folder SOC 11-5 Burma 4-15-72, NAII.

21. Martin to SS, 9 October 1972, Tel. 2446, RG 59, SNF 1970–1973, box 2141, folder POL 15-1 Burma.

22. Martin to USDS, 21 April 1972, Airgram A-63, ibid., box 2143, folder POL 23-9 Burma.

23. Irwin to US Embassies Bangkok, Rangoon, Singapore, Jakarta, Phnom Penh, Vientiane, Tokyo, 27 April 1972, Tel. 76264, ibid. Martin to SS, 3 May 1972, Tel. 1069, ibid.

24. Martin to SS, 5 May 1972, Tel. 1108, ibid.

25. Morse, *Exodus to a Hidden Valley*, 196–213.

26. Taylor to USDS, 27 June 1972, Airgram A-8, RG 59, SNF 1970–1973, box 2140, folder POL 2 Burma, NAII. Jack Foisie, "Last Missionaries Ousted by Burma," *Washington Post*, 2 September 1972. Morse, *Exodus to a Hidden Valley*, 214.

27. Martin to SS, 25 October 1972, Tel. 2581, RG 59, SNF 1970–1973, box 2143, folder 23-9 Burma, NAII.

28. Rogers to US Embassy Rangoon, 16 November 1970, Tel. 208903, ibid., folder 33-5 Burma. Rogers to US Embassies Rangoon, Bangkok et al., 14 April 1973, Tel. 069994, ibid., box 2144, folder 17 Burma-US. Unger to SS, 23 March 1973, Tel. 4704, ibid., box 2141, folder 15-1 Burma, NAII. Wendy Law-Yone, *Golden Parasol*, 190, 201–5. Martin to SS, 26 March 1973, Tel. 740, RG 59, SNF 1970–1973, box 2144, folder 17 Burma-US, NAII.

29. Gibson, *The Secret Army*, 272–75.

30. Martin to SS, 9 January 1973, Tel. 6306, RG 59, SNF 1970–1973, box 3056, folder SOC 11-5 Burma 1973, NAII. Martin to USDS, 16 January 1973, Airgram A-008, ibid.

31. Martin to SS, 5 February 1973, Tel. 313, ibid., box 2143, folder POL Burma—U 6/29/72.

32. Taylor to USDS, 5 April 1973, Airgram A-6, ibid., box 2140, folder POL 2 Burma.

33. "Section II.—Policy/Duplications," attached to Martin to USDS, 23 February 1973, Airgram A-27, ibid., box 2144, folder POL Burma-US.

34. Steinberg and Fan, *Modern China-Myanmar Relations*, 131.

35. Rogers to US Embassies Rangoon et al., 25 June 1973, Tel. 123788, RG 59, SNF 1970–1973, box 2143, folder POL 23-9 Burma—US, NAII. Martin to SS, 29 June 1973, Tel. 1510, ibid. Rogers to US Embassies Rangoon et al., 25 June 1973, Tel. 123788, ibid. Martin to SS, 29 June 1973, Tel. 1510, ibid. Far Eastern Economic Review, *Asia 1977 Yearbook* (Hong Kong: Far Eastern Economic Review, 1977), 132. CIA, Directorate of Intelligence, "Thailand: Military Actions Against Narcotics Traffickers," 23 March 1983," p. 2, CREST documents, NAII.

36. House Committee on Foreign Affairs, "The Narcotics Situation in Southeast Asia, 1973," Report, 93rd Congress, 2nd Session, 1–6. Rush to Schulz, 11September 1973, RG 59, SNF 1970–1973, box 3056, folder SOC 11-5 Burma 1973, NAII.

37. Weimer, *Seeing Drugs*, 145–46.

38. Ibid., 103–7.

39. Ibid., 146–71.

40. John A. Lacey to USDS, 21 December 1973, Airgram A-161, RG 59, SNF 1970–1973, box 2143, folder POL Burma—J 9/20/71, NAII. Steinberg and Fan, *Modern China-Myanmar Relations*, 136–39. Clipping, Daniel Southerland, "China Held Sending Troops to Burma to Help Rebels," *Washington Post*, 8 April 1974, in Allan E. Goodman Papers, box 53, folder "China—Relations with Burma," HIA.

41. Clipping, Daniel Southerland, "How Burma 'Holds Line,'" *Christian Science Monitor*, 10 April 1974, S. Walter Washington Papers, box 7, Geographical Files, 1971–74, folder Asia & the Near East File—Burma, HSTL. Defense Intelligence Note, 1 July 1975, DIADIN 1585–75, National Security Adviser, Presidential for East Asia and the Pacific, Country File, box 2, folder Burma, Ford Papers, GRFL.

42. David L. Osborn to U Ohn Kyi, 29 June 1974, no. 694, RG 84, Burma US Embassy Rangoon, Unclassified Central Subject Files, 1973, box 9, folder SOC 11-5 Narcotics, NAII. "Burma's Campaign to Combat Drug Menace, Parts 1 & 2," Robert Maher Collection, JCL.

43. Charney. *Modern Burma*, 137–38. For an account of the events surrounding the return of U Thant's body, see Andrew Selth, *Death of A Hero: The U Thant Disturbances in Burma, December 1974* (Nathan, Qld., Australia: Centre for the Study of Australian-Asian Relations, Griffith University, 1989). See also Henry Soe-Win, "Peace Eludes U Thant," *Asia Tribune*, 17 June 2008, http://www.asiantribune.com/?q=node/11810; and "Burma to Free 1,600," *New York Times*, 30 August 1976.

44. John A. Lacey to SS, 12 December 1974, National Security Adviser for East Asia and the Pacific, Country File, box 2, folder Burma—State Department Telegrams To SECSTATE-EXDIS, Ford Papers, GRFL.

45. Mike Mansfield, "Southeast Asia and U.S. Policies After Indochina: A report on Burma, Thailand and the Republic of the Philippines submitted to the President," September 1975, enclosed in Mansfield to Gerald Ford, 17 September 1975, White House Central Files, Subject Files, box 10, CO 24: Burma, Ford Papers, GRFL. Quotations in the next several paragraphs are from this source, unless otherwise indicated.

46. Rotter, *Comrades and Odds*, 249–80.

47. Mike Mansfield, *Winds of Change: Evolving Relations and Interests in Asia* (Washington, DC: Government Printing Office, 1975); Far Eastern Economic Review, *Asia 1977 Yearbook*, 134.

48. M.C. Tun, "BURMA: Cooperation on Drugs Menace," *Far Eastern Economic Review*, 2 July 1976, 55. "Working Paper: Anti-Narcotics Program for Southeast Asia," enclosed in Mathea Falco to Peter G. Bourne, 15 January 1977, CREST document NLC-63-2-12-1-6, Carter Papers, JCL.

49. Memorandum, Peter Bourne to Jimmy Carter, 6 June 1977, CREST document 63-5-19-1-6, JCL. Bourne to Tim Kraft, 6 June 1972; Kraft to Zbigniew Brzezinski, 6 June 1977; Mike Armacost to Brzezinski, 6 June 1977, all in WHCF, Subject File, Countries, box CO-13, folder CO-25 Executive 1/20/77–1/20/81, Carter Papers, JCL. Henry Kamm, "Burma Reports Gain in Its War on Opium," *New York Times*, 9 October 1977. Jimmy Carter, "Drug Abuse Message to Congress," 2 August 1977, Public Papers of the President, http://www.presidency.ucsb.edu/ws/index.php?pid=7908&st=Burma&st1=.

50. Henry Kamm, "Insurgents in Burma Lament Their Lonely Struggle," *New York Times*, 2 January 1978. Henry Kamm, "Burma Reports Gain in Its War on Opium," ibid., 9 October 1977.

51. Charney, *Modern Burma*, 140. Oral history interview with Ambassador David Osborn, 16 January 1989, Association for Diplomatic Studies, Foreign Affairs Oral History Program, Lauinger Library, Georgetown University, Washington, DC. Copy in Osborn Papers, box 6, folder "Oral History Interview," DDEL. "U.S. Envoy Denied Asylum to Suspect," *New York Times*, 23 August 1976. See also Richard Butwell, "The Burmese Way of Change," *Current History* 69 (December 1976): 206, and "Burma," in Far Eastern Economic Review, *Asia 1977 Yearbook*, 130–31.

52. Far Eastern Economic Review, *Asia 1977 Yearbook*, 134. Osborn to SS, 5 May 1977, Tel. 1260, box 3, Osborn Papers, DDEL. Henry Kamm, "Political Shape-Up Strengthens Hold of Burma's Leader," *New York Times*, 8 October 1977.

53. One official American assessment at the time was that Burma's "human rights performance is hardly better than that of most Communist states." "Human Rights in the East Asia-Pacific Area," CREST document NLC-28-17-15-10-6, Carter Papers, JCL. Mary E. King to Maurice D. Dean, 3 November 1977, CREST document NLC-129-14-15-2-5, ibid.

54. Steinberg and Fan, *Modern China-Myanmar Relations*, 139. David I. Steinberg, "The United States and Myanmar: A "Boutique Issue'?" *International Affairs* 86, no. 1 (2010): 179. Ho Kwon Ping, "To Give or Not to Give," *Far Eastern Economic Review*, 18 January 1980, 37. Author's interview with David Harr, Naperville, IL, 23 September 2011.

55. Author's interview with Ambassador Daniel O'Donohue, 9 January 2012, Dacor Bacon House, Washington, DC.

56. Mark S. Riley and Ravi A. Balaram, "The United States International Military Education and Training (IMET) Program with Burma/Myanmar: A Review of the 1980–1988 Programming and Prospects for the Future," *Asian Affairs: An American Review* 40, no. 3 (2013): 109–32.

57. Mathea Falco to Dennis DeConcini, 26 September 1978, CREST documents, NAII. John McBeth, "Drugs: The New Connections," *Far Eastern Economic Review*, 14 September 1979, 37. Edith T. Mirante, "Burma Frontier Insurgents," June 1986, WHORM: Subject Files, CO Countries, box 47, folder CO 025 (Burma), Reagan Papers, RRL. This was published by Project Maje in 1987.

58. M. C. Tun, "Long's Visit Underlines New-Look Burma-US Links," *Far Eastern Economic Review*, 25/31 December 1981, 8.

59. Proclamation, Ronald Reagan, 20 August 1982, included in Drug Abuse Policy Office, Office of Policy Development, The White House, *Federal Strategy for Prevention of Drug Abuse and Drug Trafficking 1982*, copy in RRL. CIA, Directorate of Intelligence, "Thailand: Military Actions Against Narcotics Traffickers," 23 March 1983," pp. 5, 7, CREST documents, NAII.

60. "The Asian Connection," *Newsweek*, 25 June 1984, 62–63.

61. Memorandum, David D. Gries to Director of Central Intelligence and Deputy Director of Central Intelligence, 28 June 1983, CREST documents, NAII. John McBeth and M. C. Tun, "BURMA: Goodbye to the Good Life: Ne Win's Leadership Gets a Shock Shake-up," *Far Eastern Economic Review*, 2 June 1983, 14.

62. Memorandum, David D. Gries to Director of Central Intelligence and Deputy Director of Central Intelligence, 28 June 1983, CREST documents, NAII. See also a CIA report for November 1983, which refers to Ne Win's investigation "that appears to link Tin Oo with Bo Ni's illegal smuggling and narcotics-trafficking activity." CIA, Directorate of Intelligence, "Drug Trafficking: The role of Insurgents, Terrorists, and Sovereign States: An Intelligence Assessment," November 1983, p. 10, CREST documents, NAII. Taylor, *The State in Burma*, 370-71.

63. "Burma: Record Crop From the Biggest Source," *New York Times*, 13 September 1984. CIA, "Burma: Major Political and Economic Issues" [August 1985], CREST documents, NAII. Charles E. Allen, Report, 2, enclosed in Allen to Director of Central

Intelligence, Deputy Director of Central Intelligence, 29 August 1985, CREST documents, NAII. Author's interview with Ambassador O'Donohue.

64. Quoted in "Burma: Record Crop From the Biggest Source," *New York Times*, 13 September 1984. Author's interview with Ambassador O'Donohue.

65. "Focus—Telecommunications/Office Automation: Burma Readies Itself to Enter the Computer Age," *Far Eastern Economic Review*, 31 October 1985, 74.

66. San Yu to Reagan, 5 March 1986, WHORM: Files, CO Countries, box 47, folder CO 035 (Burma), Reagan Papers, RRL. Barbara Crossette, "Burma's Eroding Isolation," *New York Times Sunday Magazine*, 24 November 1985, 138.

67. Unpublished manuscript, Edith T. Mirante, "Chemical Warfare in Burma, U.S. Involvement," 20 June 1986, WHORM: Subject Files, CO Countries, box 47, folder CO 025 (Burma), Reagan Papers, RRL (published by Project Maje in 1987). Carlton E. Turner to Ann B. Wroblaski, 4 August 1986, WHORM: Subject Files, CO Countries, box 47, folder CO 025 (Burma), Reagan Papers, RRL. Turner to Edith T. Mirante, 30 October 1986, ibid.

68. "Rebels in Burma Say Rangoon Uses Herbicide Against Them," *New York Times*, 30 November 1986. Memorandum, Melvyn Levitsky to Frank C. Carlucci, 2 March 1987, WHORM: Subject Files, CO Countries, box 47, folder CO 025 (Burma), Reagan Papers, RRL.

69. "Burma Oil Boost?" *Far Eastern Economic Review*, 18 June 1987, 9. "A Rich Country Gone Wrong," *New Yorker*, 9 October 1989, 61. Bertil Lintner, "Thein Sein Heads to the White House," *Asia Times*, 20 May 2013, http://www.atimes.com/atimes/Southeast_Asia/SEA-03-200513.html.

70. Voice of the People of Burma, "Ne Win Reported to Offer Island for U.S. Base," 16 June 1987, FBIS Daily Report, East Asia, FBIS-EAS-87-117 on 1987-06-18, under the headings Burma, Southeast Asia, p. G1. Ironically, there have been rumors for years that the Chinese had established an intelligence base on Greater Coco Island. See Andrew Selth, "Chinese Military Bases in Burma: The Explosion of a Myth," *Regional Outlook Paper #10*, Griffith Asia Institute, 2007.

71. Reagan to Ne Win, 16 March 1987, WHORM: Subject Files, CO Countries, box 47, folder CO 025 (Burma), Reagan Papers, RRL. "Talking Points for Telephone Call to U Ne Win," enclosed in Frank C. Carlucci, "Recommended Telephone Call," 11 April 1987, Presidential Handwriting File, series IV: Presidential Telephone Calls, 3/12/87–2/1/88, folder 180, box 10, Reagan Papers, RRL. The memorandum indicates that the call was made. Ne Win wrote a cordial letter of appreciation when he left.

72. "Burma Requests UN Status Downgrading," *Far Eastern Economic Review*, 12 March 1987, 8. Rodney Tasker, "BURMA: Going it Alone," ibid., 14 July 1983, 25. Burton Levin to David and Helenka Osborn, 24 August 1987, Osborn Papers, box 3, DDEL.

13. REVOLT

1. Levin to David and Helenka Osborn, 24 August 1987, Osborn Papers, box 3, DDEL. Steinberg, *Burma: The State of Myanmar*, 4–5.

2. Burton Levin, "Reminiscences of the 1988 Uprising and of the U.S. Policy Response," paper delivered at the annual meeting of the Society for Historians of American Foreign Relations, Madison, WI, 24 June 2010. Charney, *Modern Burma*, 146.

3. This event, and the entire revolution, is dramatically described in Lintner, *Outrage*.

4. Steinberg, *Turmoil in Burma*, 184–85.

5. Levin, "Reminiscences and Reflections," 9.

6. Charney, *Modern Burma*, 161.

7. Levin, "Reminiscences and Reflections," 10.

8. Levin to Osborn, 8 September 1988, box 3, folder Burma—After Retirement, Osborn Papers, DDEL.

9. Robert Pear, "Disorder in Burma leads U.S. To Draw Evacuation Plans," *New York Times*, 8 September 1988.

10. Levin to Osborn, 8 September 1988, folder Burma—After Retirement, box 3, Osborn Papers, DDEL.

11. Author's interview with Ambassador Burton Levin and Colonel John Haseman, 14 April 2014, Northfield, MN.

12. Pear, "Disorder in Burma." Robert Pear, "Burmese Revolt Seen as Spontaneous," *New York Times*, 10 September 1988; Clyde Farnsworth and Martin Tolchin, "Washington Talk: Briefing; Solarz's Long Shadow," ibid., 22 September 1988.

13. "Funds for Burma Suspended by U.S.," ibid., 23 September 1988. Elaine Sciolini, "U.S., Urging Calm in Burma, Weights Aid Cutoff," ibid., 20 September 1988. "Funds for Burma Suspended by U.S." Michael F. Martin, "U.S. Sanctions on Burma," Congressional Research Service Report for Congress, 7 February 2012, p. 4. Statement of Carol Adelman, 2 March 1989, *Foreign Assistance Legislation for Fiscal Years 1990–91* (Part 5), Hearings and Markup before the Subcommittee on Asian and Pacific Affairs of the Committee on Foreign Affairs, House of Representatives, 101st Congress, 1st Session, 309–10. Testimony of David F. Lambertson, 2 March 1989, ibid., 325.

14. "U.S. Naval Intrusion in 1988 Reported," London BBC broadcast in Burmese, 4 April 1989, Daily Report, East Asia, FBIS-EAS-89-064, 5 April 1989. Later, some did urge American military action in Burma. One was Shelby Tucker who had recently walked across northern Burma, going where no Americans had been in years. Senator Bill Cohen (R-MA) arranged for Tucker to meet with two senior NSC officials, who listened politely to his proposal that the UN Security Council prohibit international opium trafficking and threatened the use of US military action against any country that would not cooperate. This was clearly to be a pretext for the United States to restore democracy in Burma. There is no indication that the NSC considered this proposal seriously. Shelby Tucker, "Washington Meetings," enclosed in Raymond A. LaMontagne to Richard C. LaMagna, 29 September 1989, Bush Presidential Records, National Security Council, Thomas E. McNamara Files, Subject Files, GHWBL. Tucker later published his account of his Burma trek, *Among Insurgents: Walking Through Burma* (London: I. B. Tauris, 2000).

15. Interview with Ambassador Burton Levin and Colonel John Haseman. According to Levin and Haseman, the departing Americans were not initially not welcomed by the American embassy in Thailand.

16. Levin, "Reminiscences and Reflections," 10. "U.S. Viewed in Favorable Light by Demonstrators," *Bangkok Post*, 1 October 1988, in Daily Report East Asia, FBIS-EAS-88-192 4 October 1988. See also "A Rich Country Gone Wrong," *New Yorker*, 9 October 1989, 80–81.

17. Levin to Osborn, 9 December 1988, folder Burma—After Retirement (1), box 3, Osborn Papers, DDEL. Reagan to Roy D. Miller, 30 November 1988, WHORM: Subject File, CO Countries, box 47, Foler CO 025 (Burma), Reagan Papers, RRL.

18. Testimony of David F. Lambertson, 2 March 1989, *Foreign Assistance Legislation for Fiscal Years 1990–91* (Part 5), Hearings and Markup before the Subcommittee on Asian and Pacific Affairs of the Committee on Foreign Affairs, House of Representatives, 101st Congress, 1st Session, 290–99, 313, 320–21. Louis Walinsky wrote to Solarz disputing Lambertson's testimony. See "Comments on Lambertson's Testimony of March 2," enclosed in Walinsky to Solarz, 11 March 1898, Walinsky Papers, box 1, folder 1-20, Cornell University Library.

19. Charney, *Modern Burma*, 167.

20. Rodney Tasker, "Burma: Tense Weeks Ahead as Emotive Anniversaries Fall Due," *Far Eastern Economic Review*, 13 July 1989, 30. Steven Erlanger, "U.S. Embassy Reports

Torture in Burmese Jails," *New York Times*, 26 August 1989. "Burma Accuses Foreigners of Plot Against the Government," *Far Eastern Economic Review*, 21 September 1989, 14. Elie Wiesel to George H.W. Bush, 20 December 1989, Bush Papers, White House Office of Records Management (WHORM), Subject File—General, Alpha File Name, GHWBL.

21. Bush to Frederick Vreeland, 1 March 1989, Alphabetical File, folder Vreeland, Frederick, Bush Papers, White House Office of Records Management (WHORM), Subject File—General, Alpha File Name, GHWBL. Vreeland to Bush, 12 April 1989, ibid.

22. Hong Kong AFP report, "Government Rejects Nominee for U.S. Ambassador," 5 October 1990, in Daily Report. East Asia, FBIS-EAS-90-195, 9 October 1990.

23. Charney, *Modern Burma*, 176. "Burmese Military Bars U.S. Observers for Vote," *New York Times*, 27 January 1990; Steven Erlanger, "U.S. Debates Aiding Burmese in Drug Fight," ibid., 1 April 1990.

24. Hong Kong AFP, "Students Support U.S. Actions to Ban Imports," 27 April 1990, Daily Report. East Asia, FBIS-EAS-90-083, 30 April 1990, 36. Asia Watch, *Human Rights in Burma (Myanmar)* (New York: Human Rights Watch, May 1990). This report is one of the most detailed reports of conditions in Burma at this time. Draft letter, Janet C. Mullins to Lloyd Bentsen, n.d. [May 1990], Bush Papers, National Security Council, Thomas E. McNamara Files, Subject Files, GWHBL.

25. Information about Vreeland's paperwork for the position is attached to Memorandum, Sharon C. Bisdee to Chase Untermeyer, 11 May 1990, Bush Papers, Counsel's Office, White House, Appointments Files, Ambassador to the Union of Burma File, GHWBL. The phony "Biographical Information" pages submitted to the committee are available in Nomination File: Frederick Vreeland, box 31, Committee on Foreign Relations, 101st Congress, Nominations File, NA.

26. References to Cranston's accusation of lying are in Vanessa Vreeland to Bush and Barbara Bush, 21 November 1990; Vreeland to Bush, 22 November 1990; and Memorandum, Chase Untermeyer to Bush, 13 December 1990. When Bush received Vanessa Vreeland's letter, he asked Untermeyer, "what is this about being accused of 'lying'. Is he dead meat now. I feel very badly about all this." Memorandum, Bush to Untermeyer, 30 November [1990]. All in Bush Papers, WHORM, Subject File—General, Alpha File Name, GHWBL.

27. Author's interview with Marvin Ott, 24 September 2012, Woodrow Wilson International Center for Scholars, Washington, DC.

28. The stenographic transcript of the public Vreeland hearing is found in RG 46, Records of the U.S. Senate, 101st Congress, Committee on Foreign Relations, Public Transcripts, September 5–October 2, 1990, box 24, NA. Vreeland's comments are on pp. 3–9.

29. Ibid., 2–3, 9.

30. Interview with Marvin Ott, 24 September 2012. Vreeland to Bush, 22 November 1990, Bush Papers, WHORM, Subject File—General, Alpha File Name, GHWBL. Michael Wines, "U.S. Withdraws Nomination of Envoy to Myanmar," *New York Times*, 5 October 1990. Hong Kong AFP report, "Government Rejects Nominee for U.S. Ambassador," 5 October 1990, in Daily Report. East Asia, FBIS-EAS-90-195, 9 October 1990. It does not appear that Vreeland commented about narcotics in the public hearing.

31. Franklin P. Huddle, who was Deputy Chief of Mission in Rangoon from June 1990 and, after Levin left, chargé d'affaires ad interim, has a different recollection. He contends that Vreeland, egged on by senators who did not want an ambassador appointed, departed from his script and made some critical comments about Burma and perhaps said that sanctions might be appropriate at some point. When the Burmese learned of this, they withdrew their agrément, and the nomination died. In other words, he does not agree that the Burmese acted because they misattributed Cranston's remarks to Vreeland. Huddle's

sources were State Department officials who attended the hearing. Author's telephone interview with Frederick P. Huddle, 27 May 2012.

32. Interview with Marvin Ott. Telephone interview with Huddle. Both Ott and Huddle believe that one of Moynihan's staffers, Andrew Samet, whose wife was part Shan, was particularly influential. Samet was well versed in the atrocities inflicted on Burma's minority peoples and helped convinced Moynihan to resist appointing an ambassador.

33. Typescript, Testimony of David I. Steinberg, 5 February 1992, Senate Foreign Relations Committee, copy in Walinsky Papers, box 1, folder 1-31, Cornell University Library.

34. Newspaper clipping, Mya Maung, "Burma's Electoral Farce," *Christian Science Monitor*, 23 May 1990, in Osborn Papers, box 3, folder Burma—After Retirement (1), DDEL. Steinberg, *Turmoil in Burma*, 185.

35. Steinberg, *Turmoil in Burma*, 185–89.

36. Tonkin quoted ibid., 187. Draft letter to Richard A. Myint, attached to Memorandum, Sally Kelley to USDS, 17 October 1990, Bush Papers, WHORM Subject File, General, Scanned Records, folder TA 001, GHWBL.

37. David I. Steinberg believes that the military leaders really did intend to "withdraw from the political stage," though remaining influential behind the scenes. Because of fear of their past accomplishments being undone, however, along with fear of retribution, they decided not to cede power. Steinberg, *Turmoil in Burma*, 188. "Phooey to 80%," *Economist*, 21 July 1990, 29–30.

38. Bertil Lintner, "NARCOTICS 1: The Phony War," *Far Eastern Economic Review*, 28 June 1990, 20; Susuma Awanohara, "Getting Their Hands Dirty," ibid., 28 June 1990, 26.

39. Moynihan et al. to Bush, 1 October 1990, Bush Papers, National Security Council, Karl Jackson Files, Subject Files, GHWBL. "Burmese Government Cracks Down on Protesting Monks," *Far Eastern Economic Review*, 1 November 1990, 15.

40. Senator Moynihan, *Congressional Record*, vol. 137, no. 111, 102d Congress, 1st Session, 19 July 1991, S10487.

41. Richard J. Durbin et al. to Bush, 11 October 1991, Bush Papers, National Security Council, Nancy Bearg Dyke Files, Subject Files, GHWBL.

42. Press Release, The White House, Office of the Press Secretary, "Statement of the Press Secretary," 14 October 1991, ibid., WHORM Subject File, General, Scanned Records, GHBWL.

43. Statement of James K. Bishop before the Subcommittee of Asian and Pacific Affairs of the House Foreign Affairs Committee, 18 October 1991, Walinsky Papers, box 5, folder 5-20, Cornell University Library.

44. Barbara Crossette, "3 Senators Asking Action on Burmese," *New York Times*, 6 April 1992.

45. Clippings, Michele Bohana, "The New Killing Fields," *Boston Globe*, 21 April 1992; Morton Abramowitz, Richard Holbrooke, and Peter Tarnoff, "Put International Pressure on Burma," *Christian Science Monitor*, 13 April 1992; Thant Myint-U, "Bringing SLORC to Heel," *Far Eastern Economic Review*, 30 April 1992, 29. Levin quoted in clipping, "Burma's Boiling Point," *Wall Street Journal*, 10 April 1992; all in Walinsky Papers, box 1, folder 1-27, Cornell University Library.

46. Yegar, *Between Integration and Secession*, 19–30; quotation on p. 30.

47. Steinberg, *Burma's Road Toward Development*, 69.

48. Yegar, *Between Integration and Secession*, 33–67; quotation on p. 67.

49. Clipping, Susan Blaustein, "Asia's Bosnia," *New Republic*, 12 April 1993, 20, Walinsky Papers, box 5, folder 5-16, Cornell University Library.

50. Clipping, "A Glimmer in Burma," *Christian Science Monitor*, 6 May 1992, ibid., box 1, folder 1-27.

51. Clippings, Philip Shenon, "Nobelists Urge U.N. Sanctions Against Myanmar," *New York Times*, 20 February 1993, ibid., box 5, folder 5-16; Susan Blaustein, "Asia's Bosnia,"

New Republic, 12 April 1993, 21, ibid. Steven A. Holmes, "U.S. Is Criticized on Burmese Policy," *New York Times*, 21 June 1993. Author's interview with Catharin Dalpino, Washington, DC, 27 January 2012.

52. Senate Resolution 112, 103rd Congress, 1st Session. Copy in Walinsky Papers, box 5, folder 5-24, Cornell University Library. The resolution was agreed to on 27 May 1993.

53. "Clipping, "Friends of Slorc," *New York Times*, 3 December 1993, Walinsky Papers, box 5, folder 5-16, Cornell University Library.

54. Maureen Aung-Thwin, "Burma's PR Offensive," *Far Eastern Economic Review*, 26 August 1993, 22. Letters disputing Aung-Thwin's claims appeared ibid., 21 October 1993, 3.

55. Susumu Awanohara and Irene Wu, "The Junta Blinks: Burma Allows Dissident to Meeting U.S. Congressman," ibid., 3 March 1994, 26. Philip Shenon, "Detained Burmese Laureate Speaks Out to U.S. Visitors," *New York Times*, 15 February 1994. Philip Shenon, "Lawmaker Meets Again with Burmese Dissident," ibid., 16 February 1994.

56. Awanohara and Wu, "The Junta Blinks," 26.

57. Comments of Gary L. Ackerman, 29 July 1994, *U.S. Policy Toward Burma*, Hearing and Markup on H. Res. 471 Before the Subcommittee on Asia and the Pacific of the House Committee on Foreign Affairs, 103rd Congress, 2d Session, 29 July 1994 (Washington, DC: GPO, 1995), 1.

58. Steven Greenhouse, "U.S. Urges Burmese Military to Talk to Imprisoned Laureate," *New York Times*, 8 March 1994.

59. Susumu Awanohara and Irene Wu, "Foreign Relations—Hard Line, Soft Target: Washington Will Get Tough with Burmese Junta," *Far Eastern Economic Review*, 31 March 1994, 31.

60. The resolution is appended to *U.S. Policy Toward Burma: Hearing and Markup on H. Res. 471*, 156–63.

61. Clinton's decision to deemphasize cooperation on narcotics led one DEA official in Burma to sue the State Department and the CIA for tapping his telephone and forcing him out of the country, allegedly because he reported that Burma's antinarcotics campaign was successful at a time when the American government claimed the contrary. In fact, the State Department had successfully obtained the recall of three successive DEA agents in Burma, indicating a serious intergovernmental struggle over narcotics policy. Tim Weiner, "Suit by Drug Agent Says U.S. Subverted His Burmese Efforts," *New York Times*, 27 October 1994.

62. Prepared Statement of Thomas Hubbard, 29 July 1994, *U.S. Policy Toward Burma: Hearing and Markup on H. Res. 471*, 11–14.

63. Dana Rohrabacher, 29 July 1994, ibid., 34. Statement of Mike Jendrzejczyk, 29 July 1994, ibid., 40–43.

64. Michael Vatikiotis, "Burma: Catching the Wave," *Far Eastern Economic Review*, 16 February 1995, 48–52.

65. Michael Hirsh with Ron Moreau, "Making It in Mandalay," ibid., 19 June 1995, 46.

66. Albright, *Madam Secretary*, 201–2.

67. Ibid.

68. Vatikiotis, "Burma: Catching the Wave." Myint Thein, "Resistance Official Criticizes U.S. Leadership," *Sunday Post* (Bangkok), 28 May 1995, Daily Report. East Asia, FBIS-EAS-95-105, 1 June 1995, p. 58.

69. Philip Shenon, "Head of Democratic Opposition Is Released by Burmese Military," *New York Times*, 11 July 1995; "New Hope for Burmese Democracy," ibid., 13 July 1995.

70. Committee Reports, 104th Congress (1995–1996), Senate Report 104–143. http://thomas.loc.gov/cgi-bin/cpquery/?&sid=cp104oglqr&r_n=sr143.104&dbname=cp104&&sel=TOC_86776&.

71. Bertil Lintner, "Burma: A Turn for the Worse," *Far Eastern Economic Review*, 23 November 1995, 38.

72. Press Release, "Testimony of Senator McConnell on Burma Freedom & Democracy Act Before the Senate Banking Committee, 22 May 1996," copy in Walinsky Papers, box 10, folder 10-31, Cornell University Library.

73. Statement of Kent Wiedeman before the Senate Banking Committee, 22 May 1996, copy ibid. "Burma: Finance Minister on Possible U.S. Sanctions," *Asia Times* (Bangkok), 28 May 1991, 1–2, Daily Report. East Asia, FBIS-EAS-96-103, 28 May 1996, 73.

74. Philip S. Robertson, Jr., "Burma" (Washington, DC: Foreign Policy in Focus, 1 August 1997). Also available at http://www.burmalibrary.org/reg.burma/archives/199708/msg00050.html.

75. Author's interview with Eric P. Schwartz, Hubert H. Humphrey School of Public Affairs, University of Minnesota, Minneapolis, MN, 21 June 2012.

76. "Clinton Bans Burmese Leaders from U.S. in Response to Arrests," *New York Times*, 4 October 1996.

77. Steven Erlanger, "U.S. Weighs Tougher Reaction to Burmese Crackdown," ibid., 5 October 1996.

78. See Marvin Ott, "Burma: A Strategic Perspective," *Strategic Forum*, no. 92 (November 1996).

79. Tim Shorrock, "Reich Cancels Myanmar Briefing," *Journal of Commerce*, 15 November 1996, distributed on burmanet, copy in Walinsky Papers, box 10, folder 10-31, Cornell University Library. "US Senators Call for Ban on Investment in Burma," *Hong Kong Standard*, 16 (?) November 1996, copy ibid.

80. Steven Lee Myers, "Trade vs. Rights: A U.S. Debate with a Burmese Focus," *New York Times*, 5 March 1997; interview with Eric P. Schwartz.

81. Interview with Eric P. Schwartz.

82. Steven Erlanger, "Clinton Approves New U.S. Sanctions against Burmese," *New York Times*, 22 April 1997. Executive Order 13047 was published in the *Federal Register* on 22 May 1997. *Federal Register* 62 (22 May 1997): 28301–2.

83. James Guyot, "Burma in 1997: From Empire to ASEAN," *Asian Survey*, 38, no. 2, Part II (February 1998): 191. Zarni to Madeleine Albright, 29 April 1997, Walinsky Papers, box 3, folder 3-22, Cornell University Library.

84. Nigel Holloway, "Burma—Caught in the Net: U.S. Sanction Debate Moves to Cyberspace," *Far Eastern Economic Review*, 28 November 1996, 28. Clipping, John Nichols, "UW Dumps Stock Linked to Burma," *Capital Times*, 10–11 May 1997, Walinsky Papers, box 3, folder 3-22, Cornell University Library. For background on Zarni, see clipping, Sandy Barron, "Burma's Busy Networker," *The Nation* (New York), 5 January 1998, C1-C2, Walinsky Papers, box 3, folder 3-22, Cornell University Library.

85. Albright, *Madam Secretary*, 200. Author's interview with Priscilla Clapp, 15 March 2012, Washington, DC.

86. Kappiya Kan Kaung, untitled article, *New Light of Burma*, 11 August 1999. Malinowski, then the director of Human Rights Watch's Washington office, framed the article and hung it on his wall. I am grateful to him for bringing it to my attention. Steinberg, *Burma: the State of Myanmar*, xxx. In April 2014 Malinowski became assistant secretary of state for democracy, human rights, and labor.

87. "Officials Halt Burmese Dissident's Trip Again," *New York Times*, 27 July 1998; Seth Mydans, "Popular Burmese Leader Tests Wills with Junta," ibid., 30 August 2000.

88. Steinberg, *Burma: the State of Myanmar*, 243.

14. THE THAW

1. Simon Ingram, "Breakthrough in Burma—Talks Are a Start," *Christian Science Monitor*, 12 January 2001.

2. Author's interview with Clapp.

3. Interestingly, Khin Nyunt showed considerable concern for the safety of American diplomats in Rangoon during the 9/11 crisis and acted very professionally. Interview with Priscilla Clapp.

4. Joshua Kurlantzick, "Ran-goons: Why Isn't Burma on Bush's 'Axis of Evil' List?" *Washington Monthly*, April 2002, 38–41. See also Anna Husarska, "Nonviolent Protest Won't Bring Down the Dictators," *International Herald Tribune*, 14 April 2002. This column originally appeared in the *Los Angeles Times*.

5. Richard C. Paddock, "Freed Dissident Hails 'New Dawn,'" *Chicago Tribune*, 7 May 2002. The photo of Aung San Suu Kyi is on the front page of the *New York Times*, 7 May 2002. Seth Mydans, "Burmese Democracy Advocate Is Released from House Arrest," *New York Times*, 6 May 2002. Richard C. Paddock, "Freed Dissident Hails 'New Dawn,'" *Chicago Tribune*, 7 May 2002. Seth Mydans, "Freed Burmese Democracy Leader Proclaims 'New Dawn,'" *New York Times*, 7 May 2002. The *Washington Post*, for example, editorialized that the "sanctions clearly have had an effect." "Patience in Burma," *Washington Post National Weekly Edition*, 13–19 May 2002.

6. Megan Clymer, "Min Ko Naing." Rajiv Chandrasekaran, "What Next for Burma?" *Washington Post National Weekly Edition*, 13–19 May 2002. "Patience in Burma."

7. Brian Palmer, "Not So Warm a Welcome," *Newsweek*, 25 November 2002, 25. The Department of State's Bureau of Democracy, Human Rights, and Labor's statement, "Rape by the Burmese Military in Ethnic Regions," is available at http://2001-2009.state.gov/g/drl/rls/16087.htm. See also Steven Weisman, "U.S. Says Evidence Confirms Reports of Mass Rapes by Burmese," *New York Times*, 27 December 2002.

8. Aung San Suu Kyi, "What It Means to Be Truly Free," *Parade*, 9 March 2003, 4–5. "U.S. Pension Fund Chided Over Burma," *Far Eastern Economic Review*, 28 November 2002, 9.

9. Rena Peterson, "The Rangoon Squad," *Weekly Standard*, 16 June 2003, 18–19. Joe Cochrane, "The Missing Lady," *Newsweek*, 16 June 2003, 26. ASEAN Inter-Parliamentary Myanmar Caucus, "The Depayin Massacre 2 Years On, Justice Denied," 30 May 2005, available at http://www.aseanmp.org/docs/resources/Depayin%20Massacre.pdf. The Radio Free Asia report is cited in the ASEAN report, p. 2. Radio Free Asia's current estimate is found at. http://www.rfa15.org/rfas-burmese-service/. A preliminary list of the dead, injured, and detained was compiled by BurmaNet News and is available at http://www.burmanet.org/injuredlist.shtml.

10. Murray Hiebert and Shawn W. Crispin, "Getting Away with Murder," *Far Eastern Economic Review*, 19 June 2003, 18; Sarah Lyall, "Britain Says Democracy Advocate Is Held in Burmese Jail," *New York Times*, 20 June 2003.

11. Bertil Lintner, "Burma: The Military Digs In For the Long Haul," *Far Eastern Economic Review*, 25 September 2003.

12. Robert H. Taylor, "Myanmar's Political Future: Is Waiting for the Perfect the Enemy of Doing the Possible?" National Bureau of Asian Research, "Reconciling Burma/Myanmar: Essays on U.S. Relations with Burma," *NBR Analysis* 15 (March 2004): 38. Steinberg published a condensed version of his essay, entitled "Burma: Who's Isolating Whom?" in the *Far Eastern Economic Review*, 11 March 2004.

13. Adam McCarty and Paul Burke, "Burma/Myanmar: Reconciliation without Capitulation," *Harvard Asia Pacific Review* 8: (January 2005): 28–32; Murray Hiebert, "Burma: Perennial Poser," *Far Eastern Economic Review*, 25 March 2004, 22.

14. Than Shwe had come to power in 1992. In 2004 he forced Prime Minister Khin Nyunt out after only fourteen months in office. Soon thereafter Burma's ambassador to the United States was recalled, apparently because he was too close to Khin Nyunt.

15. Steinberg and Fan, *Modern China-Myanmar Relations*, 159.

16. *Human Rights in Burma: Where Are We Now and What Do We Do Next?* Joint Hearing Before the Subcommittee on Africa, Global Human Rights and International Operations And the Subcommittee on Asia and the Pacific of the Committee on International

Relations, House of Representatives, 109th Congress, 2d Session, 7 February 2006 (Washington, DC: Government Printing Office, 2006), 8.

17. Steven Lee Myers, "First Lady Makes Issue of Myanmar's Junta," *New York Times*, 6 September 2007. Hannah Beech, "Laura Bush's Burmese Crusade," *Time*, 5 September 2007. Author's interview with Aung Din, U.S. Campaign for Burma Headquarters, Washington, DC, 26 February 2012.

18. Jonathan Karl, Richard Coolidge, and Jordyn Phelps, "Front Seat to History: Cokie Roberts' Historic Chat with Michelle Obama and Laura Bush," Yahoo! News, 8 July 2013, http://news.yahoo.com/blogs/power-players-abc-news/front-seat-history-cokie-roberts-historic-chat-michelle-112829031.html?vp=1.

19. A brief summary of the Saffron Revolution and the US response is Niksch, *Burma-U.S. Relations*. For a fictional account, but one based on personal experience, about events in Burma from 1988 to 2009 with much about the Saffron Revolution, see Suragamika, *The Roadmap*.

20. Thomas Fuller, "U.N. Worker Arrested in Myanmar," printed in *Burma's Saffron Revolution*, Hearing Before the Subcommittee on East Asian and Pacific Affairs of the Committee on Foreign Relations, United States Senate, 100th Congress, 1st Session, 3 October 2007, 2. Laura Bush, ibid., 4. One of the participants at a Saffron Revolution teach-in at Northern Illinois University, Professor Eric Jones, was denied entry into Burma in 2009, despite having a valid visa. The authorities at the airport had in their hands photocopies of reports about the NIU event.

21. President Bush's address to the UN General Assembly, 25 September 2007, http://georgewbush-whitehouse.archives.gov/news/releases/2007/09/20070925-4.html.

22. *Burma's Saffron Revolution*, 3, 6, 29.

23. Ibid., 27.

24. Ibid., 53.

25. Executive Order 13448 of 18 October 2007, *Federal Register*, 23 October 2007, 60223–60226.

26. Steinberg and Fan, *Modern China-Myanmar Relations*, 334; Susan Banki, "ASEAN Goes Silent on Burma, Again," *Far Eastern Economic Review Online Forum*, 27 Nov 2007.

27. Executive Order 13464 of 30 April 2008, *Federal Register*, 2 May 2008, 24491–24493; Steven Lee Myers, "Myanmar: Sanctions on 3 Companies," *New York Times*, 2 May 2008; Interview with Aung Din.

28. Seth Mydans, "Myanmar Reels as Cyclone Toll Hits Thousands," *New York Times*, 6 May 2008; Seth Mydans, "A Reclusive Government, Forced to Ask for Help," ibid., 8 May 2008.

29. Helen Cooper and Thom Shanker, "U.S. Frustrated by Myanmar Military Junta's Limits on Aid to Wake of Cyclone," ibid., 17 May 2008; Eric Schmitt, "Gates Accuses Myanmar of 'Criminal Neglect' Over Aid," ibid., 2 June 2008; Lewis M. Stern, George Thomas, and Julia A. Thompson, "Burma in Strategic Perspective: Renewing Discussion of Options," *Strategic Forum*, October 2009, 3; Bertil Lintner, "The Burmese Way to Fascism," *Far Eastern Economic Review*, October 2007, 9; Steven Lee Myers and Thomas Fuller, "Mrs. Bush Meets with Burmese Refugees," *New York Times*, 8 August 2008.

30. Public Law 110-286, 29 July 2008. According to a Government Accounting Office report, the law was not very effective. United States General Accounting Office, Report to Congressional Committees, *International Trade: U.S. Agencies Have Taken Some Steps, but Serious Impediments Remain to Restricting Trade in Burmese Rubies and Jadeite* Report GAO-09-987 (September 2009), available at http://www.gao.gov/assets/300/296159.pdf.

31. Daniel Pepper, "Aftermath of a Revolt: Myanmar's Lost Year," *New York Times*, 5 October 2003. National Democratic Institute Press Release, "NDI Honors Archbishop Desmond Tutu, Women's League Of Burma; Focus on Struggle for Democracy in Burma," 16

December 2008, https://www.ndi.org/node/17642. Mark McDonald, "U.S. Freezes Assets of 2 Burmese Businessmen Who Backed Military Junta," *New York Times*, 17 January 2009.

32. Nicholas D. Kristof, "Sneaking In Where Thugs Rule," *New York Times*, 5 February 2009.

33. Green and Mitchell, "Asia's Forgotten Crisis: A New Approach to Burma," 155. www.foreignaffairs.com/articles/63018/michael-green-and-derek-mitchell/asias-forgotten-crisis.

34. Thomas Fuller, "U.S. and China Often Worked Closely on Myanmar, Documents Show," *New York Times*, 11 December 2010; Mark McDonald, "U.S. Diplomat Makes a Trip to Myanmar," ibid., 26 March 2009. Mark E. Manyin, Michael John Garcia, and Wayne M. Morrison, *U.S. Accession to ASEAN's Treaty of Amity and Cooperation (TAC)* (Washington, DC: Congressional Research Service, 9 May 2009), 2.

35. Carl Gershman, "Solidarity with Daw Aung San Suu Kyi and the People of Burma," 18 June 2009, National Endowment for Democracy, http://www.ned.org/about/board/meet-our-president/archived-remarks-and-presentations/061809.

36. Jim Webb, "We Can't Afford to Ignore Myanmar," *New York Times*, 26 August 2009.

37. Testimony of Kurt Campbell in *U.S. Policy Toward Burma: Its Impact And Effectiveness*, Hearing Before the Subcommittee on East Asian and Pacific Affairs of the Committee on Foreign Relations, United States Senate, 111th Congress, 1st Session, September 30, 2009 (Washington, DC: U.S. Government Printing Office, 2010), 7.

38. Seth Mydans, "Burmese Opposition Supports New U.S. Approach," *New York Times*, 25 September 2009; Thomas Fuller, "Burmese Military Leaders Allow Dissident a Rare Meeting with Foreign Diplomats," ibid.,10 October 2009.

39. The following paragraphs are based largely on Steinberg and Fan, *Modern China-Myanmar Relations*, pp. 162–265.

40. Ibid., 258.

41. Ibid., 258–59, 262.

42. Ibid., 263.

43. Ernest Z. Bower, "Why Go to Myanmar?" *Southeast Asia from the Corner of 18th and K Streets* (Center for Strategic and International Studies, Southeast Asia Program), 2, no. 20 (23 November 2011): 2. Author's interview with U Tin Oo, 9 February 2012, NLD Headquarters, Yangon.

44. Aung Din, "What Obama Can Do for Burma," *Wall Street Journal*, 1 March 2010. http://online.wsj.com/article/SB10001424052748704454304575081382142901548.html?mod=googlenews_wsj.

45. "8888: The Role of Students in the People's Uprising in Burma" (Mae Sot, Thailand: Assistance Association for Political Prisoners in Burma, n.d.[8 August 2011]), 3. http://aappb.org/2014/03/the-role-of-students-in-the-8888-peoples-uprising-in-burma/.

46. Vishal Arora, "Spike in Anti-Christian Violence Feared before Burma Elections," *Compass Direct News*, 22 January 2010, https://www.worldwatchmonitor.org/2010/01-January/14251/.

47. Thomas Fuller, "Court in Myanmar Sentences American to Prison and Hard Labor," *New York Times*, 11 February 2010. See, for example, Bo Kyi and Hannah Scott, *Torture, Political Prisoners and the Un-rule of Law: Challenges to Peace, Security and Human Rights in Burma* (Mae Sot, Thailand: Assistance Association for Political Prisoners, 14 October 2010). Available at http://aappb.org/wp/Torture_political_prisoners_and_the_un-rule_of_law.pdf.

48. David Gollust, "US: Burma Election Law 'Mockery' of Democratic Process," 10 March 2010, Voice of America, http://www.voanews.com/content/us—burma-election-law-mockery-of-democratic-process-87269337/113871.html. Mark McDonald, "U.S. Diplomat Meets with Myanmar Opposition Leader," *New York Times*, 11 May 2010.

49. National Democratic Institute, Burma's *2010 Electoral Framework: Fundamentally Undemocratic* (Washington, DC: National Democratic Institute, 2010), 4.

50. David I. Steinberg, "Is Burma on the Verge of Transformation?" *Washington Post*, 21 August 2010.

51. Feifei Sun, "Statement by President Obama on Burma's November 7 Elections," 7 November 2010, *The Page, Time,* http://thepage.time.com/2010/11/07/obama-strikes-harsh-tone-on-burma-elections/.

52. Aung Din, "What's Next for Burma's Democrats?" *Foreign Policy*, 10 December 2010, http://www.foreignpolicy.com/articles/2010/12/10/whats_next_for_burmas_democrats. Steinberg and Fan, *Modern Myanmar-China Relations*, 160.

53. Cooperative Organizations (of Burmese activist groups in several countries) to Henrik Ibsens, "An Appeal to All Nobel Prize Laureates," 10 December 2010, http://www.ifbnc.org/bur/wp-content/uploads/2010/09/Oslo-an-appeal-Letter-to-All-Nobel-Peace-Laurates.pdf. Seth Mydans, "Myanmar Hardens Stance on Opposition," *New York Times*, 21 February 2011.

54. Lalit K. Jha, "Burma Policy 'No or Limited Success': US Official," *The Irrawaddy*, 27 April 2011.

55. *Behind the Sham Election and the Difficult Road Ahead*, Hearing before the Subcommittee on Asia and the Pacific of the Committee on Foreign Affairs of the House of Representatives, 112th Congress, 1st Session, 22 June 2011 (Washington, DC: Government Printing Office, 2011), 2, 8.

56. Ibid., 22–24.

57. Thein Sein's inaugural address is available on Burmanet News at http://www.burmanet.org/news/2011/03/31/the-new-light-of-myanmar-president-u-thein-sein-delivers-inaugural-address-to-pyidaungsu-hluttaw/. Steinberg and Fan, *Modern China-Myanmar Relations*, 366.

58. See, for example, Walter Lohman and Robert Warshaw, "Do Not Back Down on Burma," *Webmemo* (Heritage Foundation), 18 September 2011, http://www.heritage.org/research/reports/2011/09/do-not-back-down-on-burma.

59. Andrew Selth, "Burma-China: Another Dam Puzzle," *The Interpreter* (Lowy Institute for International Policy), parts 1 and 2, November 2011, http://www.lowyinterpreter.org/post/2011/11/01/Burma-China-Another-dam-puzzle-%28part-1%29.aspx), http://www.lowyinterpreter.org/post/2011/11/01/Burma-China-Another-dam-puzzle-%28part-2%29.aspx. Thant Myint-U, "In Myanmar, Seize the Moment," *New York Times*, 5 October 2011.

60. The Bush administration had nominated Michael Green for the post, but the financial crisis prevented action on the nomination before the US election of 2008.

61. Steven Lee Myers and Thomas Fuller, "Detecting a Thaw in Myanmar, U.S. Aims to Encourage Change," *New York Times*, 7 October 2011. U.S. Department of State, "Special Briefing on Burma: Derek J. Mitchell" (transcript), 17 October 2011, http://www.state.gov/p/eap/rls/rm/2011/10/175572.htm.

62. Myers and Fuller, "Detecting a Thaw in Myanmar, U.S. Aims to Encourage Change."

63. David Nakamura and William Wan, "U.S., Suu Kyi Relent Amid Shifts in Burma," *Washington Post*, 19 November 2011.

64. Daw Cho Cho Kyaw Nyein, quoted in "Changes in Myanmar Impress Skeptics on Eve of Clinton Trip," *New York Times*, 30 November 2011.

65. Clymer, "China as a Factor in American Policy toward Southeast Asia"; Jin Canrong quoted in Peter Barker and Jane Perlez, "Obama's Road to Myanmar Is Paved with New Asia Intentions"; *New York Times*, 17 November 2012; Thomas Fuller and Mark Landler, "As Myanmar Eases Controls, U.S. Sees Opening," ibid., 19 November 2011. *Global Times* quoted in David I. Steinberg, "China Counter-pivots on Myanmar," *Asia Times* online, 18 March 2013, http://www.atimes.com/atimes/Southeast_Asia/SEA-01-180313.html.

66. Steinberg and Fan, *Modern China-Myanmar Relations*, 333.

67. Author's interview with Michael Thurston, US embassy, Yangon, 7 February 2012.

68. Author's interview with Ambassador Derek Mitchell, US Embassy, Yangon, 27 December 2013. Steinberg, "Aung San Suu Kyi and U.S. Policy toward Burma/Myanmar," 36.

69. Ron Gluckman, "Burmese Spring: Burma Has Repressed Its People for Decades. Now It's Ready to Play Nice with America," *Newsweek* (international edition), 12 December 2011. David Mathieson, "Burma's Reality Check," *The Mark News*, 21 December 2011, http://www.hrw.org/news/2011/12/21/burmas-reality-check.

70. Seth Mydans, "Burmese Government and Ethnic Rebel Group Sign Cease-Fire," *New York Times*, 13 January 2012. Among those released were relatives of Ne Win and former Prime Minister Khin Nyunt.

71. Thomas Fuller, "From Prisoner to Parliament in Myanmar," ibid., 2 April 2012; "Suu Kyi's Moment," *Express* (Washington, DC), 2 April 2012.

72. Steven Lee Myers and Thomas Fuller, "U.S. Moves Toward Normalizing Relations with Myanmar," *New York Times*, 5 April 2012.

73. Tom Andrews, "Lifting Sanctions on Burma's Regime would Be a Mistake," *Washington Post*, 8 April 2012.

74. Interview with Michael Thurston.

75. Interview with Derek Mitchell.

76. Mark Landler, "Advocate of Democracy In Myanmar Meets Obama," *New York Times*, 20 September 2012; Steven Lee Myers, "Myanmar's Opposition Leader Urges End to Sanctions," ibid., 19 September 2012.

77. Steven Lee Myers and Rick Gladstone, "In Further Opening, U.S. to Ease Ban on Imports from Myanmar," ibid., 27 September 2012. A particularly insightful commentary on Aung San Suu Kyi and Thein Sein is Bill Keller, "The Burmese Odd Couple," ibid., 30 September 2012.

78. Bertil Lintner, "Burma's WMD Programme and Military Cooperation Between Burma and the Democratic People's Republic of Korea," Hong Kong: Asian Pacific Media Services, April 2011, http://issuu.com/asia_pacific_media_services/docs/burma-darkpost. David Albright, Paul Brannan, Robert Kelley, and Andrea Scheel Stricker, "Burma: A Nuclear Wannabe, Suspicious Links to North Korea; High-Tech Procurements and Enigmatic Facilities," Institute for Science and International Security, 28 January 2010, http://isis-online.org/isis-reports/detail/burma-a-nuclear-wanabee-suspicious-links-to-north-korea-high-tech-procureme/.

79. For a comprehensive review of the Burma–North Korea relationship, see Lintner, "Military Cooperation Between Burma and the Democratic People's Republic of Korea."

80. Oneindia News, "Burma Builds Nuke Plant with N Korean Help: Leaks," 10 December 2010, http://news.oneindia.in/2010/12/10/burma-nuclear-missile-north-korea-wikileaks-cable.html. Bertil Lintner, "Myanmar, North Korea in Missile Nexus," *Asia Times*, 2 March 2011.

81. An account of the trip is available at http://www.dvb.no/uncategorized/military-docs/9279.

82. Andrew Selth, "Burma, North Korea and the Nuclear Question," posted 18 May 2010, East Asia Forum, http://www.eastasiaforum.org/2010/05/18/burma-north-korea-and-the-nuclear-question/. Lintner, "Myanmar, North Korea in Missile Nexus."

83. "Myanmar: Nuclear Weapons Ties with North Korea Are Denied," *New York Times*, 10 December 2011; Choe Sang-hun, "South Korea: Myanmar Pledges to Stop Buying North's Weapons," ibid., 16 May 2012. U.S. Department of the Treasury press release, 2 July 2013, http://www.treasury.gov/press-center/press-releases/Pages/jl1998.aspx. Interview with Derek Mitchell.

84. Interview with Derek Mitchell. Voice of America, "US Announces Peace Corps Program in Myanmar," 13 November 2014, http://www.voanews.com/content/us-

announces-peace-corps-program-for-myanmar/2518655.html. Kyaw Hsu Mon, "US to Train Engineers Repairing Burma's 'Death Highway,'" *The Irrawaddy*, 10 June 1014, http://www.irrawaddy.org/burma/us-train-engineers-repairing-burmas-death-highway.html.

85. John Sifton of Human Rights Watch, quoted in Peter Baker and Jane Perlez, "Obama's Road to Myanmar is Paved with New Asia Intentions," *New York Times*, 17 November 2012. David I. Steinberg, "Reflections on US-Burma Relations," *The Irrawaddy*, 15 November 2012.

86. "Obama's Burma Road," *Wall Street Journal*, 21 November 2012. Obama's speech can be viewed at http://www.youtube.com/watch?v=tTAeJJnqhbo. Author's interview with Brian Joseph, National Endowment for Democracy, Washington, DC, 31 January 2012.

87. Thomas Fuller, "Myanmar Troops Sent to City Torn by Sectarian Rioting," *New York Times*, 23 March 2013.

88. Peter Baker and Steven Lee Myers, "Obama Couples Praise for Burmese Leader with Warning Against Violence," ibid., 21 May 2013.

89. Anne Gearan, "Burma's Thein Sein Says Military 'Will Always Have a Special Place' in Government," *Washington Post*, 19 May 2013.

90. "Remarks by the President at the United States Military Academy Commencement Ceremony," 28 May 2014, http://www.whitehouse.gov/the-press-office/2014/05/28/remarks-president-west-point-academy-commencement-ceremony.

91. Author's interviews with U Tin Oo, U Thet Tun, 6 February 2012, Yangon, and James Clad, 17 April 2012, Washington, DC.

92. Robert Karr McCabe, "When China Spits, We Swim," *New York Times Magazine*, 27 February 1966, 27.

93. Jane Perlez, "Asia's 'Big Guy' Spreads Cash and Seeks Influence in Pacific Region," *New York Times*, 23 November 2014.

94. Interviews with Michael Thurston and Derek Mitchell.

95. Reuters, "U.S. Blacklists Myanmar Official Ahead of Obama Visit," 31 October 2014, http://www.reuters.com/article/2014/10/31/us-usa-myanmar-sanctions-idUSKBN0IK1XA20141031. Mark Landler, "Obama and Aung San Suu Kyi Meet Again, With Battle Scars," *New York Times*, 14 November 2014.

Selected Bibliography

Books and articles listed here are frequently cited in the notes, by author's last name and short title throughout. Occasionally cited works appear in the notes with full details on first cite, and are not listed here.

PRIMARY SOURCES

Archival Materials

American Baptist Historical Society Archives, Mercer University, Atlanta, GA.
    Papers of
    The American Baptist Mission in Burma

Columbia University, Rare Book and Manuscript Library, New York City. Papers of
    Koo, Wellington

Cornell University, Division of Rare and Manuscript Collections, Carl A. Kroch
    Library, Ithaca, NY. Papers of
    Kahin, George
    Walinsky, Louis J.

Denison University Archives, Granville, OH. Papers of
    Hicks, Lewis Ezra
    Home, Fanny Doane
    Klein, Chester LeRoy
    Mather, Ruth
    Moore, William
    Seagrave, Gordon S.
    Tin Hla, David

Dwight D. Eisenhower Presidential Library, Abilene, KS. Papers of
    Dulles, John Foster
    Eisenhower, Dwight D.
    Fitzgerald, Dennis A.
    Haggerty, James C.
    Herter, Christian A.
    Lilly, Edward
    McCann, Kevin
    Osborn, David L.

George H. W. Bush Presidential Library, College Station, TX. Papers of
    Bush, George H. W.

Gerald R. Ford Presidential Library, Ann Arbor, MI. Papers of
    Ford, Gerald R.
    Lehmann, Wolfgang J.

Harry S. Truman Presidential Library, Independence, MO. Papers of
 Acheson, Dean
 Andrews, Stanley
 Block, Ralph
 Ewing, Oscar
 Hoffman, Paul
 Roberts, Frank
 Truman, Harry S.
 Washington, S. Walter

Herbert Hoover Presidential Library, West Branch, IA. Papers of
 Hoover, Herbert.
  Photographic Records
  Scrapbooks

Hoover Institution Archives, Stanford University, Stanford, CA. Papers of
 Caraway, Paul Wyatt
 Childs, Morris (microfilm collection)
 Goodman, Allen E.
 Green, William J.
 Griffin, R. Allen
 Hill, Charles
 Hoover, Herbert
 Judd, Walter H.
 Lansdale, Edward G.
 Montgomery, John D.
 Nossal, Frederick
 Sebald, Edith (de Becker)
 Sebald, William J.

Jimmy Carter Presidential Library, Atlanta, GA. Papers of
 Carter, Jimmy
 CIA CREST Records

John F. Kennedy Presidential Library, Boston, MA. Papers of
 Goodwin, Richard N.
 Halperin, Joel L.
 Karnow, Stanley
 Kennedy, John F.
 Shriver, Sargent
 Thomson, James C., Jr.

Library of Congress, Manuscript Division, Washington, DC. Papers of
 American Medical Center for Burma

Lyndon B. Johnson Presidential Library, Austin, TX. Papers of
 Ball, George
 Johnson, Lyndon B.
 Pearson, Drew
 Soloman, Anthony M.

Myanmar National Archives, Yangon
 British Colonial Office Records (microfilm)

    Foreign Office Records
    Misc. manuscripts

National Archives, Washington, DC
    Record Group 46

National Archives II, College Park, MD
    Record Group 59
    Record Group 84
    CIA CREST database

National Archives, Kew, UK
    Foreign Office Records
    Cabinet Records
    Foreign and Commonwealth Office Records

National Archives of Australia, Canberra
    Series A461, A816, A 987, A1838, A 3300, E 887

Richard M. Nixon Presidential Library, Yorba Linda, CA. Papers of
    Nixon, Richard M. Presidential Materials
    Nixon, Richard M. Vice Presidential Materials

Ronald Reagan Presidential Library, Simi Valley, CA. Papers of
    Reagan, Ronald

US Naval Academy Library, Annapolis, MD. Papers of
    Sebald, William J.

Interviews

    Clad, James
    Clapp, Priscilla
    Dalpino, Catharin
    Daw Yin Yin Myint
    Dinger, Larry
    Harr, David
    Haseman, John
    Huddle, Frederick P.
    Hummel, Betty Lou
    Joseph, Brian
    Levin, Burton
    Malinowski, Tom
    Mitchell, Derek
    O'Donohue, Daniel A.
    Ott, Marvin
    Schwartz, Eric P.
    Thurston, Michael
    U Aung Din
    U Khin Maung Nyunt
    U Thet Tun
    U Tin Oo
    Wiedeman, Kent M.

Published Collections of Government Documents

Tinker, Hugh, ed. *Burma: The Struggle for Independence, 1944–1948: Documents from Official and Private Sources*. London: Her Majesty's Stationery Office, 1983.
US Department of State, *Foreign Relations of the United States*.

Other Printed Primary Sources (Selected)

Albright, Madeleine. *Madam Secretary: A Memoir*. New York: Miramax Books, 2003.
Aung Din. "What's Next for Burma's Democrats?" *Foreign Policy*, 10 December 2010. http://www.foreignpolicy.com/articles/2010/12/10/whats_next_for_burmas_democrats.
Aung San Suu Kyi. *Freedom from Fear and Other Writings*. London: Penguin, 1991.
——. *Letters from Burma*. New York: Penguin, 2000.
Ba Maw. *Breakthrough in Burma: Memoirs of a Revolution*. New Haven, CT: Yale University Press, 1968.
Cady, John F. *Contacts with Burma, 1935–1949: A Personal Account*. Athens, OH: Ohio University Center for International Studies, Southeast Asian Program, 1983.
Green, Michael, and Derek Mitchell. "Asia's Forgotten Crisis," *Foreign Affairs* 86 (November–December 2007): 147–58.
Knowles, James D. *Memoir of Mrs. Ann H. Judson, Late Missionary to Burmah: Including a History of the American Baptist Mission in the Burman Empire*. Boston: Lincoln and Edmunds, 1831.
Larkin, Emma. *Everything is Broken: A Tale of Catastrophe in Burma*. New York: Penguin, 2010.
——. *Finding George Orwell in Burma*. New York: Penguin, 2005.
Law-Yone, Wendy. *Golden Parasol: A Daughter's Memoir of Burma* (London: Chatto & Windus, 2013.
Lemere, Maggie, and Zoe West, eds. *Nowhere to Be Home: Narratives from the Survivors of Burma's Military Regime*. San Francisco: Voice of Witness and McSweeney Books, 2011.
Levin, Burton. "Reminiscences and Reflections on 8/8/88." *Burma Debate* (Summer 1998): 4–12.
Listowel, Earl of. *Memoirs: Burma Independence 1947–1948*. Pekhon, Myanmar: Pekhon University Press, 1998.
Maung Maung. *The 1988 Uprising in Burma*. New Haven, CT: Yale University Press, 1999.
Mirante, Edith. *Burmese Looking Glass: A Human Rights Adventure and a Jungle Revolution*. New York: Atlantic Monthly Press, 1993.
Morse, Eugene. *Exodus to a Hidden Valley*. New York: Reader's Digest Press, 1974.
Naing Luu Aung, Aung Moe Htet, and Sit Nyien Aung, eds. *Letters to a Dictator: Official Correspondence from NLD Chairman U Aung Shwe to the SLORC's Senior General Than Shwe, from December 1995 to March 1997*. Bangkok: All Burma Students' Democratic Front, 1997.
Newhall, Sue Mayes. *The Devil in God's Old Man*. New York: Norton, 1969.
Orwell, George. *Burmese Days*. New York: Harcourt, 1934.
Sargent, Inge. *Twilight Over Burma: My Life as a Shan Princess*. Honolulu: University of Hawaii Press, 1994.
Seagrave, Gordon. *Burma Surgeon*. New York: Norton, 1943.
——. *Burma Surgeon Returns*. New York: Norton, 1946.
——. *My Hospital in the Hills*. New York: Norton, 1955.

——. *Tales of a Wastebasket Surgeon*. Philadelphia: Judson, 1938.

Suragamika. *The Roadmap*. Chiang Mai, Thailand: Silkworm Books, 2012.

Taylor, Robert H., comp. *Dr. Maung Maung: Gentleman, Scholar, Patriot*. Singapore: Institute of Southeast Asian Studies, 2008.

Trumbull, Robert. *The Scrutable East: A Foreign Correspondent's Report on Southeast Asia*. New York: David McKay, 1964.

U Nu. *Saturday's Son: Memoirs of the Former Prime Minister of Burma*. New Haven, CT: Yale University Press, 1975.

Vum Ko Hau. *Profile of a Burma Frontier Man*. Bandung, Indonesia: Kilatmadju Press, 1963.

SECONDARY SOURCES (SELECTED)

Allen, Louis. "'The Escape of Captain Vivian': A Footnote to Burmese Independence." *Journal of Imperial and Commonwealth History* 19 (January 1991): 65–69.

Brumberg, Joan Jacobs. *Mission for Life: The Story of the Family of Adoniram Judson, The Dramatic Events of the First American Foreign Mission, and the Course of Evangelical Religion in the Nineteenth Century*. New York: Free Press, 1980.

Bunyanunda, Mann Mac. "Burma, ASEAN, and Human Rights: The Decade of Constructive Engagement, 1991–2001." *Stanford Journal of East Asian Affairs* 2 (Spring 2002): 118–35.

Butwell, Richard. "The Burmese Way of Change." *Current History* (December 1976): 205–8, 224.

——. *U Nu of Burma*. Stanford, CA: Stanford University Press, 1963.

Cady, John F. *A History of Modern Burma*. Ithaca, NY: Cornell University Press, 1958.

——. *The United States and Burma*. Cambridge, MA: Harvard University Press, 1976.

Callahan, Mary P. *Making Enemies: War and State Building in Burma*. Ithaca, NY: Cornell University Press, 2005.

Charney, Michael W. *A History of Modern Burma*. Cambridge, UK: Cambridge University Press, 2009.

——. "Ludu Aung Than: Nu's Burma during the Cold War." In *Connecting Histories: Decolonization and the Cold War in Southeast Asia*, ed. Christopher E. Gosha and Christian F. Ostermann, 335–55. Washington, DC: Woodrow Wilson Center Press, 2009.

Clymer, Kenton. "China as a Factor in American Policy toward Southeast Asia: A Review from the Nineteenth Century to the George W. Bush Administration," *Silliman Journal* 49, no. 1 (2008): 75–92.

——. "The Trial for High Treason of the 'Burma Surgeon,' Gordon S. Seagrave." *Pacific Historical Review* 81 (May 2012): 245–91.

——. "The United States and the Guomindang (KMT) Forces in Burma, 1949–1954: A Diplomatic Disaster." *Chinese Historical Quarterly* 21 (May 2014): 24–44.

Clymer, Megan. "Min Ko Naing, 'Conqueror of Kings': Burma's Student Leader." *Journal of Burma Studies* 8 (2003): 33–63.

Darkow, Warren Walter. "American Relations with Burma 1800–1950." M.S. thesis, University of Wisconsin, 1951.

Dudziak, Mary L. *Cold War Civil Rights: Race and the Image of American Democracy*. Princeton, NJ: Princeton University Press, 2011.

Durr, Kenneth D. *The Best Made Plans: Robert R. Nathan and 20th Century Liberalism*. Rockville, MD: Montrose Press, 2013.

Fifield, Russell H. *Americans in Southeast Asia: The Roots of Commitment*. New York: Thomas Y. Crowell, 1973.

Foley, Matthew. *The Cold War and National Assertion in Southeast Asia: Britain, the United States and Burma, 1948–62.* London: Routledge, 2010.

Gibson, Richard M., with Wenhua Chen. *The Secret Army: Chiang Kai-shek and the Drug Warlords of the Golden Triangle.* Singapore: Wiley, 2011.

Gosha, Christopher E., and Christian F. Ostermann, eds. *Connecting Histories: Decolonization and the Cold War in Southeast Asia.* Washington, DC: Woodrow Wilson Center Press, 2009.

Hess, Gary R. *The United States' Emergence as a Southeast Asian Power, 1940–1950.* New York: Columbia University Press, 1987.

Jackson, Carl T. *The Oriental Religions and American Thought.* Westport, CT: Greenwood Press, 1981.

Kaufman, Victor S. "Trouble in the Golden Triangle: The United States, Taiwan and the 93rd Nationalist Division." *China Quarterly*, no. 166 (2001): 440–56.

———. "The United States, Britain and the CAT Controversy." *Journal of Contemporary History* 40 (2005): 95–113.

Kurlantzick, Joshua. *The Ideal Man: The Tragedy of Jim Thompson and the American Way of War.* Hoboken, NJ: Wiley, 2011.

Levenstein, Susan L. ed. *Finding Dollars, Sense, and Legitimacy in Burma.* Washington, DC : Woodrow Wilson international Center for Scholars, 2010.

Lintner, Bertil. *Burma in Revolt: Opium and Insurgency since 1948.* Boulder, CO: Westview, 1995.

———. *Military Cooperation Between Burma and the Democratic People's Republic of Korea.* Hong Kong: Asia Pacific Media Services, 2011.

———. *Outrage: Burma's Struggle for Democracy.* Bangkok: White Lotus, 1990.

McCoy, Alfred W. *The Politics of Heroin: CIA Complicity in the Global Drug Trade.* 2d rev. ed. Brooklyn, NY: Lawrence Hill Books, 2003.

McLane, Charles B. *Soviet Strategies in Southeast Asia: An Exploration of Eastern Policy under Lenin and Stalin.* Princeton, NJ: Princeton University Press, 1966.

McMahon, Robert. *The Limits of Empire: The United States and Southeast Asia since World War II.* New York: Columbia University Press, 1999.

Niksch, Larry A. *Burma-U.S. Relations.* Washington, DC: Congressional Research Service, 2007.

Ott, Marvin. "Burma: A Strategic Perspective." *Strategic Forum*, no. 92 (November 1996): 1–4.

Prados, John. *Safe for Democracy: The Secret Wars of the CIA.* Chicago: Ivan R. Dee, 2006.

Rieffel, Lex, ed. *Myanmar/Burma: Inside Challenges, Outside Interests.* Washington, DC: Brookings Institution Press, 2010.

Robertson, Phil. "Burma." *Foreign Policy in Focus*, 1 August 1997.

Rotter, Andrew. *Comrades and Odds: The United States and India, 1947–1964.* Ithaca, NY: Cornell University Press, 2000.

Sacquety, Troy J. *The OSS in Burma: Jungle War against the Japanese.* Lawrence: University Press of Kansas, 2013.

Selth, Andrew. *Burma's Armed Forces: Power Without Glory.* Norwalk, CT: Eastbridge, 2002.

———. *Death of a Hero: The U Thant Disturbances in Burma, December 1974.* Brisbane: Centre for the Study of Australian-Asian Relations, Griffith University,1989.

Silverstein, Josef. *Burma: Military Rule and the Politics of Stagnation.* Ithaca, NY: Cornell University Press, 1977.

Steinberg, David I. "Aung San Suu Kyi and U.S. Policy Toward Burma/Myanmar." *Journal of Current Southeast Asian Affairs* 29, no. 3 (2010): 35–59.

———. *Burma: A Socialist Nation of Southeast Asia.* Boulder, CO: Westview, 1982.

——. *Burma: The State of Myanmar*. Washington, DC: Georgetown University Press, 2001.

——. "Burma-Myanmar: The U.S.-Burmese Relationship and Its Vicissitudes." In *Short of the Goal: U.S. Foreign Policy and Poorly Performing States*, ed. Milan Vaishnav and Robert L. Ayres, 209–44. Washington, DC: Center for Global Development, 2000.

——. *Burma/Myanmar: What Everyone Needs to Know*. New York: Oxford University Press, 2010.

——. *Burma's Road Toward Development: Growth and Ideology Under Military Rule*. Boulder, CO: Westview, 1981.

——. *Turmoil in Burma: Contested Legitimacies in Myanmar*. Norwalk, CT: Eastbridge, 2006.

Steinberg, David I., and Hongwei Fan. *Modern China-Myanmar Relations: Dilemmas of Mutual Dependence*. Copenhagen, Denmark: NIAS Press, 2013.

Taylor, Jay. *China and Southeast Asia: Peking's Relations with Revolutionary Movements*. New York: Praeger, 1976.

Taylor, Robert H. *Foreign and Domestic Consequences of the KMT Intervention in Burma*. Ithaca, NY: Southeast Asian Program, Cornell University, 1973.

——. *The State in Burma*. London: C. Hurst, 1987.

——. *The State in Myanmar*. Singapore: NUS Press, 2009.

Thant Myint-U. *The Making of Modern Burma*. Cambridge, UK: Cambridge University Press, 2001.

——. *The River of Lost Footsteps: A Personal History of Burma*. New York: Farrar, Straus and Giroux, 2006.

——. *Where China Meets India: Burma and the Closing of the Great Asian Frontier*. New York: Farrar, Straus and Giroux, 2012.

Thorne, Christopher. *Allies of a Kind: The United States, Britain, and the War Against Japan, 1941–1945*. New York: Oxford University Press, 1978.

Trager, Frank N. "Burma's Foreign Policy, 1948–56: Neutralism, Third Force, and Rice." *Journal of Asian Studies* 16, no. 1 (November 1956): 89–102.

——. "Burma: 1968—A New Beginning?" *Asian Survey*. 9 (February 1969): 104–14.

Trager, Helen G. *Burma Through Alien Eyes: Missionary Views of the Burmese in the Nineteenth Century*. New York: Praeger, 1966.

Tucker, Nancy Bernkopf. "John Foster Dulles and the Taiwan Roots of the 'Two Chinas' Policy." In *John Foster Dulles and the Diplomacy of the Cold War*, ed. Richard Immerman, 235–62. Princeton: Princeton University Press, 1990.

U Sein Win. *The Split Story: An Account of Recent Political Upheaval in Burma*. Rangoon: The Guardian Press, 1959.

Walinsky, Louis J. *Economic Development in Burma, 1951–1960*. New York: Twentieth Century Fund, 1962.

——. "The Rise and Fall of U Nu." *Pacific Affairs* 38, no. 3/4 (Autumn 1965–Winter 1965–1966): 269–81.

Weimer, Daniel. *Seeing Drugs: Modernization, Counterinsurgency, and U.S. Narcotics Control in the Third World, 1969–1976*. Kent, OH: Kent State University Press, 2011.

Wise, David, and Thomas B. Ross. *The Invisible Government*. New York: Random House, 1964.

Yegar, Moshe. *Between Integration and Secession: The Muslim Communities of the Southern Philippines, Southern Thailand, and Eastern Burma/Myanmar*. Lanham, MD: Lexington Books, 2002.

Index

Page numbers in *italics* refer to figures.